ROUTLEDGE HANDBOOK OF RUSSIAN FOREIGN POLICY

Providing a comprehensive overview of Russia's foreign policy directions, this handbook brings together an international team of scholars to develop a complex treatment of Russia's foreign policy. The chapters draw from numerous theoretical traditions by incorporating ideas of domestic institutions, considerations of national security and international recognition as sources of the nation's foreign policy. Covering critically important subjects such as Russia's military interventions in Ukraine and Syria, the handbook is divided into four key parts:

Part I explores the social and material conditions in which Russia's foreign policy is formed and implemented.

Part II investigates tools and actors that participate in policy making including diplomacy, military, media, and others.

Part III provides an overview of Russia's directions towards the United States, Europe, Asia, the Middle East, Eurasia, and the Arctic.

Part IV addresses the issue of Russia's participation in global governance and multiple international organizations, as well as the Kremlin's efforts to build new organizations and formats that suit Russia's objectives.

The *Routledge Handbook of Russian Foreign Policy* is an invaluable resource to students and scholars of Russian Politics and International Relations, as well as World Politics more generally.

Andrei P. Tsygankov is Professor of Political Science and International Relations at San Francisco State University. He has published widely in the United States, Russia, Europe, and China, and his books include *Russia's Foreign Policy* and *Russia and the West from Alexander to Putin*.

ROUTLEDGE HANDBOOK OF RUSSIAN FOREIGN POLICY

Edited by
Andrei P. Tsygankov

LONDON AND NEW YORK

First published 2018
by Routledge
2 Park Square, Milton Park, Abingdon, Oxon OX14 4RN

and by Routledge
711 Third Avenue, New York, NY 10017

Routledge is an imprint of the Taylor & Francis Group, an informa business

© 2018 selection and editorial matter, Andrei P. Tsygankov;
individual chapters, the contributors.

The right of Andrei P. Tsygankov to be identified as the author of the editorial material, and of the authors for their individual chapters, has been asserted in accordance with sections 77 and 78 of the Copyright, Designs and Patents Act 1988.

All rights reserved. No part of this book may be reprinted or reproduced or utilised in any form or by any electronic, mechanical, or other means, now known or hereafter invented, including photocopying and recording, or in any information storage or retrieval system, without permission in writing from the publishers.

Trademark notice: Product or corporate names may be trademarks or registered trademarks, and are used only for identification and explanation without intent to infringe.

British Library Cataloguing-in-Publication Data
A catalogue record for this book is available from the British Library

Library of Congress Cataloging-in-Publication Data
Names: Tsygankov, Andrei P., 1964- editor.
Title: Routledge handbook of Russian foreign policy / edited by Andrei Tsygankov.
Description: Abingdon, Oxon ; New York, NY : Routledge, 2018. | Includes bibliographical references and index.
Identifiers: LCCN 2017049656| ISBN 9781138690448 (hardback) | ISBN 9781315536934 (ebook)
Subjects: LCSH: Russia (Federation)—Foreign relations. | Soviet Union—Foreign relations.
Classification: LCC DK510.764 .R683 2018 | DDC 327.47—dc23
LC record available at https://lccn.loc.gov/2017049656

ISBN: 978-1-138-69044-8 (hbk)
ISBN: 978-1-315-53693-4 (ebk)

Typeset in Bembo
by Swales & Willis Ltd, Exeter, Devon, UK

Printed and bound in Great Britain by
TJ International Ltd, Padstow, Cornwall

DEDICATION

For the younger generation of scholars of Russian foreign policy.

CONTENTS

List of illustrations   x
List of contributors   xi
Preface   xv

PART I
Theories and conditions   1

   Introduction
   Andrei P. Tsygankov

1 International norms and identity   5
   Valentina Feklyunina

2 Global (post)structural conditions   22
   Viatcheslav Morozov

3 Power and national security   43
   Elena Kropatcheva

4 Geopolitics   60
   John Berryman

5 Nationalism   79
   Luke March

6 Petropolitics   99
   Yuval Weber

PART II
Tools and actors — 119

Introduction
Andrei P. Tsygankov

7 Diplomacy — 123
Charles E. Ziegler

8 Natural gas — 138
Boris Barkanov

9 Intelligence — 153
Mikhail A. Strokan and Brian D. Taylor

10 Military — 168
Valery Konyshev and Alexander Sergunin

11 Cyber power — 182
Julien Nocetti

12 Media and public diplomacy — 199
Greg Simons

13 The Russian Orthodox Church — 217
Nicolai N. Petro

PART III
Directions — 233

Introduction
Andrei P. Tsygankov

14 The United States — 237
Kari Roberts

15 Asia-Pacific and China — 254
Natasha Kuhrt

16 The European Union — 269
Tuomas Forsberg and Hiski Haukkala

17 Central and Eastern Europe — 282
Dmitry Ofitserov-Belskiy and Andrey Sushenstov

18	The Middle East *Philipp Casula and Mark N. Katz*	295
19	The Caucasus *Maxim A. Suchkov*	311
20	Central Asia *Mariya Y. Omelicheva*	325
21	The Arctic *Robert English and Andrew Thvedt*	338

PART IV
Organizations — 351

Introduction
Andrei P. Tsygankov

22	The United Nations *Alexander Sergunin*	355
23	The G20 *Andrej Krickovic*	367
24	European organizations *Hanna Smith*	377
25	Asian organizations *Artyom Lukin*	388
26	The Shanghai Cooperation Organization *Maria Raquel Freire*	400
27	The Eurasian Economic Union *Mikhail A. Molchanov*	410
28	The Collective Security Treaty Organization *Ruth Deyermond*	421

Index — *430*

ILLUSTRATIONS

Figures

5.1	A model for understanding the interaction between nationalism and RFP	92
6.1	Export revenues and annual percentage change, 1961–1991	107
22.1	Sustainable development: three dimensions	359

Tables

2.1	A comparative summary of theoretical perspectives on Russia	38
5.1	The main approaches to explaining nationalism and RFP	88
10.1	Russian, U.S. and Chinese military capabilities, 2015	177

CONTRIBUTORS

Boris Barkanov is a teaching assistant professor in the Political Science Department at West Virginia University. He received his PhD in political science from UC Berkeley, USA. He has been a postdoctoral fellow at the Davis Center (Harvard) and a Fulbright-Hays Scholar. His research interests include Russian politics/foreign policy, energy, and security.

John Berryman teaches International Relations at Birkbeck, University of London, and is Associate Professor of International Studies at Ithaca College, New York (London Division). His publications include 30 chapters and articles dealing with Russian foreign and security policy and he is a member of the International Institute for Strategic Studies and the Royal Institute of International Affairs.

Philipp Casula is a postdoctoral fellow of the Swiss National Science Foundation at the University of Zurich, and is currently visiting scholar at the University of Manchester, UK. His PhD thesis at Basel University analysed the domestic politics of contemporary Russia in terms of hegemony and populism. Philipp's current research interest includes the cultural history of post-colonial Russia, especially the relations of the USSR with the Middle East and their cultural representations.

Ruth Deyermond is Lecturer in Post-Soviet Security in the Department of War Studies, King's College London. Her publications include Security and Sovereignty in the Former Soviet Union (Lynne Rienner 2008).

Robert English joined the faculty of the School of International Relations at the University of Southern California in 2001. Prior to that he taught at the Johns Hopkins University School of Advanced International Studies, USA, and was also a fellow at the Institute for Advanced Study in Princeton, USA. In the 1980s, he worked as a policy analyst with the US Department of Defense and the Committee for National Security. He is the author, among other works, of *Russia and the Idea of the West: Gorbachev, Intellectuals, and the End of the Cold War* (Columbia, 2000).

Valentina Feklyunina is Senior Lecturer in Politics at Newcastle University, UK. Her publications include the monograph *Identities and Foreign Policies in Russia, Ukraine and Belarus* (co-authored with Stephen White), and articles on Russia's identity and soft power in such journals as *Europe-Asia Studies*, *British Journal of Politics and International Relations*, and *European Journal of International Relations*.

Tuomas Forsberg is Professor of International Relations at the University of Tampere, Finland. He was also deputy director and foreign policy cluster leader of the Academy of Finland Center of Excellence on Choices of Russian Modernisation at the Aleksanteri Institute (2012–17). His publications include *Divided West: European Security and the Transatlantic Relationship* (co-authored with Graeme Herd, 2006) and *The European Union and Russia* (co-authored with Hiski Haukkala, 2016).

Maria Raquel Freire is researcher at the Centre for Social Studies (CES) and Associate Professor in International Relations at the School of Economics of the University of Coimbra (FEUC), Portugal. She holds a Jean Monnet Chair and is currently director of the PhD Programme in International Politics and Conflict Resolution, CES/FEUC

Dr. Hiski Haukkala is Associate Professor of International Relations at the University of Tampere, Finland. Previously he has held positions at the Finnish Ministry for Foreign Affairs, the Finnish Institute of International Affairs and the University of Turku. He is the author of numerous books and articles on EU foreign policy. His most recent book is *The European Union and Russia* (2016, together with Tuomas Forsberg).

Mark N. Katz is a Professor of Government and Politics at the George Mason University Schar School of Policy and Government, USA, and was a visiting senior fellow at the Finnish Institute of International Affairs in 2017. He writes on Russian foreign policy, especially toward the Middle East.

Valery Konyshev is Professor of International Relations, St. Petersburg State University, Russia. He received his PhD (History) (1997) and habilitation (Political Science) (2006) from the Nizhny Novgorod State University, Russia. His fields of research and teaching include contemporary military strategy and International Relations Theory.

Andrej Krickovic is an Assistant Professor in the Faculty of World Economy and International Affairs, Higher School of Economics, Moscow. He specializes in issues of international security relations and published widely in *The Chinese Journal of International Politics, Contemporary Security Policy, Global Governance, Post-Soviet Affairs, Russia in Global Affairs*, and others.

Dr. Elena Kropatcheva is a researcher at the Institute for Peace Research and Security Policy at the University of Hamburg (IFSH), Germany. Her research interests include International Relations, European and Eurasian security policy, international security organizations, energy geopolitics, domestic and foreign policies of Russia and Ukraine.

Natasha Kuhrt is lecturer in the Department of War Studies, King's College London. Her main research interests are Russia's Asia policy, as well as broader issues of international law, sovereignty, and intervention. She has published widely on Russia's Asia policy, and her book, *Russian Policy Towards China and Japan*, based on her PhD, was published by Routledge in 2007 (paperback, 2011).

Artyom Lukin is Deputy Director for Research and Associate Professor at the School of Regional and International Studies, Far Eastern Federal University, Russia. Lukin has authored numerous chapters, papers, and commentaries on Russia's engagement with Asia. His latest book (co-authored with Rens Lee) is *Russia's Far East: New Dynamics in Asia Pacific and Beyond* (Lynne Rienner, 2015).

Luke March is Professor of Post-Soviet and Comparative Politics at the University of Edinburgh, UK. His main research interests include the politics of the European (radical) Left, and Russian domestic and foreign politics. He has published in journals including *Party Politics, Comparative European Politics, Europe-Asia Studies*, and *East European Politics*. His books include *The Communist Party in Post-Soviet Russia* (2002), *Russia and Islam: State, Society and Radicalism* (edited with Roland Dannreuther, Routledge, 2010), *Radical Left Parties in Europe* (Routledge, 2011) and *Europe's Radical Left. From Marginality to the Mainstream?* (edited with Daniel Keith, 2016).

Mikhail A. Molchanov lectures at the University of Victoria, Canada. He is Foreign Member of the National Academy of Educational Sciences of Ukraine. Dr. Molchanov has published 7 books and nearly 120 articles and book chapters. His most recent book is *Eurasian Regionalisms and Russian Foreign Policy* (Routledge, 2015).

Viatcheslav Morozov is Professor of EU–Russia Studies at the University of Tartu, Estonia. He also chairs the Council of the UT's Centre for EU–Russia Studies (CEURUS) and the Programme Committee of the Tartu Conference on Russian and East European Studies.

Julien Nocetti is a research fellow in the Russia/New independent states Centre at the French Institute of International Relations (IFRI), Paris. He focuses his Russia-related research on Russian foreign and domestic Internet policies through both top-down and bottom-up approaches. He is also a specialist in Russia's foreign policy towards the Middle East.

Dmitry Ofitserov-Belskiy is an Associate Professor at Humanities Department of National Research University Higher School of Economics (HSE), a leading analyst of the agency Foreign Policy Advisory Group.

Mariya Y. Omelicheva is an Associate Professor of political science at the University of Kansas, USA. Her research interests include Eurasian security, Russian foreign policy, democracy promotion, and terrorism/crime nexus. She is the author of *Counterterrorism Policies in Central Asia* (Routledge, 2011), and *Democracy in Central Asia: Competing Perspectives and Alternate Strategies* (University Press of Kentucky, 2015).

Nicolai N. Petro currently holds the Silvia-Chandley Professorship of Peace Studies and Nonviolence at the University of Rhode Island, USA. His scholarly work focuses on Russia, and on the role that religion, history, and cultural symbols can play in democratic development.

Kari Roberts is Associate Professor of Political Science in the Department of Economics, Justice, and Policy Studies at Mount Royal University, Canada. Her research concerns the domestic influences on Russian foreign policy toward the United States as well as American post-Cold War attitudes about Russia and their impact on the relationship.

Alexander Sergunin is Professor of International Relations, St. Petersburg State University, Russia. He received his PhD (History) from the Moscow State University (1985) and habilitation (Political Science) from the St. Petersburg State University (1994). His fields of research and teaching include Russian foreign policy thinking and making, and International Relations Theory.

Greg Simons, Associate Professor, is a senior researcher at the Institute for Russian and Eurasian Studies at Uppsala University in Sweden and a lecturer at the Department of Communication Sciences at Turiba University in Latvia. One research focus is on Russian public diplomacy and the quest for soft power.

Hanna Smith received her PhD from University of Helsinki and has been affiliated with Aleksanteri Institute, University of Helsinki specializing in Russian military and security policy and relations with European organizations. She is currently Director of Strategic Planning and Responses at the European Centre of Excellence for Countering Hybrid Threats, Helsinki.

Mikhail A. Strokan is a PhD student in Political Science at the University of Pennsylvania, USA.

Maxim A. Suchkov, Associate Professor of International Relations and Deputy Director for Research at the School of International Relations, Pyatigorsk State University, Russia. He is also the Editor of Al-Monitor's Russia-Mideast coverage and is the author of the *Essays on Russian Foreign Policy in the Caucasus and the Middle East* (Nomos, 2015).

Andrey Sushenstov is a Programme director at the Valdai Discussion Club, Moscow. He is also a political analyst and international relations scholar at Moscow State Institute of International Relations (MGIMO) and a managing partner with the Moscow-based consulting agency Foreign Policy Advisory Group.

Brian D. Taylor is Professor and Chair, Department of Political Science, Maxwell School of Citizenship and Public Affairs, Syracuse University, USA.

Andrew Thvedt has a BA from the University of South California (USC), USA and is working as a postgraduate research assistant in USC's School of International Relations.

Andrei P. Tsygankov is Professor in the Departments of Political Science and International Relations at San Francisco State University, USA. His books have been published in the United States, Europe, Russia, and China, and include *Anti-Russian Lobby and American Foreign Policy* and *Russia and the West from Alexander to Putin*.

Yuval Weber is the Kennan Institute Fellow at the Daniel Morgan Graduate School and a Global Fellow at the Woodrow Wilson Center in Washington, DC, on leave from the Higher School of Economics in Moscow, Russia, where he is an Assistant Professor in the Faculty of World Economy and International Affairs. He is a Center Associate at the Davis Center for Russian and Eurasian Studies at Harvard University, and was previously a Visiting Assistant Professor in Harvard's Department on Government.

Charles E. Ziegler is Professor of Political Science and University Scholar at the University of Louisville, USA. He is the author of over 80 professional journal articles and book chapters, and has written or edited five books, the latest of which is *Civil Society and Politics in Central Asia* (University Press of Kentucky, 2015).

PREFACE

Andrei P. Tsygankov

The importance of studying Russian foreign policy (RFP) today is as great as ever. We are living through an era of global change which Russian authorities advocate and promote. Rules and conditions of the international system are being reordered in part because the Kremlin is working tirelessly to move the world in this direction. Some regret the change and recall with nostalgia the "stability" of the post-Cold War order. Others welcome the global transition arguing that it allows more room for potential non-Western contributors. The disagreement notwithstanding, it is clear that without Russia the world would not be where it is today.

Another debate concerns conditions that shape RFP and the motives of the nation's policy makers. Some scholars and politicians view the Kremlin as predominantly a geopolitical actor that seeks to protect its sphere of influence in Eurasia and facilitate the arrival of a global multipolar balance of power. Not infrequently, members of this group advocate the notion of a new Cold War for describing Russia's behavior as aiming to undermine the West's values and interests. Others insist that as a global citizen Russia works to ensure the protection of norms and principles practiced in diplomacy and international organizations. Rather than trying to destroy the West-centered global order, Russia is determined to make it more multilateral and carve out more room for its own contribution. A large and complex country, Russia must be understood in terms of the complexity of theoretical approaches, tools and actors, geographic directions, and membership in global/regional organizations.

In recognition of this complexity, the resulting volume seeks to answer four broad questions about Russian foreign policy.

1 What are the main social and material conditions that explain change and continuity in RFP?
2 What tools and actors are especially prominent in forming and implementing RFP?
3 How is RFP conducted in various geographic and regional settings?
4 How are Russia's goals and interests realized through membership in various global and regional organizations?

With these questions in mind, the book contains four major parts. Part I explores various theoretical approaches, social, and material *conditions* in which RFP is formed and implemented. Part II investigates *tools and actors* that participate in policy making including diplomacy, military, media, and others. Part III provides an overview of RFP's *directions* toward various countries and regions such as the United States, Europe, Asia, the Middle East, Eurasia, and the Arctic. Part IV addresses the issue of Russia's participation in global governance and multiple international *organizations* operating at both global and regional levels.

The decision by Routledge to commission this volume is recognition of both the importance and the complexity of studying Russia's international behavior. I am grateful to the publisher for asking me to lead the project, being responsive to my requests, and providing helpful comments and various forms of editorial assistance along the way.

The project includes twenty-eight chapters by experts on various dimensions of RFP. The highly diverse group of contributors includes individuals of different backgrounds, career stages, nationality, gender, and places of researching and teaching about Russia, including the United States, Canada, Russia, and Europe. It has been a privilege to work with this group of scholars. I am very grateful to all for being an excellent team by meeting deadlines, incorporating comments, serving as informal reviewers of each other's work, and – most of all – for contributing comprehensive chapters on various subjects of RFP. This has been a long journey and a gratifying experience.

PART I

Theories and conditions

Andrei P. Tsygankov

Part I selects for a closer review six theoretical approaches each highlighting distinct conditions that explain Russian foreign policy (RFP) – international norms and identity, the country's position within the global political economy, international military power, geopolitics, nationalism, and energy resources. Although the selected approaches are not meant to be exclusive, they cover most of existing explanations of Russia's international behavior and should provide a comprehensive menu for those seeking to understand the nation's strategy and individual decisions.

As I approached individual contributors, I asked them (1) to assess the state of their theoretical school by identifying its most important representatives and research programs; (2) to compare the relevant school's strengths and weaknesses to those of other theoretical approaches; (3) to address potential methodological pitfalls and formulate, to the extent possible, testable hypotheses; and (4) to do so by providing empirical illustrations and examples.

In her chapter on the role of international norms and identity, Valentina Feklyunina provides an overview of constructivist research on RFP. While sharing similar assumptions about knowledge and reality, constructivists build on various subsets of social science such as psychology, sociology, and cultural studies. Feklyunina discusses four prominent research programs on RFP: studies of ideas and identity; recognition and non-recognition of Russia's identity by others; international norms; and practices and habits. For instance, some scholars analyzed the role of ideas articulated by Soviet policy entrepreneurs during the early 1970s and the late 1980s. Others researched how Russia's national identity was contested domestically in response to the West's recognition or lack thereof and how it resulted in Russia's relations with Western countries. Various episodes of Russia's assertive behavior, including the Crimean War, the early Cold War, and the annexation of Crimea following the Euromaidan revolution in Ukraine can be understood as the Kremlin's reaction to perceived Western disrespect of Russia's status, reputation, and special cultural ties. Still other scholars investigated how internationally accepted norms of sovereignty and humanitarian intervention were constructed in the Russian domestic setting. Finally, there are those who followed insights of European philosophy and neo-Marxism and studied the historically continuous role of diplomatic practices and social habits in Russia's interaction with the outside world.

Feklyunina identifies the interpretation of meanings in the selected sources as a main challenge for constructivists. She cautions against the notion of some specific "constructivist" methods and argues for pluralism of methods as long as their application is consistent with the researcher's ontological and epistemological assumptions. Feklyunina also argues for a more consistent engagement of constructivists with ethics, while preserving the scholarly objectivity. In particular, she challenges constructivist researchers to be explicit about their normative commitments and warns against seeing "the world through Russia's eyes" while reconstructing Russia's identity and worldview.

Viatcheslav Morozov seeks to establish the notion of a "thick" structure and its effects on Russia's international behavior. His chapter on (post) structural conditions of RFP partly engages with Feklyunina's analysis. In particular, Morozov reviews historical materialist and discursive approaches to RFP. Of the former, he analyzes Leninist and Trotskian approaches, the world-system perspective, and critical International Political Economy. Of the latter, he reviews approaches associated with the English School, poststructuralism, and post-colonialism. His own approach is an effort to bridge materialist and discursive dimensions in order to make sense of Russia's peculiar position within the global political economy and its implications for RFP. Morozov identifies Russia's position as that of a "subaltern empire": an exploited semi-periphery with respect to the Western core, and a capitalist colonizer with respect to Russia's Eurasian periphery. Such position explains Russia's engagement with counter-hegemonic projects such as the BRICS as well as Russia's attempts to develop Russia-influenced Eurasian Economic Union within, rather than outside, the European hegemonic space.

Morozov recognizes the limitations of the (post) structuralist approach for foreign policy analysis by proposing to combine his approach with second-image theories. The idea of combining different levels of analysis is also present in constructivism, which investigates how international norms are domestically understood and contested. Morozov shares with constructivists an interest in discourse and skepticism regarding the idea of hypothesis-testing. He proposes that researchers should aim not at "explaining specific events" but "understanding their conditions" and meanings.

The third theoretical perspective on RFP is that of international power and security. Elena Kropatcheva reviews various approaches within realism by stressing the recently developed neoclassical school. In particular, she demonstrates how realists explain Russian/Soviet empire building, claims for status, and military interventions. In all cases, the analysis begins with pressures and opportunities presented by the international balance of power to which Russia reacts defensively or offensively depending on its leaders' perceptions and constrains. For instance, realists explain Soviet "over-extension" in Afghanistan by perceived American pressures. They make sense of Russia's opposition to Nato's expansion and conflict with Georgia in August 2008 in terms of the Kremlin's perception of threat to national security and search for great power status. Here, realists overlap with constructivists who have also studied RFP as a reflection of the country's status aspirations. However, for realists the stress is always on *relative* power and security, not on mutually empowering social relations. Thus, the key to understanding Russia's military interventions in the Caucasus and Ukraine is a global competition with the United States for power and security in the anarchical environment.

According to Kropatcheva, scholars of neoclassical conviction differ from structural realists by adding domestic variables and perceptions. For instance, they argue that Western military and institutional expansion toward Russia's borders must be understood not only in terms of the threats they present for Russia's security, but also in terms of Russia's state capacity, domestic vulnerability, and special relations with neighbors. In particular, the fear of "color revolutions" heightened Russia's sense of insecurity creating the internal security dilemma. Kropatcheva therefore argues that in terms of providing a more nuanced understanding, neoclassical approaches are superior to those of structural realism. She also finds neoclassical realism well-suited for RFP analysis given its ability to incorporate domestic factors and perceptions as stressed by liberal and constructivist scholars. Along with others, she advocates multiple methods of demonstrating Russia's (in)security and power capabilities.

The geopolitical perspective as stressed by John Berryman can be broadly housed within the realist tradition of analysis, yet is distinct in highlighting geographical and spatial considerations in RFP. The often abstract notion of the international system in realism is made specific in geopolitics, which analyzes Russia as a land-based empire with a constant challenge to protect borders and preserve access to water. Berryman combines traditional geopolitics associated with thinkers such as Halford Mackinder and Alfred Mahan with some insights from critical geopolitics, although he remains more firmly rooted in traditional geopolitical approaches. Critical geopolitics analyzes traditional geographic and spatial factors in the context of social and ideological forces and perceptions. Here, geopolitics comes full circle by becoming receptive to constructivist assumptions about inter-subjectivity and social structure of knowledge.

The overall geopolitical approach is better suited for explaining continuity rather than change in RFP. Berryman acknowledges that the approach that stresses the size, topography, and spatial and strategic location can "influence or condition but not determine" international choices. Other theories and factors must account for more nuanced explanations of Russia's choices. However, Berryman's approach contributes to a historically rich description of the rising Russian state and security predicaments. He is in agreement with realists that Russia's empire-building is a product of international environment, but in his account, Russian rulers responded to Western colonial and great power aspirations in the particular geographical settings, having met some earlier resistance from nomadic tribes and seeking to gain access to the Baltic Sea in the west, the Black Sea in the south, and the Pacific Ocean in the east. In the south, Russia faced a fierce competition from the British Empire by eventually colonizing the Caucasus and Central Asia. Berryman then applies the geopolitical competition approach to RFP during the nineteenth, twentieth, and twenty-first centuries, explaining the consistent preoccupation of the Russian rulers with borders and position in the "heartland" of Eurasia. He amplifies the realist analyses of Russia's interventions in Georgia and Ukraine by describing the pervasive sense of geopolitical insecurity in the Kremlin.

The systemic conditions therefore are limited in their power to explain RFP and must be supplemented by analysis of domestic factors and institutions. Constructivism and neoclassical realism in particular indicate that they are open to integration of domestic conditions within their framework, albeit on their own terms. Constructivism believes in the logic of a social interaction between international and domestic, whereas neoclassical realism recognizes the ability of domestic to interfere with the (ultimately decisive) impact of the international.

The remaining two chapters each stress various domestic conditions. Luke March analyzes the role that nationalism plays in Russia's international behavior. He defines nationalism as the congruence of the state and national and considers theories of nationalism that stress the defining role of the international system, national and historical values, and characteristics of political regime. The latter have gained prominence in Western academic and political circles among those who attribute Russia's annexation of Crimea and international assertiveness in Europe, the Middle East, and the cyber space to a diversionary tactic to boost Putin's popularity. March recognizes nationalism's utility for regime legitimacy but objects to over-simplifying links between domestic and foreign policy. Nationalism, he argues, is a complex, multi-layered ideology that incorporates various influences and may contain both negative and positive impulses. March develops a holistic model of nationalism that incorporates analysis of official beliefs, political considerations, and mainstream non-official discourses. In particular, he demonstrates how non-official "civilizational" nationalism developed before and after Russia's intervention in Georgia in August 2008. The civilization ideology indeed influenced the regime yet in a more limited way than some would expect.

March acknowledges that even his multi-layered approach to nationalism is not sufficiently nuanced to demonstrate causation and "the degree to which such nationalist ideas actually impact policy". He calls for further research of the actual role of nationalism on RFP and proposes multiple methods for studying various layers and the real impact of nationalist ideas. March alerts readers to practical and methodological difficulties of researching beliefs and ideas, yet suggests that such research – for instance, by process-tracing and interviews with policy-makers and experts with inside knowledge – is possible.

The final chapter by Yuval Weber reviews yet another prominent approach that stresses the role of energy and explains RFP by the ways in which the political regime exploits the country's available energy resources. Weber takes issue with the war chest theory that argues the connection between growing energy revenues and international assertiveness, including military intervention. He argues that the ultimate decisive influence in foreign policy results from leader's beliefs and internal politics, whereas the revenue environment merely adds to the menu of available policy choices. Weber shows how the politically weak Soviet leader Leonid Brezhnev lost the internal battle to military hawks and had to use oil revenue to fund expansionism in the developing countries, thereby derailing détente with the West. Alternatively, the politically strong Russian leader Putin used the oil "weapon" selectively. Against the expectations of the war chest theory, he did not challenge the West when oil prices were high, but he intervened in Ukraine and Syria long after energy prices had collapsed harming the Russian economy. By warning against the simplistic "oil makes Russia aggressive" arguments, Weber's petropolitics theory shows the complexity of relations between energy and political regime and calls for researching both the political and energy sides of RFP formation.

1
INTERNATIONAL NORMS AND IDENTITY

Valentina Feklyunina

NEWCASTLE UNIVERSITY, UK

The rise of social constructivism in International Relations (IR) theory has had a major impact on studies of Russian foreign policy (RFP). Although this may also be true of foreign policy studies related to other states, constructivist studies of Russian and Soviet foreign policies played a crucial role in the emergence of social constructivism as one of the mainstream approaches to studying international politics more broadly. It is sometimes suggested that the rise of social constructivism in IR was linked to the inability of other theoretical approaches at the time to predict or explain the largely peaceful end of the Cold War (Wohlforth, 1994). While the intellectual roots of social constructivism go back long before Moscow's largely unexpected withdrawal from the Cold War (Adler, 2013; Fierke and Jorgensen, 2015), this tectonic change certainly challenged the then dominant structural and rational choice explanations of the Soviet Union's international behaviour. As argued by Guzzini (2013: 196), 'what spurred the constructivist critique was . . . that prevailing theories did not even recognize the possibility that it would happen in the first place'. It is hardly surprising that during the first post-Soviet decade the theoretical development of social constructivism in IR and the study of Soviet and RFP were often closely linked (Neumann, 1996; Checkel, 1997; Hopf, 2002).

This chapter provides an overview of the existing constructivist work on RFP and discusses some of its most significant contributions to our understanding of Russia's international behaviour. Similar to constructivist studies in IR and Foreign Policy Analysis (FPA) more broadly, the constructivist work on RFP is remarkably diverse. It encompasses studies with fairly different epistemological and methodological positions, which focus on different aspects of Russia's foreign and security policies broadly defined, ranging from the role of ideas in policy change to Russia's engagement with cultural mega projects, such as the Sochi Olympics. Some studies explicitly articulate their constructivist positions, while others avoid attaching the label of 'constructivism' – and sometimes even explicitly differentiate their approach from constructivism – but nevertheless draw on the concepts which are central to the constructivist viewpoint. The diversity of constructivist work has led to numerous attempts to identify distinct constructivist approaches. Hopf (1998: 172), for example, differentiates between conventional and critical constructivisms, while Adler (2013: 115) singles out modernist, modernist linguistic, radical (which, in Adler's view, includes a poststructuralist approach) and critical constructivisms. While these labels remain contested, they point to the continuing epistemological debate. Yet, despite their differences, constructivists generally share several key assumptions. As formulated by Guzzini (2000: 174), 'constructivism is epistemologically about the social construction of knowledge and ontologically about the (social) construction of the social world'. Thus, constructivists understand the social world, i.e. the world of social relations, as 'a project under construction, as becoming rather than being' (Adler, 2013: 113). They also recognise that our understanding of this world can never grasp the world 'as it is', because our knowledge of the world is itself socially, i.e. intersubjectively, constructed.

When applied to the study of RFP, these assumptions translate into the focus on the construction of Russia's identity and its interests, and on Russia's understanding of the world and its place in it. Despite their differences, constructivist studies emphasise the importance of the historical context and the need to open up the black box of the Russian state. It is also important to note that constructivist studies of RFP often draw on insights from other theoretical approaches in IR or other cognate disciplines, for example, historical institutionalism (Checkel, 1997), postcolonialism (Morozov, 2015), social psychology (Clunan, 2009; Larson and Shevchenko, 2010) or cultural studies (Makarychev and Yatsyk, 2014). This chapter is structured in the following way. It begins by briefly discussing some of the key constructivist assumptions as compared to other theoretical approaches in IR, and by introducing key constructivist concepts. The second section presents an overview of several major strands within the existing constructivist work on RFP, by focusing on such themes as (i) Russia's identity; (ii) recognition and non-recognition of Russia's identity by Others; (iii) norms; and (iv) practices and habits. The third section looks at various methodological challenges as they are addressed in constructivist studies of RFP. The chapter concludes by discussing possible avenues for future research.

Key assumptions: what makes constructivism constructivist?

Having initially developed as a critique of rationalist approaches, IR constructivism has rapidly become one of the main approaches to studying international politics (Ruggie, 1998; Wendt, 1999; Guzzini, 2000; Adler, 2013). Although a very broad church, constructivism includes several key assumptions that are shared by most scholars subscribing to this research tradition. Compared to rationalist approaches, including neo-realism and neo-liberalism, constructivism emphasises a deeply social nature of international interactions. Unlike rationalist assumptions about the overriding importance of material structures, such as the distribution of material capabilities, constructivists argue that 'normative or ideational structures are as important as material structures' (Reus-Smit, 2013: 224). While not denying the significance of material factors, constructivists generally believe that these factors matter not on their own but through shared meanings that actors attach to them. To quote Wendt (1995: 73), 'material capabilities as such explain nothing; their effects presuppose structures of shared knowledge, which vary and which are not reducible to capabilities'. This emphasis on *shared* knowledge points to the notion of intersubjectivity as central to the constructivist approach. Unlike psychological approaches that focus on peculiarities of cognitive processes of individual decision-makers (McDermott, 2004), constructivists are concerned with the social rather than with the individual. They see individual decision-makers as being able to 'know, think, and feel only in the context of and with reference to collective or intersubjective understandings' (Adler, 2013: 121). Thus, most constructivist studies are concerned with intersubjective understandings of identities, interests, international norms or rules as they develop and change in particular cultural and historical contexts.

In addition to their emphasis on ideational structures, constructivists generally agree that agents and structures are co-constituted. While the existing structures shape actors' identities, actors reproduce and transform these structures through their practices (Reus-Smit, 2013: 225).

To illustrate this point about co-constitution, Wendt (1995: 74) uses an example of the Cold War which he describes as 'a structure of shared knowledge'. Although it shaped identities of both the Soviet Union and the United States and was reproduced by them for several decades, 'once they stopped acting on this basis, it was "over"'. Unlike rationalist approaches that treat states as strategic actors pursuing pre-existing interests and preferences in the international realm, constructivists see states and other agents as inherently social actors whose identities and interests are constituted in the process of interaction. Although constructivists vary in their conceptualisation of identity (see, for example, Wendt, 1999; Hopf, 2002), it is, in one way or another, central to most constructivist studies. Constructivists generally agree that our understandings of who we are shape our interpretations of our interests and thus inform our behaviour (Wendt, 1999). Most constructivists also understand identity as an inherently relational concept. In other words, a socially constructed understanding of 'who we are' implies an idea of an Other – often conceptualised as an external Other, for example Europe in the case of Russia's identity (Neumann, 1996). Some constructivists have also empathised the importance of recognition or non-recognition of actors' identities by their external Others in the processes of identity and interest construction (Ringmar, 2002). At the same time, others have questioned the inevitable need for external Others, and have suggested that othering can occur in relation to multiple Others – not only in relation to external or spatial others, but also in relation to temporal Others (for example, in relation to the Soviet Union in post-Soviet Russia) or even in relation to abstract ideas (Hopf, 2002; Abizadeh, 2005).

Seeing any intersubjective understandings of social reality as closely linked to the cultural and historical contexts in which they develop, constructivists are particularly concerned with how some understandings become dominant at any particular time. Yet, this general concern coexists with significant disagreements, among other things, on *whose* understandings matter, and on how competing understandings may be linked to the state's international behaviour. Wendt (1999: 197), for example, speaks of a *state* identity and argues that 'states are real actors to which we can legitimately attribute anthropomorphic qualities like desires, beliefs, and intentionality'. However, his state-as-a-person approach has been challenged by many other constructivists and especially by poststructuralists who have focused on the domestic contestation of meanings as they are articulated by political and intellectual elites, produced and reproduced in education and in popular culture, or practised in diplomatic interactions and in everyday life (Zehfuss, 2002; Guzzini and Leander, 2005; Hopf, 2013). Adler (2013: 112) is certainly right when he argues that compared to the earlier constructivist project, more recently a growing number of constructivist work 'has moved just a little closer to critical and linguistic constructivist approaches, without uncritically adopting their ontological and epistemological arguments'.

Constructivist studies of RFP

Compared to other approaches, social constructivism has provided scholars of RFP with a framework which is particularly well suited for exploring change and continuity in Russia's interests. By seeing Russia's interests as socially constructed and historically contingent, it has challenged those explanations of Russia's international behaviour that deduce Moscow's interests from the country's geopolitical position, its political system (with an authoritarian system almost automatically implying a more assertive or even aggressive international behaviour), or its material needs. Similar to IR constructivism more broadly, constructivist studies of RFP vary in their epistemological positions, with some studies coming closer towards the positivist end of the spectrum (Checkel, 1997) and some moving towards the post-positivist end and often explicitly engaging with the poststructuralist work (Snetkov, 2014; Morozov, 2015).

Yet, despite their differences, all of these works are concerned with an attempt to understand Russian interpretations of social reality. Needless to say, this chapter cannot cover all of the studies that have either implicitly or explicitly built on the constructivist tradition. Instead it examines some of the major themes in the rapidly growing constructivist literature while inevitably omitting many other significant contributions. These themes are: (i) Russia's identity; (ii) recognition and non-recognition of Russia's identity by Others; (iii) norms; and (iv) practices and habits.

Ideas, identities and RFP

As mentioned in the introduction to this chapter, constructivism to a large extent developed as a challenger of the then dominant rationalist and materialist explanations of international behaviour. During the first post-Soviet decade, the growing focus on ideas and identities was picked up by scholars who did not necessarily associate themselves at the time with the constructivist project, but nevertheless played a major role in its development. Jeffrey Checkel's study of the role of ideas in foreign policy change, for example, differentiates his 'institutional argument that allows for an exploration of the process through which new ideas are empowered' (Checkel, 1997: ix) from the emerging constructivist literature. Unlike the constructivist focus on shared meanings, Checkel focuses on ideas which he understands as 'beliefs held by individuals' (ibid.: 130). According to Checkel, news ideas may bring about a significant change in a state's foreign policy when they are successfully promoted by policy entrepreneurs who have sufficient access to relevant decision-makers during the windows of opportunity created by a major change in the international environment. Using the method of process tracing, Checkel examines ideas articulated by Soviet and Russian policy entrepreneurs during the détente of the late 1960-early 1970 period, during Gorbachev's *Perestroika* and, finally, in the early 1990s. The role of ideational factors in RFP is also explored in an influential study of identities and foreign policies in Russia, Ukraine and Poland by Prizel (1998). Although situated in the field of nationalism, Prizel's impressive investigation of the competing understandings of Russia, Ukraine and Poland has definitely paved the way for later constructivist studies.

With the development of IR constructivism, a growing number of RFP studies have focused on the processes of identity and interest construction, and examined competing interpretations of Russian identity vis-à-vis Russia's Others and their change over time. Scholars of RFP generally agree that all major frameworks or discourses of Russia's identity, despite significant differences in their understandings of the country's past, present and future, view Europe and the 'West' more broadly as a major reference point for interpreting Russia (Morozov, 2015; Tsygankov, 2016). As argued by Iver Neumann (1996: 1) in his agenda-setting study of othering in Russia's identity formation, 'the idea of Europe is the main "Other" in relation to which the idea of Russia is defined'. Scholars of RFP also generally agree that Russia's interpretations of its historically peripheral and undecided position in or vis-à-vis Europe on the one hand, and the recognition or non-recognition of Russia's European identity by Europe and the West more broadly on the other, have been exceptionally important in shaping understandings not only of Russia's international interests, but also of its domestic goals (Zevelev, 2002; Feklyunina, 2008; Tsygankov, 2012). Finally, they largely agree that Russia's interpretations of its inclusion in or exclusion from Europe have shaped its understandings of security threats, ranging from Russia's position towards terrorism (Snetkov, 2012, 2014) to its position towards NATO enlargement (Williams and Neumann, 2000; Pouliot, 2010).

At the same time, we can identify at least three key points that have structured the identity debate. First, while most constructivists agree that understandings of identity may change both in response to external and internal factors, their empirical analysis often privileges either the external or the internal dimension. Second, studies of Russian identity differ in *where* they locate the site of identity construction. While some look at Soviet or Russian official documents and statements (Light, 2003), or focus on elite debates (Clunan, 2009; Tsygankov, 2016), others emphasise the importance of popular understandings as they are articulated in popular fiction, mass media or textbooks (Hopf, 2002, 2013), or reflected in public opinion surveys and focus groups (White and Feklyunina, 2014). Finally, studies of Russian identity differ in their attention to material factors and in the ways in which they understand their role.

Seeing domestic identity contestation as crucial to understanding Russia's international behaviour, scholars of RFP have sought to identify competing identity frameworks, discourses or schools of thought, and to account for their change over time (Neumann, 1996; Hopf, 2002; Light, 2003; Clunan, 2009; White and Feklyunina, 2014; Tsygankov, 2016). For example, Neumann's genealogy of Russia's identity debate from the Decembrist uprising of 1825 to the early 1990s points at two major identity frameworks which he labels as Romantic Nationalist and Liberal positions. More recent constructivist studies have questioned the appropriateness of interpreting Russia's identity spectrum as split between two positions reminiscent of the 19th-century debate between westernisers and slavophiles. Tsygankov (2016), for instance, suggests that Russia's identity debate in the post-Soviet period has been dominated by three rather than two 'schools of foreign policy thinking' – Westernist, Statist and Civilisationist. Tsygankov links changes in their understandings of Russia's interests and in their relative prominence in the domestic debate to the changing nature and behaviour of the 'West' as Russia's Other. Using the idea of identity coalitions that emerge and dissolve in the changing context, Tsygankov (2016: 29) demonstrates how Russia's dominant understandings of its interests have transformed from Gorbachev's 'New Thinking' of the late 1980s, to the 'Integration with the West' of the early Yeltsin years, to the 'Assertiveness' of the late 2010s, and to the understanding of Russia's interests in 'Civilisation' terms during President Putin's third term in office.

The understanding of the 'West' as Russia's most significant Other, and the focus on the elite debate have been challenged in Ted Hopf's studies of the Soviet Union's and Russia's popular identities (2002, 2012). Rather than focusing on elites, Hopf (2002: 3) emphasises the importance of 'the routine, repetitive, habitual, customary, and everyday'. According to Hopf, policy-makers, like everyone else, are limited by the existing social cognitive frameworks in what they can imagine as possible in their interpretations of the Soviet Union's and Russia's interests and in their understandings of other international actors. Hopf's variant of what he describes as a 'societal constructivism' calls for uncovering these social cognitive structures by exploring the topography of popular identities. For Hopf, studies of identities should not take for granted the significance of external others, such as Europe or the 'West', but rather they should empirically investigate which Others – external, internal, historical or even abstract – are important for any particular identity at any particular time. Having traced the topography of Soviet popular identities in 1955, Hopf (2002: 105) singles out five primary identities – class, modernity, nation, difference (New Soviet Man) and great power – that formed the social cognitive structure in Moscow at that time. Each of these identities implied different interests in relation to other international actors. Hopf's investigation of the identity topography in 1999 arrives at four competing identity discourses – New Western Russian, New Soviet Russian, Liberal Essentialist and Liberal relativist (Hopf, 2002: 157). In his more recent study of the Soviet identities at the beginning of the Cold War, Hopf (2012) explores the transformation of the dominant identity discourse in Moscow during and after Stalin's rule. Hopf shows how an alternative identity discourse of difference, which had persisted in the Soviet society during the Stalin years, allowed a major change in the Soviet understanding of itself and of others after Stalin's death.

Other constructivist works have sought to capture changes in competing understandings of Russia's identities and corresponding interpretations of interests in Russian public opinion by using public opinion surveys or focus groups (White et al., 2010). In a comparative study of competing identities in Russia, Ukraine and Belarus over the post-Soviet years, White and Feklyunina (2014), for example, identify three competing identity discourses articulated by political and intellectual elites that envisage different understandings of Russia's position vis-à-vis Europe, which they describe as 'Russia as Europe', 'Russia as part of a Greater Europe' and 'Russia as an Alternative Europe'. Focusing on Moscow's relations with the European Union (EU), White and Feklyunina demonstrate that these identity discourses not only interpret the EU differently – as primarily a normative, an economic or a geopolitical actor – but they also arrive at strikingly different assessments of the EU's ability to overcome its present challenges. Having explored the transformation of these discourses over two post-Soviet decades, White and Feklyunina examine the trajectory of these three identity frameworks and associated policy preferences in Russian opinion surveys. As argued in the study (White and Feklyunina, 2014: 248), popular understandings of Russian identity are not only important in shaping the limits of what can be imagined or seen as legitimate, but also in asserting an indirect pressure on Russia's decision-makers who have 'to generate and maintain popular legitimacy'.

While all of the studies discussed earlier acknowledge the significance of material factors in identity construction, they mostly discuss them as important in having either a constraining or an enabling effect on RFP-making. This view is challenged by Morozov (2015: 78) who suggests that material factors, and particularly economic relations, are 'the single most important factor which is not given sufficient attention in the literature discussing Russia's undecidable position in relation to Europe and the West'. Drawing on the post-colonial and poststructuralist approaches in IR and engaging with the world-systems theory, Morozov (2015) argues that Russia's ambiguous position vis-à-vis Europe and the 'West' more broadly is produced by what he describes as its identity as a 'subaltern empire'. This identity, according to Morozov, stems from the legacy of Russia's imperial past and its dominant position in its immediate neighbourhood, on the one hand, and the legacy of Russia's historical economic and normative dependence on Europe, on the other. Thus, Russia's awareness of its backwardness and its persistent claims for a great power status are to a large extent a product of a particular pattern in Russia's economic development.

Recognition and non-recognition of Russia's identity

Morozov is certainly right in pointing out that 'most of the existing approaches converge in describing Russia's position in Europe as undecidable, liminal and/or peripheral' (Morozov, 2015: 41). This fundamental uncertainty of Russia's position and Moscow's attempts to secure the recognition of its identity by its significant Others, first and foremost by the 'West', are explored in a large constructivist literature on identity recognition in Russia's relations with other international actors, especially with Europe and the 'West' more broadly. The literature also explores the importance of status recognition, honour and respect in Russia's foreign policy and Moscow's attempts at image-projection, public diplomacy and exercise of soft power.

Probably the most well-developed theme in the constructivist literature is Russia's engagement with the idea of great power-ness and Russia's search for recognition as a great power both historically and in the post-Soviet period (Zevelev, 2002; Smith, 2014; Urnov, 2014). In a seminal article on Russia's quest for such recognition, Neumann (2008) argues that the persistent salience of the great power discourse in Russia since at least Peter the Great's rule indicates the historical importance of this idea for Russia's identity. Moreover, recurrent references to this idea both in Russia's official discourse and in the elite debate suggest that Russia's attempts to secure its recognition as a great power by the established great powers have not been successful. As explained by Neumann (2008: 129), 'if an identity claim is successful, it forms part of the horizon of the political debate rather than its substance'. Unlike realist understandings of great power politics as rooted in material capabilities, a constructivist understanding emphasises the socially constructed meanings that are attached to the idea of a great power at any historical period. As demonstrated by Neumann, Russia's great power claims have historically been undermined by a persistent mismatch between the models of governance in Russia and in the 'West'. Neumann's (2008: 148) conclusion about the importance of the 'liberal standard of civilization' in the dominant definition of a great power leads him to suggest that, given the ongoing domestic developments in Putin's Russia, 'Russia will not be counted as a fully-fledged great power for decades yet'. The importance of great power aspirations in Russia's foreign policy is also underscored in Clunan's study of 'the social construction of Russia's resurgence' (Clunan, 2009). As argued by Clunan (2009: 16), 'history and status far outweighed political purpose and practicality in determining Russia's post-Soviet identity'.

Constructivist studies have also emphasised the importance of recognition or non-recognition of Russia's desired identity by the 'West' not only for RFP, but also for the country's domestic politics by strengthening or undermining the relevant identity coalitions among the Russian political elite (Splidsboel-Hansen, 2002; Tsygankov, 2016). Looking at Russia's identity debate at the turn of the 20th century and during President Putin's first term in office, several studies examine Moscow's attempts to re-interpret the country's great-powerness as that of a 'normal' great power (Zevelev, 2002; Tsygankov, 2005). Yet, Russia's reconceptualisation of its 'normal' role has proved difficult, as Moscow has struggled to gain what it sees as an appropriate recognition of its status. The mismatch between Russia's understanding of Self and its recognition has been particularly acute in Moscow's relations with Washington. As explained by Zevelev (2002: 459), 'the post-Cold War US perception of self, and its vision of the world, did not allow for the kind of bilateral relationship for which Russia was striving'. The non-recognition of Russia's 'normality' has been seen by some constructivists as contributing to Russia's difficulty in overcoming the legacy of its autocratic past and making it significantly more difficult for Russian reform-minded elites to succeed (Splidsboel-Hansen, 2002: 417).

The problem of recognition and non-recognition of Russia's identity has also become central in the rapidly developing constructivist literature on status, honour and respect (see Forsberg et al., 2014). In several agenda-setting articles, Larson and Shevchenko (2003, 2010, 2014) demonstrate the importance of status considerations both in Soviet and Russian foreign policies. Drawing on insights from the Social Identity Theory (SIT) as it developed in Social Psychology, they differentiate their approach from the constructivist tradition. Yet, their focus on identity makes their work relevant to the constructivist literature. As argued by Larson and Shevchenko (2010: 68–72), state leaders as representatives of a state in the international arena strive to maintain a positive state identity compared to relevant out-groups (other states). When faced with a humiliating defeat or any other development that has a negative effect on their status (relative standing compared to other states) and self-esteem, the state leaders attempt to improve their self-esteem by resorting to one of the identity management strategies which Larson and Shevchenko describe as social mobility, social competition and social creativity. Their analysis of the Soviet Union's adoption of a dramatically more cooperative approach under Gorbachev, for example, suggests that Gorbachev's New Thinking was an example of the social creativity strategy – an attempt to reinterpret the Soviet Union's positive identity and status when the USSR struggled to maintain its status compared to the US with material means (Larson and Shevchenko, 2003). In a later study, Larson and Shevchenko's analysis of Russia's and China's identity management strategies points at the negative consequences of status non-recognition. Seeing the 2008 Russian war with Georgia as stemming from Russia's 'sense of injury', Larson and Shevchenko (2010: 95) warn that 'the United States must learn how to treat China and Russia in ways other than as rivals or junior partners if it is to obtain their cooperation'.

Tsygankov's analysis of Russia's understandings of honour and their impact on RFP reaches similar conclusions (Tsygankov and Tarver-Wahlquist, 2009; Tsygankov, 2012). While sharing with Larson and Shevchenko the starting point that state leaders and political elites experience a psychological need to maintain positive self-esteem, Tsygankov (2012: 4) shifts the focus of attention from status to the idea of honour – a socially constructed understanding of 'what is a "good" and "virtuous" course of action' that has developed in Russia over centuries. According to Tsygankov, Russia's attempts to act according to its sense of honour have often been misinterpreted by the 'West', with the 2008 Russian-Georgian war being one of the latest examples of such misinterpretation. Emphasising the importance of recognition of Russia's identity, Tsygankov's study explains major shifts in RFP – from cooperation to a defensive reaction to assertiveness – by the varying extent to which Western nations as Russia's significant Other recognised or rejected Russia's understandings of honour and its interests stemming from those understandings. Based on a wide range of historical case-studies – from Russia's participation in the Holy Alliance that emerged in the post-Napoleon Europe to the 2008 Russo-Georgian war – Tsygankov's analysis suggests that Western recognition was a crucial factor in encouraging Moscow's cooperative approach. Thus, as argued by Tsygankov (2012: 7), the 'ability [of Western nations] to engage Moscow will only be successful when they acknowledge Russia's distinctive values, interests, and right to develop in accordance with its internal perception of honor'.

The impact of status considerations and of the psychological need for respect on RFP is further explored in a 2014 special issue in *Communist and Post-Communist Studies* edited by Heller, Forsberg and Wolf (see Forsberg et al., 2014), which takes stock of the existing status-related literature and seeks to develop a more coherent research programme. While generally agreeing on the psychological importance of status aspirations and associated grievances for Russian political elites and foreign policy decision-makers, these studies nevertheless disagree on the significance and implications of Western recognition or non-recognition of Russia's status. Forsberg's analysis of Russia's status grievances, for example, points at 'a gap of how Russia and the West perceive Russian status and in particular Western acts in honouring or ignoring it' (Forsberg, 2014: 329). The example of Russia's involvement in the crisis in and around Ukraine is particularly illustrative of this gap.

In addition to the rapidly expanding literature on status, the questions of recognition and non-recognition of Russia's identity have become central to the constructivist studies of Russia's image projection and Moscow's engagement with and exercise of soft power. These studies argue that Russia's instrumental efforts to transform its international image, and particularly its image in the 'West', can be explained not only by rational concerns with the investment climate or geopolitical considerations, but also by a need to secure a recognition of Russia's identity (Kassianova, 2001; Makarychev and Yatsyk, 2014; Kiseleva, 2015). A constructivist reading of Russia's image-projection has been particularly important in accounting for Russia's seemingly contradictory approach to public diplomacy and the idea of soft power (Feklyunina, 2012, 2016; Kiseleva, 2015). Competing understandings of Russia's identity often produce fairly different visions of what image Russia should project in the international arena and how it should engage in image-projection. While some of Russia's efforts have sought to project an image of a reliable partner, others have increasingly prioritised the image of a strong state and a great power at the expense of the idea of reliability.

Norms and RFP

The rise of social constructivism in IR has also spurred a growing literature on Russia's engagement with international norms, often understood as 'a standard of appropriate behaviour for actors with a given identity' (Finnemore and Sikkink, 1998: 891). While in the early 1990s Russia appeared to accept the dominant international norms, the subsequent growing rift between Moscow and the 'West' has led to a debate on Russia's normative understandings and their impact on its behaviour. As argued by Makarychev (2008: 30), 'Putin is not only eager to get involved in the global normative debate, but tries to use this debate to reassert Russia's leadership'. Constructivist studies have been particularly important in highlighting Russia's engagement with the norm of sovereignty and in analysing Russia's responses to the ideas of humanitarian intervention and the Responsibility to Protect (Snetkov and Lanteigne, 2015; Deyermond, 2016). Focusing on the idea of 'sovereign democracy' as it was articulated in Russia's dominant discourse in the mid-2000s, Ziegler (2012) highlights a significant clash between Russian and Western interpretations of the link between sovereignty and democracy. Russia's socially constructed understandings of sovereignty are further explored by Ruth Deyermond (2016), who demonstrates that these understandings vary depending on *whose* sovereignty it is. While Russia explicitly defends a traditional Westphalian understanding of sovereignty in relation to itself and states outside of its immediate neighbourhood, Russia's interpretation of sovereignty in relation to states of the former Soviet Union is radically different. As argued by Deyermond (2016: 982), in the post-Soviet area Moscow interprets sovereignty 'as porous in relation to Russia while remaining impermeable in relation to states outside the region'.

Constructivist studies have also discussed the implications of Russia's distinctive normative understandings for its relations with other international actors. When speaking of Russia's relationship with the EU, Makarychev (2014), for example, concludes that both actors hold 'different visions and models of international society'. Russia's apparent normative challenge to the 'West' has also raised urgent questions about any convergence between Russia's normative understandings and those of any other major non-Western powers, particularly China. While on the surface Russia's and China's approaches to sovereignty and humanitarian intervention appear to share some common ground, recent constructivist studies suggest a growing difference in Moscow's and Beijing's understandings. Looking at Russia's and China's reactions to the conflicts in Libya and Syria, Snetkov and Lanteigne (2015: 114), for instance, demonstrate that while Moscow resorts to vocal criticism of Western approaches to humanitarian intervention, Beijing refrains from explicitly opposing the dominant understandings.

Practices, common sense and RFP

Following a 'practice turn' in IR constructivism, several recent studies have made a major contribution to our understanding of what Vincent Pouliot (2010) has identified as 'the logic of practicality' in Russian foreign and security policies. In his agenda-setting monograph on NATO–Russia diplomacy in the post-Soviet period, Pouliot draws on Bourdieu to explore the role of practices in the development of security communities. Unlike the constructivist work discussed in this chapter earlier – that starts from the premise that our interests and, thus, our behaviour are shaped by our understandings of our identity – Pouliot (2010: 5) suggests that 'practices also shape the world and its meaning'. Pouliot's study examines routine diplomatic interactions between Russian and NATO representatives in the NATO–Russia Council, and seeks to recover their taken-for-granted understandings that are 'embodied' through these practices. Pouliot's analysis points at a significant gap between the taken-for-granted background understandings of Russian security practitioners about Russia's position in the world and their diplomatic practices on the one hand, and taken-for-granted understandings of NATO practitioners on the other. As argued by Pouliot (2010: 2), 'pervasive Great Power dispositions lead [Russian] security practitioners to construe their country's position as much higher in the international security hierarchy than other players in the field, especially NATO are inclined to recognize'.

In a more recent study, Neumann and Pouliot (2011) apply the practice-focused analytical framework to account for persistent symbolic struggles in Russia's relations with the 'West' which, as they argue, have characterised Moscow's engagement with its Western neighbours over the past millennium. Looking at several historical epochs – from Kievan Rus' to medieval Muskovy to the Soviet Union's and Russia's relationship with the 'West' in the 20th century – Neumann and Pouliot (2011: 106) emphasise the importance of what they refer to as Russia's 'untimely diplomatic practices'. Their argument centres on the idea of 'hysteresis' – 'a mismatch between the dispositions agents embody and the positions they occupy in a given social configuration' (Neumann and Pouliot, 2011: 109). By applying the *longue durée* approach, Neumann and Pouliot are able to demonstrate the nuanced ways in which Russia's current dispositions are shaped by its past experiences.

The focus on taken-for-granted understandings is also central to Hopf's theory of 'commonsense constructivism' which he applies to the analysis of Russia's response to the neo-liberal project in the post-Soviet period. Drawing on Gramsci's understanding of hegemony and differentiating his approach from the practice-oriented constructivism discussed earlier, Hopf (2013) calls for more attention to the common sense understandings of the masses as opposed to an exclusive focus on interpretations articulated by political elites which persist in many constructivist works. As argued by Hopf (2013: 317), 'if political elites do not take into account the taken-for-granted world of the masses, elite ideological projects would likely founder against daily practices of resistance'. Hopf's empirical analysis demonstrates a significant gap between the neo-liberal ideas adopted by Russian elites after the Soviet Union's collapse, and the common sense understandings of ordinary Russians, with the latter constituting a major challenge to the elite project on a daily basis.

Methodological considerations

As demonstrated in this brief overview of several major strands in the existing constructivist scholarship, these studies have made fairly different methodological choices. It is worth noting that the earlier constructivist literature was often criticised both by the opponents of the constructivist approach and by its 'critical friends' for its insufficient attention to methodological concerns and to empirical research (see Zehfuss, 2002). More recently, however, constructivists have made some significant contributions to the discussion of methodology and method (Klotz and Lynch, 2007; Pouliot, 2007, 2010; Lupovici, 2009; Fierke and Jorgensen, 2015). As a broad church, constructivist scholarship has relied on a variety of research methods and has utilised different types of evidence, ranging from popular fiction to statistical data. These choices, however, should be seen within a broader methodological context. While methods are usually understood as distinct 'techniques for gathering and analysing bits of data' (Jackson, 2010: 25), a methodology is a set of fundamental ontological and epistemological assumptions that prescribe how we can conduct an enquiry. To quote Pouliot (2007: 360), it 'formulates its own scientific standards and truth conditions'. Thus, the choice of methods and evidence can never be arbitrary, but should be always consistent with broader methodological commitments. If we go back to the previous section of the chapter, we will see that some constructivist studies of Russian identity(s), for example, used discourse analysis of official documents. Others, on the other hand, used historical evidence to reconstruct the practices that constituted Russian identity(s) over time. While sharing the basic assumption about the constructed and intersubjective nature of social reality, these studies proceed from fairly different conceptualisations of identity, from different views on the role of agents in the processes of social construction and from different epistemological positions. It is hardly surprising that as a result they chose different methods and types of evidence.

We can, for example, notice distinct approaches to the understanding of causality and the appropriateness of hypothesis testing. Those studies located towards the positivist end of the constructivist spectrum often ask 'why' questions, seek to uncover causal mechanisms and adopt the language of variables and hypothesis testing (Checkel, 1997, 2006; Lupovici, 2009). Studies located towards the post-positivist end of the spectrum tend to ask 'how possible' questions, speak about co-constitution rather than causality and see hypothesis testing as inappropriate. While these differences stem from distinct epistemological positions, they do not, however, constitute a rigid dividing line. As argued by Klotz and Lynch (2007: 15), the apparent difference between 'why' and 'how possible' questions in empirical research should not be taken for granted, and we should not 'preclude the possibility of causal answers to constitutive questions, or vice versa'. Thus, instead of uncritically adopting or rejecting the language of hypothesis testing, we need to ensure that if we do use hypothesis testing, our practices are consistent with our broader ontological and epistemological commitments. To illustrate this point, we can consider Hopf's use of hypotheses in his work on Soviet and Russian identities in 1955 and 1999, where 'hypotheses derived from domestic identities and their discourses are evaluated against the empirical record of Soviet and Russian understandings of external Others' (Hopf, 2002: 28).

Taking into account the diversity of constructivist approaches discussed earlier, what is distinctive about constructivist methodologies as compared to other research traditions? Since all constructivists agree that both social reality and our knowledge of social reality are socially constructed, all constructivist studies in one way or another are concerned with analysing the meanings actors attach to the world. To capture these subjective meanings, as suggested by Pouliot (2007: 359), 'a constructivist methodology should be inductive, interpretive, and historical'. Pouliot's emphasis on induction is consistent with the constructivist assumption that our understandings of ourselves and of the world are neither pre-given nor fixed, and are always in the process of re-interpretation. If we want to recover the meanings as they are understood by the actors – albeit constructivists acknowledge the limits of such recovery – we need to avoid as much as we can any imposition of our own understandings. As advocated by Hopf (2002: 9, 25), 'the researcher . . . must try to resist the categorization of meaning for as long as practicable' and 'to avoid pretheorization'. Although constructivist studies vary in the extent to which they follow Hopf's call to avoid pretheorisation (and one can argue that avoiding it completely is hardly possible), constructivists certainly treat induction more seriously than positivists.

Having inductively recovered subjective interpretations of social reality, constructivist studies must make a further step in order to interpret them. Pouliot (2007: 359) envisages this research process as proceeding from subjective knowledge to objectified knowledge through 'contextualization and historicization' – a set of steps that Pouliot refers to as a 'sobjectivist' methodology. By contextualising the inductively recovered subjective meanings, constructivist studies locate these understandings in relation to others in a particular cultural context. For instance, Hopf's analysis of popular identities in Moscow in 1955 and 1999 includes 'contextualizing the meanings of identities within texts and relating them intertextually to the vast variety of other texts for that year' (Hopf, 2002: 24). Finally, by historicising the contextualised meanings, constructivist studies locate them in a larger historical context, which allows them to trace how particular understandings of social reality become possible in particular historical circumstances. Some constructivist research projects, such as Morozov's study of Russia's identity as a 'subaltern empire', or Neumann's and Pouliot's study of the hysteresis in Russia's relations with the 'West' adopt a *longue durée* approach, which allows them to trace the transformation, as well as continuity in dominant meanings and practices in changing historical circumstances over a long period of time (Neumann and Pouliot, 2011; Morozov, 2015). Others adopt a shorter timeframe and explore contested meanings in a particular historical period, such as the early years of the Cold War or the post-Soviet period (Hopf, 2012; White and Feklyunina, 2014; Tsygankov, 2016). Yet others focus on one or several in-depth case studies, while locating them in a broader historical context, such as Forsberg's study of Gorbachev's policy towards Japan and Germany in the final years of the Cold War, or Heller's analysis of Russia's reaction to the NATO campaign in Kosovo in 1999 (Forsberg, 1999; Tsygankov, 2012; Heller, 2014; Smith, 2014).

Constructivist studies of RFP use a variety of research methods. However, they all share a primary concern with recovering subjective understandings of social reality, which generally leads them to employ interpretive methods. Some scholars, especially those who empathise the role of language in the processes of social construction, often resort to discourse or narrative analysis (e.g. Neumann, 1996; Hopf, 2002, 2010). As argued by Klotz and Lynch (2007: 19), discourse analysis is particularly well-suited for constructivist studies due to its ability to 'capture the creation of meanings and accompanying processes of communication'. Scholars of RFP have used a variety of approaches that fall under the umbrella of discourse analysis (see Milliken, 1999). Some studies have engaged with the poststructuralist discourse tradition by drawing on the variant of discourse analysis as developed, for example, by Hansen (2006) while maintaining their constructivist ontological commitments (White and Feklyunina, 2014). Others, such as Morozov's study of 'othering' in Russia's identity construction, explicitly identify with the poststructuralist tradition (Morozov, 2009). Studies adopting a *longue durée* approach have drawn on Foucault and employed the method of genealogy which allows them to trace the development of particular understandings over time, such as Neumann's investigation of Russia's identity discourses over several centuries (Neumann, 1996).

While scholars of RFP vary in their application of discourse analysis, the focus on discourses generally tends to emphasise the role of social structures in shaping or producing particular understandings of Russia's identity and interests, and to underplay the role of actors in transforming these structures. Other studies have attached more significance to agency by focusing on narratives articulated by political actors, including different groups among the Russian elite, Russian leaders, diplomats or public diplomacy practitioners (Clunan, 2009, 2014; Larson and Shevchenko, 2010; Leichtova, 2014; Tsygankov, 2016). For example, Feklyunina (2016) in her study of Russia's soft power vis-à-vis Ukraine, analyses narratives of the 'Russian World' as they were articulated by President Putin, Patriarch Kirill and Russian public diplomacy practitioners in the run-up to the 'Ukrainian' crisis. Having established the key elements of these narratives, she proceeds to explore the extent to which these narratives were accepted or rejected in competing identity discourses in Ukraine. By focusing on narratives, constructivist studies of RFP explore the role of agents in promoting particular understandings of social reality, including their interpretations of Russia's identity and interests, while acknowledging that these understandings are themselves shaped by dominant discourses. The focus on actors is even more pronounced in studies adopting the method of process tracing, such as Checkel's investigation of the role of ideas – as they were promoted by policy entrepreneurs and accepted or rejected by Soviet and Russian leaders – in the Soviet Union's and Russia's foreign policy change (Checkel, 1997).

Another method often employed in constructivist studies of RFP is semi-structured interviewing. As demonstrated in Pouliot's study of diplomatic practices in Russia's relations with

NATO (Pouliot, 2010), interviews can be particularly helpful in recovering subjective meanings of research participants when the researcher cannot rely on textual evidence or observe diplomatic practices through participant observation. In Pouliot's study, participant observation of the working meetings at the NATO-Russia Permanent Council would clearly have been more desirable than any other method. However, since the researcher could not get access to such meetings, interviews with diplomats and security experts provide an alternative strategy to recover the taken-for-granted understandings of both Russian and NATO security practitioners. Similarly to discourse and narrative analysis of textual evidence, interviews allow the researcher to gain an insight into the participants' understandings of social reality through their own voices, which is especially important for constructivist studies. When analysing popular identities and interpretations of social reality, constructivist studies have resorted not only to discourse analysis of popular texts, such as popular fiction, textbooks or mass media publications (Hopf, 2002, 2012), but also to focus groups and public opinion surveys. For example, in their comparative study of identities in Russia, Ukraine and Belarus, White and Feklyunina (2014) use focus groups to recover popular understandings of identity through the voices of participants, while using opinion surveys to establish the distributions of particular identity frameworks across the populations in individual countries and to trace their change over time.

While the methods discussed are particularly useful in recovering subjective understandings, other methods, such as macro-historical comparisons, counterfactuals or even statistical analysis, can be equally important when researchers attempt to locate these understandings in relevant cultural and historical contexts. For instance, Morozov's investigation of the patterns of Russia's economic relations with European states over several centuries is crucial in developing his argument about Russia's economic dependence on Europe and its subaltern position (Morozov, 2015). To reiterate the point made earlier in this chapter, adopting a constructivist methodology does not imply that we are limited to some specific 'constructivist' methods. Rather we can use any method as long as its application is consistent with our ontological and epistemological assumptions, and as long as it allows us to answer our research questions.

Similar to any other theoretical approach, social constructivist studies of RFP encounter a number of methodological challengers. One of the major challenges is selection of sources, whether it is about the selection of textual evidence in studies employing discourse or narrative analysis, or the selection of research participants in projects employing interviewing. Another major challenge is to do with the categorisation and interpretation of meanings in the selected texts, interview transcripts or observation notes. As argued by Hopf (2002: 25), 'for a work on identity, it is absolutely imperative that meanings remain what they mean and do not become what the researcher needs to test a hypothesis'. Hopf's warning about the danger of imposing rigid categories or our own subjective meanings on the data is important for any constructivist project. This danger is particularly evident not only when selecting or coding the data, but also when posing questions during semi-structured interviews or focus groups, or developing questionnaires for public opinion polls. At the same time, constructivists generally recognise that researchers always bring their own understandings of reality and their normative commitments into their study. Indeed, even the topics that we are interested in and the research questions that we pose, are shaped by these understandings and commitments. This recognition stems from the basic constructivist assumption that knowledge is socially constructed rather than an unproblematic reflection of an independently existing social reality. To address this major methodological challenge, constructivist studies tend to be noticeably more self-reflexive about their methodological choices compared to positivist approaches. They also tend to be more modest about their validity claims. For example, Hopf (2002: 24) speaks of 'claims to validity that I expect to be true only in relation to other interpretive claims, not to some objective reality'. Depending on their position on the constructivist spectrum, constructivists also tend to be very cautious about generalisations (Klotz and Lynch, 2007: 20). Once can agree with Hopf (2002: 31), however, that while empirical generalisations are often problematic due to constructivism's emphasis on the importance of cultural and historical contexts, constructivist studies can still make important theoretical generalisations.

Conclusions

As we have seen throughout this chapter, constructivist studies of RFP have made an invaluable contribution to our understanding of the sources of Russia's international behaviour. They have challenged explanations based on peculiarities of Russia's domestic political system, and they have convincingly argued against interpreting Moscow's behaviour as stemming from a geographically or geopolitically determined expansionist drive. By focusing on contested and evolving understandings of Russia, of its interests, of its place in the world and of its normative commitments, constructivist studies have argued against seeing Russia's interests as fixed or inherently anti-Western. At the same time, by focusing on the constitutive nature of Russia's interactions with its Others, first and foremost with Europe and the 'West' more broadly, they have called on 'Western' decision-makers to adopt a more reflexive approach towards Moscow.

To take the constructivist project forward, scholars of RFP can follow a variety of paths. Yet, three of them appear particularly promising. First, constructivist studies of RFP would benefit from more explicit and more consistent engagement with ethics. Following the constructivist logic, studies of the social construction of reality contribute to the production of this reality. Thus, studies of competing identity discourses in Russia, for example, can contribute to the reification of these discourses. To quote Guzzini (2013: 219), 'categories we use for classifying/naming people interact with the self-conception of those people'. While we cannot avoid this, we should be more reflexive about our own role in the construction of social reality. A critical engagement with the poststructuralist tradition can be particularly helpful in addressing this challenge (Dauphinée, 2007). Another ethical challenge stems from the constructivist attempt to see the world through Russia's eyes. Although this is arguably one of constructivism's main contributions to our understanding of Russia's behaviour, it also opens up the possibility that our attempt to understand Russia's views may intentionally or unintentionally turn into an apology of Moscow's international behaviour. As suggested by Morozov (2015: 4) in his discussion of Russia's attempt to position itself as representing the subaltern and challenging the hegemonic 'West' on its behalf, 'a voice claiming to speak in the name of the subaltern must not be endowed with unquestionable moral authority'. To address this challenge, constructivists could be more explicit about their normative commitments.

Second, constructivist studies of RFP could build on the existing research to develop a better understanding of popular identities, their relationship with elite identities and their role in Russia's foreign policy-making. With the rapid rise in the number of Internet users across Russia since the mid-2000s, constructivist studies of RFP could do more to explore the role of social media as sites of identity and interest construction – a research area that has produced a growing number of studies in the geopolitical research tradition (Suslov, 2014; Suslov and Bassin, 2016). Another research area that could benefit from more attention in constructivist scholarship is the role of material factors in Russia's identity construction and contestation. Studies of RFP could, for example, focus more explicitly on the role of material factors in the construction of Russia's status aspirations and Russia's status management strategies, or in Russia's engagement with the idea of soft power.

Finally, constructivist studies could enrich our understanding of RFP by experimenting with research design and methods. A larger number of comparative constructivist studies could, for example, explore peculiarities of Russia's engagement with the idea of great powerness as compared to China, Great Britain or the US, or investigate the differences and commonalities in Russia's and other states' responses to perceived humiliation. Experiments with research methods could, for example, include ethnographic research which has recently become increasingly prominent in IR studies more generally (see MacKay and Levin, 2015). Another promising direction is experimenting with a mixed-method approach. While scholars of RFP do employ qualitative and quantitative methods together, these methods often remain distinct in covering different sub-questions of the larger project. One possible way to benefit from both qualitative and quantitative insights in a more coherent and systematic manner is through applying Q-methodology (see Aalto, 2003). Although rarely used in IR studies, Q-methodology can be helpful in establishing relationships between different meanings, and can assist scholars of RFP in tracing distinct frameworks of understanding Russian identity and interests. These suggestions are only a few of the numerous ways in which social constructivism can enrich our understanding of Russia and RFP.

References

Aalto, P. (2003) 'Revisiting the security/identity puzzle in Russo-Estonian relations', *Journal of Peace Research*, 40(5), 573–591.
Abizadeh, A. (2005) 'Does collective identity presuppose an other? On the alleged incoherence of global solidarity', *American Political Science Review*, 99(01), 45–60.
Adler, E. (2013) 'Constructivism in international relations: Sources, contributions, and debates', in W. Carlsnaes, T. Risse-Kappen and B. A. Simmons (eds) *Handbook of International Relations*, 2nd ed., 112–144 (Thousand Oaks, CA: Sage).
Checkel, J. T. (1997) *Ideas and International Political Change: Soviet/Russian Behavior and the End of the Cold War* (New Haven, CT: Yale University Press).
Checkel, J. T. (2006) 'Tracing causal mechanisms', *International Studies Review*, 8(2), 362–370.
Clunan, A. L. (2009) *The Social Construction of Russia's Resurgence: Aspirations, Identity, and Security Interests* (Baltimore, MD: John Hopkins University Press).
Clunan, A. L. (2014) 'Historical aspirations and the domestic politics of Russia's pursuit of international status', *Communist and Post-Communist Studies*, 47(3), 281–290.
Dauphinée, E. (2007) *The Ethics of Researching War: Looking for Bosnia* (Manchester, UK: Manchester University Press).
Deyermond, R. (2016) 'The uses of sovereignty in twenty first century Russian foreign policy', *Europe-Asia Studies*, 68(6), 957–984.
Feklyunina, V. (2008) 'Battle for perceptions: Projecting Russia in the West', *Europe-Asia Studies*, 60(4), 605–629.
Feklyunina, V. (2012) 'Russia's foreign policy towards Poland: Seeking reconciliation? A social constructivist analysis', *International Politics*, 49(4), 434–448.
Feklyunina, V. (2016) 'Soft power and identity: Russia, Ukraine and the Russian world(s)', *European Journal of International Relations*, 22(4), 773–796.
Fierke, K. M. and Jorgensen, K. E. (2015) 'Introduction', in K. M. Fierke and K. E. Jorgensen (eds) *Constructing International Relations: The Next Generation*, pp. 3–10 (London and New York: Routledge).
Finnemore, M. and Sikkink, K. (1998) 'International norm dynamics and political change', *International Organization*, 52(4), 887–917.
Forsberg, T. (1999) 'Power, interests and trust: Explaining Gorbachev's choices at the end of the Cold War', *Review of International Studies*, 25(4), 603–621.
Forsberg, T. (2014) 'Status conflicts between Russia and the West: Perceptions and emotional biases', *Communist and Post-Communist Studies*, 47(3), 323–331.
Forsberg, T., Heller, R. and Wolf, R. (2014) 'Status and emotions in Russian foreign policy', *Communist and Post-Communist Studies*, 47(3), 261–268.
Guzzini, S. (2000) 'A reconstruction of constructivism in international relations', *European Journal of International Relations*, 6(2), 147–182.
Guzzini, S. (2013) *Power, Realism and Constructivism* (London and New York: Routledge).

Guzzini, S. and Leander, A. (eds) (2005) *Constructivism and International Relations: Alexander Wendt and His Critics* (London and New York: Routledge).

Hansen, L. (2006) *Security as Practice: Discourse Analysis and the Bosnian War* (London and New York: Routledge).

Heller, R. (2014) 'Russia's quest for respect in the international conflict management in Kosovo', *Communist and Post-Communist Studies*, 47(3): 333–343.

Hopf, T. (1998) 'The promise of constructivism in international relations theory', *International Security*, 23(1), 171–200.

Hopf, T. (2002) *Social Construction of International Politics: Identities and Foreign Policies, Moscow, 1955 and 1999* (Ithaca, NY: Cornell University Press).

Hopf, T. (2012) *Reconstructing the Cold War: The Early Years, 1945–1958* (Oxford, UK: Oxford University Press).

Hopf, T. (2013) 'Common-sense constructivism and hegemony in world politics', *International Organization*, 67(02), 317–354.

Jackson, P. T. (2010) *The Conduct of Inquiry in International Relations: Philosophy of Science and its Implications for the Study of World Politics*. (London and New York: Routledge).

Kassianova, A. (2001) 'Russia: Still open to the West? Evolution of the state identity in the foreign policy and security discourse', *Europe-Asia Studies*, 53(6), 821–839.

Kiseleva, Y. (2015) 'Russia's soft power discourse: Identity, status and the attraction of power', *Politics*, 35(3–4), 316–329.

Klotz, A. and Lynch, C. (2007) *Strategies for Research in Constructivist International Relations* (New York: ME Sharpe).

Larson, D. W. and Shevchenko, A. (2003) 'Shortcut to greatness: The new thinking and the revolution in Soviet foreign policy', *International Organization*, 57(1), 77–109.

Larson, D. W. and Shevchenko, A. (2010) 'Status seekers: Chinese and Russian responses to US primacy', *International Security*, 34(4), 63–95.

Larson, D. W. and Shevchenko, A. (2014) 'Russia says no: Power, status, and emotions in foreign policy', *Communist and Post-Communist Studies*, 47(3), 269–279.

Leichtova, M. (2014) *Misunderstanding Russia: Russian Foreign Policy and the West* (Farnham, UK: Ashgate).

Light, M. (2003) 'In search of an identity: Russian foreign policy and the end of ideology', *Journal of Communist Studies and Transition Politics*, 19(3), 42–59.

Lupovici, A. (2009) 'Constructivist methods: A plea and manifesto for pluralism', *Review of international studies*, 35(1), 195–218.

MacKay, J. and Levin, J. (2015) 'Hanging out in international politics: Two kinds of explanatory political ethnography for IR', *International Studies Review*, 17(2), 163–188.

Makarychev, A. S. (2008) 'Rebranding Russia: Norms, politics and power', *CEPS Working Document No. 283* (Brussels: Centre for European Policy Studies).

Makarychev, A. S. (2014) *Russia and the EU in a Multipolar World: Discourses, Identities, Norms* (Stuttgart, Germany: Ibidem Press).

Makarychev, A. S. and Yatsyk, A. (2014) 'The four pillars of Russia's power narrative', *The International Spectator*, 49(4), 62–75.

McDermott, R. (2004) *Political Psychology in International Relations* (Ann Arbor, MI: University of Michigan Press).

Milliken, J. (1999) 'The study of discourse in international relations: A critique of research and methods', *European Journal of International Relations*, 5(2), 225–254.

Morozov, V. (2009) *Rossiya i Drugie: identichnost' i granitsy politicheskogo soobshchestva* (Moscow: Literaturnoe obozrenie).

Morozov, V. (2015) *Russia's Postcolonial Identity: A Subaltern Empire in a Eurocentric World* (Basingstoke, UK: Palgrave Macmillan).

Neumann, I. B. (1996) *Russia and the Idea of Europe: A Study in Identity and International Relations* (London and New York: Routledge).

Neumann, I. B. (2008) 'Russia as a great power, 1815–2007', *Journal of International Relations and Development*, 11(2), 128–151.

Neumann, I. B. and Pouliot, V. (2011) 'Untimely Russia: Hysteresis in Russian-Western relations over the past millennium', *Security Studies*, 20(1), 105–137.

Pouliot, V. (2007) '"Sobjectivism": Toward a constructivist methodology', *International Studies Quarterly*, 51(2), 359–384.

Pouliot, V. (2010) *International Security in Practice: The Politics of NATO-Russia Diplomacy* (Cambridge, UK: Cambridge University Press).

Prizel, I. (1998) *National Identity and Foreign Policy: Nationalism and Leadership in Poland, Russia and Ukraine* (Cambridge, UK: Cambridge University Press).

Reus-Smit, C. (2013) 'Constructivism', in S. Burchill, A. Linklater, R. Devetak, J. Donnelly, T. Nardin, M. Paterson, C. Reus-Smit and J. True (eds) *Theories of International Relations*, 5th ed. (Basingstoke, UK: Palgrave Macmillan).

Ringmar, E. (2002) 'The recognition game: Soviet Russia against the West', *Cooperation and Conflict*, 37(2), 115–136.

Ruggie, J. G. (1998) 'What makes the world hang together? Neo-utilitarianism and the social constructivist challenge', *International Organization*, 52(4), 855–885.

Smith, H. (2014) 'Russia as a great power: Status inconsistency and the two Chechen wars', *Communist and Post-Communist Studies*, 47(3), 355–363.

Snetkov, A. (2012) 'When the internal and external collide: A social constructivist reading of Russia's security policy', *Europe-Asia Studies*, 64(3), 521–542.

Snetkov, A. (2014) *Russia's Security Policy Under Putin: A Critical Perspective* (London and New York: Routledge).

Snetkov, A. and Lanteigne, M. (2015) '"The loud dissenter and its cautious partner": Russia, China, global governance and humanitarian intervention', *International Relations of the Asia-Pacific*, 15(1), 113–146.

Splidsboel-Hansen, F. (2002) 'Russia's relations with the European Union: A constructivist cut', *International Politics*, 39(4), 399–421.

Suslov, M. D. (2014) '"Crimea Is Ours!" Russian popular geopolitics in the new media age', *Eurasian Geography and Economics*, 55(6), 588–609.

Suslov, M. D. and Bassin, M. (eds) (2016) *Eurasia 2.0: Russian Geopolitics in the Age of New Media* (New York: Lexington Books).

Tsygankov, A. P. (2005) 'Vladimir Putin's vision of Russia as a normal great power', *Post-Soviet Affairs*, 21(2), 132–158.

Tsygankov, A. P. (2012) *Russia and the West from Alexander to Putin: Honor in International Relations* (Cambridge, UK: Cambridge University Press).

Tsygankov, A. P. (2016) *Russia's Foreign Policy: Change and Continuity in National Identity*, 4th ed. (London: Rowman & Littlefield).

Tsygankov, A. P. and Tarver-Wahlquist, M. (2009) 'Duelling honors: Power, identity and the Russia–Georgia divide', *Foreign Policy Analysis*, 5(4), 307–326.

Urnov, M. (2014) '"Greatpowerness" as the key element of Russian self-consciousness under erosion', *Communist and Post-Communist Studies*, 47(3), 305–322.

Wendt, A. (1995) 'Constructing international politics', *International Security*, 20(1), 71–81.

Wendt, A. (1999) *Social Theory of International Politics* (Cambridge, UK: Cambridge University Press).

White, S. and Feklyunina, V. (2014) *Identities and Foreign Policies in Russia, Ukraine and Belarus* (Basingstoke, UK: Palgrave Macmillan).

White, S., McAllister, I. and Feklyunina, V. (2010) 'Belarus, Ukraine and Russia: East or West?' *The British Journal of Politics & International Relations*, 12(3), 344–367.

Williams, M. C. and Neumann, I. B. (2000) 'From alliance to security community: NATO, Russia and the power of identity', *Millennium: Journal of International Studies*, 29(2), 603–624.

Wohlforth, W. C. (1994) 'Realism and the end of the Cold War', *International Security*, 19(3), 91–129.

Zehfuss, M. (2002) *Constructivism in International Relations: The Politics of Reality* (Cambridge, UK: Cambridge University Press).

Zevelev, I. (2002) 'Russian and American national identity, foreign policy, and bilateral relations', *International Politics*, 39(4), 447–465.

Ziegler, C. E. (2012) 'Conceptualizing sovereignty in Russian foreign policy: Realist and constructivist perspectives', *International Politics*, 49(4), 400–417.

2
GLOBAL (POST)STRUCTURAL CONDITIONS

Viatcheslav Morozov

UNIVERSITY OF TARTU, ESTONIA

Introduction: what does structuralism mean?

In defining the scope of this chapter, I take Alexander Wendt's classic 1987 article as the starting point. Introducing the agency–structure problem, Wendt pointed out 'two truisms about social life which underlie most social scientific inquiry': the first states that 'human beings and their organizations are purposeful actors', while the second highlights the fact that 'society is made up of social relationships, which structure the interactions between these purposeful actors' (1987: 337–338). Both are equally necessary to make sense of the social world, yet at the ontological level, according to Wendt, there are three possible answers to the question about the relationship between agents and structures: one can assume that either of them is 'ontologically primitive' or give them 'equal and therefore irreducible ontological status' (1987: 339). The approach that assumes agents are ontologically primitive is labelled 'individualism', while structuralism, in turn, postulates ontological primacy of structure. Wendt himself advocates giving equal status to agency and structure – an approach that he, following Nigel Thrift, among others, defines as 'structurationist' (Wendt 1987: 336, fn2).

Another important ontological distinction concerns the view of structure as such. Ferdinand de Saussure's structural linguistics, as well as Claude Lévi-Strauss's structural anthropology and Louis Althusser's political theory viewed linguistic and social structure as fully constituted and sutured: at any given moment, the entire totality of social relationships can be described as a system of clearly defined differences which unambiguously define each position within the structure (such as the meaning of a word or an individual identity). On the contrary, authors such as Mikhail Bakhtin, Roland Barthes and Michel Foucault emphasise ambiguities always inherent in the structure, rendering it incomplete, subject to contradictory interpretations and thus prone to evolution and development (Coward and Ellis, 1977; Torfing, 1999). Poststructuralism would thus agree with the constructivist assertion that 'structure is continually in process' (Wendt, 1999: 186), but would still focus on continuous, structured patterns rather than on contingency and emergence (cf. Neumann and Pouliot, 2011: 136).

As long as this volume is concerned with Russian foreign policy, which is an empirical phenomenon rather than a theoretical issue, I cannot possibly draw a clear line between structuralism and structurationism. Similarly, I do not consistently differentiate between structuralist and poststructuralist approaches. These divisions are of secondary importance here in comparison with the basic ontological claim shared by the broad structuralist paradigm: that individual action (by a person, a state or any other agent) is always broadly conditioned by the dominant social structures in which the individual is immersed. This also leads to an epistemological preference for explanations that interpret individual action as a manifestation of broader structural patterns.

In IR terms, a structural perspective implies a strong predisposition for 'third image', system-level explanations that see each state's foreign policy as rooted in the structures of power that underlie international society as a whole. At the same time, reducing the structure to the balance of military power and polarity, as in realism and especially neorealism, is no longer the prevailing approach among structuralists. On the contrary, contemporary structuralism is characterised by ontological pluralism: structures can be seen as rooted in the economy or in discourse, sedimented in institutions or even imprinted in human bodies. This keeps open the channels for dialogue with the first- and second-image perspectives.

The key question of this review is about the contribution of structure-based explanations to our understanding of Russian foreign policy. As this chapter demonstrates, there are certain advantages in viewing structure as having an autonomous ontological status and offering a 'thick' theoretical description of how structural determination works in international politics, before engaging in the analysis of the Russian case. As with any others, structuralist accounts also have inherent limitations. In fact, the most promising way of using them seems to be by combining structuralist insights with those offered by institutionalist and constructivist approaches.

The Russian case: the general and the specific

An important advantage of the structuralist perspective pertains to the comparative dimension: in the final analysis, structure-based explanations of Russian foreign policy see it as less unique than agency-oriented accounts. This is because nation-level phenomena are seen as conditioned by deeper processes at the systemic level, bringing to the fore parallels between individual countries that are beyond reach for second-image accounts. Constructivists tell us that Europe has always played a central role for Russian national identity construction, but their theoretical tools are ill suited for going beyond this point. One has to look at the hierarchical structure of the international system to appreciate the fact that Russia's obsession with Europe has to do with the hegemonic position occupied by Europe (or the West) in capitalist modernity.

Another important consideration is that structuralist perspectives tend to embrace a critical approach to social reality. The term 'Critical Theory' is usually associated with the Frankfurt School and its leading figures – Theodor Adorno, Max Horkheimer, Herbert Marcuse and Jürgen Habermas, among others. It is distinct from positivist science in that it refuses to separate itself from practice and sets the goal of revealing inequality and injustice behind the commonsense 'truth', thus making emancipation possible. Most critical theories go back to Karl Marx, who was the first to clearly expose the *real* inequality and exploitation beneath the façade of liberal capitalist society, where everyone appears to be equal in *legal* terms.

A comparison with neorealism, on the one hand, and constructivism, on the other, could be instructive (see also a comparative summary of different approaches in Table 2.1). The original assumption of neorealism is that international structure is defined by anarchy, the primary concern of each state is survival and thus it has to rely on self-help (Waltz, 1979). In the Russian case, this implies expansion as the main strategic choice: 'expand where feasible until you come to a natural geographical frontier or the border of a strong state with which you can establish predictable relations. Take the territory now, we'll figure out what to do with it later' (Wohlforth, 2001: 228–229). Such an account is indeed plausible, yet presents only part of the story: in fact, each expansion cycle has been followed by painful adaptation, which revealed Russia's relative backwardness in terms of economic and institutional development. Strictly speaking, economic backwardness and domestic institutional deficiencies cannot be addressed from within the realist paradigm. Even less useful is it in explaining Russia's permanent concern with status: Wohlforth's (2001: 234) suggestion that Russian and Soviet leaders 'used status as an index of power' is not particularly helpful and certainly does not explain why status was invariably defined in terms of recognition by European states.

Constructivist studies of identity became one of the most popular approaches to Russian foreign policy in the post-Cold War era (see Feklyunina, this volume) specifically because of their ability to address the blind spots of neorealist theorising. 'Thick' constructivism can be classified as a type of structuralism, since it assumes that discursive structures are independent factors enabling and constraining social action. It is mostly due to this premise that constructivist research on Russian national identity has significantly enriched our understanding of the internal logic of Russia's actions and of the sources of its domestic legitimacy. The key constructivist finding is that Europe figures as the key Other in the Russian national identity discourse, and as a result, Russia strives to achieve recognition as a European great power.

At the same time, constructivist discourse analysis takes national identity discourse at face value. This is justified if one takes discourse seriously (as one definitely should), but it only works within certain limitations. Most importantly, the constructivist methodological toolkit is of little help in looking at the reasons why certain dominant articulations of national identity have been so stable over several centuries (Neumann, 1996). Consequently, even when cross-country or cross-regional comparisons are made (e.g. Neumann, 1999; Nau and Ollapally, 2012), it is difficult to account for the underlying causes of similarities and differences.

Going beyond (or below) identity requires making a choice between two views on the ontological status of discourse. Theories that gravitate towards historical materialism, such as world-system theory (WST) and the majority of critical approaches in International Political Economy (IPE) adhere to the principle of determination in the first instance by the economy. This means that in the final analysis all social processes are defined by the relations of production, which are reflected, perhaps in an indirect way, in discourses, identities, ideologies and other 'superstructural', 'ideational' phenomena.

The other, and much more diverse, group has been influenced by 'the linguistic turn' in the social sciences (Toews, 1987), as well as by institutional theory, especially by its historically inspired constructivist versions. Some of the more theoretically explicit approaches, such as poststructuralist IR or postcolonial theory, foreground discourse as the primary layer of social reality. Others prefer to focus on norms and institutions as they emerge, solidify and evolve historically. On the one hand, this concerns Russia's internal development and expansion as an empire; on the other, its interaction with and uneasy (semi-)membership in the Europe-dominated international society is in question. Even though authors working in this tradition agree that economy matters, they maintain that human action can never be reduced to any single factor alone: material production is only one element of a wider array of social reality, which is shaped by discourses, identities and institutions.

It would be premature to attempt a judgement on which of the two structuralist perspectives is more helpful in addressing Russian foreign policy. The reason is that there are hardly any studies that would go all the way from structural preconditions to foreign policy action, showing how the latter is grounded in the former. Rather, what we have at our disposal are individual pieces of the puzzle that are only beginning to fit together as a single whole. I will try to outline such a holistic perspective in the final part of this chapter, after I have reviewed the full range of the existing structuralist perspectives on Russia's position in international society. In this review,

I will often have to include works which have only tangential significance for foreign policy analysis (FPA) as applied to Russia, and even mention certain literatures that have not focused on Russia at all. This is again due to the fact that more often than not, the task of this chapter is to identify promising directions in the structuralist analysis of Russia rather than to summarise completed research, most of which still lies ahead.

Historical materialist approaches

Foundations for a historical materialist understanding of Russia's role in the world system were laid at the beginning of the twentieth century, when Marxist thinkers began to reconsider certain key elements of Karl Marx's legacy.

It was the Russian Bolsheviks, however, who – largely out of political necessity – directed their attention to the causes of Russia's 'backwardness' and its effects on institutions, ideologies and politics. Vladimir Lenin (1963 [1917]) was among the first to emphasise Russia's role as part of the global colonial system and the embeddedness of its economy in the international division of labour.

The question acquired new urgency after 1917, as the new intellectual and political elites were debating the uncertain prospects of the world proletarian revolution and the sustainability of socialism in one country. A genuine conceptual breakthrough in making sense of Russia's peripherality came with Leon Trotsky's idea of uneven and combined development, which was formulated in the course of his polemics with a fellow Bolshevik, historian Mikhail Pokrovsky. Trotsky did not invent this concept from scratch, but he certainly deserves to be credited with authorship for the crystal-clear way in which he formulates it on the first pages of *History of the Russian Revolution* (2008 [1930]).

The starting point of Trotsky's reasoning consists of two basic assumptions that had been widely accepted since Marx: first, capitalism is an ever expanding, universalising type of society which 'realises the universality and permanence of man's development'; second, different societies develop at unequal pace. Due to the globalising tendency of capitalism, backward societies face geopolitical competition on the part of the leaders: thus, 'Russia was unable to settle in the forms of the East because she was continually having to adapt herself to military and economic pressure from the West' (2008 [1930]: 4). Underdeveloped countries have the advantage of being able to imitate more advanced institutions and technologies (cf. Veblen, 1964 [1915]; Gerschenkron, 1962), but this imitation 'not infrequently debases the achievements borrowed from outside in the process of adapting them to its own more primitive culture' (Trotsky, 2008 [1930]: 4–5).

As a result of this chain of reasoning, the trivial fact of the existence of diversity is endowed with the power of a causal mechanism (Rosenberg, 2013) and a defining feature of the international (Rosenberg, 2006, 2016). In Trotsky's own formulation:

> Under the whip of external necessity . . . backward culture is compelled to make leaps. From the universal law of unevenness thus derives . . . the law of combined development – by which we mean a drawing together of the different stages of the journey, a combining of the separate steps, an amalgam of archaic with more contemporary forms.
>
> *(Trotsky, 2008 [1930]: 5)*

The 'uneven and combined development' formula captures a good deal of what other Marxists of the time – most notably, Antonio Gramsci – were writing about peripheral politics and, as shown later, can be integrated as an organic element in the neo-Gramscian and poststructuralist analysis of hegemonies and counter-hegemonies (see also Morton, 2007). It helps to make sense of Russia's difference in terms of domestic institutions, including the resource economy and the recurrence of authoritarianism. However, it does not directly translate into a theory of foreign policy.

In as much as a historical materialist understanding of Russian foreign policy is there, it should be approached through the prism of Pokrovsky's legacy. In his interpretation, the institutional growth of the Russian state and its foreign policy were driven not by tsars and their bureaucracies, but primarily by the power of commercial capital, which was the main economic force in the country prior to the rapid industrialisation of the late nineteenth to early twentieth centuries. It ruthlessly exploited the pre-capitalist sector of the economy and sustained the increasingly centralised absolutist state needed to put down the resistance of the masses (Pokrovsky, 1910–1912, 1933). The interests of commercial capital were also beyond both colonial expansion into the Eurasian periphery and the rivalry with other imperial powers, leading to repeated wars (see also Pokrovsky, 1923).

World-systems theory

The key starting point for the world-systemic perspective is international division of labour (Wallerstein, 1974), and as far as Russia is concerned, this is certainly a valid conceptual frame. As Boris Kagarlitsky (2008) has shown in his world-systemic (and Pokrovsky-inspired) overview of Russian history, the country was slotted into the emerging capitalist global order as the producer of raw materials: furs, wax, hemp, flax, later (as of late eighteenth century) grain, and in the twentieth century, oil and gas (see also Etkind, 2011: 72–90). As I have argued in my own synopsis of Russia's multifaceted dependency on the core, this pattern has never been completely broken (Morozov, 2015: 67–102).

Pointing to dependency and inequality, however, is not sufficient if one's goal is to analyse foreign policy action. Even if Pokrovsky's account might have provided the background for the understanding of imperial foreign policy, it certainly cannot be applied to the study of the post-Soviet period without a comprehensive revision. While the Russian empire engaged in colonial expansion to get access to resources, it seems that Putin's Russia spends its natural wealth on purely geopolitical pursuits. Even more importantly, world-systems theory is ill-equipped to move from structural preconditions to foreign policy steps. Its conceptual compass points in the opposite direction: it can tell us how Russia's peripherality affects its domestic developments (Simon, 2009; Lane, 2013; Christensen, 2013; Robinson, 2013) and even trace the 'developmental trajectory' of the Soviet Union from the systemic to the individual level and back (Derluguian, 2005), but it can hardly say much about the reasons why Russia's foreign policy has gone through such dramatic fluctuations, often out of sync with the degree of integration in the global economy.

A potential way forward could consist in trying to engage with these second-image explanations, taking on board their findings and trying to re-interpret them from a systemic perspective. There is a solid body of literature covering the impact of resource curse and dependent development on Russian society and politics from an institutionalist viewpoint (for most prominent examples, see Goldman, 2008; Hedlund, 2008; Jones Luong and Weinthal, 2010; Treisman, 2010; Gaddy and Ickes, 2013). The debate on these issues is ongoing also in the Russian scholarly community: apart from Kagarlitsky's work cited earlier (see also Kagarlitsky 2014), Simon Kordonsky's (2007) depiction of Russia as a society of rent-seekers organised in estates rather than classes has been rather influential. Other Russian thinkers who used to be close to the world-systems perspective have recently moved towards a more conservative position: thus, Mikhail Delyagin (2000) and Sergei Glazyev (2003) joined the nationalist Izborsk Club alongside such notorious figures like Alexander Prokhanov and Alexander Dugin. There are also studies that try to analyse Russian foreign policy in the context of resource economy and the impact of rents (Baev, 2008; Rutland, 2015; Dawisha, 2011), but these are few in number and far away from engaging with the 'big' themes at the systemic level.

In sum, we know how uneven and combined development made Russia a semi-peripheral country, we know what it means domestically, and we have started to explore how it affects its foreign policy. What is missing is a solid theory that would be able to integrate second- and third-image accounts.

Critical IPE

While it is not clear whether WST on its own can deal with these issues, there is no doubt that recent conceptual work in the field of critical IPE makes it well-prepared to tackle foreign policy as an object of study. The latter shares with the former the commitment to historical materialist ontology and to critical social enquiry.

At the same time, critical IPE does assign a significant degree of autonomy to the superstructural factors. The central role in elucidating the interplay between the material and the ideational is played by the concept of hegemony – a Gramscian term which in this line of thought is defined as 'the way one social group influences other groups, making certain compromises with them in order to gain their consent for its leadership in society as a whole', the result being that 'particular, sectional interests are transformed and some concept of the general interest is promoted' (Sassoon, 1982: 13–14). Hence, a key element of this notion is the wider idea of *universalisation* of a particular socio-economic and normative order: any social formation is based on a consensual acceptance of this order as embodying certain universal values – values which are, in fact, those of the dominant class. Hegemony is secured by means of controlling the discursive space (not just via the media, but also through education, cultural practices, organisation of urban spaces, etc.), while violent suppression of dissent happens only at the fringes of society (Forgacs, 1999; Morton, 2007: 92).

In his writings on Italian history, Gramsci explores the effects of peripherality, often drawing parallels with Russia. The added value of this approach consists in acknowledging that uneven and combined development also works at the political level: peripheral countries often feature conservative hegemonies in which both industrial and agricultural elites collude in order to control mass common sense, while the intellectual class is unable to formulate a national emancipatory agenda (Morton, 2007).

Another crucial recent contribution of critical IPE consists of the suggestion to view hegemony as a scalar phenomenon, while differentiating between dominant and nodal scales. As Bob Jessop (2006: 426) explains, 'nodal scales are non-dominant overall but nonetheless serve as the primary loci for delivering certain activities in a given spatio-temporal order or matrix'. While the dominant logic of capitalist development is global, its concrete operation can be detected and examined at the national, regional and even local, micro-social level. The national scale, however, remains of nodal significance, serving as the main playing field for the dominant dynamic that can only be understood globally (see also Morton, 2007).

This opens a way towards examining the Russian case as determined not just by the dominant global capitalist hegemonic order, but also by the national hegemony, conceived as an autonomous socio-political space. Unfortunately, this approach has so far yielded very little empirical research on Russia, with foreign policy remaining virtually unexplored. Jeremy Lester's (1995) book is very rich empirically and features an excellent theoretical introduction, but focuses exclusively on the inter-party struggle in the early post-Soviet period. The study by

Owen Worth (2005) claims to offer an IPE-based perspective, but in fact concentrates on the role played by the successive political leaders, from Lenin to Putin, while the holistic structural view is almost entirely lost.

Among the few studies that address contemporary Russia from the materialist neo-Gramscian perspective, Ted Hopf's 'commonsense constructivism' (Hopf, 2010) stands out as particularly important. In an obvious departure from his earlier writings (esp. Hopf, 2002), which emphasise the cognitive dimension of identity and its discursive construction, Hopf is developing 'a neo-Gramscian constructivism, one that . . . puts more emphasis on the material than conventional constructivists' (Hopf, 2017: 203). Accordingly, he postulates a causal connection between mass common sense and the country's peripherality: while the elites strive to bring the country closer to the West, 'common sense is hindering any Russian movement from the semi-periphery to the core of Western hegemony' and thus 'has an effect on the distribution of power in the international system' (Hopf, 2013: 348).

Unfortunately, postulating a strong equivalence between social classes and foreign policy choices does not explain the broad variety of strategies – from bandwagoning to counter-hegemonic balancing and even confrontation – chosen at different moments by semi-peripheral states, including Russia. Suggesting that common sense constantly evolves and drags the state along (Hopf, 2009) solves the problem only partially, since in this case one loses grip of the material causes of such evolution. It is not clear, for instance, why the Soviet reforms of the late 1980s produced a strong pro-Western hegemony, while the Soviet Union remained in the semi-periphery of the world system. In the subsequent decades, Russia hardly became more peripheral, but its politics gradually evolved in the conservative anti-Western direction.

To sum up, the material dimension of Russia's subordinate place in the capitalist world order remains the single most important problem which is not given sufficient attention in the existing literature on the sources of its foreign policy. The reason for that is not the lack of awareness, but rather the unavailability of conceptual tools that would allow economic and other non-ideational factors to integrate into existing accounts. As far as historical materialist position is concerned, a lot of work remains to be done integrating systemic perspectives with second-image accounts of Russian foreign policy.

Discursive and institutionalist approaches

It is remarkable that one of the first major reappraisals of Russia's post-Cold War standing, framed as a profound theoretical and historicist critique of modernity from a broadly poststructuralist perspective, was published in Moscow as far back as 1998 (Kapustin, 1998). Unfortunately, Boris Kapustin's book is little known even within Russia, in spite of the fact that he teaches at Yale and continues to publish in both Russian and English. His critique, however, was mostly addressing theories and ideologies rather than social structures, and said nothing about foreign policy. In recent years, discourse-oriented research has been paying much more attention to the economic and social dimensions, while continuing to insist that discourses, norms and identities are at least as less important as 'material' factors.

English School and its critical revisions

When it comes to the approaches that foreground identities and discourses while remaining on the systemic level of analysis, the most relevant tradition seems to be the one established by the English School. The point of departure here is the work by Headley Bull and others on the expansion of international society. Technological progress led to both military (Howard, 1984) and economic (O'Brien, 1984) superiority of Europe, which motivated other states to learn from it by adopting the standard of 'civilisation' (Gong, 1984). Even when a non-Western state does challenge Europe's pre-eminence, the aim is to redistribute benefits within the system rather than to undermine the system as such (Bull, 1984). The Russian case, as analysed by Adam Watson (1984), was a typical example of this trajectory: Russia modernised voluntarily, by its own sovereign decision, but under pressure from the expanding European international society. A similar view is offered by David Lake (2009) in his contractual theory of international hierarchy, where the latter is portrayed as a set of mutually beneficial arrangements between the stronger states safeguarding social order and the subordinates who obey the rules for the sake of predictability and security (see also Bially Mattern and Zarakol, 2016).

This image of a harmonious and one-dimensional international society is challenged by what I have suggested labelling 'critical international society literature' (see Morozov 2015: 47–51). It argues that European international society has expanded by means that were anything but peaceful and included the use of force and colonial oppression (Keene, 2002; Keal, 2003). The more powerful non-European states that more or less succeeded in achieving an insider status internalised both sets of norms and went on to engage in their own imperial pursuits (Keene, 2002: 97–119; Suzuki, 2009). Still, as Ayşe Zarakol makes clear, internalisation of the external norm leads to stigmatisation: having accepted Eurocentric hierarchies, the non-Western elites believed that 'their countries were "behind" the West in every aspect' (2011: 56). Another factor contributing to anxiety is the instability of peripheral statehood: while they integrate into the Eurocentric international society, many of the non-Western nations struggle to maintain domestic order (Ayoob, 1995, 2010).

Stigmatisation and anxiety can also be conceptualised as manifestations of ontological insecurity (Zarakol, 2010). In the most popular definition, offered by Jennifer Mitzen (who draws on Anthony Giddens), ontological security is rooted in the fundamental human need for cognitive certainty: humans are capable of overcoming the inherent uncertainty of their existence by establishing routines, which provide 'confident expectations, even if probabilistic, about the means-ends relationships that govern [the individual's] social life' (Mitzen, 2006: 345; see also Steele, 2008). In the final analysis, ontological security requires a stable relational identity – a sense of continuous selfhood that is a necessary precondition for any social action.

Both approaches can, in effect, be applied to Russia. Moreover, there are obvious overlaps between Steele's work, in particular, and the research by Anne Clunan (2009) and Andrey Tsygankov (2012) on the role of emotions, in particular self-esteem and honour, as shaping the background of Russian foreign policy-making. The more fundamental security concerns addressed by Ayoob, in their turn, come down to the fear of a total social breakdown, which has also been a persistent feature of the Russian discourse (Snetkov, 2012, 2015). As recently demonstrated by Andrej Krickovic (2016), internal vulnerabilities (real or perceived) of semi-peripheral countries can generate security dilemmas: Russia's conflict with the West over 'colour revolutions' is the best illustration of this point. Finally, Iver Neumann and Vincent Pouliot (2011) trace Russia's concern with status back to the early post-Mongol times, when Moscow tsars based their claims to a status equal to the Holy Roman Emperor on the principle of *translation imperrii* from the Golden Horde, i.e. on being direct heirs to Mongol khans. Coupled with the Russian diplomatic habitus, also rooted in the Asian tradition, this created a condition of 'hysteresis' – a mismatch between embodied dispositions and the conditions obtaining in the field of European diplomacy. This, in Neumann and Pouliot's view, explains Russia's chronic inability 'to play the field to one's advantage, through understanding the rules of the game as well as the social dispositions of other actors' (Neumann and Pouliot, 2011: 137).

Few of these studies, however, can be classified as structuralist in the sense of reaching beyond the individual country-case: they continue the constructivist tradition of analysing foreign policy through the prism of identity and thus emphasise the unique over the general. Krickovic's (2016) analysis is explicitly comparativist, but his view of international structure is relatively thin, which befits his largely neorealist theoretical framework.

As of now, Zarakol's (2011) book remains the only work that has applied the critical international society perspective to Russia in a comparative context.

Apart from the dearth of literature covering the Russian case from the critical international society perspective, another potential issue with this approach is that its view of structure is rather shallow and does not offer any ontological ground for making sense of the inequalities inherent in the international system. To recap, the sole causal mechanism for the expansion of European international society that the English School can come up with is Western technological superiority. This explains why countries that managed to escape the grip of European colonialism still feel the pressure to modernise. What is not clear is why some nations have managed to integrate into the Western core and overcome stigmatisation (contemporary Japan could be a case in point, along with a number of countries from the European periphery), while others (Russia and Turkey would be prime examples, see Morozov and Rumelili, 2012) continue to struggle with stigma and ontological insecurity. It is also difficult to explain why they cannot modernise independently, importing top technologies while keeping a distance from the Western normative order (some would argue that China has managed to follow this path). Some answers are suggested by the Foucauldian literature on global governance, which is reviewed in the next section.

Governmentality and Russia's difference

In recent decades, the legacy of Michel Foucault has been an important source of inspiration for poststructuralist IR (Kiersey and Stokes, 2011). Russia figures as a significant case in this literature: analysing its foreign policy through the prism of such concepts as governmentality and biopolitics can shed new light not just on the Russian puzzle, but also on the workings of international society as a whole.

Foucault came up with the concept of governmentality while trying to make sense of the qualitatively new form of power typical for the modern state. Its aim is not to ensure obedience, but to improve the conditions of the population. Therefore, 'it is a question not of imposing law on men but of disposing [of] things' (Foucault, 2000 [1978]: 211): the task is to make sure that society functions in a desired way without dictating to each and every person what to do at any given moment (Neumann and Sending, 2010: 8–11, 24–29).

The relevance of the concept of governmentality for the international, and for the Russian case in particular, consists in the fact that society organised around this form of power (with dominance and sovereignty still important but in the background) was never fully confined to individual states. Capitalist expansion results in all domains being ever more fully incorporated into a single world order: governmentality reaches down to the most intimate aspects of human life by taking the form of biopolitics and biopower, while international relations are increasingly conceived of in terms of 'global governance'. As Alexander Astrov puts it, '"police" begins as "international police", premised on the recognition that the conditions of international order impact the conduct of both individuals and national economies' (Astrov, 2011: 8). According to Foucault, the 1815 Congress of Vienna produced a shared understanding that:

> [t]here will be an imbalance if within the European equilibrium there is a state, not my state, with bad police. Consequently, one must see to it that there is good police, even in other states. European equilibrium begins to function as a sort of inter-state police or as right. European equilibrium gives the set of states the right to see to it that there is good police in each state.
>
> *(quoted in Neumann and Sending, 2010: 70)*

According to Neumann, this was exactly the reason for Russia's failure to be recognised as a great power. 'As seen from Europe, a Great Power cannot have state/society relations that are too different from those that at any one given time dominate European politics' (2008: 147). While it certainly had the material capability and the ambition to partake in the emerging system of great power management, the ways the country was governed were described by other Europeans, as early as in the eighteenth century, as uncivil and inappropriate. Peter I's reforms did produce a police state modelled on its European counterparts, but for some reason Russia was not able to make the crucial next step in the liberal direction by allowing its civil society to govern itself. Neither was it ever able to catch up with the evolving norms of European diplomacy – most crucially, with the idea of great power as a guarantor of international treaties (Neumann and Pouliot, 2011: 126–127). One of the most characteristic consequences of this failure was the eventual breakdown of the Vienna concert and Russia's defeat in the Crimean War, but it can also be applied to other cases, such as the Russian-Georgian War of 2008 (Astrov, 2011) and the Crimean crisis.

Neumann's argument certainly helps to understand the constitutive split within Russian national identity and the ensuing stigmatisation. It is not just due to the internalisation of an external normative order; this order remains external regardless of how Moscow behaves internationally, because recognition depends on the way the country is governed domestically. The difference between Russia and Western Europe is rooted in something more tangible than identity politics: it exists at the level of state institutions and civil society structures. It must therefore come as no surprise that when Russia felt that its own central place in the post-Soviet order was threatened by Western expansion (as in Georgia in 2008 and in Ukraine in 2014), the only type of action it could undertake was destabilising the order as such, 'reconstituting the post-Soviet space as a state of exception' (Prozorov, 2011: 41). There was simply no alternative order Russia could have attempted to promote.

There is a theoretical complication, which is missed by Neumann and Sending as they discuss the ambiguous interplay of republicanism and pastoral power in liberalism. As Astrov points out, liberal governmentality is:

> [a]n activity distinguished by its ambition to conduct the conduct of individuals themselves recognized as capable of freely conducting their own activities. But as an immediate corollary of this, comes the requirement of a prior distinction, made by way of recognition: distinction between those who, being capable of free conduct themselves, can be governed in this manner and those who, because of their ignorance of or aversion to individual freedom, can only be governed in some other way.
>
> As such, this distinction is nothing but a decision, a decision on the worth of life both as 'being and well-being'; a decision which . . . is resolutely political in so far as it presupposes the whole and gives it concrete shape by introducing divisions within it.
>
> *(2011: 15)*

This foundational decision implies a differentiation between governance and reign, analogous to the distinction between law and *nomos* in Carl Schmitt. It emphasises that before any specific act of governance, the order as such needs to be established, which includes not just an ethical-political decision on the criteria of 'well-being', but also creating the subjects of governance. 'Anarchical sovereignty', required for world governance, does not have any self-evident foundations: it results, at least to a degree, from a usurpation – such as the one that happened at the Congress of Vienna, where the future of Europe was decided upon by a narrow circle of self-appointed great powers (Astrov, 2011: 15–23). Yet this, of course, also implies that Russia's 'hierarchical inclusion' in the European international society (Prozorov, 2009) was not inevitable. Even if Russia's 'deviance' is not purely imagined, the choice of the criteria for belonging and exclusion is not in any way predetermined: this was a choice made by Europeans themselves, based on their own idea of a life worth living.

The value of sociologically inspired re-interpretations of the English School consists in adding unevenness to the otherwise flat ontology of international society. However, they tend to accept Russia being 'a laggard learner and, in that sense, inferior' (Neumann and Sending, 2010: 93) as a self-evident fact. The Bourdieu-based account developed by Neumann and Pouliot (2011) is not of much help here: they seem to argue, in effect, that the Mongol habitus has been imprinted on Russia's diplomacy, and even embodied in Russian diplomats, as the marker of Russia's non-Europeanness.[1] Postulating a definitive role played by the type of governance and associated individual dispositions, as opposed to material capabilities, in determining the status of great power removes from consideration the question of economic development and material inequality (cf. Neumann, 2008: 149, note 15). Besides, as opposed to the critical international society literature reviewed earlier, the Foucauldian governance approach has so far not engaged in any meaningful dialogue with postcolonial theory and imperial history. This is an obvious gap, given the centrality of the language of civilisation for the way in which Russia's otherness is being articulated by Western Europeans. Such a dialogue appears to be even more timely given the radical geographical refocusing and conceptual innovation that has taken place in postcolonial studies since the late 1990s.

Postcolonial theory, imperial history and internal colonisation

The idea of applying postcolonial theory to post-Soviet space, which sounded completely novel at the turn of the century (Moore, 2001) has by now inspired a wide and diverse body of scholarly work. For the most part, this research focuses on the nations colonised by Russia and the Soviet Union. While it insists on considering Russia's colonial expansion as external and thus frames it as part of foreign policy agenda, it is interested more in the consequences than in the driving forces or the relationship with identity politics. As a result, its perspective on Russian imperialism is one-dimensional: neither the causes of such conduct nor its impact on the 'domestic' social space are believed to be relevant (cf. Kołodziejczyk and Şandru, 2012).

The concept of internal colonisation, elaborated by Alexander Etkind, as well as by Dirk Uffelmann, Ilya Kukulin and others, reverses this optic by looking at the entire state formation process as a colonial experience. In doing that, it draws (often implicitly) on the vast literature on empire and imperialism. As argued by Geoffrey Hosking (1997), the Russian state had to foster Europeanised imperial elites to defend and administer the enormous overland military empire, while internal development and cohesion were never a priority. Competition with other empires was a major factor here (Lieven, 2000). Internal colonisation literature takes the rift between the elites and the masses as the point of departure and looks at how the former undertook a civilising mission in relation to the latter (Etkind, 2002, 2011).

What this approach has been able to demonstrate in a convincing way is how empire-building and internal colonisation of Russia shaped the institutional structure and conditioned the process of modernisation in imperial Russia (Hosking, 1997; Etkind, 2011; Kivelson and Suny 2016). This provides at least a partial explanation of Russia's 'laggardness' in learning from the European experience, which, according to Neumann, cost it the recognition as a European great power. It turns out that the problem was not the lack of will or the weakness of civil society as such, but the fact that Russia (all of it!) was governed as a colony. Inter alia, this made indirect liberal governance impossible, since the Russian elites viewed 'their own' population in the same way as the Western Europeans viewed Russia as a whole: as not yet civilised, not ready for self-government, waiting to be enlightened from above (cf. Etkind et al., 2012: 15; Hosking 1997: 263–285; Morozov, 2015: 154–157).

Any international problematic, however, is still largely absent from this analysis. What is highlighted is the presence of external threat as a factor contributing to the militarisation of the Russian polity and to the establishment of the empire as such. Thus, it goes along with the research design of 'second-image reversed' (Gourevitch, 1978), i.e. of looking at the international factors to explain domestic outcomes. This tradition certainly can yield valuable insights in Russian developments, as demonstrated by a number of studies that, to a greater or lesser extent, share this approach (e.g. Tsygankov, 2014).

However, at least in the case of internal colonisation, the lack of attention to the international implies serious limitations and even conceptual weaknesses. The most critical one concerns the very basic premise of the theory – that Russian colonisation was 'internal'. From a systemic viewpoint, this assertion is state-centric in its disregard for the fact that the dominant capitalist dynamic is global rather than national. As a result, it is unable to put Russian colonialism into a wider international context: instead, it focuses on how cultural differences within the country conditioned the development of the modern state. The conclusion is largely the same as the one reached by institutionalist accounts: Russian institutional landscape is deeply affected by rent capitalism, which distorts the perception of the national interest and at times leads to irresponsible foreign policy moves (Etkind, 2014).

In other words, while the conventional postcolonial critique, imperial history and internal colonisation all highlight crucially important aspects of how discourses, identities and social structures developed *within* Russian (and later Soviet) imperial domain, they are unable to account for the global context of these transformations, to see them as part of the large-scale systemic development in which Russia was a constituent part but also an actor. In order to create a coherent structuralist theory of peripheral politics, capable, inter alia, of shedding new light on Russian foreign policy, other structuralist perspectives must be brought into the picture. The concluding section will present my own subjective view of how this can be achieved.

Exploring the way forward: a subaltern empire facing Western hegemony

The overview of structuralist approaches to Russia's role in the world provided in this chapter indicates that they offer valuable insight, but so far have been unable to come up with a coherent system-level account of Russia's conduct. We know from historical materialist approaches that uneven and combined development left a characteristic mark on Russian capitalism, as well as on the role of the state and civil society. Foucauldian literature dwells on the latter point by making clear that Russia is governed in a way different from 'the standard of civilisation', which makes its long-term goal of getting accepted as a great power almost impossible to achieve. Similar to other latecomers to the Eurocentric international society, Russia ended up with a stigma and ontological insecurity. As this section demonstrates, a synthesis of these approaches could provide an understanding of the specificity of Russian identity politics in the comparative context, as an effect of the dominant dynamic of global capitalist modernity. This would amount to a holistic perspective on Russian foreign policy, not in the sense of being able to directly explain all observable empirical phenomena, but rather by placing these observations in a single, consistent theoretical framework. The key advantage, as indicated in the introductory part of this chapter, would be to de-emphasise Russia's uniqueness and to discern general patterns in the patchwork of isolated empirical facts.

Russia as a subaltern empire

This line from material semi-peripherality to discursive construction of identities and particular policies seems easy to walk when it is presented as a single brief logical chain, but not a single study has so far been able to take this way. There are pragmatic reasons for this, such as the need to cover an enormously wide field, with each segment possessing its own 'regime of truth' and distinct language. Yet more importantly, there is a leap that one has to make here from materialist ontology of WST and critical IPE to the idea of the primacy of discourse that underlies the literature on governance and ontological security. Even while some approaches, such as English School and mainstream constructivism, pretend to occupy the middle ground, in fact a more adequate way of describing their position would be as straddling the material-ideational divide without questioning the dualist ontology that underlies it.

Is there any hope, then, of developing a theory that would be able to unite, on a single ontological foundation, these diverse structuralist interpretations of Russia's international standing? It must be clear that such a theory must abandon the material-ideational dualism and embrace a monist ontology (cf. Jackson, 2008) that would view the material and the discursive as mutually constitutive. In my view, this can be done by foregrounding the concept of hegemony, which is equally prominent in historical materialist and discursive accounts of politics.

My starting point for such an endeavour would be Ernesto Laclau's assertion that 'the category of representation does not simply reproduce, at a secondary level, a fullness preceding it which could be grasped in a direct way but, on the contrary, representation is the absolutely primary level in the construction of objectivity' (2005: 115). There is no 'determination in the first instance by the economy', simply because there are no first and second 'instances'. Our ways of handling material objects – indeed, even the knowledge of what it is that we handle, the objectivity itself – is constituted by discourse to a no lesser extent than identities and norms.

This is a radical assertion, but if it is accepted, it enables one to see how uneven and combined development works to produce social orders of different scales, from the local to the global. The mechanism at work here is hegemony, understood, following the suggestion by critical IPE, as a scalar phenomenon. The dominant dynamic of capitalism never translates into concrete social practices in a direct way: it must embed itself in identities and institutions making sure that even the oppressed and the disadvantaged accept the social order and believe that their subaltern existence is full of intrinsic value. This is possible only if they perceive their way of life as part of a certain legitimate universal order – in other words, if their common sense is hegemonised, if they identify themselves with values and norms that, in an objective analysis, are not necessarily their own.

The national scale is crucial for the operation of any hegemony: it plays a nodal role in modern society, which makes the nation state the focal point of identification and decision-making. Viewed in this light, Russia's specificity results from the fact that in the course of internal colonisation the imperial elites simultaneously belonged to two hierarchically organised hegemonic spaces.

On the one hand, they were on a civilising mission in their own country and identified with Europe against their 'own' people; on the other, they belonged to an emerging nation which, as a whole, was disparaged by other Europeans as not fully civilised. The Westernisers advocated reform intended to bring Russia closer to civilisation, but European indirect governance was ill suited to the realities of peripheral, resource-oriented capitalism. The Slavophiles and their successors, contrariwise, entreated their fellow countrymen to embrace Russia's difference, but the geopolitical 'whip of external necessity' forced Russia to catch up and modernise.

In sum, the 'subaltern empire' formula seems to capture Russia's position in the interstice between two hegemonic orders of unequal scale. It emphasises that Russian periphery was colonised on behalf of the capitalist core and continues to be exploited for the benefit of global elites. Russia engages in this pursuit as a sovereign polity, which means that conflicts with the hegemon are almost inevitable. However, it is next to impossible for Russia to take the upper hand in this counter-hegemonic struggle. The reason for this is not just the technological gaps, but also the fact that Russian society and its mass common sense have been part of the global hegemonic order for too long. As the adjective 'subaltern' suggests (cf. Spivak, 1988), Russian imperialism has not developed any independent language with which to speak about its mission. Even while Russia is trying to resist Western unilateralism, it has no other language to express its resentment than the language of European civilisation.

Empirical implications

As a result, 'hierarchical inclusion' in the Eurocentric international society remains the most fundamental background condition of Russian foreign policy, which can serve as a starting point for bringing the empirical research on Russian foreign policy to a new level. Russia's development in modern times has been characterised by oscillation between attempts to internalise the global hegemonic order (by trying to follow the norms of 'civilised' foreign policy conduct, pursuing domestic reforms or both) and counter-hegemonic resentment. Imperial overstretch invariably resulted in geopolitical defeats, such as the Crimean War of 1853–56, the Russo-Japanese War of 1904–05 or the collapse of the USSR. This typically had a short-term moderating effect on foreign policy ambitions; most importantly, however, these defeats resulted in far-reaching domestic reforms: the liberation of peasants and a profound modernisation of the legal order from 1861 on, the introduction of parliamentarianism in 1906 and the pro-market, democratic reforms of the 1990s.

Nevertheless, Europeanisation always ended in disappointment, since eventually it became clear that Russia remained a liminal, in-between member of European international society. Whenever it voiced a concern about what it perceived as Western unilateralism, it was dismissed as lacking full legitimacy, not because of what Russia said, but mostly because of what it *was*: a semi-civilised peripheral nation that still had a long way to go before becoming a member of the European family. Disappointment led to resentment and eventually to another round of geopolitical rivalry with the West, as soon as Russia felt strong enough to afford that.

If background structural conditions do not change, and barring a catastrophic scenario such as a nuclear conflict between Russia and NATO, it is very likely that the current round of frantic geopolitical expansion will expire to give way to yet another cycle of pro-European modernisation. This is all the more likely now that the Russian elites, including President Putin, explicitly acknowledge the existence of technological gaps between Russia and the more developed world, even as they claim it is possible to close those gaps by relying on the domestic resources and without initiating any major institutional reforms. It is hardly possible to estimate the timing of the next turnaround or how radical it might be, but given the depth of the structural crisis in the Russian economy, it might happen earlier than most people expect. The value of the structuralist approach consists in being able to explicitly predict such an outcome by not just extrapolating the previous developments but by analysing their driving forces and thus suggesting that second-image approaches be employed in the search for symptoms of a possible change of course.

The characteristic oscillation in Russian foreign policy discourse and practice has been one of the persistent themes in the constructivist analysis of Russian foreign policy. Approaching it from a structuralist perspective allows one to assess the discursive structure of national identity as conditioned by the interplay of hegemonies and counter-hegemonies at the systemic level, which in itself is rooted in the uneven and combined development of globalising capitalism. Viewed in this light, such counter-hegemonic projects as the BRICS must be approached as based not just on the shallow anti-Westernism shared by its participants, but on a more profound similarity between their positions in the global system of production, including production of meaning (cf. Morozov, 2013b: 22–25). This, however, does not necessarily lead to any optimistic forecasts: as long as counter-hegemonic projects remain framed in the language of Western hegemony (Morozov, 2013a), they do little more than create more comfortable niches for the semi-peripheral states in the existing global order. Hence, a key indicator of potential change regarding the global role of the BRICS would not be the economic ascent of China and India, but the emergence of an alternative hegemonic discourse, whose terms of reference would be located outside the Eurocentric hegemonic field of liberal democracy.

Another characteristic illustration of subaltern imperialist foreign policy practised by Russia is Eurasian integration. This project obviously relies on the legacy of Russian and Soviet colonialism (such as the division of labour, shared cultural codes and a lot more). At the same time, it is driven by the desire to construct an independent 'pole' of the future multipolar world, which would ensure Moscow's leading position in world affairs. And yet, Eurasian Economic Union continues to be modelled on, and justified by, references to the experience of Western European integration, thus demonstrating the lack of symbolic resources at Russia's disposal and its de facto belonging to the European hegemonic space (Kazharski 2017).

Nevertheless, even though the structural forces moulding the Russian state into a subaltern empire appear to be overwhelming, international politics is never fully determined by structure alone. Early Soviet history provides a good illustration: while the 1917 revolution certainly resulted from imperial overstretch (the exhaustion from the war effort), the resulting political transformation did not fit the usual pattern. The USSR remained dependent on Western know-how and technology, but created a society based on a powerful universalist ideology, which for a while offered a convincing alternative to Western capitalism. The Soviet system eventually could not compete against liberal market democracy, but it was a major factor in global development throughout the twentieth century and left a lasting impact on Russian national identity.

The discursive landscape of contemporary Russia features no identity project even remotely similar in scale to the Soviet one. The Soviet nostalgia is strong but backward-looking, the communist idea is discredited, while the attempts to promote 'traditional values' are completely sterile in their continued orientation towards the West. The ideologues of the 'spiritual bonds' are desperately trying to prove that 'Russia is not Europe', which in fact demonstrates the persistent centrality of Europe for Russian national identity (Morozov, 2015). A structuralist third image approach to Russia's international role suggests that similar discourses are to be found elsewhere in semi-peripheral countries. Looking through this prism, it is indeed easy to see strong and revealing parallels between Russian traditionalism and nativist discourses in, for instance, South

America. In both cases, opposition to Western hegemony is presented as based on some genuine indigenous knowledge, but the existence of such knowledge seems to be an illusion (Morozov and Pavlova, 2016).

The fact that the promise of nativist discourses seems to be empty at the moment, however, does not exclude the possibility of new alternatives emerging from the semi-periphery in the future. The current moment is experienced by many as one of crisis, and crises sometimes get resolved through revolutionary breakthroughs. As in the times of Lenin and Trotsky, Russia's predicament as a semi-peripheral, subaltern empire never ceases to generate potential revolutionary situations, and Russia is by far not the only country bearing a grudge against global inequality. Discourse analysis, ethnographic research and other tools developed by constructivist social science and successfully applied in IR must be used to examine the concrete societal situations that generate social tension and might therefore constitute future 'evental sites'.

Besides, the structure of global hegemony is changing: as economic power is increasingly concentrated in the East, the symbolic power is bound to follow suit. This is acknowledged by nearly everyone in Russia and elsewhere, but it has not so far affected the structural preconditions for Russian foreign policy. The attempts to construct a 'pivot to Asia' remain largely formal, especially when it comes to securing Russia's sovereign standing as a great power or to overcome the Eurocentrism of identity politics (Lo, 2015: 132–164). However, monitoring these developments in the future is going to be an extremely revealing exercise. In particular, it is important to explore to what extent Russia becomes dependent on China as an economic superpower and how this material dependency plays out in identity politics.

Finally, the structuralist approach can offer a new perspective on the state of the debate in Russian IR scholarship. It can be demonstrated that Russian scholars use the critique of Eurocentrism, advanced by decolonial IR, in their own analysis of global affairs (Makarychev and Morozov, 2013). It would be interesting to see whether and how this positioning reflects Russia's subaltern place in the global hierarchy and which specific additional insights or blind spots it might create in the way Russian academic community contemplates world politics.

Conclusion: promises and limitations of structuralism

It must be clear by now that the main limitation of the structuralist approach, if the latter is defined as a system-level, third-image explanatory framework, is that it can hardly serve as a tool of concrete FPA. The reason for this is that it concentrates on the long-term, deep background factors that shape the conditions for policy action, rather than on everyday decision-making. However, this limitation can be converted into a strength if system-level structuralist and post-structuralist analysis is combined with second-image theories. Both constructivist identity-based accounts and institutionalist FPA could benefit from such a synergy.

On a related note, structuralism can hardly be expected to come up with falsifiable hypotheses that could be tested in empirical research. Its key contribution to the debate is related not that much to explaining specific events, but to understanding their conditions of possibility (cf. Hollis and Smith, 1990). That being said, it does not mean that structuralist approaches completely fail on the Popperian standard: they can be tested indirectly as long as they are used in defining background assumptions for concrete FPA. If and when those assumptions are found to be inadequate in the course of empirical research, this would imply the need to revise the basic premises of the structuralist image.

Another important promise held out by structuralist approaches is opening a much wider agenda for comparative research. Unlike identities and institutions, which are unique and specific to each historical context, underlying structures are shared by many countries occupying similar niches in the capitalist world-system. That being the case, we still know very little about the extent to which these structural positions are indeed identical or similar, or how they translate into discourses, identities and policies in each specific context.

As this chapter has demonstrated, serious structure-oriented research on Russian foreign policy is still largely a task for the future. There are studies which look at how the international and the domestic are related in the globalised capitalist environment, and these studies offer valuable models that can be applied and developed when looking at the Russian case (see Table 2.1). As for the specific theme of this Handbook, however, the chapter on structuralism is yet to be written.

Table 2.1 A comparative summary of theoretical perspectives on Russia

Theory	Key focus	Key ontological category	Key findings
Neorealism	International structure	Power, primarily military power	Security-driven expansion as the most typical model of Russian foreign policy
Constructivism	National identity	Discourse	Europe is the key Other in Russian identity discourse; Russia strives to achieve recognition as a European great power
Historical materialism			
World-systems theory	Global structure of production, division of labour	Economic power	Russia is a semi-peripheral country and a rent economy; rents provide resources for expansion
Critical IPE	Hierarchically organised hegemonic orders	Economic and discursive power	Russia's material position is reflected in the discursive field, including foreign policy discourse
Discursive and institutionalist approaches			
Classical English School	International society	International institutions	Russia strives to join international society and to maximise benefits from membership
Critical international society literature	International society	Institutional hierarchies and resulting insecurities	Russia is a stigmatised player, which produces ontological insecurity
Governance	International society	Governmentality as specifically modern form of power, embodied in institutions	The othering of Russia is due to the fact that it is not governed in a way befitting a European country
Imperial history and internal colonisation	Domestic	Institutions and discourses	Russian national identity and domestic institutions are a product of imperial development and internal colonisation
Poststructuralist theory of hegemony	The interplay between the international and the domestic	Hegemony (as a scalar phenomenon)	Russia as a subaltern empire facing Western hegemony; global hierarchies reflected in the domestic institutional landscape and discursive field

Glossary

Uneven and combined development – a law of capitalist development whereby the uneven development of capitalism in different countries and regions leads to the emergence in peripheral, 'backward' countries of peculiar, 'combined' institutional orders, which create specific social and political problems not experienced by the more advanced nations.

Hegemony, in the neo-Gramscian definition adopted by poststructuralists, is a form of rule based on the acceptance by a community (such as a nation) of a *particular* discursive-political order as consistent with the *universal* ideal. For example, the rule of a particular party or group is considered as legitimate because it results from a democratic procedure and thus is consistent with the universal ideal of democracy. The concept of hegemony emphasises the importance of the discursive, ideological dimension of power, as opposed to coercion.

Note

1 Another consideration is that Neumann and Pouliot's position their theory as agency-oriented, although their treatment of dispositions as embodied in behavioural patterns is certainly more structuralist than they are ready to admit.

References

Adorno, T. (1972/1976) *The Positivist Dispute in German Sociology* (London: Heinemann).
Astrov, A. (2011) 'Great Power Management without Great Powers? The Russian–Georgian War of 2008 and Global Police/Political Order', in *The Great Power (mis)Management: The Russian–Georgian War and its Implications for Global Political Order*, ed. by A. Astrov, 1–23 (Farnham, UK: Ashgate).
Ayoob, M. (1995) *The Third World Security Predicament. State Making, Regional Conflict, and the International System* (Boulder, CO and London: Lynne Rienner).
Ayoob, M. (2010) 'Making Sense of Global Tensions: Dominant and Subaltern Conceptions of Order and Justice in the International System', *International Studies* 47(2–4): 129–141.
Baev, P. K. (2008) *Russian Energy Policy and Military Power: Putin's Quest for Greatness* (London and New York: Routledge).
Bially Mattern, J. and A. Zarakol (2016) 'Hierarchies in World Politics', *International Organization*, August 2016, doi:10.1017/S0020818316000126.
Bull, H. (1984) 'The Revolt Against the West', in Bull, H. and A. Watson (eds) *The Expansion of International Society* (Oxford, UK: Oxford University Press).
Christensen, P. T. (2013) 'Russia as Semiperiphery: Political Economy, the State, and Society in Contemporary World System', in *The Political Economy of Russia*, ed. by N. Robinson (Lanham, MD: Rowman and Littlefield).
Clunan, A. L. (2009) *Social Construction of Russia's Resurgence: Aspirations, Identity, and Security Interests* (Baltimore, MD: Johns Hopkins University Press).
Coward, R. and J. Ellis (1977) *Language and Materialism. Developments in Semiology and the Theory of the Subject* (London: Routledge and Keagan Paul).
Dawisha, K. (2011) 'Is Russia's Foreign Policy That of a Corporatist-Kleptocratic Regime?', *Post-Soviet Affairs* 27(4): 331–365.
Delyagin, M. (2000) *Igeologiya vozrozhdeniya* (Moscow: Forum).
Derluguian, G. M. (2005) *Bourdieu's Secret Admirer in the Caucasus: A World-System Biography* (Chicago, IL and London: The University of Chicago Press).
Etkind, A. (2002) 'Bremia britogo cheloveka, ili Vnutrennyaya kolonizatsiya Rossii', *Ab Imperio* 1: 265–298.
Etkind, A. (2011) *Internal Colonization: Russia's Imperial Experience* (Cambridge, UK: Polity).
Etkind, A. (2014) 'Post-Soviet Russia: The Land of the Oil Curse, Pussy Riot, and Magical Historicism', *boundary 2* 41(1): 153–170.
Etkind, A., D. Uffelmann and I. Kukulin (2012) 'Vnutrenniaya kolonizatsiya Rossii: mezhdu praktikoi i voobrazheniem', in *Tam, vnutri: praktiki vnutrennei kolonizatsii v kulturnoi istorii Rossii*, ed. by A. Etkind, D. Uffelmann, I. Kukulin (Moscow: Novoe literaturnoe obozrenie).

Forgacs, D. (1999) 'National-Popular: Genealogy of a Concept', *The Cultural Studies Reader*, 2nd ed., 209–19 (London and New York: Routledge).

Foucault, M. (2000 [1978]) 'Governmentality', in *Power: Essential Works of Foucault, 1954–1984*, ed. by J. D. Faubion, 201–222 (Harmondsworth, UK: Penguin).

Gaddy, C. G. and B. W. Ickes (2013) 'Russia's Dependence on Resources', in *The Oxford Handbook of the Russian Economy*, ed. by M. Alexeev and S. Weber (New York: Oxford University Press).

Gerschenkron, A. (1962) *Economic Backwardness in Historical Perspective* (Cambridge, UK: Belknap Press).

Glazyev, S. (2003) *Blagosostoyanie i spravedlivost: Kak pobedit bednost v bogatoi strane* (Moscow: B.S.G.-Press).

Goldman, M. I. (2008) *Petrostate: Putin, Power, and the New Russia* (Oxford, UK: Oxford University Press).

Gong, G. W. (1984) *The Standard of 'Civilization' in International Society* (Oxford, UK: Clarendon Press).

Gourevitch, P. (1978) 'The Second Image Reversed: The International Sources of Domestic Politics', *International Organization* 32(4): 881–912.

Hedlund, S. (2008) 'Rents, Rights, and Service: Boyar Economics and the Putin Transition', *Problems of Post-Communism* 55(4): 29–41.

Hollis, M. and S. Smith (1990) *Explaining and Understanding International Relations* (Oxford, UK: Clarendon Press).

Hopf, T. (2002) *Social Origins of International Politics. Identities and Foreign Policies, Moscow, 1955 and 1999* (Ithaca, NY and London: Cornell University Press).

Hopf, T. (2009) 'Identity Relations and the Sino-Soviet Split', in *Measuring Identity: A Guide for Social Scientists*, ed. by R. Abdelal et al. (Cambridge, UK: Cambridge University Press), pp. 279–315.

Hopf, T. (2010) 'The Logic of Habit in International Relations', *European Journal of International Relations* 16(4): 539–561.

Hopf, T. (2013) 'Common-Sense Constructivism and Hegemony in World Politics', *International Organization* 67(2): 317–354.

Hopf, T. (2017) 'Russia Becoming Russia: A Semi-Periphery in Splendid Isolation', in *Uses of 'the West': Security and the Politics of Order*, ed. by G. Hellmann and B. Herborth, 203–230 (Cambridge, UK: Cambridge University Press).

Horkheimer, M. (1972 [1937]) 'Traditional and Critical Theory', in *Critical Theory: Selected Essays*, ed. by M. Horkheimer, 188–243 (New York: Herder and Herder).

Hosking, G. (1997) *Russia: People and Empire, 1552–1917* (Cambridge, MA: Harvard University Press).

Howard, M. (1984) 'The Military Factor in European Expansion', in *The Expansion of International Society*, ed. by H. Bull and A. Watson (Oxford, UK: Oxford University Press).

Jackson, P. T. (2008) 'Foregrounding Ontology: Dualism, Monism, and IR Theory', *Review of International Studies* 34(1): 129–153.

Jessop, B. (2006) 'Gramsci as a Spatial Theorist', *Critical Review of International Social and Political Philosophy* 8(4): 421–437.

Jones Luong, P. and E. Weinthal (2010) *Oil Is Not a Curse: Ownership Structure and Institutions in Soviet Successor States* (Cambridge, UK: Cambridge University Press).

Kagarlitsky, B. (2008) *Empire of the Periphery: Russia and the World System* (London: Pluto Press).

Kagarlitsky, B. (2014) *From Empires to Imperialism: The State and the Rise of Bourgeois Civilisation* (Abingdon, UK and New York: Routledge).

Kapustin, B. G. (1998) *Sovremennost' kak predmet politicheskoi teoriyi* (Moscow: Rosspen).

Kazharski, A. (2017) *Regionalism as an Identitary Enterprise? The Social Construction of 'Eurasian Union' and 'Russian Civilization' in Russia's Foreign Policy Discourses* (Budapest: Central European University Press).

Keal, P. (2003) *European Conquest and the Rights of Indigenous Peoples: The Moral Backwardness of International Society* (Cambridge, UK: Cambridge University Press).

Keene, E. (2002) *Beyond the Anarchical Society: Grotius, Colonialism and Order in World Politics* (Cambridge, UK: Cambridge University Press).

Kiersey, N. J. and D. Stokes (eds) (2011) *Foucault and International Relations: New Critical Engagements* (London and New York: Routledge).

Kivelson, V. A. and R. G. Suny (2016) *Russia's Empires* (Oxford, UK: Oxford University Press).

Kołodziejczyk, D. and C. Şandru (2012) 'Introduction: On Colonialism, Communist and East-Central Europe – Some Reflections', *Journal of Postcolonial Writing* 48(2): 113–116.

Kordonsky, S. (2007) *Resursnoe gosudarstvo* (Moscow: Regnum).

Krickovic, A. (2016) 'Catalyzing Conflict: The Internal Dimension of the Security Dilemma', *Journal of Global Security Studies* 1(2): 111–126.

Laclau, E. (2005) *On Populist Reason* (London: Verso).

Lake, D. A. (2009) *Hierarchy in International Relations* (Ithaca, NY: Cornell University Press).
Lane, D. (2013) *The Capitalist Transformation of State Socialism: The Making and Breaking of State Socialist Society, and What Followed* (New York: Routledge).
Lenin, V. I. (1960 [1899]) 'The Development of Capitalism in Russia', in *Collected Works*, vol. 3, 21–607 (Moscow: Progress).
Lenin, V. I. (1963 [1917]) 'Imperialism, the Highest Stage of Capitalism: A Popular Outline', in *Selected Works*, vol. 1, 667–766 (Moscow, Progress).
Lester, J. (1995) *Modern Tsars and Princes: The Struggle for Hegemony in Russia* (London and New York: Verso).
Lieven, D. (2000) *Empire: The Russian Empire and Its Rivals* (London: John Murray).
Lo, B. (2015) *Russia and the New World Disorder* (Washington, DC: Brookings Institution Press).
Makarychev, A. and V. Morozov (2013) 'Is "Non-Western Theory" Possible? The Idea of Multipolarity and the Trap of Epistemological Relativism in Russian IR', *International Studies Review* 15(3): 328–50.
Mitzen, J. (2006) 'Ontological Security in World Politics: State Identity and the Security Dilemma', *European Journal of International Relations* 12(3): 341–70.
Moore, D. C. (2001) 'Is the Post- in Postcolonial the Post- in Post-Soviet? Toward a Global Postcolonial Critique', *PMLA* 116(1): 111–128.
Morozov, V. (2013a) 'Conclusion: The Contingency of Politics and the Internationalization of Democracy', in *Decentring the West: The Idea of Democracy and the Struggle for Hegemony*, ed. by V. Morozov, 198–205 (Aldershot: Ashgate).
Morozov, V. (2013b) 'Subaltern Empire? Toward a Postcolonial Approach to Russian Foreign Policy', *Problems of Post-Communism* 60(6): 16–28.
Morozov, V. (2015) *Russia's Postcolonial Identity: A Subaltern Empire in a Eurocentric World* (Basingstoke, UK: Palgrave Macmillan).
Morozov, V. and E. Pavlova (2016) 'Indigeneity and Subaltern Subjectivity in Decolonial Discourses: A Comparative Study of Bolivia and Russia', *Journal of International Relations and Development*. doi:10.1057/s41268-016-0076-7.
Morozov, V. and B. Rumelili (2012) 'The External Constitution of European Identity: Russia and Turkey as Europe-Makers', *Cooperation and Conflict* 47(1): 28–48.
Morton, A. D. (2007) *Unravelling Gramsci: Hegemony and Passive Revolution in the Global Political Economy* (London: Pluto Press).
Nau, H. R. and D. M. Ollapally (eds) (2012) *Worldviews of Aspiring Powers: Domestic Foreign Policy Debates in China, India, Iran, Japan, and Russia* (New York: Oxford University Press).
Neumann, I. B. (1996) *Russia and the Idea of Europe. A Study in Identity and International Relations* (London and New York: Routledge).
Neumann, I. B. (1999) *Uses of the Other: 'The East' in European Identity Formation*, (Manchester: Manchester University Press).
Neumann, I. B. (2008) 'Russia as a Great Power, 1815–2007', *Journal of International Relations and Development* 11(2): 128–151.
Neumann, I. B. and V. Pouliot (2011) 'Untimely Russia: Hysteresis in Russian-Western Relations over the Past Millennium', *Security Studies* 20(1): 105–137.
Neumann, I. B. and O. J. Sending (2010) *Governing the Global Polity: Practice, Mentality, Rationality* (Ann Arbor, MI: University of Michigan Press).
O'Brien, P. (1984) 'Europe in the World Economy', in *The Expansion of International Society*, ed. by Bull, H., and A. Watson (Oxford, UK: Oxford University Press).
Pokrovsky, M. N. (1910–1912) *Russkaya istoriya s drevneishikh vremen*, with N. Nikolsky and V. Storozhev, 5 vols (Moscow: Mir).
Pokrovsky, M. N. (1923) *Diplomatiya i voiny tsarskoi Rossii v XIX stoletii* (Moscow: Krasnaya nov').
Pokrovsky, M. N. (1933) *Brief History of Russia* (London: Martin Lawrence).
Prozorov, S. (2009) 'In and Out of Europe: Identity Politics in Russian-European Relations', in *Identity and Foreign Policy: Baltic-Russian Relations and European Integration*, ed. by E. Berg and P. Ehin, 133–159 (Farnham, UK: Ashgate).
Prozorov, S. (2011) 'From *Katechon* to *Intrigant*: The Breakdown of the Post-Soviet *Nomos*', in *The Great Power (mis)Management: The Russian–Georgian War and its Implications for Global Political Order*, ed. by A. Astrov, 25–42 (Farnham, UK: Ashgate).
Robinson, N. (2013) 'The Contexts of Russia's Political Economy: Soviet Legacies and Post-Soviet Policies', in *The Political Economy of Russia*, ed. by N. Robinson (Lanham, MD: Rowman and Littlefield).

Rosenberg, J. (2006) 'Why Is There No International Historical Sociology?', *European Journal of International Relations* 12(3): 307–340.
Rosenberg, J. (2013) 'The "Philosophical Premises" of Uneven and Combined Development', *Review of International Studies* 39(3): 569–597.
Rosenberg, J. (2016) 'International Relations in the Prison of Political Science', *International Relations*, doi: 10.1177/0047117816644662.
Rutland, P. (2015) 'Petronation? Oil, Gas, and National Identity in Russia', *Post-Soviet Affairs* 31(1): 66–89.
Sassoon, A. S. (1982) 'A Gramsci Dictionary', in *Approaches to Gramsci*, ed. by A. S. Sassoon, 12–17 (London: Writers and Readers).
Simon, R. (2009) 'Upper Volta with Gas? Russia as a Semiperipheral State', in *Globalisation and the 'New' Semi-Peripheries in the Twenty First Century*, ed. by P. Moore and O. Worth (Basingstoke, UK: Palgrave Macmillan).
Snetkov, A. (2012) 'When the Internal and External Collide: A Social Constructivist Reading of Russia's Security Policy', *Europe-Asia Studies* 64(3): 521–542.
Snetkov, A. (2015) *Russia's Security Policy under Putin: A Critical Perspective* (London and New York: Routledge).
Spivak, G. C. (1988) 'Can the Subaltern Speak?', in *Marxism and the Interpretation of Culture*, ed. by C. Nelson and L. Grossberg (Basingstoke, UK: Macmillan Education).
Steele, B. (2008) *Ontological Security in International Relations: Self-Identity and the IR State* (London and New York: Routledge).
Suzuki, S. (2009) *Civilization and Empire: China and Japan's Encounter with European International Security* (London and New York: Routledge).
Toews, J. E. (1987) 'Intellectual History after the Linguistic Turn: The Autonomy of Meaning and the Irreducibility of Experience', *The American Historical Review* 92(4): 879–907.
Torfing, J. (1999) *New Theories of Discourse. Laclau, Mouffe and Žižek* (Oxford, UK: Blackwell).
Treisman, D. (2010) 'Rethinking Russia: Is Russia Cursed by Oil?', *Journal of International Affairs*, 63(2): 85–102.
Trotsky, L. (2008 [1930]) *History of the Russian Revolution* (Chicago, IL: Haymarket Books).
Tsygankov, A. P. (2012) *Russia and the West from Alexander to Putin: Honor in International Relations* (Cambridge, UK: Cambridge University Press).
Tsygankov, A. P. (2014) *The Strong State in Russia: Development and Crisis* (New York: Oxford University Press).
Veblen, T. (1964 [1915]) *Imperial Germany and the Industrial Revolution* (New York: Kelley).
Wallerstein, I. (1974) *The Modern World-System: Capitalist Agriculture and the Origins of the European World-Economy in the Sixteenth Century* (New York: Academic Press).
Waltz, K. (1979) *Theory of International Politics* (New York: McGraw-Hill).
Watson, A. (1984) 'Russia and the European States System', in *The Expansion of International Society*, ed. by H. Bull and A. Watson (Oxford, UK: Oxford University Press).
Wendt, A. (1987) 'The Agent–Structure Problem in International Relations Theory', *International Organization* 41(2): 335–370.
Wendt, A. (1999) *Social Theory of International Politics* (Cambridge, UK: Cambridge University Press).
Wohlforth, W. C. (2001) 'The Russian-Soviet Empire: A Test of Neorealism', *Review of International Studies* 27(5): 213–235.
Worth, O. (2005) *Hegemony, International Political Economy and Post-Communist Russia* (Farnham, UK: Ashgate).
Zarakol, A. (2010) 'Ontological (In)security and State Denial of Historical Crimes: Turkey and Japan', *International Relations* 24(3): 3–23.
Zarakol, A. (2011) *After Defeat: How the East Learned to Live with the West* (Cambridge, UK: Cambridge University Press).

3

POWER AND NATIONAL SECURITY

Elena Kropatcheva

INSTITUTE FOR PEACE RESEARCH AND SECURITY POLICY
AT THE UNIVERSITY OF HAMBURG, GERMANY

Introduction

Realist perspectives have been strongly present in studies of Soviet and Russian foreign policies. Especially after World War II, the popularity of realist interpretations of Soviet-Western relations was determined by the necessity of explaining the developments of the Cold War period, the distribution of power capabilities between states, deterrence strategies, and the opportunities for achieving stability and peace (see Hollis and Smith, 1990: 16–45). The development of neorealism is closely connected with the Cold War and scholarly interest in neorealism or disappointment with it reflected major trends – cooperation or conflict – in Soviet-Western relations (cf. Schörnig, 2010: 66).

Many Soviet foreign policy studies were 'atheoretical' in that they used some versions of neo-realism without, however, explicitly making a claim to being realist (Kanet, 2012: 393). They emphasized the rational and realist nature of Soviet policy and its response to the changes in the systemic environment and distribution of power (e.g. Barrington Moore, 1950; Shulman, 1963).

Because of the dissolution of the Soviet Union and the inability of realism to predict the end of the Cold War, other approaches – especially constructivism – have challenged the domination of the realist framework in studies of Russian foreign policy (Kanet, 2012: 393).

Few International Relations (IR) schools of thought have generated as many debates and criticism as realism. There have been many debates and attempts at modifications and reinterpretations within realism itself (Freyberg-Inan et al., 2009). As a result, many contemporary realist studies of Russian foreign policy have a defensive and/or exploratory character in that they try to prove the relevance of the main realist premises.

Despite theoretical challenges, competition and critique, realism has, nonetheless, survived as one of the important approaches to Russian foreign policy. This is seen in a great multitude of various 'atheoretical' studies, which refer to basic realist postulates without making a claim to being realist per se. For example, scholars note that Russia has been interested in increasing its power vis-à-vis the West (Mankoff, 2011); Russia has used its energy and other resources to project its power over its neighbours (Nygren, 2008; Newnham, 2011); Russia has challenged the US global hegemony at different levels and in different regions, by using balancing strategies (Blank and Kim, 2015) or a combination of balancing and bandwagoning (Oldberg, 2007). The number of studies which explicitly adopt different realist approaches (alone or in combination with other theoretical approaches) has been growing as well (Kropatcheva, 2012; Karagiannis, 2013; Bock et al., 2015; Splidsboel-Hansen, 2015; Becker et al., 2016).

Especially in the last few years, realist interpretations have experienced a revival within Russian foreign policy studies, owing to a more assertive, conflictive, militarized and less predictable Russian behaviour, as well as the failures of liberal approaches and institutionalism, which – in contrast to current developments – had predicted Russia's socialization and greater Russian-Western cooperation.

Finally, the popularity of the realist explanations among Russian scholars as well as politicians is an additional factor that draws scholarly interest to this theoretical school (see on IR in Russia: Sergounin, 2009; Tsygankov and Tsygankov, 2010; Romanova and Pavlova, 2012). Bertil Nygren (2012: 518) goes so far as to argue: 'Analysts are . . . advised to use the same thinking and the same perspective as these major policy-makers precisely because the quality of the prediction will improve'.

This chapter provides a review of how realism has been applied to the study of Soviet/Russian foreign policy, although – owing to the limits of this chapter – it is impossible to mention all worthy realist work on Russia. This overview of realist studies of Soviet/Russian foreign policy also reflects the main developments within realism itself, in particular the inclination to enhance structural/systemic perspectives by integrating domestic and ideational variables, in accordance with neoclassical realism (NCR).

This chapter is structured in the following way. The first section discusses some of the major realist perspectives which have been most frequently used by Russia scholars. The second section illustrates how these perspectives were applied in relation to specific questions often raised by Russia scholars. The last section summarizes the main conclusions of using realism, in general, in the area of Russian foreign policy studies, but also pays special attention to the advantages and caveats of using NCR, in particular, as the most useful and promising trend within realism (Devlen and Özdamar, 2009; Freyberg-Inan et al., 2009; Onea, 2012; Wohlforth, 2012).

Different realisms

Realism – broadly defined – is one of the oldest approaches to studying IR. Realism includes different broad theoretical and philosophical approaches, which deal with general patterns of IR, as well as more specific theories, whose goal is foreign policy analysis, e.g. neoclassical and synoptic realism, defensive, offensive, democratic, liberal, ethical, and cultural (Siedschlag, 2001; Freyberg-Inan et al., 2009; Onea, 2012; Wohlforth, 2012; Ripsman et al., 2016).

What unites all of them is the predominant focus on the exogenous factors: a state's place in the international system vis-à-vis other states and the conditions of that system itself. States are usually portrayed as guided by (largely, even though not always) rational self-interest and competing for power and resources, which are necessary to provide for the survival and security of the state.

As William C. Wohlforth (2012: 38) explains, all realist thought from Thucydides to the middle years of the Cold War – including Hans Morgenthau (1993) – is usually lumped together as classical realism, whose representatives tried to transfer 'the distilled wisdom of generations of practitioners and analysts into very general theories', without, however, always being clear, 'about when their theories applied to specific situations as opposed to general patterns'.

Kenneth N. Waltz (1979) developed the earlier realist ideas further. The focus of his analysis is at the level of the international system, within which states act 'like units' or as 'unitary actors.' Because the structure of the international system (independent variable) determines the behaviour of states, his neorealism is also called structural/systemic. Under the conditions of anarchy, states try to accumulate power vis-à-vis other states. Neorealism does not study the internal conditions of the states and leaves this as the 'black box', which may be important for understanding concrete foreign policy situations. It is not the task of neorealism to open it up, but rather to study general tendencies and systemic effects. States, which act in the anarchic system, use self-help methods (Waltz, 1979: 915). They try to create a balance of power by building up their own capabilities ('internal balancing') or aggregating their capabilities with other states in alliances ('external balancing') (Wohlforth, 2012: 40). Because changes in the distribution of power are dangerous and may lead to counterbalancing and wars, Waltz generally expects defensive strategies on the part of the states.

Those realists who, in general, agree with Waltz's balance-of-power premises can be divided into offensive and defensive (Lobell, 2016: 38). They aim to explain concrete policies of states (Lobell, 2016).

Offensive realists (e.g. Zakaria, 1998; Mearsheimer, 2014a) claim that the international system gives strong incentives for power maximization. As a result, states, even though guided by defensive motives, may act offensively in order to alter the balance of power to their benefit and to weaken competitors, inter alia by initiating expansion, wars, and revision of the international order (Lobell, 2016: 39). However, states are 'prudent territorial expanders', and 'may forgo opportunities to increase their power because the costs are too high' (Lobell, 2016: 41).

By contrast, defensive realists (e.g. Walt, 1987; Friedberg, 1988; Wohlforth, 1993) believe that states prefer cooperative and peaceful means to maximize their security, but may turn to self-defeating expansion and other – what they consider as irrational and ineffective – offensive policies because of domestic- and individual-level pathologies (Lobell, 2016: 47).

Defensive realism has given many starting points to the development of neoclassical realism (NCR). This is a sub-school within realism, which seeks to rectify the imbalance between studying the general – systemic effects and general trends in IR – and the particular – concrete foreign policies of states, paying more attention to the unit level or 'black box' (cf. Wohlforth, 2012: 39). Because of its growing popularity within Russian foreign policy studies (Kropatcheva, 2012; Nygren, 2012; Romanova and Pavlova, 2012; Simao, 2012; Splidsboel-Hansen, 2015; Becker et al., 2016), the next paragraphs explain in more detail what NCR is.

The first wave of NCR studies (though they were not labelled as such at that time) came in the 1980s (Rose, 1998: 155). The number of NCR works has grown since the end of the Cold War, owing to disappointment with neorealism. However, as Jennifer Sterling-Folker (2009a: 208) notes, even prior to these events:

> [t]here was dissatisfaction with systemic-level theorizing . . . among IR scholars who were interested in the nexus between foreign policy, history, and/or comparative politics . . . The end of the Cold War may have simply legitimized a sentiment that was already present in the discipline.

There is no single text of a 'mother/father figure who can claim to have given birth' to NCR (Sterling-Folker, 2009a: 208). Gideon Rose used this term the first time, in order to classify a group of realists who, in their works, underlined that 'the scope and ambition of a country's foreign policy is driven first and foremost by its place in the international system and specifically by its relative material power capabilities', but also emphasized the importance of the 'intervening variables at the unit level' (Rose, 1998: 146), which shape a state's actual policy responses to external stimuli.

As in the past, today many realist scholars, including Russia scholars who produce works that could be labelled as NCR, 'prefer alternative terms . . . prefer to describe their work according to another realist variant . . . or do not use the term neoclassical realism at all' (Sterling-Folker, 2009a: 208). However, the growing appeal of NCR is also reflected in the multitude of NCR studies per se (Sterling-Folker, 2009b; Onea, 2012; Sørensen, 2013; Smith, 2014; Juneau, 2015).

A neoclassical realist analysis starts with the analysis of structural/systemic variables – a state's power, its position in the international system, and its interactions with other states. The systemic nature of the main argument is consistent with the core neorealist thinking (Onea, 2012: 156).

However, during the second stage of analysis, neoclassical realists turn to 'the classical realist interest in the state, its relationship to society, and its role in determining the "national interest"' (Sterling-Folker, 2009b: 103). This is the level of intervening variables, which can be roughly grouped into two main interrelated groups: (1) perceptions/beliefs/assessments of the international position of the country and of others by decision-makers and the society; and (2) domestic factors or state-society relations – the personality of decision-makers (psychological factors), domestic power division (conflicts/consensus among coalition groups; legitimacy), features of the state (political character, ideology, nationalism, identity, narratives), and others. The growing trend has been to favour more complexity by including several intervening variables.

Most frequently, NCR acts as a 'theory of mistakes' (Schweller, 2006) by showing that the system punishes those states which allow domestic imperatives to 'overcom[e] the state and ideas interrupting accurate readings of interests' (Rathbun, 2008: 310). Even if the influence of intervening factors is presented as normal, it is temporary, and, at some point, the primacy of structural-systemic factors returns (e.g. Dueck, 2009).

Thus, the specialty of NCR is that it tries to integrate the systemic/structural, domestic, and ideational variables into an analysis in a more systematic and coherent manner, but also to show the interaction among these variables. Neoclassical realists have used domestic politics and ideational variables to flesh out the main neorealist concepts. At the same time, intervening variables are introduced to specify, not reject, the influence of the international system.

This short overview of some trends within realism shows an important development: applying realist premises to explain not only general patterns of IR, but also concrete foreign policy situations; as well as considering not only the systemic factors but also complementing the structural analysis by dealing with the 'units'. These major developments within realism are also reflected within Soviet/Russian foreign policy studies.

Soviet/Russian foreign policy through the prism of realist perspectives

This section illustrates that realist approaches have been applied to explain a number of important historic and contemporary topics concerning Soviet/Russian international behaviour: Russian/Soviet empire-building; Russia's power and status aspirations; Russia's new assertiveness in its war with Georgia in 2008; and the ongoing Ukraine crisis. This list of themes, which Russia scholars have dealt with through the prism of realism, is far from being exhaustive. They serve to illustrate when and how realist perspectives have been applied, which variables were studied, and which conclusions – about Soviet/Russian international conduct as well as strengths and weaknesses of realism – were drawn.

Russian/Soviet empire-building

One of the most important questions discussed by Russia scholars has been the motives behind Russian/Soviet empire-building. Realists have dealt with this subject as well, and the following two contributions illustrate how.

To start with, William C. Wohlforth (2001) tests whether Waltz's main premises can be applied to the case of Russian expansion. He uses a *longue durée* perspective, as Waltz's realism was not aimed at explaining specific events, but rather long-run tendencies, and draws upon abundant empirical work on Russian history. Russia's expansion is taken as a dependent variable, while the state of the international system is considered an independent variable: anarchy, both at the broader systemic level and especially in its regional dimension (regions surrounding Russia), has constantly generated security problems for Russia. These security concerns are defined as the main driving force behind Russia's expansion; they have also influenced Russian national identity and domestic political arrangements (Wohlforth, 2001: 215).

While realism is prescriptive for states to act rationally, Waltz's approach highlights adaptation and selection rather than strict rational choice (Wohlforth, 2001: 215). In accordance with this, Wohlforth (2001: 215) interprets Russia's expansion as a result of adaptation to external pressures. He writes: 'Maintaining and periodically extending this empire were, thus, necessary in order to attain and retain great-power status, which was necessary to defend the empire' (Wohlforth, 2001: 221). Thereby, Wohlforth's neorealist explanation contradicts the domestic politics approach (which explains Russian foreign policy through its domestic developments and the specific autocratic structures) and also contradicts constructivist premises. According to Wohlforth (2001: 216, 221, 223), it was the specific geopolitical context that had shaped the Russian identity and not *vice versa* – that Russia's identity had led to specific geopolitics. As a result, Wohlforth's (2001: 215) overall conclusion is that, despite all critique, 'neorealist theory turns out to have powerful explanatory leverage over the larger pattern of Russian and Soviet strategic choices'. At the same time, Wohlforth (2001: 227) also admits the limits of neorealism: a 'black box' remains a black box and 'neorealist theory cannot fully explain domestic institutions and ideas'.

Jack Snyder also studies empire-building processes by examining several case studies, including the Soviet one. He has come to the conclusion that, while realist arguments explain quite well some of the periods of the Soviet policy (e.g. Stalin's buck-passing diplomacy of the 1930s and his aggressive policies in Europe in the late 1940s), they were much weaker in dealing with other cases, such as, for example, Khrushchev's diplomatic over-assertiveness and Brezhnev's imperial overextension.

Using the premises of defensive (or what would now be called neoclassical) realism, he shows that Soviet policies were sometimes irrational and counterproductive. To develop an explanation for these Soviet policies of 'overextension' and 'self-encirclement', he not only examines their international position and systemic challenges, but also introduces an intervening variable: the Soviets' perceptions of the systemic incentives (Snyder, 1991: 229). He argues that, throughout that time, there were different schools of thought about the nature of the West's threat and whether to prefer offence or defence, which influenced Soviet foreign policy. In particular, because of misperceptions, the Soviets chose the wrong strategies and did not understand their opponents, e.g. trying to accommodate an unappeasable opponent – Hitler – (on this behaviour, characterized as underbalancing, see also Schweller, 2006). Misperceptions or 'myths of empire' also accounted for policies, which went against the systemic rules of international politics, resulting in more insecurity. Snyder (1991: 12) writes: 'States with myth-producing domestic political orders engage in preventive aggression to forestall hypothetical future threats from states that have not yet taken significant menacing actions'. Besides (mis-)perceptions, international influences (e.g. the character of an opponent, the (in)stability of the status quo, windows of opportunity and others) are also filtered through specific domestic structures (e.g. economic backwardness, self-sufficiency, inclination to expand, and risk-acceptance). His overall conclusion is: 'Realists are right in stressing power, interests, and coalition making', but they have been wrong in ignoring the role ideology/perceptions and domestic institutions play (Snyder, 1991: 19).

Summing up, while both Wohlforth and Snyder underline neorealism's strength in explaining general longer-term patterns of behaviour, they both admit that it can only account in a limited way for specific cases. This is why Snyder complements the neorealist perspective by studying domestic institutions and ideas, and shows that international aggressive behaviour may be generated by domestic sources of insecurity. At the same time, both scholars agree, in the wording of Wohlforth (2001: 227) that 'the evolution of institutions and ideas cannot be explained without reference to the causal forces neorealism identifies'.

Russia's power and status aspirations

Realists generally agree that Russia is searching for more power and influence in international relations. However, the concepts of power and influence have been most elusive and are strongly debated within realism. While most realist analyses of Russian foreign policy begin with the analysis of material indicators of power and influence, such as economic, financial and military resources, compared to those of other great powers, realist analyses have gradually started to go beyond this material understanding of power.

For example, to study Soviet foreign policy and its power aspirations, Wohlforth in his book, which was classified as NCR by Rose (1998), also introduced an intervening variable to specify what power is, that is the perceptions by the elites of power and power shifts. He worked with this modified concept of power, by analysing the dynamics of conflict and the easing of tension in Soviet–Western relations. To study perceptions, he used written sources (journals, archives, etc.) and interviews as well as the content analysis method. Wohlforth's (1993: 301–302) conclusion was:

> Each [cycle of conflict] was shaped by a change in the power relationship differently interpreted by the two sides ... In the wake of each shift, each side tried to maximize its own position. Unwilling to go to war to test the power distribution, they reached stalemates after crises, posturing and signaling until a new perceived shift led to another round.

In general, the Cold War was presented 'as an ongoing dispute between the U.S. and USSR over who had how much power and what influence over the international system they were thus entitled to exercise' (Rose, 1998: 159).

Wohlforth's perception-based approach to power is applied to studying the issue of contemporary conflict-cooperation between Russia and the West by Russia scholars adopting an NCR perspective. For example, Elena Kropatcheva (2013) considers the impact of the external variable, which was often neglected in this context – China's rise – on NATO-Russia relations. Even though China's rise leaves many questions unanswered, it has started to impact Russia's NATO policies and NATO-Russia relations. Russian foreign policy responses depend on the perceptions of global power shifts by Russian policy-makers. These perceptions have been changing: before the Ukraine crisis, not only was a hypothetical alliance with China versus NATO discussed, but also the idea of an alliance with NATO versus China was brought up. Today, in Russian foreign policy, China plays an increasingly important role in easing the pressure of Western sanctions on Russia. All in all, Russia is cooperating, competing, or even conflicting with NATO or China at the same time, depending on the issue area and broader international trends. These different patterns in Russian foreign policy are predetermined by competing domestic perceptions, but also by tactical attempts to instrumentalize these two alternatives while searching for adequate responses to external pressures.

In another article, taking the same theoretical approach, Kropatcheva (2014) explores the impact of another external factor – the 'shale revolutions' – on Russia's energy power in its foreign policy. While Russian energy policy is usually considered in the regional context (Russia's relations with the EU and the post-Soviet countries), this study has shown that, in order to understand Russia's energy power, it is necessary to place it in the broader global context as well as to consider how Russian policy-makers perceive Russia's energy power and the external challenges it faces. Then it becomes clear that Russia is not as powerful as it is often presented in the literature, and energy power capability is also about having a long-term vision as well as institutional and conceptual strength – all of which Russia lacks.

To understand Russia's power aspirations, Bertil Nygren (2012) links perceptions and domestic institutions/developments even more closely together and, thereby, introduces the special intervening variable 'Putinism', to show how intertwined domestic factors, such as specific ideational paradigms adopted by Vladimir Putin, state centralization, FSB-ization and militarization of the society, and others, impact Russia's ambitions. The 'Putinism' variable suggests that Russia's policy, aimed at increasing its global and regional role, will remain a policy of continuity, regardless of whether this policy matches the available resources (Nygren, 2012: 522).

Because power is increasingly understood by realists not only in material, but also in ideational terms, Russia scholars, who adopt realist approaches, also study not only how Russia uses material or hard-power tools to pursue its power ambitions, but also soft-power tools and international norms as a part of its *Realpolitik* (Ziegler, 2014; Becker et al., 2016).

One more important development in the concept of power by Russia realist scholars is stressing its aspiration for status or prestige (Wohlforth, 1993: 28; Mankoff, 2011: 5). Wohlforth (1993) pointed out this vital dimension of power in Soviet-US relations, observing that while the USSR was struggling to gain the status it perceived it deserved, the US was denying the USSR a greater international role, perceiving its own status to be higher. This theme is further developed in Wohlforth's later contributions (Wohlforth, 2001, 2009; Paul et al., 2014). The issue of status is used to explain historic events as well as contemporary Russian foreign policy.

For example, according to Wohlforth (2009: 44), the origins of the Crimean War illustrate how a specific material setting can create 'ambiguity about rank, setting the stage for states to fight over a minor and readily divisible issue that comes to symbolize relative status'. In this case, Russia, which saw itself throughout as defending its identity as an upholder of the status quo, became the offensive revisionist power, with painful results for it (Wohlforth, 2009: 47).

Jeffrey Mankoff also notes that Russia's foreign policy, especially in such cases as the Russian-Georgian war in 2008, is guided by whether it sees itself as a satisfied or a revisionist power. Russia has been a power dissatisfied with its international status, thus it is interested in revising the international order (cf. Mankoff, 2011: 5).[1]

Summing up, realist Russia scholars have gradually been expanding the understanding of what power means. The variable of domestic structures helps, thereby, to specify how systemic pressures on Russia's power are filtered through specific domestic conditions. The difference from diverse liberal approaches is that realists still give primacy to systemic factors. To illustrate this point, while Mankoff (2011) analyses domestic power struggles in Russian foreign policymaking and, in particular, differences between Vladimir Putin and Dmitry Medvedev during their tandem years (2008–2012), he, nonetheless, comes to the conclusion: 'Yet it is less the personality of the individual sitting in the Kremlin than the changing strategic landscape that Russia confronts that will play the most important role' in Russian foreign policy (Mankoff, 2011: 280).

Furthermore, the notion of power is expanded by Russia realist scholars by including the intervening variable of perceptions, that is, how Soviet/Russian policy-makers perceive power and international power distribution/shifts, but also by emphasizing that power means social status and prestige. While this ideational dimension of Russian foreign policy can be and is addressed within constructivist and liberal approaches, the inclusion of ideational/social variables also fits in well with the realist tradition and is not the exclusive prerogative of constructivism and liberalism (Morgenthau, 1993; Rathbun, 2008). Subjective/ideational factors have become a part of realist strategies. As a result, states pursue not only power and security in material terms, but also social status (Wohlforth, 1993; Sterling-Folker, 2002, 2009b).

The difference from liberal/constructivist approaches is that realists still connect ideational/social factors to material and systemic ones. As Wohlforth (1993: 302) notes, perceptions of power do not exist independently of material measurements and follow a broad pattern which is connected to changes in real capabilities (Wohlforth, 1993: 302). In relation to status, he observes that social status is often security-driven (Wohlforth, 2009: 31); 'actors seek to translate material resources into status' (Wohlforth, 2009: 38); 'conflicts about status depend on material capabilities and on polarity that characterizes the system' (Wohlforth, 2009: 39); and status-seeking strategies 'require persuasion' and 'the ability to persuade is linked to material capability' (Wohlforth, 2009: 55). All in all, ideational and domestic intervening variables are introduced to specify the impact of the independent – systemic/structural – variable.

Russia's new assertiveness in its war with Georgia in 2008 and the ongoing Ukraine crisis

Realism has gained popularity in recent years in attempts to explain Russian policy in relation to Georgia in 2008 and to Ukraine since 2013. Thereby, Russian foreign policy studies reflect a variety of realist variants and explanations and especially modifications and developments within realism.

Starting with the first case of the Russian-Georgian war, Emmanuel Karagiannis (2013) sees US-Russian competition both in its global context, as well as in the South Caucasus specifically, as the main cause of the 2008 Russian-Georgian war and, thereby, explicitly applies John Mearsheimer's offensive realism. The US is presented as an offshore balancer in the South Caucasus with energy interests in the region and with the geopolitical goal of preventing Russia from becoming a regional hegemon. Thus, US policy is understood as the main driving factor behind Russian assertiveness and militarization of its foreign policy. He shows that Russia responded to Georgia's military operation in South Ossetia in a well-calculated manner, using this opportunity to re-establish its hegemony without, however, going so far as to occupy other territories, because of the costs (especially the deterioration of relations with the West) being too high and the benefits being too dubious. As Karagiannis (2013) concludes, Russia needed to fight this war against a weak opponent (Georgia), in order to defend its regional position as well as to survive in the anarchical international system.

Hans Mouritzen and Anders Wivel (2012) also examine the Russian-Georgian war through a more complex – what can be classified as NCR – perspective. They explore the reactions of different actors – Russia, Georgia, the US, the EU, countries in Russia's 'near abroad', and China. In each case, they start their examination with an analysis of the systemic/structural conditions, then move onto the level of interstate relations (geopolitics) if explanations at the previous level are not satisfactory and, if still necessary, go onto the intrastate (socio-psychological factors and decision-making dynamics) level. As a result, they assess which level of analysis has a greater explanatory power in each of the cases. After having examined about forty cases, they come to the conclusion that, in the case of Russia, the purely systemic perspective works best, and other factors have played a minor role. Thus, for them, it is sufficient to use a systemic/structural perspective to understand the main driving factors behind Russia's policy (which is not true for other cases) – most importantly, the growing US influence and Georgia's closer relations with NATO.

As in the case of the Russian-Georgian war, John Mearsheimer (2016, 2014b) himself but also other leading realists (Walt, 2015; Schweller, 2017) explain Russia's recent Ukraine policy, especially its annexation of the Crimea and the ongoing destabilization strategies in the East, as a defensive reaction to the West's policies. For them, Russia's current assertive policy – in Ukraine, Georgia, or Syria – is logical and predictable, if long-term patterns of Russian-Western relations are considered.

Mearsheimer, in particular, criticizes the policies of NATO enlargement, EU expansion, and democracy promotion. Mearsheimer and other realists remind us of the fact that, from the start, realists opposed NATO's policy of 'expansion' as a mistake (Mearsheimer, 2014b, 6–7; Walt, 2016; Schweller, 2017) and predicted that Russia would counteract at some point. As Mearsheimer (in McFaul et al., 2014: 177) summarizes:

> When the United States and its allies take note of Moscow's concerns . . . crises are averted and Russia cooperates on matters of mutual concern. When the West ignores Moscow's interests . . . confrontation reigns.

Thus, realists argue in favour of a so-called 'Russia first' approach, in which the US has more interest in maintaining positive relations with Russia rather than supporting its smaller neighbours with pro-Western aspirations.

Stephen M. Walt explains that Putin is not interested 'in trying to reincorporate all of Ukraine . . . and the "frozen conflict" that now exists there is sufficient to achieve his core goal'. Both in Ukraine as well as Syria, Putin pursues goals 'equally simple, realistic, and aligned with Russia's limited means' (Walt, 2016). According to him, Putin's:

> [f]ailing is that it's all short-term . . . he is fighting a series of rearguard actions designed to prevent Russia's global position from deteriorating further, instead of pursuing a program that might enhance Russia's power and status over the longer term.
>
> *(Walt, 2016)*

Adopting the main premises of neorealism, an increasing number of scholars go beyond it, by developing neorealist concepts further and using NCR to interpret Russia's Ukraine policy. For example, Elias Götz (2016a) places Mearsheimer's neorealism into a broader temporal perspective and tests it systematically against the track record of Russia's Ukraine policy since the 1990s. He points to the gap in Mearsheimer's argument that while neorealism traditionally focuses on relations between great powers and on how smaller states react to their power games, 'the question of how larger states deal with smaller neighbours has received surprisingly little attention' (Götz, 2016a: 301). Götz's argument (2016a: 301–302) is that:

> [p]owerful states not only want to possess the greatest amount of material capabilities in their part of the world, as originally stated by Mearsheimer, but also seek to constrain the foreign-policy autonomy of smaller neighbouring countries.

They are also pursuing geopolitical and geo-economic interests.

Götz chooses 'the level of external pressure' – attempts by smaller neighbouring states to team up with great powers from other parts of the world – as an independent variable, which defines the tools and tactics by which major powers pursue and uphold their dominant regional positions. His hypothesis is that when the level of external pressure is low, the local great power will employ soft-power tools to dominate its neighbourhood; when the level of external pressure is high, it will adopt more assertive policies, including the use of force. If neighbouring states pursue multi-vector policies, then a local great power will use a mixture of soft- and hard-power tools (Götz, 2016a: 302). In the end, he comes to the conclusion that this 'simple logic goes a long way towards explaining the pattern of Russia's Ukraine policy over the last 25 years' and Russia's current Ukraine policy (Götz, 2016a: 302). However, he also brings up the neoclassical realist factor of 'state capacity' (see on this Zakaria, 1998; Schweller, 2006; Taliaferro, 2006; Foulon, 2015; Juneau, 2015) or Russia's lack of it to explain Russia's incoherent and less assertive behaviour in the late 1990s, a time of growing external pressure but internal weakness (Götz, 2016a: 316).

A number of Russia scholars also adopt NCR perspectives to emphasize the importance of the factor of perceptions in the case of Ukraine. For instance, according to Flemming Splidsboel-Hansen (2015), Russia's response to systemic inputs depends on the cognitive filters, intertwined with collective identity, which cause these systemic inputs to be interpreted by the Russian elite as well as the public in a negative way (2015: 147). Even though Russia's annexation of the Crimea was suboptimal, the way Putin 'framed' the developments in Ukraine meant he 'framed himself into a corner' from which there was only one way out – annexation of Crimea (Splidsboel-Hansen, 2015: 141).

Andrej Krickovic's (2016) approach, with his focus on the cases of Russia and China, linking international conflictive behaviour with domestic sources of insecurity, can also be classified as NCR or an adapted version of realism to non-Western realities. Thereby, he further develops the realist notion of an international security dilemma by emphasizing that it can be generated by domestic vulnerabilities. In his view, this was the case inter alia with Russia's reaction to events in Ukraine in 2013–2014. Because of its own insecurities (in particular, the problem of legitimacy and fear of 'colour revolutions' (more details in Krickovic, 2016: 8), Russia perceived the 'Euro-Maidan' and the loss of power by Victor Yanukovych as instigated by the West. As he explains further:

> Thus, the security dilemma created by Russia's internal insecurities has 'come full circle', as Russia's own concern about foreign meddling has led it to adopt policies that give rise to the same kind of fears in NATO countries . . . Thus, the two sides find themselves in the vicious circle emblematic of the security dilemma – where each side's efforts to improve its own security threaten the security of the other side.
>
> *(Krickovic 2016: 12)*

While Russia can be viewed as a weak developing state, nonetheless, it possesses significant national power (or what neoclassical realists would term 'state capacity') to engage in international security competition (Krickovic, 2016).

Finally, the role of Russia's perceptions of the developments in Ukraine, the emergence of a security dilemma, and, especially, the perceptions of Russian policy by external actors (e.g. the EU) is also discussed in contributions (Bock et al., 2015; Wigell and Vihma, 2016), which refer explicitly to Stephen Walt's modified understanding of Waltz's balance of power theory, that is his balance of threat theory (Walt, 1987). Accordingly, threats emerge under the conditions of the availability of material capabilities, important geographical location, and when a state is perceived as potentially aggressive. Thus, Russia has balanced against a potential threat of Ukraine's joining NATO, but the EU has also been balancing against the Russian threat.

Summing up, current realist analyses of Russia's policy towards Georgia and Ukraine point, first of all, to the systemic conditions which have encouraged Russia's current behaviour. Realist studies emphasize that Russia's new assertiveness was to be expected and it was only a matter of time before Russia decided to use a window of opportunity to try to restore its regional influence and, thereby, to elevate its power status in the international system. While Russia is being blamed for aggression and even imperialism, most frequently in current Western publications on the topic or in policy-making circles, the contribution of these realist studies is to point to the West's own mistakes for having neglected Russia's security and power/status concerns, for underestimating its strengths (as well as destabilization potential and 'state capacity'), and overestimating its weaknesses.

Besides general 'systemic' trends in Russian-Western relations, most Russian realist studies also point to the importance of inclusion in the analysis of regional geopolitics and geo-economics. The geopolitical approach, which specifically focuses on the impact of geography, distance, borders, physical power capabilities and instruments, and 'zero-sum' games between major powers, which compete over influence and domination in specific regions (Berryman, 2012: 531; Klieman, 2015), this is closely intertwined with realist interpretations of Russian foreign policy (for more examples, see Kropatcheva, 2011; Wigell and Vihma, 2016). The realist geopolitical/geo-economic perspectives underline that 'systemic' trends are brought into concrete regions, but these regions also have their own geopolitical/geo-economic dynamics which impact Russian foreign policy.

While the realist perspectives explain quite well the general contours of and logic behind Russia's foreign policy, as well as the systemic and regional geopolitical pressures it faces, it nonetheless leaves open some important questions. Ambivalent answers are given on Russia's choice of specific tactics and the timing of its assertiveness, even though, to be fair, other theoretical approaches, which focus on single variables, have also been unable to find exhaustive answers to Russia's assertiveness (Götz, 2016b).

For example, why did Russia annex the Crimea in 2014 and not earlier, when there were such opportunities (for example, after the Orange Revolution in 2004–2005)? In the case of South Ossetia and Abkhazia in Georgia, Russia refrained from formal annexation, so what changed between 2008 and 2014? Furthermore, in the case of Ukraine, it is not clear in the end why Russia used such aggressive tactics as it could have used milder means to pressure Ukraine to move from a more pro-Western policy towards a more pro-Russian course (as was the case in the past): both the EU and NATO lacked commitment to spend resources to support Ukraine or to accept it as a member, and Ukraine was heavily dependent on Russian energy and other financial and economic support. Moreover, realism predicts that rising power capabilities will lead to more assertive foreign policies, but in Russia's case, whether it is a rising or a declining power can be disputed, especially in the mid-2010s, owing to financial crises and low energy prices.

Finally, the main argument that it is the West that should be blamed for Russia's policy is oversimplified. Mearsheimer's critics, such as Michael McFaul (in McFaul et al., 2014) or Alexander Motyl (2015), point to the necessity of considering the factor of Russian-Ukrainian relations (or, in the first case, this would be Russian-Georgian relations) and their domestic politics and developments, including ideology. The main fault of neorealist studies in general is that they fail 'to pay much attention to states' internal structure, domestic factors, and the role of the state level in between the structure and foreign policy actions' (Foulon, 2015: 647).

Russia scholars who have applied neorealism themselves admit some of its limitations. For example, Karagiannis (2013: 88) points to 'additional factors' that likely played a role in the case of the Russian-Georgian war, for which neorealism cannot account. These can be, for example, Putin's personal antipathy toward Saakiashvili, Russian considerations of honour and prestige (as pointed out in Tsygankov and Tarver-Wahlquist, 2009; Tsygankov, 2012), and human rights concerns for ethnic Russians. Thus, as in the previous (historic) cases, the neorealist perspectives are able to explain the general logic behind Russian actions and the general patterns of Russian-Western relations, which challenged Russia to act in an offensive manner. Nonetheless, to understand the specifics of Russia's reaction, additional factors need to be included.

To fill the gaps left by neorealism, Russia scholars increasingly turn to NCR and its ability to integrate the study of perceptions/cognitive filters, state capacity, and internal vulnerabilities. NCR can also help to understand why realist thinking became dominant in the concrete constellation of external and domestic influences. All in all, NCR studies of Russian behaviour show how some neorealist arguments can and need to be further elaborated and specified, in order to increase the explanatory power of the theory.

Conclusions: the promises and caveats of applying neoclassical realism to Russian foreign policy analysis

This section starts with a summary of some general conclusions which can be drawn from this overview of the application of realism in relation to Soviet/Russian foreign policy. Because of the growing importance of the NCR perspective within the studies of Russian foreign policy, it then pays special attention to the promises and caveats of applying NCR.

As this chapter has shown, despite ups and downs within realism and all the critique it faces, realist approaches have been frequently – explicitly or implicitly – applied to explain Soviet and Russian foreign policies. Already, the few examples which it was possible to present here demonstrate that Russian foreign policy studies reflect the variety of realist approaches and major developments within realism.

Traditional systemic/structural approaches and their modified versions have been used to explicate longer and more general historic trends in Russian foreign policy (as its empire building/expansion and power/status aspirations), but also, even more, to explain concrete past and contemporary foreign policy situations (e.g. underbalancing, overextension, assertive/aggressive behaviour, costly and 'irrational' policies, shifts between conflict and cooperation). Overall, as in the past, realism is usually used to explain Russia's 'hard security' policies.

Realist approaches are a good fit for examining Russian foreign policy in different geographical and policy areas, including global and regional competition as well as cooperation, developments in the post-Soviet space, energy/economic and military policies. With their focus on exogenous factors, realist approaches have helped to turn scholars' attention to the new external developments, such as global power shifts and new technological developments, which affect Russia's power, but which are, nonetheless, sometimes neglected. Moreover, realists have started to pay more attention to Russia's soft power policies as a part of its *Realpolitik*.

The majority of realist analyses of Russian international behaviour are policy-oriented/empirical – often 'atheoretical' – studies. This practical orientation reflects the fact that realism was born out of diplomatic practice and often summarizes the common knowledge and general truths which philosophers and scholars have observed in international politics for centuries. This is why realist scholars often include policy recommendations in their analyses.

Realist studies of Russian foreign policy have also focused on theory testing, by generating realism-based hypotheses and exploring their applicability, their strengths, and their weaknesses in concrete cases. Fewer Russia scholars have made attempts at theorizing, that is, at developing some realist theoretical premises or approaches.

According to systemic/structural approaches, Russian foreign policy seems to be less surprising and more logical seen through a long-term perspective. The main motives guiding Russian foreign policy are the same (power, status, and security). What changes is tactics. This is influenced by the changes in capabilities and in the systemic strategic context. Thereby, realists underline both continuities in Russian foreign policy as well as changes, which for them are primarily systemic (and not identity changes, as, for example, for constructivists). The structural realist argument helps us to better understand international enabling factors and constraints on Russian foreign policy.

Besides considering the broader systemic context, scholars who take realist approaches to Russian foreign policy increasingly include in their analyses the factor of regional geopolitics and specific interregional power relations. In addition, the emphasis is placed on both history and geography as impacting Russian foreign policy.

Finally, an important trend within Russian foreign policy studies has been the attempt to specify the meaning of ambivalent realist concepts, especially by using NCR and by complementing the study of independent systemic variables, by incorporating the study of 'unit level' variables, such as domestic structures and ideational intervening variables. Thereby, Russian international conduct is still characterized in terms of 'traditional' realist concepts as pursuit of power, influence, and security; strategies of balancing/bandwagoning; security dilemmas; and others. However, the meanings of these concepts and the reasons behind these forms of behaviour are specified by resorting to intervening variables.

This chapter has shown that NCR offers important advantages by comparison with neorealism, while still using the logic of structural realism, but going beyond it and complementing – often overly deterministic – neorealist interpretations. As a result, a variety of available methods have been used within NCR studies of Russian foreign policy – elite interviews, process tracing, framing, content/narrative analysis, operational code analysis, and opinion polls. The broader and more flexible theoretical framework of NCR allows this methodological pluralism.

Besides having advantages vis-à-vis neorealism, as was shown throughout this chapter, NCR has some important strengths by comparison with other widespread explanations of Russian foreign policy. For example, various domestic policy approaches, which claim the primacy of domestic factors, e.g. Russia's nationalist or imperial ambitions (Bugajski, 2004), the vulnerability of the Russian regime (Stoner and McFaul, 2015; Wesslau and Wilson, 2016), the role of interest groups in Russian foreign policymaking (Dawisha, 2015; Marten, 2015), often overestimate the importance of these specific factors (Tsygankov, 2015: 294–295; Krickovic, 2016: 12) or even admit their secondary role, giving primacy to systemic factors (Charap and Welt, 2015; Marten, 2015). Re-wording Juneau (2015: 3), domestic factors 'account for tilts in foreign policy', while changes in the international balance of power can cause major shifts.

As was shown throughout this chapter, NCR does not reject, but rather integrates main constructivist categories. At the same time, NCR still prioritizes broad systemic factors and links ideational factors to material capabilities. All in all, NCR tries to show the bigger picture of how the single variables, which are studied by alternative theoretical approaches, come into interaction and shape concrete policy results.

Despite these advantages of NCR, Russia scholars have to be aware of some caveats. NCR has been characterized by its critics (including neo-realists) as a 'degenerative' research paradigm that has lost all distinctiveness vis-à-vis liberalism and constructivism (Vasquez, 1997; Legro and Moravcsik, 1999). Indeed, in practice, it is difficult to differentiate some of the studies, which claim to be NCR, from typical liberal or constructivist analyses, and the core realist argument can easily get lost among liberal/constructivist variables.

NCR is also attacked for sporadically filling the gaps left by structural realism (more details in Rathbun, 2008: 295), and for the inability to specify a priori conditions under which it can be falsified (Vasquez, 1997). One more problem is how to avoid over-complexity of research if too many explicatory variables are included.

A liberal critique is also that systemic influences are indeterminate and that it is difficult to say in advance which systemic influences have to be studied a priori. This point is admitted and debated by adherents of NCR (Onea, 2012; Ripsman et al., 2016: 2).

Perception-based NCR is dismissed for being constructivist, and constructivists point to the primacy of culture and the secondary nature of interests or consider identity and interests as being in a dialectical relationship. Neoclassical realists, however, point to the fact that because 'states and leaders are influenced by competing international and domestic norms and cultures and juggle multiple, and often conflicting identities', it would be difficult to predict their foreign policy choices, and to explain many aspects of international politics, it is necessary to consider the importance of relative distribution of material power (Ripsman et al., 2016: 6–7).

Ripsman et al. (2016) have recently tried to answer some of the most widespread criticisms and to develop some testable hypotheses and operational definitions. For example, they explain that the choice between using a structural realist explanation or working with intervening variables (as well as their choice) depends on the nature of the international environment (for example, 'restrictive' or 'permissive' conditions; the imminence of threats or opportunities; clarity of challenges) as well as the time framework of analysis. Their elaborations will be useful for future NCR studies of Russian foreign policy.

In summary, NCR is 'preferable to neorealism' (Ziegler, 2014: 592) and has many important advantages both vis-à-vis neorealism and other theoretical approaches. Those searching for a coherent and cohesive research framework or methodological purity would be looking in vain for this in NCR. Research, using single variables, helps us to better understand the individual factors which are involved in the process of Russian foreign policy-making. However, we also need a second strand of research – an integrative IR framework – which tries to bring single variables into a larger picture of how Russian foreign policy is made. This is what NCR attempts to do. At the same time, the main challenge remains that the core of the structural/systemic argument has to remain at the centre of the analysis, while it needs to be clear why and how intervening variables were chosen, and in which way they specify the structural/systemic argument.

Application of NCR to the Russian case can help not only to improve the understanding of Russian foreign policy in its complexity and international-domestic interaction, but also to further develop NCR postulates. NCR can help address a variety of topics – the unpredictability of Russia's actions, its suboptimal 'irrational' policies, and the shifts between cooperation and conflict as well as continuity and change, as these are shaped by the dynamic relationship between external and intervening variables. The NCR studies on Russian foreign policy should take a longer-term comparative perspective by including different historical periods, geographical areas, and issue areas so as to better contextualize and understand Russian international behaviour. All in all, despite the aforementioned serious caveats, the promises of NCR are strong enough for NCR analyses of Russian foreign policy to be pursued.

Note

1 For more on states that are satisfied or dissatisfied with status see, for example: Schweller 2006.

References

Barrington, MJ 1950, *Soviet politics: the dilemma of power – the role of ideas in social change*, Harvard University Press, Cambridge, MA.

Becker, ME, Cohen, MS, Kushi, S and McManus, IP 2016, 'Reviving the Russian empire: the Crimean intervention through a neoclassical realist lens', *European Security*, vol. 25, no. 1, pp. 112–133.

Berryman, J 2012, 'Geopolitics and Russian foreign policy', *International Politics*, vol. 49, no. 4, pp. 530–544.

Blank, S and Kim, Y 2015, 'Russia and Latin America: the new frontier for geopolitics, arms sales and energy', *Problems of Post-Communism*, vol. 62, no. 3, pp. 159–173.

Bock, AM, Henneberg, I and Plank, F 2015, '"If you compress the spring, it will snap back hard": the Ukrainian crisis and the balance of threat theory', *Canada's Journal of Global Policy Analysis*, vol. 70, no. 1, pp. 101–109.

Bugajski, J 2004, *Cold peace: Russia's new imperialism*, Center for Strategic and International Studies, Washington, DC.

Charap, S and Welt, C 2015, 'Making sense of Russian foreign policy', *Problems of Post-Communism*, vol. 62, no. 2, pp. 67–70.

Dawisha, K 2015, *Putin's kleptocracy: who owns Russia?* Simon & Schuster, New York.

Devlen, B and Özdamar, Ö 2009, 'Neoclassical realism and foreign policy crises', in A Freyberg-Inan, E Harrison and P James (eds), *Rethinking realism in international relations. Between tradition and innovation*, John Hopkins University Press, Baltimore.

Dueck, C 2009, 'Neoclassical realism and the national interest: presidents, domestic politics, and major military interventions', in SE Lobell, NM Ripsman and JW Taliaferro (eds), *Neoclassical realism, the state, and foreign policy*, Cambridge University Press, Cambridge, UK.

Foulon, M 2015, 'Neoclassical realism: challengers and bridging identities', *International Studies Review*, vol. 17, no. 4, pp. 635–661.

Freyberg-Inan, A, Harrison, E and James, P (eds) 2009, *What way forward for contemporary realism?* John Hopkins University Press, Baltimore, MD.

Friedberg, AL 1988, *The weary titan. Britain and the experience of relative decline, 1895–1905*, Princeton University Press, Princeton, NJ.

Götz, E 2016a, 'Neorealism and Russia's Ukraine policy, 1991-present', *Contemporary Politics*, vol. 22, no. 3, pp. 301–323.

Götz, E 2016b, 'Putin, the state, and war: The causes of Russia's near abroad assertion revisited', *International Studies Review*, doi: 10.1093/isr/viw009.

Hollis, M and Smith, S 1990, *Explaining and understanding international relations*, 1st edition, Clarendon Press, Oxford, UK.

Juneau, T 2015, *Squandered opportunity. Neoclassical realism and Iranian foreign policy*, Stanford University Press, Stanford, CA.

Kanet, R 2012, 'Russia in the new international order: theories, arguments and debates', *International Politics*, vol. 49, no. 4, pp. 393–399.

Karagiannis, E 2013, 'The 2008 Russian-Georgian war via the lens of offensive realism', *European Security*, vol. 22, no. 1, pp. 74–93.

Klieman, A (ed.) 2015, *Great powers and geopolitics. International affairs in a rebalancing world*, Springer, London.

Krickovic, A 2016, 'Catalyzing conflict: the international dimension of the security dilemma', *Journal of Global Security Studies*, doi: 10.1093/jogs/ogw002.

Kropatcheva, E 2011, 'Playing both ends against the middle: Russia's geopolitical energy games with the EU and Ukraine', *Geopolitics*, vol. 16, no. 3, pp. 553–573.

Kropatcheva, E 2012, 'Russian foreign policy in the realm of European security through the lens of neoclassical realism', *Journal of Eurasian Studies*, vol. 3, no. 1, pp. 30–40.

Kropatcheva, E 2013, 'NATO–Russia relations and the Chinese factor: an ignored variable', *Politics*, vol. 34, no. 2, pp. 149–160.

Kropatcheva, E 2014, 'He who has the pipeline calls the tune? Russia's energy power against the background of the "shale revolutions"', *Energy Policy*, vol. 66, pp. 1–10.

Legro, JW and Moravcsik, A 1999, 'Is anybody still a realist?', *International Security*, vol. 24, no. 2, pp. 5–55.

Lobell, SE 2016, 'Realism, balance of power, and power transitions', in TV Paul (ed.), *Accommodating rising powers. Past, present, and future*, Cambridge University Press, Cambridge, UK.

Mankoff, J 2011, *Russian foreign policy. The return of great power politics*, 2nd edition, Rowman & Littlefield Publishers, Inc., Toronto.

Marten, K 2015, 'Informal political networks and Putin's foreign policy: the examples of Iran and Syria', *Problems of Post-Communism*, vol. 62, no. 2, pp. 71–87.

McFaul, M, Sestanovich, S and Mearsheimer, JJ 2014, 'Faulty powers. Who started the Ukraine crisis?', *Foreign Affairs*, 17 October, pp. 167–178.

Mearsheimer, JJ 2014a, *The tragedy of great power politics*, updated edition, WW Norton & Company, London.

Mearsheimer, JJ 2014b, 'Why the Ukraine crisis is the West's fault. The liberal delusions that provoked Putin', *Foreign Affairs*, September/October.

Mearsheimer, JJ 2016, Defining a new security architecture for Europe that brings Russia in from the Cold, *Military Review*, vol. 96, no. 3, pp. 27–31.

Morgenthau, HJ 1993, *Politics among nations: the struggle for power and peace*, McGraw-Hill, Boston, MA.

Motyl, AJ 2015, 'The surrealism of realism: misreading the war in Ukraine', *World Affairs*, January/February, viewed 12 February 2017, www.worldaffairsjournal.org/article/surrealism-realism-misreading-war-ukraine.

Mouritzen, H and Wivel, A 2012, *Explaining foreign policy. International diplomacy and the Russo-Georgian war*, Lynne Rienner Publishers, London.

Newnham, R 2011, 'Oil, carrots, and sticks: Russia's energy resources as a foreign policy tool', *Journal of Eurasian Studies*, vol. 2, no. 2, pp. 134–143.

Nygren, B 2008, *The rebuilding of greater Russia. Putin's foreign policy towards the CIS countries*, Routledge, London.

Nygren, B 2012, 'Using the neo-classical realism paradigm to predict Russian foreign policy behavior as a complement to using resources', *International Politics*, vol. 49, no. 4, pp. 517–529.

Oldberg, I 2007, 'Russia's great power ambitions and policy under Putin', in R Kanet (ed.), *Russia. Re-emerging great power*, Palgrave MacMillan, Basingstoke, UK.

Onea, T 2012, 'Putting the "classical in neoclassical realism: neoclassical realist theories and US expansion in the post-Cold War', *International Relations*, vol. 26, no. 2, pp. 139–164.

Paul, TV, Larson, DW and Wohlforth, WC (eds) 2014, *Status in world politics*, Cambridge University Press, New York.

Rathbun, B 2008, 'A rose by any other name: neoclassical realism as the logical and necessary extension of structural realism', *Security Studies*, vol. 17, no. 2, pp. 294–321.

Ripsman, NM, Taliaferro, JW and Lobell, SE 2016, *Neoclassical realist theory of international politics*, Oxford University Press, Oxford, UK.

Romanova, T and Pavlova, E 2012, 'Towards neoclassical realist thinking in Russia?' in A. Toje and B. Kunz (eds), *Neoclassical realism in European politics*, Manchester University Press, Manchester, UK.

Rose, G 1998, 'Neoclassical realism and theories of foreign policy', *World Politics*, vol. 51, no. 1, pp. 144–172.

Schörnig, N 2010, 'Neorealismus', in S. Schieder and M. Spindler (eds), *Theorien der Internationalen Beziehungen*, 3rd edition, Leske + Budrich, Opladen, Germany.

Schweller, RL 2006, *Unanswered threats*, Princeton University Press, Princeton, NJ.

Schweller, RL 2017, 'Policy Series. A third-image explanation for why Trump now: a response to Robert Jervis's "President Trump and IR theory"', *The International Security Studies Forum*, 8 February, https://issforum.org/roundtables/policy/1-5m-third-image#_ftnref48.

Sergounin, A 2009, 'Russia: IR at a crossroad', in AB Tickner and O Wæver (eds), *International Relations scholarship around the world*, 223–241, Routledge, London.

Shulman, M 1963, *Stalin's foreign policy reappraised*, Harvard University Press, Cambridge, MA.

Siedschlag, A (ed.) 2001, *Realistische Perspektiven internationaler Politik*, Leske + Budrich, Opladen, Germany.

Simao, L 2012, 'Do leaders still decide? The role of leadership in Russian foreign policymaking', *International Politics*, vol. 49, no. 4, pp. 482–497.

Smith, NR 2014, 'The EU's difficulty in translating interests into effective foreign policy action: a look at the Ukrainian crisis', *Baltic Journal of European Studies*, vol. 4, no. 1, pp. 54–68.

Snyder, J 1991, *Myths of empire. Domestic politics and international ambition*, Cornell University Press, Ithaca, NY and London.

Sørensen, CTN 2013, 'Is China becoming more aggressive? A neoclassical realist analysis', *Asian Perspective*, vol. 37, pp. 363–385.

Splidsboel-Hansen, F 2015, 'Framing yourself into a corner: Russia, Crimea, and the minimal action space', *European Security*, vol. 24, no. 1, pp. 141–158.

Sterling-Folker, J 2002, *Theories of international cooperation and the primacy of anarchy. Explaining U.S. international policy-making after Bretton Woods*, State University of New York Press, Albany.

Sterling-Folker, J 2009a, 'Forward is as forward does. Assessing neoclassical realism from a traditions perspective', in A Freyberg-Inan, E Harrison and P James (eds), *Rethinking realism in international relations. Between tradition and innovation*, John Hopkins University Press, Baltimore, MD.

Sterling-Folker, J 2009b, 'Neoclassical realism and identity: peril despite profit across the Taiwan Strait', in SE Lobell, NM Ripsman and JW Taliaferro (eds), *Neoclassical realism, the state, and foreign policy*, Cambridge University Press, Cambridge, UK.

Stoner, K and McFaul, M 2015, 'Who lost Russia (this time)? Vladimir Putin', *The Washington Quarterly*, vol. 38, no. 2, pp. 167–187.

Taliaferro, JW 2006, 'State building for future wars: neoclassical realism and the resource-extractive state', *Security Studies*, vol. 15, no. 3, pp. 464–495.

Tsygankov, A 2012, *Russia and the West from Alexander to Putin: honor in international relations*, Cambridge University Press, Cambridge, UK.

Tsygankov, A 2015, 'Vladimir Putin's last stand: the sources of Russia's Ukraine policy', *Post-Soviet Affairs*, vol. 31, no. 4, pp. 279–303.

Tsygankov, AP and Tarver-Wahlquist, M 2009, 'Duelling honors: power, identity, and the Russia-Georgia divide', *Foreign Policy Analysis*, vol. 5, no. 4, pp. 307–326.

Tsygankov, AP and Tsygankov, PA 2010, 'Russian theory of International Relations', in RA Denemark (ed.), *International Studies Encyclopedia*, Wiley-Blackwell Publishers, Hoboken, NJ.

Vasquez, JA 1997, 'The realist paradigm and degenerative versus progressive research programs: an appraisal of neotraditional research on Waltz's balancing proposition', *The American Political Science Review*, vol. 91, no. 4, pp. 899–912.

Walt, S 1987, *The origins of alliances*, Cornell University Press, Ithaca, NY.

Walt, SM 2015, 'Who is a better strategist: Obama or Putin? Pitting a former KGB agent against a former community organizer and seeing what happens in Syria', *Foreign Policy*, 9 October, viewed 21 March 2017, http://foreignpolicy.com/2015/10/09/who-is-a-better-strategist-obama-or-putin.

Walt, SM 2016, 'What would a realist world have looked like?' *Foreign Policy*, 8 January.

Waltz, KN 1979, *Theory of International Politics*, McGraw-Hill, New York.

Wesslau, F and Wilson, A 2016, 'Russia 2030: A story of great power dreams and small victorious wars', *ECFR Policy Brief*, 23 May.

Wigell, M and Vihma, A 2016, 'Geopolitics versus geoeconomics: the case of Russia's geostrategy and its effects on the EU', *International Affairs*, vol. 92, no. 3, pp. 605–627.

Wohlforth, WC 1993, *The elusive balance of power: power and perceptions during the Cold War*, Cornell University Press, Ithaca, NY.

Wohlforth, WC 2001, 'The Soviet-Russian empire: a test of neorealism', *Review of International Studies*, vol. 27, no. 5, pp. 213–235.

Wohlforth, WC 2009, 'Unipolarity, status competition, and great power war', *World Politics*, vol. 61, no. 1, pp. 28–57.

Wohlforth, WC 2012, 'Realism and foreign policy', in S Smith, A Hadfield and T Dunne (eds), *Foreign policy. Theories, actors, cases*, 2nd edition, Oxford University Press, Oxford, UK.

Zakaria, F 1998, *From wealth to power*, Princeton University Press, Princeton, NJ.

Ziegler, CE 2014, 'Russia in Central Asia: the dynamics of great-power politics in a volatile region', *Asian Perspective*, vol. 38, pp. 589–617.

4
GEOPOLITICS

John Berryman

UNIVERSITY OF LONDON, UK

The chapter[1] provides a broad overview of the fluctuating connections between the controversial and ambiguous field of modern geopolitics and Russia. Given the pivotal significance of the Russian challenge within the early hypotheses of Mahan and Mackinder, the chapter first explores those distinctive geographical and spatial considerations that helped shape the development of the Russian Empire. The place of geopolitics in the Cold War is then reviewed, including both its policy orientation and the exchanges between the proponents of geopolitical realism and liberal internationalism. In conclusion, the chapter examines the post-Cold War renaissance of geopolitics, reviewing both theoretical developments and policy implications for Russian foreign policy.

Imperial geopolitics: Mahan and Mackinder

Although commentators have employed geopolitical reasoning from the days of Herodotus and Thucydides, the term 'geopolitics' was coined in 1899 by the Swedish political scientist, Rudolf Kjellen, at a point when the first fully inter-connected 'closed' global international system of states was emerging in which any significant changes in the global balance of power would unavoidably trigger 'zero-sum game' struggles between rival great powers (Osterud, 1988; Black, 2009: 107–110).

As continental Europe's greatest powers, Imperial Germany and the Russian Empire attracted the attention of two of the founders of modern 'classical' geopolitics: Rear-Admiral Alfred T. Mahan (1840–1914) and Sir Halford Mackinder (1861–1947). Having served two terms as president of the United States Naval War College, Mahan's studies had focused on the geostrategic importance of sea-power. However, in his geopolitical study, *The Problem of Asia*, published in 1900 (new ed., 2003), he drew attention to the 'vast uninterrupted mass of the Russia Empire' within the mega-continent of Eurasia and concluded that Russia would seek to use its land power to secure better access to the sea. In Mahan's judgement, the containment of Russia (and probably its ally France) would require an extensive naval and land coalition (Mahan, 2003: 20–22, 68, 107–109). By 1910 he no longer saw Imperial Germany as the natural partner in such a coalition to contain Russia, but instead advocated Anglo-American cooperation to contain what he saw as the greater danger of Imperial Germany's bid for mastery of Europe (Sprouts and Sprouts, 1962: 318–325).

In his famous lecture, 'The Geographical Pivot of History', delivered at the Royal Geographical Society in London on 25 January 1904, the British geographer, Halford Mackinder, argued that the 'Columbian age' of overseas imperial rivalry between maritime powers such as Britain, France, Spain and the Netherlands was coming to an end. Fearful of the challenge posed to the global status of the British Empire by the rise of large continental powers, which by combining both land power and sea power might prove to be virtually impregnable, Mackinder pointed at the size, central geographical location, resource abundance and even distinctive morphology of Imperial Russia, which he saw to be the current occupant of a critical geographical 'Pivot Area' of Eurasia and world politics, surrounded by a vast 'Inner Marginal Crescent' which had nurtured the great civilizations of Europe, the Middle East, India and China. (Mackinder, 1904: 436–437; Parker, 1982: 147–158; Hauner, 1992, chapter 6). Subsequently fearful that Germany, or a German-Russian combination, might add 'oceanic frontage' to the 'resources of the great continent' and come to dominate the Pivot Area, he welcomed the formation in 1907 of the Anglo-French-Russian Triple *Entente* to contain Imperial Germany (Sprouts and Sprouts, 1962: 326–329; Heffernan, 2000: 32–36).

Witnessing the defeat of both Germany and Russia in World War I, in his 1919 book, *Democratic Ideals and Reality: A Study in the Politics of Reconstruction*, Mackinder renamed the Pivot Area as the 'Heartland' of Eurasia and identified the east-central European states emerging from the former Austro-Hungarian and Ottoman empires as constituting an unstable 'Strategic Annexe', stretching between the Baltic and the Black Sea and the Caucasus. Judging that these states would remain the geopolitical target of both German and Russian designs, Mackinder urged the victorious Allied powers to support their development, issuing his famous dictum, 'Who rules East Europe commands the Heartland: Who rules the Heartland commands the World-Island [Eurasia plus Africa]: Who rules the World-Island commands the World'. And having served as British High Commissioner to South Russia in 1919–20, in a scheme prepared for the British Cabinet he urged the establishment of additional 'buffer states' such as White Russia (Belarus), Ukraine, Georgia, Armenia, Azerbaijan and Daghestan. Although these latter proposals failed to win the support of a war-weary British government, his observations with respect to east-central Europe uncannily anticipated western inter-war efforts to construct an anti-Soviet eastern *cordon sanitaire*, the reversal of this process was the establishment of a Soviet sphere of influence in the region at the end of World War II, and the post-Cold War geopolitical contests for the allegiance of the east-central European states and the successor states of the 'post-Soviet space' (Mackinder, 1919; Parker, 1982: 163–175, 220; Blouet, 1987: 164–177; Sloan, 1999: 30–31; Kaplan, 2012: 68–74; Ashworth, 2014: 141–143).

Mahan and Mackinder have been portrayed as western imperialist commentators, worried by the growing strength of Russia and Germany, whose writings reflect an 'offensive racism' and are divorced from the reality of the twenty-first century (Rieber, 1993: 317; Bassin and Aksenov, 2006: 111–112; Hobson, 2012: 43, 124–130; Kaplan, 2012: 69). For English navalists such as Andrew Lambert and Chris Parry, and the Russian international relations analyst, Sergei Karaganov, Mackinder's expectations that railways would displace the sea-based transport of world trade were misplaced (Lambert, 1995: 194; Karaganov, 2013; Parry, 2014, chapter 2). For Paul Kennedy and John Darwin, however, Mackinder's identification of the way industrialization was shifting the balance of forces in the world towards the potential of large continental powers with a network of railways able to mobilize vast resources has proved superior to Mahan's faith in the efficacy of sea power (Kennedy, 1983: 83–85; Darwin, 2007: 19, 300). Whatever the balance of this equation, Mackinder's 'Heartland thesis' remains the most intensively debated grand proposition of geopolitics (Parker, 1982: 159–162; Sloan, 1999; Coones,

2005; Gray, 2005; Hooson, 2005; Kaplan, 2012: 61). In the light of his geopolitical propositions, to what degree did special geographical and spatial factors shape the distinctive pattern of development of what Mackinder termed 'the Russian tenant of the Pivot region' (Mackinder, 1904: 437)?

Russia: the geopolitics of periphery

The rise of Russia

Following the rule of Kievan Rus from the ninth to the thirteenth century, the subsequent two and a half centuries of rule by horsemen of the Mongol-Turkic hordes delayed Russia's development at a time when the remainder of Europe was experiencing the Renaissance. Released from the 'Tatar Yoke' (*Tataro-Mongolskoye Igo*), the rulers of the Grand Duchy of Muscovy confronted a harsh and predatory international environment within a vast flat Eurasian plain lacking natural geographical barriers. Compensating for its geographical vulnerability by means of territorial expansion, Moscow's location proved to be ideally suited as a point from which deep thrusts could be launched against rivals (Wohlforth, 2001: 217; Trenin, 2002: 32–33; Le Donne, 2004: 4). Meeting negligible resistance from nomadic tribes, Russian rule was quickly extended eastward across the relatively empty flatlands of Siberia to the Pacific Ocean, incorporating a third of the Asian landmass into what was by culture and history a European state. Assured of a relatively stable eastern hinterland, Russia was then able to turn west and wage successive wars with the declining Polish-Lithuanian, Swedish, Ottoman and Persian kingdoms (Kennedy, 1988: 120).

By the eighteenth century Imperial Russia had secured ice-free footholds on the Baltic and Black Seas. Although these outlets provided only constrained and limited access to the world's oceans through the 'choke-points' of the Danish and Turkish Straits and the mouth of the Mediterranean, which realistically Russia could never hope to control, by comparison with the sharply different and conflictual regions of Europe, divided from each other by mountain ranges and rivers, Russia's occupation of the Northern Eurasian land-mass made for homogeneity and unity. Russia's vast space (*prostranstvo*) therefore came to be seen as a guarantor of the wider stability of the Eurasian land-mass (Bogaturov, 1993: 32–34). Yet despite the enhanced security provided by its 'strategic solitude' on the periphery of Europe and its interior lines of communication, Russia's speedy mobilization and despatch of adequate forces to points of strategic deployment along its enormous borders in sufficient time proved to be difficult (Kokoshin, 1998: 111). Like other continental empires, Imperial Russia therefore sought to protect its vulnerable western and southern borders by fostering protectorates, spheres of influence, and buffer zones or borderlands in contiguous territories. These privileged positions helped to protect Russia's 'Heartland' from intrusion (Curzon, 1907; Thaden, 1984; Le Donne, 1997; Munkler, 2007).

Following Russia's further annexation of predominantly Muslim territories in the Caucasus and Central Asia through the nineteenth century, an asymmetric 'Great Game' was conducted between the British Empire and the Russian Empire as Whitehall sought to contain and even cut back the enormous territories of its Russian rival. It generated only one great-power war, the so-called 'Crimean War' of 1853–1856, the focus of which was the protracted siege by the combined forces of Britain, France, Turkey and Sardinia, of the great naval bastion of Sevastopol on the Crimean peninsula, home of Russia's Black Sea fleet (Jelavich, 1974; Gillard, 1977; Hauner, 1992, chapter 5; Lambert, 1995, 2011; Berryman, 2017a).

By the end of the nineteenth century, Russia had acquired some 17 million square kilometres of new territories and 18,000 kilometres of borders over the preceding 300 years, a scale of expansion which no other state has matched. The Russian Empire therefore found itself the world's largest country and the third largest empire in history. Imperial Russia's vast interior helped it frustrate the invading *Grande Armée* of Napoleon, underpinned its claim to great power status, and was a source of pride and self-identity for many of its peoples. However, military defeat in the Crimean War and the Russo-Japanese War underlined that territorial size per se was not to be equated with power, especially since the empire had become a huge multinational conglomerate of 170 million, comprising well over 100 different nationalities plus religious minorities. Ruling so diverse a population in an era of growing ethno-nationalism would prove to be an intractable challenge for the authorities in both Imperial Russia and the USSR (Wesson, 1974; Fuller, 1992: 452; Lieven, 2003: 274–287).

Imperial Russia and Imperial Germany: the road to war

Thanks to their joint participation in the partition of the Polish Kingdom, and the containment of Revolutionary and Napoleonic France, the post-1815 settlement saw the establishment of the 'Holy Alliance' of the conservative monarchies of Prussia and the Russian and Habsburg Empires. However, in return for Russia's military intervention in support of the Habsburg Empire, crushing the Hungarian Revolt in 1849, Austria 'astonished the world with its ingratitude' by supporting Russia's enemies in the Crimean War, turning St Petersburg firmly against Vienna. As a consequence, thanks to the benevolent neutrality of Russia, in two wars with Austria and France Otto von Bismarck was able to forge a Prussian-dominated united Germany (Lieven, 2015: 26). Concerned to isolate France, apart from establishing the Dual Alliance with Austria-Hungary in 1879 and widening the agreement to include Italy in the Triple Alliance of 1882, Bismarck established a *Dreikaiserbund* (Three Emperor's League) 1873–1878 and a Three Emperors Alliance 1881–1887 to hold together the three empires of Russia, Germany and Austria-Hungary. Only in 1890 did disagreements over a German grain tariff and a boycott of Russian bonds precipitate Bismarck's dismissal by the new Kaiser.

In the short term, Berlin's refusal to renew the secret 1887 Reinsurance Treaty with Russia pushed St Petersburg to recognize the geopolitical logic of a security arrangement with republican France, directed exclusively to contain Imperial Germany – a significant breach in the Bismarckian system. By 1894 diplomatic and military agreements were reached between St Petersburg and Paris (Fuller, 1992: 350–360; Schimmelpenninck, 2006: 567). While German power was a source of concern in St Petersburg, fears of the spectacular acceleration of Russian power fuelled consideration within Berlin of preventive war with Russia (and its ally France). It has been suggested that had the opportunity offered by Russia's military defeat in the Russo-Japanese War been seized, Germany almost certainly would have won such a war (Copeland, 2000, chapter 3; Lieven, 2016: 12–17). Nonetheless, critics have argued that a Russo-German military clash was not inevitable and that a shift by Russia away from its traditional alliances with conservative powers on its borders towards the 'fateful alliance' with France was a misstep in empire geopolitics which in 1914 propelled Imperial Russia into an unnecessary and disastrous war (Kennan, 1984; Fuller, 1992: 360; Burbank and Cooper, 2010: 356; Tsygankov, 2012: 89–93).

Soviet-German geopolitics 1917–1947

Brest-Litovsk

Although Imperial Russia's military and economic effort in World War I exceeded many expectations, with the political collapse of the home front in February 1917 and the seizure of power by the Bolsheviks in October, Russia's military position became unsustainable (Jones, 2002; Lieven, 2002: 286). Confronting the advance of German forces on Petrograd, to buy time for expected revolutionary developments within Germany, in March 1918 Lenin insisted upon the need to sign the Treaty of Brest-Litovsk which would require Russia to relinquish all the western territories it had acquired since the seventeenth century. Over the next eight months, 1 million German and Austro-Hungarian troops occupied the former Russian territories of Finland, Poland, the Baltic, Ukrainian and Belorussian provinces, plus Crimea and Georgia. With its grain and coal, Ukraine was Germany's greatest prize. As Andreas Hillgruber emphasizes, 'The Russian recognition of Ukraine's separation exacted at Brest-Litovsk represented the key element in German efforts to keep Russia perpetually subservient' (Hillgruber, 1981: 47). In the event, despite the transfer of one-third of its *Ober-Ost* forces (40 divisions) to the western front, unable to secure victory Germany was forced to relinquish its eastern territories, vindicating, albeit in an unexpected fashion, Lenin's colossal gamble (Kennedy, 1988: 351; Herwig, 2014: 326, 369–374).

The geopolitics of Soviet-German relations

If the grand concepts of Mackinder were overlooked within Imperial Russia, which was developing its own geopolitical traditions, after 1917 his concepts were dismissed on ideological grounds as 'false science' (*lzhenauka*), providing 'a bourgeois reactionary conception which [used] selectively interpreted facts of physical and economic geography for the formation and propagation of the aggressive policies of imperialist states' (Parker, 1982: 148, 184; Hauner, 1992, chapter 7). In Weimar Germany, however, a large school of *Geopolitik* was established at the Institute for Geopolitics in Munich under the direction of Karl Haushofer (1869–1946), a Professor of Geography in the University of Munich. Drawing on Mackinder's 'Heartland thesis', earlier 'organic state' theories of Friedrich Ratzel and Rudolf Kjellen, and inspired by Germany's brief occupation of the Ukraine, Crimea and the Baltic states in 1918, Haushofer's institute sought to rebut the hated 1919 Versailles *Diktat* and shape German geopolitical designs to re-secure *Lebensraum* to the East. Moreover, concluding that the defeat of both Russia and Germany in World War I had enabled the western sea powers to secure their world hegemony, Haushofer looked to the possibility of establishing a 'Heartland' German-Russian-Japanese transcontinental bloc 'from the Elbe to the Amur' which could challenge the Anglo-Saxon sea powers (Parker, 1982: 176–182, 1985: chapter 5; Hauner, 1992, chapter 8; Deudney, 1997: 93–96; Black, 2009: 126–135; Hobson, 2012, chapter 7; Kelly, 2016: 49–52).

Soviet-German relations initially followed the Bismarckian tradition of German-Russian cooperation as trade and secret military cooperation agreements were signed, followed by the 1922 Treaty of Rapallo re-establishing diplomatic relations between Berlin and Moscow. Without abandoning its revolutionary anti-capitalist perspectives, Moscow sought 'peaceful coexistence' with the established international order, stabilizing its borders by negotiating non-aggression and friendship treaties with its neighbours. Following Hitler's accession to power in 1933, although the possibility of closer Soviet-German ties was never completely shelved, Soviet diplomacy initially focused on securing a defensive pact with London and Paris to contain Nazi Germany. Thanks to western anti-Bolshevism and failure to secure the right of passage for Soviet forces to transit the 'buffer states' of Poland or Romania to gain access to Germany, by the summer of 1939 it was clear that this track had failed. Having kept his options open until the very last moment, a cautious but flexible Stalin now abandoned pursuit of collective security and turned to a balance of power strategy to enable the Soviet Union to stand on the periphery and stay out of any forthcoming war. August 1939 therefore saw the signing of the Nazi-Soviet

Non-Aggression Pact, opening the way to the German-Soviet invasion and fourth partition of Poland, thereby facilitating subsequent Nazi expansion westward. However, Germany's swift conquest of most of western Europe in 1940 dramatically reduced the 'breathing space' (*peredyshka*) which the Soviet Union had hoped could be utilized would be available to prepare its western defences. On 22 June 1941, without concluding hostilities with Britain, Hitler unleashed *Operation Barbarossa*, his 'war of annihilation' (*Vernichtungskrieg*), on the Soviet Union. For Moscow, the respite provided by the Non-Aggression Pact had therefore lasted only twenty-two months (Nation, 1992; Kissinger, 1994; Raack, 1995; Roberts, 1995; Weeks, 2002; Tsygankov, 2012, chapters 7, 10; Moorhouse, 2014). Having welcomed Germany's earlier military and economic cooperation with the USSR and the signing of the Nazi-Soviet Pact, following the opening of *Operation Barbarossa* Haushofer now looked to the forging of a German-Russian-Japan bloc by force rather than by alliance (Weigert, 1942; Hauner, 1992: 177; Herwig, 1999).

For John Darwin:

> As the German armies tore into Russia and raced across the Ukraine, a huge geopolitical revolution was under way. There was every sign that within a year the Germans would control the Soviet land mass west of the Urals, as well as the Caucasus with its supplies of oil. They would have built an empire on the grandest of scales. They would command what Mackinder had called the 'heartland' and be the dominant power in continental Eurasia, driving Britain (and America) to its maritime fringes and the Outer World beyond.
>
> *(Darwin, 2007: 419).*

In the event, operating at the end of their extended lines of communication, German armed forces met stubborn resistance from Soviet armed forces, buttressed by a formidable Soviet military-industrial complex located east of the Urals, deep within the 'Heartland' (Hauner, 1992: 194–196). And following the victories of Stalingrad and Kursk, Soviet forces drove west to the heart of Germany, opening the way for the consolidation of a huge new Soviet geopolitical salient in east-central Europe containing 95 million people, more than half the population of the USSR itself, which dwarfed Imperial Russia's post-1815 Polish salient (Kennedy, 1988: 469; Kramer, 1996). With the British withdrawal from India in 1947, the USSR therefore emerged as 'unquestionably the greatest single power in Eurasia with far more capacity to influence events throughout the continent than either the British or Russian governments had possessed in the nineteenth century' (Gillard, 1977: 180).

Cold War geopolitics

The containment consensus

Following America's entry into World War Two, in 1942 a study of *America's Strategy in World Politics* (Spykman, 2007) by Nicholas Spykman (1893–1943) updated Mackinder's Heartland thesis, renaming the vast 'Inner Marginal Crescent' as the 'Rimland' and reversing Mackinder's dictum into: 'Who controls the Rimland rules Eurasia; who rules Eurasia controls the destinies of the world'. And drawing on his understanding of Britain's grand strategy of off-shore balancing in relation to the balance of power in Europe, Spykman urged the US to bolster the 'Rimland' states in both Europe and East Asia to maintain a balance of power in post-war Eurasia (Haslam, 2002: 178–181; Spykman, 2007; Ashworth, 2014: 209–213; Bew, 2016: 196).

Notwithstanding the titanic Soviet victory in its 'Great Patriotic War', in the judgement of the American career diplomat and Russia specialist, George Kennan, the ideologically aggressive but dysfunctional Soviet system looked likely to collapse in some ten to fifteen years. In his influential 1947 article in *Foreign Affairs* he therefore advocated a 'long term, patient but firm and vigilant containment of Russian expansive tendencies . . . by the adroit and vigilant application of counterforce at a series of constantly shifting geographical and political points, corresponding to the shifts and manoeuvres of Soviet policy' (X, 1947: 575–576). Concerned to prevent the resources and military-industrial potential of Eurasia passing into the control of a single hostile power, but recognizing that Russia's rulers had always sought to insulate Russia from outside influence by establishing buffer zones along its borders, Kennan argued that the United States should accept the reality of the Soviet sphere of influence in east-central Europe and concentrate on blocking Soviet penetration of the neighbouring 'Rimland' states of Western Europe and Japan (Kaplan, 2012, chapter VI; Kennan, 1967: 246–251). His recommendations accorded closely with the conclusions reached by the policy studies of the Truman administration, and for the next half century US Cold War Grand Strategy was based on the 'containment consensus' – the view that in relation to Eurasia the United States was an island power with inferior resources and that its position would not be secure if the markets and raw materials of Eurasia and the 'Rimland' states fell under the domination of a hostile single power or group of powers (Gaddis, 1982, chapter 2; Layne, 2006; Iseri, 2009; Petersen, 2011, chapter 3).

Pursuing an active military geostrategy, Washington mobilized a global maritime coalition and established a chain of alliances (NATO, CENTO, SEATO) along the Rimland of Eurasia, which together with US air and naval bases, circumscribed the reach of the land fortress of the USSR. In an echo of the earlier Anglo-Russian 'Great Game', the Cold War became a contest between 'the insular *imperium* of the United States and the "Heartland" *imperium* of the Soviet Union . . . for control/denial of control of the Eurasian-African "Rimlands"' (Gray, 1977: 14). By virtue of its strategic isolation in the remote American hemisphere, the United States was seen to pose no direct threat to the security of the Eurasian Rimland states. As an off-shore balancer, the United States was thereby able to offer attractive security guarantees to these Eurasian states. By contrast, the continental geopolitical proximity of the immense landmass of the Soviet Union was perceived to pose a potential security threat to the neighbouring Rimland states (Walt, 1987: 23–24, 277; Levy and Thompson, 2010).

Geopolitics in America and the Soviet Union

Tainted by its connections with the *Geopolitik* of the Third Reich, with the exception of the works of Robert Strausz-Hupe and Saul Cohen, for almost three decades after World War II the academic study of geopolitics in the United States was shunned (Black, 2009: 147–151; Kaplan, 2012: 82–88; Bew, 2016: 193). However, with the spread of Cold War rivalry to the Third World and America's rapprochement with China in the 1970s, President Nixon's German-born National Security Adviser, Henry Kissinger, began to use geopolitics as a synonym for an unemotional *realpolitik* pursuit of what he termed 'global equilibrium', while studies by the Polish-American scholar, Zbigniew Brzezinski, the English scholar, Colin Gray, and NATO examined the geopolitics of the Cold War (Gray, 1977, 1988; Zoppo and Zorgbibe, 1985; Brzezinski, 1986; Haslam, 2002: 162; Black, 2009: 151–158; Bew, 2016: 240–241, chapter 15). By contrast, although the ideological and geostrategic 'Brezhnev Doctrine' provided justification for the Soviet intervention in Czechoslovakia in 1968, within the Soviet Union geopolitics was still seen to provide little more than an intellectual rationale for Washington's Cold-War strategy of 'encirclement' of the socialist world (Vigor, 1985; Hauner, 1992, chapter 9; Kolossov and Turovsky, 2002: 143, 163 n. 7).

Post-Cold War geopolitics

International theory and geopolitics in the West

Since the peaceful transition of 1989 seemed to demonstrate the possibility of peaceful change and the superiority of non-realist approaches to international relations, neoliberal international relations scholars argued that in the emerging interdependent globalized post-Cold War world gains through commerce were displacing gains through the acquisition of territory. It was argued that much as nuclear deterrence had diminished the strategic significance of territory in international security, geo-economics had supplanted a backward-looking geopolitics (Richardson, 1993; Rosecrance, 1999; Fettweis, 2003; Grygiel, 2006; Wohlforth, 2006: 265–266; Guzzini, 2012, chapter 1; Jackson and Sorensen, 2016: 103–107). Indeed, the post-modern project of European integration required that member states of the European Union (EU) turn their backs on both geopolitical precepts and the balance-of-power system as an ordering mechanism in Europe (Buzan and Wæver, 2003: 361–362; Cooper, 2004). The American liberal-internationalist scholar, Daniel Deudney consequently dismissed geopolitics as a slippery amalgam of the natural and social sciences, a heterogeneous body of insights that had failed to coalesce into a rigorous set of social-scientific propositions, while Charles Clover of the *Financial Times* concluded that 'few modern ideologies are as whimsically all-encompassing, as romantically obscure, as intellectually sloppy, and as likely to start a third world war as the theory of "geopolitics"' (Deudney, 1997; Clover, 1999: 9).

In response to these criticisms, defenders of 'classical' geopolitics argued that, notwithstanding the globalization of economic activity and the emergence of significant transnational and non-state actors, territorially based and defined states still constitute the basic building blocks of the international system. In this view, the perspective provided by geopolitics did not rest simply on the grand reductionist concepts of Mackinder but demonstrated ways in which the exercise of international political power was shaped and limited by geographical and spatial imperatives (Gray, 1996; Owens, 1999; Grygiel, 2006; Walton, 2007, chapter 1). Moreover, providing a focus on the interaction of geographical and political forces in the social construction of geographical space, it was argued that both 'classical' and 'critical' post-modern geopolitics complemented the ideational emphasis of the new social constructivist approach to the study of international relations, recognizing that perceptions of international realities by policymakers and opinion-formers were shaped not just by power political imperatives but also by historically rooted and geographically shaped foreign policy calculations and security identities (Goldstein and Keohane, 1993, chapter 1; Hopf, 2002; Suny, 2007: 35–36; Jackson and Sorensen, 2016, chapter 8. For critiques of critical geopolitics see Kelly, 2006; Guzzini, 2012: 13–16; Kelly, 2016: 55–62). By moving beyond the parsimonious propositions of neo-realist structural theory, geopolitics has therefore helped fill something of a gap, advancing understanding of foreign policymaking, strategic culture and international security (Croft, 2008: 505; Buzan and Hansen, 2009; Lantis and Howlett, 2016).

Geopolitics in Russia

Two years after the termination of the Cold War the self-liquidation of the USSR created a black hole in the very centre of Eurasia. It was as if the geopoliticians' Heartland had been suddenly yanked from the global map' (Brzezinski, 1997: 87).Thanks to the eruption of ethnic and national rivalries generated by the new geographical configurations arising from the breakup of the national-federal structures of both the USSR and Yugoslavia, Moscow found itself operating within a Eurasian environment 'shot through with geopolitical manoeuvring to a degree unseen at the present stage in any other part of the world' (Buzan and Wæver, 2003: 414). Since the new external boundaries of the Russian Federation and many of the fourteen post-Soviet successor states had not been designed to be international boundaries but had been drawn to serve administrative and political functions in the periods of imperial and Soviet rule (Rieber, 2007: 257). The contest for control of Eurasia therefore re-emerged as the great prize of post-Cold War geopolitics (Rieber, 2007, p. 257; Mead, 2014).

Over the next five years, as Russia reduced its military forces from 3 million to 1 million, more than 1 million former Soviet troops, civilian personnel and family members withdrew 1,500 kilometres east from former Warsaw Pact states and Soviet republics, characterized by one RAND analyst as 'one of the most extensive and least appreciated force withdrawals in modern times' (Lambeth, 1995: 94). And much as 12 million Germans found themselves located outside the borders of defeated Germany in 1918; after 1991 25 million Russian nationals were now located outside the borders of the Russian Federation, half of them in Ukraine and the rest in the other thirteen post-Soviet republics. Like Weimar Germany, Russia therefore looked to geopolitics to help explain and articulate its new international identity and provide some guidance as to its national destiny and foreign policy (Erickson, 1999; Goble, 2005; Guzzini, 2012, chapter 3).

Seeking to theorize Russia's political identity and place in the post-Soviet space, since the late 1990s the geopolitical discourse within the Russian Federation has ranged from specialist academic studies, university textbooks and policy-oriented polemics, to poems and geopolitical or military-political novels. Two interrelated and mutually reinforcing discourses on geopolitics and Eurasianism have emerged (Morozova, 2009: 68). In the Yeltsin years it was argued that since Russia could no longer pretend to be a global power with a capacity to exercise significant influence in Latin America, Africa and parts of Asia, if it wished to remain a great power it needed to remain the strategic axis of Eurasia. Pointing up the historical legacy of Imperial Russia and the USSR, Russia's natural resources, hegemonic size and central locational position within continental Eurasia, statist commentators and policy makers such as Sergei Rogov, Andranik Migranyan and Yevgeni Ambartsumov advocated a pragmatic geopolitics, emphasizing the importance of maintaining Russia as a multinational Eurasian great power, while Alexei Bogaturov, one of Russia's leading international relations scholars, concluded that 'henceforth Russia's stabilizing function is naturally converted from a predominantly European one into a properly Eurasian one' (Bogaturov, 1993: 41; Kerr, 1995; Kolossov and Turovsky, 2002; Solovyev, 2004; Bassin and Aksenov, 2006; Zheltov and Zheltov, 2009; Tsygankov, 2016: 69). By contrast, the civilizational geopolitics of Vladimir Tsymbuskii, Gennady Zyuganov and Nikolai Nartov proposed that Russia focus on its development as an autarkic ethno-civilizational 'island' (*ostrov*) within Eurasia. Tsymburski urged that Russia abandon its efforts to incorporate the Caucasus and Central Asia within its geopolitical body, while Kamaludin Gadzhiev advocated new security structures for the region (Zyuganov, 1997; Gadzhiev, 2000; Tsygankov, 2003, 2011; Tsymburskii, 2007; Nartov and Nartov, 2016). Meanwhile 'hard-line' Eurasianists such as Aleksandr Dugin and Aleksei Mitrofanov insisted on the continued land-sea opposition of Atlanticism and Continentalism and advocated a Eurasian continental coalition of Russia, Germany, Iran and possibly Japan (Dugin, 1997, 2011, 2014; Mitrofanov, 1997; Tsygankov, 1998; Laruelle, 2008; Clover, 2016). Dismissing Eurasianism as 'a dead-end: a pretentious neither-nor position [that] erects an unnecessary barrier on the Russian-European border, while doing nothing to strengthen Russia's position in Asia, or even the greater Middle East', Dmitri Trenin has argued that Russia should stress its European identity and seek to engineer its gradual integration into a Greater Europe (Trenin, 2002: 36, 311). How far have these contrasting geopolitical perspectives helped to shape and guide Russia's post-Cold War foreign policy?

The geopolitics of Russian foreign policy

From Cold War to cold peace: the Yeltsin years 1992–1999

Following a 60 per cent fall in Soviet GDP between 1985–1991, the resignation of Soviet President Gorbachev and the implosion of the USSR in December 1991, it could be expected that the exaggerated expectations of Gorbachev's Western-inspired liberal-institutionalist 'new political thinking' would be abandoned. However, looking to secure substantial Western financial assistance and a swift integration of Russia into Western institutions, President Yeltsin and his Foreign Minister, Andrei Kozyrev, judged that they had little option but to follow the Western-oriented accomodationist grand strategy of Gorbachev while proposing that the security governance of a 'Greater Europe' be based on the non-bloc pan-European Conference on Security and Co-operation in Europe (CSCE), established by the 1975 Helsinki Accords. In the event, despite assurances by some Western policymakers of the desirability of developing such pan-European security institutions, for both the Bush and Clinton administrations the post-Cold War enlargement of NATO was seen to provide the only reliable geostrategic instrument to deter a 're-imperializing' Russia, block any attempts by the EU to serve as the primary security actor in Europe, and thereby enable the United States to maintain its preponderant influence in Europe (Layne, 2006, chapter 5; Shifrinson, 2016). As Henry Kissinger emphasized in 1994:

> America is an island off the shores of the large landmass of Eurasia whose resources and population far exceed those of the United States. The domination by a single power of either of Eurasia's two principal spheres – Europe or Asia – remains a good definition of strategic danger for America . . . [and] . . . Russia, regardless of who governs, sits astride the territory Halford Mackinder called the geopolitical heartland.
>
> *(Kissinger, 1994: 813–814)*

For his part, mindful of the central geographic position and size of Germany, and echoing Mackinder's concerns as to its hegemonic potential, Zbigniew Brezinski argued that provided Germany's interests remained congruent with or sublimated within the EU or NATO, Europe could continue to serve as the Eurasian bridgehead for US power (Brzezinski, 1997: 42, 73–74, 86).

With the crumbling of the 'Atlanticist' strategy, in December 1995 Kozyrev was dismissed and over the next four years a 'Eurasianist' geopolitical consensus prevailed under Russian Foreign Minister and Prime Minister Yevgeny Primakov. Although reliance on geopolitics to the detriment of geo-economics contributed to the failure of his grand design of a tripolar partnership of Russia with India and China, unable to block NATO enlargement, Primakov was nonetheless able to secure the signing in 1997 of the *Founding Act on Mutual Relations, Cooperation and Security between NATO and the Russian Federation*, which provided assurances (albeit carefully qualified) that NATO had no immediate intention of deploying nuclear weapons or permanently stationing substantial combat forces on the territory of new NATO member states. In March 1999 Poland, the Czech Republic and Hungary entered NATO against the backdrop of a three-month bombardment of Russia's 'ally' Serbia by 1,200 NATO aircraft, an operation less about relieving the suffering of the Albanian people and more about Washington demonstrating the ability of NATO to conduct a successful operation without the authorization of the UN Security Council. On New Year's Eve 1999, Acting President Vladimir Putin assumed power (Trenin, 2002: 308; Wohlforth, 2006: 271–278; Berryman, 2009: 167–169, 2017b: 168–170; Tsygankov, 2016: 27–28, 127–130).

From cold peace to a new Cold War? The Putin years 2000–2017

Although Moscow had earlier warned that NATO membership for the Baltic states might trigger Russia's deployment of tactical nuclear weapons in Kaliningrad, March 2004 saw the 'big bang' entry into NATO of Bulgaria, Romania, Slovenia, Slovakia and the three Baltic states of Estonia, Latvia and Lithuania, followed in May by the even more extensive enlargement of the EU. Having witnessed the limits of Primakov's 'Eurasianist' foreign policy, Putin had adopted a centrist course of pragmatic realism, looking to preserve Russia's territorial integrity and enhance its commanding presence within the post-Soviet space (Morozova, 2009; Karaganov, 2013). However, recognizing that Russia's international position was still weak, he chose not to pick a fight he could only lose. NATO's military infrastructure accordingly moved east along the Baltic Sea to the very border with Russia within 100 miles of Russia's second city of St Petersburg, enclosing Russia's exclave of Kaliningrad. Meanwhile the entry to NATO and the EU of Romania and Bulgaria ensured that by 2007 both institutions now had an enhanced presence in the Black Sea region. In view of the eastward extension of the spheres of influence of these two major Western institutions, from which Russia was firmly excluded, Moscow concluded that prospects for the construction of some form of a Euro-Russian confederacy of 'Greater Europe' from Lisbon to Vladivostok were now remote. Russia was once more consigned to geopolitical isolation on the periphery of Europe (Berryman, 2009: 169–173; Yost, 2014: 227–229).

Alarmed by what it perceived to be the role of the United States in the 'Colour' revolutions in Georgia (2003) and Ukraine (2004), and the efforts (albeit unsuccessful) of the United States to persuade its European partners to offer NATO membership to Ukraine and Georgia at the April 2008 Bucharest NATO summit, the rash authorization by Georgian President, Mikheil Sakaashvili, of a military attack on South Ossetia in August 2008 offered Moscow the opportunity to utilize its locally superior military assets to block Georgia's membership of NATO. At the conclusion of a strictly limited five-week Russo-Georgian war, Moscow recognized the independence of the breakaway republics of South Ossetia and Abkhazia, and two Russian military brigades were deployed in these territories, together with units of the Russian Black Sea Fleet in the Abhazian port of Ochamchira (Berryman, 2011: 233–239; Bugajski and Assenova, 2016: 326–331). With Georgia's prospects of entry to NATO remote, Ukraine now became the focus of attention.

Given Berlin's efforts in both world wars to secure Ukraine as a vital counter-weight to Russia, in the fluid post-Cold War geopolitical environment Ukraine once more came to be seen as a potential 'pivot state' on the Eurasian chessboard – its status derived not just from the sensitive strategic location of its 1,925 kilometre land border with Russia, only a few hundred miles from Moscow, but from the deep internal divisions within Ukraine between communities enjoying different civilizational identities. In view of the evident determination of the Washington and Ukrainian political elites to override popular opposition and lever Ukraine into NATO, Moscow began to consider the possibility of supporting Crimean irredentism and to play with ideas of a major geopolitical redesign of the northern Black Sea region in which Russian-majority territories in eastern and southern Ukraine, extending beyond Crimea and Odessa to include even Transnistria, would secede from Ukraine and Romania (Trenin, 2011: 46, 100;

Berryman, 2015: 186, 197–201; Tsygankov, 2015: 10–12). Although the 2010 announcement by the new government of President Yanukovych that Ukraine would no longer seek NATO membership restored a measure of equilibrium, the Eastern Partnership (EaP) initiative of the EU to advance its 'civilizational choice' into its 'shared neighbourhood' with Russia by offering Association Agreements (AA), was seen by Moscow to be another zero-sum effort to advance the West's sphere of influence, this time geo-economic and piously geo-ideational in character (Charap and Colton, 2017: 29–30, 95–100).

Caught between Brussels and Moscow, the rejection by Yanukovych of the AA in November 2013 triggered protests which climaxed in an armed coup in Kyiv which swept away the EU-brokered crisis settlement of 21 February 2014 and ousted elected President Yanukovych. Worried that far-right elements exercising significant control of security structures within the new authorities in Kyiv might in short order terminate Russia's basing agreements in Crimea and apply for NATO membership, buttressed by a hastily organized referendum in the Crimean peninsula, Putin authorized swift pre-emptive armed intervention to secure Crimea and Sevastopol, and subsequently provided covert military support to deny Kyiv the ability to smash the separatist revolt by the 8 million-strong largely Russian population of the Donbas (Putin, 2014; Berryman 2015: 200–203; Tsygankov, 2015: 14–15). For liberal Western observers it was 'nonsense to think that Moscow had no viable alternatives to the use of force; none was seriously tried after the fall of Yanukovych', while the Kremlin's allegations that NATO aimed to bring Ukraine into its fold was 'a self-serving falsehood', but one which was 'nevertheless a reality to the Russian leadership' (Merry, 2016: 42–43; Lo, 2015: 20; Nixey, 2015: 35). For realists, by contrast, Putin's response was not an expression of Russian expansionism or imperial nostalgia but rather reflected the unsurprising determination of a great power to take pre-emptive actions as it might deem necessary to deny potentially hostile powers the discretionary availability of military and naval facilities on territory geopolitically proximate to its borders – in the case of the Crimea the vital naval base of Sevastopol and the other 189 military bases on the peninsula (Ruhl, 1997; Berryman, 2011: 239, 2017a: 63; Marshall, 2015: 13–18). As the realist scholar, John Mearsheimer, put it, 'Washington may not like Moscow's position, but it should understand the logic behind it. This is Geopolitics 101: great powers are always sensitive to potential threats near their home territory' (Mearsheimer, 2014: 82).

Generating security concerns among the sixteen states which enjoy common borders with the Russian Federation, Russia's open challenge to the post-Cold War and post-Soviet settlement in Europe has triggered something of a 'New Cold War.' NATO has authorized rotational, and thereby quasi-permanent, troop reinforcements, heavy weapons deployments, and enhanced military exercises in those eastern member states close to or on the borders of Russia, while NATO naval and air forces in the Baltic and Black Seas have been reinforced. In response, new divisions have been added to Russia's Western and Southern Military Districts, the tempo of large-scale 'snap' military exercises has been stepped up and *Iskander*-M short range surface-to-surface ballistic missile platforms, S-400 *Triompf* anti-aircraft systems and K-300 *Bastion*-P coastal defence anti-ship cruise missiles have been deployed to create Anti-Access/Area Denial (A2/AD) bastions in the Crimea, the Kaliningrad region and the Arctic, while the Russian air force has undertaken increasingly assertive reconnaissance patrols in the Baltic, Black and North Seas and the Arctic. The dangers posed by these new military postures and exercises of NATO and Russian forces are therefore clear (Trenin, 2016a; Berryman, 2017a, 2017b). And within the context of a highly charged media war, Western accusations of the threat to Europe posed by Russia's 'neo-imperialist geopolitical project' have been met with Kremlin suggestions that economic sanctions are part of a Western geo-economic strategy to weaken Russia and prepare the way for regime change and possibly even the break-up of the Russian Federation (Van

Herpen, 2014; Tsygankov, 2015: 16–21; Bugajski and Assenova, 2016: 4–10; Legvold, 2016: 118–119; Trenin, 2016b, chapter 1). What then are the prospects for Russia and Eurasian security following the Ukraine crisis, and what judgements can be reached as to the worth of the notoriously ambiguous literature of geopolitics?

Conclusions

Since Europe's post-Cold War security architecture has been built on the foundations of two institutions – the EU and NATO – which do not include Russia, it has been recognized that, unlike the peaceful incorporation of France into the Concert of Europe after 1815 or the successful re-integration of Germany and Japan into the international community after 1945, the treatment of Russia at the end of the Cold War has represented something of a missed opportunity (Deudney and Ikenberry, 2009–10; Menon and Rumer, 2015: xix, 162). It is therefore suggested that a new European security system is required with Russia and Ukraine as key players (Tsygankov, 2015: 21). However, building on the 'Normandy format' of Russia, Germany, France and Ukraine responsible for the political management of the Ukraine crisis, a Concert-style framework for conflict resolution by regional powers has been proposed, together with suggestions of a wider Eurasian security framework embracing the EU, OSCE, Eurasian Economic Union (EAEU), the Shanghai Cooperation Organisation (SCO) and China's 'One Belt One Road' (Trenin, 2016b: 104–110; Berryman 2017b: 179–181). Since prospects for the construction of any such new security arrangements are remote, it has been suggested that Georgian and Ukrainian membership of the EU but not NATO may provide a geopolitically sensitive way forward (Berryman, 2011: 239–240; Kissinger, 2014; Lo, 2015: 163; Wolff, 2015: 1117–1121).

Thanks to the economic sanctions of the US, EU and some other states, and the reciprocal Russian economic sanctions, the volume of EU-Russia trade and Russia's trade with Ukraine has dropped by more than half, and China has been able to gain wider access to Russian energy, other natural resources and military technology and is now Russia's biggest trading partner. Arguing that Russia has the potential to retain its civilizational attachment to Europe but economically attach itself more fully to East Asia, Sergei Karaganov has urged that Russia look to turn itself from a peripheral European state into a great Asian-Pacific Eurasian one, constructing a Greater-Eurasia partnership open to Europe (Kaplan, 2012: 179; Bugajski and Assenova, 2016, chapter 6; Trenin, 2016b: 65–68; Gabuev, 2017; Karaganov, 2017). While Beijing currently displays no wish to undertake the role of security manager in Inner Eurasia, in the longer term it is possible that enjoying unimpeded access to the world's oceans and with substantial human and natural resources, China may supplant Russia as the new geopolitical 'Pivot' in Eurasia. Although there are those in Washington who look to the possibility of US-Chinese security management of eastern Eurasia, so long as the United States pursues Mackinder's geopolitical imperative of denying a single power or combination of powers preponderance over the entire Eurasian land mass, a new contest between China and the United States for mastery of Eurasia can be expected. In such a circumstance, Russia may align with China or look to assume the role of a balancer (Karaganov, 2013; cf. Trenin, 2014).

With respect to the recent 'renaissance' of geopolitics within both academia and the media, while providing a corrective to the claims of post-modern globalism, the validity and relevance of the grand propositions of Mackinder are still contested, while the grandiose claims of 'hard line' Eurasianism have likewise failed to convince (Kortunov, 2015). However, a more policy-oriented variant of neoclassical geopolitics has suggested that the size, topography, resource endowments, and spatial and strategic locations of states can influence, but not determine, national politics, international relations and grand strategy (Guzzini, 2012: 70; Kelly, 2016:

23, 167; Ortmann and Whittaker, 2016; Youngs, 2017: 21–25, 34). Employed as 'strategic realism with attention to geography' or 'standard-issue *realpolitik* with special attention to attaining influence over particular countries or areas', such a geopolitical lens can continue to provide useful insights into contemporary international relations and Russian foreign policy (Deudney, 2000: 100; Charap and Colton, 2017: 29).

Note

1 The chapter builds on Berryman 2012.

References

Ashworth, L. M. (2014) *A History of International Thought: From the origins of the modern state to academic international relations.* London and New York: Routledge.

Bassin, M. and Aksenov, K. E. (2006) Mackinder and the Heartland theory in post-Soviet geopolitical discourse. *Geopolitics* xi(1): 99–118.

Berryman, J. (2009) Russia, NATO enlargement and the new lands in between. In: R. E. Kanet (ed.) *A Resurgent Russia and the West: The European Union, NATO and Beyond.* Dordrecht, The Netherlands: Republic of Letters Publishing, pp. 161–186.

Berryman, J. (2011) Russia, NATO enlargement, and 'regions of privileged interests'. In: R. E. Kanet (ed.) *Russian Foreign Policy in the 21st Century.* Basingstoke, UK: Palgrave Macmillan, pp. 228–246.

Berryman, J. (2012) Geopolitics and Russian foreign policy. *International Politics* 49(4): 530–554.

Berryman, J. (2015) Russian grand strategy and the Ukraine crisis: An historical cut. In: M. Sussex and R. E. Kanet (eds) *Power, Politics and Confrontation in Eurasia: Foreign Policy in a Contested Area.* Basingstoke, UK: Palgrave Macmillan, pp. 186–209.

Berryman, J. (2017a) Crimea: Geopolitics and tourism. In: D. R. Hall (ed.) *Tourism and Geopolitics: Issues and Concepts from Central and Eastern Europe.* Wallingford, UK: CABI, pp. 57–70.

Berryman, J. (2017b) Russia and the European security order: Impact and implications of the Ukraine crisis. In: R. E. Kanet (ed.) *The Russian Challenge to the European Security Environment.* Basingstoke, UK: Palgrave Macmillan, pp. 167–188.

Bew, J. (2016) *Realpolitik: A History.* Oxford, UK: Oxford University Press.

Black, J. (2009) *Geopolitics.* London: The Social Affairs Unit.

Blouet, B. W. (1987) *Halford Mackinder: A Biography.* College Station, TX: Texas A & M University Press.

Bogaturov, A. (1993) The Eurasian support of world stability. *International Affairs* (Moscow) (2 February), pp. 32–44.

Brzezinski, Z. (1986) *Gameplan: A Geostrategic Framework for the Conduct of the US-Soviet Contest.* Boston, MA: The Atlantic Monthly Press.

Brzezinski, Z. (1997) *The Grand Chessboard: American Primacy and Its Geostrategic Imperative.* New York: Basic Books.

Bugajski, J. and Assenova, M. (2016) *Eurasian Disunion: Russia's Vulnerable Flanks.* Washington, DC: The Jamestown Foundation.

Burbank, J. and Cooper, F. (eds) (2010) *Empires in World History: Power and the Politics of Difference.* Princeton, NJ and Oxford, UK: Princeton University Press.

Buzan, B. and Wæver, O. (2003) *Regions and Powers: The Structure of International Security.* Cambridge, UK: Cambridge University Press.

Buzan, B. and Hansen, L. (2009) *The Evolution of International Security Studies.* Cambridge, UK: Cambridge University Press.

Charap, S. and Colton, T. J. (2017) *Everyone Loses: The Ukraine Crisis and the Ruinous Contest for Post-Soviet Eurasia.* London: The International Institute for Strategic Studies.

Clover, C. (1999) Dreams of the Eurasian Heartland: The reemergence of geopolitics. *Foreign Affairs* 78(2): 9–13.

Clover, C. (2016) *Black Wind, White Snow: The Rise of Russia's New Nationalism.* New Haven, CT and London: Yale University Press.

Coones, P. (2005) The Heartland in Russian history. In: B. W. Blouet (ed.) *Global Geostrategy: Mackinder and the Defence of the West.* London and New York: Frank Cass, pp. 64–89.

Cooper, R. (2004) *The Breaking of Nations: Order and Chaos in the Twenty-first Century.* London: Atlantic Books.
Copeland, D. C. (2000) *The Origins of Modern War.* Ithaca, NY and London: Cornell University Press.
Croft, S. (2008) What future for security studies? In: P. D. Williams (ed.) *Security Studies: An Introduction.* London and New York: Routledge, pp. 499–511.
Curzon, G. N. (1907) *Frontiers.* Oxford, UK: The Clarendon Press.
Darwin, J. (2007) *After Tamerlane. The rise and fall of global empires, 1400–2000.* London: Penguin.
Deudney, D. (1997) Geopolitics and change. In: M. W. Doyle and G. J. Ikenberry (eds) *New Thinking in International Relations Theory.* Boulder, CO: Westview, pp. 91–123.
Deudney, D. (2000) Geopolitics as theory: Historical security materialism. *European Journal of International Relations* 6(1): 77–107.
Deudney, D. and G. J. Ikenberry (2009–10) The unravelling of the Cold War settlement. *Survival* 51(6): 39–61.
Dugin, A. G. (1997) *Osnovy geopolitiki. Geopoliticheskoe budushchee Rossii.* [Foundations of Geopolitics. The Geopolitical Future of Russia]. Moskva: Arktogeya.
Dugin, A. G. (2011) *Geopolitika.* [Geopolitics]. Moskva: Akademycheskii Proekt.
Dugin, A. G. (2014) *Eurasian Mission: An Introduction to Neo-Eurasianism.* Milton Keynes, UK: Aktos Media Ltd.
Erickson, J. (1999) 'Russia will not be trifled with': Geopolitical facts and fantasises. In: C. S. Gray and G. Sloan (eds) *Geopolitics, Geography and Strategy.* London and Portland, OR: Frank Cass, pp. 242–268.
Fettweis, C. J. (2003) Revisiting Mackinder and Angell: The obsolescence of great power geopolitics. *Comparative Strategy* 22(2): 109–129.
Fuller, W. C. (1992) *Strategy and Power in Russia 1600–1914.* New York: The Free Press, Macmillan.
Gaddis, J. L. (1982) *Strategies of Containment: A Critical Appraisal of Postwar American National Security Policy.* Oxford, UK: Oxford University Press.
Gadzhiev, K. S. (2000) *Vvedeniye v geopolitika* [Introduction to Geopolitics]. Moskva: Logos.
Gillard, D. (1977) *The Struggle for Asia 1828–1914: A Study in British and Russian Imperialism.* London: Methuen.
Goble, P. (2005) In Moscow, geopolitics is the scientific communism of today. *Radio Free Europe/ Radio Liberty (RFE/RL) Newsline,* 11 August, www.rferl.org/content/article/1143457.html. Accessed 23 January 2017.
Goldstein, J. and Keohane, R. O. (eds) (1993) *Ideas and Foreign Policy: Beliefs, Institutions, and Political Change.* Ithaca, NY and London: Cornell University Press.
Gray, C. S. (1977) *The Geopolitics of the Nuclear Era: Heartlands, Rimlands, and the Technological Revolution.* New York: Crane, Russack.
Gray, C. S. (1988) *The Geopolitics of Super Power.* Lexington, KY: The University Press of Kentucky.
Gray, C. S. (1996) The continued primacy of geography. *Orbis* 40(2): 247–259.
Gray, C. S. (2005) In defence of the Heartland: Sir Halford Mackinder and his critics a hundred years on. In: B. W. Blouet (ed.) *Global Geostrategy: Mackinder and the Defence of the West.* London and New York: Frank Cass, pp. 17–35.
Grygiel, J. J. (2006) *Great Powers and Geopolitical Change.* Baltimore, MD: Johns Hopkins Press.
Guzzini, S. (ed.) (2012) *The Return of Geopolitics in Europe? Social Mechanisms and Foreign Policy Identity Crises.* Cambridge, UK: Cambridge University Press.
Haslam, J. (2002) *No Virtue Like Necessity: Realist Thought in International Relations since Machiavelli.* New Haven, CT and London: Yale University Press.
Hauner, M. (1992) *What Is Asia To Us? Russia's Asian Heartland Yesterday and Today.* London and New York: Routledge.
Heffernan, M. (2000) *Fin de siècle, fin du monde?* On the origins of European geopolitics, 1890–1920. In: K. Dodds and D. Atkinson (eds) *Geopolitical Traditions: A Century of Geopolitical Thought.* London and New York: Routledge, pp. 27–51.
Herwig, H. H. (1999) Geopolitik: Haushofer, Hitler and Lebensraum. In: C. S. Gray and G. Sloan (eds) *Geopolitics: Geography and Strategy.* London and New York: Frank Cass, pp. 218–241.
Herwig, H. H. (2014) *The First World War: Germany and Austria-Hungary 1914–1918.* 2nd Edition. London: Bloomsbury Publishing.
Hillgruber, A. (1981) *Germany and the Two World Wars.* Cambridge, MA: Harvard University Press.
Hobson, J. M. (2012) *The Eurocentric Conception of World Politics: Western International Theory, 1760–2010.* Cambridge, UK: Cambridge University Press.

Hooson, D. (2005) The Heartland: Then and now. In: B. W. Blouet (ed.) *Global Geostrategy: Mackinder and the Defence of the West*. London and New York: Frank Cass, pp. 165–172.

Hopf, T. (2002) *Social Construction of International Politics: Identities and Foreign Policies, Moscow 1955 and 1999*. Ithaca, NY: Cornell University Press.

Iseri, E. (2009) The US grand strategy and the Eurasian Heartland in the twenty-first century. *Geopolitics* 14(1): 26–46.

Jackson, R. H. and G. Sorensen (2016) *Introduction to International Relations: Theories and Approaches*. 6th Edition. London and New York: Routledge.

Jelavich, B. (1974) British means of offence against Russia in the nineteenth century. *Russian History* (1): 119–135.

Jones, D. R. (2002) The Imperial Army in World War I, 1914–1917. In: F. W. Kagan and R. Higham (eds) *The Military History of tsarist Russia*. Basingstoke, UK: Palgrave Macmillan, pp. 227–248.

Kaplan, R. D. (2012) *The Revenge of Geography: What the Map Tells us About Coming Conflicts and the Battle Against Fate*. New York: Random House.

Karaganov, S. (2013) The map of the world: Geopolitics stages a comeback. *Russia in Global Affairs*. 19 May. At http://eng.globalaffairs.ru/pubcol/The-map-of-the-World-Geopolitics-Stages-a-Comeback-159747, Accessed 23 January 2017.

Karaganov, S. (2017) Russia's victory, new contest of nations. *Russia in Global Affairs*, 31 March. At: http://eng.globalaffairs.ru/pubcol/Russia's-Victory-of-Nations-18641. Accessed 3 May 2017.

Kelly, P. (2006) A critique of critical geopolitics. *Geopolitics* 11: 24–53.

Kelly, P. (2016) *Classical Geopolitics: A New Analytical Model*. Stanford, CA: Stanford University Press.

Kennan, G. F. (1967) *Memoirs 1925–1950*. Boston, MA: Little, Brown.

Kennan, G. F. (1984) *The Fateful Alliance: France, Russia, and the Coming of the First World War*. Manchester, UK: Manchester University Press.

Kennedy, P. (1983) *Strategy and Diplomacy 1870–1945*. London: Fontana.

Kennedy, P. (1988) *The Rise and Fall of the Great Powers: Economic Change and Military Conflict from 1500 to 2000*. London: Fontana.

Kerr, D. (1995) The new Eurasianism: The rise of geopolitics in Russia's foreign policy. *Europe–Asia Studies* 47(6): 977–988.

Kissinger, H. (1994) *Diplomacy*. London: Simon & Schuster.

Kissinger, H. (2014) How the Ukraine crisis ends. *The Washington Post*, 5 March. At www.washingtonpost.com/opinions/henry-kissinger-to-settle-the-ukraine-crisis. Accessed 23 April 2017.

Kokoshin, A. A. (1998) *Soviet Strategic Thought, 1917–1991*. Cambridge, MA: The MIT Press.

Kolossov, V. and F. Turovsky (2002) Russian geopolitics at the fin-de-siècle. *Geopolitics*. Special Issue, *The Changing Geopolitics of Eastern Europe*. Dawn, A. H. and R. Fawn (eds), 6(1): 141–164.

Kortunov, A. (2015) The splendours and miseries of geopolitics. *Russia in Global Affairs*, 16 January. At: http://eng.globalaffairs.ru/book/The-Splendours-and-Miseries-of-Geopolitics-17258. Accessed 27 January 2017.

Kramer, M. (1996) The Soviet Union and Eastern Europe: Spheres of influence. In: N. Woods (ed.) *Explaining International Relations since 1945*. Oxford, UK: Oxford University Press, pp. 98–125.

Lambert, A. D. (1995) The shield of empire. In: J. R. Hill (ed.) *The Oxford Illustrated History of the Royal Navy*. Oxford, UK: Oxford University Press, pp. 161–199.

Lambert, A. D. (2011) *The Crimean War: Britain's Grand Strategy against Russia, 1853–1856*. 2nd Edition. Farnham, UK: Ashgate.

Lambeth, B. S. (1995) Russia's wounded military. *Foreign Affairs* 74(2): 86–98.

Lantis, J. S. and Howlett, D. (2016) Strategic culture. In: J. Baylis, J. J. Wirtz and C. S. Gray (eds) *Strategy in the Contemporary World: An Introduction to Strategic Studies*, 5th Edition. Oxford, UK: Oxford University Press, pp. 84–101.

Laruelle, M. (2008) *Eurasianism: An Ideology of Empire*. Baltimore, MD: John Hopkins University Press.

Layne, C. (2006) *The Peace of Illusions: American Grand Strategy from 1940 to the Present*. Ithaca, NY and London: Cornell University Press.

Le Donne, J. P. (1997) *The Russian Empire and the World, 1700–1917: The Geopolitics of Expansionism and Containment*. New York: Oxford University Press.

Le Donne, J. P. (2004) *The Grand Strategy of the Russian Empire, 1650–1831*. Oxford, UK: Oxford University Press.

Legvold, R. (2016) *Return to Cold War*. Cambridge, UK: Polity Press.

Levy, J. S. and W. R. Thompson (2010) Balancing on land and at sea. *International Security* 35(1): 7–43.

Lieven, D. (2003) *Empire: The Russian Empire and Its Rivals*. London: Pimlico.
Lieven, D. (2015) *Towards the Flame: Empire, War and the End of Tsarist Russia*. London: Allen Lane.
Lieven, D. (2016) Foreign intervention: The long view. In: T. Brenton (ed.) *Historically Inevitable? Turning Points in the Russian Revolution*. London: Profile Books, pp. 11–28.
Lo, B. (2015) *Russia and the World Disorder*. London and Washington, DC: Chatham House and Brooking Institution Press.
Mackinder, H. J. (1904) The geographical pivot of history. *The Geographical Journal* 23(4): 421–437.
Mackinder, H. J. (1919) *Democratic Ideals and Reality: A Study in the Politics of Reconstruction*. London: Constable and Co. Ltd.
Mahan, A. T. (2003) *The Problem of Asia: Its Effect upon International Policies*, New Paperback Edition. With a new introduction by Francis P. Sempa. New Brunswick, NJ: Transaction Publishers.
Marshall, T. (2015) *Prisoners of Geography. Ten Maps That Tell You Everything You Need To Know About Global Politics*. London: Elliot and Thompson Ltd.
Mead, W. R. (2014) The return of geopolitics. *Foreign Affairs* 93(3): 69–79.
Mearsheimer, J. (2014) Why the Ukraine crisis is the West's fault. *Foreign Affairs* 93(5): 77–89.
Menon, R. and Rumer, E. G. (2015) *Conflict in Ukraine: The Unwinding of the Post-Cold War Order*. Cambridge, MA: The MIT Press.
Merry, W. (2016) The origins of Russia's war in Ukraine: The clash of Russian and European 'civilizational choices' for Ukraine. In: E. Wood, W. E. Pomeranz, E. W. Merry, M. Trolyubov (eds) *Roots of Russia's War in Ukraine*. New York: Columbia University Press, pp. 27–50.
Mitrofanov, A. (1997) *Shagi novoi geopoltiki* [Steps toward a new geopolitics]. Moskva: Russki vestnik.
Moorhouse, R. (2014) *The Devil's Alliance: Hitler's Pact with Stalin, 1939–1941*. London: Bodley Head.
Morozova, N. (2009) Geopolitics, Eurasianism and Russian foreign policy under Putin. *Geopolitics* 14(4): 667–686.
Munkler, H. (2007) *Empires: The Logic of World Domination from Ancient Rome to the United States*. Cambridge, UK: Polity Press.
Nartov, N. A. and Nartov, B. H. (2016) *Geopolitika* [Geopolitics]. 6th Edition. Moskva: Unity.
Nation, R. C. (1992) *Black Earth, Red Star: A History of Soviet Security Policy, 1917–1991*. Ithaca, NY and London: Cornell University Press.
Nixey, J. (2015) Russian foreign policy towards the West and western Responses. In: K. Giles, P. Hanson, R. Lyne, J. Nixey, J. Sherr and A. Woods (eds) *The Russian Challenge*. Chatham House Report. London: The Royal Institute of International Affairs, pp. 33–39.
Ortmann, S. and Whittaker, N. (2016) Geopolitics and grand strategy. In: J. Bayliss, J. J. Wirtz and C. S. Gray (eds) *Strategy in the Contemporary World: An Introduction to Strategic Studies*. 5th Edition. Oxford, UK: Oxford University Press, pp. 299–316.
Osterud, O. (1988) The uses and abuses of geopolitics. *Journal of Peace Research* 25(2): 191–199.
Owens, M. T. (1999) In defense of classical geopolitics. *Naval War College Review* 52(4): 60–78.
Parker, G. (1985) *Western Geopolitical Thought in the Twentieth Century: Past, Present and Future*. London and Sydney: Croom Helm.
Parker, W. H. (1982) *Mackinder: Geography as an Aid to Statecraft*. Oxford, UK: Clarendon Press.
Parry, C. (2014) *Super Highway: Sea Power in the 21st Century*. London: Elliot and Thompson.
Petersen, A. (2011) *The World Island: Eurasian Geopolitics and the Fate of the West*. Santa Barbara, CA: Praeger.
Putin, V. (2014) Direct line with Vladimir Putin. 17 April. At http://eng.kremlin.ru/news/7034. Accessed 23 January 2013.
Raack, R. C. (1995) *Stalin's Drive to the West, 1938–1945: The Origins of the Cold War*. Stanford, CA: Stanford University Press.
Richardson, J. L. (1993) The end of geopolitics? In: R. Leaver and J. L. Richardson (eds) *The Post-Cold War Order: Diagnoses and Prognoses*. Canberra: Allen & Unwin in association with the Department of International Relations, Australian National University, pp. 39–50.
Rieber, A. J. (1993) Persistent factors in Russian foreign policy: An interpretive essay. In: H. Ragsdale (ed.) *Imperial Russian Foreign Policy*. Cambridge, UK: Cambridge University Press, pp. 315–359.
Rieber, A. J. (2007) How persistent are persistent factors? In: R. Legvold (ed.) *Russian Foreign Policy in the Twenty First Century and the Shadow of the Past*. New York: Columbia University Press, pp. 205–278.
Roberts, G. (1995) *The Soviet Union and the Origins of the Second World War: Russo-German Relations and the Road to War, 1933–1941*. Basingstoke, UK: Macmillan.

Rosecrance, R. (1999) *The Rise of the Virtual State: Wealth and Power in the Coming Century*. New York: Basic Books.
Ruhl, L. (1997) The historical background of Russian security concepts and requirements. In: V. Baranovsky (ed.) *Russia and Europe: The Emerging Security Agenda*. Oxford, UK: Oxford University Press for the Stockholm International Peace Research Institute, pp. 21–41.
Schimmelpenninck, D. Van Der Oye (2006) Russian Foreign Policy. In: D. Lieven (ed.) *The Cambridge History of Russia. Volume II Imperial Russia, 1689–1917*. Cambridge, UK: Cambridge University Press, pp. 554–574.
Shifrinson, J. R. I. (2016) Deal or no deal? The end of the Cold War and the U.S. offer to limit NATO expansion. *International Security* 40(4): 7–44.
Sloan, G. (1999) Sir Halford Mackinder: The Heartland theory then and now. In: C. S. Gray and G. Sloan (eds) *Geopolitics, Geography and Strategy*. London and New York, pp. 15–38.
Solovyev, E. G. (2004) Geopolitics in Russia: Science or vocation? *Communist and Post-Communist Studies* 37(1): 85–96.
Sprouts, H. and M. (1962) *Foundations of International Politics*. Princeton, NJ: D. Van Nostrand.
Spykman, N. J. (2007) *America's Strategy in World Politics: The United States and the Balance of Power. With a New Introduction by Francis Sempa*. New Brunswick, NJ: Transaction Publishers.
Suny, R. G. (2007) Living in the hood: Russia, empire, and old and new neighbours. In: R. Legvold (ed.) *Russian Foreign Policy in the Twenty-first Century and the Shadow of the Past*. New York: Columbia University Press, pp. 35–76.
Thaden, E. C. (1984) *Russia's Western Borderlands, 1710–1870*. Princeton, NJ: Princeton University Press.
Trenin, D. (2002) *The End of Eurasia: Russia on the Border between Geopolitics and Globalization*. Washington, DC: Carnegie Endowment for International Peace.
Trenin, D. (2011) *Post-imperium: A Eurasian Story*. Washington, DC: Carnegie Endowment for International Peace.
Trenin, D. (2014) Russia's Great Power Problem. *Carnegie Moscow Center*. 28 October. At http://carnegie.ru/2014/10/28/russia-s-great-power-problem/hsxm. Accessed 23 April 2017.
Trenin, D. (2016a) Russia and NATO must communicate better. *Carnegie Moscow Center*, 8 August. At http://carnegie.ru/commentary/2016/08/08/russia-and-nato-must-communicate-better/j3hi. Accessed 23 April 2017.
Trenin, D. (2016b) *Should We Fear Russia?* Cambridge, UK: Polity Press.
Tsygankov, A. P. (1998) Hard-line Eurasianism and Russia's contending geopolitical perspectives. *East European Quarterly* XXXII(3): 315–334.
Tsygankov, A. P. (2003) Mastering space in Eurasia: Russia's geopolitical thinking after the Soviet break-up. *Communist and Post-Communist Studies* 36(1): 101–127.
Tsygankov, A. P. (2011) The Heartland no more: Russia's weakness and Eurasian meltdown. *Journal of Eurasian Studies* 1: 1–9.
Tsygankov, A. P. (2012) *Russia and the West from Alexander to Putin*. Cambridge, UK: Cambridge University Press.
Tsygankov, A. P. (2015) Vladimir Putin's last stand: The sources of Russia's Ukraine policy. *Post-Soviet Affairs* 31(4): 2–25?
Tsygankov, A. P. (2016) *Russia's Foreign Policy*. 4th Edition. Lanham, MD: Rowman & Littlefield.
Tsymburskii, V. L. (2007) *Ostrov Rossiya: Geopoliticheskie i Khronopoliticheskie Raboty 1993–2006* [Island Russia: Geopolitical and Chronopolitical Essays 1993–2006]. Moskva: Rossiiskaya Politicheskaya Entsyklopedia.
Van Herpen, M. H. (2014) *Putin's Wars: The Rise of Russia's New Imperialism*. Lanham, MD: Rowman & Littlefield.
Vigor, P. (1985) The Soviet view of geopolitics. In: C. E. Zoppo and C. Zorgbibe (eds) *On Geopolitics: Classical and Nuclear*. Dordrecht, The Netherlands: Martinus Nijhoff, pp. 131–139.
Walt, S. (1987) *The Origins of Alliances*. Ithaca, NY: Cornell University Press.
Walton, C. D. (2007) *Geopolitics and the Great Powers in the Twenty-first Century: Multipolarity and the Revolution in Strategic Perspective*. London and New York: Routledge.
Weeks, A. L. (2002) *Stalin's Other War: Soviet Grand Strategy, 1939–1941*. Lanham, MD: Rowman & Littlefield.
Weigert, H. W. (1942) *German Geopolitics. Pamphlets on World Affairs. America Faces the War No. 10*. London and New York: Oxford University Press.

Wesson, R. G. (1974) *The Russian Dilemma: A Political and Geopolitical View*. New Brunswick, NJ: Rutgers University Press.

Wohlforth, W. C. (2001) The Russian-Soviet empire: A test of neo-realism. *Review of International Studies* 27 (Special Issue, December): 213–235.

Wohlforth, W. C. (2006) Heartland dreams: Russian geopolitics and foreign policy. In: W. Danspeckgruber (ed.) *Perspectives on the Russian State in Transition*. Princeton, NJ: Liechtenstein Institute on Self Determination, pp. 265–281.

Wolff, A. T. (2015) The future of NATO enlargement after the Ukraine crisis. *International Affairs* 93(5): 1103–1121.

X. (pseud. George Kennan) (1947) The sources of Soviet conduct. *Foreign Affairs* XXV(July): 566–582.

Yost, D. S. (2014) *NATO's Balancing Act*. Washington, DC: United States Institute of Peace.

Youngs, R. (2017) *Europe's Eastern Crisis: The Geopolitics of Asymmetry*. Cambridge, UK: Cambridge University Press.

Zheltov, V. V. and Zheltov, M. V. (2009) *Geopolitika: Istoria i Teoria* [Geopolitics: History and Theory]. Moskva: Vuzovskii Uchebnik.

Zoppo, C. E. and Zorgbibe, C. (eds) (1985) *On Geopolitics: Classical and Nuclear*. Dordrecht, The Netherlands: Martinus Nijhoff.

Zyuganov, G. (1997) *Geografiia Pobedy. Osnovy Rossiiskoi Geopolitiki*. [The Geography of Victory: Foundations of Russian Geopolitics]. Moskva: u.p.

5
NATIONALISM[1]

Luke March

UNIVERSITY OF EDINBURGH, UK

'Nationalism' is one of the most poorly understood themes in the analysis of Russian foreign policy (RFP). Many accounts do not recognise the concept, arguing that RFP is rational, pragmatic and interest-based. For others, nationalism has become ever more dominant in Putin-era politics. However, accounts that investigate nationalism and foreign policy specifically in depth are relatively few. Indeed, most either look at nationalism as one, often marginal, offshoot of RFP generally, or have an explicit domestic focus (e.g. nationalist intellectuals, movements, political parties or subcultures) with little direct engagement with RFP. Many accounts that do engage with nationalism and RFP do so in a normative, alarmist and stereotypical way, where nationalism is an omnipresent but ill-defined threat, conflated with aggression, imperialism and general mischief-making.

Such divergent approaches have very different implications for such central questions as what motivates RFP, what is the role of domestic politics therein, what are the factors of continuity and change in Russian and Soviet foreign policy, and what are the implications of specific foreign policy actions (especially towards Ukraine after the 2014 annexation of Crimea). Unpicking the role of nationalism is thus (or should be) a central concern.

This chapter discusses different approaches to nationalism and RFP. In the first section, it outlines definitional issues and justifies the concept of nationalism used. The second section then analyses the strengths and weaknesses of the main approaches towards nationalism and RFP espoused by the main theoretical 'schools' of RFP analysis (realist, constructivist and liberal approaches). The following section argues that only multilevel and theoretically eclectic regime-focussed approaches which explicitly explore the intersections between nationalism, domestic and foreign policy, can give a sufficiently measured, nuanced and non-normative analysis; the fourth section outlines some testable hypotheses resulting from this approach; the fifth highlights some future areas for research; and the final section concludes.

This chapter's over-riding argument is that nationalism is a valuable but often misrepresented focus of RFP research. First, nationalism cannot be a parsimonious prism through which to interpret the *entirety* of RFP, and above all foreign policy behaviour. Second, prevalent approaches which attribute homogeneity and uniformity to nationalism as somehow 'drivers' of foreign policy are among the most simplistic and contentious. Third, this notwithstanding, nationalism provides a vital addition to the palette of approaches to understanding RFP.

Its main virtue is its ability, when accurately defined and utilised, to identify the linkages between domestic values, regime structures and foreign policy discourses.

'Nationalist' foreign policy: defining the undefinable?

There is a significant conceptual problem with identifying nationalism as practised by states, rather than non-state groups. As John Breuilly argues (1993: 10–11), 'nationalist' states are in the eye of the beholder: those whose policies defend 'national interests' and which other states might regard as 'assertive' or 'aggressive' are so universal that 'governmental nationalism' is a meaningless category unless there is an obvious, direct link between government and a nationalist movement. As outlined later, in Russia such an obvious link has rarely existed. The problem is compounded because many analysts approach nationalism in a profoundly normative, even Orientalist way (Laruelle, 2014). Indeed, there has long been a central argument that Russian nationalism is uniquely negative, revanchist and aggressive, alongside a research stream exposing the individuals or ideas who support such views (e.g. Yanov, 1995; Allensworth, 1998). Adding to the complexity is the tendency for states to refer to their own nationally-oriented policies as 'patriotic', reserving 'nationalist' to describe other states' similar policies, a tendency from which Russia provides no exception.

For the purposes of this analysis, I adopt a broad and non-normative definition that '*nationalism is primarily a political principle that holds that the political and the national unit should be congruent*' (Gellner, 1983: 1). As such, nationalism argues for 'the recognition of a people (nation) [*narod (natsiia)*] as the source of state power and the main agent [*sub"ekt*] of the political system' (Verkhovskii and Pain, 2012: 52; cf. Laine, 2017: 223). A nationalist policy asserts: (1) that there exists a nation with an explicit character; (2) that the interests/values of this nation take priority over those of other nations; and (3) that the nation must be as independent/sovereign as possible (Breuilly, 1993: 2). Therefore, with a nationalist foreign policy, we would expect ideational tendencies reflecting these principles, in particular evidence of messianism, exclusionism or chauvinism, inasmuch as the interests of the core nation are seen as pre-eminent, not only in relation to domestic ethnic groups but foreign ones as well.

Specifically concerning Russia, we might regard a nationalist foreign policy as one that aligns ideationally with the foreign policy preferences of nationalist groups, even if such groups' direct influence on policy outcomes is indistinct. Russian nationalist groups are themselves so divided that it only makes sense to talk of Russian nationalism*s* in the plural. The principal division was traditionally between multi-ethnic imperialist 'empire-savers' and ethno-nationalist 'nation-builders' (Szporluk, 1989). However, with further subdivisions, the increasing salience of ethno-nationalism and the co-mingling of these ideal types, this division is now too simplistic (Kolstø, 2016a; Laruelle, 2017a). Broadly, however, such groups can be regarded as belonging to a 'hard-line nationalist' camp who wish to defend (ethnic) Russian cultural norms, language and religion and insist on Russia's national uniqueness and independence (Tsygankov, 2009). As outlined further later, many see Russia's 2014 annexation of Crimea as an archetypal example of nationalist foreign policy, inasmuch as it was partially justified on the basis of defending ethnic Russians and reuniting the ethnic Russian nation allegedly divided by arbitrary borders.

Nationalism also needs to be conceptually distinguished from patriotism. For many, these are antithetical concepts: 'good' patriotism is counterposed to chauvinistic nationalism (Gries et al., 2011). However, for the purposes of this study, they should be seen as ontologically separate even if practically intertwined concepts. Patriotism entails individual feelings towards the community (e.g. pride in one's country), whereas nationalism involves group feelings towards the state (primarily, the desire for the state to represent the nation) (Baker, 2012). So, patriotism need not be political, whereas nationalism is so by definition. The distinction is important in the Russian context, since the state's 'managed nationalism' described later essentially attempts to defuse nationalism's mobilisational potential in favour of a depoliticised patriotism that reinforces acquiescence in the status quo.

Approaches to nationalism and foreign policy: driver or driven?

This section outlines the chief conceptual approaches to the role of nationalism in RFP, outlining their main strengths and weaknesses. Of course, any such categorisation is schematic and somewhat simplistic. Far from all analysts declare an overt theoretical position, neither is everyone consistent across their body of work. Many works approach nationalism from an area-studies rather than IR perspective, and thus address very specific aspects of the issue (e.g. the rise of hate crime, the role of skinhead groups, the ideology of the Russian Orthodox Church), without attempting to make many broader inferences about the regime, still less about foreign policy (e.g. Mitrofanova, 2012; Pilkington et al., 2013). However, the following presents a viable heuristic framework for understanding the main tenets of the most prevalent views.

Realism and the non-importance of ideology

Realist (or geopolitical) approaches are probably the most influential among scholars of RFP, but are also those that say least about nationalism. It is well known that classical realism's main concern is with system-level factors, and there is little emphasis put either on considering domestic factors generally, or prising open the black box of foreign-policy making in particular (Pursiainen, 2000).

Such approaches conceptualise state policy in terms of stable, rational national interests focussed on issues of 'hard' security, geopolitics and economic gain. Specifically, many regard RFP as 'based on classic realist notions of international politics in which states pursue their conception of national interests without fear of favour' (Sakwa, 2016: 120). Such 'classically realist' geopolitical axioms include balance-of-power and spheres of influence, embedded in a Hobbesian mindset of a zero-sum conflict of all against all (e.g. Lo, 2003; Mankoff, 2009). Realist analyses have little truck with more subjective, values-based motivations, including ideational factors and national identity generally or nationalism specifically. 'Russia Inc.' is viewed as a pragmatic, cynical and non-ideological power, focussed on economic self-interest above all (Trenin, 2007).

Central to realist views of RFP is long-term continuity. Churchill's view that the key to the Soviet enigma is 'national interest' might equally apply to post-Soviet politics, irrespective of domestic fluctuations. Even Russia's 2014 Crimea intervention, which to some is 'nationalist' foreign policy par excellence, is regarded as largely more of the same. According to Mearsheimer (2014: 81), it is 'Geopolitics 101: great powers are always sensitive to potential threats near their home territory'; in this case threats posed by Western expansion via NATO to Sevastopol. Others have highlighted how the Ukrainian crisis indicates realist postulates need to be brought even more to the centre of analysis than hitherto (e.g. Kotkin, 2016).

Realist approaches' intuitive plausibility is reinforced by the evident utilisation of geopolitical guiding tenets in official RFP doctrine, which traditionally evince 'very rational language and . . . formal strategies' (Forsberg and Pursiainen, 2017: 12). An emphasis on pragmatism and sober rationality are also central to elite justifications of RFP, particularly during crisis periods. For example, following the 2008 Russo-Georgian war, Foreign Minister Sergei Lavrov reiterated that the only ideology determining foreign policy was 'common sense and the supremacy of international law' (Lavrov, 2008).

However, realist approaches look far less robust under the microscope. In particular, they make the fundamental mistake of taking official discourse at face value, rather than investigating its role in regime legitimation and self-justification. After all, analysts were not confined to using Marxist-Leninist lenses to interpreting Soviet ideology; it was accepted that the degree to which Soviet conduct followed ideological postulates needed investigation, not a priori acceptance (Robinson, 1995).

In particular, the idea that Russia has 'permanent' interests as a great power is a staple of contemporary state discourse. As Putin put it in his Millennium Manifesto, Russian greatpowerness is 'preconditioned by the inseparable characteristics of its geopolitical, economic and cultural existence. They determined the mentality of Russians and the policy of the government throughout the history of Russia and they cannot but do so at present' (Putin, 1999). Striving to return to a supposedly deserved 'rightful' status forms the crux of the contemporary foreign policy consensus (Lukyanov, 2016). However, such arguments are anachronistic, neatly homogenising history to further regime legitimacy. That the national interests of an ideological superpower (the USSR), the much smaller and weaker (geopolitically and economically) contemporary Russia and the Tsarist Empire can be reduced to fundamentally continuous greatpowerness is more act of faith than serious analysis.

Certainly, several analysts hold that the Soviet system reflected nationalist elements alongside Communist principles, with particular resemblance to the policies of Nikolai I. According to Robert Tucker (1991: 29), the Leninist system was 'a kind of neo-czarist order that called itself "socialist"'. For David Brandenburger (2010) the Stalin period in particular was marked by 'Russocentric Etatism', whereby Marxism-Leninism was downgraded in favour of Russian historical themes. However, such continuity is much overstated. It is more accurate to see Russocentric geopolitics and Marxism-Leninism coexisting in what Vladislav Zubok (2009) calls the 'revolutionary-imperial paradigm'. Recent research shows that Soviet leaders took ideology very seriously (Gould-Davies, 1999). Generally, neither geopolitical nor ideological components lent themselves to unthinking expansionism. Indeed, Soviet interventions in Hungary, Czechoslovakia and Afghanistan (especially the latter) were undertaken reluctantly and somewhat reactively after much Politburo debate (Zubok, 2009). Indeed, the 2014 annexation of Crimea appears much more precipitate in comparison and hardly shows a historical reflex.

Moreover, whereas realism has broad-brush explanatory power, it cannot explain the detailed evolution of post-Soviet RFP. Certainly, identifying the common thread of a pushback against Western (especially NATO and EU) incursion into Russia's sphere of influence broadly explains how Russia has subverted 'coloured revolutions' in its 'near abroad' and why it intervened directly in Georgia and Ukraine to reinforce 'red lines' preventing their movement Westwards. However, this does not explain exceptionality and inconsistency, e.g. why Putin acquiesced in NATO expansion in the early 2000s, why Russia intervened militarily in Ukraine in 2014 but not in 2004–2005, or why Russia actively helped oust Kurmanbek Bakiev in Kyrgyzstan in 2010 (Götz, 2016). Most strikingly, realism fails to account for why the West is construed as an existential threat, when both NATO and the EU are divided, often weak and decreasingly expansionist, with, in particular, NATO enlargement to Ukraine barely realistic after 2008 (Macfarlane, 2016). In contrast, the rise of China, especially its encroachment to Russia's south and east, and its rising economic and military power, which ought certainly to figure highly in any 'objective' list of Russia's security threats, has not been securitised in Russian discourse (Kaczmarski, 2012).

Overall, many realist accounts still take insufficient account of subjective domestic motivations. Official regime discourse is accepted at face value, and is assumed to be constant and not fundamentally domestically contested. Most curiously, given his status as one of the foremost analysts of Russian politics, Richard Sakwa's *Frontline Ukraine* (2015) lacks substantive focus on Russian domestic politics. This account's coverage of nationalism is limited to 'monist' Ukrainian nationalism, whose virulence is allegedly deleterious to Ukraine's Russian-speakers, as argued by Russia's official discourse.

Certainly, some more nuanced realist accounts do acknowledge the role of domestic constituencies. In particular, neo-classical realism accords a role for regime factors as intervening variables in translating external, geopolitical incentives into domestic politics (Simão, 2012; Charap and Welt, 2015). This is potentially a useful prism for examining how nationalist politicians and interest groups intervene in foreign policy making in response to external factors (Laruelle, 2015).

However, even neo-classical realism gives insufficient credence to the role of domestic factors in interpreting and shaping, as well as being shaped by, external pressures. For instance, an otherwise sophisticated account inspired by neo-classical realism argues that Vladimir Putin is little more than a '"transmitter" responsible for translating geopolitical imperatives into foreign-policy behavior' (Götz, 2016: 17). This view clashes diametrically with most scholarly approaches to Russian domestic politics who argue that Putin's role is absolutely pivotal. As regards nationalism, Laruelle (2015: 88) sees it more as a *post hoc explanation* for foreign policy discourse than a direct driver of the RFP agenda. Whereas this has a strong kernel of truth, it downplays the extent to which nationalist ideas may inform mainstream discourse and thereby reflexively affect policy making in a more diffuse and long-term way.

Constructivism and the centrality of identity

In contrast to realist accounts, constructivist approaches do put ideational factors, including values, identity and status, far more to the fore (e.g. Clunan, 2009; Tsygankov, 2010). They highlight how 'national interests' are themselves subjective, contested, emotional and strongly ideational. A vital claim is that national identity debates are central; in particular, the West is the significant Other in interlocution with which Russian identity is constructed. Aspirations towards Western recognition of Russia's Great Power status, and of associated national values, especially sovereignty, are constants in Russia's relationship with the West and explain the fluctuating and frictional nature of this interaction. This also helps explain how China, whose role in Russian identity construction is minimal and largely uncontested, is not construed as a security threat. So for constructivists, security threats, and national interests *in toto*, are 'what states make of them'.

Many constructivists do not dwell on nationalism explicitly. However, their emphasis on ideational factors indicates significant potential overlap with the topic at hand. For instance, authors have highlighted how Russian assertiveness has been underpinned by a new focus on 'soft power' from c. 2007 onwards, which seeks to promote Russia as a 'value centre' (Monaghan, 2008a; Feklyunina, 2016). Among such values, Russian culture and language, and the notion of *Russkii mir* (Russian World) have taken increasingly prominent roles. In this way, RFP has taken an increasingly 'civilisational turn' since the late 2000s, whereby its formerly realist *Weltanschauung* has been increasingly infused with ideas of Russian exceptionalism, informed by a focus on Russian linguistic, cultural and spiritual uniqueness (Tsygankov, 2016). Arguably, this made assertive defence of Russian speakers in Ukraine unavoidable (Zevelev, 2014).

Furthermore, several constructivist authors do accord prominence to nationalist discourses. In particular, there are three generally accepted foreign policy tendencies, whose interaction drives foreign policy articulation: the liberals/Westernisers, statists/pragmatic nationalists and the aforementioned hard-line nationalists/civilisationalists (Tsygankov, 2009). This latter camp is represented among most parliamentary political parties (especially the Liberal Democrats [LDPR] and Communists [KPRF]) as well as among the non-party elite. For most of the Putin era the statists (among which he is counted) were the most influential group and the nationalists the least (Zevelev, 2014). Despite giving them occasional rhetorical concessions, the authorities have generally regarded nationalist policies as geopolitically confrontational and economically counterproductive (Tsygankov, 2009). However, the rise of the civilisationalist discourse may show changes afoot. In particular, the statists' emphasis on anti-Western *ressentiment* (the sense of envy that reinforces particularistic pride and xenophobia as parts of national identity) indicates that the statists are closer to the nationalists than often assumed (Smith, 2012). The Putin circle has developed a visceral anti-Western conspirology (Zygar', 2016). Such proclivities allow nationalist ideas (usually, but not exclusively, pragmatic ones) to act as 'conceptual "road maps"' steering foreign policy (Jackson, 2003: 173).

Accordingly, the main relevance of constructivist approaches is in prioritising the role of identity debates in RFP, which are focussed predominantly on Russia's relationship with the West, and in seeing nationalists as active participants in them. However, whereas unlike realism, constructivism does explicitly focus on the domestic/foreign policy interaction, it also suffers from a macro-level approach that helps identify general trends but is often insufficiently fine-grained to understand the twists and turns of foreign policy making. For example, the focus on Europe as Russia's Other potentially obfuscates the many convolutions of Kremlin policy, from the explicit pro-Europeanism of Putin's early years, partially recaptured in the Medvedev interregnum, to the increasing emphasis on Russian exceptionalism and non-European essence in Putin's fourth term. Arguably, the discursive focus obscures more accurate and nuanced attention towards domestic policy shifts. For instance, Laruelle (2015) argues that there is no nationalist 'school' in Russian politics with direct impact on foreign policy. The 'hard-line nationalist' camp is thus more a heuristic ideal type than an accurate depiction of policy influence.

The normativity of liberalism

'Liberal' approaches do not necessarily correspond to 'neoliberal institutionalist' IR theories (focussing on international co-operation), and they rarely display as cohesive a theoretical position as the two aforementioned approaches (indeed their epistemology is often implicit). However, this group encompasses those influenced by democratisation/transition theories, which critique Russia for its increasing authoritarianism (Shevtsova, 2014; Stoner and McFaul, 2015). Such viewpoints focus more explicitly on domestic politics than the previous two, and bring the role of nationalism therein much more to the fore. That said, the implications of the liberal stance are more problematic inasmuch as there is a normative focus that leads to potential inaccuracy and exaggeration.

As regards domestic policy, liberals see nationalism as playing a core role. They generally regard it as on the rise, since it is associated with a general trend towards increasing elite repression and/or manipulation of the political space. Specifically, the elite uses and abuses nationalism to mobilise regime support by creating an image of national crisis and external enemies, a 'besieged fortress' that creates a 'rally round the flag effect', mobilising disparate constituencies around the national leadership in a quasi-war footing, and simultaneously delegitimising the domestic opposition as unpatriotic quislings (Shevtsova, 2015a). Indeed, the Putin-era Kremlin has periodically attacked its domestic opponents as 'unpatriotic' fifth-columnists, a tendency particularly marked in the immediate aftermath of the 2014 Crimea annexation.

Furthermore, the Kremlin's active propagation of nationalist actors has helped move nationalism from the Yeltsin-era political margins to the Putin-era mainstream. Most notorious are the nationalist/imperialist ideologues and 'shock jocks' who have increasing visibility as regime cheerleaders and/or ideologues. Most column inches have been devoted to the propagandist Aleksandr Dugin, the progenitor of modern neo-Eurasianism (e.g. Umland, 2007). Some have gone as far as to attribute him direct policy influence as 'Putin's brain' (Barbashin and Thoburn, 2014). Many assert that Eurasianism underpins an allegedly increasingly concrete new regime ideology (Laqueur, 2015; Clover, 2016). At the same time, the Kremlin has actively encouraged quasi-nationalistic GONGOs such as Nashi and Molodaya gvardiya, and has developed often ambiguous relations with a range of other, more hard-line groups such as *Russkii obraz* (Russian image).

A cardinal example of the apparently inexorable rise of nationalism has been Putin's so-called 'conservative turn' after 2012. The regime increasingly distinguished itself from Western liberalism by emphasising 'biopolitical conservatism', i.e. 'traditional values' such as spirituality, the nuclear family and patriotism (Makarychev and Yatsyk, 2014). This had a domestic dimension (e.g. new legislation against blasphemy, 'gay propaganda', and increased restrictions on the extra-parliamentary opposition) but also a more marked foreign policy dimension, with the securitisation of identity and civilisational values (Zevelev, 2016). A common view, albeit one that ignores a lot of continuities, was that 'Russia's foreign policy ha[d] undergone a "paradigm shift" from state-driven foreign policy to one driven by ethno-nationalist ideas' (Tsygankov, 2015: 279–280).

The conservative turn had a plausible domestic rationale, i.e. Putin's weakening support after the 2011–2012 electoral protests, particularly among more educated, urban strata, necessitated reinforcing his support among more traditionalist rural and small-town electorates, and administratively and discursively marginalising the liberal opposition as unpatriotic degenerates, a campaign most visible in the victimisation of the 'Pussy Riot' collective in 2012.

Liberal views (e.g. Treisman, 2014; Shevtsova, 2015b) see the Crimean escapade as an extension of these domestic tactics: the use of a 'short, victorious war' as a diversionary tactic to boost Putin's flailing popularity. As with the Georgian war in 2008, Putin's poll-ratings hit stratospheric heights in the aftermath of an intervention that reinforced Russia assertiveness and its return as a Great Power to be reckoned with.

Such views are clearly right to focus on nationalism's utility for regime legitimacy. There is a long tradition of the Russian state utilising nationalist themes and groups for societal consolidation. In the Tsarist era, Official Nationality, Uvarov's Triad of Orthodoxy, Autocracy and Nationality, was intended to challenge the appeal of revolutionary liberalism (Riasanovsky, 1959), while at the turn of the 20th century, the regime actively fostered nationalist groups to intimidate anti-regime challengers (Laqueur, 1994). In the Brezhnev era, regime conservatives tolerated and protected nationalist figures in order to buttress the Party's declining Marxist-Leninist legitimacy (Mitrokhin, 2003), while in the Gorbachev period, Kremlin conservatives were again the protégés of a new generation of Russophile groups (Dunlop, 1993).

However, such accounts generally over-emphasise these links, assuming that they are rising inexorably. In contrast, the Medvedev interregnum coincided with the mothballing of the Nashi group, while Western analysts paid more attention to Dugin's apparent rise than they did to his 2014 dismissal as head of the Sociology Department at Moscow State University. Neither did they note the rehabilitation of 'liberal' figures (e.g. Kudrin and Kirienko) to the Kremlin after 2015 (Laruelle, 2017a). Moreover, they exaggerate the utility of regime-sponsored nationalism. There are significant doubts as to whether regime legitimacy in 2012–2013 was so weak as to necessitate a risky diversionary manoeuvre. The impact of the 2011–2012 protests is contestable and in any case, by early 2014, Putin had silenced the domestic opposition (Tsygankov, 2015).

Liberal views are strongest when they concentrate in detail on domestic regime functions without over-reliance on transitological frameworks. For example, several works use the term 'managed nationalism' to highlight how Kremlin policy and nationalist groups inter-relate (Horvath, 2014; Laine, 2015). This concept focusses on how the Kremlin's use of nationalism is profoundly instrumental, and nationalism can be encouraged as well as actively oppressed, whenever it suits regime goals.

Among the most productive accounts are those that reject the realist view of the state as unified actor and probe the ways in which nationalism maps onto Russia's complex informal elite networks. For Kimberley Marten (2015), Russian policy making is opaque, contradictory, shambolic and often self-defeating by nature, which is explained by the contestation of self-interested regime networks who have no strategic view in mind, let alone a united conception of 'national interests'. Where nationalism fits in is that 'assertive' nationalism is usually bluster designed to signify strength for disciplining domestic networks. However, regime networks' self-interest results in risk-aversion beneath the bluster. For Marten (2015: 83), Russia's annexation of Crimea was only possible since it was a 'low-risk' endeavour, given 'its overwhelming ethnic Russian majority, its long history as a Russian imperial subject, and its rather arbitrary re-designation from a Russian to Ukrainian Soviet territory under Nikita Khrushchev'.

A similar, but more developed, view is offered by Henry Hale (2016). He broadens the regime's use of nationalism from simply expediency or legitimacy to a fundamental question of elite survival – the function of patronal presidents (i.e. those whose core role is as patrons of rent-seeking networks). From this perspective, whereas previously Putin had relied sparingly on domestic nationalism because it was politically risky, his 'conservative turn' raised its prominence. It thereby solved a fundamental problem of regime stability after 2011, by delegitimising liberal constituencies, by giving Putin's third term a revived political narrative and by consolidating elites around the president. Similarly, Neil Robinson (2017: 360) highlights how the 'conservative turn' provided an answer to the regime's long-term modernisation dilemmas, by attempting to shift 'the ground of what counted as success in state building from issues of functionality towards vague and indeterminate goals based on a cultural rather than an administrative conception of the state'. These perspectives help understand Russia's involvement in Ukraine, which, according to Hale (2016: 247), hit the 'sweet spot' of Russian nationalism: 'enhancing Russia's purity from the perspective of narrowly ethnic Russian nationalists while also restoring Moscow's control over more lands of the former USSR'. Thus it consolidated multiple elite groups, public opinion and opposition nationalist groups round the regime.

Liberal approaches often also emphasise the international spill-over of domestic politics. By inverting Kantian democratic peace theory, they argue that increasing domestic authoritarianism/nationalism engenders aggressive/assertive foreign policy. Allegedly, Russia is offering a coherent ideology to challenge Western liberal-democratic values. Nationalism is seen as intrinsically linked to this ideology. As Edward Lucas has argued (2009: 14), the 'ideological conflict of the New Cold War is between lawless Russian nationalism and law-governed Western multilateralism'. Such views highlight the role of anti-Western ideologues and the alleged prominence of Eurasianism to indicate that the regime's foreign policy views are increasingly motivated by anti-Western nationalism (Laqueur, 2015; Clover, 2016). Similarly, the rise of the GONGOs is associated with a demonstrable 'preventive counter-revolution' against Western liberalism as encouraged by the early 2000s Colour Revolutions in Georgia, Ukraine and Kyrgyzstan (Horvath, 2012). After the Crimean intervention, it appears that domestic and foreign policy discourses have become fused around a nationalist core (e.g. Galeotti and Bowen, 2014). Symptomatic in this regard has been Russia's indirect support for nationalist groups in the Donbas, as well as often less concrete encouragement for a panoply of right-wing populist groups in Europe, chiefly Marine Le Pen's Front National (Pomerantsev, 2015). Such examples would most clearly show domestic nationalism underpinning Russian malfeasance, not just in the post-Soviet space but across the EU more widely.

These approaches rightly highlight the increased visibility of nationalist figures and themes in Russia's foreign as well as domestic policy. Furthermore, there are strong theoretical arguments for positing a link between illiberalism and nationalism. Arguably, illiberal nationalism is inherent to authoritarian or semi-authoritarian systems, which lack the representative institutions and cultures of compromise that might digest nationalism into milder forms. As Michael Mann argues (1995: 62), 'mild nationalism . . . is democracy achieved, aggressive nationalism is democracy perverted'. There is no a priori reason to think that such 'aggressive' nationalism would not affect foreign policy.

However, liberal approaches often fail to provide a nuanced investigation of links between domestic and foreign policy. Implicitly, a direct relationship is often assumed (i.e. that foreign policy simply reflects domestic). To that end, the role of nationalist thinkers is often de-contextualised, with the visibility and declared influence of nationalists taken at face value. This leads to truisms that are seldom questioned, e.g. Aleksandr Prokhanov being 'Nightingale of the General Staff', or Aleksandr Dugin being an influential 'Kremlin advisor'. In reality, such figures do not advise the Kremlin directly, and their influence is much more diffuse. It remains an open question as to whether Kremlin links with foreign 'nationalists' are driven by ideological or pragmatic motivations (Shekhovtsov, 2015).

Often, liberal approaches attribute nationalism a barely warranted causative power. They tend to see it as a largely homogeneous, undifferentiated ideology. Implicitly or otherwise, they view it as characterised by an unchanging primordial anti-Westernism, whereas more constructivist approaches would emphasise that mutability, contestation and division are far more characteristic of it. Similarly, liberal approaches can use some highly normative terms with little attempt at accurate definition. For example, van Herpen (2015) regards the party of power 'United Russia' and the various pro-Kremlin GONGOs as examples of 'chauvinist ultranationalism'. An extreme example is Kuzio (2017), in whose work nationalism is a catch-all term for all kinds of nefarious behaviour: not just foreign policy aggression but extra-judicial murder, corruption, etc.

Overall, liberal approaches' value is in bringing domestic regime type and motivations to the fore, in particular highlighting the regime's use of nationalist forces in power consolidation. These approaches are stronger in the analysis of domestic than foreign politics. In the former, they identify the functionality of nationalism for regime electoral and legitimacy purposes. In the latter, they highlight the increasing role of nationalist intellectuals and ideas as potentially underpinning more assertive foreign policy agendas. However, in both cases, the liberal approach can be simplistic and selective, highlighting examples of nationalist influence outside broader policy-making contexts, and seeing nationalism as a reflexively anti-Western phenomenon.

The main strengths and weaknesses of all the above perspectives are summarised in Table 5.1. Clearly, they all have some validity. Realist approaches highlight the interest-based discourses that dominate Russian foreign policy, among which nationalism, at least until the 'conservative turn', has played a minor role; constructivist approaches show how Russian 'national interests' are subjectively constructed and domestically contested; nationalist ideas have played significant roles in such contestation and appear to be gaining traction; liberal approaches show how the 'rise' of nationalism is related to increasing illiberalism in domestic and foreign policy (albeit they exaggerate its role). What is largely lacking, however, are more holistic approaches that acknowledge both the contested and diverse nature of Russian nationalisms and which seek explicitly to address their interaction with the multilevel nature of Russian policy making. The next section focusses on two such approaches and how they might be developed further.

Table 5.1 The main approaches to explaining nationalism and RFP

	Main explanations	Main strengths and weaknesses
Realist explanations	RFP motivated by material capabilities and global/regional balance of power; little role for ideologies generally and nationalism specifically Western threats to Russian sphere of influence (NATO, Coloured Revolutions, EU)	Strengths: identifies main themes of Russian doctrine and official discourse; explains RFP 'red lines' towards NATO Weaknesses: uncritical approach; no explanation for growing ideational factors; absence of threat-perception towards China
Constructivist explanations	Focus on domestic contestation of RFP, in which Russian nationalists play a key but subordinate role RFP motivated by search for Great Power recognition, status, prestige and honour	Strengths: explains Russian focus on West as Other; brings ideational factors to the fore; explains growing focus on civilisation and soft power; explains domestic contention Weaknesses: generic approach that does not sufficiently explain link between discourse and policy; sees nationalists as undifferentiated whole
Liberal explanations	RFP has domestic sources; rise of nationalism explained by regime's authoritarianism and attempt to divert attention from domestic policy failures Nationalism linked to foreign policy assertion. Russia seeks both to prevent democratic contagion in its immediate neighbourhood and challenge Western liberalism more broadly	Strengths: focus on regime utilisation of nationalism for legitimacy/expediency; explains 'conservative turn' Weaknesses: normative approach that exaggerates unity and strength of nationalism; exaggerates and reifies nationalism as eternally rising; subjective view of policy failure

Source: Author, inspired by Götz (2016).

Towards a holistic model of nationalism and RFP

There have been several recent works linking the study of nationalism to regime dynamics in a more detailed and holistic fashion. Kolstø and Blakkisrud (2016) focus on the role of nationalist groups and national identity, while Cadier and Light (2015) address domestic and foreign policy in the aftermath of the conservative turn. These are detailed and theoretically eclectic edited volumes (albeit drawing most on liberalism and constructivism, and in Cadier and Light's case the Foreign Policy Analysis tradition). Both see nationalism as on the rise and (particularly the latter) conclude both that foreign policy is an extension of domestic policy, and that nationalism plays a great role within the latter. However, only two approaches explicitly aim to provide a multilevel conceptual model for Russian nationalism's policy-making role, Luke March (2012a, 2012b) and Marlène Laruelle (2017a). The ensuing analysis will outline how these complementary works can provide a road-map for future research.

Like several aforementioned accounts, March sees Kremlin's overall approach as 'managed nationalism'. He further argues that managed nationalism is consistent with the Kremlin's general approach to civil society, sometimes described as 'managed pluralism' (Balzer, 2003). This is the way in which the regime sets the agenda for 'healthy' socio-political competition and stigmatises those outside this agenda. Managed nationalism permits nationalism that does not fundamentally challenge the authoritarian state, which gives an inbuilt advantage to illiberal and even extremist forms, but is generally inimical to any liberal nationalism that critiques the state. This managed nationalism consists of three interlocking spheres (March, 2012a):

1. *Official nationality* is named because it is functionally equivalent to Tsarist Official Nationality in terms of being only quasi-nationalist (state interests are prior to the nation's) and in its broader aim of co-opting patriotic sentiment in the interests of preserving internal and external regime stability against foreign threats. It is contained in official Kremlin statements, such as presidential addresses and foreign policy doctrines that articulate the *gosudarstvennik* (statist) position. This is a relatively moderate, pro-European, secular and pragmatic conservatism most cogently articulated in the doctrine of 'sovereign democracy'.
2. *Cultural nationalism* is principally the mainstream intellectual and media discourse and symbols that aim to reinforce the historical, moral and social aspects of a distinct Russian 'national' way of life and thereby build a sense of national solidarity.
3. *Political nationalism* is simply domestic electoral and social mobilisation around nationalist motifs.

The regime actively shapes the relationship between these three spheres: official nationality sets down the parameters for the cultural and political sphere that are allowed some autonomy within (and occasionally, beyond) these limits as long as they do not fundamentally challenge it. Furthermore, managed nationalism has a long historical tradition and echoes the way the Kremlin over the ages has periodically used nationalist sentiment while trying to remain autonomous from it. Kremlin policy is very rarely nationalist per se (cf. Tuminez, 2000).

This is a paradoxical process; the Kremlin sometimes encourages nationalism, but sometimes has to rein in nationalist forces, often with oppressive methods. Increasingly during the Putin regime, the need to encourage nationalism in the cultural and political realm has conflicted with the Kremlin's officially restrained policy, risking creating a self-sustaining momentum to which the Kremlin has to respond.

Supporting some constructivist views of a 'civilizational turn', we can see that, even prior to the more recent 'conservative turn', a dominant theme of both cultural and political nationalism had become 'civilisational nationalism', which emphasises the uniqueness of Russian 'civilisation' and contrasts it against the Western 'Other' (especially pro-Western governments in Georgia, Ukraine and Moldova) (Shnirel'man, 2007). This civilisational nationalism often directly contradicts the pro-European, modernist and pragmatic elements of official nationality. This tendency also gives support to the liberal view of the regime's domestic legitimacy as relying on a 'besieged fortress' paradigm.

The 'rise' of nationalism can be explained partly as a legitimating device against perceived external threats (e.g. Coloured Revolutions) and domestic policy problems (the focus on external enemies makes a convenient distraction). As Laruelle (2015) argues, state-created nationalism is mainly used instrumentally as a post hoc policy justification. But March's approach also emphasises that nationalism is dialectical. The Kremlin is a keen observer (as well as manipulator) of public opinion (Zygar', 2016: 239). Given state control of the electronic media, a vicious circle of 'civilisational nationalism' is created. The state allows such nationalism to dominate the public space. Undoubtedly, this must re-inform Kremlin policy by creating a demand to which it then has to respond.

Indeed, March (2012b) shows how the 'mission creep' of civilisational nationalism grew before and after Russia's intervention in Georgia in 2008. Hard-line nationalists were the dominant cheerleaders for assertive solutions before and during the conflict. Moreover, Aleksandr

Dugin reputedly trained South Ossetian militias in the run-up (Spiegel Online, 2008). Regime and nationalist policies coincided, albeit briefly (e.g. the October–November 2006 campaign against Georgians was 'the first incident of officially endorsed ethnic discrimination in contemporary Russia' (Kozhevnikova, 2007)). Furthermore, regime and nationalist discourses (e.g. the assertion of Georgian intervention in South Ossetia as 'genocide') were briefly symbiotic. The war gained Putin and Medvedev their then-highest public approval ratings and briefly endowed Medvedev with the nationalists' seal of approval. Moreover, this period had long-term effects, with civilisational nationalism appearing in the 2008 foreign policy concept for the first time, with the declaration that global politics were taking on a 'civilisational dimension'. However, the 'Five-Day War' also showed the paradoxicality of state-sponsored nationalism. The Kremlin was aware of nationalism escaping state control, and President Medvedev warned about the dangers of domestic extremism even during the conflict. An incipient crackdown on domestic nationalist groups intensified until Putin's return in 2012 and until then the Kremlin, its increased emphasis on soft power and *Russkii mir* notwithstanding, tried to reassert the golden rule of a pragmatic, interest-based foreign policy that indicated a continued hesitancy about prioritising ideational factors abroad.

The main strength of March's approach is that it links nationalism clearly to regime dynamics. In this case, factors include a long-term campaign of 'othering' Georgians, ad hoc policy improvisation as well as Medvedev's weak domestic legitimacy (Monaghan, 2008b). It further helps explain evident contradictions in state policy (i.e. attempts to utilise and repress Russian nationalism simultaneously). Moreover, such a multilevel approach can draw to different degrees on the aforementioned theoretical approaches, which at a macro-level appear mutually contradictory. For example, it shows the essential validity of realist approaches in explaining the formal elements of RFP (especially the focus on NATO expansion as a threat, a more plausible motivation in the Georgian intervention than in the Crimean annexation). However, it makes clear that the realist approach does not explain domestic contestation over identity issues, which is better approached via a constructivist lens. As liberal approaches argue, March indicates how the regime has an interest in manipulating nationalism. However, contrary to these accounts, it shows that when nationalism directly impacts RFP, this occurs in a much more exceptional and limited fashion.

March's approach does have weaknesses. Although it can map the interaction between nationalism and domestic and foreign policy in some detail, it remains somewhat broad-brush. This is an inevitable corollary of the opacity of the Russian foreign policy process, but the approach is also predominantly discursive. It can explain temporal shifts in regime rhetoric and thereby show potential congruence between nationalist and regime ideas. However, it cannot show causation or whether nationalist ideas directly impact specific foreign policy decisions.

Laruelle (2017a) argues that more precise analysis needs to focus less on ideas and ideologues than the policy locus of nationalists, both in terms of interaction with elite groups and in more specific legislative outcomes. In doing so, she argues that the role of nationalists is much more constrained than often understood. They are just one of several interest groups, and not a unified one at that. The Kremlin generally keeps a distance from them, and utilises their ideas as one of several 'doctrinal products' on the 'ideological market' (Laruelle, 2017b). There is definitely evidence of increasing interaction with nationalists in the emergence of conservative ideology, although not all of this can accurately be regarded as nationalist. However, Laruelle (2015) identifies only limited evidence of direct, consistent nationalist impact on RFP (policy towards compatriots).

Laruelle (2017a) further identifies three main strata promoting a nationalist agenda. These are: (1) *nonstate actors* (unregistered parties, social movements and social media/internet networks), including the National Bolsheviks, skinhead groups and the 'national democrats' (Aleksei Naval'nyi et al.), who want the Russian nation to rise up against the Putin regime; these groups are anti-system, but may have regime patrons; (2) *parastate actors*, who 'operate under the state umbrella, in the gray zone of the Kremlin's "ecosystem" of interest groups, lobbies, and personal connections' (2017a: 90). Such groups have their own interests and ideologies, and include the main Duma parties, the Russian Orthodox Church, Orthodox businessmen (e.g. Vladimir Yakunin and Konstantin Malofeev), as well as different governmental branches and the military industrial complex; and (3) finally, there are state actors, primarily the President and Presidential Administration. Laruelle argues that this focus on groups and strategies allows a comprehensive assessment of the mobilisational potential of Russian nationalism. This approach is not unproblematic (e.g. the 'parastatal' groups, particularly the MIC, might be considered elements of the state). However, it does focus on the essential pluralism of Russian nationalism, its contested nature and its different roles at multiple levels. Laruelle's argument is that nationalism is growing at grassroots level and receives increasing sympathy from some parastatal groups, but is so far limited by state co-optation and the antipathy of most groups to grassroots anti-regime ethnonationalism.

While Laruelle's approach does not directly engage with March's and has a different focus (more policy-oriented, but without explicitly mentioning RFP), it is largely complementary to it. This is especially so in its analysis of official nationality (what Laruelle calls 'state nationalism'), which like March, Laruelle regards as inclusive, instrumental and 'an eclectic piece of bricolage' (2017a: 96). This state nationalism posits the state as 'the symbol, embodiment, and quintessence of the nation' (p. 95) and draws on a range of ideologies, not just nationalism. It is a flexible mélange of ideas that 'guarantees stability in exchange for political loyalty and deference; and . . . embodies historical continuity in the face of regime changes and collapses' (p. 95). As such, it again recalls Tsarist Official Nationality. Convincingly, Laruelle argues that a state master-narrative is not unique to Russia. What is more noteworthy is 'that the nation's master narrative is intimately articulated and instrumentalized by the regime to secure its legitimacy and to marginalize opponents, real or imagined' (p. 95). Contrary to liberal accounts, this is not 'an inherent and essentialist Russian nationalism . . . but the state's use of the national grand narrative it produces in domestic political struggle is a critical characteristic of the regime' (Ibid.). Laruelle's approach is also clearly compatible with regime network accounts, inasmuch as it argues for pluralist and conflictual regime interests.

Using March and Laruelle's accounts as bases, and drawing on the aforementioned theoretical approaches, we can outline a plausible model for how nationalism affects RFP that could form the basis for further research. This model is outlined in Figure 5.1.

This model has a constructivist underpinning, evidenced in the number of bidirectional arrows showing a reflexive relationship between, for example, public opinion and state discourses and the central importance of the latter. More specifically, although international geopolitical factors are of vital importance (top left box), unlike in a similar model by Götz (2016) which has a neo-classical realist framework, they do not have causative effect, reflecting the constructivist view that there are no 'objective' national interests independent of domestic contestation. The changing global/regional balance-of-power, and in particular the increasing prominence of Western influence in the 'near abroad' via NATO/EU expansion and the Coloured Revolutions have become vital to the regime's threat perceptions. But these threats are mediated both by public opinion (bottom left box) and crucially by the Kremlin (top right). Their salience has changed over time. For instance, of particular importance appear to be Putin's feelings of personal betrayal at a whole range of Western policies (especially regime change in Iraq and Syria and Western support for Russia's opposition), as well as a shared Russian elite perception that Coloured Revolutions were engineered by Western security services rather than social change (Zygar', 2016).

Luke March

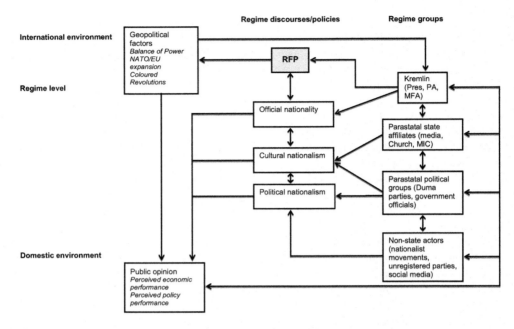

Figure 5.1 A model for understanding the interaction between nationalism and RFP

The second column represents the mechanisms of 'managed nationalism' as outlined by March, i.e. a range of interlocking discourses under the direct control of the state that seek to police public discourse over national values and to actively mould public opinion. As aforementioned, official nationality provides the parameters for cultural and political nationalism, although there is also a feedback loop from these to the official doctrine (e.g. the spillover of civilisational nationalism into official nationality and thence foreign policy). However, whereas the upwards arrow from official nationality indicates that this stands at the nexus between domestic and foreign policy, so nationalist discourse can thereby directly affect (and be affected by) RFP, this model does not assume that this is the main driver of RFP. The Kremlin retains direct and independent control over both official nationality and RFP. This reflects that (a) the Kremlin can usually limit any spillover of more grassroots nationalism into official nationality and 'turn off the tap' where necessary and that (b) many other Kremlin proclivities (doctrinal and personal) go directly into RFP, including personal pique and ad hoc improvisation.

The third column represents the regime groups outlined by Laruelle, and shows their input into nationalist discourse and policy making. Once again, the model is top-down, with policy making centred on the Kremlin. However, in common with regime network models, the 'presidential vertical' is made of divergent and competing groups. Again, the Kremlin sets down the general parameters, but they have certain autonomy in interceding in public discourse. I have divided Laruelle's 'parastatal' groups into *state affiliates* and *political groups*. The former are opinion formers (such as the ROC, media and the MIC), whose influence will be predominantly in the sphere of cultural nationalism. The latter include Duma political parties and government ministers, who also intercede into cultural nationalism. However, since they actively link their view of nationalism with their political campaigns, they are also part of the political nationalism realm. Non-state actors generally have little or no access to state media and are generally excluded from official licence to influence public debates over nationality or other issues, and are therefore influential in the political nationalism discourse only.

Public opinion plays an important role in this model. The public can assess geopolitical factors directly (e.g. via the internet and social media), but clearly in Russia's media environment, will be receptive to managed nationalism as it is promoted via the dominant pro-Kremlin (especially electronic) media. The model shows how the different elements of the regime are influenced by public opinion, particularly to the degree that it reflects assessments of the regime's political and economic performance. How they respond to such information cannot be predicted, but, consistent with the liberal model, negative public assessments of regime performance provide an incentive to accentuate the importance of nationalism both in the domestic and foreign policy sphere.

Summing up, the above model provides a flexible, multilevel schema for understanding how nationalist discourses and regime interests interact. It highlights the important but variable role of nationalism in domestic discourse, and shows how it is a vital but far from decisive element in foreign policy. It is necessarily not conclusive but should provide a useful framework for future studies.

Towards testable hypotheses?

Nationalism's dialectical and discursive nature makes it difficult to subject rigorously to the discipline of hypotheses. Nevertheless, detailed analysis of how it interacts with the regime and policy-making realm along the lines of the model in Figure 5.1 could be instructive in illustrating the following propositions:

1. Nationalism is a socially constructed phenomenon, not a primordial entity. Therefore the role of nationalism in Russian foreign policy is not constant, nor doomed to rise inexorably.
2. (A linked issue) nationalism is not unitary: it is contested and multilevel. Consequently, official nationality is demonstrably different from the view-points of leading nationalist ideologues, but is itself the product of contestation between regime networks.
3. The oft-quoted leading nationalist ideologues are just one of several loose foreign policy tendencies, but do not amount to a coherent, united, let alone dominant nationalist 'school' in foreign policy.
4. Nationalism rarely impacts foreign policy directly. It is certainly part of the ideological arsenal of foreign policy makers. However, the default official position of Russian foreign policy is a pragmatic Realist world-view based on interests.
5. Typically, the regime tries to utilise nationalism instrumentally for domestic legitimacy; it tries both to exploit and to limit such nationalism, but not always successfully.
6. When nationalism does impact foreign policy more directly, this is in conditions of regime instability, when its domestic legitimacy is threatened, and outside systemic factors (e.g. Coloured Revolutions, NATO expansion) make elites feel vulnerable.
7. Following such crises, the regime tries to reassert control over the nationalist agenda.
8. However, the 'bait-and-switch' tactic risks provoking nationalist groups and demands in wider society, that then prove difficult to control.

Future questions and themes

Testing the above propositions is not easy, and needs a multilevel approach with detailed investigation both of regime dynamics and policy making. Approaches that are derived too closely from system-level theories of IR are unlikely to be revealing.

The main weakness afflicting all approaches to RFP is lack of access to the policy-making 'black box'. Despite official secrecy, demystifying the RFP-making process to identify intentions, not just outcomes, and to isolate the real (not alleged) role of nationalists is vital. Interviewing policy makers and experts with inside knowledge is clearly difficult, but in principle methodologically possible and essential. For instance, there are still major divergences between the 'collective Putin' view of the president as largely an arbiter of elite interests (Götz, 2016) and those who see him as having the last word on essential decisions (Zygar', 2016).

In the probable absence of much necessary information, there is still scope for familiar investigations into the role of nationalist thinkers and think-tanks, and of nationalist ideas in public debates. Recent research is beginning to focus on newer groups and figures (such as the Izborskii Club and the *Sputnik i Pogrom* blog) (e.g. Laruelle, 2016). However, Laruelle is right to propose moving away from focussing on ideologues towards policy processes. This chapter's model can be tested and developed in order to systematise and link such research directions, particularly if it is applied to within-case comparisons over space and time (cf. Götz, 2016). Analysing the development of Russia's policy towards different post-Soviet states will help theorise the degree to which 'nationalism' is a consistent feature of its policy, or rather, as is probable, only those most attracted by the Western 'Other'.

Similarly, since the Russian regime's relationship with nationalism is a moving target, there is scope for reviewing over-hasty contemporaneous assumptions with the benefit of hindsight. For example, immediately after the 'conservative turn' and Crimean annexation, it became axiomatic that Russian nationalism had become a mainstream element in RFP-making for the first time. However, a longer-term view indicates first, that the miscegenation of nationalism and foreign policy had already started with the 2008 Russo-Georgian conflict; second, that after the Crimean intervention, the familiar pattern of elite repression of nationalism reasserted itself, with the sidelining of nationalist groups at home and in the Donbas (Kolstø, 2016b), and the de-escalation of Ukraine as a subject of public concern. Therefore in the *longue durée*, the Crimean intervention might look far less exceptional.

Moreover, research in the ideational development of Russian nationalism and foreign policy might usefully develop more sophisticated methods of process-tracing and discourse analysis in order to avoid more impressionistic accounts of the alleged influence of nationalist ideas on debate (Beach and Pedersen, 2013; Götz, 2016). A recent paper by Frear and Mazepus (2017), which traces the ideational themes in official policy documents, shows a usefully replicable and simple methodology.

Another highly relevant theme is Russia's direct sponsoring of nationalists abroad. Russia's aid to the Donbas rebellion remains more dominated by sensationalist journalistic accounts than serious analysis and fuller accounts of the so-called 'nationalist international' remain forthcoming (Shekhovtsov, 2018). This work is focussed on the radical right, but there is need also to focus on the European radical left, who retain a Russophile constituency. There are many questions to explore, such as the role of ideology versus instrumentality, and the nature of support, be it financial, logistical or moral.

Overall, there remains a compelling need for more nuanced and less normative accounts of nationalism that do not assume a priori that Russian nationalism is bad and aggressive (Laruelle, 2014). Indeed, the degree to which Russian nationalism is sui generis and predisposed to authoritarian and aggressive overtones needs to be a research question corroborated by extensive data rather than a normative truism. To this end, there is clearly scope for analyses that explore the impact of nationalism on foreign policy in a comparative context, not solely via single-country case studies.

Conclusion

The above analysis has surveyed the disparate field of nationalism and foreign policy. It has argued that focussing on nationalism is an important element to understanding contemporary RFP, providing that it is understood as a multifaceted and multilevel phenomenon interlinking different discursive and policy fields, domestic and foreign, but not a homogenous variable that in any way 'drives' RFP, either in general or towards the West.

Many approaches to Russian nationalism are derived (explicitly or not) from macro-level IR theories. These provide insights, but struggle to offer a sufficiently nuanced and flexible account able to address the variable role of nationalism in RFP. In particular, realist accounts largely dismiss nationalism's function, whereas liberal accounts largely exaggerate it as an ideological underpinning for regime actions. Constructivist approaches are better at showing how nationalist views interact with domestic national identity debates; however, they tend to exaggerate the homogeneity of nationalist constituencies, while lacking sufficient attention to how nationalists interact with policy processes.

Only multilevel accounts which focus on how nationalism interacts with regime policy making, legitimacy and intra-regime networks can fully identify the nationalism-RFP nexus, and only by taking account of both the ideational influence of nationalism and the policy context of its proponents. This is a topic needing detailed longitudinal empirical investigation and comparative analysis, and this chapter has provided a model that will help illuminate this research direction. Fortunately or otherwise, the recent direction of the Russian regime indicates that the topic of Russian nationalism and foreign policy is unlikely to lose salience any time soon.

Note

1 Thanks to the Aleksanteri Institute, University of Helsinki, for a Fellowship in April 2016 which contributed substantially towards this chapter. Many thanks are also due to Hanna Smith and Veera Laine, for comments on earlier drafts.

References

Allensworth, W., 1998. *The Russian question: nationalism, modernization, and post-Communist Russia*. Rowman & Littlefield, Lanham, MD.
Baker, J., 2012, 'As loved our fathers: The strength of patriotism among young Newfoundlanders', *National Identities* vol. 14, pp. 367–386.
Balzer, H., 2003, 'Managed Pluralism: Vladimir Putin's Emerging Regime', *Post-Soviet Affairs* vol. 19, pp. 189–227.
Barbashin, A., Thoburn, H., 2014, 'Putin's brain. Alexander Dugin and the philosophy behind Putin's invasion of Crimea', *Foreign Affairs*, 31 March. Available at: www.foreignaffairs.com/articles/russia-fsu/2014-03-31/putins-brain.
Beach, D., Pedersen, R.B., 2013, *Process-tracing methods: foundations and guidelines*, University of Michigan Press, Ann Arbor, MI.
Brandenberger, D., 2010, 'Stalin's populism and the accidental creation of Russian national identity', *Nationalities Papers* vol. 38, pp. 723–739.
Breuilly, J., 1993, *Nationalism and the state*, Manchester University Press, Manchester, UK.
Cadier, D., Light, M. (eds), 2015 *Russia's foreign policy ideas, domestic politics and external relations*, Palgrave Macmillan, Basingstoke, UK.
Charap, S., Welt, C., 2015, 'Making sense of Russian foreign policy', *Problems of Post-Communism* vol. 62, pp. 67–70.
Clover, C., 2016, *Black wind, white snow: the rise of Russia's new nationalism*, Yale University Press, New Haven, CT.
Clunan, A.L., 2009, *The social construction of Russia's resurgence: aspirations, identity, and security interests*, Johns Hopkins University Press, Baltimore, MD.

Dunlop, J.B., 1993, *The rise of Russia and the fall of the Soviet empire*, Princeton University Press, Princeton, NJ.
Feklyunina, V., 2016, 'Soft power and identity: Russia, Ukraine and the "Russian world(s)"', *European Journal of International Relations*, vol. 22, pp. 773–796.
Forsberg, T., Pursiainen, C., 2017, 'The psychological dimension of Russian foreign policy: Putin and the annexation of Crimea', *Global Society*, vol. 31, pp. 220–244.
Frear, M., Mazepus, H., 2017, *A new turn or more of the same? A structured analysis of recent developments in Russian foreign policy discourse*, EU-STRAT Working Paper 3, Freie Universität Berlin, Berlin.
Galeotti, M., Bowen, A.S., 2014, 'Putin's empire of the mind', *Foreign Policy*, 21 April. Available at: https://foreignpolicy.com/2014/04/21/putins-empire-of-the-mind/.
Gellner, E., 1983, *Nations and nationalism*, Basil Blackwell, Oxford, UK.
Götz, E., 2016, 'Putin, the state, and war: the causes of Russia's Near Abroad assertion revisited', *International Studies Review*. doi:10.1093/isr/viw009.
Gould-Davies, N., 1999, 'Rethinking the role of ideology in international politics during the Cold War', *Journal of Cold War Studies*, vol. 1, pp. 90–109.
Gries, P.H., Zhang, Q., Crowson, H.M., Cai, H., 2011, 'Patriotism, nationalism and China's US policy: structures and consequences of Chinese national identity', *The China Quarterly* vol. 205, pp. 1–17.
Hale, H.E., 2016, 'How nationalism and machine politics mix in Russia', in P. Kolstø and H. Blakkisrud (eds), *The new Russian nationalism*, pp. 221–248, Edinburgh University Press, Edinburgh, UK.
Horvath, R., 2014, 'Russkii Obraz and the politics of "managed nationalism"', *Nationalities Papers*, vol. 42, pp. 469–488.
Horvath, R., 2012, *Putin's preventative counter-revolution: post-Soviet authoritarianism and the spectre of velvet revolution*, Routledge, Abingdon, UK.
Jackson, N.J., 2003, *Russian foreign policy and the CIS*, Routledge, Abingdon, UK.
Kaczmarski, M., 2012, 'Domestic sources of Russia's China policy', *Problems of post-Communism*, vol. 59, pp. 3–17.
Kolstø, P., 2016a, 'The ethnification of Russian nationalism. Imperialism, ethnicity and authoritarianism 2000–2015', in P. Kolstø and H. Blakkisrud (eds), *The new Russian nationalism*, pp. 18–45, Edinburgh University Press, Edinburgh, UK.
Kolstø, P., 2016b, 'Crimea vs. Donbas: how Putin won Russian nationalist support – and lost it again', *Slavic Review* vol. 75, pp. 702–725.
Kolstø, P., Blakkisrud, H., (eds) 2016, *The new Russian nationalism: imperialism, ethnicity and authoritarianism, 2000–2015*, Edinburgh University Press, Edinburgh, UK.
Kotkin, S., 2016, 'Russia's perpetual geopolitics: Putin returns to the historical pattern', *Foreign Affairs*, vol. 95, pp. 2–9.
Kozhevnikova, G., 2007, *Radical nationalism in Russia and efforts to counteract it in 2006*. Available from: www.sova-center.ru/en/xenophobia/reports-analyses/2007/05/d10896/ [11 July 2017].
Kuzio, T., 2017, *Putin's war against Ukraine: revolution, nationalism, and crime*, CreateSpace Independent Publishing, Toronto.
Laine, V., 2015, *Managed nationalism. Contemporary Russian nationalistic movements and their relationship to the government*, Finnish Institute of International Affairs, Helsinki.
Laine, V., 2017, 'Contemporary Russian nationalisms: the state, nationalist movements, and the shared space in between', *Nationalities Papers*, vol. 45, pp. 222–237.
Laqueur, W., 1994, *Black Hundred: rise of the extreme right in Russia*, HarperCollins, New York.
Laqueur, W., 2015, *Putinism: Russia and its future with the West*, Thomas Dunne, New York.
Laruelle, M., 2014, '"Russkii natsionalism" kak oblast' nauchnikh issledovanii', *Pro et Contra*, vol. 62, pp. 54–72.
Laruelle, M., 2015, 'Russia as a "divided nation," from compatriots to Crimea', *Problems of Post-Communism*, vol. 62, pp. 88–97.
Laruelle, M., 2016, 'The Izborsky Club, or the new conservative avant-garde in Russia', *The Russian Review*, vol. 75, pp. 626–644.
Laruelle, M., 2017a, 'Is nationalism a force for change in Russia?' *Daedalus* vol. 146, pp. 89–100.
Laruelle, M., 2017b, 'Putin's regime and the ideological market: a difficult balancing game', available from: http://carnegieendowment.org/2017/03/16/putin-s-regime-and-ideological-market-difficult-balancing-game-pub-68250 [7 April 2017].
Lavrov, S., 2008, 'Litsom k litsu s Amerikoi: Mezhdu nekonfrontatsiei i konvergentsiei', available from: www.profile.ru/politics/item/56173-litsom-k-litsu-s-amerikoi-mezhdu-nekonfrontatsiei-i-konvergentsiei-56173 [26 June 2017].

Lo, B., 2003, *Vladimir Putin and the evolution of Russian foreign policy*, Wiley-Blackwell, Oxford, UK.
Lucas, E., 2009, *The new Cold War: how the Kremlin menaces both Russia and the West*, Bloomsbury, London.
Lukyanov, F., 2016, 'Putin's foreign policy: the quest to restore Russia's rightful place', *Foreign Affairs*, www.foreignaffairs.com/articles/russia-fsu/2016-04-18/putins-foreign-policy.
Macfarlane, S.N., 2016, 'Kto Vinovat? Why is there a crisis in Russia's relations with the West?', *Contemporary Politics* vol. 22, pp. 342–358.
Makarychev, A., Yatsyk, A., 2014, *A new Russian conservatism: domestic roots and repercussions for Europe*, Barcelona Centre for International Affairs, Barcelona.
Mankoff, J., 2009, *Russian foreign policy: the return of great power politics*, Rowman & Littlefield, Lanham, MD.
Mann, M., 1995, 'A political theory of nationalism and its excesses', in S. Periwal (ed.), *Notions of nationalism*, pp. 44–63, Central European University Press, Budapest.
March, L., 2012a, 'Nationalism for export? The domestic and foreign-policy implications of the new "Russian idea"', *Europe-Asia Studies*, vol. 64, pp. 401–425.
March, L., 2012b, 'Nationalist grievance and Russian foreign policy: the case of Georgia', in M.R. Freire and R. Kanet (eds), *Russia and its near neighbours*, pp. 63–88, Palgrave Macmillan, Basingstoke, UK.
Marten, K., 2015, 'Informal political networks and Putin's foreign policy: the examples of Iran and Syria', *Problems of Post-Communism*, vol. 62, pp. 71–87.
Mearsheimer, J.J., 2014, 'Why the Ukraine crisis is the West's fault: the liberal delusions that provoked Putin', *Foreign Affairs*, vol. 93, pp. 77–89.
Mitrofanova, A., 2012, 'The new nationalism in Russia', *Hérodote*, vol. 144, pp. 141–153.
Mitrokhin, N., 2003, *Russkaya partiya: Dvizhenie Russkikh natsionalistov v SSSR 1953–1985*, Novoe Literaturnoe Obozrenie, Moscow.
Monaghan, A., 2008a, '"An enemy at the gates" or "from victory to victory"? Russian foreign policy', *International Affairs*, vol. 84, pp. 717–733.
Monaghan, A., 2008b, *The Russo-Georgian conflict: immediate report*, NATO Defense College, Rome.
Pilkington, H., Garifzianova, A., Omel'chenko, E., 2013, *Russia's skinheads*, Routledge, Abingdon, UK.
Pomerantsev, P., 2015, 'The Kremlin's information war', *Journal of Democracy*, vol. 26, pp. 40–50.
Pursiainen, C., 2000, *Russian foreign policy and International Relations Theory*, Ashgate, Aldershot, UK.
Putin, V., 1999, 'Russia at the turn of the millennium', available from: http://pages.uoregon.edu/kimball/Putin.htm [26 June 2017].
Riasanovsky, N., 1959, *Nicholas I and official nationality in Russia, 1825–1855*, University of California Press, Berkeley, CA.
Robinson, N., 1995, 'What was Soviet ideology? A comment on Joseph Schull and an alternative', *Political Studies*, vol. 43, pp. 325–332.
Robinson, N., 2017, 'Russian neo-patrimonialism and Putin's "cultural turn"', *Europe-Asia Studies*, vol. 69, pp. 348–366.
Sakwa, R., 2015, *Frontline Ukraine: crisis in the borderlands*, IBTauris, London.
Sakwa, R., 2016, 'Russian neo-revisionism and dilemmas of European integration', in R.E. Kanet and M. Sussex (eds), *Power, politics and confrontation in Eurasia: foreign policy in a contested region*, pp. 111–134, Palgrave Macmillan, Basingstoke, UK.
Shekhovtsov, A., 2015, 'The Kremlin's marriage of convenience with the European far right', available at: www.opendemocracy.net/od-russia/anton-shekhovtsov/kremlin%E2%80%99s-marriage-of-convenience-with-european-far-right [30 June 2017).
Shekhovtsov, A., 2018, *Russia and the Western far right: Tango Noir*, Routledge, Abingdon, UK.
Shevtsova, L., 2014, 'Falling into Putin's trap', *The American interest*, 10 March, www.the-american-interest.com/2014/03/10/falling-into-putins-trap/.
Shevtsova, L., 2015a, 'Forward to the past in Russia', *Journal of Democracy*, vol. 26, pp. 22–36.
Shevtsova, L., 2015b, 'The Kremlin is winning', *The American Interest*, 12 February, www.the-american-interest.com/2015/02/12/the-kremlin-is-winning/.
Shnirel'man, V., 2007, 'Tsivilatsionnyi podkhod kak natsional'naya ideya', in M. Laruelle (ed.), *Sovremennye Interpretatsii Russkogo Natsionalizma*, pp. 217–248, ibidem-Verlag, Stuttgart, Germany.
Simão, L., 2012, 'Do leaders still decide? The role of leadership in Russian foreign policymaking', *International Politics*, vol. 49, pp. 482–497.
Smith, H., 2012, 'Domestic influences on Russian foreign policy: status, interests and ressentiment', in M. Freire and R. Kanet (eds), *Russia and its near neighbours*, pp. 39–62, Palgrave Macmillan, Basingstoke, UK.
Spiegel Online, 2008, 'Road to war in Georgia: the chronicle of a Caucasian tragedy', 25 August, www.spiegel.de/international/world/road-to-war-in-georgia-the-chronicle-of-a-caucasian-tragedy-a-574812.html.

Stoner, K., McFaul, M., 2015, 'Who lost Russia (this time)? Vladimir Putin', *The Washington Quarterly*, vol. 38, pp. 167–187.

Szporluk, R., 1989, 'Dilemmas of Russian nationalism', *Problems of Communism*, vol. 38, pp. 15–35.

Treisman, D., 2014, 'The two Putins', available at: www.cnn.com/2014/03/03/opinion/treisman-two-putins/index.html [29 June 2017].

Trenin, D., 2007, *Getting Russia right*, Carnegie Endowment for International Peace, Washington, DC.

Tsygankov, A.P., 2009, 'From Belgrade to Kiev. Hard-line nationalism and Russia's foreign policy', in M. Laruelle (ed.), *Russian nationalism and the national reassertion of Russia*, pp. 189–202, Routledge, Abingdon, UK.

Tsygankov, A.P., 2010, *Russia's foreign policy: change and continuity in national identity*, Rowman & Littlefield, Lanham, MD.

Tsygankov, A.P., 2015, 'Vladimir Putin's last stand: the sources of Russia's Ukraine policy', *Post-Soviet Affairs*, vol. 31, pp. 279–303.

Tsygankov, A.P., 2016, 'Crafting the state-civilization: Vladimir Putin's turn to distinct values', *Problems of Post-Communism*, vol. 63, no. 3, pp. 146–158.

Tucker, R.C., 1991, 'Czars and Commiczars', *New Republic*, vol. 204, pp. 29–35.

Tuminez, A.S., 2000, *Russian nationalism since 1856: ideology and the making of foreign policy*, Rowman & Littlefield, Lanham, MD.

Umland, A., 2007, 'Alexander Dugin, the issue of post-Soviet fascism, and Russian political discourse today', *Russian Analytical Digest*, vol. 14, pp. 2–4.

van Herpen, M., 2015, *Putin's wars: the rise of Russia's new imperialism*, Rowman & Littlefield, Lanham, MD.

Verkhovskii, A., Pain, E., 2012, 'Civilizational nationalism: the Russian version of the "special path"', *Russian Politics and Law*, vol. 50, pp. 52–86.

Yanov, A., 1995, *Posle El'tsina: 'Veimarskaya Rossiya'*, KRUK, Moscow.

Zevelev, I., 2014, 'Granitsy russkogo mira. Transformatsiya natsional'noi identichnosti i novaya vneshnepoliticheskaya doktrina Rossii', *Rossiya v global'noi politike* vol. 2, www.globalaffairs.ru/number/Granitcy-russkogo-mira—16582.

Zevelev, I., 2016, *Russian national identity and foreign policy*, CSIS Center for Strategic and International Studies, Washington, DC.

Zubok, V.M., 2009, *A failed empire: the Soviet Union in the Cold War from Stalin to Gorbachev*, University of North Carolina Press, Chapel Hill, NC.

Zygar', M., 2016, *All the Kremlin's men: inside the court of Vladimir Putin*, PublicAffairs, New York.

6
PETROPOLITICS

Yuval Weber

HIGHER SCHOOL OF ECONOMICS, MOSCOW

Introduction

The Russian Federation has been a petrostate for its entire legal existence.[1] Russia's reliance on energy resources to generate hard currency, undergird the industrial economy, and project influence abroad extends further back into Tsarist times when Baku was a leading center of oil production under the Nobel brothers and a young Joseph Stalin was agitating amongst *nefty-aniki* [oil workers]. The contemporary literature on energy in Russian politics and statecraft is understandably voluminous (see, inter alia, Gustafson, 1989, 2012; Lane, 1999; Ellman, 2006; Goldman, 2008; Sakwa, 2008a, 2008b; Gaidar, 2010; Alekperov, 2011; Gaddy and Ickes, 2011; while Hewett 1984, 1988 are classic older works), but it often misidentifies how "energy" has influenced Russian domestic political outcomes and foreign policy formulation. This chapter specifies the connections between oil, war, and foreign policy in petrostates generally and Russia specifically. I show that foreign policy formulation and implementation relies much more on elite politics rather than a simple "oil weapon" correlation.

This chapter introduces a theory of *petrostate* foreign policy formulation to clarify just how oil booms and busts shape Russia's foreign policy decisions. By focusing on internal (and informal) political dynamics faced by Leonid Brezhnev and Vladimir Putin at the time each experienced an oil boom, I show that contra to the war chest theory (also known as the "oil weapon") that claims otherwise, energy revenues do not make Russia immediately more aggressive in terms of militarized interstate disputes. Increases in energy revenues do expand the menu of foreign policy options, but when or how that is expressed is a function of that leader's political strength. Brezhnev's relative political weakness allowed subordinates to pursue countervailing expansionism in the Third World parallel to his focus on détente with the West, whereas the use of force abroad and expansion of diplomatic commitments has happened much more slowly and deliberately under Putin's leadership. This contrasts with conventional wisdom of Russian foreign policy and energy, which often draws a direct and mechanical link from oil booms and busts to more, or less, conflict abroad. The emphasis on internal and informal politics challenges two hidden assumptions usually ascribed to petrostates: they are always aggressive, limited only by fiscal resources, and their leaders possess no agency in the foreign policy decision-making process.

I provide a petropolitics theory of foreign policy formulation and implementation in which energy revenues interact with pre-existing foreign policy preferences and leadership strength.

I draw this theory from two sources: the studies of informality in Russian politics and the current state of the "resource curse" literature, which, not to put too fine a point on it, has largely debunked the "curse" aspect. Since Sachs and Warner (1995) observed the correlation that "states with a high ratio of natural resource exports to GDP in 1971 had abnormally slow growth rates between 1971 and 1989," petropolitics scholars now hold that energy resources are more usefully thought of as fiscal resources and not as physical commodities. Since fiscal resources are inherently political resources, the presence or absence of energy resources means the presence or absence of political resources for leaders to redistribute. What matters is the executive's patronal strength at the time of revenue shock, regardless of political regime type. As an influx or shortfall of fiscal resources enters a political environment, a strong leader will be able to control redistribution of rents or policy positions while effectively infinite financial and policy demands beset a weak leader.

The chapter concludes by evaluating the challenges posed by the current expansionist foreign policy course on a Russian state still reliant on the redistribution of oil rents for regime continuity. First, trends in the international energy market (decreased demand interacting with increased supplies of conventional and shale oil, as well as transition towards increased use of natural gas) offer few easy solutions. Second, the military and diplomatic expansionism of recent years has tested the Putin-era social contract. The underlying strategic paradox is that absent another oil boom, the Russian leader will have to evaluate a difficult trade-off: increased diplomatic commitments in Ukraine and Syria are central to domestic legitimacy, but they inhibit economic growth by isolating Russia from the international economy. Retrenchment would alleviate economic difficulties, but, like Mikhail Gorbachev before him, identify the limits of Russian capabilities and potentially provoke a domestic backlash – particularly from the security elite.

Petrostate foreign policy formulation: where does oil cause states to go to war?

The debate over petrostate foreign policy formulation and implementation is whether oil has an independent, causal effect on a petrostate's foreign policy. Does the price of oil lead to more frequent and more extensive usages of coercive diplomacy, as measured in militarized interstate disputes, or do high prices of oil lead to expansion of military capabilities, but not necessarily more aggressive actions? I review here the empirical evidence and theoretical basis of this mechanical explanation of petrostate foreign policy and other familiar arguments linking oil to war in Russia, and provide a more modest petropolitics theory in the next section. By distinguishing what petropolitics scholars have shown from what critics of Russian foreign policy claim, I show in studies of Brezhnev's and Putin's tenures that oil does – eventually – lead to more expansionist foreign policy, but only after interacting with pre-existing foreign policy preferences and the strength of Russian executives relative to their political coalitions.

The war chest theory is a familiar one (Lamborn, 1983). Sometimes called "the oil weapon" (Stegen, 2011), it holds that energy prices and foreign policy outcomes are correlated, so that the price of oil determines the petrostate's aggressiveness. An increase in revenues means an increase in capabilities, leading petrostates to demand more from their adversaries, whereas a decrease in revenues leads states to seek diplomatic solutions to settle disputes as well as to demand less from adversaries. In effect, the price of oil determines the frequency and extent a petrostate employs coercive diplomacy in its foreign relations.

Cross-national data do not confirm this mechanical correlation. The war chest has been found to have a significant effect only on certain types of international conflict: revolutionary and other political environments where state capacity is weak. Statistical results have been confirmed only by excluding settled great powers such as Russia. Morrison (2009) reviewed the existing oil and conflict literature and found two contradictory arguments, oil "leads simultaneously to increased risk of civil conflict and exceptional regime stability." He shows that:

> [h]ypotheses linking oil to civil conflict implicitly assume a government with weak state capacity, while those linking oil to regime stability assume a government with strong state capacity . . . [showing] that oil's tendency to spur civil conflict disappears in the context of strong state capacity, and that oil's tendency to stabilize political regimes disappears in the context of weak institutions.

Colgan (2013, 2014) similarly showed that oil money allows revolutionary leaders the resources to expand conflict abroad to protect political changes at home, as ready oil revenues reduce the risk of domestic punishment and lessen opportunity cost of disruption through dispersal of excess rents. Ross (2012) reviews, inter alia, the literature on oil and civil conflict, finding an effect only occurs under specific conditions: when there are abundant resources far from state power, and where insurgencies have already been in operation for a number of years.

The war chest theory finds support from the universe of cases where petrostates are revolutionary or otherwise fragmented, but does it describe Russia? Critics of Russian foreign policy often claim that the war chest tells a convincing story. Starting with the Yom Kippur oil shock flooding Soviet coffers with petrodollars, we can observe expansionism in the Third World during the 1970s, pullback from there and Eastern Europe in the 1980s as oil prices crashed, abdication of an international role during the similarly lean 1990s, and finally a resurgence of sorts during the past ten years following the boom of the 2000s. The actual data do not fit as neatly. The Soviet Union might have been quite ideologically oriented, but it was a settled great power with numerous interests by the time energy made a fiscal impact on foreign policy decision-making – as well as engaging in major and smaller wars long before becoming a major oil exporter once more.

Militarized interstate disputes (MIDS) associated with the Soviet Union spike in the late 1960s, providing some superficial support for the war chest theory. Yet the actual disputes from those years collated by the *Correlates of War* Project are overwhelmingly geolocated in Southeast Asia and the western edge of the Middle East, meaning that Soviet use of force abroad is due to the Vietnam War and the wars between Israel and its neighbors, two critical Cold War theaters (Palmer et al., 2015).

The war chest theory also has a difficult time explaining direct changes later on – MIDS' decline in the 1970s when the USSR enjoyed an initial influx of energy revenues, and increase in the early 1980s when the price of oil went bust as lingering wars of decolonization provided another theater for superpower competition. Retrenchment pursued by Mikhail Gorbachev from 1987 onwards only occurred after he had consolidated power at home, and was a surprise to the Soviet establishment even though the price of oil had gone bust much earlier in the decade (Lewin, 1991; Brown, 1997). Even after the collapse of the Soviet Union, the war chest had a difficult time explaining Russian foreign policy. Although state capacity was at its weakest since perhaps the German invasion of World War II or the Civil War, Russia engaged in a tremendous number of disputes across the former Soviet Union as its boundaries resettled. Those early Russian MIDS were numerous but low profile for an international audience, such as intervention in Tajikistan's civil war. More recent MIDS, detailed below in the case study on Vladimir Putin, have been much more high profile, concentrated in wars with Georgia, Ukraine, and Syrian rebels, but those have occurred in wildly differing revenue environments (Palmer et al., 2015).

Brown (2011) and Stulberg (2007) provide solid neoclassical realist interpretations of the war chest that sidestep polemical demonization of Russia, but the war chest falls short theoretically on the whole. It implies that capabilities cause outcomes – foreign policy preferences are endogenous to capabilities – so that having more money causes more expansive foreign policy behavior. This strips away agency from policymakers and leads to a conclusion that any arbitrary executive will behave identically to any other. These assumptions are not borne out. Expansionism to the Third World existed alongside détente efforts to reduce international tension. An aggressive military posture by the Soviet Union continued well into the 1980s past oil bust liquidity crunches, with perestroika scholars and participants arguing that a non-Gorbachev status quo could have seen the Soviet Union survive for a number of years more – albeit with a likelihood of even greater collapse (Miller, 2016). Expansion into Georgia and Ukraine in 2008 and 2014 respectively, occurred after specific challenges to the regional status quo and not upon a positive revenue shock, while intervention in Syria has continued even under a serious recession in Russia (Adams, 2017).

The war chest directly emphasizes the independent power of revenues and asks the observer to believe that having any leader at the helm makes no difference to Russian foreign policy. A competing approach emphasizes leaders as individuals with pre-existing foreign policy preferences who exploit energy shocks to pursue idiosyncratic foreign policy courses (Balzer, 2005). This approach argues that leaders at the helm of organizations drive decisions, which ignores the informality at the basis of Russian governance as argued by Keenan (1986) and Ledeneva (1998, 2006, 2013). The clear drawbacks to such an explanation are first, that leaders pursue different strategies at different times, and second, attributes near-magical powers to colorful or mysterious individuals, diminishing the cut and thrust of internal politics leaders must master to achieve and retain their positions, as shown by Breslauer's (1982) classic work on pluralism in Soviet governance and Anderson's (1993) clever evaluation of public politics in the Soviet Union. With particular reference to Russia, the variation in regime type and the shallowness of formal political institutions have meant that the most successful politicians are the ones that can exploit the weakness of their rivals and build informal networks.

Over-reliance on revenues and diminishment of politics for the war chest theory and the reverse problem for personality-driven arguments leave both explanations incomplete and unbalanced. The petropolitics theory of petrostate foreign policy formulation augments and links both explanations to argue that energy resources help determine the menu of choices available to policymakers, but that the content of those choices is driven by internal politics, foreign policy preferences of the executive, and his political subordinates and supporters. Since the mid-1960s, positive or negative energy revenue shocks have created varying revenue environments in which Russian policymakers have greater or fewer policy options available to them. The political strength of the executive relative to those subordinates and supporters determines the manner in which Russian leaders make foreign policy decisions. Weaker executives subject to greater political pressure, like Leonid Brezhnev, accede to the preferences of others in determining which strategies to follow to stay in office, while stronger executives like Vladimir Putin are better able to shape policy closer to their own preferences. The revenue environments determine the menu of choices, but internal politics drives which decisions are made and how.

Politics and energy conditions

Central to petropolitics and defining the inputs and outputs of petrostate foreign policy is to distinguish between oil and gas, review the institutional turn in the resource curse literature, and finally provide a theory of foreign policy in Russia. In short, the idea of energy being a "curse" has largely been debunked, and the war chest's applicability to Russia is similarly limited, so a theory of energy revenues and foreign policy in Russia must run through familiar models of political behavior. The theory provided here is drawn from the contemporary literature, which argues that developmental outcomes from energy revenue influxes or shortfalls – booms and busts – are contingent upon the political environment that exists prior to the revenue shock, not to anything specific about oil. Similarly, the petropolitics theory of petrostate foreign policy formulation offered later in this chapter concentrates on the executive's political strength or weakness at the time an exogenous resource boom or bust actually occurs.

Whereas natural gas is a capital-intensive business centered on building incredibly costly pipelines and supporting logistical infrastructure that can run into the billions (Stevens, 2009), oil is a far different business. It is an easily transportable commodity, whose very mobility means that it is extracted, refined, shipped away, and sold to the highest bidder anywhere in the world. Oil is a global commodity whose price is set by the market and whose principal purpose is earning money – fungible for any purpose – for its producer.

The differentiation between oil and gas, and the pace by which either provides revenue, informs the conceptual transition towards treating oil as an explicitly political resource and represents the final debunking of the resource curse thesis, so named by Auty (1993: 1), who noted: "Resource-rich countries fail to benefit from a favourable endowment, [and] they may actually perform worse than less well-endowed countries. This counterintuitive outcome is the basis of the resource curse thesis." When the oil industry transitioned ownership from private Western oil interests to indigenous national oil companies in the mid-1960s, economists and officials in the Middle East and elsewhere assumed that gaining such lucrative resources would improve developmental outcomes. Many expected states to export valuable commodities to make up for a shortfall of domestic investable capital while also attracting foreign direct investment, but economic and social indicators were unfortunately as bad or worse than before (Sachs and Warner, 1995).

That states with natural resources often performed less well on economic, social, and political indicators than originally anticipated led scholars to search for a causal explanatory theory in effectively three stages: purely economic explanations, then revisionist literature focusing on the corrosive effects of energy resources on the state, and finally contemporary research arguing that oil merely magnifies the effects, positive or negative, of the institutions already in place at the time of discovery and exploitation. That last point provides the insight for petrostate foreign policy: revenue from oil exports magnifies the positive or negative aspects of the foreign policy formulation process already in place.

Economic explanations for poor development outcomes focused on issues such as Dutch Disease, revenue volatility, excessive borrowing, and other monetary and fiscal maladies (Karl, 1997: ch. 2). These explanations failed to explain divergence in development outcomes of resource-rich countries, where some petrostates such as Indonesia and the Gulf states seemed to be stable and others such as Norway demonstrably benefitted from natural resource exports.

The state corrosion argument looked inside the state for clues on what was going wrong. Karl (1997) argued that energy resources corrode state institutions by quickly and durably generating rent seeking, which incentivizes officials to weaken regulatory and extractive capabilities. Politicians then distribute oil rents to powerful organized interests that double as bureaucratic and private sector allies, making the state less of a vehicle to drive development goals and more of a milk cow to be sucked dry (Karl, 1997: 91). Rent competition degrades political institutions associated with and responsible for successful development outcomes, such as robust taxation and redistribution systems, transparent and effective bureaucracies, political decisions made on behalf of a universal electorate, that lead individuals to overwhelm public institutions for private gain and inhibit the provision of public goods. Ross (1999: 297) provided further support for state-centered explanations, dismissing cognitive and societal explanations. The former violates because the basic rationality assumption of leadership contends, "that resource booms produce a type of short-sightedness among policymakers," and the latter because they impute an implausible level of influence by non-state actors over the state when commodities and their rents are controlled by the state.

Ross's review left state-centered explanations as the main viable route to understanding the political effects of energy resources, but continued variation of development and democratization outcomes across petrostates led scholars to investigate the role played by political institutions. Instead of looking at the state as an overwhelmed object, petrostate scholars narrowed in on the state of political institutions at the time of a revenue shock. Rosser (2006) and Weinthal and Luong (2006) offered exhaustive review articles that explicitly challenged the transformative value of energy resources and expressly provided institutional accounts of political and economic capacity at the time of discovery. Smith (2007: 1) stated directly: "oil rents have effects on institutions that vary systematically according to the circumstances of oil's entry as a major export commodity. Where rentier state/resource curse theorists have asked whether a country is oil-rich, I ask *when*."[2] Smith's work marked a turning point by labeling energy resources as explicitly political resources, that is, as revenue or the promise of revenue by politicians to current or potential supporters. In this vein, Luong and Weinthal (2010) published a book boldly titled *Oil Is Not a Curse* that demonstrated wide variation in the selection of ownership structure of oil and gas sectors by several post-Soviet governments in response to political incentives.

Petropolitics theory fits extremely well with approaches to Russian politics based on informal governance and networks. In the historiographical debates between depictions of Russian rulers as Iron Tsars dictating outcomes to subordinates (Pipes, 1974), versus more contingent interpretations of individuals balancing interests of myriad power brokers and interest groups (Keenan, 1986), petropolitics clearly fits in the latter tradition. Petropolitics asks how strong a leader is relative to her political supporters at the moment energy revenues become noticeably plentiful or noticeably absent, and how does she handle that influx or shortfall relative to the foreign policy preferences of her *okruzhenie* [inner circle]?

Recent literature on Russian politics has illuminated many aspects of both questions. Hale (2005, 2010, 2014) argues that "patronal politics" – patronage networks defined by illiberalism and punctuated by color revolutions – shape the post-Soviet Eurasian space. He argues against the transitology and neo-patrimonialist literatures, so that instead of transitions inevitably leading to democratic states defined by political competition or neo-patrimonial networks of principals relying on agents, Eurasia is a series of patronal networks. Hale depicts stable systems as ones where leaders, subordinates, and the public in general do not anticipate substantive political changes; instability and color revolutions result when there is an expectation that the future does not look like the present. "Single pyramids of power" thus cut across formal political institutions to shape future expectations of political behavior for those inside and outside the pyramid of power. In modern Russian political history, we are familiar with the phrase "vertical of power" [*vertikal vlasti*] to describe Vladimir Putin's efforts to eliminate sources of formal or informal opposition to his rule, which Hale would say is the construction of a single pyramid of power. In Hale's account and in similar approaches, such as McGlinchey (2011), the opportune exploitation of financial resources provided by energy exports allows the leader to distribute rents as necessary to safeguard power from competition so that the present can be iterated indefinitely into the future.

Hale uses the pyramid metaphor, but another prominent recent work, Marten (2015), employs a network metaphor to understand how Russian leaders consolidate and retain power. Although Marten notes that scholars point to the necessity of formal political institutions in providing information to national leaders on sub-national leadership performance, channeling elite conflict, shaping local outcomes, and attracting individuals with policy expertise to government

(Gel'man, 2012; Reuter and Robertson, 2012), the bulk of attention has been to informality in Russian governance. Kryshtanovskaya (2005) traces the generational origins of contemporary Russian elites, and her co-authored work with White (White and Kryshtanovskaya, 2011) looks into Putin's placement of personal acquaintances into government over his rule, which itself dovetails with Petrov's (2011) assertion that the current Russian government is a privatized facade for the KGB. Huskey (2004a, 2004b) has written extensively about Putin's shaping of cadre policy as a revival of the Soviet-era nomenklatura system to provide the leadership with pre-vetted bureaucrats. Ledeneva's research into *sistema* [system] argues that "individual players in the game matter more than bureaucratic rules or laws, because powerful individuals can use, bend, and create rules to serve their interests in a game that lacks overall coherency and consistency" (Marten, 2015: 72, describing Ledeneva's research).

If the first question of petropolitics is how strong is the leader relative to her supporters, then the second question is how that leader handles the foreign policy preferences of those supporters given that even strong leaders cannot get too far ahead of their supporters? Marten shares with Hale a focus on how leaders actually construct the pyramids or networks that insulate them from domestic and international political and economic competition. She describes strong leaders of informal networks very carefully as astute accumulators of wealth, pursuing foreign policy as simply another avenue for self-enrichment and self-protection (Marten, 2015: 74–77).

When applied to foreign policy formulation and implementation, we can formulate a basic conceptual model of foreign policy formulation and execution in a petrostate where leaders are not only bound by informality, but must respond to an exogenous revenue shock to test against the actual episodes in Russian history that can be tested. Following the literature above, I assume that (1) the executive wishes to remain in office (or help choose her successor), (2) she is not omnipotent but relies on political supporters to exercise policy decisions, and (3) trade-offs exist between self-enrichment, military spending, domestic consumption, and potential diplomatic commitments.

In turn, we can generate simple hypotheses on how leaders in petrostates will formulate and implement foreign policy upon positive or negative revenue shocks. A strong leader in a petrostate can face down pressure from subordinates to change foreign policy and stay in power upon a noticeable revenue shock, positive or negative. A strong leader can, counter-intuitively, change specific foreign policies fairly frequently, because she can pursue a single overarching strategy. Yet a weak leader has much less room to maneuver; facing a positive or negative shock, she is unable to withstand pressure from political supporters to alter foreign policy without running the risk of disaffected supporters seeking a new leader to form an opposing pyramid of power.

Does oil make Russia more aggressive?

The petropolitics theory of petrostate foreign policy formulation furnishes a simple argument that foreign policy decisions in petrostates depend on the internal political dynamics in place at the time of the revenue shock. Not merely that a shock occurs or that a specific leader is in place, but the political strength of the leader – at the time the money starts rolling in unexpectedly or does not come in as expected – explains foreign policy outcomes. This theory provides for a much simpler analysis of Russian foreign policy from the leadership tenure of Leonid Brezhnev onwards.

The case studies below contrast expansion under the leadership of Leonid Brezhnev to more selective expansion and accommodation under Vladimir Putin. The differing political dynamics at the time of the revenue shock – Brezhnev was weak, and Putin was not – explain the differences in policy options selected. Brezhnev, weak relative to Politburo and military hawks, failed to stop Soviet expansion into the Third World. That alternative foreign policy brought détente to an end as U.S. policymakers countered the "arc of crisis" by starting a peacetime arms buildup that the Soviet Union could not match (Westad, 2005). Putin, strong relative to the oligarchs and other Yeltsin-era political players prior to the mid-2000s oil boom, has overseen an expansion of Russian diplomatic interests and power projection abroad – but after some years and fairly selectively. Putin's ongoing political strength has also allowed Russia to maintain and increase its presence in Ukraine and Syria long after energy prices have collapsed and recession continues to harm the Russian economy. I do not address the retrenchment of Mikhail Gorbachev in great detail, but the negative revenue environment of the early 1980s carried on for years without a change in Soviet foreign policy, until he consolidated enough power to withstand pressure from defense hawks to retrench Soviet interests abroad.

Leonid Brezhnev

Leonid Brezhnev became General Secretary of the Communist Party through a palace coup as a compromise candidate amongst the plotters and this defined his political weakness for years (Bacon and Sandle, 2002).[3] Brezhnev found himself subject to policy pressures from powerful corners whom he had to placate or else face the same fate as his predecessor, Nikita Khrushchev. In time he acceded to an interventionist policy in the Third World that served to confound his own preferred foreign policy course of détente with the West (Ouimet, 2003).[4] A revenue boom and weak leadership interacted to produce a foreign policy orientation further away from his personal preferences and closer to Politburo and military hawks. This section outlines Brezhnev's political weakness, the revenue shock, the interaction of both, and the foreign policy outcome: an "arc of crisis" that led to U.S. challenges of the Soviets across the Third World and a ruinous arms race.

The palace coup (Tompson, 1991) that unseated Khrushchev had many sources,[5] but key among them was his attempt to break the power of the economic ministries and regional Party secretaries, the previously dominant bureaucratic hierarchies (Markevich and Zhuravskaya (2011) specifically refer to Khrushchev's efforts as trying to transform the Soviet Union from a traditional unitary-form hierarchy to a multidivisional-form organization to marginalize the Stalinist bureaucratic core. Brezhnev worked to reverse those so-called *sovnarkhoz* reforms and reestablish neo-Stalinist institutions and norms. The result was an institutional environment where those around Brezhnev were collectively much stronger than he was even if he could attack any single opponent (Yanov, 1977).[6] Both Brezhnev and the Politburo members knew that the way he came in – deposing the previous leader – could be the way he could go out, which Roeder (1993) used to explain the leader's painstaking efforts to signal collegiality and reassure potential rivals that he was not another leader who would, or would try, to amass too much power too quickly, as Stalin did and Khrushchev tried. As long-time Soviet Ambassador to the United States Anatoly Dobrynin (1995: 219) put it:

> A general secretary of course had many ways of persuasion to carry his ideas through the Politburo, but he was always careful not to antagonize the other members unnecessarily. After all, they could always revolt and replace him, as they did with Khrushchev.

As the Party consolidated oligarchical control, Brezhnev and his Foreign Minister, Andrei Gromyko, pursued détente with the United States to improve economic relations with the West (Garthoff, 1995). Yet Brezhnev's political weakness created a puzzling outcome where official state organs pursued accommodation with the West while hawks in the military and ideologues in the International Department of the Communist Party pushed for higher military expenditures and a more aggressive role abroad in the Third World. This split provided for two mutually

Petropolitics

exclusive grand strategies. The Foreign Ministry conducted the country's official diplomatic relations and pursued détente, while the International Department of the Party, responsible for managing relations with foreign communist parties and movements of national liberation, treated the Third World as a growth opportunity regardless of relations with the United States.

Overseen by Boris Ponomarev, protégé of chief ideologist Mikhail Suslov, Dobrynin (1995: 401–405) described the policy rivalry:

> To understand our sometimes bizarre policy in the Third World, it is important to know how the decision-making mechanism in foreign affairs operated in the Kremlin. On a day-to-day basis it was the Foreign Ministry who gave recommendations for dealing with current problems. In practice that mainly meant Gromyko himself, and as a rule all his suggestions were accepted. He was a recognized authority, especially in dealing with the West and the United States in particular, and he stubbornly defended his position in this field during Politburo meetings. Overall he was a cautious man who opposed any serious confrontation with the United States if the vital interests of the Soviet Union were not involved. But the Third World was not his prime domain. He believed that events there could not in the final analysis decisively influence our fundamental relations with the United States; that turned out to be a factor he definitely underestimated.

This is the environment into which energy revenues started to become noticeable. Figure 6.1 demonstrates the impact of energy exports in the mid to late-1960s and marks what may be the first attempt to define when the Soviet Union became a petrostate.[7] The data show petroleum export revenues expressed in terms of nominal U.S. dollar amounts and as an annual percentage change.

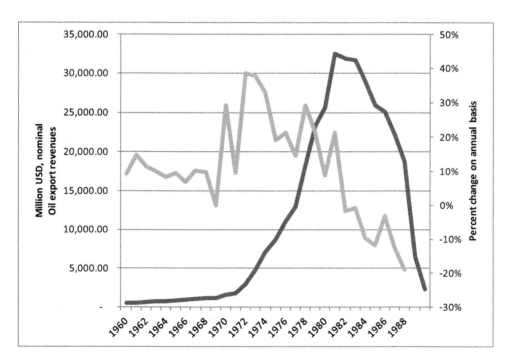

Figure 6.1 Export revenues and annual percentage change, 1961–1991

I then converted the export amounts into domestic prices, which would have been more immediate to Soviet leaders for their decision-making. From these domestic price figures, I divided the domestic price rubles by the size of the economy (of which more below) to achieve the rough figures to ascertain the second criterion of the petrostate definition: revenues from their export equal to or above 5% of GDP.[8] The size of the Soviet economy is still unknown with complete confidence, but best available estimations of the size and growth of the economy from Khanin (Harrison, 1993), the Central Intelligence Agency (Bergson, 1991), and Kuboniwa (1997) all indicate that the Soviet Union irrevocably became a petrostate sometime in late 1974 or early 1975, but that as early as 1969, something changed. Producers in the developing countries wrested pricing control away from the international oil companies; while the Soviet Union was not a member of OPEC, it benefitted from the rise in prices alongside the increased export opportunities to the West at a time when relations with the developing world grew more contentious. From 1970 to 1971, the value of fuel exports as a percentage of the economy grew by more than 25% over the previous year, which should have alerted Politburo members that more revenue was coming into the system. It is likely that energy resources became apparent to decision-makers in 1970–1971 with this big jump, rather than in 1974–1975.

The strength of the Soviet establishment and the weakness of its leader led to foreign policy actions further away from Brezhnev's preferences, but not immediately as the war chest might suggest. A change in internal deliberations regarding the possibility of revolution in the Third World following rapprochement in Europe came from two sources, the military and the ideologues. By Brezhnev's middle years (1969–1975), nuclear settlements and relative peace in Europe led the military establishment to engage in revisionist ideology to justify new great power concerns. Military newspapers argued that given the "change in the balance of forces in the international arena in favor of socialism [i.e. the increasing wealth of the Soviet Union], another possibility is also increasing more and more – that of preventing the development of local wars into an enormous clash on a worldwide scale" (Katz, 1982: 68). This change of warfare thinking meant that the military and their advocates in the Party believed that the USSR could now control the size of conflict abroad and make foreign policy gains for itself without fear of world war (Katz, 1982: 69). The military and the military-industrial complex pushed for and received increases in arms deals, "training of revolutionary forces by Soviet military advisors," buildup of the Soviet Navy to gain and hold military bases abroad, and transport and support for allied troops.

Increased military spending overlapped with individuals in the International Department of the Communist Party, a holdover from the early days of the revolution when two foreign policy operations emerged. One was the preexisting Foreign Ministry that interacted with other governments in traditional diplomacy, but the other was a Party body responsible for coordinating relations with foreign communist parties and national liberation movements. This International Department had declined in importance with the dissolution of the Comintern and Cominform bodies, but in the political environment of Brezhnev's CPSU came back to project national power abroad in the Third World. Dobrynin, a détente supporter, lamented this alternative foreign policy line for the marginal importance of the areas and clients being supported, and the blowback it engendered:

> Our Foreign Ministry traditionally was not really involved with the leaders of the liberation movements in the Third World, who were dealt with through the International Department of the party, headed by Secretary Boris Ponomarev. He despised Gromyko; the feeling was mutual . . . Under the slogan of solidarity, [Suslov] . . . his zealous followers in the party managed to involve the Politburo in many Third World adventures. The KGB supported him in this because many of the party contacts in that area

were handled through their agents. Many professional Soviet diplomats opposed our deep involvement in these remote areas, but who would openly object when all this was done in the name of the party? Some diplomats, myself included, tried on their own in informal conversations to minimize the damage in the West. We explained to our Western colleagues that all these actions were spontaneous and not necessarily part of any Soviet grand plan to deliberately undermine the world positions of the West. But this was hardly persuasive when viewed against our adventurous involvement in remote regions, and it raised a negative reaction in the United States.

(Dobrynin, 1995: 401–405)

The increase in energy revenues increased the menu of capabilities and allowed the pursuit of countervailing policies. Although expansionism did not commence immediately, pressure on Brezhnev did. The Soviet Union soon found itself pursuing détente while simultaneously supporting anti-colonial wars of liberation and specific sides in civil wars across the Third World. The profusion of foreign policy tools permitted by energy revenues and Brezhnev's inability to stop an alternative foreign policy resulted in an increased set of diplomatic commitments across the world, eventually including the decision to invade Afghanistan to support a local client against political rivals.[9] Intervention in Afghanistan solidified U.S. fears that the Soviet Union was attempting to increase its power in West Africa, the Horn of Africa, and the Middle East, giving credence to National Security Advisor Zbigniew Brzezinski's characterization of an "arc of crisis" (Lenczowski, 1979). Jimmy Carter lamented Soviet actions that seemingly confirmed the hawkish viewpoint of Brzezinski and led to undesirable outcomes such as delaying SALT II and boycotting the 1980 Summer Olympics to be held in Moscow (Carter, 2010: 282, 382–384, 486). The impossibility of separating those different policies created confusion in the assessment of Soviet grand strategy by the United States, as the United States was obliged to counter "military adventurism" (Gelman, 1984). Energy resources expanded the menu of capabilities and eventually led to foreign policy expansionism even under the most propitious circumstances; expansion proceeded neither immediately nor mechanically as suggested by the war chest.

Vladimir Putin

Russian foreign policy under the leadership of Vladimir Putin displays even more clearly the petropolitics theory of petrostate foreign policy formulation. As an appointed successor to Yeltsin and a relative unknown, Putin appeared, like Brezhnev, to be a compromise candidate between Yeltsin's ruling clique and the oligarchs who had grown wealthy and powerful in the preceding decade, a modest individual dwarfed by the bureaucratic challenges of running Russia (Shevtsova, 2010; Hill and Gaddy, 2013). Like the Brezhnev period, Russia experienced a sustained energy revenue boom during Putin's tenure. Unlike Leonid Brezhnev, the positive revenue shock occurred after Putin had already consolidated considerable political control and eliminated rivals remaining from the Boris Yeltsin period. Putin was then (and continues to be) in a much stronger political position relative to subordinates, has controlled redistribution far more effectively than his predecessors, and has varied foreign policy expansion and accommodation far more selectively. In contrast to the war chest explanation, Russian foreign policy expansion under Putin has not directly followed positive revenue shocks, but has been in response to challenges emerging from Putin's grand strategy course of returning Russia to the great power ranks. The domestic political strength of Putin can be observed directly as Russian power projection into Ukraine and Syria has not wavered even as energy prices have steadily declined, and the Russian economy has entered what appears to be a fairly durable era of stagnation.

The details of Vladimir Putin's journey, from relative obscurity to the top of Russian power are quite well known (Putin et al., 2000). Scholarly analysis of the transition from Yeltsin to Putin initially assessed Putin as a caretaker of the system subject to intense political pressure from his ostensible subordinates. Observers reasoned at the time that without any independent source of authority, natural constituencies, or explicit political views, Putin would rule at the pleasure of those with the informal, but real, political power, and the real, but poorly understood, economic power (Shevtsova, 1999; Herspring, 2005).[10] After all, throughout the 1990s, Putin had accomplished each role assigned to him without drawing any undue attention or articulating any independent policy positions (Sakwa, 2008b; Hill and Gaddy, 2013: ch. 5).

Putin took control of the political environment through a popular war in Chechnya (Lapidus, 2002) and by revealing what he had been doing in addition to fulfilling his official duties: gathering compromising information on the oligarchs individually and as a group during his various positions in the presidential administration dealing with state property and as the head of the security services (Gaddy and Ickes, 2005, 2011). Armed with this *kompromat*, he then presented the oligarchs individually and, in July 2000 as a group, with a revision of the expected contractual relationship. Putin was not to serve at their discretion, but as their ruler instead (Reynolds, 2000). In exchange for them acceding to his authority, he would not look into financial affairs of the previous decade. In this extraordinary meeting that defines the critical juncture where power began to shift from the oligarch class to Putin, those who accepted and paid their taxes would be part of the system, but those who defied him could expect criminal tax investigations up to an including dispossession, prison, and exile. The threat was credible – surprise *maskirovka* investigations by machine-gun wielding tax police had already begun (Bowen, 2013). On the face of it, the threat was also reasonable, given the uncertainty and insecurity oligarchs had in their dealings with each other.[11] By coopting this elite group, protecting the Yeltsin family from prosecution through decree, and demonstrating to the public that at least one individual could bring order to government, Putin addressed the sources of political pressure and potential opposition, building his power vertical. Putin also coopted economic and political liberals with ambitious reform plans (Bohlen, 2000) and "solved" the Chechnya problem by coopting one of the warlords, Akhmad Kadyrov, to attack the others with state support (Lapidus, 2002). The patron–client relationship even survived Kadryov's assassination when the latter's son Ramzan took power and helped shape a more explicit medieval-style exchange of federal fealty for local control (Sharafutdinova, 2010).

By exploiting the insecurity and uncertainty of the political and economic elite, and the exasperation and frustrations of the public, Putin did not create any new political structures but instead generated his own legitimacy to fulfill the capacity of a super-presidential system inherited from Yeltsin. He cleared out his rivals and built massive public support, reducing political pressure to manageable levels. The resource boom followed serendipitously, and the country's leadership substituted increased living standards for public accountability (Shevtsova, 2010).

I have argued elsewhere that the goal of contemporary Russian grand strategy under Vladimir Putin is not to make the country a superpower as it once was, but to secure its position as one of several regional hegemonic powers, specifically the BRICS grouping plus the United States and Germany (Weber, 2015). The intent is to revise the international order so that great powers coordinate on issues of transnational importance and provide order within their sphere of influence, which would return Russia to the position of power negotiated by Mikhail Gorbachev and George H.W. Bush at the Malta Summit in 1989 that brought the Cold War to an end. That 1989 world barely got going before the Soviet Union collapsed at the end of 1991. The sum effect of Russian foreign policy under Putin has been to restore Russia to the category of great power and make the international order look more post-Cold War than post-Soviet.

Independent of whether challenging the international and regional political orders or attempting to generate a hierarchical Eurasian order is advisable, the question is whether expansionism under Putin followed immediately or with a delay and in response to specific challenges. The oil money increased the menu of options available to Putin, but when and why he selected expansion has been based on the underlying strategic goal.

A short review of Russian diplomatic and military expansion since the mid-2000s makes the petropolitics story clearer. First, a minor territorial dispute with China over islands near Khabarovsk that had led to a brief war in 1969 were resolved to China's satisfaction in 2004 (Fravel, 2005) when the war chest theory would predict that Russia would be *more* inclined to take a hard line.

Second, the war with Georgia emerged from a serious dispute over the potential expansion of NATO into areas that Putin considered the Russian sphere of influence along its own borders (Asmus, 2010). At the April 2008 NATO general meeting, U.S. President George W. Bush advocated extending a Membership Action Plan (MAP) to Ukraine and Georgia, but was rejected by German Chancellor Angela Merkel and French President Nicolas Sarkozy due to fears of destabilizing NATO relations with Russia – especially since Putin attended the talks and directly "warned President Bush and other alliance leaders that their plan to expand eastwards to Ukraine and Georgia 'didn't contribute to trust and predictability in our relations'" (Evans, 2008). NATO members did not extend a MAP to Georgia or Ukraine, but decided to review the decision at the following December summit. Georgia's Minister for European Integration, Giorgi Baramidze, hailed the decision as a historic moment for the country to move out of Russia's sphere of influence: "The decision to accept that we are going forward to an adhesion to NATO was taken and we consider this is a historic success" (NATO, 2008).

The clear commitment problem posed by NATO expansion represented a redline security issue for a Russian leader publicly opposed to membership for former Soviet republics outside of the Baltic states. The expectation that it would happen at some undefined point in the future regardless of Russia's concerns set the stage for conflict, which duly occurred later that August (Allison, 2009). Russian advance in support of Abkhazia and South Ossetia stopped only after five days of fighting, by which time Russia had successfully expanded its foreign policy reach by using force abroad, defending clients, handing an assured defeat to a country it considered a pesky irritant, and making a geopolitical statement that it would not countenance the expansion of NATO further into its borderlands (Asmus, 2010). That was possible because of energy revenues, but the energy revenues did not cause that war.

Third, and further out from the resource boom of the mid-2000s, Russian foreign policy expansionism has occurred in relation to challenges that would hinder Russia's ability to become a great power while maintaining Putin's ability to keep his *sistema* in place. Quite obviously, the annexation of Crimea, the support for separatist rebels in Ukraine, and the intervention into the civil war in Syria on behalf of the government of Bashar Al-Assad represent an attempt to revise the international order (Sakwa, 2014; Menon and Rumer, 2015; Krickovic and Weber, 2017). The resource bust from 2013 onwards shows that these interventions, whatever their strategic purpose, have occurred as the energy revenues have fallen flat. If it were energy revenues driving Russian foreign policy, then we would observe Russia retrenching from those two conflicts and seeking accommodation with Ukraine and decreasing its support to Assad. The continued presence of Russia abroad while leaders at home mull over ways to improve economic performance demonstrate that the menu of policy options for Russian policymakers has shrunk, but what drives foreign policy decision-making is not energy revenues.

The petropolitics theory of foreign policy formulation also explains Mikhail Gorbachev's retrenchment of diplomatic commitments. While space considerations limit in-depth analysis of Gorbachev's tenure, the bottom fell out of incoming energy revenues prior to Gorbachev's ascension to the top spot in in March 1985. The war chest argument would have predicted retrenchment of foreign policy commitments sometime in 1981–1982 under Brezhnev, Andropov, or Chernenko, while the leadership approach of Russian foreign policy would have predicted Gorbachev to maintain the foreign policy of the gerontocratic Politburo. What the petropolitics theory would predict is that the negative revenue environment would have reduced his menu of options in improving the political and economic health of the Soviet Union, and that Gorbachev would have used the internal political capital of his unusual candidacy (including massive public support) to overcome political pressure from hawks (often the same people from the Brezhnev period) to retrench Soviet interests abroad. The war chest argument would have only captured the retrenchment without noting Gorbachev's "New Thinking," and the leadership approach could only retroactively assign a motive for Gorbachev's actions.

Oil resources have not made Soviet or Russian leaders more aggressive as the conventional wisdom suggests or the war chest argument predicts. Increased revenues expand the menu of options available to leaders, but when and why they permit expansion reflects on internal politics. Brezhnev proved unable to restrain hawks in the Politburo and military seeking expansion, whereas Putin responded to specific (or self-declared) security threats. Gorbachev responded to a negative revenue environment, but only after shaping the internal political environment.

Conclusion

Petropolitics makes a simple claim regarding foreign policy formulation: strong leaders withstand financial and policy pressures from their subordinates in ways weaker counterparts cannot. Leaders who have already consolidated power can maintain policy consistency whether an oil boom or bust produces a revenue influx or shortfall of revenues. The oil boom of the mid-2000s will define modern Russia until the end of Vladimir Putin's time in power and likely far beyond. The Russian president had already consolidated power to a considerable extent by the time the money started rolling, but he seized the opportunity to form a relatively durable state apparatus, raise domestic consumption, and rebuild the military. He has retained power through a powerful state security apparatus that has effectively inserted the state at each level of the economy, and by maintaining a coalition of state security personnel, government employees, vulnerable economic groups, and various conservative social groups. Perhaps most importantly, over the nearly two decades of direct and indirect power, Putin has made many friends and associates around him very wealthy.

Energy resources paid for this durable political coalition, and from this position of strength, Putin has pursued a simple but far-reaching grand strategy: revise the international order to replace the U.S. hegemonic position with a series of regional powers (the BRICS, Germany, and the United States) coordinating on issues of transnational importance such as climate change and Islamist terrorism while providing public goods such as security in their own regions. The oil money increased Russian diplomatic and military capabilities so that the strategy of becoming a great power appeared feasible, and Putin's political strength allowed him to cycle through various foreign policies to work towards that goal. After failing to form a partnership with the United States after offering assistance in the wake of the September 11, 2001 attacks, and failing to stop the invasion of Iraq through balancing with France and Germany, Putin's speech at the 2007 Munich Security Conference revealed explicitly that Russia was prepared to use all means to revise the international order and be acknowledged as a relevant international player. The subsequent expansionism into the Caucasus, Eastern Europe, and the Middle East over the next decade generated Russia's international credibility and domestic legitimacy, but it has also revealed the fragility of the social contract in Russia.

The expansionist foreign policy is very popular at home, but it has come at a very high price. It inhibits economic growth by isolating Russia from the international economy due to the sanctions associated with Crimea, support for rebels, and the consequences of shooting down the MH17 jetliner over the Donbas. Unrelatedly, but with terrible timing, a bust in the energy market interacted with the sanctions regime to threaten Putin's ability to claim the future will look like the present.

A series of difficult choices confront the president and his power vertical. A muscular role abroad is central to justifying privation at home through a sense of patriotism and being surrounded by foreign enemies. The social contract in which increased domestic consumption flows downwards to the population in return for quiescence flowing upwards to the state itself relies upon a tacit assumption that the leader and his government are working hard to reform the economy while maintaining the country's dignity. Corruption scandals belie this assumption, and popular dissatisfaction with the poor state of the economy has tested Putin's political strength. Shifting existing rents and benefits from the privileged members to society at large would introduce challenges to Putin's rule from the inside. Foreign policy retrenchment would alleviate economic difficulties, but, like Mikhail Gorbachev before him, identify the limits of Russian capabilities and potentially provoke a domestic backlash. Doing nothing and hoping the status quo holds means that the only savior is an exogenous fiscal shock of another oil boom or some other black swan event.

The paradox of Putin's Russia is that a tremendous amount of wealth and property have shifted from one group to another during his rule, and Putin's soft treatment of his predecessor is not guaranteed to be a precedent for his successor. The grand strategy of reasserting Russia's great power status reflects traditional foreign policy objectives for the country. Vladimir Putin now needs the latter grand strategy to be successful to generate sufficient political legitimacy to maintain his political coalition and protect the wealth and property transfer underpinning his rule, yet the very strategy challenges the international order and risks regime-ending blowback.

Notes

1 I define "petrostate" as a state exporting 2 million or more barrels of oil per day valued at 5% or more of gross domestic product. For a more detailed definition, see note 8.
2 Emphasis in original.
3 They describe Brezhnev as providing a stability of cadres, balancing interests, and paling in comparison to Stalin: "In other words, although Brezhnev's hold on power increased through his term in office, the way in which this power was exercised did not approach a one-person dictatorship owing to factors such as his leadership style, the existence of networks of political patrons and their clients, and the physical and mental decline of Brezhnev particularly from around 1977 onwards" (p. 8).
4 Ouimet's biography of the "Brezhnev Doctrine" advances a novel revisionist argument for the tough line against within-bloc ideological deviation. He argues that maintaining within-Pact rigidity allowed the Soviets to pursue détente with the West carefully and on their own terms, with a lower chance of defection from their allies. Brezhnev is portrayed as being very motivated to succeed in the détente policy with the idea of reducing military spending in the medium term and allowing greater inter-bloc cooperation.
5 Such as policy inconsistency ("harebrained schemes"), relaxation of control over society, backing down in the Cuban Missile Crisis, losing China in the Sino-Soviet split, pursuing "peaceful co-existence," etc.
6 "Both Stalin and Khrushchev were – or considered themselves – masters of the Plenum; therefore, they were fearless; therefore, they were strong leaders. Brezhnev feels like a prisoner of the Plenum; therefore, he is a weak leader. Judge for yourself. He can crush any one of the prefects individually with almost

no difficulty, but when they are assembled together they are suddenly transformed into a mysterious, unpredictable, almost mythical force that it is unthinkable to fight against. That is the price that Brezhnev has to pay for preserving the political machine created by Stalin" (Yanov, 1977: 40).
7 For a fuller description of the methodology, see Weber (2017).
8 There is as yet no accepted definition for a petrostate. I adopt and adapt Demkiv's (2012) definition: a state that "[produces] two million or more barrels of oil per day and/or where oil rents are over 10% of GDP. The second criterion in the definition suggests that the country is not economically diversified and depends heavily on oil revenues for its budget. The first part of the definition suggests a benchmark for the amount of oil production that is vital in the global energy market." The data Demkiv uses from the World Bank only go back to 1990 for Russia. I would like to extend the data much further back. Demkiv cites Kennedy (2008), who defines petrostates as "having an average of more than 5% of GDP from fuel exports during the period 1965–2001." As the amount of relatively reliable data available from the Soviet period is less than that of post-communist Russia, I follow the measure adopted by Kennedy to ensure uniformity across the sample of cases while retaining the notion of the petrostate being economically undiversified and reliant on the export of energy resources in the national budget.
9 A former aide to Konstantin Chernenko, Vadim Pechenev, noted "that strategic decisions in the Soviet Union during Brezhnev's last years were taken by six senior members of the Politburo – Suslov, Ustinov, Gromyko, Andropov, Chernenko, and Brezhnev (with Brezhnev himself, for health reasons, playing the least active part of the six)" (Brown, 1997: 56).
10 Yeltsin and those around him viewed Putin as a sort of podestà. In medieval Genoa and other Italian city-states, local oligarchs would hire an outsider to enforce rules and cooperation by maintaining the balance of power via the implicit threat of allying with those who would be threatened. As Greif (1994, 2006) has shown, this was an early attempt to create a self-sustaining political institution to commitment problem. The key element to the self-sustaining aspect of the political institution was that the podestà had a fixed term and was supposed to leave the commune once his services were no longer required.
11 Putin's behavior mirrors, to an extent, the logic of the obsolescing bargain first explored by Vernon (1971). The oligarchs resemble the multinational enterprises that make investments in a host county, i.e. President Putin. As the oligarchs came to depend on Putin to protect their fixed assets, the bargaining power shifted to Putin and the original bargain obsolesced into irrelevancy.

References

Adams, K 2017, *The price of Russia's support of Syria is steep*, 7 April 2017, *Marketplace*, NPR. www.marketplace.org/2017/04/07/world/price-russia-s-support-syria-steep.
Alekperov, VI 2011, *Oil of Russia: past, present, & future*. East View Press, Minnetonka, MN.
Allison, R 2009, 'The Russian case for military intervention in Georgia: international law, norms and political calculation', *European Security*, vol. 18, no. 2, pp. 173–200.
Anderson, RD 1993, *Public politics in an authoritarian state: Making foreign policy during the Brezhnev years*. Cornell UP, Ithaca, NY.
Asmus, R 2010, *A little war that shook the world: Georgia, Russia and the future of the West*. Macmillan, New York.
Auty, RM 1993, *Sustaining development in mineral economies: the resource curse thesis*, Psychology Press, Hove, UK.
Bacon, E, Sandle MA (eds), 2002, *Brezhnev reconsidered*, Macmillan, New York.
Balzer, H 2005, 'The Putin thesis and Russian energy policy', *Post-Soviet Affairs*, vol. 21, no. 3, pp. 210–225.
Bergson, A 1991, 'The USSR before the fall: how poor and why', *The Journal of Economic Perspectives*, vol. 5, no. 4, pp. 29–44.
Bohlen, C 2000, 'Putin's team hammers out a plan to untwist, level and streamline russia's Economy', *New York Times*, 2 April. Available from www.nytimes.com/2000/04/02/world/putin-s-team-hammers-out-a-plan-to-untwist-level-and-streamline-russia-s-economy.html?_r=0.
Bowen, A 2013, 'The Russian tax man: return to the bad old days?', *The Interpreter*, November 16. Available from www.interpretermag.com/the-russian-tax-man-return-to-the-bad-old-days/.
Breslauer, GW 1982, *Khrushchev and Brezhnev as leaders: building authority in Soviet politics*, Allen & Unwin, London.
Brown, A 1997, *The Gorbachev factor*, Oxford UP, Oxford, UK.
Brown, JD 2011, *The energy impact theory of foreign policy: an analysis of Soviet Union and Russian Federation, 1970–2010*, PhD thesis, University of Aberdeen, UK.

Carter, J 2010, *White House diary*, Macmillan, New York.
Colgan, JD 2013, *Petro-aggression: when oil causes war*, Cambridge UP, Cambridge, UK.
Colgan, JD 2014, 'Oil, domestic politics, and international conflict', *Energy Research & Social Science*, vol. 1, pp. 198–205.
Demkiv, A 2012, *Political instability in petrostates: The myth or reality of oil revenue as petrostate stabilizer*, PhD thesis, Rutgers University, NJ.
Dobrynin, AF 1995, *In confidence: Moscow's ambassador to America's six cold war presidents (1962–1986)*, Times Books, New York.
Ellman, M (ed.), 2006, *Russia's oil and natural gas: bonanza or curse?* Anthem Press, London.
Evans, M 2008, 'Vladimir Putin tells summit he wants security and friendship', *The Times* (London), April 5. Available from www.thetimes.co.uk/tto/news/world/article1974064.ece.
Fravel, MT 2005, 'Regime insecurity and international cooperation: explaining China's compromises in territorial disputes', *International Security*, vol. 30, no. 2, pp. 46–83.
Gaddy, CG, Ickes, BW 2005, 'Resource rents and the Russian economy', *Eurasian Geography and Economics*, vol. 46, no. 8, pp. 559–583.
Gaddy, CG, Ickes, BW 2011, 'Putin's protection racket', in Korhonen, I & Solanko, L (eds), *From Soviet plans to Russian reality*. WSOY pro Oy, Helsinki.
Gaidar, Y 2010, *Collapse of an empire: lessons for modern Russia*. Brookings Institute, Washington, DC.
Garthoff, R (1995) *The great transition: American-Soviet relations and the end of the Cold War*. Brookings, Washington, DC
Gelman, H 1984, *The Brezhnev Politburo and the decline of détente*, Cornell UP, Ithaca, NY.
Gel'man, V 2012, 'Subversive institutions, informal governance, and contemporary Russian politics', *Communist and Post-Communist Studies*, vol. 45, no. 3, pp. 295–303.
Goldman, MI 2008, *Petrostate: Putin, power, and the new Russia*. Oxford UP, New York.
Greif, A 1994, 'On the political foundations of the late medieval commercial revolution: Genoa during the twelfth and thirteenth centuries', *The Journal of Economic History*, vol. 54, no. 2, pp. 271–287.
Greif, A 2006, *Institutions and the path to the modern economy: lessons from medieval trade*, Cambridge UP, Cambridge, UK.
Gustafson, T 1989, *Crisis amid plenty: the politics of Soviet energy under Brezhnev and Gorbachev*, Princeton UP, Princeton, NJ.
Gustafson, T 2012, *Wheel of fortune*, Harvard UP, Cambridge, MA.
Harrison, M 1993, 'Soviet economic growth since 1928: the alternative statistics of GI Khanin', *Europe-Asia Studies*, vol. 45, no. 1, pp. 141–167.
Hale, HE 2005, 'Regime cycles: democracy, autocracy, and revolution in post-Soviet Eurasia', *World Politics*, vol. 58, no. 1, pp. 133–165.
Hale, HE 2010, 'Eurasian polities as hybrid regimes: the case of Putin's Russia', *Journal of Eurasian Studies*, vol. 1, no. 1, pp. 33–41.
Hale, HE 2014, *Patronal politics: Eurasian regime dynamics in comparative perspective*, Cambridge UP, Cambridge, UK.
Herspring, DR (ed.), 2005, *Putin's Russia: past imperfect, future uncertain*, Rowman & Littlefield, Lanham, MD.
Hewett, EA 1984, *Energy economics and foreign policy in the Soviet Union*. Brookings Institute, Washington, DC.
Hewett, EA 1988, *Reforming the Soviet economy: equality versus efficiency*. Brookings Institute, Washington, DC.
Hill, F, Gaddy, C 2013, *Mr. Putin: operative in the White House*. Brookings Institute, Washington, DC.
Huskey, E 2004a, 'From higher party schools to academies of state service: the marketization of bureaucratic training in Russia', *Slavic Review*, vol. 63, no. 2, pp. 325–348.
Huskey, E 2004b, 'Nomenklatura lite? The cadres reserve in Russian public administration', *Problems of Post-Communism*, vol. 51, no. 2, pp. 30–39.
Karl, T 1997, *The paradox of plenty: oil booms and petro-states*. UC Press, Berkeley, CA.
Katz, MN 1982, *The Third World in Soviet military thought*, Johns Hopkins University Press, Baltimore, MD.
Keenan, EL 1986, 'Muscovite political folkways', *The Russian Review*, vol. 45, no. 2, pp. 115–181.
Kennedy, R 2008, *Lifting the curse: distribution and power in petro-states*, PhD thesis, The Ohio State University, Columbus, OH.
Krickovic, A, Weber, Y, 2017, 'Commitment issues: the Syrian and Ukraine crises as bargaining failures of the post-Cold War international order', *Problems of Post-Communism*, vol. 64, nos. 3/4, pp. 167–188.

Kryshtanovskaya, O 2005, *Anatomy of the Russian elite*, Zakharov Publishing House, Moscow.

Kuboniwa, M 1997, 'Economic growth in postwar Russia: estimating GDP', *Hitotsubashi Journal of Economics*, vol. 38, no. 1, pp. 21–32.

Lamborn, A 1983, 'Power and the politics of extraction', *International Studies Quarterly*, vol. 27, no. 2, pp. 125–146.

Lane, DS 1999, *The political economy of Russian oil*, Rowman & Littlefield, Lanham, MD.

Lapidus, GW 2002, 'Putin's war on terrorism: lessons from Chechnya', *Post-Soviet Affairs*, vol. 18, no. 1, pp. 41–48.

Ledeneva, AV 1998, *Russia's economy of favors: blat, networking and informal exchange*, Cambridge UP, Cambridge, UK.

Ledeneva, AV 2006, *How Russia really works: the informal practices that shaped post-Soviet politics and business*, Cornell UP, Ithaca, NY.

Ledeneva, AV 2013, *Can Russia modernise? Sistema, power networks and informal governance*, Cambridge UP, Cambridge, UK.

Lenczowski, G 1979, 'The arc of crisis: its central sector', *Foreign Affairs*, vol. 57, no. 4, pp. 796–820.

Lewin, M 1991, *The Gorbachev phenomenon: a historical interpretation*, UC Press, Berkeley, CA.

Luong, PJ, Weinthal, E 2010, *Oil is not a curse: ownership structure and institutions in Soviet successor states*, Cambridge UP, Cambridge, UK.

Markevich, A, Zhuravskaya, E 2011, 'M-form hierarchy with poorly-diversified divisions: a case of Khrushchev's reform in Soviet Russia', *Journal of Public Economics*, vol. 94, pp. 730–748.

Marten, K 2015, 'Informal political networks and Putin's foreign policy: the examples of Iran and Syria', *Problems of Post-Communism*, vol. 62, no. 2, pp. 71–87.

McGlinchey, E 2011, *Chaos, violence, dynasty: Politics and Islam in Central Asia*, University of Pittsburgh Press, Pittsburgh, PA.

Menon, R, Rumer, EB 2015, *Conflict in Ukraine: the unwinding of the post-cold war order*, MIT Press, Cambridge, MA.

Miller, C 2016, *The struggle to save the Soviet economy: Mikhail Gorbachev and the collapse of the USSR*, UNC Press Books, Chapel Hill, NC.

Morrison, KM 2009, *Oil, conflict, and stability*. University of Pittsburgh, Pittsburgh, PA.

NATO Summit Bucharest 2008, available from www.summitbucharest.ro/en/doc_189.html.

Ouimet, MJ 2003, *The rise and fall of the Brezhnev doctrine in Soviet foreign policy*, UNC Press Books, Chapel Hill, NC.

Palmer, G, D'Orazio, V, Kenwick, M, Lane, M 2015, 'The MID4 dataset, 2002–2010: Procedures, coding rules and description', *Conflict Management and Peace Science*, vol. 32, no. 2, pp. 222–242.

Petrov, N 2011, 'The excessive role of a weak Russian state', in M Lipman and N Petrov (eds), *Russia in 2020: scenarios for the future*, pp. 303–328. Carnegie Endowment for International Peace, Washington, DC.

Pipes, R 1974, *Russia under the old regime*. Penguin, New York.

Putin, VV, Gevorkyan N, Timakova N, Kolesnikov, A 2000, *First person: an astonishingly frank self-portrait by Russia's President Vladimir Putin*, trans. CA Fitzpatrick, Public Affairs, London.

Reuter, OJ, Robertson, GB 2012, 'Subnational appointments in authoritarian regimes: evidence from Russian gubernatorial appointments', *The Journal of Politics*, vol. 74, no. 4, pp. 1023–1037.

Reynolds, M 2000, 'Putin reaches out to oligarchs', *Los Angeles Times*, April 29. Available from http://articles.latimes.com/print/2000/jul/29/news/mn-61087.

Roeder, PG 1993, *Red sunset: the failure of Soviet politics*, Princeton UP, Princeton, NJ.

Ross, ML 1999, 'The political economy of the resource curse', *World Politics*, vol. 51, no. 2, pp. 297–322.

Ross, ML 2012, *The oil curse*, Princeton University Press, Princeton, NJ.

Rosser, A 2006, 'The political economy of the resource curse: a literature survey', Institute of Development Studies, Brighton, UK.

Sachs, JD, Warner, AM 1995, 'Natural resource abundance and economic growth', National Bureau of Economic Research, No. w5398. www.hks.harvard.edu/centers/cid.

Sakwa, R 2008a, *Putin: Russia's choice*, 2nd edn, Routledge Press, Abingdon, UK.

Sakwa, R 2008b, 'Putin and the oligarchs', *New Political Economy*, vol. 13, no. 2, pp. 185–191.

Sakwa, R 2014, *Frontline Ukraine: crisis in the borderlands*. IB Tauris, London.

Sharafutdinova, G 2010, 'Subnational governance in Russia: how Putin changed the contract with his agents and the problems it created for Medvedev', *Publius: The Journal of Federalism*, vol. 40, no. 4, pp. 672–696.

Shevtsova, LF, 1999, *Yeltsin's Russia: myths and reality*, Carnegie Endowment, Washington, DC.

Shevtsova, LF, 2010, *Putin's Russia*. Carnegie Endowment, Washington, DC.
Smith, B 2007, *Hard times in the lands of plenty*, Cornell UP, Ithaca, NY.
Stegen, KS 2011, 'Deconstructing the "energy weapon": Russia's threat to Europe as case study', *Energy Policy*, vol. 39, no. 10, pp. 6505–6513.
Stevens, P 2009, *Transit troubles: pipelines as a source of conflict*. Chatham House, London.
Stulberg, A 2007, *Well-oiled diplomacy: strategic manipulation and Russia's energy statecraft in Eurasia*, SUNY Press, Albany, NY.
Tompson, WJ 1991, 'The fall of Nikita Khrushchev', *Europe-Asia Studies*, vol. 43, no. 6, pp. 1101–1121.
Vernon, R 1971, *Sovereignty at bay*, Basic Books, New York.
Weber, Y 2015, 'Are we in a Cold War or not? 1989, 1991, and great power dissatisfaction', *E-IR*. Available from www.e-ir.info/2016/03/07/are-we-in-a-cold-war-or-not-1989-1991-and-great-power-dissatisfaction/.
Weber, Y 2017, 'When did the Soviet Union become a petrostate?' *manuscript*.
Weinthal, E, Luong, PJ 2006, 'Combating the resource curse: an alternative solution to managing mineral wealth', *Perspectives on Politics*, vol. 4, no. 1, pp. 35–53.
Westad, OA, 2005, *The global Cold War: Third World interventions and the making of our times*, Cambridge UP, Cambridge, UK.
White, S, Kryshtanovskaya, O 2011, Changing the Russian electoral system: inside the black box. *Europe-Asia Studies*, vol. 63, no. 4, pp. 557–578
Yanov, A 1977, *Detente after Brezhnev: the domestic roots of Soviet foreign policy*, UC Press, Berkeley, CA.

PART II

Tools and actors

Andrei P. Tsygankov

Part II analyzes tools and actors on which Russia relies in achieving its foreign policy objectives. In particular the part assesses the potential and actual role of diplomacy, energy, intelligence, military, cyber capabilities, media and public diplomacy, and the Russian Orthodox Church.

Each contributor proposes an approach to analyzing a particular policy instrument by situating it within existing literature on the topic. Such approach allows the author to (1) compare the analyzed tool to other instruments in terms of its potential and foreign policy effectiveness; (2) assess whether it became more or less important over time; (3) discuss important issues generated by its application; and (4) reflect on future questions and themes related to continued use of the instrument under discussion.

In his chapter on the role of diplomacy in RFP, Charles Ziegler argues that the Russian government primarily relies on the traditional diplomacy involving state-to-state negotiations by professionals. He describes principles of Russian diplomacy as those defending realist ideas in international relations including protection of sovereignty, non-interference in internal affairs, and great power status and respect. Moscow has been generally skeptical of humanitarian intervention and the United Nations-endorsed Responsibility to Protect (R2P). Ziegler notes that Russia has been especially adamant in rejecting foreign interferences and defending its position of a great power in the post-Soviet space. Moscow has been more open to global governance, multilateral cooperation, and the search for collective solutions in areas that did not affect its vital security in the Eurasian region. Whenever the traditional norms clashed with the R2P norm, Russia sought to back its position by arguments and various methods of statecraft including military, energy diplomacy, and media. Russian diplomacy has been flexible in style and skilled in both coercive and soft power methods.

In the post-Cold War era, Russian diplomacy evolved from being cooperative toward becoming more assertive in the 1990s. This change was expressed in policies of Foreign Ministers Andrei Kozyrev and Yevgeni Primakov and reflected Russia's disappointment with the Western nations' policies such as NATO's military intervention against Serbia, Russia's traditional ally. Under Vladimir Putin – in partial recognition of Russia's growing material strength – Russian diplomacy obtained a strong coercive dimension by relying on the threat of economic sanctions or military force, rather than persuasion. The coercive tactics, Ziegler maintains, has been only partly successful in defending Russia's objectives as it alienated some allies and consolidated foreign opposition to the Kremlin. Since the second half of 2000s, Russia has also adopted new, technologically advanced forms of diplomacy including reliance on internet, media, and non-governmental organizations. However, the international agenda of the latter organizations continued to comply with Russian state priorities.

Boris Barkanov continues with the theme of energy in RFP by considering the role of natural gas. He argues that rather than seeking to disrupt the global energy market and the dominance of Euro-Atlantic region, Russia has sought to adjust to conditions of Western "unipolarity". It has done so by pursuing the state-driven strategy of *Gazprom*'s penetration downstream and restructuring the Eurasian gas market to assist with Russia's objective of integration with European markets.

Barkanov's assessment of Russia's natural gas strategy is mixed and based on analysis of *Gazprom*'s interaction with Germany, Ukraine, and China. Gazprom has been successful in Germany by obtaining sizable stakes in *Wintershall*-related companies and fields and completing the Nord Stream pipeline in a consortium with Western companies. However, in the 2010s Gazprom faced serious complications related to cancellation of the South Stream pipeline and the crisis over Ukraine. Gazprom failed to purchase Ukrainian energy infrastructure or make it accept Russia's preferred gas price. The Kremlin is now interested in bypass routes and prospects for Russia's gas integration following the Euromaidan revolution are "bleak". Russia's "pivot" to China accelerated after the West had imposed sanctions against the Russian economy, but progress has been modest. Gazprom has accepted the pricing formula with China's CNPC and agreed to build a new pipeline from Eastern Siberian fields. Overall, however, access of Russian energy companies to the Chinese market has been limited and China's terms have prevailed.

Another prominent tool of RFP is the role of intelligence and security services. In their chapter, Mikhail Strokan and Brian Taylor acknowledge difficulties with researching the security services' highly secretive activities, yet they call for a more theoretical, comparative, and generalizable framework for thinking about the topic. Dispensing with clichés such as a "KGB state" and "spookocracy" requires analyzing the role of security services over time and in comparison with other agencies and tools of RFP. Strokan and Taylor analyze the role and division of labor between various security agencies in the Soviet and post-Soviet period, stressing their relations with the political authorities. They find that intelligence agencies have been traditionally "more successful in the scientific and technical sphere than in political analysis".

Strokan and Taylor find it difficult to assess the importance of the security services in the overall foreign policy toolkit, but provide a discussion that suggests their relatively large role, because "Russia is on a weaker footing vis-à-vis the West in the military and economic realm". In particular, the so-called "active measures" were on display in the war in Ukraine when intelligence services performed very well on a tactical level providing accurate information on Ukrainian military. However, they were much less successful in anticipating political change in the country. Scholars of Russian security services trace the latter failure to security officers' confrontational mentality and tendency to ignore mass sentiments. Traditionally, *siloviki* attribute revolutions and public protests to activities of foreign intelligence services such as the CIA, not to internal causes. In addition to participating in military operations, security services were involved in counter-terrorism, cyber-attacks, and covert operations.

Valeri Konyshev and Alexander Sergunin analyze the role of the military in RFP. Although Russian military is sometimes viewed as poorly controlled and aggressive, they see such position as unnecessary alarmist. In their perception, the military in Russia is largely under civilian control and is generally exploited as a last resort when other means of foreign policy are no longer available. Against some expectations, it was Vladimir Putin who oversaw the reform that established control over the military under Anatoly Serdyukov's leadership as Defense Minister. The reform made the armed forces adequate to domestic and foreign threats in terms of both size and technological capabilities. Russia's perception of threat has evolved considerably since the 1990s and today incorporates developments such as internal instability, terrorism, regional conflicts, expansion of NATO, deployment of the U.S. ballistic missile system in Europe, and several other military technological advancements by the Western armies.

It was also under Putin that the Russian army was deployed in Eurasia and outside in defense of international objectives. In particular, the army was used in Georgia, Ukraine, and Syria. Although the nature and extent of military involvement differed in each case, Konyshev and Sergunin find that in all of these cases the use of force came as a last resort due to the failure of diplomacy and other means to bloc Georgia and Ukraine's integration with the Western economic and military organizations and prevent the Syrian regime from collapse. In the authors' assessment, the military is especially effective when it is used in combination with soft power tools. The authors also observe the overall trend toward the declining role of the military in RFP, but they acknowledge dangers of relying on new military tactics of asymmetrical or "hybrid warfare".

Another prominent tool that has been recently scrutinized by observers concerns Russia's cyber power. Julian Nocetti introduces the topic and argues against the notion of Moscow's offensive foreign policy aiming to deploy cyber capabilities in order to destroy the West's global information dominance. Rather, he maintains, Russia uses the cyber realm for defensive purposes and seeks to bring Western powers, particularly the United States to negotiate rules in digital and information spaces. Such rules are yet to be established, as Moscow and Washington disagree on their approach to the issue. While Russia emphasizes the importance of "digital sovereignty", the United States views the topic in terms of technology and free access to information. Russia has adopted several versions of the Doctrine on Information Security stressing threats of information warfare and dangers stemming from foreign governments' exploiting information and communication technologies for undermining state "sovereignty, political independence, and territorial integrity". In 2014, Putin famously referred to the Internet as a "CIA project".

Nocetti documents how Russia's perception of information changed in the 2000s and especially in the early 2010s in response to domestic protests and the Arab Spring in 2011. The Kremlin viewed both developments as reflecting the West's attempts to undermine Russia's political system and raised the spectrum of fear and the need to confront the perceived U.S. digital dominance. The new fear found its expression in two types of policy. One of them included measures to develop information and cyber expertise for asserting Russia's interests with respect to Western countries and those in the Eurasian region such as Ukraine and others. The other policy was to promote within the framework of the Shanghai Cooperation Organization the norm of "cyber-sovereignty" in contrast to the U.S. advocated "cyber-freedom". Overall, Nocetti finds cyber power to be on the rise in the RFP toolkit, although Russia has not yet been successful in its effort to regulate the Internet.

In addition to the potentially coercive tools, Russia has increasingly built expertise in media and public diplomacy to assist in promoting the nation's interests. Greg Simons' chapter studies the extent to which practices of media and public diplomacy in Russia reflect the "contextual intelligence" of the state. He argues that Moscow has been quite successful in breaking the West's media and information monopoly especially considering Russia's significantly more limited capabilities. The overall purpose of the Kremlin was not to fight a new Cold War of values with the West, but rather to establish Russia's own narrative and expose flaws of anti-Russian propaganda in the United States and other Western countries. One example of the latter discussed by Simons was the BBC2-aired mockumentary depicting a possible outbreak of a nuclear war in the Baltics. Through various conventional and digital media and activities of non-governmental organizations, Russia increased its visibility in the global information space and undermined the credibility of the Western media narrative.

Simons attributes Russia's relative success in the area of media and public diplomacy to their flexible and non-ideological nature along with a commitment to realization of concrete goals and interests. At the same time, he acknowledges constrains and limitations of Russia's public diplomacy, some of which have to do with excessive reliance on state support and others with lacking awareness of the target audience and weakness of a message for a global community.

Finally, any discussion of RFP would be incomplete without investigating the role played by the Russian Orthodox Church (ROC). Nicolai Petro argues that the ROC acts in partnership with the state, rather than subordinate to it. Historically the Church and the state often shared values and had overlapping interests. Today the ROC seeks to establish what it always wanted from the state – not separation of church and state, but a "separation of sphere of competencies" expressed with the notion of symphonia. Petro demonstrates the similarity of the Church's worldview with that of the state by highlighting ideas of spiritual and civilizational distinctiveness, global cultural diversity, traditional family, and defense of Christian and Russian values. He illustrates his argument with the case of *Russki mir*, or the Russian world.

The narrative of *Russki mir* was endorsed and supported by both the Church and the state and developed over 2007–2017 as an alternative to the narrative of nationally minded discourses and a spiritual complimentary to Russia's special relations with neighbors such as Ukraine and Belarus. The difference between the Church and the state views, however, concerns the question of national identity and sovereignty. Petro argues that the ROC's eschatological mission is broader that than of the Russian state and extends to the larger community of those associated with Kievan Rus. Petro also maintains that however difficult the question of Russia-Ukraine reconciliation may be, the ROC remains the only institution opposing the nationalist narrative inside Ukraine. The Church has consistently called upon all its followers to refrain from confrontation and violence and to seek peaceful resolution within ROC values.

7
DIPLOMACY[1]

Charles E. Ziegler
UNIVERSITY OF LOUISVILLE, USA

Introduction

In the quarter century since the collapse of the Soviet Union, Russian diplomacy has evolved from a passive, Western-orientation to a muscular, multilateral and assertive posture. In the immediate post-perestroika years, Russian diplomacy reflected the nascent democratic character of the new Russia, and the search for a new post-Soviet identity. Under the guidance of Foreign Minister Andrei Kozyrev, Russia sought acceptance in the Western liberal democratic order. Kozyrev, committed to the democratization of Russia, viewed the global environment following the collapse of the USSR as friendly and supportive, which he argued would promote the domestic reform process. The absence of foreign hostility would marginalize conservative forces, while providing assistance for Russia's economic transformation. The task of Russian diplomacy was to integrate the country into the Western liberal economic order, becoming "a reliable partner in the community of civilized states" (Kozyrev, 1992: 9, 1995).

While much has been written about Russian foreign policy, little attention has been paid to the actual practice of Russian diplomacy. This chapter starts with a definition of diplomacy, and discusses the major principles and the style of Russian diplomacy. The next section traces the evolution of Russian diplomatic practice from the early Soviet period through the Cold War. Diplomacy in the post-communist era foundered as Russia's leaders searched for ways to integrate the new Russian state into a U.S.-dominated international order. Russia's early, cooperative diplomacy toward the West was soon replaced with a multilateral and more sophisticated approach under former Soviet academic and intelligence chief Evgeniy Primakov.

Primakov's successor, career diplomat Igor Ivanov, continued Primakov's legacy and further professionalized the Russian diplomatic service in the late Yeltsin and early Putin years. Under Foreign Minister Sergei Lavrov, Russian diplomacy became more assertive and confrontational, reflecting the leadership style of Vladimir Putin. In the Putin-Lavrov period of the 2000s, Russian diplomacy stressed multilateral approaches and network diplomacy. Following Putin's return to his third presidential term in 2012, Russian diplomacy became more coercive, relying increasingly on sanctions and the threat of military force to achieve foreign policy aims. The final section provides a broader historical perspective, and summarizes the mixed record of Russian diplomacy.

Principles, style, and conditions of Russian diplomacy

Diplomacy and the Russian perspective

Diplomacy as a concept has a wide range of meanings. Many use the term as synonymous with international relations or the entirety of foreign policy (Kissinger, 1994; Ivanov, 2002; Primakov, 1999); for others it has a much narrower meaning, excluding the use of economic instruments or physical force (Hamilton and Langhorne, 2000). Scholars and practitioners distinguish between the traditional form of "high diplomacy" involving state-to-state negotiations conducted by seasoned professionals, and the more inclusive public diplomacy that incorporates a broad range of non-state actors in international relations (see Chapter 12 by Greg Simons on media and public diplomacy). Here I focus primarily on high diplomacy as practiced by the Russian government that, in recent years, has evolved to include modern forms of network diplomacy.

According to classical realism, diplomacy is the means by which states achieve their objectives short of war. The tasks of diplomacy are to determine the state's interests and objectives (which are constrained by power), assess the objectives of other nations, determine to what extent these objectives are compatible, and employ the best means suited to pursue national interests. Experienced diplomats use a mixture of persuasion, compromise and the threat of force in pursuing their goals (Morgenthau, 2006: 539–541). Diplomacy is a profession, staffed by experts in foreign languages and cultures who are adept at bargaining, and who use their skills to negotiate their country's interests (Berridge, 2001: 1–5).

Historically, diplomats have served as the chief representatives of their sovereign states abroad; foreign ministers and ambassadors today continue to serve as the voice and face of their countries in the international arena. The classical realist Hans Morgenthau subdivided this primary function into symbolic representation, legal representation, and political representation (Morgenthau, 2006: 542–545). The first of these deals with the ceremonial or prestige aspects of representation, the second relates to legally binding treaties and documents, while the third involves shaping and implementing foreign policy together with gathering information. In addition to the representation functions emphasized by Morgenthau, Christer Jonsson (2002) lists communicating national interests and goals, bargaining, and negotiation as major aspects of diplomacy.

If traditional diplomacy consists largely of representing individual state interests in the international arena, globalization has elevated the governing function – defined as multilateral cooperation to solve collective action problems – to equal importance (Sending et al., 2011). For Russia, however, the representative function is primary. Global governance is distinctly secondary, despite frequent statements about the importance of multilateral approaches. Russian diplomacy since the late 1990s has been very effective at promoting and representing Russian national interests; defending key principles of sovereignty, non-interference in internal affairs, and respect for Russia as a great power; recognizing the former Soviet space as a privileged sphere of Russian influence; and addressing Russia's vital security concerns in the Eurasian region, including limits on NATO and EU expansion eastward. Moscow's contributions to global governance have been marginal, or even obstructive, in response to U.S. and European global governance initiatives.

Moscow's skeptical position on humanitarian intervention and the Responsibility to Protect (R2P), adopted by the United Nations at its 2005 Summit, is a prominent example of this reluctance to engage in global governance (Ziegler, 2016). The R2P norm as promoted by liberal democratic actors in the West clashes with key Russian principles of sovereignty and non-interference in internal affairs. Similarly, by annexing Crimea and destabilizing southeast Ukraine, Russia violated Western principles of global governance and international law, OECD principles, and the Budapest Memorandum signed in 1994. From Moscow's perspective these actions are historically justified and vital for national security – they reinforce Russia's position as a great power in the post-Soviet space. Russia is reasserting hegemony in this area of vital national interest, and rejects Western criticism. But Russian leaders do not reject global governance wholesale. The Kremlin is willing to engage international institutions and observe legal processes beyond the post-Soviet periphery, as illustrated in its constructive Arctic policy (Maness and Valeriano, 2015).

Some analysts view diplomacy as the peaceful conduct of statecraft at the very highest levels; for others, diplomacy on occasion involves coercion. Coercive diplomacy – defined as "efforts to persuade an opponent to stop and/or undo an action he is already embarked upon" – is primarily defensive, and is generally related to crisis situations. The tools of coercive diplomacy include threats, sanctions, incentives, and the judicious and exemplary application of limited force. Bargaining and communication (on two levels – between words and actions) are closely coordinated with the threat of force (George, 1991: 4–7, 10). Coercive diplomacy is highly context dependent:

> Its effectiveness is a function of the type of provocation, the magnitude and depth of the conflict of interests, actors' images of the destructiveness of war, the degree of time urgency, the presence or absence of allies on either side, the strength and effectiveness of leadership, and the desired post-crisis relationship with the adversary.
>
> *(Levy, 2008: 540)*

Traditional "club" diplomacy is a largely secretive, hierarchical negotiation process conducted among a select few high-level representatives of the state. This hierarchic form of diplomacy is being displaced by flatter, more open and inclusive interactions termed "network" diplomacy (Heine, 2013). Network diplomacy has emerged in a globalized world where communications are instantaneous and the number of players in foreign policy has expanded dramatically. Non-governmental organizations (NGOs), corporations, and various multinational institutions play an important role in public diplomacy. Contemporary Russian practice contains elements of both club and network diplomacy, to be discussed later.

Political institutions, domestic politics, and diplomacy

In Russia's political system the President is instrumental in setting the main contours of Russian foreign policy. According to Article 80 of the Russian Federation Constitution, the President is the head of state and represents the country in international relations. Since assuming the presidency in 2000, Vladimir Putin has centralized policy-making in his office. The Minister of Foreign Affairs and various high-level officials of the Ministry coordinate and implement the details of foreign policy, but policy is closely coordinated with the President, who sets foreign policy guidelines. As one knowledgeable specialist puts it, "There is almost no space for involvement in foreign policy decision-making for the Federal Assembly (Parliament) and a rather small space for the Ministry of Foreign Affairs. Russian diplomats are managers rather than artists" (Tkachenko, 2017).

Russian diplomacy under Putin has reflected his approach to the world. For example, after the September 11, 2001 terrorist attacks on the United States, Putin offered Russian support to

President George W. Bush and Russian diplomacy followed his lead. Six years later, convinced that Bush had been weakened by the Iraq adventure and angered by U.S. support for the color revolutions, Putin delivered his 2007 Munich speech condemning the United States for unilateralism and the hyper-use of force. Russian diplomacy subsequently reflected this more aggressive approach. It also reflects the unpredictability of Russian foreign policy, which is subject to the personal whims of Putin.

As with most chief executives, the Russian President frequently engages in summit diplomacy. High-profile meetings enhance the leader's image abroad, and confirm Russia's great power status for domestic audiences. By inviting Boris Yeltsin to the G-7 meetings in 1994, the leading industrial states were signaling their willingness to include Russia in the club. Conversely, after Russia flouted international norms by annexing Crimea and supporting separatists in southeastern Ukraine, President Putin was excluded from the summit meetings. To minimize this slight, Russian media have played up Putin's participation in G-20, Shanghai Cooperation Organization (SCO), and BRICS forums, together with his bilateral summits and hosting ASEAN leaders at Sochi in 2016.

There is a close link between Russian foreign policy and domestic politics. As Russia transitioned from centrally planned state socialism toward a capitalist market economy, foreign policy adjusted to prioritize economic diplomacy as a tool to promote development and modernization. One specialist estimates that about half of all activity conducted by the Foreign Ministry's geographic departments is linked to trade and investment (Zonova, 2016: 340). The Ministry has a Department of Economic Cooperation tasked with coordinating trade and investment activities, and promoting Russia's integration in the global economy through such mechanisms as the World Trade Organization. Russian energy diplomacy is often conducted at the very highest levels, as in negotiations over the Nord Stream natural gas pipeline (between Putin and former German Chancellor Gerhard Schröder), and the Power of Siberia gas pipeline finalized by Putin and Chinese President Xi Jinping in early 2014.

Maintaining a prominent presence on the world stage enhances the legitimacy of Russian leaders, who can point to their diplomatic successes as evidence that Russia is a respected major player in global affairs. Soviet leaders valued détente so highly because the United States in effect acknowledged parity with the Soviet Union, recognizing its status as a co-equal superpower. Similarly, Foreign Minister Lavrov's article on the historical background of Russian foreign policy refers to Russia's "special role in European and global history", and quotes Henry Kissinger as stating that "Russia should be perceived as an essential element of any new global equilibrium" (Lavrov, 2016).

In foreign policy, military capabilities are closely linked to diplomatic influence. Russia's military weakness in the 1990s resulted from the collapse of the economy and ineffective political institutions. Under these conditions, foreign policy tended to be more accommodating (Tsygankov, 2012). One example is the development of pacific diplomacy between NATO and Russia in the immediate post-communist period, to the point that the possibility of using force in the relationship became unthinkable (Pouliot, 2010). However, the dismissive attitude toward Russia expressed by NATO officials nurtured resentment and a determination to reassert Russia's interests more vigorously once the power balance had been restored.

As Russia has modernized its military under Putin, its diplomatic approaches have become more assertive and confident. Russian diplomacy is very much realist in orientation, power-oriented and premised on defending the country's national interests. In addition, there is a clear hierarchy whereby more powerful states are accorded respect, while smaller and less powerful countries are frequently dismissed as inconsequential. Respect and status are very important for Russia – top leaders consistently assert that Russia must be treated as an equal great power by other states. Much of the resentment of NATO's expansion eastward derives not so much from an existential security threat posed by the admission of new member states, but because NATO did not take Russian interests seriously in the 1990s (Pouliot, 2010; Tsygankov, 2012).

Since NATO's assault on Serbia in 1999, Russian leaders have been fixated on the principle that state sovereignty should be inviolable. Following the West's support for Kosovo's declaration of independence in 2008, against the express wishes of Serbia, Russia politicized its approach to diplomatic recognition. Immediately after the brief Russo-Georgian war in August 2008, Dmitri Medvedev's government extended diplomatic recognition to the breakaway territories of Abkhazia and South Ossetia, citing a parallel to Kosovo's status. Russia has refused to recognize Kosovo and upon annexing Crimea in March 2014, asserted that in this case self-determination trumped sovereignty (Churkin, 2014). During earlier negotiations on Kosovo's status, Putin dismissed the U.S. claim that Kosovo was a unique situation, positing instead a universal model that equated it with the Georgian territories (Socor, 2006). If Europe and the United States applied a certain model of self-determination in the Balkans, the reasoning went, then Russia was fully justified in applying the same logic to the former Soviet space.

The need for full equality and respect in foreign affairs leads to a strategy of reciprocity in Russian diplomacy – whether positively or negatively (Glasser, 2013a). Foreign Minister Sergey Lavrov has described "normal" diplomatic relations as characterized by respect, and criticized the Barack Obama administration for being obsessed with American U.S. exceptionalism and leadership, and for a tendency to impose values by force rather than example ("Sergey Lavrov", 2017). In his controversial speech to the 2007 Munich Security Conference, Putin rejected a unipolar world with only one sovereign, where countries like Russia were constantly being lectured about democracy and with the United States imposing its policies on other nations. Democratic equality, Putin suggested, should extend to the realm of international relations (Putin, 2007).

Russia's reciprocity strategy was evident in 2012 when the U.S. Congress passed the Magnitsky Act designed to punish Russian officials for the death of lawyer Sergei Magnitsky. Encouraged by presidential aide Vyacheslav Volodin, a vocal critic of the United States, the Russian Duma responded by banning adoptions of Russian children by Americans (Zygar, 2016: 240–245). Although Foreign Minister Lavrov personally opposed the adoption ban (his ministry had just concluded an adoption agreement with the United States), he later observed in an interview: "You always reciprocate. Positively, negatively, but this is something which you cannot change. It was not invented by us. It is the law of international relations. Reciprocity is the key" (Glasser, 2013b).

To summarize, Russian diplomacy defends the key principles of inviolable state sovereignty, promotes recognition of Russia as a great power with a Eurasian sphere of influence, demands respect in international affairs, seeks to restrain U.S., NATO and EU advances, and asserts Russia's right to participate in major global forums and institutions. Russian diplomatic methods include both cooperation and coercion, and reciprocity is a key strategy in preserving Russian honor. Finally, Russian diplomacy after the collapse of the Soviet Union was forced to adjust to conditions of economic crisis, limited military capabilities, and a unipolar world dominated by the United States. As chaotic democratization under Yeltsin gave way to consolidated authoritarianism under Putin, Russian diplomacy became more centralized, secretive, and assertive. The next section briefly reviews how present-day Russian diplomacy has been influenced by seventy years of Soviet diplomatic practices and institutions.

From the Cold War to the 1990s

Following a short period of revolutionary idealism, where Bolshevik leaders rejected traditional bourgeois diplomacy and sought to undermine the bourgeois international order, Soviet diplomacy reverted to a more typical European style of conducting foreign affairs (Kocho-Williams, 2012). Soviet diplomacy was soon tasked with promoting the country's national interests, rather than the cause of proletarian internationalism, although foreign policy behavior was conceptualized through the ideological prism of Marxism-Leninism.

The Soviet Ministry of Foreign Affairs was highly professional, with diplomats well schooled in foreign languages and history. In 1934 the Diplomatic Academy of the USSR was founded under the Commissariat of Foreign Affairs to train Soviet diplomats. Toward the end of WWII, the Moscow State Institute of International Relations (MGIMO) was established to educate students for careers in foreign affairs. Both institutions survived into the post-communist era and continued to train foreign service professionals. The USSR had diplomatic legations in virtually every country in the world, and this policy of great-power engagement has continued in the post-communist era. Diplomacy was a vital tool in the Cold War struggle with the United States.

Much of this Soviet foreign policy bureaucracy would be carried over into the post-communist period – with Cold War thinking and a residual Marxist-Leninist worldview evident among older diplomats. The foreign ministry also inherited a centralized, top-down form of decision-making characterized by a high level of formality and secrecy (Pouliot, 2010: 134–138). In the Soviet period all major foreign policies were formulated by the Communist Party's Politburo, and decisions of the Party leadership were above criticism. Mikhail Gorbachev's "new thinking" in foreign policy sought to de-ideologize Soviet foreign policy, to open it up to more critical scrutiny, and to admit foreign policy failures, as in the invasion and occupation of Afghanistan. In today's Russia, the President and his closest advisors dominate foreign policy decision-making, much like the Politburo in Soviet times, and certain issues are no longer open to critical discussion.

Studies of Russian diplomacy

There are many excellent studies of Russian foreign policy, but very little has been written specifically on Russian diplomacy in the post-communist period. Former Foreign Minister Igor Ivanov's *The New Russian Diplomacy* (2002) is useful as an overview of Russian foreign policy positions a decade after the collapse of the USSR. Evgeniy Primakov's *Gody bol'shoi politiki* (1999, translated as *Russian Crossroads*, 2004) provides insights into Primakov's tenure as Foreign Minister, including his energetic efforts to contain NATO expansion, Russia's negotiations on Iraq and Kosovo, and U.S.-Russian relations.

Russia's first post-communist Foreign Minister, Andrei Kozyrev, expressed his thoughts on foreign policy in several works from the 1990s. In his 1995 book *Preobrazhenie*, Kozyrev outlined the transformation of Russian foreign policy from the messianic, ideological, and confrontational practices of the Soviet period, to the more cooperative and pragmatic diplomacy of his tenure. Soviet foreign policy concentrated on the good of the state, while the new Russian diplomacy had as its basic goals defending the rights of citizens, guaranteeing the country's security, and creating favorable conditions for economic development. Kozyrev defended his engagement with the West, which some denigrated as unduly "romantic", as not only natural but also necessary to break completely with the imperial Soviet past.

Kozyrev emphasized the importance of a friendly international environment for the new Russia, and the need to work together with international financial institutions such as the World Bank, International Monetary Fund (IMF), and General Agreement on Tariffs and Trade (GATT) for Russia to complete successfully its transformation to democracy and become a normal great power. The central tasks of Russian diplomacy were to improve the everyday life of Russian citizens, and reconstitute ties with the former republics – the Commonwealth of

Independent States (Kozyrev, 1992). In another essay Kozyrev stressed the need for a close strategic partnership with the United States based on mutual trust and conducted in the framework of a multipolar world and inclusion of Russia in the G-7 forum (Kozyrev, 1994).

Within the academic literature, Tatiana Zonova's work on Russian diplomacy is very useful. Zonova, a faculty member at MGIMO holding diplomatic rank of Counsellor 1st class, surveys the range of Russian diplomatic activities and discusses new trends in Russian diplomatic practice (Zonova, 2016). Elsewhere, Zonova has analyzed the historical Byzantine tendencies that infused Soviet and Russian diplomatic culture with messianic elements distinct from the modern European model (Zonova, 2007).

Recent work on coercive diplomacy illustrates how Russia is able to combine enhanced military capabilities with skilled diplomacy to shape international affairs, punching well above its weight globally. Stanislav Tkachenko, professor at St. Petersburg State University, notes the complexity of Russia's coercive diplomacy, its *"respect for sovereignty as the highest value in the international arena"*, and a preoccupation with preserving the status quo near Russia's borders (Tkachenko, 2017; emphasis in the original). Ryan Maness and Brandon Valeriano (2015) find Russia's use of coercive diplomacy to be situational, influenced by context and history. Coercive diplomacy – including military force, cyber attacks, and energy leverage – has been evident in Russia's relations with Georgia, Ukraine, Estonia, and Moldova, former republics of the USSR that Moscow considers to be within Russia's sphere of influence. Maness and Valeriano argue that Russia's heavy-handed coercive tactics encourage neighboring states to align more closely with the West, resulting in diplomatic failures.

Russian diplomacy in the 1990s

The new Russian diplomacy has been oriented toward reasserting Russian national interests long ignored by the West. Former Foreign Minister Igor Ivanov (1998–2004), in an oblique criticism of Kozyrev, described Russia's approach to the post-Cold War order eloquently: "Probably the main Russian illusion of the 1990s was a romantic vision of the world after the Cold War" (Ivanov, 2011). A key diplomatic goal at this time was avoiding Russia's isolation, by using diplomacy to make up for the lack of economic clout or military prowess in foreign policy. In a world order dominated by the United States, promoting multipolarity became a means of limiting U.S. power. Evgeniy Primakov's efforts at restoring the balance of power during his tenure as Foreign Minister (1996–1998) earned him a reputation as Russia's consummate diplomat – professional, experienced, a realist and pragmatist dedicated to advancing Russia's interests abroad by strengthening alliances with the non-Western powers.[2]

A key priority of Russian diplomacy from the beginning was to provide the conditions for Russia's economic development and economic reform through integration into the global economy (Ivanov, 2002: 141–149). During the 1990s, the Russian economy suffered from hyperinflation, unemployment, and the stress of transitioning toward a market economy. Russia's economic diplomacy was tasked with encouraging foreign investment, making foreign markets more accessible to Russian exports, developing economic ties with the Asia Pacific Economic Cooperation (APEC) and Association of Southeast Asian Nations (ASEAN) members, and preserving economic links to the former Soviet republics. Participation in the World Trade Organization (WTO) was a top priority – Russia eventually acquired WTO membership, but only after eighteen years of arduous negotiations. As the economy improved, Russian diplomacy prioritized the re-integration of the post-Soviet space through the Customs Union, and later the Eurasian Economic Union.

Russia's diplomats faced the daunting challenging of reorienting their country's foreign policy in the midst of political transition, major economic reforms, and virtual political anarchy.

Russia's Ministry of Foreign Affairs was charged with establishing diplomatic ties to the fourteen new states on Russia's border, while contending with the Defense Ministry freelancing foreign policy in the Caucasus, Moldova, and elsewhere.[3] A central problem was the question of Russia's national and foreign policy identity, which in the earliest years was oriented toward joining the Western world. But Moscow's perspective quickly evolved in a different direction. By the mid-1990s many Russian elites became disillusioned with the West, believing that Russian weakness in the 1990s led the West to take advantage of Russia, to humiliate it while ignoring Russian interests.

Soviet diplomacy was premised on the ideas of Marxism-Leninism, and Russia inherited much of this legacy, including personnel, institutions, and experiences. The Marxist-Leninist ideology that had shaped Soviet foreign policy was abandoned, but a democratic ideology never really took hold. In the more liberal political atmosphere of the 1990s, however, new foreign policy actors emerged – the state Duma, independent media, business groups, regional officials, and public opinion – effectively decentralizing the conduct of foreign policy (Ivanov, 2002: 21). Under Putin's leadership, power to shape foreign policy gravitated toward the presidency – no other institution has as significant a role in Russian diplomacy. The State Duma has a Committee on International Affairs, for example, but it lacks the policy-making or oversight authority to constrain either the President's office or the Ministry of Foreign Affairs.

The new post-communist Russian diplomatic corps retained much of the Soviet foreign policy structure and personnel (Ivanov, 2002: 21). However, like many other government bureaucracies, the new Russian Ministry of Foreign Affairs experienced a significant decline in budget and personnel following the collapse of the Soviet Union. Some thirty-two embassies and consulates were closed, and many talented younger diplomats – especially those with good language skills – left for more lucrative employment in the private business sector. Women found professional advancement in the diplomatic service highly limited (Zonova, 2016). Yelena Biberman's survey of international affairs students in Russia found that careers in the Foreign Ministry were unattractive not because of low salaries, but rather due to their perception that power was concentrated in the ruling elite, and their belief that the Foreign Ministry lacked autonomy in policy-making (Biberman, 2011). This concentration of power stemmed from Vladimir Putin's determination to rebuild the "power vertical" in Russian politics, to address the weakness of a decentralized, nearly feudalistic polity.

This weakness was evident on the international stage. Many conservatives and nationalists in Russia decried the country's subservient position in relations with the West. In his memoirs Evgeniy Primakov describes a conversation that Andrei Kozyrev had with Richard Nixon in 1992, shortly after the breakup of the Soviet Union, as related by Nixon Center director Dmitri Simes. Russia's young Foreign Minister assured Nixon of Russia's commitment to universal human values and told the ex-President he would be very appreciative of any assistance in identifying Russia's national interests. Nixon, the consummate realist, was clearly embarrassed by the question, which he regarded as hopelessly naïve and idealistic (Primakov, 1999: 210–211). This exemplified for many Russians the weakness of Russian diplomacy under Kozyrev, who seemed to many Russian nationalists more determined to transform his country into a client state of the United States than to build a partnership based on equality.[4]

Evgeniy Primakov personified the turn away from Kozyrev's Western orientation toward greater multilateralism in foreign policy. Primakov's strategy of creating the best possible conditions for a severely weakened Russia to pursue internal reforms, while avoiding isolation and preserving an international balance of power favorable to Russia's interests, was modeled on the diplomatic precedent set by Prince Aleksandr Gorchakov, who served as foreign minister (1856–1882) to Tsar Alexander II in the aftermath of the Crimean War (Ivanov, 2002: 26–27).

Foreign Minister Sergei Lavrov has repeatedly praised Gorchakov for restoring Russian influence in the nineteenth century solely through diplomacy, without resort to force. And like his Soviet counterpart Andrei Gromyko, Lavrov personifies Russian opposition to U.S. policies, earning the nickname "Mr. Nyet" (Glasser, 2013a). Russian diplomacy under Putin and Lavrov, while assertive, has also been highly pragmatic, realist, and until Putin's third presidential term, largely non-ideological, tailored solely to the defense and promotion of Russian state interests.

Using Gorchakov as his model, Primakov sought to restore Russia's global influence in the 1990s, balancing the United States by strengthening Russia's ties with China and India. Lavrov has continued to pursue Primakov's multipolar diplomacy, while constraining the exercise of U.S. power through the United Nations and other international institutions. In 2015, to honor Primakov, the government created the Moscow Primakov Center, with Henry Kissinger and a phalanx of Russian dignitaries in attendance for the opening. His name was attached to the prestigious Institute of World Economy and International Relations (IMEMO), and in 2016 the Gorchakov Fund held a series of "Primakov Readings" marking the legacy of the Russian statesman.

Russian diplomacy in the 2000s

In the early years of Vladimir Putin's presidency, Russia largely continued the cooperative diplomacy toward the West pursued by Yeltsin's administration, albeit leavened with Primakov's multipolar diplomacy. Putin demonstratively supported the United States in its war on terror following the September 11, 2001 attacks, overruling his generals to approve U.S. military deployments to Central Asia. However, with the U.S. invasion of Iraq in 2003, and the succession of color revolutions in Georgia, Ukraine, and Kyrgyzstan (2003–2005), Russian policy shifted toward confrontation.

The most prominent backlash to U.S. unilateralism was Putin's 2007 speech to the Munich security forum, which took Western leaders by surprise. By that time Russia was developing the economic and military capabilities to back up its diplomatic maneuvering to gain acceptance as an equal partner. But the effectiveness of Russia's material capabilities cannot rest solely on energy resources and military might. Russian leaders realized that to maintain Russia's status as a great power the country would also need to develop its soft power, or non-material capabilities. Former Foreign Minister Ivanov advocated pursuing a "smart" foreign policy – one that was more flexible and backed by expert advice, with better inter-agency coordination, incorporating civil society institutions and public-private partnerships. Ideas, Ivanov stressed, could confer a decisive advantage in a globalizing world. These non-material dimensions of foreign policy had been underestimated or neglected by the traditional diplomacy of the past (Ivanov, 2011). Network diplomacy exemplifies this new strategy.

Network diplomacy

Foreign Minister Lavrov first advanced the concept of "network diplomacy" in 2006, though the concept may be traced back to the system of flexible alliances advocated by Count Gorchakov in the nineteenth century. The idea is purely pragmatic, to move beyond the bloc politics of the Cold War and engage any combination of states based on coincident interests. Network diplomacy, Lavrov claimed, is aimed at solving common problems and is not directed against any particular state or organization. One major configuration Lavrov specified was the Russia-EU-U.S. partnership. This triangle was not directed against China, but rather could cooperate with China on issues of mutual concern such as North Korea's nuclear weapons program.

Similarly, Lavrov asserted, a network like the BRICS was not directed against the interests of the United States or the EU (Umerenkov, 2006). Following the annexation of Crimea and deterioration of relations with the West, Russia's network diplomacy focused more on the Shanghai Cooperation Organization, the Collective Security Treaty Organization (CSTO), and the Russia-China-India triangle, groupings that excluded Western powers.

For Russia, network diplomacy aligns with the primary goal of shifting the global order away from U.S. dominance, and toward a more balanced, multipolar system. The Shanghai Cooperation Organization and the BRICS process are examples of diplomatic successes because they include non-Western powers China and India, and so constitute the realization of Primakov's Eurasian vision. These organizations, together with the CIS and CSTO, form the new ideal of network diplomacy. Lavrov has identified the Iran nuclear agreement, the deal to eliminate Syria's chemical weapons, and terrorism as issues where collective action is needed (Lavrov, 2016).

These diplomatic initiatives may be considered a form of global governance, but it is governance on Russia's terms. Russian support for the United Nations, for example, can be viewed as a form of network diplomacy and support for global governance. Since Russia has a veto in the UN Security Council, however, and can work with shifting coalitions of like-minded states in the UN General Assembly to realize foreign policy goals, this global institution provides Moscow with an effective means of restraining U.S. power.

Personal diplomacy

In the decade after the collapse of the Soviet Union, personal diplomacy at the highest levels augured well for bilateral relations between Russia and the United States. Presidents Bill Clinton and Boris Yeltsin personally met eighteen times over the eight years that Clinton was in office, and developed a close friendship. A second regular line of diplomatic communications was the Gore-Chernomyrdin commission, proposed by Andrei Kozyrev and headed by U.S. Vice President Al Gore and Russia's Premier Viktor Chernomyrdin. The commission dealt with IMF conditionality provisions (a sore spot with Chernomyrdin), energy development, joint space exploration, and Russia's nuclear deal with Iran. Through these high-level channels the principals negotiated a number of major agreements, including securing Ukraine's nuclear weapons, withdrawing Russian troops from the Baltic states, and institutionalizing Russia's relationship to NATO (Talbott, 2002: 5–9, 84–86).

As Russian diplomacy, like Russian politics, was recentralized under Vladimir Putin, his penchant for secrecy and lack of any significant institutional constraints made foreign policy more unpredictable. Putin established close personal relations with some leaders – former German Chancellor Gerhard Schröder and Italian Prime Minister Silvio Berlusconi, most notably. Schröder had criticized the U.S. invasion of Iraq, while Berlusconi admired Putin's macho authoritarian style of leadership. With other world leaders Putin had tense relations, including President Barack Obama, who early in his first term chided Putin for "having one foot in the old ways of doing business and one foot in the new", and Schröder's successor Angela Merkel, famously intimidating her with his black Labrador (Blomfield, 2009; Smale and Higgins, 2017).[5] Putin's extensive experience as the leader of Russia, and his intelligence training, give him an edge in personal diplomacy. One senior U.S. intelligence officer remarked on how Putin's KGB training helps him discern vulnerabilities in others and exploit them to his advantage during negotiations (Morell, 2016).

Russian diplomacy in the early years of the Yeltsin administration was fairly idealistic, but under Putin it became far more pragmatic in advancing Russian interests. U.S.-style moralism, which resists engaging with certain international actors (rogue states, for example), is absent from

Russian diplomatic practice. Indeed, Putin sought to reestablish close ties with states that had been effectively abandoned following the breakup of the USSR, and he made a point of courting leaders hostile to Washington. These included Venezuelan President Hugo Chavez, Syria's Bashar al-Assad, and North Korea's Kim Jong-il. Curiously, while the Chinese-Russian strategic partnership is critical to Moscow's foreign policy, and both leaders describe ties as the best in history, Putin's personal relationship with President Xi Jinping is not very warm (Baev, 2016).

Classical diplomacy attaches great importance to developing long-term personal relationships based on understanding each other's national interests. During Yeltsin's time in office U.S. Secretary of State Madeleine Albright and Russian Foreign Minister Igor Ivanov worked together productively during the Balkan crises of the 1990s. As Ivanov and Albright observed years afterward at a conference on U.S.-Russia relations, understanding and respecting the other side's national interests will lead to trust and respect, even if the sides have serious differences.[6] Echoing this point, Secretary of State Condoleezza Rice noted "Personal relationships do matter . . . I came to trust that Sergei Ivanov was someone who was going to deliver on what he said he would do, and I think he believed the same about me" (Roxburgh, 2013: 45). U.S. Secretary of State John Kerry and Sergei Lavrov had a warm relationship, notwithstanding the tensions between Obama and Putin. But even the closest personal relationships cannot surmount competing national interests, which often lead great powers to engage in more forceful diplomacy.

Putin's coercive diplomacy

Coercive diplomacy relies on threat of force, rather than persuasion, and it includes economic, trade, and visa sanctions, in addition to a willingness to use military force in at least a limited capacity. Russia's weakness and its determination to limit U.S. influence along its periphery has led Moscow to move quickly from coercive diplomacy to a demonstration of military power (as in Ukraine and Georgia), rather than engage in more extended efforts at diplomatic persuasion (Tkachenko, 2017). Russia has at times used large-scale coercive diplomacy against Georgia, Ukraine, and Turkey. These actions are designed primarily to limit U.S. power in Russia and throughout the former Soviet space, to oppose infringements on Russian sovereignty, and to protect its perceived sphere of interests. Tkachenko claims that given Russia's disadvantageous position after the Cold War:

> Russian leaders simply do not believe that non-violent coercive diplomacy will lead to effective change of the existing status quo for one favourable to Russian interests. This perception is based on the view that even the most talented negotiators are not able to "renegotiate" the consequences of the collapse of the USSR and change Russia's image as a country defeated by the West in the Cold War. The Russian Federation needs another type of argumentation to insist on changing the post-Cold War status quo.
>
> *(Tkachenko, 2017: 121)*

Russia's coercive diplomacy seeks to create a new multilateral balance of power in the regional, if not the global, order. The goal is to force the United States to accept certain changes in the status quo favorable to Russia, namely the frozen conflicts in Georgia and Moldova, Russia's annexation of Crimea, and limits on Kiev's authority in southeastern Ukraine. Russia's coercive diplomacy has been applied along the country's periphery, and beyond that to Syria, but not much further. Conventional military power is sufficient to allow Moscow to exercise a regional form of coercive diplomacy, but Russia has neither the capability nor the inclination to extend its reach globally.

Diplomacy is effective only if it is backed up by the prospect of credible verbal or non-verbal signaling, substantial economic power (needed for imposing sanctions or providing incentives), and a willingness and ability to use military force. Russia has modernized its military forces since the Georgian war (2008), giving it sufficient capabilities to back up coercive diplomacy regionally (Trenin, 2016). Diplomacy alone was not sufficient to ensure that Georgia and Ukraine remained outside NATO, a key goal for the Kremlin. President George W. Bush had pushed membership for both states at the April 2008 NATO summit in Bucharest, and while France and Germany were opposed, the Bucharest Summit Declaration expressed support for their eventual membership (Baker, 2008). Lavrov asserted NATO membership for either country was a critical threat to Russian national security, and blamed the events in Ukraine on NATO's 2008 ("Dragging Ukraine", 2014). Similarly, Syria exemplifies the new Russian strategy of coercive diplomacy backed by a demonstration of military capabilities, while calling for the destruction of terrorists and an eventual negotiated settlement.

Generally, more powerful states are better positioned to make use of coercive diplomacy. Russia uses coercive diplomacy not only against weaker states such as Georgia, Ukraine, and Kyrgyzstan, but is increasingly using intimidation against stronger entities like the United States, the EU, and NATO. Diplomacy, especially coercive diplomacy, is an essential dimension of Russia's hybrid warfare strategy, which incorporates a range of measures, many of them non-kinetic, to disrupt and weaken a potential opponent. These include cyber attacks, trolling, disinformation, and similar methods that are especially effective against open democratic systems.

Russia uses secretive instruments of coercive diplomacy in tandem with public diplomacy, which relies on a country's soft power, or cultural attractiveness. As communications technologies have advanced, public diplomacy – the practice of influencing public opinion among publics in foreign nations using governmental and non-governmental organizations – has moved into prominence as a form of soft power (Melissen, 2005; Nye, 2008). Russia's government utilizes a network of organizations to advance Russian interests abroad, including RT (formerly Russian Television), Sputnik, Rossotrudnichestvo (Federal Agency for the CIS Region, Compatriots Living Abroad, and International Humanitarian Cooperation), Russkii Mir (Russian World), and the Russian Orthodox Church. Russia's public diplomacy and media are discussed at length in Chapter 12; here I will simply note that the Kremlin is skillfully using modern forms of public diplomacy to complement Russia's successful traditional diplomacy.

Conclusion and assessment

Russia's Ministry of Foreign Affairs has a proud tradition dating back to September 1802, when it was established under Tsar Alexander I. Russian diplomats have rediscovered Tsarist imperial practices, and routinely praise Russia's contribution to European statecraft. Foreign Minister Lavrov has heralded Russia's central contribution to the defense of Europe and preservation of civilization, while noting the continuity of Russian history and diplomatic traditions. Russia's great historical mission, the Foreign Minister claimed, was to serve as a bridge between East and West. The Russian Revolution and communist rule resulted in tremendous violence, Lavrov acknowledged, but on the positive side the Soviet state played a vital role in defeating fascism and promoting decolonization and the right of self-determination. Russia's diplomatic experience provided "the basis for moving vigorously forward and asserting our rightful role as one of the leading centers of the modern world, and as a source of values for development, security and stability" (Lavrov, 2016).

Historical continuity may be discerned in Russia's current promotion of stability and opposition to revolutionary movements or popular protests that threaten authoritarian government, which recalls the Holy Alliance of conservative monarchies sponsored by Alexander I. Popular uprisings near Russia's borders threaten Russia's sovereignty and territorial integrity, much as French revolutionary ideas threatened Europe's monarchies in the nineteenth century. The Kremlin has enlisted Russia's Orthodox Church, led by Patriarch Kirill, to promote Russia's image as guardian of conservative Christian values, and to legitimize the regime's actions in Ukraine and Syria (Cichowlas, 2017). This search for a new unifying Russian national idea based on religion recalls the symphonia tradition of close collaboration between church and state of the pre-Petrine era (Zonova, 2007).

James Sherr (2013) suggests that historically Russian diplomacy has exhibited calculated ambiguity about what was domestic and what was foreign. The historical messianism of Moscow as the Third Rome, Soviet efforts to spread communism internationally, and the Kremlin's current paternalistic approach toward compatriots in the former republics exemplify this relationship. Close linkages between foreign and domestic politics are evident in the dominance of President Putin, together with a few close associates, as chief decision maker, and the degree to which national interests reflect elite group interests (Lo, 2015: 3–37).

Russian diplomacy also reflects political culture, most notably the pride in national greatness, recognition as an influential major power, and the importance of preserving honor in international relations, aspects of Russian foreign policy that have endured for centuries (Tsygankov, 2012). To honor Russia's diplomatic service, in 2002 President Putin decreed a Diplomatic Worker's Day, marking the 200th anniversary of Russia's Foreign Ministry.[7] In his congratulatory remarks to Foreign Ministry personnel marking the 2017 holiday, Putin said, "Russia's diplomacy has a long and glorious history and our diplomats have always remained true to their professional duties and served the homeland with honor."[8] Russian diplomacy pragmatically expresses Russian national interests, as realism would suggest, but it also reflects the quest for international respect and defends a distinct Russian national identity, dimensions neglected by a purely realist approach.

Russian diplomacy is in a process of transition away from the traditional high diplomacy of the Soviet era, and the diplomacy of weakness of the 1990s, toward a multifaceted and complex diplomacy balancing effective traditional mechanisms with newer, more nimble forms of diplomacy. It builds on pre-revolutionary and Soviet traditions, and is tightly controlled by President Putin, who is assisted by a small group of foreign policy elites. Russia's professional diplomatic corps has played an important role in restoring the country to a position of prominence in world affairs, though a tendency to resort to coercive diplomacy and intimidation has heightened tensions with the West, and contributed to Russia's isolation. Russian diplomacy has been more successful with the non-Western world, through an extensive network of multilateral institutions that either exclude or constrain U.S. and European actions.

The skill and professionalism of Russia's diplomatic corps has served the country well, enabling the Kremlin to exercise a larger global influence than its economic or military capabilities would suggest. Nonetheless, in the absence of effective long-term domestic reform, economic and demographic factors will constrain Russia's foreign policy options. Diplomacy can only partially compensate for these structural weaknesses. Moreover, Russia's increasing reliance on coercive diplomacy has often proved counter-productive, alienating friends and strengthening opposition to the Kremlin's aggressive tactics.

Notes

1 I am indebted to Andrei Tsygankov and Kenneth Yalowitz for their helpful comments on an earlier version of this chapter.
2 See the commemorative speech by Foreign Minister Lavrov to the Gorchakov Fund, 1 December 2016, at http://gorchakovfund.ru/en/news/19893/.

3 I am indebted to Ambassador Kenneth Yalowitz for this insight.
4 A different perspective may be found in Sidorova (2017). Galina Sidorova is a journalist who served as Kozyrev's political advisor from 1992–1995. She has high praise for Kozyrev, though she is very critical of Lavrov for "dumbing down" Russian foreign policy and his slavish devotion to Putin's foreign policy line.
5 For an extended discussion of Putin's relationship with Angela Merkel, see Mushaben 2017. Mushaben notes that for all his misogyny, Putin has great respect for Merkel's leadership.
6 At https://sfs.georgetown.edu/secretary-state-madeleine-albright-foreign-minister-russia-igor-ivanov-discuss-u-s-russia-relations/.
7 The precise date of the holiday was also meant to commemorate the *Posolsky Prikaz* (roughly, Foreign Office) set up under Ivan IV in 1549.
8 http://en.kremlin.ru/events/president/news/53849.

References

Baev, Pavel. 2016. "Mistrust Sets Low Ceiling for Russia-China Partnership: Deconstructing the Putin-Xi Jinping Relationship." *Ponars Eurasia Policy Memo 447*, at www.ponarseurasia.org/memo/mistrust-sets-low-ceiling-russia-china-partnership-deconstructing-putin-xi-jinping-relationship.

Baker, Peter. 2008. "Bush Pressing NATO to Set Membership Path for Ukraine, Georgia." *Washington Post*, 2 April, at www.washingtonpost.com/wp-dyn/content/article/2008/04/01/AR2008040100686.html.

Berridge, G.W., Maurice Keens-Soper, and T.G. Otte. 2001. *Diplomatic Theory from Machiavelli to Kissinger* (Basingstoke: Palgrave Macmillan).

Biberman, Yelena. 2011. "The Politics of Diplomatic Service Reforms in Post-Soviet Russia." *Political Science Quarterly* 126(4), 669–680.

Blomfield, Adrian. 2009. "Vladimir Putin rejects Barack Obama's claim he has one foot in the past." *The Telegraph*, 3 July, at www.telegraph.co.uk/news/worldnews/barackobama/5734243/Vladimir-Putin-rejects-Barack-Obamas-claim-he-has-one-foot-in-the-past.html.

Churkin, Vitaly. 2014. Statement on the UN General Assembly Resolution on Crimea, GA/11493, 27 March, at www.un.org/press/en/2014/ga11493.doc.htm.

Cichowlas, Ola. 2017. "Patriarch Kirill: From Ambitious Reformer to State Hardliner." *The Moscow Times*, 14 April, at https://themoscowtimes.com/articles/patriarch-kirill-from-ambitious-reformer-to-state-hardliner-57725.

"Dragging Ukraine into NATO negative for European security – Lavrov." 2014. *RT*, 14 May, at https://www.rt.com/news/158908-lavrov-russia-ukraine-nato/.

George, Alexander L. 1991 *Forceful Persuasion: Coercive Diplomacy as an Alternative to War* (Washington, DC: U.S. Institute of Peace).

Glasser, Susan B. 2013a. "Minister No: Sergei Lavrov and the blunt logic of Russian power." *Foreign Policy*, 29 April, at http://foreignpolicy.com/2013/04/29/minister-no/.

Glasser, Susan B. 2013b. "'The Law of Politics' According to Sergei Lavrov." *Foreign Policy*, 29 April, at http://foreignpolicy.com/2013/04/29/the-law-of-politics-according-to-sergei-lavrov/.

Hamilton, Keith and Richard Langhorne. 2000. *The Practice of Diplomacy: Its Evolution, Theory and Administration* (London: Routledge).

Heine, Jorge. 2013. "From Club to Network Diplomacy." In Andrew F. Cooper, Jorge Heine, and Ramesh Thakur, eds. *The Oxford Handbook of Modern Diplomacy* (Oxford, UK: Oxford University Press).

Ivanov, Igor. 2002. *The New Russian Diplomacy* (Washington, DC: Bookings Institution Press).

Ivanov, Igor. 2011. "What Diplomacy Does Russia Need in the 21st Century?" *Russia in Global Affairs*, 29 December, at http://eng.globalaffairs.ru/number/What-Diplomacy-Does-Russia-Need-in-the-21st-Century-15420.

Jonsson, Christer. 2002. "Diplomacy, Bargaining and Negotiation." In Walter Carlsnaes, Thomas Risse, and Beth A. Simmons, eds. *Handbook of International Relations* (London: Sage).

Kissinger, Henry. 1994. *Diplomacy* (New York: Simon and Schuster).

Kocho-Williams, Alastair. 2012. *Russian and Soviet Diplomacy, 1900–39* (London: Palgrave Macmillan).

Kozyrev, Andrei. 1992. "Russia: A Chance for Survival." *Foreign Affairs* 71(2), 1–16.

Kozyrev, Andrei. 1994. "The Lagging Partnership." *Foreign Affairs* 73(3), 59–71.

Kozyrev, A.V. 1995. *Preobrazhenie* (Moscow: Mezhdunarodnye otnosheniia).

Lavrov, Sergei. 2016. "Russia's Foreign Policy in a Historical Perspective." *Russia in Global Affairs*, 30 March, at http://eng.globalaffairs.ru/number/Russias-Foreign-Policy-in-a-Historical-Perspective-18067.

Levy, Jack S. 2008. "Deterrence and Coercive Diplomacy: The Contributions of Alexander George." *Political Psychology* 29(4), 537–552.

Lo, Bobo. 2015. *Russia and the New World Disorder* (London: Chatham House).
Maness, Ryan C. and Brandon Valeriano. 2015. *Russia's Coercive Diplomacy: Energy, Cyber, and Maritime Policy as New Sources of Power* (Basingstoke, UK: Palgrave Macmillan).
Melissen, Jan, ed. 2005. *The New Public Diplomacy: Soft Power in International Relations* (Basingstoke, UK: Palgrave Macmillan).
Morell, Michael J. 2016. "I Ran the CIA. Now I'm Endorsing Hillary Clinton." *New York Times*, 5 August, at www.nytimes.com/2016/08/05/opinion/campaign-stops/i-ran-the-cia-now-im-endorsing-hillary-clinton.html.
Morgenthau, Hans J. 2006. *Politics Among Nations*, seventh edition (New York: McGraw Hill).
Mushaben, Joyce Marie. 2017. *Becoming Madam Chancellor: Angela Merkel and the Berlin Republic* (Cambridge, UK: Cambridge University Press).
Nye, Joseph S. Jr. 2008. "Public Diplomacy and Soft Power." *Annals of the American Academy of Political and Social Science* 616(1), 94–109.
Pouliot, Vincent. 2010. *International Security in Practice: The Politics of NATO-Russia Diplomacy* (Cambridge, UK: Cambridge University Press).
Primakov, Evgeniy. 1999. *Gody bol'shoi politike* (Moscow: Sovershenno Sekretno). An English version is *Russian Crossroads: Toward the New Millennium*. Trans. Felix Rosenthal (New Haven, CT: Yale University Press, 2004).
Putin Vladimir. 2007. "Speech and the Following Discussion at the Munich Conference on Security Policy," 10 February. http://en.kremlin.ru/events/president/transcripts/24034.
Roxburgh, Angus. 2013. *The Strongman: Vladimir Putin and the Struggle for Russia* (London: I.B. Tauris).
Sending, Ole Jacob, Vincent Pouliot and Iver B. Neumann, 2011. "The Future of Diplomacy," *International Journal* 66(3), 527–542.
"Sergey Lavrov: The Interview." 2017. Interview by Paul Saunders, *The National Interest*, 29 March, at http://nationalinterest.org/feature/sergey-lavrov-the-interview-19940?utm_source=CGI%20Daily%20Russia%20Brief&utm_campaign=2ec5bbee8b-EMAIL_CAMPAIGN_2017_03_31&utm_medium=email&utm_term=0_814a2b3260-2ec5bbee8b-281714293&mc_cid=2ec5bbee8b&mc_eid=20913c9efa.
Sherr, James. 2013. *Hard Diplomacy and Soft Coercion: Russia's Influence Abroad* (London: Chatham House).
Sidorova, Galina. 2017. "Under the Aegis of the Foreign Ministry." Trans by Arch Tait (January) Henry Jackson Society and Radio Free Europe/ Radio Liberty, at http://henryjacksonsociety.org/wp-content/uploads/2017/01/Under-the-Aegis-of-the-Foreign-Ministry-.pdf.
Smale, Alison and Andrew Higgins. 2017. "Putin and Merkel: A Rivalry of History, Distrust, and Power." *New York Times*, 12 March, at www.nytimes.com/2017/03/12/world/europe/vladimir-putin-angela-merkel-russia-germany.html?_r=0.
Socor, Vladimir. 2006. "Putin on Kosovo and Post-Soviet Conflicts: Destructive Ambiguity." *Eurasia Daily Monitor*, 2 February, at https://jamestown.org/program/putin-on-kosovo-and-post-soviet-conflicts-destructive-ambiguity/.
Talbott, Strobe. 2002. *The Russia Hand: A Memoir of Presidential Diplomacy* (New York: Random House).
Tkachenko, Stanislav. 2017. "The Coercive Diplomacy of Vladimir Putin (2014–2016)," in *The Russian Challenge to the European Security Environment*, Roger E. Kanet, ed. (London: Palgrave Macmillan).
Trenin, Dmitri. 2016. "The Revival of the Russian Military." *Foreign Affairs* 95(3), 23–29.
Tsygankov, Andrei P. 2012. *Russia and the West from Alexander to Putin: Honor in International Relations* (Cambridge, UK: Cambridge University Press).
Umerenkov, Evgeniy. 2006. "Ministr inostrannykh del Rossii Sergey Lavrov: 'Setevaia diplomataia' seichas vostrebovana kak nikogda." *Izvestiia*, 28 December, at http://izvestia.ru/news/320459.
Ziegler, Charles E. 2016. "Russia on the rebound: using and misusing the Responsibility to Protect." *International Relations* 30(3), 346–361.
Zonova, Tatiana V. 2007. "Diplomatic Cultures: Comparing Russia and the West in Terms of a 'Modern Model of Diplomacy'." *The Hague Journal of Diplomacy* 2(1), 1–23.
Zonova, Tatiana V. 2016. "Russian Post-Soviet Diplomacy." In Costas M. Constantinou, Pauline Kerr and Paul Sharp, eds. *The Sage Handbook of Diplomacy* (Los Angeles, CA: Sage).
Zygar, Mikhail. 2016. *All the Kremlin's Men: Inside the Court of Vladimir Putin* (New York: Public Affairs).

8
NATURAL GAS

Boris Barkanov

WEST VIRGINIA UNIVERSITY, USA

Introduction

This chapter utilizes realist political economic theory to make sense of Russian natural gas policy (henceforth policy). The contribution is to clarify the relationship between economics and politics in Russian policy by situating it within the broader historical and theoretical question of Russia's strategic adjustment to unipolarity. This facilitates an alternative interpretation of the 2006 and 2009 Russo-Ukrainian gas wars to the academically and politically influential geopolitical "weapon" view.

The argument is threefold. First, policy is best understood as reflecting a stage in Moscow's strategic adjustment to unipolarity that emerged at the turn of the 20th century, and focused on geo-economics, the use of state power to craft international markets. Second, policy specifics originated in the business strategy of Russia's dominant gas company, *Gazprom*, which was consistent with the state's general goal of shaping markets to promote Russian economic integration on favorable terms. Third, this strategy saw mixed success depending on the character of strategic interactions. When the latter soured due to Russia's partners' policies, Moscow reacted by prioritizing position and control over profits, which is consistent with a geo-economic strategy. This empowered Euro-Atlantic hawks whose securitizing moves (Wæver, 1995; Buzan et al., 1998) layered geopolitical dynamics over relations with the EU, which had its own geo-economic agenda to create competitive markets. In this sense, the strategy backfired. The 2014 Maidan revolution, Russia's unrecognized annexation of Crimea, and the Donbass war (henceforth, the Ukrainian crisis), marked the failure of geo-economics in Ukraine and seriously disrupted energy and broader political relations with the EU, as geopolitical tendencies became more pronounced.

The argument is applied to post-2000 policy toward Germany and Ukraine. Gas merits our attention because Russia's relative power – based on proportion of world reserves, production, and imports into Europe – is particularly prominent. This power advantage implies that policy drivers, whatever they may be, should find maximal expression in this sector. These intrinsically important cases present full spectrum outcome variation: success (Germany) and failure (Ukraine). Ukraine also displays across-time variation.

The discussion begins by examining the literature on Russian energy policy from a realist political economic perspective to highlight gaps in our knowledge concerning the relationship between power, wealth, and state strategy under unipolarity. After describing Russia's and Gazprom's strategies, the analysis turns to the empirical cases. To fill out the picture globally, Russia's "pivot to China" is also examined.

The conclusion summarizes the role of gas in Russian strategy and the reasons for its variable success.

Weapon or what?

The role of energy in Russian foreign policy is an emotive issue. Despite general agreement that energy is central to Russian foreign policy, Moscow is a consequential energy actor particularly relative to Europe, and Russian energy relations see some admixture of profit-seeking and power politics (Stent, 2008: 78–79), research is mired in controversy.

An important axis of debate concerns how energy policy relates to high politics. Reminiscent of Hirschman's (1980) famous study of Hitler's economic strategy in southeastern Europe, the voluminous energy "weapon" literature (Smith, 2004, 2008; Baran, 2007; Goldman, 2008; Orbán, 2008; Umbach, 2010; Blank, 2011; Lucas, 2014; Jonsson and Seely, 2015) interprets Russian policy as an effort to leverage international economic structural dependencies to enhance its power and influence for geopolitical ends.

Analysis focuses on the discursive constitution of "energy superpower" (Bouzarovski and Bassin, 2011), how asymmetrical interdependence affects the security and independence of Russia's energy partners (D'Anieri, 1999), and the consequences for EU/NATO cohesion (Blank, 2011), U.S. influence (Leverett and Noël, 2006; Kubicek, 2013), and the global order (Cohen, 2009; Bouzarovski and Bassin, 2011). The state's prominent policy role and conflicts with neighbors, especially Ukraine, support the inference of power-seeking motives, while energy prices (Nygren, 2008; Snegovaya, 2015) and balance of power perceptions explain variation (Orbán, 2008).

This view is contested by research highlighting positive sum outcomes associated with Moscow's long-term economic priorities (Tsygankov, 2006), commercial/economic goals in the energy sphere (Stern, 2006b; Aalto et al., 2012; Abdelal and Mitrova, 2013), mutual dependence on EU markets (Closson, 2009; Oliker et al., 2009; Stern et al., 2009: 60; Casier, 2011), and the difficulties of exercising gas market power (Finon and Locatelli, 2008). Some argue that a geopolitical focus obscures more serious political economic dilemmas (Luciani, 2006; Milov et al., 2006; Stern 2006a, 2009; Jaffe and Soligo, 2008; Noël, 2008). Domestic constraints raise doubts about strategy and policy coherence (Monaghan, 2007; Legvold, 2008; Balmaceda, 2013). Others focus on how commercial, institutional, and ideational factors produce behavior and outcome variation (Hancock, 2006; Stulberg, 2007, 2012, 2015).

A significant body of work suggests Russian policy is reactive (Shadrina, 2010: 17; Aalto et al., 2012). EU market liberalization – also "political" – portends major risks (Goldthau, 2012; Godzimirski, 2013: 153–154; Hulbert and Goldthau, 2013) associated with "security of demand" (Yenikeyeff, 2006), relationships in Europe (Abdelal, 2015), and Russia's financial well-being, energy security, institutional development, and political culture (Feklyunina, 2008; Meulen, 2009). The result is a growing EU-Russia "energy security dilemma" (Monaghan, 2006; Krickovic, 2015), partly the result of EU hawks' attempts to securitize energy, disrupting decades-long successful cooperation (McGowan, 2011; Raszewksi, 2012).

These correctives to the "weapon" perspective are insightful from a business, political economic, and IR perspective. However, they reproduce the politics-economics dichotomy or do not explicitly theorize this conceptually complicated relationship. Moreover, research neglects how a key systemic factor – a unipolar distribution of power – has influenced Russia's strategic posture and policy.

This work differs from previous research by examining these lacunae directly. Realism highlights two systemic factors – anarchy and the distribution of power – that are central to understanding world politics and political economy. Second, it allows a more sophisticated, historically sensitive approach to the relationship between power and wealth. Three interrelated questions structure the analysis: How do power and plenty relate under anarchy? What are the macro-incentives associated with unipolarity? Under contemporary unipolarity, are state strategies likely to be primarily geopolitical (the subordination of economic goals to high politics) or geo-economic (the use of state power to advance economic goals)?[1]

For realists, separating politics from economics is an artifact of liberal thinking. Politics and energy are inextricably linked (Shaffer, 2009: 1), as are power and plenty generally (Viner, 1948). World politics influences international economic relations due to anarchy, while economic prowess is essential to long-term power (Grieco, 1990; Kirshner, 1999). Economic resources can yield security and political dividends (Hirschman, 1980). However, politics shapes economics too. States create domestic markets (Heckscher, 1934; Polanyi, 1944), a process shaped by anarchical danger (Gerschenkron, 1962; Snyder, 1990), while the most powerful states – hegemons – create international economic orders (Kindleberger, 1973; Gilpin, 1981; Ruggie, 1983).

The economics-politics relationship varies historically. During the Cold War, pursuing wealth followed the high politics of bipolarity (Luttwak, 1990; Gowa, 1994). Hegemonic realists emphasize that unipolarity – the overwhelming and unambiguous concentration of power in a single state – creates different incentives (Wohlforth, 2009). The unipole's power advantages render geopolitical competition futile and risky.

Unipolarity dampens geopolitical competition, but the incentives for geo-economic strategies are ambiguous. States are likely to focus on long-term economic development to meet domestic expectations or eventually catch up. Ruthless inter-state competition for a bigger, better piece of the pie supports geo-economic strategies – states' leveraging power for wealth – and the emergence of status/positional concerns (Schweller, 1999). However, secondary states have to be careful that geo-economic competition, especially with the unipole, its allies, and states courting them stays within bounds; there is a fine line between competing and provoking unipolar animus (Wohlforth, 2003).

To summarize, under unipolarity, geopolitical strategies are unlikely to survive (hypothesis 1). Economics will be prioritized; however, state power is deployed to shape markets in self-regarding ways (hypothesis 2). Competitive interactions make positional goals salient (hypothesis 3).

Energy in Russian foreign policy

Geopolitics to geo-economics

As hegemonic realists predict, by 2000 Moscow recognized the futility of geopolitical competition. Strategic adjustment reflected an explicit repudiation of a misguided policy that wasted limited resources. This was not just a rhetorical shift, but informed important changes in strategic thinking and policy (SVOP, 2000; Larson and Shevchenko, 2010; Pouliot, 2010; Tsygankov, 2013).

The new strategy reflected the 'economisation' of Russian foreign policy (Pirani, 2009a: 8–9) to promote economic growth and modernization (Tsygankov, 2006). This meant supporting Russian business to increase revenues, advance integration through deepening commercial relations, and to find a niche in a competitive, globalizing economic (SVOP, 2000). In the post-Soviet space, gas became the main integration vehicle (Mitrova, 2014). This contrasted with Primakov's unsuccessful mobilization of Russian business for geopolitical goals (Stulberg, 2007; Tsygankov, 2013).

Moscow did not reject the power-laden view of international relations that became dominant under Yeltsin (Mlechin, 2007). It saw the international economy as a ruthless competition between state-supported firms. As Putin remarked, "nobody is going to especially help us ... We must fight ... for a place under the economic sun" (Putin, 2002). Russia would continue Yeltsin's integration project to support growth, modernization, and become a "normal great power" (Tsygankov, 2005). However, Russia would be not a passive economic object of neo-liberal engineering promoted by Western powers, but a purposive subject attuned to its own needs and striving to shape the terms of its integration advantageously. This meant developing a coherent foreign policy that leveraged commercial and political resources to Russia's economic benefit. Geo-economics was a multi-sectoral strategy, but natural resources and infrastructure acquired "strategic" importance because they comprised Russia's competitive advantage (Grigoriev and Chaplygina, 2003).

Considered a legitimate project for a state aspiring to an influential role internationally, geo-economics was mimicking Western powers which have close relations with firms (Krasner, 1978; Mitchell, 1991; Yergin, 1991) and play hardball. Yeltsin's Russia experienced firsthand Western use of financial aid in the 1990s to shape Russian policy, including energy. The Baku-Tbilisi-Ceyhan pipeline, dubious commercially, became reality with U.S. support, breaking Russia's Caspian oil export monopoly.

The leadership did not necessarily have a scientific understanding of Western states' IPE policy; these were schemata that informed Russian understandings of appropriate behavior. This makes legible Putin's refrain, that "When we fight for our interests, we look for the most acceptable methods ... We see how the United States defends its interests ... what methods ... they use" (Abdullaev, 2006).

This was Moscow's understanding of economic cooperation in a competitive world. Russia assumed leadership by creating markets and this was appropriate behavior even if it ruffled feathers. Thus, Presidential aide Igor Shuvalov claimed that:

> We are telling Europe: you are leading on some things. But we have raised the bar of leadership in a different area ... at a substantial risk ... but successfully so far. We have already become involved in conflicts, we are making progress ... we know how to act in the future.
>
> *(Nezavisimaya Gazeta, 2006)*

Gazprom's strategy

Having rebuilt its domestic influence, the state coopted Gazprom, whose pre-existing strategy oriented geo-economics in the gas sector. Three components stand out. First, Gazprom wanted to grow its European business by penetrating downstream. Forced to sell to national monopolies "at the border" during the Cold War, the exporter sought to enter the distribution/retail segments where margins were thought to be higher (Stern, 2005: 111; Vavilov and Trofimov, 2016a: 85). Eventually, it proposed swapping upstream for downstream assets, or "asset swaps".

Second, Gazprom was interested in acquiring some ownership control in midstream pipelines. Ownership minimizes transportation costs (Vavilov and Trofimov, 2016b: 113). Controlling market access conditions would interest any large supplier. This had special significance for Gazprom since transport pipelines had been coterminous with the Soviet state. With the collapse, Gazprom became dependent on Ukraine's transit monopoly to Europe, prompting Russia to seek ownership control over Kyiv's gas transport system (GTS) (D'Anieri, 1999: 81; Pirani, 2007: 20) and build bypass pipelines (i.e. Yamal-Europe through Belarus and Poland).

Pipeline policy also aimed to protect markets. Gazprom argued that U.S. efforts to bring Central Asian gas to Turkey and Europe through bypass pipelines (i.e. Trans-Caspian pipeline) harmed its business (*Petroleum Report (Interfax)*, 1999). Europe's subsequent *Nabucco* project exacerbated these worries. Additional pipelines bring incremental supply, lowering prices. As pipelines are expensive, this creates a first-mover advantage. By accelerating its own projects (Blue Stream/Turkey; South Stream/southeast Europe), Gazprom rendered competing routes financially unattractive. It also signed long-term contracts with Central Asian exporters, locking-in volumes consumers hoped would be supply alternatives (Barkanov, 2014).

Third, Gazprom valorized business relationships. Personal relations are important for business everywhere, and relationship-based practices are especially resonant in Russian political culture. One-on-one deals also allowed Gazprom to leverage its size.

In practice, Gazprom's strategy boiled down to protecting and growing its market through vertical integration from gas deposit to final consumer based on business-to-business ties. The major change concerned the state's strategic shift to geo-economics. Previously, the state helped Gazprom when necessary. Under Putin, Gazprom's business became a vehicle for promoting the state's top strategic priority: using statecraft to influence the terms of Russia's international economic integration and most immediately to structure the Eurasian gas market to the advantage of Russia's largest firm.

Mixed results

Europe

Gazprom first entered the German market in the 1990s (Stern, 2005). With Chancellor Merkel and President Putin's blessing, Gazprom made several "win-win" deals. Between 2007–2009, Germany's chemical conglomerate BASF and E.ON Ruhrgas AG (E.ON) each acquired minority stakes – roughly 25% – in Severneftegazprom, a Gazprom subsidiary holding the license to the *Yuzhno-Russkoye* field in Yamal-Nenets Autonomous Okrug ("Yuzhno-Russkoye", n.d.). The firms could add a portion of the field's gas to their reserve balance, an important metric for investors (Tomberg, 2007). Earlier, E.ON Rurhgas had acquired a majority stake (69.34%) in the OGK-4 power company, making it vertically integrated in Russia ("Acquisition of Majority Stake in OGK-4 Signed and Sealed – E.ON SE", 2007). Despite diverging from the EU's preferred modus operandi, upstream investment was possible for western investors.

In exchange, Gazprom's share in BASF grand-daughter Wingas GmbH, a gas trading, distribution, transit, and storage company, went from 35% to roughly 50%. Gazprom purchased a 49% stake in two Libyan oil concessions owned by BASF daughter Wintershall Holding AG. Later it invested in Wintershall's North Sea fields. From E.ON, the company received a 49% share in the financial asset ZAO Gerosgaz ("Yuzhno-Russkoye", n.d.).

In 2011, a multinational consortium of Gazprom, Wintershall, and E.ON, N.V. Nederlandse Gasunie (Netherlands) and GDF SUEZ SA (France) ("Who We Are", n.d.) completed the Nord Stream pipeline transporting gas under the Baltic Sea directly to Germany. With these "asset swaps", Gazprom became vertically integrated from well-head to consumer.

Nord Stream was justified by expected demand growth and lower transportation costs due to shorter distance and the absence of transit payments. The pipeline had significant consequences (Abdelal, 2015: 565) including eliminating transit risk due to Russia's relations with Ukraine,

Belarus, and Poland, whose leverage it reduced. Not surprisingly, Polish Foreign Minister Radek Sikorski called it the new Ribbentrop-Molotov pact (Kramer, 2009).

Recent European developments

Conflict with the EU's geo-economic agenda to create competitive markets, and geopolitics have upset Russo-European relations. Gazprom is negotiating to settle a contentious anti-trust case opened by DG Competition in 2012 (Golubkova and Chee, 2016). U.S. shale gas, liquid natural gas (LNG), and growing EU regional spot markets challenge its long-term contract-based business model (Stern and Rogers, 2014).

With major state support, Gazprom successfully negotiated the South Stream pipeline project under the Black Sea, advancing vertical integration in southeastern/central Europe. By 2010, Russia had signed intergovernmental agreements with Bulgaria, Serbia, Hungary, Greece, Slovenia, Croatia, and Austria. Construction started in December 2012. Unlike Nord Stream, a TEN-E priority project with limited exemptions from competition directives, South Stream was at odds with EU legislation and the EC ("Russia Says South Stream Project Is Over", 2014).

The Ukrainian crisis complicated Gazprom's strategy by freezing EU-Russia gas relations. EU pressure made Bulgaria shelve South Stream (Stern et al., 2015: 4) In response, Gazprom negotiated an alternative route with Turkey that was canceled after Turkey shot down a Syria-destined Russian bomber crossing its borders. Ankara's subsequent apology allowed intensified pipeline negotiations to resume (Makhneva, 2016).

Gazprom is also negotiating Russo-German capacity expansion: Nord Stream II. A shareholders' agreement was signed at the 2015 Vladivostok Economic Forum, where Gazprom and Wintershall concluded another asset swap (Socor, 2015). EU geo-economic (implications for competition) and geopolitical (lost revenues/leverage for Ukraine) concerns make the expansion controversial. Gazprom's access to OPAL, the German on-shore extension which it owns with Wintershall, is also in question (Beckman, 2016; *Platts News*, 2016).

After South Stream's cancellation, Gazprom announced that it no longer sought downstream assets, provoking speculation about a changed European strategy (Stern et al., 2015). Recent German developments suggest the shift may be geographically limited. However, the broader context is troublesome. In May 2014, Russia concluded a major Chinese gas deal (discussed later), while Europe's largest economies met in Rome to reduce Russian gas dependence. Post-Maidan Russo-European relations were in deep crisis. Energy strategic cooperation, previously a dominant theme, may be over.

Russo-Ukrainian gas wars

The orthodox view – that Russia's 2005–2006 price increases were a geopolitical reaction to punish the Orange government – is problematic. It ignores broader pricing trends toward Ukraine (Pirani, 2009b: 93) within the CIS (Pirani et al., 2010: 6), including a price war with Belarus (Stern, 2006b: 11), and domestically (Mitrova, 2009; 25), which predicted an eventual price increase (Abdelal, 2013). It neglects Ukraine's transit policy, a key sub-sectoral factor that precipitated conflict (Stern, 2006b: 6). Misperceiving its power, Ukraine leveraged its transit near-monopoly to conduct "brinkmanship" to extract better terms of trade, betting correctly that Moscow would be blamed, damaging its reliable supplier reputation. Ukraine's dictating terms raised positional concerns in Moscow, which did not blink (Shaffer, 2009: 44).[2]

The crisis had been "brewing" throughout 2005. Under Kuchma, Ukrainian domestic opposition and commercial disagreements slowed cooperation. However, supply/transit terms were successfully negotiated, obviating crisis. Upon assuming power, the Yushchenko government unilaterally modified a GTS consortium agreement which later collapsed. The pre-existing trade deal was disrupted after Naftogaz raised transit tariffs inviting Gazprom to reopen the gas pricing question, access to Ukrainian gas storage came into question, and Prime Minister Tymoshenko "waged an aggressive campaign" against the transit intermediary Rosukrenergo, in which Gazprom was a partner. Facing Ukrainian intransigence, Russia escalated while offering off-ramps on its own terms, but Kyiv feared "becoming permanently ensnared in Gazprom's ambitions". With no contract on January 1, Gazprom stopped Ukrainian supplies while continuing to ship European gas (Stern, 2006b; Pirani, 2007; Pirani, 2009b; Hadfield, 2012; Abdelal, 2013; O'Sullivan, 2013; Malygina, 2014; Vavilov and Trofimov, 2016a).

Earlier, Ukraine had threatened to siphon transit gas for its own use (*BBC Monitoring Service*, 2005). European shortfalls suggested it was following through. After a day of shortages, Gazprom increased volumes to protect its reputation. The January 4 agreement was a complicated compromise that favored Russia, including Gazprom's downstream advance (Stern et al., 2009).

Close examination of 2006–2008 indicates that the 2009 gas war resulted from similar disagreements exacerbated by Ukrainian elite conflict over who would partner with Gazprom to extract rents through intermediary firms on the Ukrainian market. With Timoschenko's April 2007 return as prime minister, state-owned companies, including Naftogaz, voided sales contracts with Ukrgaz-Energo, jeopardizing earlier agreements. February 2008 saw a new Putin-Yuschenko deal, but faltering negotiations led Gazprom to reduce volumes. Again, Naftogaz warned it could not assure European transit without Russian supply guarantees. Another agreement emerged that advanced Gazprom's downstream penetration directly by eliminating intermediaries. In October, a Tymoshenko-Putin memorandum and Gazprom-Naftogaz agreement elaborated the deal; notably Naftogaz partnered with Gazprom in the lucrative European re-export business (Balmaceda, 2009; Stern et al., 2009).

Ukraine experienced chronic difficulties paying for gas imports (Abdelal, 2013: 433). Relations deteriorated in November when Naftogaz failed to settle its debts and rejected Gazprom's proposal for alternative payment (Balmaceda, 2009), jeopardizing the previously agreed contract to be signed at the month's end. Again, Russia and Gazprom applied pressure. Criticized for not warning customers in 2005, Gazprom also sent a delegation to European capitals, including Brussels. Financing was made available to cash-strapped Naftogaz which eventually made payment, but late and not including Gazprom fines/penalties that it contested. In a December 31 letter, Naftogaz CEO Oleg Dubyna threatened that if supplies were cut, transit gas to Europe could be confiscated under Ukrainian law.

Gazprom and Tymoshenko claimed a last-minute compromise was torpedoed when President Yushchenko blocked negotiations. Yushchenko denied this. Former Energy Minister Yuri Boiko blamed Tymoshenko for delaying Ukraine's debt repayment. An unprecedented two-week crisis with major European shortages ensued, and the subsequent agreement overwhelmingly favored Russia (Pirani, 2009c; Stern et al., 2009; Vavilov and Trofimov, 2016a).

Recent developments

Despite improved relations after Yanukovych's 2010 presidential election, negotiations "proceeded cautiously", with "fault lines" keeping relations pragmatic and self-interested. Skeptical about transit reliability, Russia lost interest in Ukraine's GTS, preferring bypass routes. April 2010 witnessed the Kharkiv accords. In an obvious geopolitical linkage, a state-funded gas discount was exchanged for a long-term lease extension for Russia's Black Sea fleet (Pirani et al., 2010). In connection with Ukraine's participation in Russia's broader geo-economic project, the Eurasian Economic Community (EEC), Gazprom overlooked non-payment and accumulated debt, offering additional price discounts (Stern et al., 2015). Yanukovych's inability to manage pressure from Russia's EEC and the EU's Eastern Partnership provoked the Maidan uprising (Barkanov, 2015).

After Crimea's annexation, Russia canceled the Kharkiv discount. Negotiations in 2014 were tense, but European mediation prevented crisis. Diminished market power from changing southeast European markets also restrained Russia (Stulberg, 2015). Already declining with Gazprom's exorbitant price, Ukrainian gas demand collapsed due to a deep economic crisis and post-Maidan efforts to reduce gas dependency (Bershidsky, 2016). In November 2015, Kyiv suspended purchases (Rapoza, 2016). In 2016, EU-brokered discussions to cover winter shortfalls recommenced (*Bloomberg.com*, 2016). Nevertheless, Kyiv remains determined to move closer to the EU. Russo-Ukrainian relations are worse than ever, making prospects for gas integration bleak.

Pivot to China

Gas negotiations with China began in the 1990s, intensifying after the 2004 strategic co-operation agreement. In 2006, the Sakhalin-1 consortium (with Rosneft and ExxonMobil) and CNPC concluded an export deal. However, it was blocked by Gazprom, whose sales to China would take nearly a decade to agree (Henderson, 2011; Henderson and Mitrova, 2016).

There are obvious complementarities supporting bilateral trade. Gas can contribute to meeting China's expected long-term demand growth and regional development needs, which it links to political stability. Its supports Beijing's ecologically driven "energy revolution". In 2014, relatively cheap and domestically available coal met nearly two-thirds of primary energy demand. But coal exacerbates environmental woes that are becoming socially and politically acute. As U.S. naval superiority facilitates maritime blockades, Russian "onshore" pipeline gas is attractive because of its immunity to potential supply disruptions should conflict between China and the United States emerge.

China's large market offers Russia an alternative to Europe, where Gazprom faces stagnating demand, major regulatory challenges, and geopolitical risk. It is the closest major market for otherwise commercially stranded East Siberian gas. Finally, trade promotes state priorities such as developing scarcely populated regions and pivoting to Asia (Henderson, 2011; Chang, 2014; Jaffe et al., 2015; Paik, 2015; Henderson and Mitrova, 2016).

Haggling over commercial details hindered agreement. Price – where consumer/producer interests conflict directly – was key. Emphasizing the magnitude of necessary investment, Gazprom insisted on European equivalent prices, proposing a methodology linking price to oil or high-priced, Asian LNG gas. Any price concessions create incentives for renegotiations with other consumers in Europe and Asia. China suggested a link to coal and later to the domestic market, expecting convergence with world prices. Regulated domestic consumer prices also create a price ceiling. Complicating negotiations further, price depends on financing arrangements, including prepayment, preferential loans, or upstream direct investment (Henderson, 2011; Chang, 2014; Paik, 2015; Henderson and Mitrova, 2016).

Another disagreement concerned the pipeline route. Russia prioritized the Altai route, bringing West Siberian gas to Western China, because the Russian segment would be shorter and gas would come from already developed, albeit distant deposits. Because West Siberia supplies Europe, in theory, this would make Russia a "swing producer" able to create competition between the two regions (Chow, 2015). Moscow mentioned this in 2006 when EU energy relations became strained after the 2006 gas war. "Swing production" could ensure Gazprom against difficulties in Europe, but West Siberia currently has sufficient gas for east and west, blunting Gazprom's power (Stern, cited in Paik, 2015).

For China, Central Asian (especially Turkmen) imports make Altai less desirable. Unenthusiastic about becoming embroiled in Russo-European disputes, it was also leery of Altai's security of supply and financial consequences. China preferred the Power of Siberia pipeline from East Siberian fields (Chayanda and Kovykta) to China's northern Bohai Bay region. Closer to key markets, it promises cheaper transportation and diversifies routes away from the politically volatile Xinjiang region (Henderson, 2011; Paik, 2015).

In the context of mutual efforts to create leverage, disagreement over bargaining power prevented a deal. For Gazprom, rising demand and expensive alternatives justified a higher price. Wary of monopsonies, it envisioned connecting the *Power of Siberia* pipeline to the proposed Vladivostok LNG terminal to facilitate entering additional markets, particularly Japan, whose gas demand grew after Fukushima. However, the tremendous transport distance and liquefaction costs made this uneconomical. Russia is also courting India (Henderson, 2011; Chow, 2015; Henderson and Mitrova, 2016).

Meanwhile, China cultivated various alternatives, including pipeline gas from Central Asia and Myanmar, domestic conventional and non-conventional supplies, and LNG from Australia and Indonesia (contracted in the early 2000s). New LNG is expected in the early 2020s particularly from North America (United States and Canada), East Africa (Mozambique and Tanzania), and Australia (Henderson and Stern, 2014).

Frustrated with Gazprom's slow negotiations, the government broke its LNG export monopoly to include YLNG and Rosneft, making possible deals with its Russian competitors Novatek and Rosneft. By January 2014, Novatek had sold a 20% stake in Yamal LNG (YLNG) to the China National Petroleum Corporation (CNPC). It subsequently negotiated a 20-year agreement to sell 18% of YLNG's capacity. Later, the Silk Road Fund acquired a 9.9% stake, and together with Chinese banks provided $13 billion in project financing. Lobbying by Rosneft's President/Chairman Igor Sechin, an ex-deputy prime minister overseeing energy, was instrumental. Rosneft also seeks pipeline exports to China. This rekindled debate over Gazprom's dominant gas market position which seemed unassailable a decade earlier (Henderson and Mitrova, 2016).

Clearly, domestic pressure was making agreement approximating China's preferences likely. The Ukrainian crisis tipped the scales. High-level meetings, one-third of which included President Putin, spiked in 2014 (Henderson and Mitrova, 2016). May 2014 saw Gazprom and CNPC finally agree on the *Power of Siberia* project, purportedly worth $400 billion for gas averaging 38 bcm annually over 30 years. Paik's (2015) price estimate is $9.9–$10.8/mmbtu. Russian officials claimed it approximated Germany's, among the lowest in Europe. Most concluded that Gazprom's expectations were disappointed, although apparently both parties could be satisfied at $10/mmbtu, the Central Asian equivalent (Henderson and Stern, 2014). The pricing formula mirrors traditional European contracts. Unlike other Russian firms (e.g. Rosneft, Novatek, Sibur), Gazprom declined CNPC's request for upstream equity participation and a $25 billion dollar loan, preferring cheaper state financing and smaller Chinese loans instead. This is consistent with reports that post-sanctions Chinese financing has been "armed robbery" and more burdensome than evading sanctions in the EU. Deliveries were expected in 2018–2019, but delays up to 2021 – from demand uncertainty and decline in (oil-based) prices – have been reported (Henderson and Mitrova, 2016).

Several other projects are emerging. In November 2014, a non-binding, Altai Memorandum of Understanding adumbrating contractual terms and an implementation schedule was concluded (Henderson and Mitrova, 2016). As a second, high volume project, Altai would undermine Central Asian and expensive LNG prices. With competing Russian and U.S. gas "pivots to Asia", Altai was potentially a "significant blow to IOCs" and a "game changer" for Asian gas markets (Paik, 2015). However, low prices have precluded a deal and jeopardized its future (Henderson and Mitrova, 2016).

In June 2016, Gazprom declined CNPC's "integrated contract" foreseeing joint investment in production, pipeline construction/operation, and exports. This contrasts with its "asset swap" strategy in Europe, where relationships are a source of valuable influence (Abdelal, 2015).

In the medium term, Asian gas markets are likely to be very competitive (Henderson and Stern, 2014). Unless Chinese shale development stalls or becomes uneconomical (at oil prices below $50), Russia is unlikely to enjoy long-term political leverage, with optimistic scenarios forecasting a maximum 20% market share (Jaffe et al., 2015).

Russia's Chinese gas strategy has not been consistent. Gazprom's extended and unsuccessful bargaining has delayed market entry, ironically catalyzing something it long resisted: consideration of alternative, non-monopolistic market structures at home and abroad. Geopolitics created the final impetus for a deal. Finally, sales to China, though probably less lucrative, would be a financial alternative to Europe, pre-empting Russia's economic isolation. Otherwise, achievements have been limited.

Geo-economics and its limitations

What does this tell us about how Russia views natural gas power? Gazprom's revenues are very important but appear subordinated to the goal of maintaining position and control when strategic interactions sour. Invited to play chicken by Ukraine, Russia did not back down and even upped the ante by applying pressure, exacerbating conflict. States covet position, reputation, and control, and this is consistent with geo-economic motives. These only appear geopolitical if we ignore the role of power in creating markets implicit in the facile economics-politics distinction. One exception is the clear geopolitical linkage in the 2010 Kharkiv agreement. Even here, broader relations emphasized economic cooperation, and the state, not Gazprom, picked up the tab.

Second, outcomes depended on the character of strategic interaction. Russia's strategy required bargaining with actors who had competing preferences. Moscow has used the gas trade to both incentivize and compel its partners to do business on its preferred terms. In Germany, conflicts of interest were cooperatively resolved, generating success. In Ukraine, crisis was avoided under Yanukovych (and Kuchma) when competing interests were resolved through compromise agreements that advanced Russia's geo-economic goals.

Meanwhile, Yuschenko's aggressive bargaining raised positional concerns, inviting pressure and retaliation, culminating in the 2006 conflict. This was not punishment for geopolitical waywardness, but reflected the Orange government's overplaying its hand. When Ukraine agreed to play ball on Russia's terms after losing the 2006 war, conflict was managed as deals that advanced Gazprom's downstream advance were crafted. Unfortunately, this was not enough to avoid the 2009 war which erupted despite available win sets due to Ukrainian domestic political struggles.

The results of gas geo-economics have been mixed. The most significant achievement are deepening ties with Western European states and especially Germany, in connection with the Nord Stream project and its potential expansion. Nevertheless, these are exceptional accomplishments that stand out amongst other attempts that were mostly unsuccessful (Vavilov and Trofimov, 2016a). After initial success, the strategy failed in Ukraine as Kyiv moved closer to the EU and shut Russia out. Success in China has also been modest.

Russia's strategy was not interpreted as such in the West. Geo-economic goals and the conflict with Ukraine were misinterpreted by Western hawks, supporting securitizing moves that transposed relations into the realm of high politics. Geopolitics became increasingly salient, making what was essentially a geo-economic conflict between Russia and the EU more onerous. As a result, mutual alienation rather than integration obtained, making the geo-economic strategy more difficult. Germany was exceptional because Gazprom's ties to local firms – who narrated developments favorably for the government – pushed in the other direction (Abdelal, 2013).

Finally, the Ukrainian crisis has transformed the character of international relations and geopolitical logics are re-emerging. Although Russian domestic politics mattered, a Chinese gas deal was struck because of developments in Europe that made Russia willing to pay a geopolitical premium. Russia's movement toward China became more urgent, and so China's terms prevailed.

This alone does not represent the end of unipolarity, Russian and Chinese "multipolarity" rhetoric notwithstanding. Unipolarity is a global systemic structure constituted by the material balance of power based on relative military and long-term technological/economic capabilities. Whether recent changes constitute a structural transformation in this sense is debatable. The alternative interpretation is that U.S. long-term global power remains unrivaled, but the long-awaited hard balancing has begun. Within-structure processes means unbalanced unipolarity is giving way to balanced unipolarity, which may be more stable.

Notes

1 This distinction is consistent with Luttwak but the focus is on the relationship between politics and economics (Luttwak, 1990).
2 See also Abdelal (2013, 2015).

References

Aalto, Pami, Dusseault, David, Kivinen, Markku and Kennedy, Michael D. 2012. "How Are Russian Energy Policies Formulated? Linking the Actors and Structures of Energy Policy." In *Russia's Energy Policies: National, Interregional and Global Levels*, edited by Pami Aalto. Cheltenham, UK: Edward Elgar Publishing.
Abdelal, Rawi. 2013. "The Profits of Power: Commerce and Realpolitik in Eurasia." *Review of International Political Economy* 20(3): 421–56.
Abdelal, Rawi. 2015. "The Multinational Firm and Geopolitics: Europe, Russian Energy, and Power." *Business and Politics* 17(3): 553–576.
Abdelal, Rawi, and Tatiana Mitrova. 2013. *U.S.-Russia Relations and the Hydrocarbon Markets of Eurasia*. Cambridge, MA: Davis Center for Russian and Eurasian Studies, Harvard.
"Acquisition of Majority Stake in OGK-4 Signed and Sealed - E.ON SE." 2007. *EON.com*. October 15.
Balmaceda, Margarita. 2009. "Intermediaries and the Ukrainian Domestic Dimension of the Gas Conflict." *Russian Analytical Digest* 53: 9–14.
Balmaceda, Margarita. 2013. *The Politics of Energy Dependency: Ukraine, Belarus, and Lithuania between Domestic Oligarchs and Russian Pressure*. Toronto: University of Toronto Press.
Baran, Zeyno. 2007. "EU Energy Security: Time to End Russian Leverage." *The Washington Quarterly* 30(4): 131–44.
Barkanov, Boris. 2014. "The Geo-Economics of Central Asian Gas: The Evolution of Russian-Turkmen Relations in Natural Gas (1992–2010)." In *Export Pipelines from the CIS Region: Geopolitics, Securitization, and Political Decision-Making*, edited by Heinrich and Pleines. Stuttgart, Germany: Ibidem-Verlag.
Barkanov, Boris. 2015. "Crisis in Ukraine: Clash of Civilizations or Geopolitics." In *Eurasia Rising? Power, Politics and Institutions in a Contested Region*, edited by Matthew Sussex and Roger E. Kanet. Vol. 1. Basingstoke, UK: Palgrave Macmillan.
BBC Monitoring Service. 2005. "Ukrainian Gas Company Warns Russia over Low Gas Supplies," July 1.

Beckman, Karel. 2016. "Can Nord Stream 2 Be Stopped?" *EnergyPost.eu*. April 14.
Bershidsky, Leonid. 2016. "How Ukraine Weaned Itself Off Russian Gas." *Bloomberg View*, January 12.
Blank, Stephen. 2011. "Russian Energy and Russian Security." *Whitehead Journal of Diplomacy and International Relations* 12(1): 173–88.
Bloomberg.com. 2016. "Russia-Ukraine Gas Talks Make Little Progress as EU Mediates," December 9.
Bouzarovski, Stefan, and Mark Bassin. 2011. "Energy and Identity: Imagining Russia as a Hydrocarbon Superpower." *Annals of the Association of American Geographers* 101(4): 783–94.
Buzan, Barry, Ole Wæver, and Jaap de Wilde. 1998. *Security: A New Framework for Analysis*. Boulder, CO: Lynne Rienner.
Casier, Tom. 2011. "Russia's Energy Leverage over the EU: Myth or Reality?" *Perspectives on European Politics and Society* 12(4): 493–508.
Chang, Felix. 2014. "Friends in Need: Geopolitics of China-Russia Energy Relations." Philadelphia, PA: Foreign Policy Research Institute.
Chow, Edward. 2015. "Russia-China Gas Deal and Redeal." Washington, DC: CSIS.
Closson, Stacy. 2009. "Russia's Key Customer: Europe." In *Russian Energy Power and Foreign Relations: Implications for Conflict and Cooperation*, edited by Jeronim Perovic, Robert W. Orttung, and Andreas Wenger. London and New York: Routledge.
Cohen, Ariel. 2009. "Russia: The Flawed Energy Superpower." In *Energy Security Challenges for the 21st Century: A Reference Handbook*, edited by Gal Luft and Anne Korin. Santa Barbara, CA: Praeger Security International.
D'Anieri, Paul J. 1999. *Economic Interdependence in Ukrainian-Russian Relations*. Albany, NY: SUNY Press.
Feklyunina, Valentina. 2008. "The 'Great Diversification Game': Russia's Vision of the European Union's Energy Projects in the Shared Neighbourhood." *Journal of Contemporary European Research* 4(2): 130–48.
Finon, Dominique, and Catherine Locatelli. 2008. "Russian and European Gas Interdependence: Could Contractual Trade Channel Geopolitics?" *Energy Policy* 36(1). www.sciencedirect.com/science/article/pii/S0301421507003795.
Gerschenkron, Alexander. 1962. *Economic Backwardness in Historical Perspective*. Cambridge, UK: Belknap Press.
Gilpin, Robert. 1981. *War and Change in World Politics*. Cambridge, UK: Cambridge University.
Godzimirski, Jakub M. 2013. *Russian Energy in a Changing World: What Is the Outlook for the Hydrocarbons Superpower?* Farnham, UK: Routledge.
Goldman, Marshall I. 2008. *Petrostate: Putin, Power, and the New Russia*. Oxford, UK: Oxford University Press.
Goldthau, Andreas. 2012. "Emerging Gas Governance Challenges for Eurasian Markets after the Shale Gas Revolution." In *Dynamics of Energy Governance in Europe and Russia*, edited by Kuzemko et al. New York: Palgrave Macmillan.
Golubkova, Katya and Foo Yun Chee. 2016. "Gazprom Aims for Amicable Solution in EU Antitrust Case." *Reuters*, March 9.
Gowa, Joanne S. 1994. *Allies, Adversaries, and International Trade*. Princeton, NJ: Princeton University Press.
Grieco, Joseph M. 1990. *Cooperation Among Nations: Europe, America, and Non-Tariff Barriers to Trade*. Ithaca, NY: Cornell University Press.
Grigoriev, Leonid, and Anna Chaplygina. 2003. "Looking into the Future." *Russia in Global Affairs* 2. http://eng.globalaffairs.ru/number/n_846.
Hadfield, Amelia. 2012. "Energy and Foreign Policy: EU-Russia Energy Dynamics." In *Foreign Policy: Theories, Actors, Cases*, edited by Steve Smith, Amelia Hadfield, and Tim Dunne. Oxford, UK: Oxford University Press.
Hancock, Kathleen J. 2006. "The Semi-Sovereign State: Belarus and the Russian Neo-Empire." *Foreign Policy Analysis* 2(2): 117–36.
Heckscher, Eli F. 1934. *Mercantilism*. London: Allen & Unwin.
Henderson, James. 2011. *The Pricing Debate over Russian Gas Exports to China*. Oxford, UK: Oxford Institute for Energy Studies.
Henderson, James, and Tatiana Mitrova. 2016. *Energy Relations between Russia and China: Playing Chess with the Dragon*. Oxford, UK: Oxford Institute for Energy Studies.
Henderson, James, and Jonathan Stern. 2014. "The Potential Impact on Asian Gas Markets of Russia's Eastern Strategy." Oxford, UK: Oxford Institute for Energy Studies.
Hirschman, Albert O. 1980. *National Power and the Structure of Foreign Trade*. Berkeley, CA: University of California Press.

Hulbert, Matthew, and Andreas Goldthau. 2013. "Natural Gas Going Global? Potential and Pitfalls." In *The Handbook of Global Energy Policy*, edited by Andreas Goldthau. Oxford, UK: Wiley-Blackwell.

Jaffe, Amy Myers, and Ronald Soligo. 2008. "Militarization of Energy: Geopolitical Threats to the Global Energy System." *Part of Energy Forum Study & working paper series The Global Energy Market: Comprehensive Strategies to Meet Geopolitical and Financial Risks: The G8, Energy Security, and Global Climate Issues.* www.bakerinstitute.org/research/militarization-of-energy-geopolitical-threats-to-the-global-energy-system/.

Jaffe, Amy Myers, Kenneth B. Medlock, and Meghan L. O'Sullivan. 2015. "China's Energy Hedging Strategy: Less Than Meets the Eye for Russian Gas Pipelines." *National Bureau of Asian Research*. Washington, DC.

Jonsson, O, and R Seely. 2015. "Russian Full-Spectrum Conflict: An Appraisal After Ukraine." *Journal of Slavic Military Studies* 28(1): 1–22.

Kindleberger, Charles P. 1973. *The World in Depression: 1929–1939.* Berkeley, CA: University of California.

Kirshner, Jonathan. 1999. "The Political Economy of Realism." In *Unipolar Politics: Realism and State Strategies after the Cold War*, edited by Ethan B Kapstein and Michael Mastanduno. New York: Columbia University Press.

Kramer, Andrew E. 2009. "Russia Gas Pipeline Heightens East Europe's Fears." *The New York Times*, October 12.

Krasner, Stephen D. 1978. *Defending the National Interest: Raw Materials Investments and U.S. Foreign Policy.* Princeton, NJ: Princeton University Press.

Krickovic, Andrej. 2015. "When Interdependence Produces Conflict: EU–Russia Energy Relations as a Security Dilemma." *Contemporary Security Policy* 36(1): 3–26.

Kubicek, Paul. 2013. "Energy Politics and Geopolitical Competition in the Caspian Basin." *Journal of Eurasian Studies* 4(2): 171–80.

Larson, Deborah Welch, and Alexei Shevchenko. 2010. "Status Seekers: Chinese and Russian Responses to U.S. Primacy." *International Security* 34(4): 63–95.

Legvold, Robert. 2008. "Russia's Strategic Vision and the Role of Energy." *NBR Analysis* 19(2): 9–22.

Leverett, Flynt, and Pierre Noël. 2006. "The New Axis of Oil." *The National Interest* 84: 62–70.

Lucas, Edward. 2014. *Renewed Focus on European Energy Security.* Washington, DC: Senate Foreign Relations Committee Subcommittee on European Affairs.

Luciani, Giacomo. 2006. "Is Russia a Threat to Energy Supplies?" *Oxford Energy Forum* 2006: 4–10.

Luttwak, Edward N. 1990. "From Geopolitics to Geo-Economics: Logic of Conflict, Grammar of Commerce." *The National Interest* 20: 17–23.

Makhneva, Alyona. 2016. "Turkish Stream Gas Pipeline Set for Revival." *Moscow Times*, July 27.

Malygina, Katerina. 2014. "The Struggle over Ukraine's Gas Transit Pipeline Network through the Lenses of Securitisation Theory." In *Export Pipelines from the CIS Region: Geopolitics, Securitization, and Political Decision-Making*, edited by A. Heinrich and H. Pleines. Stuttgart, Germany: Ibidem-Verlag.

McGowan, Francis. 2011. "Putting Energy Insecurity into Historical Context: European Responses to the Energy Crises of the 1970s and 2000s." *Geopolitics* 16(3): 486–511.

Meulen, Evert Faber Van Der. 2009. "Gas Supply and EU–Russia Relations." *Europe-Asia Studies* 61(5): 833–56.

Milov, Vladimir, Leonard L. Coburn, and Igor Danchenko. 2006. "Russia's Energy Policy, 1992–2005." *Eurasian Geography and Economics* 47(3): 285–313.

Mitchell, Timothy. 1991. "The Limits of the State: Beyond Statist Approaches and Their Critics." *American Political Science Review* 85(1): 77–96.

Mitrova, Tatiana. 2009. "Natural Gas in Transition: Systemic Reform Issues." In *Russian and CIS Gas Markets and Their Impact on Europe*, edited by Simon Pirani. Oxford and New York: Oxford University Press.

Mitrova, Tatiana. 2014. "The Geopolitics of Russian Natural Gas." Houston, TX: Center for Energy Studies, Baker Institute, Rice University.

Mlechin, L M. 2007. *Evgeniĭ Primakov.* Moskva: Molodaia gvardiia.

Monaghan, Andrew. 2006. "The Power of Oil and Gas." *Pro et Contra* 10(2–3): 1–13.

Monaghan, Andrew. 2007. "Russia's Energy Diplomacy: A Political Idea Lacking a Strategy?" *Southeast European and Black Sea Studies* 7(2): 275–88.

Nabi Abdullaev. 2006. "Sochi Summit Yields No Energy Pact." *The Moscow Times*, May 26.

Nezavisimaya Gazeta. 2006. "Interview with Presidential Aide Igor Shuvalov (Part 1)," May 23.

Noël, Pierre. 2008. *Beyond Dependence: How to Deal with Russian Gas.* London: European Council on Foreign Relations.

Nygren, Bertil. 2008. "Putin's Use of Natural Gas to Reintegrate the CIS Region." *Problems of Post-Communism* 55(4): 3–15.

Oliker, Olga, Keith Crane, Lowell H Schwartz, and Catherine Yusupov. 2009. *Russian Foreign Policy Sources and Implications*. Santa Monica, CA: RAND.

Orbán, Anita. 2008. *Power, Energy, and the New Russian Imperialism*. Westport, CT: Praeger Security International.

O'Sullivan, Meghan L. 2013. "The Entanglement of Energy, Grand Strategy, and International Security." In *The Handbook of Global Energy Policy*, edited by Andreas Goldthau. Oxford, UK: Wiley-Blackwell.

Paik, Keun Wook. 2015. *Sino-Russian Gas and Oil Cooperation: Entering into a New Era of Strategic Partnership?* Oxford, UK: Oxford Institute for Energy Studies.

Petroleum Report (Interfax). 1999. "Blue Stream Becoming Foreign Policy Priority," October 6.

Pirani, Simon. 2007. *Ukraine's Gas Sector*. Oxford, UK: Oxford Institute for Energy Studies.

Pirani, Simon. 2009a. "Introduction." In *Russian and CIS Gas Markets and Their Impact on Europe*, edited by Simon Pirani. Oxford, UK: Oxford University Press.

Pirani, Simon. 2009b. "Ukraine: A Gas Dependent State." In *Russian and CIS Gas Markets and Their Impact on Europe*, edited by Simon Pirani. Oxford, UK: Oxford University Press.

Pirani, Simon. 2009c. "The Russo-Ukrainian Gas Dispute, 2009." *Russian Analytical Digest* 53: 2–8.

Pirani, Simon, Jonathan Stern, and Katja Yafimava. 2010. *The April 2010 Russo-Ukrainian Gas Agreement and Its Implications for Europe*. Oxford, UK: Oxford Institute for Energy Studies.

Platts News. 2016. "European Commission Delays Ruling on New *Gazprom* Bid for German Gas Link Opal Use," July 14.

Polanyi, Karl. 1944. *The Great Transformation*. New York: Farrar & Rinehart, Inc.

Pouliot, Vincent. 2010. *International Security in Practice: The Politics of Nato-Russia Diplomacy*. New York: Cambridge University Press.

Putin, Vladimir. 2002. "Presidential Address to the Federal Assembly." *President of Russia*. April 18. http://en.kremlin.ru/events/president/news/53379.

Rapoza, Kenneth. 2016. "Ukraine's Naftogaz Breaks with Russia's *Gazprom* . . . Again." *Forbes*. April 1.

Raszewksi, Slawomir. 2012. "Security and the Economics of Energy in Northeast Europe." In *Dynamics of Energy Governance in Europe and Russia*, edited by Kuzemko et al. New York: Palgrave Macmillan. http://public.eblib.com/choice/publicfullrecord.aspx?p=912232.

Ruggie, John. 1983. "International Regimes, Transactions and Change." In *International Regimes*, edited by Stephen Krasner. Ithaca, NY: Cornell University Press.

"Russia Says South Stream Project Is Over." 2014. *EurActiv.com*. December 2.

Schweller, Randall. 1999. "Realism and the Present Great Power System." In *Unipolar Politics: Realism and State Strategies after the Cold War*, edited by Ethan B Kapstein and Michael Mastanduno. New York: Columbia University Press.

Shadrina, Elena. 2010. "Russia's Foreign Energy Policy, Norms, Ideas, and Driving Dynamics." *PEI Electronic Publications*. Turku, Finland: Turku School of Economics.

Shaffer, Brenda. 2009. *Energy Politics*. Philadelphia, PA: University of Pennsylvania Press.

Smith, Keith C. 2004. *Russian Energy Politics in the Baltics, Poland, and Ukraine: A New Stealth Imperialism?* Washington, DC: CSIS.

Smith, Keith C. 2008. *Russia and European Energy Security: Divide and Dominate*. Washington, DC: CSIS.

Snegovaya, Maria. 2015. "Think of Russia as an Ordinary Petrostate, Not an Extraordinary Superpower." *Washington Post*.

Snyder, Jack. 1990. "Averting Anarchy in the New Europe." *International Security* 14(4): 5–41.

Socor, Vladimir. 2015. "Nord Stream Expansion Agreed, Wintershall Swapped to *Gazprom* (Part One)." *The Jamestown Foundation*. September 10.

Stent, Angela. 2008. "An Energy Superpower? Russia and Europe." In *The Global Politics of Energy*, edited by Kurt Campbell et al. Washington, DC: Aspen Institute.

Stern, Jonathan, Simon Pirani, and Katja Yafimava. 2015. "Does the Cancellation of South Stream Signal a Fundamental Reorientation of Russian Gas Export Policy?" Oxford, UK: Oxford Institute for Energy Studies. www.oxfordenergy.org/publications/the-russo-ukrainian-gas-dispute-of-january-2009-a-comprehensive-assessment/.

Stern, Jonathan. 2005. *The Future of Russian Gas and Gazprom*. Oxford, UK: Oxford University Press.

Stern, Jonathan. 2006a. "Is Russia a Threat to Energy Supplies?" *Oxford Energy Forum* 2006: 4–10.

Stern, Jonathan. 2006b. "The Russian-Ukrainian Gas Crisis of January 2006." Oxford, UK: Oxford Institute for Energy Studies.

Stern, Jonathan. 2009. *Future Gas Production in Russia: Is the Concern about Lack of Investment Justified?* Oxford, UK: Oxford Institute for Energy Studies.

Stern, Jonathan, Simon Pirani, and Katja Yafimava. 2009. *The Russo-Ukrainian Gas Dispute of January 2009.* Oxford, UK: Oxford Institute for Energy Studies.

Stern, Jonathan, and Howard Rogers. 2014. "The Dynamics of a Liberalised European Gas Market." Oxford, UK: Oxford Institute for Energy Studies.

Stulberg, Adam N. 2007. *Well-Oiled Diplomacy: Strategic Manipulation and Russia's Energy Statecraft in Eurasia.* Albany, NY: State University of New York Press.

Stulberg, Adam N. 2012. "Strategic Bargaining and Pipeline Politics: Confronting the Credible Commitment Problem in Eurasian Energy Transit." *Review of International Political Economy* 19(5): 808–36.

Stulberg, Adam N. 2015. "Out of Gas?: Russia, Ukraine, Europe, and the Changing Geopolitics of Natural Gas." *Problems of Post-Communism* 62(2): 112–30.

SVOP. 2000. "Strategy for Russia: Agenda for the President, -2000." Vagrius: Moscow.

Tomberg, Igor. 2007. "Two Aspects of Russian-German Asset Swap Agreements." *RIA Novosti*, December 20.

Tsygankov, Andrei P. 2005. "Vladimir Putin's Vision of Russia as a Normal Great Power." *Post-Soviet Affairs* 21(2): 132–58.

Tsygankov, Andrei P. 2006. "If Not by Tanks, Then by Banks? The Role of Soft Power in Putin's Foreign Policy." *Europe-Asia Studies* 58(7): 1079–99.

Tsygankov, Andrei P. 2013. *Russia's Foreign Policy: Change and Continuity in National Identity.* London: Rowman & Littlefield.

Umbach, Frank. 2010. "Global Energy Security and the Implications for the EU." *Energy Policy* 38(3): 1229.

Vavilov, Andrei and Trofimov, Georgy. 2016a. "A Phantom Energy Empire." In *Gazprom: An Energy Giant and Its Challenges in Europe*, edited by A Vavilov and D Nicholls. Springer.

Vavilov, Andrei and Trofimov, Georgy. 2016b. "The Struggle for Pipelines." In *Gazprom: An Energy Giant and Its Challenges in Europe*, edited by A. Vavilov and D. Nicholls. New York: Springer.

Viner, Jacob. 1948. "Power Versus Plenty as Objectives of Foreign Policy in the Seventeenth and Eighteenth Centuries." *World Politics* 1(1): 1–29.

Wæver, Ole. 1995. "On Security." In *Securitization and Desecuritization*, edited by Ronnie Lipschutz, 46–86. New York: Columbia University Press.

"Who We Are." n.d. Nord Stream *AG*.

Wohlforth, William C. 2003. "Russia's Soft Balancing Act." In *Fragility and Crisis*, edited by Richard J Ellings, Aaron L Friedberg, and Michael Wills. Seattle, WA: National Bureau of Asian Research.

Wohlforth, William C. 2009. "Unipolarity, Status Competition and Great Power War." *World Politics* 61(1): 28–57.

Yenikeyeff, Shamil. 2006. "Is Russia a Threat to Energy Supplies?" *Oxford Energy Forum* 2006: 4–10.

Yergin, Daniel. 1991. *The Prize: The Epic Quest for Oil, Money, and Power.* New York: Simon & Schuster.

"Yuzhno-Russkoye." n.d. *Gazprom.com*.

9
INTELLIGENCE

Mikhail A. Strokan

UNIVERSITY OF PENNSYLVANIA, USA

Brian D. Taylor

SYRACUSE UNIVERSITY, USA

The security services are commonly portrayed as one of the most powerful actors in Russian politics. Many observers believe that president Vladimir Putin's background in the Soviet KGB (State Security Committee) is an important guide to his worldview, and his reliance on the KGB and its successor organizations for many top personnel has further solidified the view that Russian security services are one of the dominant, if not *the* dominant, political actors today. The perceived influence of the security agencies often is linked directly to the powerful role of the KGB in Soviet politics. Indeed, in the absence of Communist Party control, many argue that the security services have increased their influence relative to the Soviet era. Putin's Russia is, in this view, a "KGB state" (Marten, 2017; see also Anderson, 2006; Bateman, 2014).

It is therefore surprising that there has been relatively little detailed scholarly analysis of the role of the security services in Russian foreign policy. Most academic works on Russian foreign policy discuss the security services only in passing, and the most prominent and influential accounts on the topic have been written by journalists, think tank analysts, and independent scholars, rather than university professors. This relative scholarly neglect is noteworthy given the high degree of speculation about the role of Russian security services in the domestic politics of other states in recent years. In particular, accusations of Russian interference in the 2016 US presidential election became one of the world's biggest stories, and similar claims were made about Russian meddling in multiple European states (e.g., Galeotti, 2017c). Although the role of the security services in Russian foreign policy is big news, as a scholarly matter it is a marginal concern.

This chapter reviews the state of the English-language literature on Russian security services and foreign policy. Although we know quite a bit about certain aspects of the foreign policy actions of the security services, we still lack a coherent, generalizable framework for thinking about the topic. Future scholarship on the topic would be helped by more systematic comparison to the role of intelligence agencies in the foreign policy process in other countries, and greater integration into general approaches to the study of Russian foreign policy. Explicit statements of underlying assumptions, and clear criteria for assessments of influence and performance (successes and failures), would help advance the accumulation of knowledge. It also would help clarify how useful it is to think of Putin's Russia as a KGB state, a contentious issue in the literature on Russian domestic politics but a relatively underdeveloped debate in writings on Russian foreign policy.

There are several obvious reasons why academic research on the Russian security services and their role in foreign policy remains a niche concern. First, there is the conventional rule of thumb that one should not go looking for the secret services if you don't want them to come looking for you. Second, data on secret activities are, by definition, hard to come by, and even harder to verify using multiple sources. Unlike in the parable of the drunk searching for his keys not where he lost them, but under the streetlight because it's easier to see, studying the security services basically requires that one go looking for information in dark and poorly lit locations. Third, the study of intelligence more generally is often atheoretical and not comparative. Finally, to the extent that we have detailed scholarly work on the role of the security services in authoritarian countries, the focus is usually on their domestic role in protecting the regime, rather than on their international and foreign policy role.

The chapter proceeds as follows. First, we note some of the central themes in the general literature on intelligence and security services as it relates to foreign policy. Second, we examine the role of the KGB in Soviet foreign policy. Third, we describe the organization of Russia's security services and provide some background on the literature on their domestic influence. Fourth, and centrally, we analyze the Russian security services as a foreign policy guide and tool. We discuss their mandate and role, and their activities as it relates to analysis and operations. The final section summarizes our key points, and suggests some future directions for the academic study of the foreign policy role of Russia's security services.

The study of intelligence and the security services

State security services are studied in one of two basic ways, either as externally oriented organizations that contribute to the formulation and implementation of foreign and security policy, or as internally oriented bureaucracies that play a role in protecting the state against internal threats, such as espionage or terrorism or, in authoritarian regimes, any potential threat to the ruling authorities. This division of labor reflects the organization of political science as a discipline, in which international relations and comparative politics are treated as separate fields. International relations work on security services is usually thought of as the study of "intelligence." Intelligence as a field of study can refer to certain kinds of information (especially secret), to a set of missions (collecting and analyzing information, counter-intelligence, covert action), to a process (the "intelligence cycle"), or to specific organizations (Johnson, 2007: 1–5). Intelligence research focuses on organizations like the United States Central Intelligence Agency (CIA), MI-6 in the United Kingdom, and the Russian Foreign Intelligence Service (*Sluzhba Vneshney Razvedki*, or SVR). When security services are studied as internally oriented bodies, the focus is rarely described as "intelligence"; rather, the topic is regime or state security, or law enforcement. Typical examples include the US Federal Bureau of Investigation (FBI), Britain's MI-5, and the Russian Federal Security Service (*Federal'naya Sluzhba Bezopasnosti*, or FSB). Experts on comparative politics are interested in topics like state power, coercion, surveillance, and repression.

Multiple experts have noted that the study of intelligence is poorly integrated into mainstream international relations research. Indeed, the British historian Christopher Andrew (2004: 170) observes that intelligence "is all but absent in most contemporary international relations theory." Further, comparative foreign policy studies often ignore the way in which intelligence agencies are not just information sources for policy-makers, but also potential tools for executing policy in the form of covert action (Scott and Jackson, 2004: 141–142).

Much work on intelligence is atheoretical and focused on a single country. Studies of the United States and the United Kingdom dominate the literature, and this work is frequently historical or focused primarily on organizational structures and processes. Peter Gill (2007: 86–89) notes that intelligence studies "need to get serious about theoretically informed comparative work." Gill suggests greater attention to levels of analysis issues. Using this approach, work at the individual level would focus on cognition and perception, that at the small group level would examine issues of social psychology and "groupthink," and that at the organizational level would engage with the literature on bureaucratic politics and organizational culture. More broadly, work at the societal level would explore the effects of regime type (democratic, authoritarian, and mixed or "hybrid" regimes), and transitions from one regime type to another, on intelligence. Systematic, comparative studies of intelligence "successes" and "failures" would also be valuable.

Internally focused work on the security services is motivated by a different set of concerns. In democracies, issues of oversight and accountability have been a core topic, given the secret nature of intelligence and security work, and documented cases of past abuse of power, including in established democracies. Research on security services in authoritarian regimes usually examines their role in regime protection and domestic repression. For example, studies of Middle Eastern politics have emphasized the role of the security services in maintaining authoritarianism in so-called Mukhabarat (intelligence) states (Kamrava, 2000; Bellin, 2004). Much work on both Soviet and post-Soviet Russian security services is in a similar vein, analyzing the internal repression role of these agencies and evaluating their influence in domestic politics (for a survey, see Renz, 2012).

This chapter, consistent with the theme of the volume, focuses primarily on the international roles of the Russian intelligence and security services. For the most part the literature on this topic is not connected to broader debates in international relations theory and does not employ a comparative framework or make explicit assessments of similarities and differences to other countries. One reason for this may be because Russia generally lacks a scholarly community in the social sciences that studies intelligence. Further, existing research tends to focus more on outputs than organizational dynamics, given the paucity of information about internal practices. To put it differently, the primary concern is about missions and activities, rather than the intelligence cycle as an analytical and decision-making process.

The KGB and Soviet foreign policy[1]

The collapse of the Soviet Union represented both a challenge and an opportunity for the study of Russian security services and foreign policy. It was a challenge because the KGB as an organization was dismantled and broken into multiple parts (outlined in the next section). Further, the broader context in which Russian security services operated changed fundamentally: communism as an economic system, single-party rule as a political system, and the Soviet Union itself ceased to exist. The Russian economy and the polity became relatively more open, and the country more connected to the outside world. Thus, it became unclear how much of what we thought we knew about Soviet intelligence was still relevant.

The opportunity is that the collapse of the Soviet Union and the KGB generated a great deal of new information about the Soviet secret services and their role in foreign policy. Some of this information came through the opening of archives in various post-communist states, some from memoirs by former spies and political figures or interviews with these individuals, and some from documents and notes smuggled out of the Soviet Union or Russia by former KGB officials, most notably a former KGB archivist, Vasili Mitrokhin. This material can provide a baseline of knowledge about the role of the security services in Soviet foreign policy, and thus help scholars assess the degree of continuity between the Soviet and post-Soviet period.

We emphasize four general conclusions from recent research on Soviet intelligence. First, intelligence analysis – arguably the most important part of what these agencies did – largely failed at its primary task: provide an accurate picture of what your enemies are up to. Instead, analysis was shaped to meet the preconceptions of Soviet leaders. One officer noted that the guiding principle was, "Blame everything on the Americans, and everything will be OK" (Andrew and Mitrokhin, 1999: 214; see also Andrew and Mitrokhin, 2005: 21, 488). Raymond Garthoff (2015: 99) notes that the Soviet intelligence services gathered a lot of useful information, but that they were weaker at political analysis. He concludes, "Intelligence did not contribute to understanding the adversary." Rather, Soviet leaders encouraged this tendency to distort intelligence analysis by signaling that they were pleased with reports that fit their ideological preconceptions (Andrew and Gordievsky, 1990: 583–605; Garthoff, 2015: 61–63, 97). On the other hand, Soviet intelligence agencies were generally more successful in the scientific and technical sphere than in political analysis, because information about science and technology "was not distorted by the dictates of political correctness" (Andrew, 2000: 56). The KGB and the main military intelligence directorate (*Glavnoye Razvedyvatel'noye Upravleniye*, or GRU) were able to penetrate vital industries in the West, such as defense, space, and computing (Andrew and Gordievsky, 1990: 621–623; Andrew and Mitrokhin, 1999: 131, 186–188, 215–222).

Second, major shifts in Soviet foreign policy were driven by leadership turnover, not changing perceptions of the outside world due to intelligence work. The views of the top Soviet leaders were generally independent of the work of Soviet intelligence services. Most centrally, perhaps, the dramatic shift in Soviet foreign policy heralded by Gorbachev's New Thinking was not at all due to input from the KGB. Gorbachev, in fact, ordered the KGB in 1985 to stop distorting intelligence to fit ideological preconceptions (Andrew and Mitrokhin, 1999: 214–215, 555; Garthoff, 2015: 82–83, 99).

Third, the success of so-called "active measures" – "overt and covert actions to exercise influence in foreign countries" (Scott, 2004: 323) – is difficult to judge, because the KGB tended to take credit for positive political developments overseas, even if they played little actual role in bringing them about. For example, a KGB spy in Norway boasted that he had prevented the Nobel Peace Prize committee from awarding the 1978 prize to Soviet dissident Yuriy Orlov, phoning a top member of the Politburo in the middle of the night to pass on the good news (Andrew and Mitrokhin, 1999: 329–330). The Nobel that year went to Anwar Sadat and Menachem Begin for the Egyptian-Israeli peace deal, hardly a surprising choice. In general, it appears active measures were more successful in the developing world than in the West, primarily because tales of malign US and CIA influence were perceived as more credible by both masses and elites in the developing world, in part because the United States did often interfere in the internal affairs of other states (Andrew and Gordievsky, 1990: 587, 630–632; Andrew and Mitrokhin, 1999: 19, 428; 2005: 14–15, 32, 267, 483).

Fourth, bureaucratic competition between the KGB and the GRU was a common feature of Soviet foreign intelligence work. In foreign embassies, both the KGB and the GRU would have representatives, and they would send their reports back through their own channels, while diplomatic traffic traveled on a third channel back to the Ministry of Foreign Affairs (Kozyrev, 2017). In general, the GRU and the KGB did not collaborate in the collection or analysis of intelligence. For example, they had separate responsibilities for the type of signals intelligence (SIGINT) that they would collect, rather than pooling their results. If their responsibilities overlapped, for example in the area of preparations for wartime sabotage, they would clash (Andrew and Mitrokhin, 1999: 213, 337, 361).

General findings about the work of Soviet intelligence – about relative successes and failures depending on the topic and region, about the politicization of intelligence, about bureaucratic conflict between services, and so on – could serve as the basis for both cross-national and cross-temporal comparison. Certain kinds of temporal analysis, such as work on path dependency and historical legacies (see, for example, Beissinger and Kotkin, 2014; Taylor, 2014), would provide a broader theoretical framework for analyzing the work of Russian security services and its influence on foreign policy.

The security services in post-Soviet Russia

Both the KGB and the Soviet Union ceased to exist in December 1991. After the failed August 1991 hardliner coup against Gorbachev, led by KGB head Vladimir Kryuchkov, both Gorbachev and Russian President Boris Yeltsin independently supported plans to break the KGB into multiple parts. Most consequentially for this chapter, the First Chief Directorate, responsible for foreign intelligence, was separated from the domestic parts of the KGB and renamed the Foreign Intelligence Service (SVR). This separation between foreign and domestic intelligence already had some standing in the KGB, especially because the First Chief Directorate moved its headquarters from the main KGB building at Lubyanka in the center of Moscow to the suburbs in the 1970s (Albats, 1994: 294–359; Knight, 1996: 29–61; Soldatov and Borogan, 2010: 12–14).

The main domestic secret service, after several reorganizations and name changes, became the FSB. The FSB took over domestic and military counterintelligence, counterterrorism, internal surveillance, economic crimes, and other domestic security missions. Although in theory the separation between the SVR and the FSB, the foreign and domestic, is clear, in practice it is not so straightforward. This is true especially because the FSB does not limit its activity to Russia. At first FSB activities outside Russia were primarily confined to other post-Soviet states. The SVR, as part of its coordination with KGB successor organizations in the so-called "near abroad," had agreed not to spy on these countries (and vice-versa), a position reaffirmed in 2016 by current SVR Director Sergey Naryshkin (2016). The FSB had made no such promise, so a directorate was created to manage FSB activity in the post-Soviet space. Over time the FSB expanded its work to other external states (Soldatov and Borogan, 2010: 209–212).

The other Russian security service involved in foreign policy is the GRU, which is the military intelligence component of the Ministry of Defense. There are also a range of other security and law enforcement agencies that have primarily an internal focus, such as the Ministry of Internal Affairs (MVD, responsible for the police), the Federal Guards Service (FSO, responsible for leadership security and domestic analysis), and the National Guard (Rosgvardiya), created in 2016 with the formal role of fighting terrorism and organized crime. Some of these agencies have responsibilities that straddle the domestic/foreign divide, such as the MVD's migration role and the counter-terrorism role of the National Guard, a responsibility shared with the FSB.

The internal functions of Russia's "power ministries," such as the FSB and the MVD, have received relatively more scholarly attention than the external and foreign policy roles of Russia's security services. This is particularly true because of Putin's secret service background, and the widespread perception that the Russian government is dominated by *siloviki*, the Russian term for those officials with backgrounds in security, military, and law-enforcement bodies, and particularly *chekisty*, those with a background in the security services. This literature is primarily about domestic politics, touching on topics such as state building, the nature of the political regime, and the importance of informal politics (Kryshtanovskaya and White, 2003, 2009; Anderson, 2006; Renz, 2006, 2012; Rivera and Rivera, 2006, 2014, 2017; Soldatov and Borogan, 2010, 2015; Taylor, 2011, 2014, 2017; Bateman, 2014; Soldatov and Rochlitz, 2018; Marten, 2017).

This internally focused scholarship on the Russian power ministries and the *siloviki*, especially the FSB, tends not to deal with foreign intelligence and foreign policy. The one obvious way this literature intersects with the standard literature on intelligence services is on the issue of oversight and accountability of the security services. The weakness of democratic control over the Russian security services, and the extremely limited degree to which other branches of government, such as parliament and the courts, can exercise oversight, is a theme that unites writing on the internal and external role of the security services (Kramer, 2002; Tsypkin, 2007). Furthermore, some of this work, particularly research which argues that the security services dominate the state, draws little distinction between operations taken at home to secure the rule of Putin and his team, and those taken abroad. In the rest of our discussion, we focus primarily on the external and foreign elements of the work of Russia's security services, rather than these domestic issues.

The security services as a foreign policy guide and tool

Intelligence agencies serve both as a guide and a tool of foreign policy (Scott and Jackson, 2004). Typically, this distinction is thought of as one between the analytical and operational roles of the secret services. We first discuss the formal mandate and role of Russia's security services, before turning to an enquiry into their analytical and operational roles.

Mandate and role

According to the foundational law on foreign intelligence, the law that regulates Russian security services' actions abroad, the official goals of modern Russian intelligence are "to provide the Russian president, the Federal Assembly, and the government with intelligence information necessary for decision-making," as well as "to provide conditions for the successful realization of Russian Federation policy in the field of security," and "to assist the economic development, scientific and technological progress of the country and military-technological security of the Russian Federation" ("O vneshney razvedke," 1996: s.5). The same law names three institutions responsible for achieving these goals and conducting foreign intelligence: the SVR; "bodies of foreign intelligence of the Ministry of Defense," meaning the GRU; and the FSB.

The law on foreign intelligence is almost solely dedicated to the role and authority of the SVR, which makes it de jure the main foreign intelligence agency of Russia if compared to the GRU and the FSB. When the law was adopted in 1996, the SVR arguably was also the de facto most powerful security service of Russia, a direct descendent of the prestigious and elite KGB First Chief Directorate. In 1994 Yeltsin gave a speech at SVR headquarters in which he stressed its central role in foreign policy and in providing for Russia's security (Donaldson and Nogee, 2005: 167). Then-SVR Director Yevgeniy Primakov took the agency somewhat out of the shadows by promoting SVR analytic reports on important foreign policy issues. His conservative line trumped pro-Western politicians of the early Yeltsin era and promoted a more powerful role for *chekisty* in foreign policy (Kozyrev, 2017).

The SVR is responsible for gathering intelligence information in "political, economic, military-strategic, scientific-technological and ecological spheres" ("O vneshney razvedke," 1996) using different types of secret communications, SIGINT, human intelligence (HUMINT), and other methods of gathering information outside of Russia. Anderson (2007) maintains that HUMINT has grown in importance since the Soviet collapse due to a degradation of more technical means. In this regard it is worth noting that, although some KGB documents were declassified (archives), KGB spy networks all across the globe were never revealed (Waller, 1994: 143), and the security services maintained their personnel in foreign embassies of the new Russia (Kozyrev, 2017). It is important to note that the SVR inherited only a small part of

SIGINT capabilities, those that the Soviet Union possessed abroad. Most of the SIGINT capacity was located within Russian borders, and apparently after 2003 the bulk of KGB capability in this realm was transferred to the FSB (Khinsteyn, 2003; Galeotti, 2010: 124; Soldatov and Borogan, 2010: 20), although some experts believe the GRU acquired significant pieces of it as well (Galeotti, 2017b; Golts, 2017).

The FSB, as noted earlier, is primarily a domestically oriented body. On the other hand, it also has foreign policy responsibilities and the authority to conduct foreign intelligence, and it seemingly has expanded its international work under Putin (Soldatov and Borogan, 2010: 209–212). Thus, it has both HUMINT and SIGINT capabilities, and undertakes both analytical and operational missions related to foreign policy.

In contrast with the FSB and the SVR, the GRU has preserved its name and, in many respects, its structure since Soviet times. It is important to stress that the GRU is not an independent security service or agency – it is an integral part of the Ministry of Defense. GRU goals presented on the official website (Ministry of Defense of the Russian Federation, n.d.) almost entirely replicate those mentioned for the SVR in the law on foreign intelligence. According to Russian security expert Aleksandr Golts (2017), the GRU is the largest entity among intelligence agencies because it has its personnel in almost all military bases across Russia and in almost all Russian embassies across the globe, so HUMINT is a key part of its work. The GRU also plays a pivotal role in technological intelligence (TECHINT), involving both imaging intelligence (IMINT) and SIGINT. The GRU is responsible for spy satellites (Hendrickx, 2005).

Regardless of the fact that the GRU, the FSB, and the SVR all have the authority to conduct operations abroad, each has its own typical – at least as it is understood by researchers and experts – functions and spheres of responsibility. The GRU is mostly interested in military and technological developments of foreign nations and their military plans, while the SVR and the FSB are focused on political and economic issues. Moreover, the focus of the SVR is usually on larger strategic issues in countries other than former USSR republics, while the FSB is considered to be working with rather tactical developments in political and economic life, with special attention to on the so-called "near abroad." However, this does not mean that if the SVR, for example, recruits a foreign military officer, they will "pass" this source to the GRU. Competition between agencies is considerable, and it forces them to transcend their "typical" spheres of responsibility, thereby blurring them. Thus, the GRU might gather political and economic reports, while the FSB might work far from the near abroad gathering military secrets, just because it can (Golts, 2017).

The heads of both the FSB and the SVR report directly to the Russian president. At least in theory the chain of command for the GRU runs from the president to the Minister of Defense to the Chief of the General Staff to the head of the GRU. Some observers contend that the head of the GRU can also report directly to the president in some circumstances (Galeotti, 2016b: 2; Tsypkin, 2007: 277). Experts agree that the president is the dominant actor controlling the foreign intelligence services, with little role for parliamentary or public oversight (Knight, 1996: 120; Kramer, 2002; Tsypkin, 2007). Further, the Law on State Secrets makes it easy for the intelligence agencies to impede investigations through their broad powers of classification (Soldatov and Rochlitz, 2018: 87). This lack of civilian and societal control beyond the president makes it difficult for researchers interested in studying intelligence failures, particularly on a comparative basis, since mistakes are easier to conceal from outsiders than in more open political systems.

Information and analysis

Informing the leadership about foreign affairs is a key role of the secret services, and therefore information and analysis are core themes in discussions of the security and intelligence services' influence on Russian foreign policy. Crucial research questions include the process by which the political leadership receives intelligence reports, the weight of this information in decision-making, and the quality of these reports. For example, there does not seem to be an organized process for bringing together reports from divergent agencies that may conflict with each other, at least within the intelligence community. It seems that is left up to the president and the Security Council to sort through this information. Tsypkin (2007: 277) observes that Russia lacks a system for creating any type of "collective judgment" of the different agencies, like there is with the US system of creating "national intelligence estimates." Rather, each service reports separately and directly.

Competition among different agencies for the president's ear seems to be a frequent aspect of intelligence analysis. The SVR appeared to take a lead role in the 1990s, including with a series of public reports on such key issues as nuclear proliferation, NATO expansion and its effect on Russian security, and the struggle for political and economic influence in the former Soviet space between Russia and Western powers. Tsypkin (2007: 278) argues that these reports largely restated the Russian government position on these issues, whereas others see the public nature of these reports – in sharp contrast to past KGB practice – as a reflection of a battle between traditionalist and pro-Western forces inside the Russian government (Knight, 1996: 131; Donaldson and Nogee, 2005: 167; Kozyrev, 2017).

Under Putin, most analysts maintain that the FSB has significant influence in terms of providing information and analysis. Soldatov and Rochlitz (2018: 102) contend that, in the absence of Communist Party oversight, the analytical and forecasting department of the FSB has an even more dominant role than the KGB had in the Soviet period. The FSB, they state, "enjoys a near monopoly with respect to the provision of intelligence to the Kremlin." Further, in their view the FSB director himself has an enormous role in controlling the flow of information to President Putin. Golts (2017) agrees with this analysis about the dominant role of the FSB in providing analysis and information to the president, and goes somewhat further, suggesting that Putin and other top decision-makers are not interested in open source information, relying solely on classified information received from security and intelligence agencies.

Scholars have argued that KGB analysis provided to the Soviet leadership was politicized and ideological, designed to reinforce rather than challenge the prevailing worldview. What about in post-Soviet Russia? Most experts argue that the security services share and reinforce the anti-Western and illiberal views of Putin and his close associates who share KGB backgrounds, such as Security Council Secretary Nikolay Patrushev. For example, Mark Galeotti (2017c), probably the most prolific Western expert on Russia's security services, argues that the FSB became the dominant source for the Kremlin by tailoring its reports to Putin's pre-existing worldview. He quotes a former SVR officer claiming that "our mistake was to keep talking about the world as it is, not as he would like it to be." Further, he claims that the SVR and the GRU have now learned "to flatter Putin's prejudices and assumptions." Soldatov and Rochlitz (2018: 100) claim that the FSB "utterly failed" to predict the events that brought about the 2014 Ukrainian "Euro-Maidan" revolution because they were focused solely on the elites and ignored mass sentiments. This failure led the FSB to blame the West for the Ukrainian crisis. More generally, Skak (2016) concludes that Russian strategic culture is heavily influenced by *chekisty*, who blame foreign intelligence services like the CIA for fomenting "colored revolutions" in the post-Soviet space, with Russia as an ultimate target.

This description of the dominant worldview among the political leadership and the security services is echoed by others. Taylor (2017: 54), for example, notes, "It is generally believed that *siloviki* tend to be statist and illiberal, favoring a hard line at home and a confrontational foreign policy abroad." One organizational embodiment of this worldview is the Russian Institute for

Strategic Studies (RISI), a state-sponsored think tank linked to the SVR that claims to provide analysis for the president and the Security Council. Leonid Reshetnikov, a retired SVR general who was the director of RISI until early 2017, gave several public interviews in which he articulated hardline views, claiming that the United States was behind the 2014 revolution in Ukraine because it sought to make Ukraine a base for deploying missile defense and nuclear weapons, and that the ultimate goal of US policy is to overthrow Putin and dismember Russia (Panyukov, 2015). Some observers, however, suggest that it is a mistake to attribute too much influence to RISI, which adopted far-right views that were too extreme to influence Russian foreign policy (Bershidsky, 2017).

Tsypkin (2007: 278–279) cautions that it is hard to evaluate the quality of security service analysis because almost all of their work is classified and thus not accessible. He states, "It is difficult to judge whether external intelligence agencies report to the political leadership as objectively as they can, or provide intelligence-to-please, or twist intelligence reports to serve their institutional interests, or all of the above." This is one of the challenges of conducting research on topics and agencies that are deliberately kept in the dark. Both the process of providing analysis, and the quality of information, therefore, remain opaque, making it hard to provide a detailed accounting of intelligence success and failures.

Foreign operations

Russian security services do not only provide the government with information for decision-making, they also execute operations abroad in order to assist in achieving foreign – and sometimes domestic – policy objectives (Galeotti, 2016b: 5). In recent years the use of "active measures" to influence politics in other states has received considerable attention, but Russia's security services perform other foreign policy operations, including counter-terrorism and support for military operations. The secret nature of these foreign operations often makes it difficult to judge how large a tool they are in the overall foreign policy toolkit, compared to more open activities such as diplomacy, the overt use of military force, arms sales and transfers, and trade.

One area in which relatively more information is available is counter-terrorism. The FSB plays a central role in domestic counter-terrorism analysis and operations, including as a law-enforcement body with core responsibilities in this area. The head of the FSB is also the chair of the National Antiterrorism Committee. Terrorism, of course, is an issue that blurs the divide between domestic and foreign policies, since people and ideas can cross state borders to carry out or inspire terrorist attacks. The Chechen Wars, and the broader problem of North Caucasus extremism, have been central to the development of counter-terrorism capabilities by the Russian security services (Pokalova, 2015).

Involvement in counter-terrorism operations at home led the FSB to extend its "counteroffensive beyond national boundaries," including the use of "extrajudicial assassinations of terrorists abroad" (Soldatov and Borogan, 2010: 193). Soldatov and Borogan (2010: 193–238) provided a detailed account of multiple assassinations outside the country linked to Russian security services, including the killing of the Chechen warlord Zelimkhan Yandarbiyev in Qatar in 2004. Legislation to authorize assassinations by the security services abroad was initially absent, but was passed by the parliament in 2010.

Counter-terrorism cooperation is one component of Russian foreign policy. Russia is often represented in international fora by former or acting security officers. Both the Commonwealth of Independent States (CIS) and the Shanghai Cooperation Organization (SCO) have anti-terrorism centers in which the FSB plays a prominent role. According to Soldatov and Borogan (2010: 221), the Regional Antiterrorist Structure of the SCO "began carrying out abductions across national boundaries and outside standard judicial procedures, much like the infamous CIA practice of extraordinary rendition."

Perhaps the most controversial and spectacular assassination linked to the Russian security services was the murder of former FSB officer Aleksandr Litvinenko with the radioactive substance polonium in London in 2006. The official British inquiry (Owen, 2016) concluded that it was a "strong probability" that the operation was conducted by the FSB, and that it was "probably" approved by Putin himself. The Russian government has strenuously denied any involvement in this assassination, and other ones as well.

The spectrum of foreign operations abroad was never limited to counter-terrorism and extrajudicial assassinations and abductions. Recently, the use of so-called "active measures" by the Russian security services has become a matter of not only journalistic attention but even hearings in the US Congress (Osnos et al., 2017; *Disinformation*, 2017). In this context the focus has been on computer hacking and propaganda. Allegations of Russian security service involvement apply primarily to the GRU and the FSB, who are said to be responsible for a series of cyber attacks against not targets in the United States and elsewhere.[2] Experts suggest the use of active measures has increased in recent years (Soldatov and Rochlitz, 2018: 106 and Galeotti argues that even international criminal networks – RBOC (Russian Based Organized Crime) – are partially under the control of Russian intelligence and should be considered part of the toolkit (Galeotti, 2017a).

This recent attention to Russian active measures and the role of the security services as a tool of foreign policy suggest the need for greater research on this issue. With respect to scholarship about the influence of the security services on Russian domestic politics, there is a lively debate about whether Putin's Russia is a "neo-KGB state," or whether this characterization is overblown. At the level of Russian foreign policy, however, there seem to be few scholars questioning the general perception that the security services are one of Putin's most important and capable foreign policy tools, although former insiders (Kozyrev, 2017) caution that their role should not be overstated.

For scholars some of the most interesting questions about active measures are the comparative ones: how do current Russian active measures compare to past-Soviet operations, to similar covert activities undertaken by other countries, and to other possible tools in the Kremlin foreign policy toolkit? Mark Kramer (2017) argues that recent Russian active measures are very similar to those used by the KGB and the GRU during the Cold War. Both in terms of the overarching goal of undermining the Western liberal democratic order, and the means (albeit adapted to the cyber age), Kramer sees strong continuity between Soviet and Russian foreign policy. This straight-line connection between the Soviet past and the Russian present is commonplace in analysis of the Russian security services (Knight, 2000; Tsypkin, 2007; Bateman, 2016; Marten, 2017). In partial contrast, some specialists (Taylor, 2011; Galeotti, 2016b) stress both the proliferation of competing security services and the rise of commercial and corrupt motives for security service activity, which mark important differences from the Soviet past.

What about comparisons to other states? Galeotti (2017b) contends that comparisons to Western agencies like the CIA and MI-6 are misleading, in particular because Russian security services "are on a wartime footing . . . in terms of their missions, interactions, and mindsets." Galeotti does not specify when this shift to a wartime footing took place, although from context it is clear he means at some point under Putin. He claims that this stance has led Russian security services to be much more risk-taking than their Western counterparts, and the feeling of being under direct threat from the West leads to an "unprecedentedly high tempo and visibility of Russian active measures." In general, his view is shared by many other analysts, although often only implicitly (Waller, 1994: 9–10; Bateman, 2016: 24). The significant gap in comparative studies is that the comparison is generally limited only to the Western security services.

Finally, in terms of comparison to other tools of foreign policy, this issue is probably the one least likely to be explored, perhaps because experts on Russian foreign policy often ignore the security services, and experts on the security services are often more domestically focused. Still, several analysts have suggested that Russian security services play a relatively large role in foreign policy compared to other tools, because Russia is on a weaker footing vis-à-vis the West in the military and economic realms. In this respect, active measures are treated as a relatively cheap and effective tool, and an area of Russian comparative advantage (Galeotti, 2017b; Rumer, 2017).

One final way in which Russian security services can be used as a tool for foreign policy objectives is as direct participants in military operations. This goes beyond simply the use of military intelligence collected by the GRU to inform the conduct of military operations. Rather, we are interested in the covert use of security service personnel for war-fighting, which could be seen as just another active measure, but probably deserves separate discussion.

The war in Ukraine is most frequently discussed in this respect. Since the beginning of the crisis over Crimea, the term "hybrid warfare" became popular among analysts in the West. This term implies a complex of measures undertaken in various fields, from disinformation to real physical force by the Russian military. An integral part of "hybrid warfare" includes the intelligence and security services operations. Critics of the use of the term have argued, rather convincingly, that a combination of multiple forms of war – conventional, irregular, information, psychological, and so on – is hardly new or unique (Kofman and Rojanksy, 2015; Galeotti, 2016a). Regardless, the term seems to have stuck.

Several detailed studies of Russian operations in Crimea and Eastern Ukraine highlight the important role of security and intelligence services (Mitrokhin, 2015; Kofman et al., 2017). Apparently all three main security services – the FSB, the GRU, and the SVR – had operatives in Ukraine prior to the fall of the Viktor Yanukovych government in 2014, as well as afterwards during the annexation of Crimea and the start of irregular operations in the Donbas (or Donbass) region of southeast Ukraine (Galeotti, 2016b: 4; Golts, 2017; Kofman et al., 2017: 60, 68). Much of the analytical work done so far simply seeks to piece together from multiple journalistic and online sources the best available picture of Russian security service activity in Ukraine, given the covert nature of these actions. Although Russia eventually admitted its direct role in the Crimean events, it has consistently denied military involvement in the separatist war in Donetsk and Lugansk.

A larger task, beyond trying to describe factually what role Russian security services played in Ukraine, is to assess the success or failure of these activities. This is a standard question in intelligence studies, and some preliminary conclusions have been offered. Galeotti (2016b: 14) argues that in both Crimea and Donbas, the Russian intelligence agencies performed extremely well on a tactical level, providing accurate information on Ukrainian military forces' deployments and preparations, down to specific judgments on "the willingness of individual officers to fight." He also credits them with successful political and informational active measures. Kofman et al. (2017: esp. 60, 67–68) suggest that operations in Eastern Ukraine were improvised and incoherent, positing that this may have been due to competition and lack of coordination between the FSB, the GRU, and the SVR. Soldatov and Rochlitz (2018) see the events in Ukraine as a larger strategic failure for the FSB, since the scale of the crisis apparently took them by surprise.

This final point about the role of the Russian security services in terms of policy-making towards Ukraine raises a larger and important question: how much influence do they have over key foreign policy decisions? For example, was the SVR or the FSB asked to provide an assessment of how the United States, the EU, and NATO might respond to the annexation of Crimea and, if so, what did they say? Putin's own testimony ("Krym. Put' na Rodinu," 2015) suggests that it was a small-group decision taken quickly in response to rapidly changing events in Ukraine, one involving only four or five people. According to other accounts (e.g., Bukkvoll 2016: 273–276), this small group was dominated by close Putin associates with backgrounds in the Leningrad KGB, who at the time were head of the FSB, Secretary of the Security Council, and chief of the Presidential Administration. This image of a highly centralized and informal decision-making process in foreign policy is consistent with more general accounts of elite Russian politics (e.g., Kononenko and Moshes, 2011; Ledeneva, 2013). If accurate, this suggests that the influence of security service personnel is more likely individual than institutional, and a product of their closeness to Putin rather than the bureaucratic weight of the agency they lead (Soldatov and Rochlitz, 2018). Another important and related research question is whether the security services, to the extent that they have formal or informal influence over key foreign policy decisions, tend to be more hawkish than other key actors. This hawkish outlook is frequently assumed, and seems consistent with public statements of key chekisty, but it is harder to demonstrate conclusively in crucial episodes, such as Ukraine and Syria.

Conclusion: future scholarship

Researching the role of the security services in Russian foreign policy is extremely difficult. This is true because of the nature of the subject and because of the nature of the Russian political system, both of which make good data hard to come by. These formidable obstacles are compounded by the highly politicized debates surrounding the topic, and the current poor state of relations between Russia and the West.

Despite these difficulties, and academic incentives that further discourage social science research on the topic – the study of intelligence and the security services are relatively marginal concerns that lack well-developed, cross-national theories – a determined group of scholars, analysts, and journalists have created a solid body of literature. As outlined earlier, a considerable amount is known about the main Russian security and intelligence services and their various missions related to foreign policy.

Big gaps, however, still remain in our knowledge. Information about the more technical aspects of foreign intelligence work, sometimes referred to as TECHINT and involving both imaging and signals intelligence, is almost entirely inaccessible. Important questions include how TECHINT is shared (if at all) across various agencies, how it is combined with HUMINT, and, more generally, the "intelligence cycle" of collecting, analyzing, and disseminating intelligence.

The difficulties in researching bureaucratic processes (although see Galeotti 2016b; Soldatov and Rochlitz, 2018; Tsypkin 2007) may help explain why the greatest attention seems to be to activities and operations. Covert operations and active measures also make for more exhilarating reading than studies of organizational procedures and small-group decision-making below the level of the political leadership. One potential pitfall of this focus, however, is that it may create a bias toward the dramatic and rare over the routine, and also garner more attention for apparent successes rather than hidden failures. Scott and Jackson (2004: 159) note that some popular culture treatments of intelligence in the West, such as the *Bourne* movies starring Matt Damon, treat these services as "malign, all-powerful, and all-pervasive." One sometimes gets a similar feeling reading about the Russian intelligence services, particularly writing that stresses the influence of *chekisty* and their hostile and aggressive orientation toward the West.

This is not to suggest that these portrayals of the Russian security services are necessarily wrong. In many respects they are probably correct. Rather, the problem is that the overall impression created by this work could be tendentious and lead to an over-estimation of Russian foreign policy proficiency. In an interview with the online Russian paper *Gazeta.ru*, Galeotti (2016c) suggests that Russia isn't getting its best out of its intelligence services. This is because of competition between services, a basically non-existent inter-agency process, politicization, and a failure to allow alternative data and interpretations to reach the political leadership.

One possible way forward for the study of Russian security services and foreign policy is to bring implicit assumptions about their role and influence into the open, stating them in a more generalizable way that allows for comparison both to the Soviet past and to the role of intelligence in foreign policy in other states. A similar approach could also bring out differences across levels of analysis (individual, small group, organizational, and the state as a whole) and issue areas. Moving in this direction might also help to integrate the study of the security services into more general accounts of Russian foreign policy and international relations.

Notes

1 We thank Whitney Baillie for research assistance for this section.
2 Cyber operations as a component of Russian foreign policy are covered elsewhere in this volume, so they will not be discussed further here.

References

Albats, Y., 1994. *KGB: State within a State*. London: IB Tauris.
Anderson, J., 2006. The Chekist takeover of the Russian state. *International Journal of Intelligence and counterintelligence*, 19(2), pp. 237–288.
Anderson, J., 2007. The HUMINT Offensive from Putin's Chekist State. *International journal of Intelligence and Counterintelligence*, 20(2), pp. 258–316.
Andrew, C., 2000. The Mitrokhin Archive. *The RUSI Journal*, 145(1), pp. 52–56.
Andrew, C., 2004. Intelligence, international relations and'under-theorisation'. *Intelligence & National Security*, 19(2), pp. 170–184.
Andrew, C. and Gordievsky, O., 1990. *KGB: The Inside Story*. London: Hodder & Stoughton.
Andrew, C. and Mitrokhin, V., 1999. *The Mitrokhin Archive: The KGB in Europe and the World*. London: Allen Lane.
Andrew, C. and Mitrokhin, V., 2005. *The World Was Going Our Way: The KGB and the Battle for the Third World*. New York: Basic Books.
Bateman, A., 2014. The political influence of the Russian security services. *The Journal of Slavic Military Studies*, 27(3), pp. 380–403.
Bateman, A., 2016. The KGB and its enduring legacy. *The Journal of Slavic Military Studies*, 29(1), pp. 23–47.
Beissinger, M. and Kotkin, S. eds., 2014. *Historical Legacies of Communism in Russia and Eastern Europe*. Cambridge, UK: Cambridge University Press.
Bellin, E., 2004. The robustness of authoritarianism in the Middle East: Exceptionalism in comparative perspective. *Comparative Politics*, pp. 139–157.
Bershidsky, L., 2017. Another reason to avoid rushing on Russia's election role. *Bloomberg*, April 20, 2017.
Bukkvoll, T., 2016. Why Putin went to war: Ideology, interests and decision-making in the Russian use of force in Crimea and Donbas. *Contemporary Politics*, 22(3), pp. 267–282.
Disinformation: A Primer in Russian Active Measures and Influence Campaigns. 2017. Hearings before the Select Committee on Intelligence, United States Senate, 30 March. www.intelligence.senate.gov/hearings/open-hearing-disinformation-primer-russian-active-measures-and-influence-campaigns, and www.intelligence.senate.gov/hearings/open-hearing-intelligence-matters-1.
Donaldson, R.H. and Nogee, J.L., 2005. *The Foreign Policy of Russia: Changing Systems, Enduring Interests*. New York: M.E. Sharpe.

Galeotti, M., 2010. "Terrorism, crime and the security forces." In Galeotti, M. ed., 2010. *The Politics of Security in Modern Russia*. Farnham, UK: Ashgate, pp. 123–145.

Galeotti, M., 2016a. Hybrid, ambiguous, and non-linear? How new is Russia's 'new way of war'? *Small Wars & Insurgencies*, 27(2), pp. 282–301.

Galeotti, M., 2016b. Putin's hydra: Inside Russia's intelligence services. *European Council on Foreign Relations Policy Brief*.

Galeotti, M., 2016c. "Vlasti Rossii ignoriruyut dannye svoei vneshnei razvedki." *Gazeta.ru*, May 16, 2016.

Galeotti, M., 2017a. Crimintern: How the Kremlin uses Russia's criminal networks in Europe. *European Council on Foreign Relations*, April 18, 2017.

Galeotti, M., 2017b. Russian intelligence is at (political) war. *NATO Review*, 2017. www.ecfr.eu/publications/summary/putins_hydra_inside_russias_intelligence_services.

Galeotti, M., 2017c. The spies who love Putin. *The Atlantic*, January 17, 2017.

Garthoff, R.L., 2015. *Soviet Leaders and Intelligence: Assessing the American Adversary During the Cold War*. Washington, DC: Georgetown University Press.

Gill, P., 2007. "Knowing the self, knowing the other: The comparative analysis of security intelligence." In Johnson, L.K. ed. *Handbook of Intelligence Studies*. London and New York: Routledge, pp. 82–90.

Golts, A. 2017. *Interview with M. Strokan*. 3 March, Washington, DC.

Hendrickx, B., 2005. Snooping on radars: A history of Soviet/Russian global signals intelligence satellites. *Journal of the British Interplanetary Society*, 58(2), pp. 97–133.

Johnson, L.K., 2007, "Introduction." In Johnson, L.K. ed., 2007. *Handbook of Intelligence Studies*. London and New York: Routledge, pp. 1–14.

Kamrava, M., 2000. Military professionalization and civil-military relations in the Middle East. *Political Science Quarterly*, 115(1), pp. 67–92.

Khinsteyn, A., 2003. "FAPSI razdelili na troikh," *Moskovskiy Komsomolets*, 31 March.

Knight, A., 1996. *The KGB's Successors: The Spies Without Cloaks*. Princeton, NJ: Princeton University Press.

Knight, A., 2000. The enduring legacy of the KGB in Russian politics. *Problems of Post-Communism*, 47(4), pp. 3–15.

Kofman, M., Migacheva, K., Nichiporuk, B., Radin, A., Tkacheva, O. and Oberholtzer, J., 2017. *Lessons from Russia's Operations in Crimea and Eastern Ukraine*. Santa Monica, CA: RAND Corporation.

Kofman, M. and Rojansky, M., 2015. A closer look at Russia's "Hybrid War." *Kennan Cable*, 1(7), pp. 1–8.

Kononenko, V. and Moshes, A. eds., 2011. *Russia As a Network State: What Works in Russia When State Institutions Do Not?* Berlin: Springer.

Kozyrev, A. 2017. *Interview with M. Strokan*. 12 April, Washington DC.

Kramer, M., 2002. Oversight of Russia's Intelligence and Security Agencies: The Need and Prospects of Democratic Control. *PONARS Policy Memo*, 281. www.ponarseurasia.org/memo/oversight-russias-intelligence-and-security-agencies-need-and-prospects-democratic-control.

Kramer, M., 2017. The Soviet roots of meddling in US politics. *PONARS* Eurasia Policy Memo, 452. www.ponarseurasia.org/memo/soviet-roots-meddling-us-politics.

"Krym. Put' na Rodinu, "2015. *Online documentary film*. Available from: www.youtube.com/watch?v=t42–71RpRgI. [Accessed 29 May 2017].

Kryshtanovskaya, O.G. and White, S., 2003. Putin's militocracy. *Post-Soviet Affairs*, 19(4), pp. 289–306.

Kryshtanovskaya, O.G. and White, S., 2009. The sovietization of Russian politics. *Post-Soviet Affairs*, 25(4), pp. 283–309.

Ledeneva, A.V., 2013. *Can Russia Modernise? Sistema, Power Networks and Informal Governance*. Cambridge, UK: Cambridge University Press.

Marten, K., 2017. The "KGB state" and Russian political and foreign policy culture. *The Journal of Slavic Military Studies*, 30(2), pp. 131–151.

Ministry of Defense of the Russian Federation. n.d. *Glavnoye Upravleniye General'nogo Shtaba Rossiiskoi Federatsii*. [Online]. [Accessed 29 May 2017]. Available from: http://structure.mil.ru/structure/ministry_of_defence/details.htm?id=9711@egOrganization.

Mitrokhin, N., 2015. Infiltration, instruction, invasion: Russia's war in the Donbass. *Journal of Soviet and Post-Soviet Politics and Society*, 1(1), pp. 219–250.

Naryshkin, S., 2016. Interview. "Sluzhba, kotoroy ne vidno. Eksklyuzivnyy reportazh 'Vestey v subbotu' iz shtab-kvartiry SVR." *Vesti.ru*, 8 October.

O vneshney razvedke 1996. Moskva: Sobranie zakonodatelstva Rossiiskoi Federatsii.

Osnos, E., Remnick, D., and Yaffa, J., 2017. Active measures. *The New Yorker*, 6 March.
Owen, R., 2016. *The Litvinenko Inquiry: Report into the Death of Alexander Litvinenko*. www.litvinenkoinquiry.org/.
Panyukov, M, 2015. "Leonid Reshetnikov: Rusofoby proderzhatsya na Ukraine eshche maksimum 20 let," *Kom'somolskaya Pravda*, 11 October.
Pokalova, E., 2015. *Chechnya's Terrorist Network: The Evolution of Terrorism in Russia's North Caucasus*. Tunbridge Wells, UK: ABC-CLIO.
Renz, B., 2006. Putin's militocracy? An alternative interpretation of Siloviki in contemporary Russian politics. *Europe-Asia Studies*, 58(6), pp. 903–924.
Renz, B., 2012. "The Russian power ministries and security services." In Gill, G. and Young, J. eds. *Routledge Handbook of Russian Politics and Society*. London and New York: Routledge, pp. 209–219.
Rivera, S.W. and Rivera, D.W., 2006. The Russian elite under Putin: Militocratic or bourgeois? *Post-Soviet Affairs*, 22(2), pp. 125–144.
Rivera, D.W. and Rivera, S.W., 2014. Is Russia a militocracy? Conceptual issues and extant findings regarding elite militarization. *Post-Soviet Affairs*, 30(1), pp. 27–50.
Rivera, D.W. and Rivera, S.W., 2017. The militarization of the Russian elite under Putin: What we know, what we think we know (but don't), and what we need to know. *Problems of Post-Communism*, pp. 1–12. Online https://doi.org/10.1080/10758216.2017.1295812.
Rumer, E., 2017. Russian active measures and influence campaigns. Testimony, U.S. Senate Select Committee on Intelligence, March 30, 2017.
Scott, L., 2004. Secret intelligence, covert action and clandestine diplomacy. *Intelligence & National Security*, 19(2), pp. 322–341.
Scott, L. and Jackson, P., 2004. The study of intelligence in theory and practice. *Intelligence & National Security*, 19(2), pp. 139–169.
Skak, M., 2016. Russian strategic culture: The role of today's Chekisty. *Contemporary Politics*, 22(3), pp. 324–341.
Soldatov, A. and Borogan, I., 2010. *The New Nobility: The Restoration of Russia's Security State and the Enduring Legacy of the KGB*. New York: PublicAffairs.
Soldatov, A. and Borogan, I., 2015. *The Red Web: The Struggle Between Russia's Digital Dictators and the New Online Revolutionaries*. New York: PublicAffairs.
Soldatov, A. and Rochlitz, M., 2018. "The Siloviki in Russian politics." In Treisman, D., ed. *The New Autocracy: Information, Politics, and Policy in Putin's Russia*. Washington, DC: Brookings Institution Press.
Taylor, B.D., 2011. *State Building in Putin's Russia: Policing and Coercion after Communism*. Cambridge, UK: Cambridge University Press.
Taylor, B.D., 2014. "From police state to police state? Legacies and law enforcement in Russia." In Beissinger, M. and Kotkin, S. eds., 2014. *Historical Legacies of Communism in Russia and Eastern Europe*. Cambridge, UK: Cambridge University Press, pp. 128–151.
Taylor, B.D., 2017. The Russian Siloviki & political change. *Daedalus*, 146(2), pp. 53–63.
Tsypkin, M., 2007. "Terrorism's threat to new democracies: The case of Russia." In Bruneau, T.C. and Boraz, S.C., 2007. *Reforming Intelligence: Obstacles to Democratic Control and Effectiveness*. Austin, TX: University of Texas Press, pp. 269–300.
Waller, J.M., 1994. *Secret Empire: The KGB in Russia Today*. Boulder, CO: Westview.

10
MILITARY

Valery Konyshev and Alexander Sergunin

ST. PETERSBURG STATE UNIVERSITY, RUSSIA

Introduction

The military's role in Moscow's present-day world policies is a popular theme both in the Russian and international scholarship. However, upon closer examination, this topic, in fact, has not been extensively studied.

The bulk of the literature is, in fact, devoted to the study of civil-military relations in post-Soviet Russia (Herspring, 1996; Chaldymov, 2001; Maslyuk, 2001; Stepanova, 2001; Ulrich, 2002; Taylor, 2003; Betz, 2004; Knoph, 2004; Isakova, 2005: 159–194; Danilova, 2007; Gomart, 2008; Pallin, 2009: 15–48; Renz, 2011) rather than how the military affects Russia's foreign policy making. The second type of works focuses on Russian military reforms and their implications for Moscow's security policies in various regions of the planet (Taylor, 2003; Isakova, 2005: 195–229; Pallin, 2009: 49–63; Barabanov, 2011; Bartles, 2011; Lannon, 2011; McDermott, 2011; McDermott et al., 2011; Makarychev and Sergunin, 2013; Gressel, 2015; Russell, 2015; Golts and Kofman, 2016). A third group of authors has studied the state of affairs of the Russian armed forces and their military capabilities at present and in the foreseeable future (Taylor, 2003; Galeotti, 2010; McDermott et al., 2011; Persson, 2016). Few scholarly works examine the role which the military actually plays in Russia's foreign policy making and implementation (Betz, 2004; Isakova, 2005; Allison et al., 2006: 36–40; Sergunin, 2008, 2016: 167–194; Pallin, 2009: 15–48).

The scholarship on the Russian military can be divided to two groups – Alarmists and Pragmatists. On the Alarmist side there are those arguing that Russia's military is poorly controlled and aggressive. Here, there are also those who believe that Putin is dependent on the military and exploits their instincts for diversionary politics and regime stability (Betz, 2004: 151–156; Knoph, 2004; Isakova, 2005: 159–194; Pallin, 2009: 15–48; Renz, 2011; Golts and Kofman, 2016: 13–19). For instance, for them, Russia's Ukrainian and Syrian policies are both predicated on Putin's survival tactics (Marten, 2015). On the Pragmatist side, the authors argue that Russia remains largely defensive and, while not being a Western-style democracy, is controlled by civilian authorities (Allison et al., 2006: 36–40; Gomart, 2008: 6–10). In a certain sense, Putin has continued Russia's historical tradition: the absence of successful military coups implies that Tsars were firmly in charge in the army, not the other way around (Taylor, 2003).

This study aims to argue that civilian control was largely established following the post-Cold War years although civil-military relations in Russia are still not fully in line with Western democratic standards and remain an object of criticism from the foreign policy-making and expert communities. One more point is that the military's role in Russian foreign policy is quite limited; the use of military force is seen as a last resort, when other – non-military – means are exhausted, and it is done in a rather limited/selective way.

Along with the general research objective (which role does the military play in Moscow's foreign policy?), there are several specific purposes of this study:

- How can the military (hard power) instruments be compared to other – soft power – tools (diplomacy, energy, city-twinning, compatriots, NGOs, research, educational and cultural cooperation, etc.) in terms of achieving Moscow's international policy objectives?
- How has the role of the Russian military in international affairs evolved since the end of the Cold War? Has it become more or less successful across time and relative to some other key political actors?
- What future questions and themes of the military in Russia's foreign policy are likely to arise?

Threat perceptions, doctrines

In the 1990s, there were certain discrepancies between foreign policy and military doctrines with regard to threat perceptions and the use of military force. For example, the Russian foreign policy concept of 1993 ('Kontseptsiya vneshney politiki', 1993) did not see any serious threats to Russia's security except those coming from the developing world. The document emphasized Russia's commitment to political and diplomatic methods and negotiation rather than to the use of military force, the admissibility of the limited use of force in strict accordance with international law to ensure national and international security and stability. In general, the document can be characterized as liberal and pro-Western in its spirit. In contrast, the Russian military doctrine of 1993 described systematically and at length both external and internal sources of military threats to the country (Yeltsin, 1994). Still, the document represented a radical departure from Soviet strategic thinking. The new doctrine did not identify the United States and NATO as primary sources of military danger. Rather, it warned against provoking a new confrontation by violating the strategic balance, i.e. military build-up in the regions adjacent to Russia and NATO expansion. The proliferation of weapons of mass destruction (WMD) and international terrorism were given a rather important status. This brought Russia closer to leading Western countries, which also consider these phenomena to be the most dangerous international developments.

The new reading of military threats has led to new approaches to military strategy, as well as to an appropriate organization and training of the armed forces. The document called for a re-targeting of the Russian armed forces from large-scale war to low intensity conflicts. The main aim of the use of the armed forces and other services in armed conflicts and local wars, the doctrine said, was "to localize the seat of tensions and stop hostilities at the earliest possible stage, in the interests of creating conditions for a peaceful settlement of the conflict on conditions suiting the interests of the Russian Federation" (Yeltsin, 1994: 9).

The doctrine, however, did not exclude the possibility of large-scale war. It mentioned that under certain conditions, armed conflicts and local wars can develop into an all-out war. According to the document, the priority was to develop the armed forces and other services designed to deter aggression, as well as mobile elements, which can be quickly delivered and deployed in the required area and can carry out mobile operations in any region where the security of Russia might be threatened. Military operations should be carried out by peacetime groups of forces (those which organized for peace-time conditions, i.e. have incomplete personnel and arsenals; in the war-time period they are reorganized to be fully fledged military units), deployed in the conflict area. In case of need, they might be strengthened by a partial deployment and re-deployment of forces from other regions.

Furthermore, the military doctrine of 1993 recognized multiple dangers stemming from domestic developments and laid a legal foundation for the use of the armed forces in internal conflicts such as Chechnya. The doctrine also clarified Russia's nuclear policy, declaring that the goal of nuclear policy is to avert the threat of a nuclear war by deterring aggression against Russia and its allies. Therefore, nuclear weapons were seen as a political deterrent to nuclear or conventional aggression. This marked the shift in Russian strategic thinking to a Western-like concept of deterrence, compensating for conventional weakness. The most distinct departure of the new Russian nuclear doctrine from the Soviet one was Russia's abandonment of the principle of no-first-use (introduced by Leonid Brezhnev in 1982). At the same time, the document promised that Russia would never use its nuclear weapons against any member of the Non-Proliferation Treaty of 1968 if it is not aligned with a nuclear state against Russia (Yeltsin, 1994: 6). NATO members and nuclear states fell under these categories.

The 1993 military doctrine was a path-breaking document which laid basic foundations for Russia's defense philosophy in the post-Cold War period. This doctrine is regularly being updated but its main underpinnings remain intact. Moreover, this document has affected the Russian national security and foreign policy concepts developed under the Yeltsin, Putin, and Medvedev regimes.

However, the second Chechen war, NATO military intervention in Kosovo, and NATO's eastward enlargement (all in 1999) prompted the Kremlin and the new Russian President Vladimir Putin to revise its national security and foreign policy strategies. For instance, the national security and foreign policy concepts of 2000 elevated the importance and expanded the types of external threats to Russian security: the weakening of the OSCE and the UN; weakening Russian political, economic, and military influence in the world; further eastward expansion of NATO, including the possibility of foreign military bases or deployment of forces on Russian borders; proliferation of WMD and the means for their delivery; weakening of the CIS, and escalation of conflicts on CIS members' borders; and territorial claims against Russia (Putin, 2000a: 4, 2000b). They argued that, contrary to multi-polar tendency, the United States and its allies under the guise of multilateralism had sought to establish a uni-polar world outside of international law.

In addition to these threat perceptions, the military doctrine of 2000 pointed to a new threat of an information war against Russia as an important factor of the contemporary security environment in the world (Putin, 2000c). This document described in detail the nature of contemporary and future wars, distinguishing the following trends: use of high-precision and non-contact weapons, attacks throughout the whole enemy's territory, involvement of irregular forces, and high risk of the use of WMD. The doctrine defined different types of possible armed conflicts: intra-state, local, regional, and large-scale.

The military's threat perceptions have also significantly affected Russia's national security and foreign policy documents of the Medvedev and the third Putin administrations – national security strategy of 2009, foreign policy concepts of 2008 and 2013, and military doctrine of 2010. The latter document, however, paid more attention to the challenges posed by the military reform, socio-economic aspects of the Russian military strategy and defense diplomacy, rather than to purely strategic issues (Medvedev, 2010).

The Ukrainian crisis of 2014 has further shifted Moscow's threat perceptions toward the hard security problematique. On December 26, 2014, an updated version of the Russian military doctrine was signed by President Putin (Putin, 2014). The new doctrine highlighted NATO's build-up and expansion toward the Russian borders as being the main external dangers to Russia's security. Other threats mentioned in the document include the development and deployment of the U.S. ballistic missile defense (BMD) systems, the implementation of the 'global strike' doctrine, plans to place weapons in space, deployment of high-precision conventional weapons systems as well as evolving forms of warfare such as, for example, information warfare. For the first time, the protection of Russia's national interests in the Arctic in peacetime was assigned to the Russian armed forces.

The doctrine showed increased Russian interest in improving its own ability to use precision conventional weapons. For the first time, the concept of non-nuclear deterrence was introduced in the document. This became a reflection of the fact that most of the military threats that Russia faces now are of a non-nuclear character and can be successfully met with conventional means. But the central question of when Moscow might feel compelled to use nuclear weapons seems unchanged: in the case of WMD attack or use of conventional forces threatening the existence of state (Putin, 2014). In general, however, the new version of the military doctrine retained its defensive nature.

The new doctrine differed from the previous one in treating internal threats to the country as military ones. The new document stated that "the destabilization of the domestic political and social situation in the nation" and even "information-related activity aimed at influencing the population, primarily the country's young citizens, with the goal of undermining the historical, spiritual and patriotic traditions in the area of defending the Fatherland" (Putin, 2014). Some Western experts believe that such a broad interpretation of internal threats may lead to perceptions of any political opposition as an activity requiring a military response (Sinovets and Renz, 2015: 2).

In late July 2015 Putin approved a new version of Russia's maritime doctrine that included both naval and civilian components (Putin, 2015a). The novelty of the document was that it emphasized the priority of the North Atlantic and Arctic where NATO activities and international competition for natural resources and sea routes continued to grow and required Russia's 'adequate response'. Along with the naval forces, the nuclear icebreaker fleet will be substantially modernized by 2020.

On December 31, 2015, Russian President Vladimir Putin approved a new national security strategy (NSS-2015). The doctrine paid great attention to the internal aspects of Russia's security. Particularly, security threats such as terrorism, radical nationalism and religious fanaticism, separatism, organized crime and corruption were identified. As for the external threats, the NSS-2015 accused the West of causing the Ukrainian crisis. The document noted a threat emanating from the biological weapons. "The network of U.S. biological military labs is expanding on the territories of countries neighboring Russia," it said. The NSS-2015 underlined that "Russia's independent foreign and domestic policy" has been met with counteraction by the United States and its allies. The new NSS also declared that Russia has demonstrated the ability, "to protect the rights of compatriots abroad" (Putin, 2015b). The doctrine has received a rather hostile reaction from the Western expert community (Lynch, 2015; Payne and Schneider, 2016).

On November 30, 2016, a new version of the Russian foreign policy concept was approved by the Kremlin. In contrast with the previous version of 2013, the new document underscored the increasing role of force (including its military component) in present-day international relations as a result of growing tensions between various international actors and the instability of the world's political and economic systems (Putin, 2016). However, the paper is based on the assumption that the threat of a large-scale nuclear war is still highly improbable. The document underlined the need to complete the process of demarcation of Russia's land and maritime boundaries, and delimitation of continental shelves to eliminate a potential source of conflict with foreign countries.

It should be noted that the military doctrine of 2014, maritime doctrine of 2015, NSS-2015, and foreign policy concept of 2016 mark the culmination of a rather long process in deteriorating relations between Moscow and the West and in how the Russian security elite perceives security threats and challenges. On the other hand, these documents signal that Moscow is still open to cooperation with its Western and other foreign partners.

Decision-making

The Ministry of Defense (MoD) of the Russian Federation was formally established on March 16, 1992, with President Yeltsin fulfilling the role of minister. On 18 May he was replaced by General Pavel Grachev, a former Commander of the Soviet Airborne Forces, who played a critical role in obstructing the August 1991 coup d'état attempt.

A dramatic change took place in civil-military relations in post-Soviet Russia in the early 1990s. Soviet-era controls and supervisory agencies were eroded, but no authoritative civilian institutions and conventions about the limits on military involvement in political matters have emerged to take their place. There were some hopes that a sort of civilian control over the military would be established. Some experts suggested the appointment of a civilian Defense Minister who would be a President's representative among the military establishment rather than a representative of the military elite in the entourage of the President.

According to this view, the Defense Minister should deal with issues such as military R&D and the defense budget, while strategic planning and operational control over the armed forces and military training should be the General Staff's responsibilities. There were also some more radical proposals such as the withdrawal of the General Staff from the MoD, its re-subordination to the Defense or Security Council, and the assumption by this body of the role of chief coordinator of all 'power' agencies' activities.

At the same time, the weakness of central authority and the lack of a sound decision-making system in the first half of the 1990s meant that the Russian military establishment enjoyed considerable autonomy and was able to gradually increase its influence on security policy. Its links with civilian politicians and expatriate communities provided the defense establishment with additional channels of influence on Russian decision-making. Along with Kozyrev, the Defense Minister became a member of the Security Council's Inter-Agency Foreign Policy Commission in December 1992. The General Staff dominated the process of drafting military doctrine in 1992–93. According to some accounts, at a meeting of the Security Council on February 28, 1993, Yeltsin asked the high-ranking military leaders to draft not only military-technical sections but also the political chapter of the new military doctrine – a prerogative which in principle belonged to the Security Council or the President himself (Malcolm et al., 1996: 253). The final version of the doctrine reflected military rather than civilian preferences.

In the 1990s, the Ministry of Foreign Affairs' (MFA) neglect of relations with the former Soviet Union republics effectively invited the MoD to take the leading role in conflict management in the post-Soviet space (Baev, 1996: 38). The MoD often prevailed over other foreign policy institutions in Russia's relations with the Baltic States and the states of the South Caucasus (Crow, 1993). The MoD officials also opposed military intervention in the former Yugoslavia. Deputy Defense Minister Georgy Kondratyev announced in late April 1993 that Russia would not send additional peace-keeping forces there. Both Defense Minister Grachev and then Commander in Chief of the CIS Armed Forces, Marshal Yevgeny Shaposhnikov protested against the use of military force in settling the conflict (Crow, 1993: 50). Furthermore, the MoD was quite independent in decisions on military agreements and cooperation with foreign countries. Finally, the military exercised its autonomy in expressing criticism, alongside the Foreign Intelligence Service, of plans to expand NATO and the possibility of replacing the UN with NATO in peace-keeping activities in the CIS area (*Nezavisimaya Gazeta*, 1 August 1992).

It was President Putin who was able to establish an effective civilian control over the armed forces. In 2007, he appointed Anatoly Serdyukov, a former furniture salesman and tax inspector with no background in defense issues, to be Russia's first really civilian Defense Minister. According to Mankoff (2009: 57–58), the appointment of a complete outsider like Serdyukov signaled how little trust the Kremlin had in the upper ranks of the military. Yuri Baluevsky's (an outspoken critic of Serdyukov's reforms) departure as chief of the General Staff in mid-2008 was likewise connected to attempts by the MoD to rein in the military's autonomy and subject it to modernization in line with a perception of the country's civilian leadership that the military has failed to adapt to new realities and adequately confront the range of non-traditional security threats facing Russia in a globalizing world.

Under Serdyukov (2007–2012), the Russian armed forces had undergone the most serious structural changes in the post-Soviet era. In contrast to the Yeltsin administrations who tried simply to downsize the huge Soviet-born military monster, the Putin-2 (2004–2008), Medvedev (2008–2012), and Putin-3 (from 2012 to the present) teams intended to create a principally new army. The Kremlin aimed to make the armed forces adequate to the nature of domestic and external threats to Russia's military security on the one hand, and to Russia's economic, technical, demographic, and intellectual capabilities, on the other.

The priority was to develop the armed forces and other services designed to deter aggression, as well as mobile elements, which could be quickly delivered and deployed in the required area(s) and carry out mobile operations in any region where the security of Russia might be threatened. Special attention was paid to enhance the interoperable abilities of the armed forces. The core idea of the Russian military reform was the transformation of the armed forces from a conventional mobilization army to a permanently combat-ready force (Taylor, 2003; Isakova, 2005: 195–229; Pallin, 2009: 49–63; Barabanov, 2011; Bartles, 2011; Lannon, 2011; McDermott, 2011; McDermott et al., 2011; Makarychev and Sergunin, 2013; Gressel, 2015; Russell, 2015; Golts and Kofman, 2016).

The new round of reforms under Defense Minister Sergey Shoygu (since 2012) includes the creation of five Joint Strategic Commands (North, South, Central, East, West) and a National Defense Management Center as the highest command and control body of Russia's armed forces; further modernization of strategic and conventional forces; improvement of control over planning, production, and testing of new weapons; development of plans to expand permanent military presence abroad (in addition to the Russian bases in Armenia, Kyrgyzstan, Syria, and Tajikistan, negotiations has started with Cuba, Vietnam, Venezuela, Nicaragua, Singapore, and others).

The coordination of long-term planning on military policy is done through the Security Council where the Defense Minister has a permanent seat, while the chief of the General Staff is a member of the Council. The MoD has a key role, and especially the General Staff, but from the composition of the Security Council Interdepartmental Commission on Military Security it is clear that military security encompasses the activity of a large number of ministries, services, and agencies. The chief of the General Staff heads the Commission (www.scrf.gov.ru/about/commission/MVK_VB_members/).

The Military-Industrial Commission is something of a hybrid president-government coordination vehicle. The President has chaired the Commission since 2014, while Deputy Prime

Minister Dmitry Rogozin is deputy chair. In this Commission the ministers of finance, industry and trade, and economic development are represented as well as the heads of the so-called power ministries and their deputies (including the MoD) (http://docs.cntd.ru/document/420219875). Within the government, Rogozin is responsible for questions pertaining to the defense industry, export control, international military-technical cooperation, civil defense, mobilization, and proposing systems to prepare the young for military service.

A system of parliamentary oversight over the military was effectively established under the Putin and Medvedev administrations (Allison et al., 2006: 38). Formally speaking, the Defense Minister is accountable to the Federal Assembly and should report to each of the two chambers on a regular basis (as other ministers do). In practice, the activities of the MoD are most closely considered by specialized committees on defense and security.

As for the MoD's role in decision-making, some experts believe that while after the collapse of the Soviet Union the MoD initially had a great deal of influence over the foreign policy direction of the country, Foreign Minister Evgeny Primakov who took this position in February 1996 "helped to seize the initiative that the military had increasingly been taking away from civilian authorities . . . and took considerable powers away" from the Defense Ministry (Tsygankov, 2016: 117).

Under three Putin and Medvedev administrations, the MoD has continued to lose its influence on foreign policy decision-making. The role of the military declined to the point where "the military had little influence in foreign policy formation" (Sakwa, 2008: 374). Part of this declining role in foreign policy can also be credited to the fact that the MoD had many domestic priorities including the war in Chechnya and the military reform process (Sergunin, 2008: 67, 2016: 175–176). Despite this decline of influence in areas of foreign policy, the areas of national security and disarmament still remained areas where the MoD retained influence. Within the MoD itself there are many branches that have responsibilities towards these areas of policy, particularly because "to a large extent [they] dominate the discourse because of their monopoly on technical expertise" related to the issues of arms control and disarmament (Sokov et al., 2009: 7). Areas such as missile defense and nuclear reductions talks are strongly influenced by the MoD because of their technical knowledge of the subjects being addressed.

Prior to the Ukrainian and Syrian crises, the President had assigned the MoD predominantly internal missions such as military reform, the war in Chechnya, etc. Even the CIS collective security system, including peacekeeping operations in the post-Soviet space and in the Balkans, were no longer the MoD's preferential areas. The ministry looked often more like a decision-taker, an instrument of implementing policies, rather than a decision-maker (Pacer, 2016: 10–11).

During the Syrian and Ukrainian crises, the most important decisions on the use of military force were also prescribed by political priorities of Kremlin. According to Bloomberg (Meyer and Arkhipov, 2015), the military plan of intervention in Syria was pushed by Sergey Ivanov (the then head of the Presidential Administration) and Nikolay Patrushev (Security Council's secretary), rather than by Defense Minister Sergey Shoygu.

Besides, Russia's decision-making system significantly rests on personal loyalty to a political leader (Averkov, 2012; Gomart, 2008: 1–2) as was the case with the last two Defense Ministers (Serdyukov and Shoygu) who didn't represent any influential policy or military elites and had no political ambitions of their own. This also demonstrates the political leadership's view of the military as an important but secondary actor in the decision-making process. As the President himself and his team have signaled many times, defense policies are framed mainly through the interaction of the Presidential Administration and Security Council, on the one hand, and the Federal Assembly (Russia's parliament), on the other.

To summarize, there were ups and downs in the defense agency's influence on the decision-making process. Being created and properly institutionalized later than many other Russian governmental bodies, the MoD and General Staff have had to wage permanent bureaucratic warfare to secure their interests and authority. This often resulted in open confrontation with the MFA and presidential structures as well as inconsistencies in Russia's security and foreign policies in the world. In the 1990s, the military establishment managed to retain its positions in areas such as CIS military integration, peace-keeping in the post-Soviet space and Balkans, arms control, military-technical cooperation with foreign countries, and military-to-military contacts. The military lobby's influence increased in the periods when the President badly needed the army's support in domestic political struggles and decreased when the Kremlin's positions were more-or-less stable. As Putin enjoys stable domestic support, the MoD's impact on decision-making could rise only as result of a decline in relations between Russia and West.

Military power as a foreign policy tool

Russia has implemented far-reaching military reforms to create more professional and combat-ready armed forces that can swiftly deploy abroad, backed by expertise in non-conventional warfare tactics such as subversion and propaganda (Gressel, 2015). The West has misunderstood these reforms – focusing on shortcomings in equipment – and, as a result, has underestimated Russia's military capacity, as shown by its response to the Ukrainian and Syrian crises. Russia could now overwhelm any of the countries in the post-Soviet sphere if they were isolated from the West.

Assessing the fighting power of the Russian armed forces, military analysts try to find out what kind of military assets are available for three overall missions: operational-strategic joint inter-service combat operations (JISCOs), stand-off warfare, and strategic deterrence. The experts note that Russia possesses (and will retain in the foreseeable future) a large ground operations-centric force. The Russian military is able to launch at least one – possibly two – large-scale JISCOs, with thousands of vehicles and aircraft and around 150 000 servicemen in each (Persson, 2016: 192).

The experts also believe that Russia's military capability – both conventional and nuclear – is likely to continue to improve. As Russian military intervention in Syria and counter-measures to NATO's recent military build-up show, the emphasis will be put on obtaining new naval platforms for launching long-range cruise missiles as well as additional Iskander-M brigades.

Russia's military assets for strategic deterrence will most likely continue to increase during the 2020s. Apart from the ability to perform JISCOs and stand-off warfare, Russia will be able to maintain a substantial operational strategic nuclear weapons force. The organization in a triad will probably remain during the next ten-year period, with the land-based Strategic Missile Forces as the backbone. The number of deployed intercontinental missiles will decrease but, with more multiple-warhead missiles, the overall number of warheads is likely to remain the same. A larger share of these will be deployed on mobile launchers. The capability – and the strategic importance – of the SSBN fleet will increase if the introduction of Bulava missiles and the Borei class submarines can be carried out (http://militaryrussia.ru/blog/topic-338.html). The strategic bomber fleet of modernized aircraft may shrink slightly towards the mid-2020s, and there are significant uncertainties regarding deliveries of new strategic bomber aircraft.

Although NATO's military advantage over Russia is undermined by low combat-readiness, understaffing, and the need to coordinate between countries, Russia's military potential is still insufficient to pose a serious threat to Europe. Moreover, as Moscow's threat perception assessment demonstrates, the Kremlin has no aggressive ambitions in this region. Its strategic forces aim to deter other nuclear powers (first and foremost the United States) while conventional forces are comparable or even inferior to the U.S./NATO and Chinese ones (see Table 10.1) and are designed for defensive missions as well.

In the post-Soviet era, Russia has systematically used military force to achieve its political aims. In the 1990s, Moscow intervened militarily in the local conflicts in the post-Soviet space to manage or stop them, as well as for peace-keeping and peace-enforcement purposes (Nagorny Karabakh, Abkhazia, South Ossetia, Tajikistan, and Transnistria). In August 2008, Moscow used its armed forces to stop Georgia's invasion of South Ossetia. In 2014–15, the Kremlin used military force to take over Crimea and support the breakaway republics in Donbass. Finally, Moscow intervened in the Syrian conflict to prevent the fall of the Assad regime and defeat international terrorism in this country.

It should be noted that in all cases, Russian uses of military force since the early 1990s share a fundamental similarity: the Kremlin used its military, first and foremost, to achieve foreign policy goals. The military objectives were driven by the policy mission; in other words, there have been no purely military goals. According to Charap (2016: 1–2), Russia's use of force is best understood as a means of coercion. He uses Thomas Schelling's theory of military coercion developed in his classic *Arms and Influence* (2008) to explain Moscow's approach to the use of military force as a foreign policy tool. Schelling classifies coercive military acts as either deterrence, aimed at preventing adversary behaviors, or compellence – threatening or taking action to force the adversary to induce compliance (Schelling, 2008: 79).

The Russian cases of the use of military force clearly were acts of both deterrence and compellence. For example, in March 2014 the Federation Council, the upper chamber of the Russian parliament, provided President Putin with the permission to use armed forces on the Ukrainian territory until the "normalization of the situation" in this country. This was a clear message to the new regime in Kiev to prevent it from using force against the Autonomous Republic of Crimea, which had decided to hold a referendum on secession.

On other occasions, such as the peace enforcement operation in South Ossetia (August 2008) and alleged operations against the Ukrainian army at Ilovaisk (August 2014) and Debaltsevo (January-February 2015), this did not result in the total defeat of the Georgian and Ukrainian forces but did demonstrate Moscow's willingness and ability to force Tbilisi and Kiev to change their behavior. Russia's intention was not just to change the Georgian and Ukrainian military's behavior; it also forced their political leaders to the negotiating table as well as to stop hostilities and produce ceasefire agreements.

One should understand the military component of Russian policy as one element of a broader coercive bargaining process related to political outcomes. The Georgia and Ukraine cases were elements of Russia's campaign to block these countries' integration in the Western military and economic structures. The Syria intervention is part of the international bargaining process over the civil war that dates from 2011. In all these cases the use of force came as a last resort. Russia tries to achieve its objectives by using diplomacy, economic pressure, threats, etc., and only when it still has not succeeded does it resort to the military tool. It should also be noted that Moscow has only intervened when the stakes were perceived to be high relative to other regional or global crises. Worst-case scenario outcomes in either Syria and especially Ukraine would have been very detrimental for Russia's security (as seen by the Kremlin). All above coercive bargaining processes that reached the threshold for the use of force were thus tied into Russia's core national security concerns (Charap, 2016: 3). In addition, Moscow's objective has been to prevent or reverse (perceived) geopolitical loss, not to make new geopolitical gains. Russia wanted to restore the status quo in South Ossetia, return Ukraine to its orbit after it drifted away in the wake of the February 2014 coup, and sustain the regime in Syria from rebel/international terrorist overthrow.

Table 10.1 Russian, U.S. and Chinese military capabilities, 2015

Item	Russia	U.S.	China
Military expenditure, U.S. $bn	65.6	597.5	145.8
Military personnel			
Active	1,013,628[a]	1,381,250	2,333,000
Civilian	889,423[a]	14,850	–
Reserve	2,000,000	840,500	510,000
Conventional forces			
Army			
MBT[b]	2,700	2,384	6,540
RECCE[c]	1,200	1,900	250
AIFV[d]	5,400	4,559	3,950
APC[e]	6,000	16,377	5,020
ARTY[f]	4,180	5,923	13,178
Navy:			
Tactical submarines	49	57	57
Principal surface combatants	35	98	74
Aircraft	186	1,123	346
Helicopters	185	563	103
Air force:			
Aircraft	1,090	1,442	2,306
Helicopters	669	129	53
Strategic forces			
Submarines	13	14	4
Bombers	76	90	62
ICBM[g]	332	450	

[a] – 2017
MBT[b] – main battle tank
RECCE[c] – reconnaissance vehicle
AIFV[d] – armored infantry fighting vehicle
APC[e] – armored personnel carrier
ARTY[f] – artillery
ICBM[g] – intercontinental ballistic missile

Sources: The International Institute for Strategic Studies 2016; Interfax 2017 https://news.mail.ru/politics/29239264/?frommail=1

Russian military operations in many cases share several important characteristics. Moscow has used just enough military force to achieve policy goals, but not more. Coercion was conducted by degree, in measured doses. According to Schelling (2008: 173), the objective of coercive warfare is to "make the enemy behave," not to annihilate him. For example, Moscow's peace enforcement operation in South Ossetia (August 2008) started only when the Georgian troops invaded this breakaway republic and killed the Russian peacekeepers. It continued until the pre-conflict status quo was restored but it did not aim to oust the Saakashvili regime in Georgia. In Eastern Ukraine, Russia's alleged interventions near Ilovaisk and Debaltsevo only came when the Donbass rebels were on the verge of catastrophic failure. These interventions, if they happened, were quite limited; no high-end capabilities were employed, and the majority of the Russian forces concentrated at the Russian-Ukrainian border never crossed it. As soon as Kiev agreed to the ceasefire negotiations in Minsk, the Russian troops left Donbass and were moved from the border.

Interestingly, Russia has portrayed the use of military force in all these cases as consistent with international law. In South Ossetia, Moscow referred to Russia's legitimate right for peace enforcement operations to force Georgia to comply with previous international agreements. In Crimea, the Russian-Ukrainian agreements on the Black Sea Fleet basing and the principle of self-determination were invoked. In Donbass, the Kremlin denied the fact they had intervened militarily as such and claimed they were providing humanitarian assistance to the people of the Donetsk and Lughansk republics who had suffered from the Ukrainian blockade. In Syria, Moscow points out that in contrast to the U.S.-led coalition, the Russian military were formally invited by Damascus.

These arguments are important for Moscow in terms of legitimizing the use of force and keeping its image as a responsible international actor who plays by the rules established by the UN and other international organizations.

It should be noted that the Kremlin is cognizant of the limits of the use of military force; it understands that coercion can sometimes produce resistance rather than restraint or compliance (as in the cases of Ukrainian and Syrian opposition). That's why Moscow always tries to use diplomatic and political instruments in parallel or in addition to military tools.

Conclusions

Several conclusions emerge from the above analysis.

First, the military was an important determinant of Russia's foreign policy in the post-Soviet era and will remain so for the foreseeable future. The military influences Russia's foreign policy by shaping the elites' threat perceptions, forging foreign and national security policy doctrines, partaking in the decision-making process, and using military force to achieve geopolitical goals.

Furthermore, under the Putin and Medvedev administrations, Moscow managed to exercise an impressive military reform which resulted in becoming more efficient, and having better equipped and trained armed forces. This may provide the Russian political leadership with additional incentives to use military force and coercion in achieving its geopolitical goals.

The nature of civil-military relations in Russia has substantially changed since the 1990s. It was President Putin who was able to bring the military under strict political control and introduce some important elements of parliamentary and public oversight. These relations, however, are still not fully in line with Western democratic standards and, for this reason, foreign strategists and military analysts remain critical about the state of affairs in this field.

There have been ups and downs in the military's role in Russia's foreign policy decision-making since the late 1990s, but the general trend is that this role continues to steadily decline. With the exception of purely military issues, the MoD and General Staff look more like decision-takers rather than decision-makers in the foreign policy domain. The military is considered just one of Russia's foreign policy instruments, rather than the only or main one.

The Kremlin uses military coercion as a last resort when other non-military means are exhausted, and does it in a limited way to try to dissuade its opponents from hostile actions or compel them to comply with certain Russian requirements rather than to completely defeat or destroy the opposition.

In this sense, the military (hard power) instruments complement rather than exclude or clash with the soft power tools in terms of achieving Moscow's international policy objectives. When used in combination, military and non-military means reinforce each other and make Moscow's foreign policy even more effective. It is also important for the Kremlin to provide its military/coercive actions with a legitimacy from the point of view of international law.

Several questions related to the role of the military in Russia's foreign policy will remain on the future political agenda. First, Russia's military reform and further changes in civil-military relations still have unfinished business, and it is unclear how these reforms will proceed in the foreseeable future. It also remains to be seen how the Ukrainian and Syrian crises will affect Russia's strategic thinking, particularly Moscow's threat perceptions and foreign policy and national security doctrines. There are also some concerns regarding Moscow's potential inclination to use military force as the seemingly simplest way to resolve its foreign policy problems. A possible excessive reliance by the Kremlin on the use of military coercion may occur once other available means (economic, diplomatic, cultural, etc.) have been limited under the conditions of economic hardship and growing international isolation. Western and some post-Soviet countries are also intrigued by Moscow's intent to use so-called 'hybrid warfare' against them, albeit the Kremlin accuses its foreign opponents of doing the same. It should be noted that the 'hybrid warfare' tactics and strategies blur the boundaries between real and virtual wars, and bring both sides to the brink with all its dangerous consequences.

References

Allison, R, Light, M and White, S 2006, *Putin's Russia and the enlarged Europe*, Chatham House, London.
Averkov, V 2012, Prinyatiye vneshnepoliticheskih resheniy v Rossii [Foreign policy decision making in Russia], *Mezhdunarodnye protsessy* [International Trends], vol. 10, no. 2: 111–124 (in Russian).
Baev, P 1996, *The Russian army in a time of troubles*, Peace Research Institute Oslo, Oslo.
Barabanov, M ed. 2011, *Russia's new army*, Center for Analysis of Strategies and Technologies, Moscow.
Bartles, CK 2011, 'Defense reforms of Russian defense minister Anatolii Serdyukov', *The Journal of Slavic Military Studies*, vol. 24, no. 1: 55–80.
Betz, D 2004, *Civil-military relations in Russia and Eastern Europe*, RoutledgeCurzon, London and New York.
Chaldymov, NA ed. 2001, *Aktual'nye voprosy razvitiya voenno-grazhdanskikh otnosheniy* [Topical issues of the military-civil relations], Koventri, Moscow (in Russian).
Charap, S 2016, 'Russia's use of military force as a foreign policy tool. Is there a logic?' *PONARS Eurasia Policy Memo*, no. 443, www.ponarseurasia.org/sites/default/files/policy-memos-pdf/Pepm443_Charap_Oct2016_4.pdf.
Crow, S 1993, *The making of foreign policy in Russia under Yeltsin*, Radio Free Europe/Radio Liberty Research Institute, Munich and Washington, DC.
Danilova, NY 2007, *Armiyai obshestvo: printsipy vzaimodeistviya* [The army and the society: the principles of interaction], Norma, St. Petersburg (in Russian).
Galeotti, M, ed. 2010, *The politics of security in modern Russia*, Ashgate Publishing, Aldershot, UK.
Golts, A and Kofman, M 2016, *Russia's military assessment, strategy, and threat*, The Center on Global Interests, Washington, DC.
Gomart, T 2008, *Russian civil-military relations: Putin's legacy*, Carnegie Endowment for International Peace, Washington, DC.
Gressel, G 2015, *Russia's quiet military revolution, and what it means for Europe*, European Council on Foreign Relations, Berlin (ECFR Policy Brief no. 143).
Herspring, D 1996, *Russian civil-military relations*, Indiana University Press, Bloomington, IN.
Interfax 2017, Shat vooruzhennykh sil RF s iulya uvelichitsya do 1,9 mln chelovek [RF's armed forces personnel will increase by 1,9 mln since July]. https://news.mail.ru/politics/29239264/?frommail=1.
The International Institute for Strategic Studies 2016, *The Military Balance 2016*, London.
Isakova, I 2005, *Russian governance in the twenty-first century. Geo-strategy, geopolitics and governance*, Frank Cass, London and New York.
Knoph, J 2004, *Civilian control of the Russian state forces: a challenge in theory and practice*, Swedish Defense Research Agency, Stockholm.
'Kontseptsiya vneshney politiki Rossiyskoi Federatsii' [Foreign Policy Concept of the Russian Federation] 1993, *Diplomaticheskiy Vestnik* (Special Issue), January: 3–23 (in Russian).

Lannon, GP 2011, 'Russia's new look army reforms and Russian foreign policy', *The Journal of Slavic Military Studies*, vol. 24, no. 1: 26–54.

Lynch, D 2015, 'Russia updates national security strategy to respond to "new emerging military threats"', *International Business Times*, 5 May, www.ibtimes.com/russia-updates-national-security-strategy-respond-new-emerging-military-threats-1909770.

Makarychev, A and Sergunin, A 2013, 'Russian military reform: institutional, political and security implications', *Defense and Security Analysis*, vol. 29, no. 4: 320–328.

Malcolm, N, Pravda, A, Allison, R and Light, M 1996, *Internal factors in Russian foreign policy*, The Royal Institute of International Affairs and Clarendon Press, Oxford, UK.

Mankoff, J 2009, *Russian foreign policy. The return of great power politics*, Rowman & Littlefield Publishers, Lanham, MD.

Marten, K 2015. 'Putin's choices: explaining Russian foreign policy and intervention in Ukraine', *The Washington Quarterly*, vol. 38, issue 2: 189–204.

Maslyuk, SG 2001, *Voenno-grazhdanskie otnosheniya v Rossii: istoriya i sovremennost'* [Military-civil relations in Russia: past and present], Prava cheloveka, Moscow (in Russian).

McDermott, R 2011, *The reform of Russia's conventional armed forces: problems, challenges and policy implications*, The Jamestown Foundation, Washington, DC.

McDermott, R, Nygren, B and Pallin, CV, eds. 2011, *The Russian armed forces in transition – economic, geopolitical and institutional uncertainties*, Routledge, Abingdon, UK.

Medvedev, D 2010, Voennaya doktrina Rossiyskoy Federatsii [The Military Doctrine of the Russian Federation], http://prezident.rf/ref_notes/461 (in Russian).

Meyer, H and Arkhipov, I 2015, 'Putin's gamble: Syria move born of hopes of coming in from cold', *Bloomberg*, 2 October, www.bloomberg.com/news/articles/2015-10-02/putin-s-gamble-syria-move-born-of-hopes-of-coming-in-from-cold.

Pacer, V 2016, *Russian foreign policy under Dmitry Medvedev, 2008–2012*, Routledge, Abingdon, UK.

Pallin, CV 2009, *Russian military reform. A failed exercise in defense decision making*, Routledge, Abingdon, UK.

Payne, KB and Schneider, MB 2016, 'Russia's new national security strategy: stark realities confronting the West', *RealClear*, 12 February, www.realcleardefense.com/articles/2016/02/12/russias_new_national_security_strategy_109016.html.

Persson, G, ed. 2016, *Russian military capability in a ten-year perspective – 2016*, FOI, Stockholm.

Putin, V 2000a, 'Kontseptsiya natsionalnoy bezopasnosti Rossiyskoi Federatsii' [The national security concept of the Russian Federation], *Nezavisimaya Gazeta*, 14 January: 4–5 (in Russian).

Putin, V 2000b, Kontseptsiya vneshney politiki Rossiyskoi Federatsii [Foreign policy concept of the Russian Federation], 28 June, www.scrf.gov.ru/documents/25.html (in Russian).

Putin, V 2000c, Voennaya doktrina Rossiyskoi Federatsii [The Military Doctrine of the Russian Federation], www.ipmb.ru/1_3.html (in Russian).

Putin, V 2014, Voennaya doktrina Rossiyskoy Federatsii [The Military Doctrine of the Russian Federation], http://static.kremlin.ru/media/events/files/41d527556bec8deb3530.pdf (in Russian).

Putin, V 2015a, Morskaya doktrina Rossiyskoy Federatsii [Maritime Doctrine of the Russian Federation], http://statc.kremlin.ru/media/events/files/ru/uAFi5nvux2twaqjftS5yrIZUVTJan77L.pdf (in Russian).

Putin, V 2015b, O strategii natsional'noi bezopasnosti Rossiyskoi Federatsii [On the National Security Strategy of the Russian Federation]. www.scrf.gov.ru/documents/1/133.html (in Russian).

Putin, V 2016, Kontseptsiya vneshnei politiki Rossiyskoi Federatsii [The foreign policy concept of the Russian Federation], http://publication.pravo.gov.ru/Document/View/0001201612010045?index=0&rangeSize=1 (in Russian).

Renz, B 2011, 'Civil-military relations and Russian military modernization', in McDermott, R, Nygren, B and Pallin, CV, eds, *The Russian armed forces in transition: economic, geopolitical and institutional uncertainties*, Routledge, Abingdon, UK, pp. 196–204.

Russell, M 2015, *Russia's armed forces: reforms and challenges*, European Parliamentary Research Service, Brussels.

Sakwa, R 2008, *Russian politics and society*, 4th edition, Routledge, Abingdon, UK.

Schelling, T 2008, *Arms and Influence*, Yale University Press, New Haven, CT and London.

Sergunin, A 2008, 'Russian foreign-policy decision making on Europe', In Hopf, T, ed., *Russia's European choice*, Palgrave Macmillan, Basingstoke, UK, pp. 59–93.

Sergunin, A 2016, *Explaining Russian foreign policy behavior: theory and practice*, Ibidem-Verlag, Stuttgart, Germany.

Sinovets, P and Renz, B 2015, 'Russia's 2014 military doctrine and beyond: threat perceptions, capabilities and ambitions', *NATO Research Paper*, no. 117. www.ndc.nato.int/news/news.php?icode=830.

Military

Sokov, N, Yuan, J, Potter, WC and Hansell, C 2009, 'Chinese and Russian perspectives on achieving nuclear zero', In Hansell, C and Potter, WC, eds, *Engaging China and Russia on nuclear disarmament*, James Martin Center for Nonproliferation Studies, Monterey, CA, http://cns.miis.edu/opapers/op15/op15.pdf.

Stepanova, EA 2001, *Voenno-grazhdanskie otnosheniya v operatsiyakh nevoennogo tipa [Military-civil relations in the non-combat operations]*, Human Rights, Prava chelovek, Moscow (in Russian).

Taylor, B 2003, *Politics and Russian Army. Civil-military relations, 1689–2000*, Cambridge University Press, Cambridge, UK.

Tsygankov, A 2016, *Russia's foreign policy: change and continuity in national identity*, 4th ed., Rowman and Littlefield, New York.

Ulrich, M 2002, *Democratizing Communist militaries: the cases of the Czech and Russia armed forces*, University of Michigan Press, Ann Arbor, MI.

Yeltsin, B 1994, 'The basic provisions of the military doctrine of the Russian Federation', *Jane's Intelligence Review* (Special Report), no. 1: 6–12.

11
CYBER POWER

Julien Nocetti

FRENCH INSTITUTE OF INTERNATIONAL RELATIONS, PARIS

Introduction

In June 2016, at the height of the Democratic National Convention in Pennsylvania, WikiLeaks disclosed some 20,000 emails revealing how the machinery of the Democratic Party had favored presidential elections' candidate Hillary Clinton and multiplied low blows to discredit the latter's opponent, Bernie Sanders, which aroused great confusion in the United States. U.S. law enforcement agencies then suspected Russian hackers, and opened an investigation on the existence of a large-scale covert influence operation by the Kremlin to meddle in the November presidential voting. A few months later, in October, the White House publicly acknowledged the implication of the Russian government in these cyberattacks, while the U.S. director for national intelligence described the Russian covert influence campaign as "ambitious" and designed to counter U.S. leadership in international politics (Priest et al., 2016; Rid, 2016).

A couple of years before, Russia's annexation of Crimea and the outburst of hostilities between pro-Russian separatists and loyal Ukrainian forces in Eastern Ukraine, gave rise to a particularly intense "information war" between Moscow and the West (labelled here as the United States and the European Union). Information warfare is perceived in Moscow as adapting to the situation in which Russia believes itself to be towards Western countries: a no-declared war, no peace context, but a permanent state of conflict which requires the use of alternative tools to weaken both the will and the capabilities of the enemy (Franke, 2015).

Both of these examples demonstrate how Russia uses the cyber realm for geopolitical advantage. This includes Russia's cyber capabilities and espionage motivation and its use of the Internet for information warfare. Truly, the cyber and information realms have been carefully integrated into Russian foreign policy's doctrines and practice, all the more so as Internet access has skyrocketed throughout the globe since the late 2000s, de-multiplying the latter's potential for reaching strategic objectives.

First amongst these, the Russian decision-makers are driven by a mostly defensive and risk-averse approach towards information and communications technologies (ICTs): they seek above all to counter any spillover of "Arab Spring"-like events to Russia and post-Soviet republics, thus seeing the Internet as a profoundly disruptive technology that threatens not only government-to-government relations but also, and more importantly, the stability and integrity of nations. In other words, domestic concerns do impact the formulation of Russia's foreign policy, which is not a new phenomenon in itself but is considerably accelerated by the dissemination of networked technologies. The Kremlin's conception of cyber and information is thus a mostly *defensive* one, which is explicitly reflected in all Russian recent "security doctrines" and "foreign policy concepts."

Second, Russia, as a country seeking to challenge the international consensus on a number of issues since the mid-2000s, is eager to shift the Western narrative over the current global governance regime of the Internet, over which the United States still retains considerable leverage. Here, the Internet is a *subject* of international relations – all the more contentious since former National Security Agency (NSA)'s subcontractor Edward Snowden's disclosures on the United States' massive global electronic surveillance revealed a new form of "U.S. hegemony" in the eyes of the Kremlin. This approach underpins two major features: first is portraying the Internet as a dangerous place and instrument in the hands of a hostile United States – somewhat emphasizing Moscow's largely neo-Hobbesian view of international politics. Second is a U.S.-centric cyber/information foreign policy, driven by both a deep anti-Americanism persisting in the top Russian foreign policy and security elites, and a will to position Russia as an exclusive interlocutor to Washington in key international negotiations on, most notably, cyber norms. On the "information" level, Moscow seeks to stir up widespread distrust in the Western political system and values – understood as rule-of-law-based democracy. On the "cyber" level, Russia is eager to challenge NATO member states' reactions and capacities, while blurring the lines between cybersecurity and the Russian concept of information security.

This chapter does not seek to recount exhaustively the whole Kremlin's cyber and information policies during the "Putin years." Instead it first aims at comprehending in a novel way our understanding of Russia's foreign policy: indeed "things digital and cyber" have long been neglected, even largely ignored, in all the major works published on Russian foreign policy since the late 2000s.[1] This carelessness is all but restricted to Russia: it is also visible in the wider academic debate in international affairs (Powers and Jablonski, 2015) – although important works have recently been published, mostly in the United States (Mueller, 2010; Kramer and Müller, 2014; McCarthy, 2015; Owen, 2015; Segal, 2016). In such a context, overlapping Internet studies with the analysis of Russia's foreign and security policies appears necessary, and should help us in "reloading" our understanding of Moscow's initiatives, moves, and maneuvering towards the West and in a more general sense in the international arena – where information and cyber-related "events" frequently occur.

This chapter's second aim is to analyze Russia's "foreign internet policy" combining cyber and information elements – which is surprisingly a new approach – thus providing a *holistic view* of Russian "cyber power." While in the United States (and Europe) cyber security has been conceived of in a technical way, focusing on the security of hardware and software, i.e. not determining what content and information should be allowed online, Russia rather envisions "information security," thus encompassing the cognitive layer of cyberspace – in other words, *content*. That difference is key: mixing the *cyber* instrument and the *information* tool, even granting more significance to information, Moscow once again blurs the boundaries in order to shape a quickly evolving cyberspace/Internet governance along its sole national interests.

Terminology and concepts

It should be no surprise that "cyber power" is inherently a U.S. concept, which has been defined as "the ability to use cyberspace to create advantages and influence events in all the operational environments and across the instruments of power" (Kuehl, 2009). In a more general sense it can be described as the ability to control and apply typical forms of control and domination of cyberspace. Others approach the issue primarily from a military perspective (Starr, 2009). A slightly broader view is offered by Joseph Nye, who considers the most important application of soft (cyber) power to be outward-facing, influencing nations, rather than inward-facing. Just who has cyber power often relates back to questions of capabilities and resources. As Nye (2010) notes, "power depends on context and cyber power depends on the resources that characterize the domain of cyberspace." Traditional global powers such as the United States, China, and Russia seem to be the most dominant cyber actors because they have the resources, manpower, and money to support massive cyber operations (Valeriano and Maness, 2015: 25).

What is compelling about cyber power is the ability of the tactic to bleed into other arenas, suggesting that it is not a new and separate domain. What happens in cyberspace does not stay in cyberspace. Weakness displayed in the cyber arena can influence how states interact in all areas and levels; this has an impact on trust between states and corporations (Valeriano and Maness, 2015: 27).

The Russian equivalent to "cyber power" (*kiber sila*) is not used by Russian officials and academics – although it can sometimes be employed at think tank gatherings and forums in Moscow, but mostly in reference to the United States' own cyber power.[2] Generally speaking, "cyber" as a separate function or domain is not a Russian concept. The delineation of activities in the cyber domain from other activities processing, attacking, disrupting, or stealing information is seen as artificial in Russian thinking.[3]

However, the official Russian narrative and policy cannot but hide an ultimate goal which appears close to what has been described as *cyber power*. To the author, a top-Russian official in charge of international information security at the Ministry of Foreign Affairs once said that "Those in control of ICTs will be in control of financial flows, and then, world politics,"[4] suggesting a clear consciousness of the Internet's disruptive role in international politics as well as it being a new and huge source of power.

The phrase "cyber warfare" in Russian writing describes foreign concepts and activities, which do observe this distinction between information activities on computers and networks and those "in real life." Consequently, searches for "cyber" in Russian sources primarily return references to Western doctrine and thinking. It follows that any research on Russian capabilities and intentions which includes the word "cyber" risks providing fundamentally misleading results.

This includes above all the Russian view of *cyber security*, to which the Russians prefer the term *information security* (*informatsionnaya bezopasnost'*), which emphasizes the holistic span of information, where cyber is one component along with others. The Russians see information as being either artificial or natural. Cyber is artificial and is seen as the technical representation of information. In addition to what would be included in cyber, information also includes thoughts in one's head and information in books and documents. Further, they see a logical assumption that a discussion should encompass all information, and not just a subset (i.e. cyber) (Streltsov, 2010).

In other words, according to Russian experts, the U.S. terms *cyber security* and *cyberspace* are primarily technological, whereas the Russian terms for *information security* and *information space* are seen as having broader philosophical and political meanings.[5] The technology is perceived as only one of many components in Russia's understanding of information security and is not considered to be the most important one.[6] The Russian word most equivalent to the English "security" (*bezopasnost'*) denotes "protection"; their view of security of information includes therefore several dimensions: human, social, spiritual, and technical factors. Conversely, the main priorities for U.S. cyber security policy are to safeguard domestic technologies from disruptions, unauthorized access, or any other kind of interference.[7]

In the Russian construct, *information warfare* is not an activity limited to wartime. It is not even restricted to the "initial phase of conflict" before hostilities begin, which includes information preparation of the battle space (Antonovich, 2011). Instead, it is an ongoing activity of the state of relations with the opponent (Heickerö, 2010); "in contrast to other forms and methods of opposition, information confrontation is waged constantly in peacetime" (Slipchenko, 1998; Panarin, 2006, 2012) For Russia, contest with the West in the information domain has already begun. Ongoing information warfare is "a regular feature of the country's news and current affairs coverage."[8]

At the same time, some Russian authors while discussing the permanent nature of information confrontation have drawn a distinction between its nature in peacetime and wartime. According to this categorization, peacetime is mostly characterized by covert measures, reconnaissance, espionage, building capacities, and degrading those of the adversary, and maneuvering for advantage in information space. Wartime measures, by contrast, are deliberately aggressive, and include "discrediting [adversary] leadership, intimidating military personnel and civilians . . . falsification of events, disinformation, and hacking attacks" (Malyshev, 2000; Sharavov, 2000) Furthermore, "the main effort is concentrated on achieving political or diplomatic ends, and influencing the leadership and public opinion of foreign states, as well as international and regional organizations" (Donskov and Nikitin, 2005). If measured by these criteria, recent Russian activities in the information domain would indicate that Russia already considers itself to be in a state of war.[9]

Crucially, information warfare can cover a vast range of different activities and processes seeking to steal, plant, interdict, manipulate, distort, or destroy information. The channels and methods available for doing this cover an equally broad range, including computers, smartphones, real or invented news media, statements by leaders or celebrities, online troll campaigns, text messages, vox pops by concerned citizens, YouTube videos, or direct approaches to individual human targets.[10]

The Internet, cyber, and information in Russia's worldview

State-centrism (emphasis on state sovereignty) and anti-Americanism (pushing for "de-Westernizing" the Internet, fed by a quest for international recognition and prestige) are the "heart and lungs" of Russia's vision and policy on Internet-related issues at both domestic and global levels. On a "practical level," Russia considers information to be *militarized*, the aim being to reach informational superiority over the adversary (Gorbachev, 2013).

De-Americanizing the Internet

In recent years, global issues connected to the Internet and its uses have vaulted into the realm of "high politics." Amongst these, Internet governance has long been ignored and restricted to small silos of experts; however, the leaks disclosed by Edward Snowden in June 2013 triggered a massive response to the historical "stewardship" of the Internet by the United States, destabilized foreign relations, and impacted geopolitics of cyberspace (Segal, 2016). Today, international politics has blended with individual actions (from Julian Assange's WikiLeaks to Edward Snowden) and the development of multinational corporations in a way never seen before. Stakes are high indeed: today 2.5 billion people are connected, and by 2030, the Internet is likely to represent 20% of the world's GDP (Dean, 2012). Beyond mere figures, Internet governance sharpens everyone's appetite – from big corporations to governments, as the Internet has taken such a place in our lives, and from freedom of expression to privacy, intellectual property rights to national security (Nocetti, 2014a). Data encryption, as well as data localization, have more recently emerged as significant and contentious policy issues between the states-corporations-citizens' triangle (Farrell and Newman, 2016; Nocetti, 2016).

Unsurprisingly, a number of countries including Russia have been criticizing U.S. "hegemony" over the Internet (infrastructures, "critical resources" such as protocols, the domain names system, or normative influence, etc.). To a large extent, the Internet is the ambivalent product of the U.S. culture and the expression of its universalist and expansionist ideology. As U.S. policymakers emphasized the importance of winning the battle of ideas both during the Cold War and in the post-2001 period, the ability to transmit the United States' *soft power* via communications networks has been perceived as vital. U.S. policymakers have viewed the "free flow of information" as a means to by-pass authoritarian governments to allow the United States to "tell its story" directly to the people, allowing the targeted populations to understand that U.S. foreign policy is benign and thereby wean them away from radical ideologies (McCarthy, 2011).

Consequently, in recent years, particularly since the Arab uprisings in 2011, governments around the world have become more alert to the disruptive potential of access to digital communications. Thus the line between *technical* and *political* governance is being increasingly blurred by predominantly – but not exclusively – authoritarian governments who fear the "subversive power" of networked technologies from both a political and economic perspective (Yakushev, 2010, 2013). Demographic factors are also put forward: by the 2020s, the Internet's center of gravity will have moved eastwards – already in 2012, 66% of the world's Internet users were living in the non-Western world.[11] However, the reasons for questioning U.S. supremacy also lie in these countries' defiance towards the current Internet governance system, which is accused of favoring the sole interests of the United States (Nocetti, 2014b). As a result of these conceptions, *Moscow has been advancing the "internationalization" of Internet governance* at both regional and international levels since the mid-2000s. Russia, like China and some Middle Eastern nations, considers much of the U.S. stance on cyber politics to be hypocritical: while preaching the tearing down of "digital borders" that have emerged in some authoritarian countries, U.S. intelligence organizations have been recording and exploiting metadata without any oversight (Gomart, 2013: 102).

The Kremlin fully considers the Internet as a foreign policy item, and strives to take the lead on global cyber governance and security issues as international contention increasingly arises surrounding the membership, mandates, and supervision of the institutions for cyber management. Reflecting its views on the international system and law, Moscow upholds a traditional understanding of sovereignty and the principle of non-intervention at the core of its policy towards global Internet matters. This results in portraying cyberspace as a territory with virtual borders which correspond to real state borders, and in extending the remit of international laws to the Internet space. As a consequence, Russia is actively involved in promoting international norms that should guide states' behavior in cyberspace on the global arena, thus reflecting a mostly state-centric approach to Internet-related issues (see later) (Nocetti, 2015).[12]

The militarization of information

In contrast to the common Western view of the Internet as an enabler and facilitator, many Russian analysts, experts, and commentators are guided by a much better established perception of insecurity online, and a greater openness to considering the Internet as a vulnerability (*Antirossiyskiy vector*, 2016). The Russian intelligence services publicly stress the potential for a detrimental effect on national security arising from being connected to the Internet.

The functional ("war on information warfare against Russia") and the geopolitical contexts are closely intertwined. The foreign policy doctrine treats information as a dangerous weapon: it is a cheap, universal weapon, with unlimited range; it is easily accessible and permeates all state borders without restrictions. The information and network struggle (more frequently, the information-psychological struggle), including its extreme forms, such as information-psychological warfare and netwars, are means the state uses to achieve its goals in international, regional, and domestic politics, and also to gain a geopolitical advantage.

On 29 December 2014, the Security Council of the Russian Federation published a new version of the Military Doctrine of the Russian Federation. The comments accompanying the Russian doctrine emphasized the importance of informational operations in contemporary conflicts, and the inclusion of information into the country's defensive arsenal (Security Council, 2014).

By emphasizing the need for a reassessment of the global situation (the struggle of the world's leading countries for their interests are characterized by indirect actions, exploiting the potential for protest among local populations, radical and extremist organizations, as well as private military companies), the Security Council reiterated the anti-NATO and anti-American mantra which has constantly been present in successive editions of the Doctrine.

The new Doctrine conceives of information as a national security instrument amongst others. This is not new in Russia's approach – both the 2000 Military Doctrine and Doctrine on Information Security already emphasized that precise aspect. However, information warfare now features prominently in several sections of the Doctrine, which proves how fundamental the information factor has become in recent conflicts. Indeed, one of the main external military threats is identified as "the use of ICTs in a political-military purpose in order to act, against international law, sovereignty, political independence and territorial integrity of states, and to threaten international peace and security, and world and regional stability."

The Doctrine states a number of examples of information uses described earlier, as "the combined use of military force with political, economic, informational and other means, leading to an intense use of the protest potential of the population." This particular scenario, which imagines the population ganging up against its political leaders, is recurring in how Russians understand information warfare. This Doctrine also enumerates other informational threats as encouraging the youth to give up their historical, spiritual, and patriotic traditions, or to disturb governmental agencies and information infrastructures.

The new elements introduced in the Doctrine clearly suggest a blurring of the lines between external and internal threats. For some scholars, these signal the "militarization" of the Kremlin's domestic and foreign policies. By mobilizing and sensitizing the public to the threat from the West, the Kremlin legitimizes its military policy on both the domestic and international arenas (Darczewska, 2015: 12). The message to foreign audiences is more nuanced: the Doctrine supplies the so-called opinion-makers, and in practice the moderators with informational campaigns.

The significance of the domestic factor

As a relatively young nation-state that has been experiencing a potent feeling of insecurity since the chaotic 1990s transition to a free market economy and pluralism, Russia has thus been adopting a threat-oriented lens towards the Internet. By extension, the country's Internet policy conveys a long-lasting security fear. This feeling stems in part from the complex interactions between state authorities and the media ecosystem since the 1980s, when Soviet leaders tolerated increased access to previously suppressed information, thus opening the "information gates" to the masses. In the 2000s, with Russia striving for full sovereignty and struggling against the "permeability" of its neighborhood, President Vladimir Putin gradually saw the information revolution – driven by the considerable growth in domestic Internet access – as one of the most pervasive components of the U.S. expansionism in the post-Soviet sphere, most notably in Russia itself.

However, officials have long paid modest attention to the Russian Internet's development, supporting its benefits for the country's economy while tolerating some spaces online for dissenting activities (Etling, 2010). The first legal online restrictions were imposed in 2002–2003 on condition of fighting "extremism." In parallel, SORM-II, the technical system used by several law enforcement agencies to intercept and analyze the contents of telecommunications within Russia, extended its reach to monitoring the Internet.[13]

The authorities' approach drastically changed from 2011 when they observed citizens from some Arab countries mobilizing and coordinating their protest actions through networked technologies. These events – known as "Arab Spring" – did profoundly impact the minds of Russian political and security elites. Reflecting on the sustained use of digital technologies – microblogs such as Twitter, video platforms such as YouTube, and social networks such as Facebook – in the revolutionary processes in Tunisia, Libya, and Egypt, the Kremlin and Russian law enforcement agencies started to monitor closely the impact of the political use of networked technologies upon social mobilization and democratic transition (Nocetti, 2012). The events in the Arab world did clearly reawaken the authorities' fear of "regime change" initiated from abroad, i.e. by the United States, through the use of digital tools.

These international developments inspired many in Russia who demanded substantial political changes after a decade of Vladimir Putin's rule characterized by rising living standards for the population guaranteed by the state in exchange for (most) political freedoms (Parker, 2014). During the years of Dmitry Medvedev as President of Russia (2008–2012), the Internet served as a substitute to the public sphere in Russia, equivalent to the role played by literature in the nineteenth century and independent media in the 1980s (Pipenko, 2010). Digital technologies have indeed been used by citizens in a "creative" way for mobilization purposes around a particular cause, addressing the politicians directly to solve such issues, thus going beyond both the legal online restrictions that have been imposed since 2002–2003, and overcoming the traditional distrustful attitude toward institutions among Russian society (Sidorenko, 2011). Overall, Internet users have become skillful in circumventing "legislative" obstacles online or at least mitigating their consequences. They learned to move their profiles quickly or duplicate them on Western social networks when popular blog platforms such as LiveJournal were subject to denial-of-service (DDoS) attacks. They massively use services such as TOR, and traditionally resort to humor to make a mockery of political authorities (Kastoueva-Jean and Nocetti, 2012).

The 2011–2012 election cycle in Russia – a parliamentary ballot in December 2011 and a presidential vote in March 2012 – reawakened Russian leaders' anxiety over the Internet's potential for political disruption. Indeed, the political leadership feared a ripple effect in the countryside, as mass protests in its biggest cities were mostly coordinated on and facilitated by the use of digital technologies (Bode and Makarychev, 2013). Likewise, the Kremlin felt irritated by the fact that the Internet enables citizens to circumvent government-controlled "traditional" media, most importantly television.[14]

More strikingly, the scandal which involved the National Security Agency (NSA) around Edward Snowden's leaked documents revived the push for tighter controls over the Internet in Russia, on the basis that the transnational companies' privacy policies (Google, Facebook, Twitter, etc.) pose a threat to Russia's digital sovereignty – and consequently national security. Several members from both houses of the parliament suggested locating in Russia all servers having Russian citizens' personal data, and started a media campaign to bring global Web platforms under Russian jurisdiction – either requiring them to be accessible in Russia by the domain extension ".ru", or obliging them to be hosted on Russian territory (Zheleznyak, 2013).

Though not specific to Russia, plans to promote national networking technology, set up a secure national email service, and encourage regional Internet traffic to be routed locally, are well in the spirit of the times in Moscow. All these claims tend to legitimize and revive the years-old call for a "national operating system" that would reduce Russian dependency on Microsoft Windows.

In April 2014 Vladimir Putin publicly assimilated the Internet into a "CIA project." Rumors about an Internet "kill switch" being devised in Russia came after "cyber exercises" reportedly revealed vulnerabilities in the Russian Internet's security infrastructure preparedness against potential external aggression (Golitsyna, 2014). This produced calls for the creation of a self-contained system duplicating the root domain name system (DNS) architecture to keep the Russian Internet running in case of emergency, either externally – which is no longer seen as hypothetical in the current belligerent geopolitical context – or, in case of civil disorder and/or extremist action, internally.[15]

The assumption that digital technologies are used by the West to topple regimes in countries where the opposition is too weak to mobilize protests has thus come to define the Kremlin's approach to the Internet both in Russia and globally. *Domestic factors therefore play a crucial role in shaping Russia's Internet policies.* Fundamentally, Russia has been adopting an "inside-outside" approach towards the Internet: (draft) laws and public speeches go hand-in-hand with policy initiatives at the regional (i.e. near abroad) and global level, while international events impact Russia's policy-making in this regard. For some, this approach cannot be split away from the inherently authoritarian nature of the Russian regime, which would perpetuate a century-long tradition of muzzling dissenting voices, whatever the medium used.[16] For others, this strategy can be explained by the fact that Russia is a relatively young nation-state still insecure about its sovereignty, hence the stronger commitment to a backwards-looking, sovereigntist approach to Internet governance (Mueller, 2013).

Beyond the "Arab Spring" and Snowden syndromes, it is clear that Russia has deep concerns on the principle of uncontrolled exchange of information in cyberspace, and over the presumption that national borders are of limited relevance there (Giles, 2012). "Content as threat" pertinently informs the Russian perception that digital technologies can be used as tools *against* Russia. In Russian documentation this is expressed as the "threat of the use of content for influence on the socio-humanitarian sphere."

This overall defensive mindset and stance led to a questioning of the reshaping of Russian foreign and security policies through cyber. The cyber domain is conceived of as an asymmetric weapon, in an unequal balance of power as Russia's conventional means remain inferior to NATO's. Back in 2007 Vladimir Putin claimed, "Our answers have to be based on intellectual superiority; they will be asymmetric and less costly." In short, the Russian strategy is one of a "cross-domain coercion"[17] that combines propaganda, cyberattacks, and the use of both conventional and nuclear forces, in an action aimed at blurring the distinction between war and peace, and preventing any quick and coordinated reaction from Western leaders. The successive hacks, leaks, dissemination of "fake news" are thus seen as complementary to the use of strategic bombers, missile defense systems, or tanks. In other words, the traditional vehicles for Russian power – the military, energy – are no longer sufficient to explain the transformation of Russian power. Cyber and information instruments do not contradict other foreign policy tools; they complement them, as Chief of Staff Valery Gerasimov clearly wrote in his articles (Gerasimov, 2013).

Government funding has been increasing in parallel with the Kremlin's interest in cyberspace. The appointment of Sergei Shoigu as Minister of Defense in November 2012 seemingly translated into a progressive and constant interest in strengthening both Russian capabilities and "human resources" dealing with cyber and information (Turovskiy, 2016).

The successive Russian military involvements in Georgia, and later in Crimea, Eastern Ukraine, and Syria, were the opportunity to test the country's enhanced capabilities in information and cyber. These were reflected in particular in the long-announced creation of "Information Troops," effective from February 2017 and which gather diverse profiles from hackers, specialists in sociolinguistics, psychology, and networks.

Moscow's cyber diplomacy in practice

Russia wants to position itself in an *exclusive dialogue with the United States on defining norms in cyberspace*. On the one hand, the Kremlin noticed that since the annexation of Crimea in 2014 the United States dropped their strategic dialogue with Moscow on cyber security in favor of China – to the point of signing with Beijing a pact of non-aggression in cyberspace in 2015. *The redefinition of Internet geopolitics in favor of a China-U.S. "duopoly" irritates Russia*, which still considers itself as a cyber superpower. On the other hand, the Kremlin did not hide its irritation towards Barack Obama's reluctance to agree on a "Code of conduct" that would rule cyber war operations. Pushed by Russia, such an agreement would replace debates within the United Nations – a red line for the U.S. administration. *Moscow and Washington remain antagonistic on their approach towards cyber security*: unlike the United States that gives priority to technology and networks, the Russians want to include in any future agreement the cognitive layer of cyberspace.

Reshaping the debate on cyber norms

In little more than a generation, the Internet has become the substrate of the global economy and governance worldwide. The convergence of the data economy, robotics, the Internet of Things, and (tomorrow) artificial intelligence overwhelms not only industrial production but also societies and the world's balance of power. All of this increasing interdependence implies vulnerabilities that governments and non-governmental actors can exploit. In such a volatile context, *Russia posits that the set of norms that governed state behavior before the rise of the Internet did not translate to state behavior in an Internet age* – in other words, a new digital age required new norms.

As a consequence, Russia has been pro-actively engaged in norm-promotion through international institutions. Now a highly contentious issue (Bradshaw, 2014), global Internet governance has seen a constant Russian involvement to introduce security concerns into previously unpoliticized or mostly technical issues and forums (Nocetti, 2015).

As a case in point, Russia and the Russian-speaking countries of the former Soviet Union have adopted a wide-ranging engagement with forums such as the International Telecommunications Union (ITU) and the Internet Governance Forum (IGF) to promote policies that synchronize with national-level laws surrounding information security. Vladimir Putin himself several times pleaded that global cyberspace should be governed by international institutions operating under the United Nations – and that the ITU was the best placed institution to regulate the Internet. Notably, every year since 1998, Russia has put forward resolutions at the United Nations to prohibit "information aggression," which is widely interpreted to mean ideological attempts, or the use of ideas, to undermine regime stability.

In a 2011 letter to the United Nations General Assembly outlining a proposal for an "International Code of Conduct for Information Security," the Russian coalition (gathering China, Uzbekistan, and Tajikistan) proposed a codification of this concept, stipulating that states subscribing to the Code pledge to "not use information and communications technologies and other information and communications networks to interfere with the internal affairs of other states or with the aim of undermining their political, economic and social stability."

At roughly the same time, a *Draft Convention on International Information Security* was released at an "international meeting of high-ranking officials responsible for security matters" in the Russian city of Yekaterinburg. The draft neatly illustrates many divergences between Russian and Western preconceptions about the nature of the Internet and the basic assumptions on how it should be governed.

Taken together, the two documents propose to significantly strengthen the power of the state in cyberspace vis-à-vis non-government actors, introducing raw security concerns. But they also provide an alternative vision for hesitant countries that may lean naturally toward state-dominated models of governance, and that side with Russia – and China – in decrying the destabilizing potential of the Internet and cyberspace more broadly.

At the regional level, Moscow uses regional organizations and forums to disseminate its views on cyberspace policies and the norms it seeks to push internationally. One illuminating example is the Shanghai Cooperation Organization (SCO).[18] The SCO aims to share information and coordinate policies around a broad spectrum of cultural, economic, and security concerns, among them cyberspace policies. Generally speaking, experts see the SCO as a regional vehicle of "protective integration" against international norms of democracy and regime change, with shared information policies being seen as critical to that end.[19] Since 2009, SCO member states are bound by an agreement on "cooperation in the field of ensuring international information security"; and more recently, the SCO issued a statement on "information terrorism," which drew attention to the way in which the countries have a shared and distinct perspective on Internet security policy. The Code of Conduct discussed earlier was proposed by SCO states, which formulated global standards for "unacceptable state behavior" in cyberspace.

The BRICS format is also used as a vehicle for cooperation on cyber issues. At the policy level, the BRICS states have all shown an interest in Internet governance and cyber security. Yet there is a difference in prioritization. There was no joint BRICS proposal for a Code of Conduct on information security. Despite the increased institutionalization of BRICS as a coalition, and despite various proposals contesting the U.S. role regarding the Internet, the group is splintered, and formal proposals have been submitted either through IBSA (India-Brazil-South Africa) or the SCO (Ebert and Maurer, 2013). Generally speaking, the key differences are informed by states favoring an intergovernmental approach based on international cooperation and those preferring to adopt a strict "sovereigntist" cyber policy.

The Russia/China/U.S. triangle

Increasingly active in forging new alliances and trying to reformulate norms and standards, Russia has also been engaged in an up-and-down cyber diplomacy with the United States (Markoff and Kramer, 2009; White House, 2013b). Clearly, while endeavoring to shape the international dialogue on cyberspace, *the aim for Moscow is to "bilateralize" cyber security and cyber warfare issues with Washington, reflecting a quest for an exclusive and direct dialogue on par with the United States* on this issue.

There is clear evidence that the dialogue between the two countries is not easy – they both have diverging approaches toward the security of cyberspace, and have reacted differently to major international events surrounding Internet governance and cyber security. Bilateral consultations particularly focused on reaching a consensus on critical terminology defining cyber/information security, as both governments have had different priorities from each other on the issue. Beyond agreements on terminology, both governments have turned to a series of confidence-building measures, including the establishment of a "cyber-hotline" between the U.S. cyber security coordinator and the Russian deputy secretary of the Security Council, should there be a need to directly manage a crisis situation arising from an ICT security incident. The step was taken on the fringe of the G-8 Summit in Northern Ireland in June 2013 (White House, 2013a) – just when leaked details of network surveillance and espionage programs by the NSA were stirring up international concern about how deep U.S. intelligence is reaching into IT operations worldwide. A month later was announced the formation of a bilateral presidential group on information security, tasked with easing tensions between both capitals and carrying on the implementation of confidence-building measures (Chernenko, 2013).

Russia views the major world economies' build up of their potential for information warfare with great concern. As stressed by official Russian documents, this development could lead to a new arms race in the information sphere and raises the threat of foreign intelligence services penetrating Russia through technical means, such as global information infrastructure. Consequently, Russia vehemently wants to restrict offensive cyber weapons (Croft, 2012; Peck, 2013). In this respect, the increasingly institutionalized dialogue with Washington also serves as a way to call for the prevention of cyberspace militarization. Indeed, while the United States has said they want a peaceful cyberspace, *Moscow accuses Washington of militarizing the Internet* through the establishment of a Cyber Command and the development of offensive capabilities such as *Stuxnet* (PIR-Tsentr, 2016).

More broadly, Russia criticizes the constant rise in the U.S. budget for cyber operations.[20] As far as norms are concerned, the U.S. concept of counter-measures sounds worrisome to Moscow. The Kremlin, as Beijing, is opposed to a key notion in Washington: the extraterritoriality of counter-measures, i.e. the possibility for a state attacked by another state via servers domiciled in a third country to respond to these servers.[21]

It is clear that recent global Internet governance and security venues have shown a portability of Cold War policies into the twenty-first century cyber arena (Gross, 2012; Klimburg, 2013). Using the nuclear non-proliferation treaty as an appropriate precedent, others note that a global consensus on cyber security could be best achieved by pursuing deterrence strategies (Choucri, 2012: 173). Russia has conspicuously opted for the first strategy, which enables its policy-makers to follow Moscow's long-standing foreign policy objective of promoting legally binding international treaties, whilst in this case developing its own cyber capabilities.[22]

Though largely U.S.-centric, Russia's international cyber policy has also sought to focus on China following the Russian "turn to the East" fostered by the Kremlin since 2014 (Trenin, 2016). The bilateral relationship has attracted speculation about whether it will continue to deepen into an alliance. The cybersecurity deal signed in 2015 between Moscow and Beijing seemed to mark further Sino-Russian cooperation in another arena – cyberspace. The pact has two key features: mutual assurance on non-aggression in cyberspace and language advocating cyber-sovereignty. The two sides agreed on a range of trust- and confidence-building measures and joint "promotion of norms of international law in order to ensure national and international information security," especially under the auspices of the platforms of the relevant international organizations: the United States, OSCE, and ITU. The agreement looks like an ambitious attempt at setting the rules of the game in cyberspace at a time when no such consent on norms of behavior seems currently feasible at a global level. Also, the Russia-China deal can be seen as a response to the 2015 U.S. cyber defense strategy, which directly identifies Russia and China among its key adversaries – both countries "have developed advanced cyber capabilities and strategies," while only mentioning the need for keeping a dialogue with China.

The two sides have not experienced big public fallout on mutual hacking so far,[23] which makes what seems like a non-aggression pact look more like a pre-emptive declaration of understanding, making a special point of this consensus to the external world.

Nevertheless, cyber-espionage is not the core of the Sino-Russian cybersecurity cooperation. Much like Russia and China's combined effort to oppose a U.S.-dominated world order, the insistence on "cyber-sovereignty" is a shared strategic interest that contrasts with the U.S. advocacy for "cyber freedom." This was further emphasized at the Wuzhen World Internet Conference, an annual meeting organized by Chinese government agencies first held in 2014, where Chinese politicians – including President Xi Xinping – together with Russian guests (high-level officials, experts) also forcefully promoted a norms-driven approach to cyberspace governance.

However, *for the Chinese the highest priority remains their strategic dialogue on cyberspace with the United States*. Beijing and Washington signed a non-aggression pact in cyberspace in autumn 2015 following years of negotiations on highly contentious issues between the two sides (cyberwarfare, cyber espionage) (Austin and Gady, 2012; Lieberthal and Singer, 2012). *The redefinition of global Internet geopolitics along a Sino-U.S. axis is not seen favorably in Moscow* – that might be a reason why the Russians "flex their muscles" in terms of cyber aggressions worldwide in order to test U.S. and NATO capabilities and reactions, and to reshape the cyber norms' debate. Moscow's U.S. election-related activities brought the importance of Russia's conceptualization of information security front and center in the United States, possibly making it harder for Washington to separate cyber security from information security.[24]

Russia's interference in the 2016 U.S. presidential election

Russian involvement in the U.S. presidential election, as formally alleged by the Obama administration, represented a turning point in U.S.-Russia relationships and in international politics – at least as regards state conduct in cyberspace. The theft of a vast amount of data in mid-2016 belonging to the Democratic National Committee and other political organizations was allegedly the work of Russian hacker groups. Although Russian cyber operations are surrounded with high secrecy, some groups labelled as "APT 28" and "APT 29," also known respectively as "Cozy Bear" and "Fancy Bear," gained public attention during the election campaign as well as being under Washington's high scrutiny, as these are allegedly tied to Russian intelligence services. Barack Obama took the unprecedented step of imposing sanctions on the chiefs of the Main Intelligence Directorate (GRU) and the FSB (Jones, 2017). The alleged attacks from Moscow combined the technological dimension and intelligence-gathering capabilities of twenty-first-century hackers with the art of propaganda familiar with Cold War-era tactics.[25]

Overall, Russian interference in the U.S. election perfectly illustrated how the Russians view cyber, i.e. as an embedded part of the broader concept of information operations. Russian maneuvers aimed less at influencing the outcome of the election than at the perceptions (*soznanie*) Americans have about the reliability of their rulers and institutions. Sowing a general distrust towards the U.S. political system, directing voters toward candidates more lenient vis-à-vis Russian *Weltanschauung* and objectives, keeping the idea that Western leaders are indecisive, weak, divided: that is the longer-term Russian strategy. Moscow's larger goal is to strengthen the doubt in public opinion toward Western policies and values: liberal democracy, multiculturalism, and interventionism under the guise of "responsibility to protect."

Less costly than "traditional warfare," information and cyber instruments also prove considerably harder to be attributed to governments. In the case of the U.S. election, the Obama administration took several months to publicly attribute the hacks and leaks to Moscow – nevertheless an unprecedented move given the escalation risks such a step can carry, all the more opening both a legal and technical "Pandora's box" for further cyber damage.

Conclusion

The cyber realm is becoming a salient topic in international relations – no one doubts that. Russia so far has had a rather subtle "use" of the Internet/cyber instrument in its foreign policy, which remains under-estimated in academic and policy-oriented analyses. Like in other international issues, in cyberspace Russia does not have permanent allies. All Moscow's alignments are situational and conditional, serving primarily Russia's regional interests or, most notably, its world-order goals. *There is no Russian "grand strategy" related to cyber policy. Instead, the Kremlin constantly maneuvers, seizes opportunities wherever they are, and quickly reacts to international events.* The Snowden disclosures in 2014 immediately come to mind: in welcoming on its soil the U.S. whistleblower, Russia not only caused a major diplomatic blow to Washington, it also signaled a shift in the geopolitics of cyberspace, the consequence of which are still meaningful.

One of the major differences between Russia and the West on cyberspace is that the Russians primarily consider the cognitive layer of the network, i.e. the contents. The key word is *information*. In the Russian conceptual framework, this information can be stored anywhere and transmitted by any means – so information in print media, or on television, or in somebody's head, is subject to the same targeting concepts as that held on an adversary's computer or smartphone. Similarly, the transmission or transfer of this information can be by any means: so introducing corrupted data into a computer across a network or from a flash drive is conceptually no different from placing disinformation in a media outlet, or causing it to be repeated in public by a key influencer. *This holistic approach has also been underestimated – or misunderstood – in the West*, which has always been keen to create a clear separation between cybersecurity and information security.

Will the 2016 U.S. presidential election be a game-changer in the future? For the first time in history, the cyber tool has been directly accused of playing a pre-eminent role in determining the outcome of a vote through the meddling of a foreign power – Russia. Relying on both cyber-attacks and information operations, a confident Russia may use these as a particularly potent foreign policy instrument wherever it needs to dictate its interests. In other words, hydrocarbon pipelines and conventional military instruments are no longer sufficient to illustrate twenty-first-century Russian power: cyber power is definitely a core element in this triad.

Notes

1 The author stresses the following books Lo, 2015; Tsygankov, 2013; Allison, 2013; and Mankoff, 2009.
2 Author's experience during closed seminars and internet forums, Moscow, April 2013, November 2014 and April 2015.
3 Author's interview with the deputy director of Moscow State University's Institute for Information Security Issues (IISI), Moscow, 13 December 2012.
4 Author's informal talk on the sidelines of an international seminar in Garmisch-Partenkirchen, Germany, 23 April 2013.
5 Author's interview with the deputy director of Moscow State University's Institute for Information Security Issues (IISI), Moscow, 20 October 2011 and 13 December 2012.
6 Author's discussions with Russian experts and officials, Moscow, July and October 2011. See also Giles (2012).
7 Author's discussion with an American official, Krakow, 29 September 2015. See also the U.S. *International Strategy for Cyberspace*, The White House, May 2011.
8 As described in a BBC Monitoring media survey (Ennis, 2016).

9 Multiple indicative examples include computer network operations targeting the U.S. in a practically overt manner, and Russia's new lack of concern at accompanying damage to its international reputation (Blake, 2016).
10 Closed seminar at IFRI, Paris, 10 March 2017.
11 Data collected from www.internetworldstats.com (as of 15 February 2014).
12 On Russia's activities on norms-making at the United Nations, see Maurer, 2011.
13 For a comprehensive analysis of early restrictive legislations over the internet in Russia, see Alexander, 2004.
14 However, television has so far remained the main source of information for a majority of Russians.
15 Even though a special Security Council meeting reassured that "no internet switch off" or state takeover is planned, it would be right to assume the further strengthening of Russia's internet at the level of critical cyber infrastructure as part of the national security capacities.
16 Author's interviews with academics in Moscow, December 2012 and February 2013.
17 The expression was coined by Dmitry Adamsky, 2015.
18 The Organization comprises China, Kyrgyzstan, Kazakhstan, Russia, Tajikistan, and Uzbekistan. India, Iran, Mongolia, Afghanistan and Pakistan have observer status, and Belarus, Turkey, and Sri Lanka are considered dialogue partners.
19 Author's interview with a Russian academic, Moscow, October 2011. Read also Allison, 2008.
20 Indeed, the 2014 budget request includes a 20% increase from 2012; the U.S. Cyber Command is reportedly expanding by more than fivefold (Negroponte et al., 2013: 35).
21 Author's talk with a French official, 29 September 2015.
22 Author's interview with a Russian expert on information security, Moscow, February 2013.
23 Russia's security firm Kaspersky Lab estimated that cyber-espionage attacks by "Chinese-speaking" groups against Russian targets increased 300 percent from December 2015 to February 2016.
24 Informal discussions of the author with American and British experts, Ditchley, 18 November 2016.
25 See, for instance, declassified U.S. Department of State (1981) reports on Soviet "active measures."

References

Adamsky, Dmitry. 2015. "Cross-Domain Coercion; The Current Russian Art of Strategy," Ifri, *Proliferation Papers* No. 54, November.
Alexander, Marcus. 2004. "The Internet and Democratization: The Development of Russian Internet Policy," *Demokratizatsiya* 12, 4: 616.
Allison, Roy. 2008. "Virtual Regionalism, Regional Structures and Regime Security in Central Asia," *Central Asian Survey* 27, 2: 185–202.
Allison, Roy. 2013. *Russia, the West, and Military Intervention*, Oxford, UK: Oxford University Press.
Antirossiyskiy vektor: zarubezhe SMI v 2015 g. 2016. Moscow: Rossiyskiy Institut Strategicheskikh Isledovaniy.
Antonovich, P. 2011. "Cyberwarfare: Nature and Content," *Military Thought* 20, 3: 35–43.
Austin, Greg and Franz-Stefan Gady. 2012. "Cyber Detente between the United States and China. Shaping the Agenda," New York: East-West Institute.
Blake, Aaron. 2016. "The CIA Concluded that Russia Worked to elect Trump. Republicans Now Face an Impossible Choice," *The Washington Post*, 9 December.
Bode, Nicole and Andrei Makarychev. 2013. "The New Social Media in Russia: Political Blogging by the Government and the Opposition," *Problems of Post-Communism* 60, 2: 53–62.
Bradshaw, Samantha, Laura DeNardis, Fen Osler Hampson, Eric Jardine and Mark Raymond 2014. "The Emergence of Contention in Global Internet Governance," *The Centre for International Governance Innovation, Paper presented at the 9th Annual GigaNet Symposium, Istanbul*, 1st September. https://papers.ssrn.com/sol3/papers.cfm?abstract_id=2809835.
Chernenko, Yelena. 2013. "RF i SShA popytayutsiya snizit' napryazhenie v seti", *Kommersant'*, 22nd July.
Choucri, Nazli. 2012. *Cyberpolitics in International Relations*, Cambridge, MA: MIT Press.
Croft, Adrian. 2012. "Russia Says Many States Arming for Cyber Warfare," Reuters, 25 April.
Darczewska, Jolanta. 2015. "The Devil is in the Details: Information Warfare in the Light of Russia's Military Doctrine," OSW, *Point of View* 50, May.
Dean, David, Sebastian Digrande, Dominic Field, Andreas Lundmark 2012. "The Internet Economy is Growing More than 10 percent Per Year in the G-20 Nations." www.bcg.com/publications/2012/technology-digital-technology-planning-internet-economy-g20-4-2-trillion-opportunity.aspx.

Donskov, Yu and O. Nikitin. 2005. "Mesto i rol' spetsial'nykh informatsionnykh operatsij pri razreshenii voennykh konfliktov," *Voyennaya mysl'* 6: 17–23.
Ebert, Hannes and Tim Maurer. 2013. "Contested Cyberspace and Rising Powers," *Third World Quarterly* 34, 6: 1054–1074.
Ennis, Stephen. 2016. "Russia's Fixation with 'Information War,'" BBC News, 26 May.
Etling, Bruce, Karina Alexanyan, John Kelly, Robert Farris, John G Palfrey Jr and Urs Gasser, 2010. "Public Discourse in the Russian Blogosphere: Mapping RuNet Politics and Mobilization," Massachusetts, MA: Harvard University, Berkman Center for Internet & Society, October.
Farrell, Henry and Abraham Newman, 2016. "The Transatlantic Data War," *Foreign Affairs*, January/February. Online. www.foreignaffairs.com/articles/united-states/2015-12-14/transatlantic-data-war.
Franke, Ulrik. 2015. "War by Non-Military Means. Understanding Russian Information Warfare," Swedish Defence Research Agency (FOI), *Report*, March.
Gerasimov, Valery. 2013. "Tsennost' nauki v predvidenii", *Voenno-promychlennij kurier*, 27 February.
Giles, Keir. 2012. "Russia and Cyber Security," *Naçao e Defesa* 5, 133: 69–88.
Golitsyna, Anastasia. 2014. "Soviet bezopasnosti obsudit otkluchenie Rossii ot global'nogo interneta," *Vedomosti*, 19 September.
Gomart, Thomas. 2013. "De quoi Snowden est-il le nom?" *Revue des deux mondes*, December.
Gorbachev, Yuri. 2013. "Kibervoina uzhe idet," *Novoe voennoe obozrenie*, 13, 12–18 April.
Gross, Michal Joseph. 2012. "World War 3.0," *Vanity Fair*, May.
Heickerö, R. 2010. "Emerging Cyber Threats and Russian Views on Information Warfare and Information Operations," *Swedish Defence Research Establishment (FOI)*.
Jones, Sam. 2017. "Russia Mobilises an Elite Band of Cyber Warriors", *Financial Times*, 23 February.
Kastoueva-Jean, Tatiana and Julien Nocetti. 2012. "Le LOL, nouvel avatar de la contestation en Russie", *Les Echos*, 8 November.
Klimburg, Alexander. 2013. "The Internet Yalta," Center for a New American Security, *Commentary*, 5th February
Kramer, Franklin, Stuart Starr and Larry Wentz (eds), 2009. *Cyber Power and National Security*, Washington, DC: National Defense University Press.
Kramer, Jan-Frederik and Benedikt Müller (eds), 2014. *Cyberspace and International Relations. Theory, Prospects and Challenges*, Berlin: Springer.
Kuehl, Dan. 2009. "From Cyberspace to Cyberpower: Defining the Problem," in Franklin Kramer, Stuart Starr and Larry Wentz (eds), 2009. *Cyber Power and National Security*, Washington, DC: National Defense University Press.
Lieberthal, Kenneth and Peter W. Singer. 2012. *Cybersecurity and U.S.-China Relations*, New York: Brookings Institution, February.
Lo, Bobo. 2015. *Russia and the New World Disorder*, New York: Brookings Institution, and London: Chatham House.
Malyshev, V. 2000. "Ispol'zovanie vozmozhnostey sredstv massovoy informatsii v lokal'nikh vooruzhen-nykh konfliktakh", *Zarubezhnoye voyennoye obozreniye*, 7: 2–8.
Maurer, Tim. 2011. "Cyber Norm Emergence at the United Nations: An Analysis of the UN's Activities Regarding Cyber-security," *Discussion Paper 2011-11*, Cambridge, MA: Belfer Center for Science and International Affairs, Harvard Kennedy School, September.
Mankoff, Jeffrey. 2009. *Russian Foreign Policy: Return to Great Power Politics*, New York: Council on Foreign Relations and Rowman & Littlefield.
Markoff, John and Andrew Kramer. 2009. "In Shift, U.S. Talks to Russia on Internet Security," *The New York Times*, 12th December.
McCarthy, Daniel. 2011. "Open Networks and the Open Door: American Foreign Policy and the Narration of the Internet," *Foreign Policy Analysis*, 7, 1: 89–111.
McCarthy, Daniel. 2015. *Power, Information Technology, and International Relations Theory. The Power and Politics of US Foreign Policy and the Internet*, Basingstoke, UK: Palgrave Macmillan.
Mueller, Milton. 2010. *Networks and States: The Global Politics of Internet Governance*, Cambridge, MA: MIT Press.
Mueller, Milton. 2013. "Are We in a Digital Cold War?" *Paper presented on 17th May at the GigaNet workshop The Global Governance of the Internet: Intergovernmentalism, Multistakeholderism and Networks*, Graduate Institute, Geneva. www.internetgovernance.org/2013/07/19/are-we-in-a-digital-cold-war/.

Negroponte, John, Samuel Palmisano, Adam Segal (eds.). 2013. *Defending an Open, Global, Secure, and Resilient Internet*, Council on Foreign Relations, Independent Task Force Report No. 70, June. www.cfr.org/report/defending-open-global-secure-and-resilient-internet.
Nocetti, Julien. 2012. "Russie: le web réinvente-t-il la politique?" *Politique étrangère*, 77, 2, Summer: 277–289.
Nocetti, Julien. 2014a. "Puissances émergentes et internet: vers une 'troisième voie'?" *Politique étrangère*, 4, Winter: 44–51.
Nocetti, Julien. 2014b. "Global'noe upravlenie Internetom: pochemu eto tak vazhno," *Rossijskij Soviet po Mezhdunarodnym delam*, 29 July.
Nocetti, Julien. 2015. "Contest and Conquest: Russia and Global Internet Governance," *International Affairs* 91, 1, January: 121–125.
Nocetti, Julien. 2016. "Vojna za Internet-dannye nachalas," Rossijskij Soviet po Mezhdunarodnym delam, 22 March.
Nye, Joseph. 2010. *Cyber Power*, Harvard Kennedy School: Belfer Center for Science and International Affairs, May.
Owen, Taylor. 2015. *Disruptive Power: The Crisis of the State in the Digital Age*, New York: Oxford University Press.
Panarin, I. 2006. *Informatsionnaya voyna i geopolitika*, Moscow: Goryachaya liniya
Panarin, I. 2012. "Vtoraya mirovaya informatsionnaya voyna – voyna protiv Rossii," *Kirill i Mefodiy*, 10 January
Parker, Emily. 2014. *Now I Know Who My Comrades Are: Voices from the Internet Underground*, New York: Sarah Crichton Books.
Peck, Michael. 2013. "Russia Says Cyberspace Is New Theater of War," Forbes.com, 20 August.
Pipenko, Maria. 2010. "Russian Blogosphere as a Public Sphere," *Journal of Siberian Federal University*, 4, 3: 526–535.
PIR-Tsentr. 2016. "Pravo voyny i kiber prostranstvo," PIR-Tsentr, 6 April.
Powers, Shawn and Michael Jablonski. 2015. *The Real Cyber War: The Political Economy of Internet Freedom*, Champaign, IL: University of Illinois Press.
Priest, Dana, Ellen Nakashima, Tom Hamburger. 2016. "U.S. Investigating Potential Covert Russian Plan to Disrupt November Elections," *The Washington Post*, September 5.
Rid, Thomas. 2016. "How Russia Pulled Off the Biggest Election Hack in U.S. History," *Esquire*, October 20.
Security Council. 2014. "Ob itogakh operativnogo soveshchaniya Soveta Bezopasnosti Rossiiskoy Federatsii po voprosu 'O vnesenii utocheniy v Voennuyu doktrinu Rossiiskoy Federatsii", Security Council of the Russian Federation, 20 December, accessible at www.scrf.gov.ru/news/838.html.
Segal, Adam. 2016. *The Hacked World Order: How Nations Fight, Trade, Maneuver, and Manipulate in the Digital Age*, New York: PublicAffairs.
Sharavov, I. 2000. "K voprosu ob informatsionnoy voyne i informatsionnom oruzhii", *Zarubezhnoye voyennoye obozreniye*, 10: 2–5.
Sidorenko, Alexey. 2011. "Blogery i gosudarstvo, tsifrovoy dualizm v Rossii," Ifri, *Russie.Nei.Visions* No. 63, December.
Slipchenko, V.I. 1998. "Future War (A Prognostic Analysis)," January.
Starr, Stuart. 2009. "Toward a Preliminary Theory of Cyberpower," In Franklin Kramer, Stuart Starr and Larry Wentz (eds), *Cyber Power and National Security*, Washington, DC: National Defense University Press.
Streltsov, A. 2010. *Gosudarstvennaya informatsionnaya politika: osnovy teorii*, Moscow: MTsNMO.
Trenin, Dmitri. 2016. "Aziatskaya politika Rossii: ot dvustoronnego podkhoda k global'noy strategii," Ifri, *Russie.Nei.Visions* No. 94, June.
Tsygankov, Andrei. 2013. *Russia's Foreign Policy: Change and Continuity in National Identity*, New York: Rowman & Littlefield, 3rd edition
Turovskiy, Daniil. 2016. "Rossijskie vooruzhennye kibersily", *Meduza*, 7 November.
U.S. Department of State. 1981. "Forgery, Disinformation, Political Operations", U.S. Department of State, Bureau of Public Affairs, *Special Report* No. 88, October. www.cia.gov/library/readingroom/docs/CIA-RDP84B00049R001303150031-0.pdf.
U.S. International Strategy for Cyberspace. 2011. The White House, May. https://obamawhitehouse.archives.gov/sites/default/files/rss_viewer/international_strategy_for_cyberspace.pdf.

Valeriano, Brandon and Ryan C. Maness. 2015. *Cyber War versus Cyber Realities: Cyber Conflict in the International System*, New York: Oxford University Press.

Yakushev, Mikhail. 2010. "Upravlenie Internetom: politiki i geopolitiki," *Indeks Bezopasnosti*, 2, 93, Summer.

White House. 2013a. "Joint Statement by the Presidents of the USA and the Russian Federation on a New Field of Cooperation in Confidence Building," The White House: Office of the Press Secretary, 17th June. https://obamawhitehouse.archives.gov/the-press-office/2013/06/17/joint-statement-presidents-united-states-america-and-russian-federatio-0.

White House. 2013b. *Fact sheet: U.S.-Russian cooperation on information communications technology security*, The White House's Office of the Press Secretary, 17th June. https://obamawhitehouse.archives.gov/the-press-office/2013/06/17/fact-sheet-us-russian-cooperation-information-and-communications-technol.

Zheleznyak, Sergei. 2013. "My dolzhny obespechiy' 'tsifrovoj suverenitet," *Ekonomika I Zhizn'*, 19th June.

12
MEDIA AND PUBLIC DIPLOMACY

Greg Simons

UPPSALA UNIVERSITY, SWEDEN

Introduction

When approaching issues in international political and foreign policy, actors need to attain the right balance and equilibrium in their approach with regards to competing priorities, opposing ideologies and differing approaches aimed at leveraging power (McClory, 2016: 12). Values and interests are important factors in shaping and determining the perception of policy makers and directions in foreign policy and practice; however, this is only part of the equation. Those opposing values and interests of other foreign policy actors are critical in shaping responses and reactions, such as has been witnessed in Ukraine during and after Euromaidan (Tsygankov, 2015). When taken at a more practical level, "the policies and practices of public diplomacy reflect the 'contextual intelligence' of the state" (Hayden, 2012: 277).

Public diplomacy (PD) is intended to engage in public debates, influence public opinion and shape relationship dynamics (Sevin, 2015). It does this in order to help realise a state's efforts in foreign policy goals and objectives. This is achieved through a government communicating interactively with an international audience ('Government to People' or G2P). This chapter seeks to trace the use of media-based communication (including social media and Internet-based) within its PD, which is linked to foreign policy aims and objectives as outlined in the 2013 Russian Foreign Policy conceptual document. This document has been subsequently updated in 2016. It is an intention of this chapter to analyse and examine the conceptual/theoretical means, the operational mechanism and the desired/intended foreign policy outcomes.

Unlike many authors within the current period of confrontation between Russia and the West, it is not the intention of the author to assign any ethical or moral value in support of or against what is happening. Rather it is the intention to account for what transpires and why it does so. The current state-state level of political conflict and diplomatic impasse that exists between Russia and the West means that other means and channels of communication and audience are needed and sought. Mass media, and especially Internet-based and social media, offer an opportunity for interactive G2P forms of communication. This communication is dialogic, rather than monologic, in nature, which enables a more effective means of influence and persuasion (Simons, 2015b). The question to be investigated is how are foreign policy, communication means and event/issue opportunities coinciding in global events? It is not the intent of the author to engage in content analysis of media-based communications, but rather the results that are transpiring from the information and communication strategies used.

Before addressing this question, the chapter will begin with a brief overview of the current state of research on Russian public diplomacy and soft power. There is a significant split in opinion and characterisation of Russian efforts, which is indicated by the words and terms that are used to describe Russia's efforts in this field. This is followed by an overview of how Russian PD has evolved over time in the post-Cold War world. Not only do means and approach differ, but so do the objectives, goals and foreign policy framework. The next section deals with an attempt by Russia to break the global US hegemony and bring back 'multi-polarity' within the international political system. The strengths and weaknesses, threats and opportunities are explored in turn. Possible future trends and prospects of Russian foreign policy in the PD can develop and evolve.

Current state of art in research

The current state of political and diplomatic relations between the West and Russia is depicted as being located somewhere between competition and conflict between the blocks within a geopolitical context. Tsygankov (2016) notes that throughout history, Russia has either tried to imitate or compete with the West; it has never ignored events and processes that have taken place in that space. Tsygankov (2015: 19) states that "the values/interests nexus is helpful in understanding the foreign policy of great powers such as Russia. In addition, one must consider interaction with other large states that compete with Russia for influence in Europe and Eurasia". There are those that depict the current situation as being a New Cold War (Lucas, 2014; Osipova, 2015; Legvold, 2016). A New Cold War narrative is not realistic at this stage, but it does serve a purpose. It attempts to recreate a familiar narrative, together with the associated struggle, values, villains and heroes. The current conflict/competition is much more pragmatically based (on geopolitical influence) than ideological in nature. In addition, a great asymmetry exists in terms of tangible military power (such as size of armed forces and defence budgets) of the West and Russia.

This increasing competition has been seen for some time already in events and processes occurring in post-Soviet space, such as the increasing tensions that led to an armed conflict in Georgia in 2008 that was based within competing and interacting frames and perceptions of power and security between Georgia and Russia (Tsygankov and Tarver-Wahlquist, 2009). This current state of being in the 21st century has been explained in geopolitical terms by some:

> The United States is struggling to hold on to the position of sole superpower, and is hesitant to accept rapidly rising multipolar world order. Russia, on the other hand, is still reeling from the abrupt demise of the Soviet Union, seeking restoration of its regional power and demanding recognition as an actor of global significance with legitimate interests that others should respect. While there are concrete economic and security interests at stake, perceptions play an equally important part in shaping the distrust and tensions plaguing the relationship between the two former superpowers.
>
> *(Osipova, 2015: 41–42)*

The above description of the current problems in the relations between the United States and Russia is also valid and applicable to the wider global diplomatic and political trends and events. One of the intellectual problems in the current study of public diplomacy within foreign policy is the deliberate and inaccurate assigning of labels to an opponent's/competitor's international communication attempts. This issue is related to the rhetorical attempts to shape perception and public opinion through contests and competitions concerning messenger credibility. Within the current geopolitical conflict, it is very evident in how Russian communications are worded. There is in some cases, more talk about "weaponised information" and "propaganda" (Lucas and Nimmo, 2015) or a "firehose of falsehood" (Paul and Matthews, 2016), the use of disinformation and conspiracy theories (Missiroli et al., 2016) than about public diplomacy and international broadcasting.

There is a tendency to apply subjective and selective labelling to the international communication programmes of different countries. As noted in an opinion article appearing in *The Guardian*, "the impression is given is that our governments engage in truthful 'public relations', 'strategic communication' and 'public diplomacy' while the Russians lie through 'propaganda'". It is also noted in the same article, these claims and assertions lack sufficient academic support.[1] Together, these forms of information presentation represent examples of the narrative of a return to the Cold War. This has caused an increase in the interest of Russian foreign policy, public diplomacy and notions of soft power.

A specific example of an expression of this increased interest in Russia's concepts and practice of PD and soft power is in a special issue of the journal *Politics* in late 2015, edited by Michael Barr and Valentina Feklyunina and featuring the theme of *The Soft Power of Hard States*. There a strong link or association being established between Russian foreign policy and the development of soft power strategies in the special issue. Sergunin and Karabeshkin (2015) argue that Russia does possess elements of soft power, and the attractiveness of its use has been heightened by the poor image of Russia. However, there are a number of apparent problems in terms of the institutional structure for realising soft power, as there is evident stove piping with the duplication of functions and responsibilities. Kiseleva (2015: 325) goes further, stating that the current conflict between Russia and the West "pushes policy makers in Russia to frame Russian soft power in geopolitical terms, as a counterforce to the West and its detrimental soft power, meant to defend Russian national interests". Thus an influence on Russia's perception and behaviour is the geopolitical competition with the West.

Another line of academic thought and construction is to lump together 'like-minded' international actors, and one of those is seen in increasingly creating a comparison with China. Often there are similar arguments and logic that are found in the examples that are mentioned immediately above. Wilson (2015: 287) argues that:

> [b]oth the Kremlin and Beijing consider that the soft power methods of the West present nothing less than an existential threat, and conceive of a soft power policy as the outcome of state initiatives rather than the product of autonomous civil society.

This is in a similar vein to the arguments of Kiseleva (2015), where soft power is seen as a resource of the state to defend itself against the West. This implies the need to engage in an active form of communication with a somewhat modified 'political technology' in order to engage in an information war.

The weakness of Russia is its reputation and image, which was raised by Sergunin and Karabeshkin (also see Simons, 2011, 2013). Given the generally less than favourable image of Russia in Western publications, there is a consequent motivation to develop media assets to carry the foreign policy message. Rawnsley (2015) has noted that Russia has set aside significant time and resources in developing its international broadcasting capacity, which is forming an integral part of their PD efforts. These assets are intended to rectify what are deemed as being informational distortions, but increasingly as a means to expose those weak points in the West (in terms of issues and policies). These are attempts to enter into the global conversation and attempt to influence opinion and perception, which is a competition of credibility among the communicators in a crowded marketplace of ideas.

The PD evolution in the post-Cold War world

PD is a communication-based activity which is widely interpreted and defined by the academic and practitioner communities. One possible definition that captures the essence of it is "referring to the communication-based activities of states and state-sanctioned actors aimed at non-state groups in other countries with the expectation of achieving foreign policy goals and objectives" (Sevin, 2015: 563). PD can therefore be viewed as being an extension to traditional state-to-state diplomacy. British diplomat Tom Fletcher captured the essence of diplomacy. In his words on his Twitter feed he stated that "diplomacy is Darwinian".[2] That is, diplomacy is something that is continually evolving in order to adequately meet the challenges of a constantly changing environment, if it is to be successful in meeting policy goals and objectives. There is a dual influence of politics and technology upon how diplomacy is practised. An ever-increasing use of mass media within the framework of PD is being observed:

> Mediatization theory raises the stakes of this general approach by arguing that the profound integration of media in to everyday life allows for radical new configurations of practices surrounding the representations of identities and relationships.
> *(Pamment, 2014: 259)*

This form of communication enables a direct form of G2P communication. It opens up possibilities for a direct line of communication with a foreign public, which is interacted with in order to influence and shape their perceptions, opinions and political relationships. Fominykh observes that "in practical terms, both countries are carrying out their 'soft' power policy in the form of vast information efforts, including positive interpretation of their foreign policies and, quite recently, wide use of the Internet" (2010: 69). Media channels are a medium of outreach to global publics, and the Internet in particular is able to by-pass the gatekeeping mechanisms that exist in traditional mainstream media.

At a time when government-to-government forms of communication between Western governments and Russia are in a politically dysfunctional state of being, diplomacy conducted through media enables agenda building, socialisation and strategic coordination (Pamment, 2014: 277). This is done through engaging an audience in policy or issue debates. Socialisation occurs with a growing sense of projected familiarity with elements of another culture, identity and way of thinking. The aspect of strategic coordination refers to the information/communication programme being used as a supporting element to the political programme (policy aims and objectives).

The academic community in Russia quickly understood the need to develop their own variant of soft power as a means to counter the US use of it. There was a question of discussing and deriving adequate ways and means of creating and using soft power. One of the means was a wider use of educational and humanitarian cooperation. Dolinksy from Russkiy Mir commented that "today, Russian public diplomacy is geared towards tactical tasks; at the present level of conceptualisation of goals and institutional development, it is unable to deal with strategic aims. To succeed, this segment of state policy should be systematised and institutionalised" (Fominykh, 2010: 73–74). One of the significant constraints on Russia PD efforts is the negative image of the country. Different institutions have been created in order to generate a more positive image and reputation of the country internationally. In particular, the use of language and culture have been used to draw the attention and interest of international publics (Fominykh, 2010: 74). Culture should be part and parcel of any PD effort:

> Cultural diplomacy, which has been defined as "the exchange of ideas, information, art, and other aspects of culture among nations and their peoples in order to foster mutual understanding," is the linchpin of public diplomacy; for it is in cultural activities that a nation's idea of itself is best represented.
>
> *(Department of State, 2005: 4)*

In spite of there being a superficial lack of readily apparent soft power aspects to Russia, it does exist. Russian classical literature and arts, language and sport, provide some basis that is viewed favourably by some audiences (Simons, 2015b). In addition to the dimension that involves external communication to foreign audiences, culture and identity are key to how a country defines itself, including Russia. The internal communication among citizens of a country requires an effective dialogue in order to capture the essence of a country to which citizens can mostly agree, and this makes the external communication easier owing to an internal agreement and psychological cohesion on national markers of culture and identity. One of the biggest gaps in how soft power is perceived by Joseph Nye, the concept's founder, and Russia is that the Russian state attempts a top-down approach and not the grassroots and civic society origins found in the United States:

> Soft power is always something that society chooses for itself in the knowledge that the choice is voluntary and appealing. Soft power is not built by decree from on high, but takes shape naturally and over a period of many years. In the choice between a point of no return and a turning point in the realisation of potential, the latter looks more constructive and promising.[3]

The argument is about having a soft power that is perceived as being more genuine and representative of the people of a country, rather than as a 'contrived' image representation created by a government and communication specialists. Russia has forgone the integration of ideology into their foreign policy communications and interactions, and instead has adopted an approach based upon the realisation of concrete goals and interests (Ivanov, 2001; Simons, 2014). Interestingly, the Russian military has been working on developing its own soft power concept, which is based in part on the experience and work of the Foreign Ministry as a counter to hybrid warfare threats.[4] Other scholars have noted the more pragmatic and realistic approach of matching goals with a realistic appraisal of the political situation and environment:

> However, since the early 2010s, the course of pragmatic cooperation has demonstrated limitations, as Western nations declined to recognise Russia's distinct security interests and values . . . Putin's new vision of Russia as a state-civilisation with distinct interests and values since 2012 sought to compensate for the weaknesses of Medvedev's cooperative and West-centric approach.
>
> *(Tsygankov, 2016: 28)*

Thus the political environments domestically and internationally forced a rethink at times as to whether the current strategy of the day is sufficient for the purposes of attaining Russia's foreign policy objectives. Fominykh recognised by 2010 that "in any rivalry with the United States, the Russian Federation should move towards categories of a higher order – *universal* ideas and values – and make them attractive to wide foreign audiences" (2010: 74). Russia's values tend to be somewhat distinct from many other countries. "Russian values and ideas include an authentic concept of spiritual freedom inspired by Eastern Christianity and the idea of a strong, socially protective state capable of defending its own subjects from abuses at home and threats from abroad" (Tsygankov, 2014: 2). Lavrov (2016) also spoke of Russia's unique set of values and the long historical antagonism to defend its borders from different foreign invaders, which echoes the views expressed by Tsygankov. In its current form, Russian PD situates Russia as being in opposition to US global hegemony and the associated policies, such as regime change (MID, 2013; Simons, 2014, 2015a). Andrei Manoilo, a geopolitical expert in Russia, believes that the US has been somewhat unsuccessful in adapting and countering Russian foreign policy owing to its asymmetry:

> Yes, the Americans are still expecting symmetric responses from us, expecting that we respond to a strike with a strike. You know, we are very lucky to have Sergey Lavrov as foreign minister. He is a Gorchakov-style diplomat and leader of the department of foreign policy in Russia. Lavrov participates actively in making foreign-policy decisions in Russia.[5]

Here Manoilo alludes to the success of Russian foreign policy in terms of effective leadership and strategies. Namely, this is the coincidence of a very effective leader of foreign policy, together with a viable strategy during a difficult period. It also points to an attempt to establish and play the rules of their own 'game' rather than to follow reactively the US lead.

Organisationally speaking, there has been a shake-up of public diplomacy organisational structures and also touching operational aspects. In addition to the formal state-based instruments of diplomacy and PD, the Russian Foreign Ministry maintains and cultivates relations with NGOs, where these organisations interact on various international topics. This also functions at the formal level. On 7 May 2012, President Putin signed into law *On Measures to Implement the Foreign Policy Course of the Russian Federation*,[6] which specifically mentions a role for civil society (including NGOs) in the foreign policy process. In 2012 some 250 events within the framework of Foreign Ministry and NGO interaction were held. Relations with the Public Chamber are developing, and *Rossotrudnichestvo*[7] maintains relations with some 150 NGOs. There are currently some 5,000 officially registered NGOs involved in foreign policy, of which 859 possess an international status.[8] These serve as a means for helping to develop and influence the information environment.

Two such NGOs were founded by the President of Russia. On 2 February 2010, President Medvedev signed decrees that established the *Alexander Gorchakov Fund to Support Public Diplomacy* (http://gorchakovfund.ru/) and the *Russian International Affairs Council* (http://russiancouncil.ru/en/). Both organisations are located within the structure of the Foreign Ministry, and the Russian International Affairs Council is also associated with the Ministry of Education. The funding for these organisations comes from the state budget.[9] The President of the Russian International Affairs Council, Igor Ivanov, noted that with regard to the active participation of society and public organisations in international affairs "Russia is seriously lagging behind other countries and, consequently, it is at a disadvantage in the formation of public opinion abroad".[10] In 2013 there was a major revamping of Russia's international media by presidential decree, which had significant effects upon RT, Voice of Russia and RIA Novosti. A new institution was created, Russia Today, with Dmitry Kiselyov as its head (known for his conservative and anti-Western views).[11] The effect and likely intention was to bring in a much more consistent and uniform message and narrative across state-controlled media outlets engaged in PD.

The very latest iteration of Russian Foreign Policy Concepts (MID, 2016), progresses from where MID 2013 left off. Instead of speaking about the necessity to challenge the dangerous excesses of US foreign policy, it speaks of fundamental changes occurring in the international system. This is namely the relative decline of Western dominance and the emergence of a multipolar international system. There is the stressed need for Russia to protect her interests and objectives in this environment, but also to cooperate with other actors within mutual interests and goals.

The return of multi-polarity in the global system of public diplomacy and foreign affairs

From the perspective of political marketing, an election can be characterised as a competitive form of political communication that creates a sense of conflict and competition between competing political images, reputations and brands. As the opposing sides lobby their offerings and cause, the outcome is decided by whose communications resonate the most with the target audience (Newman, 1999). This particular political conflict/competition is played out in the public information space via various channels of media carrying political communication in a global geopolitical context. One of the current threats facing Russia, according to the Minister of Foreign Affairs, is "a distorted view of the international situation and Russia's international standing" (2016: 1). This competition and conflict is readily observable in the public information space, where different outlets and channels of communication play out this 'election' of credibility and popularity.

This final point of observation and commentary speaks of other possible reasons for an increasing level of soft power potential. Fyodor Lukyanov, chief editor of *Russia in Global Affairs*, stated:

> [c]ulture is, of course, always important and Russia has a powerful cultural arsenal . . . But when it comes to short-term changes, the comparison of this year to last, the position in the ranking is not determined by eternal values but by specific political actions.[12]

Therefore, a country's hard arsenal can be an asset if used appropriately at the right moment in time. Some surveys have produced unexpected results too, such as a YouGov poll on the world's top 20 most admired men. Vladimir Putin came in at number six on the global list, a higher ranking than both the Dalai Lama and Pope Francis.[13] In spite of receiving an overwhelmingly negative coverage in mainstream Western media, Putin is still an attractive political figure for different political publics, those who see him as representing a challenge to global US hegemony and others that see him as being an upholder of traditional values (Simons, 2015c). This means that the issue of politics and even the use of hard power can play a positive role in Russia's soft power potential if events, issues and reputations are managed more deliberately and effectively.

In a 2016 global soft power survey, Russia ranked 27th out of the 30 top countries (McClory, 2016: 37). Russia was a new entry in this rating system in 2016, in spite of a negative image projected through mainstream Western politics and mass media. One of the suppositions for this ranking was based upon the vast cultural soft power that is possessed by Russia. The news of this ranking sparked an immediate debate. One argument was that the element of Russian (the other elements being government and engagement) culture is proving decisive. "Soft power use[s] attraction and persuasion to change minds and influence behaviour. Its sources include culture, political values and positive global engagement". McCloy noted that one of the constraints on Russia's performance is negative reporting and news about the country.[14] Others evaluated the outcome of the top 30 ranking as being helped through the use and development of international broadcasting media, and a large number of foreign university students (some 185,000 of them in 2014–15). A binary vision of global popularity was also offered. "In the diplomatic sphere, Russia's recent success in Syria is part of particular note in a world dominated by an ideology of American exceptionalism, which regards Russian foreign policy as audacious and unacceptable".[15] It is important to note that foreign policy does not exist in a bubble beyond the borders of the country concerned.

Russian foreign policy is not something that remains disconnected from Russia's domestic policy; ideally there should be some form of connection between the public and the country's foreign policy. In the context of the current period of competition and conflict with the West, Russia's foreign policy shapes the self-perception of not only the political elites, but also of ordinary Russians. By reasserting its position in international affairs, there has been an increased sense of patriotism that has grown through the perception that Russia is gaining her 'rightful' place and respect in the world.[16] Russia's relations with the West are determined by the sum effect of the sides' attitudes and interactions. "Russia cooperates with the Western nations when its fundamental values and interests are not challenged. When they are challenged, Russia tends to turn to nationalist and assertive foreign policy, especially if it possesses sufficient power capabilities" (Tsygankov, 2014: 2). This assertion is especially evident in the West's and Russia's interactions and rhetoric concerning Ukraine and Syria. In line with this, the United States and Russia seemingly form each other's Other, and the rising and waning fortunes of the other exert some sort of flow on effect.

In the global debate about the relationship between the West and Islam, the United States faces many negative challenges and perceptions, such as the Abu Ghraib scandal, US policies on the Israeli-Palestinian issues and the Iraq War in 2003. All of these have come together to damage US credibility and its power to persuade. They see their political salvation in "cultural diplomacy . . . [as] a means by which we may engage and influence that debate" (Department of State, 2005: 3). Russia can learn lessons from this approach too, especially given its image and reputation that is projected by the West. A similar diplomatic and reputational challenge is faced. A relative weakness of one actor may be exploited by an opponent as their strength. As in an election outcome, the contest is not always about the best possible candidate, but also potentially in some situations, the least worst.

Russia has positioned itself, within the contextual alignment of its foreign policy, as a challenger to the US-led global hegemony. One of the challenges that is faced by Russia in this sphere is how to approach the perceived threat of regime change that emerges via branded revolutions and 'democracy promotion'. These events are staged within the informational space that potentially affects the perception and behaviour of the targeted audiences (Sussman, 2010), which is seen as a risk and a threat to Russian state security. In order to meet this challenge, Russia needs to be able to negate the effects of its rivals and to 'sell' their own story to a sceptical global public. Communicating messages through mass media forms a critical element of the foreign policy goals. Frames are created in order to identify a problem and subsequently to offer a possible solution. When covering political events, issues and actors, a systematic approach is taken: (1) to define effects or conditions as being problematic; (2) identifying causes; (3) then to convey moral judgement; and finally, (4) to endorse certain remedies or improvements (Entman, 2004: 5). This conflict is seen clearly being played out in the public information sphere through media coverage of key events and processes.

Russian international broadcasting efforts have drawn a lot of attention and some revealing analysis. The annual budget of the Broadcasting Board of Governors (BBG) is US$730 million per annum; currently RT's is US$307 million. Jeff Shell the chairman of BBG noted in a recent media interview that "there's no question we're badly underfunded and don't have enough money to compete with our adversaries". In spite of RT's budget being lower, the article noted "the Russian operation is more focussed and efficient". The article elaborated further, "the network also appears to be dominating in the 'new media' sphere . . . RT has emerged as the world's top TV news network on You Tube, having garnered more than 3 billion views across its channels on the site".[17] The United States also characterises the current global situation as a geopolitical conflict. A significant point from this article is that international broadcasting efforts within PD need to focused and efficient and not just on a bigger scale. Otherwise the message becomes lost in an overcrowded market place of communicated ideas.

The presence of RT in the international broadcasting scene has caused a lot of interest and speculation as to its supposed levels of success and its abilities to influence audiences. A difference of opinion exists, which can be seen in the literature. One line of thought characterises RT as "competing aggressively" with the United States for global hearts and minds (Seib, 2010; Dale et al., 2012). Given the increasing competition for attention and influence in international affairs, RT does fulfil a function of getting the national narrative into the international arena in order to create a sense of familiarity with Russia and its policies. This creates the interpretation by some observers as creating a fine line between propaganda and public diplomacy (Rawnsley, 2015). There are those that see and project RT as being a threat by undermining the global information space with 'unreliable' information. RT's format, style and content have been dismissed, in some instances, as consisting of the use of 'conspiracy theories' (Yablokov, 2015). Sometimes different realities simply do not add up, causing some kind of dissonance. "US security services have fingered the channel as a key player in the Kremlin's efforts to sway Western politics. But inside its offices, RT seems a far cry from what the US says it is – and what it aspires to be".[18] For all of the opinions expressed, it is easy to understand the Measure of Activity of RT, but much more difficult to gauge with any precision the Measure of Effect.

At times, Western analysis of Russian foreign policy is tinged with assumptions and projections that are simply not there. As these assertions appear, there can be little of substance to support these claims, other than the fact that the claim has been made. An article by Natalie Nougayrède that appeared in *The Guardian* falls into this category. "The president (Putin) has never forgotten the Afghan debacle of the 1980s and demands redemption in Syria".[19] Putin is not a solitary actor in all of Russia's domestic and foreign affairs; the high level of personalisation is not credible. The connection to the reality of the Russian engagement in Syria is at best tenuous. These factors include supporting a long-term Soviet and now Russian ally to counter the threat of the latest evolution of 'Colour Revolutions', and the geopolitical context that demands Russia support this ally (unlike permitting the regime change that took place in Libya) in order to retain any possibility of influence and credibility in the region as a serious actor. Others tend to conflate propaganda and public diplomacy, seeking to undermine any possible legitimacy in Russian policy or interests through a series of carefully selected rhetorical labels:

> To the extent Russia's propaganda effort is effective, it poses challenges to key foreign policy goals of the Euro-Atlantic alliance. These foreign policy goals are to deter further aggression (either military or ideological) by Russia in former Soviet territories and elsewhere, encourage the growth of strong civil societies and democratic political institutions in the region, and improve the image of the United States and its European allies as potential economic and political partners.
>
> *(Gerber and Zavisca, 2016: 79)*

The above demonstrates the use of creating information on a certain subject or object; if that information becomes sticky it is transformed into knowledge. In this regard, knowledge serves as a form of conventional 'wisdom'. In this case, the narrative of this information is that Russia is to be contained (military and ideologically) and the United States is likely to be the benefactor of any changes in zones of influence. This is in keeping with Tsygankov's (2016) contention of an era of competition between Russia and the West, but also demonstrates that this is a far from one-way process. The idea of an information war existing within the context of a New Cold War does exist in both Russia and the West, where media is at the forefront. Scores are kept by some analysts and commentators, such as Russia's apparent victory in the media narrative on Ukraine among former Soviet Republics.[20] Ivan Timofeev notes "each party insists that it is on the defensive in terms of information policy, seeking merely to counter hostile information distribution. All sides tend to significantly overstate the possibilities of their neighbours in terms of information war and its outcome".[21] Other attempts include trying to shut down the permissible discourse (enforcing a spiral of silence) and open empathy with the Russian position:

> Russia's European "understanders" legitimise Moscow's Eurasian ambitions and the right to defend its interests and those of its "compatriots" by force and annexation. Some commentators predict that a "Fifth International, a loose collection of anti-status quo forces is emerging out of the chaos of the Ukraine conflict".
>
> *(Makarychev and Braghiroli, 2016: 6)*

This is a means to undermine the credibility of an actor, and does not take into account the level of validity of what is communicated. At times, an opponent may have valid points, which is difficult to accept within the context of a geopolitical information war that is based upon perception and credibility. An article concerning the views of Stephen Cohen reinforces this point; as controversial as he may be, he does make some valid points.[22] An attempt is made by the sides to create a binary reality of right and wrong, truth and lies, information and propaganda. It not only concerns getting one's own message across, but attempting to cripple the opponent's communication credibility. The creation of East Stratcom can be seen as an institution created with this specific purpose in mind. The EU announced "an attempt to start trying to win hearts and minds in eastern partnership countries" through "launching a rapid-response team to counter what it considers biased Russian media reports".[23] NATO has been taking a similar approach, making use of such slogans as the Kremlin's "weaponisation of information". In 2016 NATO produced a 23-page document to analyse the issue.[24] Within this information war, mockumentaries have made an appearance. One of these was aired on BBC2 in early 2016. *World War Three: Inside the War Room* portrayed the scene of hybrid war in the Latgale province in Latvia becoming a nuclear war. The airing of this drew harsh critique, including from the Latvian Foreign Minister who denounced the film as "rubbish".[25] These are all part of an attempt to follow the path noted earlier from Entman (2004): (1) define effects or conditions as problematic; (2) identify causes; (3) convey moral judgement; and (4) endorse certain remedies or improvements.

In spite of the information war and the dominant narrative of the Russian threat and Russian aggression, the results do not equate to an effort to make those labels sticky. This is often the result of a contextual perception of realities. "Most Europeans see Russia as a 'minor' threat compared to Islamic State, the refugee crisis or other issues". The Pew study found a great deal of dramatic differences between the opinions and perceptions of the different European countries surveyed.[26] Other surprising results have been witnessed in the Ukraine issue, which has been considered a PD disaster for Russia. In 2016 the Razumkov Centre ran a survey on who was responsible for the war in Ukraine. Of respondents, 9 per cent blamed only Kyiv, 33 per cent blamed both Moscow and Kyiv, and 48 per cent blamed only Moscow.[27] One situation does not necessarily dictate a permanent future path in foreign policy.

Unlike events in Ukraine, Russia's military engagement in Syria was perceived in a more positive light. This was in spite of the negative coverage in many mainstream Western media outlets that used similar narratives to those associated with events in Ukraine. Western leaders and media made many dire predictions and were proven wrong by a quick political decision and decisive military action. This forced the United States into having to acknowledge Russian interests and objectives in the country.[28] One article marked this as a significant turning point in global politics as an emerging multipolar world order.[29] Perhaps even more importantly, it signalled that the global narrative on Syria had been lost by the United States and was gained by Russia,[30] which in practical terms meant that the United States was forced to respond to a now more Russian-led narrative on the Syrian conflict. Some 71 per cent of respondents in a poll (27,000 respondents) in the UK supported the Russian military intervention in Syria, in spite of overwhelmingly critical media coverage.[31] A YouGov poll conducted in the United Kingdom in 2015 saw 59 per cent of respondents supportive of the UK and the United States cooperating with Russia in Syria to fight ISIS,[32] and this is running contrary to the message coming from mainstream Western politicians that stated categorically that they would not cooperate. In this regard, media coverage of Russia's military intervention in Syria has acted according to Pamment's (2014) account of mediatisation of PD: (1) engaged in agenda building; (2) brought about a level of socialisation of the international public; and (3) performed the role of strategic coordination.

Russia maintains that it is fighting a defensive informational war in its foreign policy, which contradicts the mainstream Western political narrative that it is fighting an offensive war. This contest has been clearly seen in the competing narratives of competing public diplomacy messages of these actors. One political analyst, Dmitry Abzalov, has characterised a transformation of Russia's diplomatic relations: "Unlike previous years, when Moscow was in a defensive pattern of diplomatic relations, now it plays a more active role in the world".[33] But the results can be described as being somewhat 'mixed'. A recent Pew Research poll has found that 90 per cent of Americans view Russia's power and influence as a threat, and that 72 per cent polled believe that Russia hacked the Democratic National Committee and Hillary Clinton's campaign. However, this has not translated into an angry response toward Russia and Putin. Instead, Putin's favourability has increased slightly in comparison with two years ago. This is found in terms of an expressed grudging respect being shown.[34] Therefore, even though audiences in the United States were not necessarily consuming information from Russian PD sources, and did tend to believe the projected threats, they did not feel threatened, especially among Republican and conservative voting segments (thus tending to support the observations in Simons, 2015c; see also Laruelle, 2015).

At the same time that Russia seeks to look for an identity for its foreign policy, there are changes in identity that are occurring in the wider world, which may actually assist Russian foreign policy goals and objectives without being an official part of it. Ivan Timofeev notes the massive changes in identity and culture that are taking place in the world, especially after Brexit and the election of Donald Trump. The United States' very identity and shared cultural or political foundations are being shaken by what he terms "pragmatic nationalism".[35] In spite of public attempts by his opponents to portray Trump as being a puppet of Putin via mass media and social media, US cultural conservatives tend to be much more sympathetic to Russia and its leader as geopolitical concerns are not top of their agenda – social issues are their greatest concern. A Gallup poll from February 2017 revealed that support among US Republicans for

Vladimir Putin has increased from 12 per cent in 2015 to 32 per cent now.[36] This should not necessarily be seen as a success of Russian public diplomacy, but rather a failure of social politics in the West that has assisted Russia's image and reputation through people to people interaction.

Constraints on Russian PD

The author approached two people working within Russian PD, Dr Ivan Timofeev[37] the Director of programmes at the Russian International Affairs Council, and Dr Anna Velikaya[38] a PD expert with the Alexander Gorchakov Foundation. Both Timofeev and Velikaya were asked the same question: what are the main constraints on Russian PD? There was some agreement and divergence evident in the answers given.

According to Dr Timofeev, he saw three primary constraints faced by Russian PD. These were financial in nature, a lack of professional workers, and the third point was a heavy dependence on state institutions. Therefore, the focus is on the internal components that are necessary for the creation and implementation of PD programmes – finance, personnel and organisational structures.

A broader range of issues was identified by Dr Velikaya. She named one of the constraints as being the manner in which Russia approached their target audiences. "Till recently Russian PD initiatives were focused on inter-governmental relations or projects with cultural intelligentsia while neglecting the work with civil society and the expert community: NGOs, policy and decision makers, International Relations scholars". This observation echoes the criticism of Timofeev's third point. Both of these criticisms are in line with Nye's understanding and vision of the active participation and involvement of grass roots society in helping to realise soft power potential. To back this critique, she noted that Russia had backed the Ukrainian elite and had invested some US$200 billion in their economy, whereas the US invested US$5 billion in civil society. The results of Euromaidan have proved the Russian strategy to be ineffective in the strategy employed by their geopolitical rival. The knock-on effects of the events in Ukraine have had a negative knock-on effect on Russian PD efforts in the wider region.

Another weakness identified was a lack in the "prioritisation of the target audience". This means a more deliberate and effective approach to identifying key public segments. Further, "the weak point of Russian PD is the focus on civil, people to people and cultural diplomacy, while the[re is a] lack of track II diplomacy initiatives". Velikaya also noted that the approach to PD is often taken from the perspective of the assumption of how a particular audience views Russia and not the way that they really perceive the country and people.

A number of potential approaches were given in order to address those current weaknesses in Russian PD. These include:

> [t]he work with compatriots could be shifted towards work with scholars, journalists and decision-makers who can become bridges between their home country and the society that they are successfully integrated in, or government scholarships for the international students could cover not only the university tuition fee, but also living expenses.

Velikaya's focus differed from Timofeev as she placed much more emphasis on the nature and quality of the communication and subsequent relationships that are formed with foreign publics.

These reflections by Timofeev and Velikaya seem to not point to a New Cold War or a symmetrical confrontation of values, but rather it involves political rivalry that occurs within the realm of information and perception. In order to compete successfully in such an environment,

Russia needs to get its message directly to global publics in an unfiltered form. This not only involves impersonal communication via mass media, but also more personal P2P-based diplomacy. The constraints and obstacles outlined by Timofeev and Velikaya make this task ever more problematic.

Possible future trends and prospects

"The dominance of hierarchical, state-to-state classical diplomacy is fading away as networks increasingly determine the direction of global events" (McClory, 2016: 21). The easiest and most expedient way to reach and influence those global networks is through expanding one's digital diplomacy footprint. The trend being indicated in research (Simons, 2015a), with state-state level diplomacy in disarray between Russia and the West, is that the logical step is to communicate with foreign publics, especially via social media, which would facilitate not only dialogic communication but also relationship building.

Drs Timofeev and Velikaya were both asked a second question, which concerned their personal predictions of possible future trends and tendencies in Russian PD. Timofeev gave three predictions – that it "will be affected negatively by political conjuncture"; second that "it may be marginalised by information warfare"; and third, "it will be increasingly concentrated in state institutions". Velikaya, on the other hand, predicted a more legalistic-moralistic approach to international problems by Russian PD. "Russia insists that coercive democratisation can bring nothing but harm to the states with their specific way of development, the nation state is the only reliable guarantor of the world order". She pointed out that Russia has reaped some gains from conducting a foreign policy line from the 2013 foreign policy doctrine that situated Russia as a counter to the US policy of regime change. But she feels there is room for improvement including tapping further potential. "The Russian position on Syria, Iraq and Libya was warmly welcomed by millions of people all over the world, but Russia has much untapped potential in offering its own framework of international engagement through public diplomacy methods". Thus it is not only about standing in opposition to something, but being able to offer an attractive alternative. Velikaya also foresaw the big countries of the Eurasian partnership becoming a key region of focus for Russian PD efforts.

Conclusion

The current state of international relations has not yet seen a return to a New Cold War, in spite of some stating this to be the new 'old' reality. What is evident is an information war through diplomatic and mass media channels that involves lobbying and influencing international audiences with clashing and competing sets of norms and values. Russia projects itself as fighting a defensive information war against the US-led West, and positions itself in the 'market' of international actor positions as being a benevolent force and a challenger niche to some aspects of US foreign policy. This defensive challenger positioning does have some advantages over the incumbent United States – there is a growing discontent across the left and right of the political spectrum (Simons, 2015c) of the effects of foreign and domestic policy in the West, including regime change/foreign military interventions, immigration and value systems. By positioning itself as a 'defensive' actor, the implication is that it is reacting to an injustice that has been imposed by an 'offensive' actor. An emerging problem is the increasingly politicised and hyperbolic nature of the media and information space, for example seen in the accusations concerning Russia's alleged hacking of the DNC and power grid with little credible evidence to hand.[39] This has had the effect of creating a very problematic and toxic information environment.

A lot of the processes and events that have been detailed in this chapter are hedged within a framework and context of geopolitics. Russia's foreign policy is seemingly intrinsically linked to domestic policy. It has contextualised its foreign policy position as being in opposition to the excesses and instability caused by US policy, especially in reference to the role played by regime change and hybrid warfare. The link between foreign and domestic policy appears to be the desire to avert the use of regime change or hybrid war (such as the Colour Revolutions and Arab Spring) being possibly used against the government of the Russian Federation. Thus in some regards, the current foreign policy direction can be seen as a preventative strategy.

Russia projects itself as a unique civilisational force, created under specific historical circumstances. This seems to be a means to legitimise and justify its adherence to a special developmental and civilisational path (in likeness to the US 'exceptionalism' narrative). A question to ask could be: does this help or hinder an international public from empathising with the Russian perspective and policy agenda? Empathy is based on a sense of familiarity, but some of what Russia conveys to the outside world is the sense of the Russian enigma. The 2013 Russian foreign policy doctrine and some media communications do emphasise Russia's geopolitical position as being in opposition to the United States. However, it remains to be seen whether Russia will retain this oppositional stance or go further and adopt the position of Fominykh (2010) and create a universal set of ideas and values that compete with their geopolitical rivals.

Even though culture and other 'soft' aspects have been traditionally associated as core to any country's soft power potential, other aspects that have been considered 'hard', such as the decisive use of politics and military force, can also have an impact on a country's perceived attractiveness in the short term. In answer to how are foreign policy, communication means and event/issue opportunity coinciding in global events, Russia has a number of problems, not least of which is its brand and reputation which place constraints upon its operational choices. However, the use of new media has meant that the playing field has been slightly levelled as it enables a clear and dialogic channel of communication directly with international publics. It gives the ability to define certain conditions and effects as problematic (such as Syria), it identifies the causes (US foreign policy for example), conveys moral judgement (it is not ethical to use force to impose 'democracy' upon another state), and endorses certain remedies or improvements (opposing US global hegemony and military intervention in Syria).

Any strengths that Russian PD messaging has are due to weaknesses in US messaging. This is owing to how publics perceive and interpret events. For example, the United States framed the Syrian conflict within the Arab Spring and a battle between democracy and dictatorship, freedom and oppression, in order to justify regime change (Simons, 2016). However, Russian intervention was possible due to public perception not of human values, but security concerns (rising levels of terrorism and the refugee crisis).

Notes

1 Robinson, P., *Russian News May be Biased – But so is Much Western Media*, The Guardian, www.theguardian.com/commentisfree/2016/aug/02/russian-propaganda-western-media-manipulation, 2 August 2016 (accessed 3 August 2016).
2 Tom Fletcher, https://twitter.com/tfletcher/status/274445685628231680, 30 November 2012 (accessed 18 July 2016).
3 Ivanova, N., *How to Re-Brand Russian Soft Power*, Russia Direct, http://www.russia-direct.org/opinion/how-re-brand-russian-soft-power, 10 August 2015 (accessed 10 August 2015).
4 *Russian Military Experts to Develop 'Soft Power' Concept – Reports*, Sputnik News, https://sputniknews.com/russia/20160301/1035564527/russia-soft-power-hy Как Россия будет использовать «мягкую силу» против ДАЕШ и «цветных революций» brid-warfare.html, 1 March 2016 (accessed 2 March

2016); Бочкарёв, В., *Как Россия будет использовать «мягкую силу» против ДАЕШ и «цветных революций»*, Русская Правда, http://ruspravda.info/Kak-Rossiya-budet-ispolzovat-myagkuyu-silu-protiv-DAESH-i-tsvetnih-revolyutsiy-19443.html, 9 March 2016 (accessed 9 March 2016).

5 Piirsalu, J., *FSB Information Warfare Specialist: Russia Will Quickly Establish Private Military Units*, www.diplomaatia.ee/en/article/fsb-information-warfare-specialist-russia-will-quickly-establish-private-military-units/, Diplomaatia, No. 154/155, June 2016.

6 To read this document please go to www.mid.ru/brp_4.nsf/0/76389FEC168189ED44257B2E0039B16D.

7 Full name Federal Agency for the Commonwealth of Independent States Affairs, Compatriots Residing Abroad, and International Humanitarian Cooperation (Ministry of Foreign Affairs, Russian Federation -- is a federal executive authority, carrying out functions for rendering public services and management of state property in the area of providing for and developing the international relations of the Russian Federation and CIS member states, other foreign states, as well as within the field of international humanitarian cooperation (from www.linkedin.com/company/rossotrudnichestvo).Website found at http://rs.gov.ru/.

8 Shakirov, O., *Russian Soft Power Under Construction*, e-International Relations, www.e-ir.info/2013/02/14/russian-soft-power-under-construction/, 14 February 2013 (accessed 12 June 2013).

9 *Russia builds up its public diplomacy structures*, Centre for Eastern Studies, www.osw.waw.pl/en/publikacje/eastweek/2010-02-10/russia-builds-its-public-diplomacy-structures, 10 February 2010 (accessed 26 January 2013).

10 *Roundtable on Public Diplomacy*, Russian International Affairs Council, http://russiancouncil.ru/en/inner/?id_4=512, 21 June 2012 (accessed 26 January 2013).

11 Davydova, A., *Putin Takes a Hard Line on Soft Power With New Broadcaster*, The Conversation, http://theconversation.com/putin-takes-a-hard-line-on-soft-power-with-new-broadcaster-21401, 13 December 2013 (accessed 20 January 2017).

12 Yegorov, O., Russia *Ranks Among Top 30 Countries Worldwide in Terms of Soft Power*, Russia Beyond the Headlines, http://rbth.com/international/2016/06/15/russia-ranks-among-top-30-countries-worldwide-in-terms-of-soft-power_603091, 15 June 2016 (accessed 17 June 2016).

13 Blair, O., *Vladimir Putin More Admired Across the World Than Dalai Lama and Pope Francis, According to Poll*, The Independent, www.independent.co.uk/news/people/vladimir-putin-more-admired-across-the-world-than-dalai-lama-and-pope-francis-according-to-poll-a7020261.html, 9 May 2016 (accessed 11 May 2016).

14 Vladimirova, A., *Increasing Soft Power of Russia*, Blogs, Russian International Affairs Council, http://russiancouncil.ru/en/blogs/political-power/?id_4=2528, 20 June 2016 (accessed 20 June 2016).

15 Ryan, D., *Russia's Appearance on Global 'Soft Power' Ranking Shouldn't Come as a Total Shock*, Re-thinking Russia, http://rethinkingrussia.ru/en/2016/06/russias-appearance-on-global-soft-power-ranking-shouldnt-come-as-a-total-shock/, 22 June 2016 (accessed 27 June 2016).

16 Koshkin, P., *Russia's National Identity Through the Lens of the Kremlin's Foreign Policy*, Russia Direct, www.russia-direct.org/qa/russias-national-identity-through-lens-kremlins-foreign-policy, 2 August 2016 (accessed 2 August 2016).

17 Taylor, G., *Russian, Chinese Propaganda Muffling U.S. Government's Message to World*, The Washington Times, www.washingtontimes.com/news/2016/jan/3/russian-chinese-propaganda-muffling-us-governments/, 3 January 2016 (accessed 4 January 2016).

18 Weir, F., *Inside the Belly of Russia's 'Propaganda Machine': A Visit to RT News Channel*, The Christian Science Monitor, www.csmonitor.com/World/Europe/2017/0117/Inside-the-belly-of-Russia-s-propaganda-machine-A-visit-to-RT-news-channel, 17 January 2017 (accessed 19 January 2017).

19 Nougayrède, N., *Pity Aleppo as Putin Drops His Bombs to Salvage Russian Pride*, The Guardian, https://www.theguardian.com/commentisfree/2016/aug/07/aleppo-putin-russia-afghan-syria, 7 August 2016 (accessed 8 August 2016).

20 Esipova, N. & Ray, J., *Information Wars: Ukraine and the West vs. Russia and the Rest*, HIR, http://hir.harvard.edu/information-wars-ukraine-west-vs-russia-rest/, 6 May 2016 (accessed 10 May 2016).

21 Timofeev, I., *Russia and the West: An Information War?*, Valdai Club, http://valdaiclub.com/a/highlights/russia-and-the-west-an-information-war/, 6 June 2016 (accessed 6 June 2016).

22 Tamkin, E., *Vladimir Putin's American Apologists Have a Point*, The Week, http://theweek.com/articles/599579/vladimir-putins-american-apologists-have-point, 24 January 2016 (accessed 26 January 2016).

23 Panichi, J., *EU Declares Information War on Russia*, Politico, www.politico.eu/article/russia-propaganda-ukraine-eu-response-disinformation/, 27 August 2015 (accessed 31 August 2015).

24 Emmott, R., *NATO Looks to Combat Russia's 'Information Weapon': Document*, Reuters, www.reuters.com/article/us-nato-reform-idUSKCN0V51RU, 27 January 2016 (accessed 28 January 2016).
25 *Latvia Up in Arms Over BBC's Russian Invasion Drama*, AFP in Space Daily, www.spacedaily.com/reports/Latvia_up_in_arms_over_BBCs_Russian_invasion_drama_999.html, 4 February 2016 (accessed 6 February 2016).
26 Rettman, A., *Few Europeans See Russia as 'Major' Threat*, EU Observer, https://euobserver.com/foreign/133815, 14 June 2016 (accessed 15 June 2016).
27 Goble, P., *Why Only 48% of Ukrainians Blame Moscow Alone for the War in the Donbas?*, Euromaidan Press, http://euromaidanpress.com/2016/06/09/survey-48-blame-moscow-alone-for-war-in-the-donbass-new-survey-finds/, 9 June 2016 (accessed 13 June 2016).
28 Cohen, J., *Why and How Russia Won in Syria*, Reuters, http://blogs.reuters.com/great-debate/2016/03/15/why-and-how-russia-won-in-syria/, 15 March 2016 (accessed 29 September 2016).
29 Dal Santo, M., *Russia's Success in Syria Signals an Emerging Multipolar World Order*, The Interpreter, www.lowyinterpreter.org/post/2016/04/06/Russias-success-in-Syria-signals-an-emerging-multipolar-world-order.aspx, 6 April 2016 (accessed 6 April 2016).
30 Slane, R., *Reclaiming the Media Narrative After Russian Intervention in Syria – by Russell O'Phobe*, Blogmir, www.theblogmire.com/reclaiming-the-media-narrative-after-russian-intervention-in-syria-by-russell-ophobe/, 14 October 2015 (accessed 14 October 2015).
31 Virtue, R., *More than 70% SUPPORT for Vladimir Putin's Bombing Campaign Despite Middle East Tensions*, Express, www.express.co.uk/news/uk/611495/Vladimir-Putin-bombing-campaign-poll-support-syria-middle-east, 13 October 2015 (accessed 29 September 2016).
32 Majority Support for Cooperation with Russia on Syria, YouGov, https://yougov.co.uk/news/2015/10/01/cooperation-russia-syria/, 1 October 2015 (accessed 29 September 2016).
33 *'Current Reality' Prompts Changes to Russia's New Foreign Policy Concept*, Sputnik, https://sputniknews.com/world/201612041048152594-russia-foreign-policy-concept/, 4 December 2016 (accessed 5 December 2016).
34 Bershidsky, L., *Putin Starts to Win American Minds, if Not Hearts*, Bloomberg, www.bloomberg.com/view/articles/2017-01-18/putin-starts-to-win-american-minds-if-not-hearts, 18 January 2017 (accessed 20 January 2017).
35 Timofeev, I., *Russian Identity: Making the Impossible Possible*, Valdai Club, http://valdaiclub.com/a/highlights/russian-identity-making-the-impossible-possible/, 18 April 2017 (accessed 18 April 2017).
36 Weaver, C. & Seddon, M., *US Conservatives Keep Faith With Putin Despite Trump Travails*, Financial Times, www.ft.com/content/94869390-2102-11e7-a454-ab0442897719, 18 April 2017 (accessed 20 April 2017).
37 An email was sent to Dr Timofeev on 28 September 2016 and a reply was received on 29 September 2016.
38 Dr Velikaya was contacted via Facebook messenger on 28 September 2016 and a reply received on the same day.
39 Henningsen, P., *The Fake News About Fake News*, Consortium News, https://consortiumnews.com/2016/11/30/the-fake-news-about-fake-news/, 30 November 2016 (accessed 20 January 2017).

References

Dale, H. C., Cohen, A. & Smith, J. A., 2012, 'Challenging America: How Russia, China, and Other Countries Use Public Diplomacy to Compete with the U.S.', *The Heritage Foundation*, No. 2698, 21 June.
Department of State, September 2005, *Cultural Diplomacy: The Lynchpin of Public Diplomacy*, Report of the Advisory Committee on Cultural Diplomacy, Washington DC.
Entman, R. M., 2004, *Projections of Power: Framing News, Public Opinion, and U.S. Foreign Policy*, Chicago, IL: University of Chicago Press.
Fominykh, A., 2010, 'Projecting "Soft Power": American and Russian Public Diplomacy in Post-Soviet Central Asia', *Regional Politics: Central Asia and the Caucasus*, 11(3), pp. 66–77.
Gerber, T. P. & Zavisca, J., Summer 2016, 'Does Russian Propaganda Work?' *The Washington Quarterly*, pp. 79–98.
Hayden, C., 2012, *The Rhetoric of Soft Power: Public Diplomacy in Global Contexts*, Lanham, MD: Lexington Books.
Ivanov, I., 2001, 'The New Russian Identity: Innovation and Continuity in Russian Foreign Policy', *The Washington Quarterly*, 24(3), pp. 5–13.

Kiseleva, Y., 2015, 'Russia's Soft Power Discourse: Identity, Status and the Attraction of Power', *Politics*, 35 (3/4), pp. 316–329.
Laruelle, M., 2015, 'Dangerous Liaisons: Eurasianism, the Far Right, and Putin's Russia', in Laruelle, M. (Ed.), *Eurasianism and the European Far Right: Reshaping the Europe-Russia Relationship*, Lanham, MD: Lexington, pp. 1–31.
Lavrov, S., 3 March 2016, 'Russia's Foreign Policy: Historical Background', *Russia in Global Affairs*, Document No. 408. www.mid.ru/en/foreign_policy/news/-/asset_publisher/cKNonkJE02Bw/content/id/2124391.
Legvold, R., 2016, *Return to the Cold War*, Cambridge, UK: Polity Press.
Lucas, E., 2014, *The New Cold War: Putin's Russia and the Threat to the West*, New York: Bloomsbury Publishing.
Lucas, E. & Nimmo, B., November 2015, *Information War: What Is It and How To Win It?* CEPA Infowar Paper No. 1. http://infowar.cepa.org/files/?id_plik=1896.
McClory, J. (Ed.), 2016, *The Soft Power 30: A Global Ranking of Soft Power*, London, Portland.
Makarychev, A. & Braghiroli, S., August 2016, *Russia 'Understanders' in Europe: Discourses, Communication, Consequences*, Ponars Eurasia Policy Memo No. 435. www.ponarseurasia.org/sites/default/files/policy-memos-pdf/Pepm435_Makarychev-Braghiroli_August2016.pdf.
Missiroli, A., Andersson, J. J., Gaub, F., Popescu, N. & Wilkins, J-J., July 2016, *Strategic Communications: East and South*, Issue Report No. 30, Paris, European Union Institute for Security Studies. www.iss.europa.eu/sites/default/files/EUISSFiles/Report_30.pdf.
Newman, B., 1999, *The Mass Marketing of Politics: Democracy in an Age of Manufactured Images*, Thousand Oaks, CA: Sage.
Osipova, Y., October 2015, 'US–Russia Relations in the Context of Cold War 2.0: Attitudes, Approaches, and the Potential of Public Diplomacy', in Albright, A., Bachiyska, K., Martin, L. & Osipova, Y., eds., *Beyond Cold-War Thinking: Young Perspectives on US-Russia Relations*, Washington, DC: Centre on Global Interests, pp. 41–58.
Pamment, J., 2014, 'The Mediatization of Diplomacy', *The Hague Journal of Diplomacy*, 9, pp. 252–280.
Paul, C. & Matthews, M., 2016, *The Russian 'Firehose of Falsehood' Propaganda Model: Why it May Work and Options to Counter it*, PE 198, RAND Corporation. Santa Monica, CA
Rawnsley, G. D., 2015, 'To Know Us is to Love Us: Public Diplomacy and International Broadcasting in Contemporary Russia and China', *Politics*, 35(3/4), pp. 273–286.
Russian Ministry of Foreign Affairs (MID), 2013, 18 February, *Concept of the Foreign Policy of the Russian Federation*, Approved by President of the Russian Federation V. Putin on 12 February 2013, Document no. 303. www.mid.ru/en/foreign_policy/official_documents/-/asset_publisher/CptICkB6BZ29/content/id/122186.
Russian Ministry of Foreign Affairs (MID), 2016, 1 December, *Foreign Policy Concept of the Russian Federation*, Approved by President of the Russian Federation V. Putin on 30 November 2016, Document no. 2232-01-12-2016. www.mid.ru/en/foreign_policy/official_documents/-/asset_publisher/CptICkB6BZ29/content/id/2542248.
Seib, P., 2010, 'Transnational Journalism, Public Diplomacy, and Virtual States', *Journalism Studies*, 11(5), pp. 734–744.
Sergunin, A. & Karabeshkin, L., 2015, 'Understanding Russia's Soft Power Strategy', *Politics*, 35(3/4), pp. 347–363.
Sevin, E., 2015, 'Pathways of Connection: An Analytical Approach to the Impacts of Public Diplomacy', *Public Relations Review*, 41, pp. 562–568.
Simons, G., Summer/Fall 2011, 'Attempting to Re-Brand the Branded: Russia's International Image in the 21st Century', *Russian Journal of Communication*, 4(3/4), pp. 322–350.
Simons, G., October 2013, *Nation Branding and Russian Foreign Policy*, UI Occasional Papers, #21. www.ui.se/globalassets/ui.se-eng/publications/ui-publications/nation-branding-and-russian-foreign-policy-min.pdf.
Simons, G., 2014, 'Russian Public Diplomacy in the 21st Century: Structure, Means and Message', *Public Relations Review*, 40, pp. 440–449.
Simons, G., 2015a, 'Taking New Public Diplomacy Online: China and Russia', *Journal of Place Branding and Public Diplomacy*, 11, pp. 111–124.
Simons, G., 2015b, 'Perception of Russia's Soft Power and Influence in the Baltic States', *Public Relations Review*, 41(1), pp. 1–13.
Simons, G., 2015c, 'Aspects of Putin's Appeal to International Publics', *Global Affairs*, 1(2), pp. 205–208.

Simons, G., 2016, 'News and Syria: Creating Key Media Moments in the Conflict', *Cogent Social Sciences* 2, pp. 1–16.

Sussman, G., 2010, *Branding Democracy: U.S. Regime Change in Post-Soviet Eastern Europe*, New York: Peter Lang.

Tsygankov, A., 18 December 2014, 'The Sources of Russia's Ukraine Policy', Analysis, *Russian Analytical Digest*, No. 158. www.css.ethz.ch/content/dam/ethz/special-interest/gess/cis/center-for-securities-studies/pdfs/RAD-158.pdf.

Tsygankov, A., 2015, 'Vladimir Putin's Last Stand: The Sources of Russia's Ukraine Policy', *Post-Soviet Affairs*, 31(4), pp. 279–303.

Tsygankov, A., 2016, *Russia's Foreign Policy: Change and Continuity in National Identity*, 4th Edition, Lanham, MD: Rowman & Littlefield.

Tsygankov, A. & Tarver-Wahlquist, M., 2009, 'Duelling Honours: Power, Identity and the Russia-Georgia Divide', *Foreign Policy Analysis*, 5, pp. 317–326.

Wilson, J. L., 2015, 'Russia and China Respond to Soft Power: Interpretation and Readaptation of a Western Construct', *Politics*, 35 (3/4), pp. 287–300.

Yablokov, I., 2015, 'Conspiracy Theories as a Russian Public Diplomacy Tool: The Case of *Russia Today* (RT)', *Politics*, 35 (3/4), pp. 301–315.

13
THE RUSSIAN ORTHODOX CHURCH

Nicolai N. Petro

UNIVERSITY OF RHODE ISLAND, USA

Since the collapse of the Soviet Union, the Russian Orthodox Church (ROC) has emerged as an influential actor in both Russian domestic and foreign policy. This chapter explores the relationship between church and state in Russia. It examines the scholarly debate over the actual role of the ROC in Russian foreign policy, as well as arenas for potential for conflict and cooperation between the church and the state in foreign policy.

Is the ROC a tool of the state?

A fundamental question needs to be addressed at the very outset. Does it even make sense to discuss the role of the ROC in Russian foreign policy?[1] For many scholars this topic does not exist. According to this view, there can be no foreign policy influence of the ROC because it is not an autonomous political and social actor.

Most books published about the ROC in recent years argue that little has changed Church-state relations since the collapse of the Soviet Union. For one group of scholars the ROC is a reliable tool of the state (Knox, 2004; Mitrofanova, 2005; Blitt, 2011; Papkova, 2011; Fagan, 2013). Since there is no distinguishable ROC foreign policy agenda, it need not be examined separately from the state's own foreign policy agenda.

A second group grants the ROC some autonomy, but contends that its freedom of movement is severely constrained (Marsh, 2004; Payne, 2010; Curanović, 2012; Richters, 2012). Its foreign policy agenda is therefore of interest only as an expression of what has already been decided within state institutions. For both groups the foreign policy agenda of the ROC derives entirely from the Russian state.

There is much in Russian history that supports this view, which makes its uncritical acceptance today so dangerous. Rather than looking at how relations have changed since the collapse of communism, most scholars have tended to fall back on familiar stereotypes.

The most common stereotype is the casual assumption that because the ROC supports the Russian state in many arenas, such support must derive from its subordination to the state, rather than a similarity of views. As a result, the actual views of the ROC on social partnership are generally dismissed, since it is assumed that the state would instruct the ROC to insist that it was not subordinate to the state, in any case. The argument is thus non-refutable.

A *prima facie* case for the autonomy of the ROC in foreign policy, however, can easily be made by pointing to religious priorities that have become part of the Russian foreign policy agenda. Professional diplomats are notably reluctant to adopt "values agendas" of this sort because it complicates their work. When this happens in the case of religious or human rights concerns, therefore, it is generally viewed as an indirect measure of the influence of these outside actors on state policy.

I, however, propose that we go even further and take seriously not just the Church's social agenda, but also its eschatological agenda. I believe this sheds new light on how the Church deals with issues of political conflict and where it will draw the line on cooperation with civil authorities. In areas where the social interests of the Church and the state overlap, the weight of the ROC in society is now such that it cannot be simply ignored. Moreover, as that weight has grown, the ROC has gained greater autonomy, pursuing its own agenda, and becoming a true partner of the Russian state.

To demonstrate the rise of this influence, I will briefly discuss the Orthodox approach to politics, then explore how this approach affects Russian foreign policy thinking through the concept of the *Russky mir*, or Russian World. Finally, I will look at areas where the agendas of the ROC and the Russian government are likely to diverge over time.

The historical Orthodox attitude to politics

Within the broad framework of Christian political thought, Orthodoxy's perspective on proper church–state relations derives from the Eastern Roman or Byzantine Empire. Since it was in the Eastern Roman Empire that the Christian doctrine of church–state relations were first formalized, this gives it several specific characteristics.

While the Patriarch of Rome (the Pope) faced the difficult task of preserving the Church in the face of the collapse of political institutions so vividly described by St. Augustine, the Patriarch of Constantinople held onto his place of honor within Byzantine society, even during times of conflict with the Basileus (for a good overview, see Gvosdev, 2000). Church–state relations therefore evolved very differently in the Eastern and Western halves of Europe.

In the West the Church struggled to survive the collapse of the state and to preserve its independence from state control, once it had been re-established. The march of Western progress, from the Renaissance, to the Reformation, to the Enlightenment, has been widely equated with the rise of the modern concepts of personal liberty and individual freedoms (Swidler, 1986; Casanova, 2003). The loss of "Christendom" – the social and political manifestation of a common Christian social ideal – is usually seen as a small price to pay for the establishment of individual freedom and modern relations between church and state.

By contrast, the pattern of church–state relations that emerged in the East presumed that the Patriarch and Basileus should continue to work together to accomplish God's purpose on Earth. As described in Roman Emperor Justinian's (482–565) *Sixth Novella*, their respective spheres of competence might overlap, but remained distinct:

> There are two greatest gifts which God, in his love for man, has granted from on high: the priesthood and the imperial dignity. The first serves divine things, the second directs and administers human affairs . . . if the priesthood is in every way free from blame and possesses access to God, and if the emperors administer equitably and judiciously the state entrusted to their care, general harmony will result, and all that is beneficial will be bestowed upon the human race.
>
> *(Meyendorff, 1968: 48)*

The ideal relationship between church and state was thus one of *symphonia*, or harmony, between religious and state institutions. Though this ideal was rarely achieved, it thrived in the East because that is where Greek culture survived, after the fall of Rome. By the time of the Reformation, much of the Middle East and Greece was under Ottoman rule, and Russia had emerged as the "Third Rome." As the last surviving ruler of an Orthodox country, it fell to the princes of Moscow, according to this legend, to preserve the "one true faith."

Peter the Great's reign created a new caste of people, more sympathetic to Western patterns of development. It also leaves the ROC in a subordinate position to the Tsar, and unable to exercise its customary tutelary function over the state and its regents. Peter the Great's reign thus marks the end of *symphonia* and the beginning of modern, Imperial Russia.

Over the next two centuries the intellectual elite drifted away from the weakened and isolated Church, embracing Western ideas that seem to provide ways to overcome Russia's backwardness. Among the most ambitious and radical solutions is Marxism.

The victory of the Bolsheviks in 1917, as we know, led to an all-out assault on the Church that nearly ended in its extinction. On the eve of the Russian revolution, the ROC had more than 55,000 churches and more than 66,000 priests. Two decades later, in 1939, the ROC had just 300 open churches and roughly as many priests ('Russkaya pravoslavnaya tserkov', 2016). While the regime failed to achieve its declared objective of a totally atheist population, the effort left profound wounds in the country's historical and cultural tapestry.

A quarter century after the collapse of the Soviet regime, the situation is strikingly different. Survey data shows that between 1991 and 2008 the share of Russian adults considering themselves orthodox has grown from 31% to 72%, while the share not considering themselves religious dropped from 61% to 18% (Romeo, 2015). Today the ROC has more than 34,000 churches and more than 35,000 priests ('Russkaya pravoslavnaya tserkov', 2016). If we are to believe a 2011 Ipsos survey of 23 European countries, Russia has become the most religious country in Europe (Weir, 2011).

This "miracle of the rebirth of faith in our secular age," as the Patriarch of Moscow and All Rus, Kirill (Gundyaev) calls it, has been accompanied by a seven-fold increase in corporate philanthropy, and a level of social activity that has made the ROC, in the words of former Russian president Dmitry Medvedev, "the largest and most authoritative social institution in contemporary Russia" (Anishyuk, 2011; 'Slovo Svyateishego Patriarkha Kirilla', 2016). It would seem that the rise of Orthodoxy has been good not only for business, but for political stability as well.

Many analysts, however, regard this new found piety as superficial, since the vast majority of Orthodox do not attend church regularly and do not follow strict religious practices. But as Stephen Prothero (2008) has shown, religious literacy is on the decline almost everywhere, including the United States. What is different in Russia, and what makes it such a remarkable social phenomenon, is the conflation of confessional attachment with national identity, something that Jerry Pankhurst calls "the confessionalisation of political culture" (Pankhurst and Kilp, 2013: 228).

Modern day *symphonia*

Today the ROC insists on the validity and importance of *symphonia* in church-state relations, and routinely touts the Eastern Roman Empire as a model in this regard. According to the Patriarch of Moscow, modern day *symphonia* allows the Church and the state to "spiritually coordinate their service" to society, even when they are formally separate institutions (Mite, 2004).

While many elements of the relationship have yet to be perfected, the Church is very clear about how it would like this partnership to evolve. First, it says, instead of a separation of church and state, there should be a "separation of sphere of competencies." Second, spiritual and secular authorities should cooperate in areas of common interest and mutual benefit. Third, whereas in the past the Church has been relatively passive, today it needs to be more assertive and work alongside the government to create a healthy spiritual and moral social climate, social peace and solidarity. Central to its teaching is the concept of the *co-authorship* of policy with the state (Kirill, 2009).

Additionally, the state should have a special relationship with the ROC because not all religions carry the same weight in Russian society. Sometimes this is justified in terms of the singular importance of Orthodoxy in Russian history ('Doklad Patriarkha Moskovskogo', 2013). At other times, Patriarch Kirill has suggested that the state should follow the established pattern of relations among Russia's four established religions, based on the length of their historical presence, population, civic position, and contribution to the formation of the common national culture ('Vystuplenie Svyateishego Patriarkha Moskovskogo', 2009). This should lead to more extensive state interaction with minority religions in those regions of where they predominate, and with the ROC throughout the Russian Federation as a whole.

Although the parameters of this relationship are still being worked out, it is already clear, from the experience since the late 1990s, that the new *symphonia* takes for granted that Russia is a pluricultural, multi-confessional, and democratic society. But while the ROC now explicitly endorses the view that church and state are properly separate institutions, it insists that no such distinction should be made between the Church and society.

While this formulation removes the ROC from all *formal* aspects of the political process, it *reinforces* its role as the moral guide and spokesman for society. As Fr. Vsevolod (Chaplin), the controversial former head of the Synodal Department for Church and Society Relations, put it, "[the Church] cannot but have a position that would give it the right to speak to those in power, in all spheres of public life, in fulfillment of its prophetic role . . . as the voice of God in politics, in economics, and in any social processes" ('Vsevolod Chaplin', 2012).

How does this approach to politics carry over into foreign affairs?

What implications does this grandiose social agenda have for foreign affairs? As a non-state actor, the ROC is limited in its ability to promote any specific foreign policy agenda; neither can it explicitly promote religious views through state organizations. Instead it "piggybacks" on state institutions, promoting moral and cultural values that both the ROC and the Russian state share.

The foreign relations of the ROC reflect the closeness of relations with traditional religions in different regions of the globe. In descending order of intimacy, they go from traditionally Orthodox countries, to traditionally Catholic countries, to traditionally Muslim countries, to traditionally Protestant and now predominantly secularized countries, and finally to non-Christian countries.

Overlaid onto a regionally based view of Russian foreign policy, the resulting matrix of corresponding areas of canonical and political responsibility looks something like this:

ROC regionalization	RFP regionalization
Traditionally Orthodox societies	Former Soviet Union and parts of Eastern Europe
Traditionally Catholic societies	Southern Europe and Latin America
Traditionally Muslim Societies of Central Asia and Iran	North Africa and the Middle East
Traditionally Protestant, secular societies	Northern Europe and North America
Traditionally non-Christian societies	Asia and parts of sub-Saharan Africa

There is obviously a high degree of correspondence between the two, but the non-congruence of what I referred to earlier as the social and eschatological agendas means that their interests will never fully coincide. For one thing, the avowed priority of Russian foreign policy is the pursuit of the national interest, whereas the avowed priority of the ROC is the salvation of mankind.

At first blush, these seem like such different realms that it is not even clear why they would ever overlap. The link between the two, as Andrei Tsygankov (2012) has pointed out, lies in Russia's sense of honor – the basic moral principles that are popularly cited within a culture as the reason for its existence, and that inform its purpose when interacting with other nations. While a nation's sense of honor overlaps with present day interests, it cannot be reduced to the present day national interest alone, because political leaders must also respond to culturally imbedded moral ideals.

A nation's sense of honor, therefore, serves as a baseline for what might be called the *long-term national interest* which, for Russia, revolves around three constants: first, sovereignty or "spiritual freedom"; second, a strong and socially protective state that is capable of defending that sovereignty; and third, cultural loyalty to those who share Russia's sense of honor, wherever they may be. Each of these involves, correspondingly, the defense of Orthodox Christianity, the defense of the ROC, and the defense of Orthodox Christians around the world.

To be clear, government institutions are in the driving seat when it comes to responding to immediate foreign policy concerns. But when it comes to shaping Russia's long-term strategy, these culturally embedded ideals play a prominent role. Having re-assumed its traditional role as the supreme arbiter of morality in Russian society, the ROC has become a key actor in shaping this strategy.

So far, we have focused on the theoretical and cultural framework within which the ROC and the Russian state operate. One critical example illustrates just how the ROC shapes Russia's long-term foreign policy agenda – Ukraine.

Before the current crisis with Ukraine, and in the absence of any other actors willing to provide a culturally rooted vision of Russian-Ukrainian relations, the ROC promoted the idea that Russia, Ukraine, and Belarus constitute a distinct community, a Holy Rus (*Svyataya Rus*), or a Russian World (*Russky mir* or *Rus'kii mir*), that shares a common spiritual destiny ('Doklad Patriarkha Moskovskogo', 2013).

The Russian World: a political and religious project

It is no coincidence that the ROC has taken the lead in the development of the concept of a *Russky mir*, or that Ukraine has emerged as its key focus. It is, after all, a vision that explicitly looks beyond Russia's present borders, to the larger canonical domain of the ROC. It was part of the ROC's response to fragmentation of its pastoral community that occurred with the collapse of the USSR.

For several years after the collapse, the majority of ROC parishes were actually outside the Russian Federation. Responding to this unique historical circumstance, the ROC began emphasizing spiritual unity over the divisions that had been created by new national borders.

The term "Russky" in "Russky mir" is neither a geographical nor an ethnic concept. It is a spiritual identity born in the cradle of civilization of Ukrainians, Russians, and Belarussians – Kievan *Rus* ('Vystuplenie svyateishego Patriarkha Kirilla', 2009). When Kievan *Rus* adopted Christianity from Constantinople in 988, Church hierarchs say, the Eastern Slavs were consecrated into a single civilization and given the task of constructing Holy Rus.

That mission has survived throughout Russian history. It survived the religious persecutions of the Soviet era, and continues today in democratic Russia (Ryabykh, 2010). The core of this community resides in Russia, Ukraine, and Belarus (at other times, Patriarch Kirill has also added Moldova and Kazakhstan), but it can refer to anyone who shares the Orthodox faith, a reliance on Russian language, a common historical memory, and a common view of social development ('Vystuplenie svyateishego Patriarkha Kirilla', 2009).

In June 2007, president Putin helped to inaugurate the *Russky mir Fund*, a state sponsored entity that promotes Russian language and culture throughout the world ('Stenograficheskiy otchet', 2007). The use of the same term in both a secular and religious context has led to considerable confusion. While there is some overlap, there are also important differences.

As used by the state, the term *Russky mir* is a typical public relations initiative. It strives to popularize Russia and the use of Russian abroad. It is an element of Russia's "soft power," increasing her influence among neighboring states, and improving Russia's image as a global power. From the state's perspective, the ROC can be a useful tool for these purposes.

As used by the Church, the term *Russky mir* is God's project, since it is by God's design that these nations were baptized into one civilization. The ROC thus sees it efforts as the realization of God's plan – the establishment of Holy Rus. To achieve this ideal the Church, here and now, seeks to reverse the secularization of post-Soviet society, a task that Patriarch Kirill has termed the "second Christianization" of Rus ('Patriarch Kirill challenges Church', 2010). From the ROC's perspective, the Russian government, and every other government within its canonical territory, can be useful tools for this purpose.

Public reaction to the Patriarch's use of the phrase has been mixed. It has aroused the most controversy in Ukraine, where the Greek-Catholic (Uniate) church and the non-canonical Ukrainian Orthodox Church of the Kievan Patriarchate (UOC-KP) dismissed it outright, while the Ukrainian Orthodox Church that is in communion with the Moscow Patriarchate (UOC-MP), which serves approximately half of all Christians in Ukraine, has been cautiously receptive.

The latter suggests that national identity should, ultimately, be less important to a religious person than religious identity. As Metropolitan Paul (Lebed), head of the Kiev-Pechersk Laura, one of Orthodoxy's oldest monasteries, put it:

> [t]o earn the right to call ourselves Holy Rus we must strive to make ourselves holy . . . the venerable Hilarion called our land Rus back in 1051. In this sense we are all Russians. But there is a state called Ukraine on this earth, and I am its citizen. In this sense, we are all Ukrainians. I see no contradiction here. As a Ukrainian I would note that there is no particular merit to being part of a nation. It is deeds that are called for.
> *(Taksyur, 2016)*

But, just as this issue highlights the long-term goals of the Church, it also illustrates the ROC's limited ability to affect immediate policy decisions. The very different approaches to the crises in Crimea and Donbass illustrate these limitations.

Most analysts view the annexation of Crimea as a reaction to the opportunity to secure a strategic advantage for Russia in the Black Sea region. Some feel it was an understandable move given the hostility of the Maidan leadership, while others argue that there was no prospect of such hostility ever actually threatening Russian interests.

To this end, Putin constructed a narrative that portrayed the annexation of Crimea as both a defense against imminent threats to the Russian identity of this region, and a return to its proper Russian cultural sphere – an objective close to the Russian World. Later, during his December 4, 2014 speech to the Federal Assembly, Putin explicitly melded the geopolitical and the religious aspects of the Crimean annexation together, saying:

For Russia, Crimea, ancient Korsun (Khersones), Sebastopol have enormous civilizational and sacral meaning – just as the Temple Mount in Jerusalem has for those who profess Islam and Judaism . . . this territory is strategically important because it is the spiritual source of the formation of our multifaceted but monolithic Russian nation and centralized Russian state. It was in this very place, in Crimea, in ancient Khersones, or as Russian chroniclers called it, Korsun, that Prince Vladimir was baptized, and [he] then baptized all of Rus.

('Krym imeet sakral'noe znachenie', 2014)

Yet with respect to the uprising in Donbass, which evolved nearly simultaneously, Putin took a very different position.

Rather than encouraging separatism there, Russian officials quickly distanced themselves from the rebels, offering them nothing but statements about the need to respect the will of the people. When the rebels scheduled their own referendum on secession, president Putin publicly urged them not to hold it. Russia did conduct military exercises near the Ukrainian border in late February, but returned these troops to their barracks in late April, <u>after</u> the beginning of Kiev's anti-terrorist military campaign. In May, Putin recognized the legitimacy of Ukrainian presidential elections, and most importantly, at the end of June, just as the Ukrainian military campaign in the East was ramping up, Putin asked the Russian parliament to rescind his authority to use troops outside Russia.

In the case of Crimea, Russian culture and Orthodox religion were used to popularize a policy that had already been deemed in the strategic interests of the nation, whereas in the case of Donbass similar appeals were ignored (some observers even say suppressed) because they did not correspond to Russia's strategic interests. The ROC had no discernible impact on immediate policy choices in either instance.

In the long term, however, the question of how to reconcile Russia and Ukraine is still very much on the agenda, and the ROC is the only institution providing a comprehensive alternative to the post-Maidan Ukrainian narrative. It does so by rallying the global Orthodox community behind the UOC-MP, which openly condemns the government's military operations in Eastern Ukraine and refers to the conflict as a "civil war," and by expanding cooperation with the Roman Catholics to establish a pan-European Christian social agenda.

Its most dramatic international success to date is the Joint Declaration of Pope Francis I and Patriarch Kirill signed in Havana on February 12, 2016. The two church leaders came up with a formula for reconciliation on the contentious issue of Catholic proselytism in Ukraine. While the Catholic Church deplores the "uniatism" of the past, "understood as the union of one community to the other, separating it from its Church," the ROC acknowledges that "the ecclesial communities which emerged in these historical circumstances have the right to exist and to undertake all that is necessary to meet the spiritual needs of their faithful" (Petro, 2016).

Second, Pope Francis publicly indicated his hope that schisms within the Orthodox church "may be overcome through existing canonical norms," phrasing that clearly puts the Pope on the side of the Synaxis of the world's Orthodox primates, held in Geneva (January 21–27, 2016), which did not invite the UOC-KP to participate in the historical Pan-Orthodox Church Council that took place in August 2016 (Petro, 2016).

Finally, when referring to the hostilities in Ukraine, the Pope and Patriarch called upon their followers "to refrain from taking part in the confrontation, and to not support any further development of the conflict." This too is a notable step toward the view of the canonical Ukrainian Orthodox Church, which is the only one in Ukraine that has refused to support the Ukrainian government's "anti-terrorist operation" in Eastern Ukraine.

In response, the Ukrainian government has thrown its full support behind the non-canonical Ukrainian Orthodox Church of the Kievan Patriarchate and the Ukrainian Greek-Catholic Church (UGCC). The latter identifies the independence of Ukraine and the resurgence of the UGCC with Paschal theology, while the head of the former has defined the ROC, and its relations with the state, as aberrations spawned by Satan (Denysenko, 2015).

In this struggle for the hearts and minds of Ukrainians, the official Ukrainian press now commonly associates the term "Russian World" with separatism, while in the rebellious Eastern provinces the terms "Russian Spring" and "Russian World" are often seen as synonyms. As Fr. Nicholas Denysenko (2015) observes:

> The irony of the intensity of the current religious narratives in Ukraine is that one is doomed no matter where they attend church. Those belonging to the UGCC are hopelessly nationalistic and seek the destruction of canonical Orthodoxy. Those belonging to the UOC-KP are schismatic and enjoy no support within global Orthodoxy. Those belonging to the MP are opponents of Ukraine and keep company with the likes of Cain, Pharaoh, and Judas . . . the space of each church is occupied by scandalous sinners even as they champion old and new saints as models one should pattern their lives after.

These efforts to politicize the religious meaning of the *Russky mir* ("against the will of its authors," Denysenko notes), appear to be succeeding in inflaming national and religious animosity, but the ROC Church shows no signs of abandoning the concept.

To ignore the spiritual development of the people God has entrusted to the pastoral care of the Russian Church, Patriarch Kirill has said repeatedly, would be to go against God's will [ослушаться самого Бога] ('Vystuplenie svyateishego Patriarkha Kirilla', 2009). Moreover, it has also had some successes. As the influence of the ROC in Russian society has grown, it has influenced political speech. Among the many examples, let me highlight just one – President Putin's address in Kiev on the occasion of the 1025th baptism of Rus in 2013 ('Konferentsiya', 2013). This was also Putin's most recent visit to Ukraine.

His remarks reflect nearly every religious motif of the *Russky mir* including: the decisive spiritual and cultural significance of the baptism of Rus; the uniqueness of Orthodox values in the modern world; deference to Kiev's historical significance (before the revolution, he says, it was known as "the second cultural and intellectual capital after St. Petersburg," ahead of Moscow); and public recognition of Ukraine's right to make any political choice it wishes which, however, "in no way erases our common historical past" ('Konferentsiya', 2013).

In conclusion, it is worth highlighting that the transnational perspective implicit in *Russky mir* puts the ROC at odds with one of the cornerstones of international politics – state sovereignty. While the Church says it respects the sovereignty of states, it takes no position on its merits ('Vystuplenie svyateishego Patriarkha Kirilla', 2009). Nation-states are neither good nor bad *per se*. They are merely the current framework within which God intends the Church to accomplish the restoration of Holy Rus (Ryabykh, 2010).

The ROC sees the *Russky mir* as a spiritual complement to national sovereignty – one that allows people to see their common heritage not as a threat to independence, but as a valuable resource in a globalizing world. The Byzantine Empire served as such a model in the past. Today, says Kirill, the European Union and the Commonwealth of Nations (formerly known as the British Commonwealth) serve the same purpose ('Vystuplenie svyateishego Patriarkha Kirilla', 2009).

That is also why, according to the ROC, there should be multiple political and cultural centers in the world, a view that coincides with Russia's official foreign policy position.

The *Russky mir* is one such center because it provides "a system of values which is the basis for several modern states" (Ryabykh, 2010).

The ROC as a foreign policy actor

If we take seriously the eschatological nature of the Church's mission, how might we best describe its foreign policy goals? Simply put, it is to save souls. Within its canonical territory it does so by promoting the re-baptism of Rus; beyond its canonical territory it does so by working alongside religious organizations in other countries to promote "all that is good in relations among peoples . . . [and] be a force for peacemaking" ('V zavershenie vizita', 2016).

The partnership between Church and state therefore naturally extends to foreign policy, where the ROC seeks to heighten the role of religious diplomacy and assist in the construction of a multipolar world that respects diverse cultural worldviews (Lipich, 2004). In every nation of the globe, Patriarch Kirill ('Metropolit Kirill otvetil', 2005) has said, the Church's task is to make that particular nation "a carrier of Orthodox civilization."

In his 2009 address to Russian Civil Service Academy, Patriarch enumerated an extensive list of areas where the ROC should collaborate with state institutions. These include:

> [c]oncern for the moral upbringing of young people, support for the institution of the family, fighting drug addiction, alcoholism and other dangerous vices, preventing crimes, caring for those in prisons, preserving cultural inheritance, overcoming national and religious intolerance, assisting the preservation of social peace and harmony, opposing the rise of radical and extremist attitudes, opposing pseudo-religious movements, helping to resolve international conflicts, promoting interreligious and intercultural dialogue both within the state and globally, as well as in international organizations.
>
> *('Vystuplenie Svyateishego Patriarkha', 2009).*

Taking note of "our common aspiration for the preservation of out spiritual and cultural identity of our brothers and sisters," the Patriarch identified the following areas of foreign policy where the ROC could assist:

- Improving the situation of Orthodox churches around the globe;
- Improving contacts with Russians living abroad;
- Expanding the dialogue of religious communities in Russia with state structures and international organizations;
- Promoting a positive image of Russia, its history, culture, and religion abroad.

To this end, the ROC and the Ministry of Foreign Affairs have set up a number of standing committees to coordinate their activities. One area where cooperation has proven fruitful is in re-establishing relations with Georgia, after the conflict of August 2008. It is worth noting that the ROC opposed the wishes of the Russian state, which was promoting the territorial, cultural, and religious autonomy of Abkhazia and South Ossetia from Georgia ('Russia church says', 2011). Instead, it deferred to the wishes of the Georgian Patriarchate and continued to recognize the latter's jurisdiction in these disputed regions ('Obmen "tserkovnymi poslami"', 2009).

With respect to its eschatological agenda, the ROC has succeeded not only in focusing the Russian foreign policy establishment's interest on the defense of Orthodox communities around the globe which, given tensions in Ukraine, Syria, and Palestine would arguably coincide with

Russia's national interest, but in Christian moral values in general. Its greatest success in this arena was Putin's 2013 speech to the Valdai Club, in which he underscored the importance of traditional religious values to human dignity, and asserted that the abandonment of traditional Christian values had led to a moral crisis in the West. Russia, Putin said, intends to counter this trend by defending Christian moral principles, both at home and abroad (Putin, 2013).

In the future we can expect the ROC's influence over the long-term agenda of Russian foreign policy to manifest itself in advocacy for the concerns of Orthodox Christians, even if they are not Russian citizens, and in the promotion of Christian moral and social values in international fora. Where it does not have direct access to such fora, it will use Russian state channels to promote this agenda.

In the promotion of Russian culture and language abroad, however, its eschatological mission differs from that of the Russian state. Whereas the state seeks to promote Russian national interest and culture, the ROC seeks to promote the larger identity and culture associated with Kievan *Rus*. This distinction, the result of a theologically steeped view of how that conflict should be resolved, could become significant in long-term Russian-Ukrainian relations.

Since the Church views the conflict as a civil war within the *Russky mir*, it cannot be resolved by isolating Ukraine from Russia. The only permanent solution is for the Ukrainian government to admit the pluricultural nature of Ukrainian society and, in effect, admit that Ukraine is an integral part of the *Russky mir*. From the Church's perspective, this is the only way to achieve harmony and reconciliation both within Ukrainian society, and between Ukraine and Russia.

But the Church's most important success has been to transform relations with the state from subordination to meaningful partnership. Today the ROC provides intellectual and moral support to state policies not because it has to, but because it wants to. Indeed, to the extent that there is a moral framework guiding Russian foreign policy, it is the Church's moral framework. The Church promotes it because it is convinced that helping the Russian government to create a "congenial international order" will assist the Church in its threefold salvific mission – to save individual souls, to save all national cultures that have been baptized into Christ, and to save all mankind.

The ROC as a source of future conflict

Having reviewed the benefits that each side derives from a harmonious church-state relationship, let us look at some potential areas of conflict.

The first is that Orthodox Christianity sees no intrinsic value in political beliefs or actions ('Obshchestvennaya deyatel'nost', 2011; 'Praktika zayavalenii', 2011). As Archbishop Anastasios (Yannoulatos) notes, the Orthodox tradition has no set preference for one form of politics over another because those things that are ultimately needful, right, and proper, lie beyond the ken of politics. Yet, while the Church does not see itself as a *political* actor, it does sees itself as actively engaged in society. As Patriarch Kirill explains:

> We cannot, through our silence, seemingly support the positions . . . that are deadly for people's souls. Without entering into political battle, we must remain true to our religious worldview, including in giving our assessment of the actions of political actors . . . [especially those] whose program documents express ideas contrary to the teachings of the Church.
>
> *(Yannoulatos, 2003: 74)*

This implies that ROC support for government policy is conditional upon its judgement about the spiritual benefit of that policy.

Second, the ROC does not see itself as just one constituency among many in society. It is, rather, the very "soul of the people and, at its deepest level the Church represents its people externally" ('V zavershenie vizita', 2016). Its purview therefore exceeds that of any other social groups, even the government, for while the government speaks to the values of society in the present, the Church speaks for the eternal values of Holy Rus. As the Patriarch put it:

> From the time of the Baptism of Rus to the present, the Church bears a special responsibility for the spiritual and moral well-being of the people . . . Concern for the people's souls is the main component of the Church's service in the past, present, and future.
>
> *('Doklad Patriarkha Moskovskogo', 2013)*

Third, the ROC accords itself a special privilege in offering social solutions ('Vsevolod Chaplin', 2012). This solution is to "Churchify" all aspects of society. To quote the patriarch, "The Church has a clear vision of reality, revealed to the world by God himself, and it is our mission to bring this vision to our contemporaries, with full confidence in its unique correspondence to the truth" ('Doklad Patriarkha Moskovskogo', 2013). The ROC therefore cannot support policies, no matter how socially beneficial, that result in movement away from the ideal of Holy Rus. What the Russian Orthodox is looking for can best be described as the modernization of society without its secularization.

One thing that will probably not be a source of friction between the state and the Church is the issue of democracy, particularly in the form of a Protestant style movement that pits the Church against the state. That is not because the Church itself does not value personal freedom. Indeed, as Nicolas Berdyaev (1926) points out, freedom is essential to the Church's goal of Churchification and the task both sides have set themselves is to work together in harmony). It would therefore be quite out of character for either of them to disagree publicly. Rather, they will simply work separately in arenas where their interest do not coincide, and in concert where they do.

Paradoxically, the establishment of broadly harmonious and mutually supportive relations between Church and state in Russia has itself become a source of conflict with the West, for it leads to conclusions that some in the West find troubling.

For example, Vladimir Putin's high popularity ratings reflect the popularity of his social and political agenda, which are popular precisely because they have the blessing of the ROC. The success of the Putin Plan, the Putin Model, or Putinism, thus derives from its public embrace of religion in general, and of the ROC in particular. The socially cohesive influence of the latter can be seen in surveys showing that Patriarch Kill is more commonly identified as the "spiritual leader [and] moral mentor" of the entire Russian nation than he is as the head of a single religious confession ('Patriarkh Kirill: chetyre goda', 2013).

Putin's unpopularity in the West, and his extraordinarily high levels of support in Russia, thus stem from the same source – the popularity of the traditional social values being advocated by the ROC.

Such disagreements are often summarized in Western literature as "the values gap." And while the examples typically given are Russia's failure to abide by international (read Western) standards, they often can be traced to deep seated cultural disagreements about the role that religious institutions should play in shaping both values and policies. Simply put, many in the West regard partnership between church and state as reactionary, whereas many in Russia regard its absence as a sign of moral decay. According to such logic, conflict between Russia and the West is inescapable until Russia fundamentally alters its values.

I feel this conclusion is premature. After all, this is not the first time that religious differences have played a role in international relations, and as many astute observers have argued, it has not always been a negative role. Most of these studies look askance at the ROC, but it is worth asking if there is the potential to transform the ROC from a source of conflict into a source of reconciliation with the West.

The ROC as a source of conflict resolution

There are two ways in which the ROC might become a source of reconciliation between Russia and the West. One is by focusing greater attention on peacemaking activities, something that unites most major religious institutions, and also helps to expand our notions of traditional diplomacy. The other is to help dismantle the notion of "the values gap."

Douglas Johnston, a former diplomat, has co-authored several books and articles on what he terms "religious diplomacy." He views religious or "faith-based" diplomacy as particularly well suited to "nonmaterial identity-based conflicts," for it focuses attention on the transformative impact of appeals on the basis of shared spiritual convictions or values. Such appeals allow the participants to appreciate the "emotional stakes" involved in a conflict (Johnston, 1994: 3, 5).

Vendley and Little (1994: 308) provide examples of the ways in which various religious traditions disentangle themes of peace from themes of conflict. In this way, they argue, religions allow us to "turn back to appropriate histories" and work out possible connections that can lead to solutions. Edward Luttwak (1994: 10) argues that in the process of conflict resolution, introducing the authority of religion can allow parties to concede assets by portraying concession as an act of deference to religion.

Finally, R. Scott Appleby (2003: 231) describes religion as "the missing dimension of statecraft." Retrieving it involves: (1) identifying the genius of each religious tradition, and its ways of producing social harmony; (2) accessing the mystical, experiential, syncretistic dimensions of faith traditions; (3) engaging scholars, theologians, others who view conflict resolution as a normative commitment of their religious tradition; (4) developing experts on conflict resolution within religious communities; and (5) drawing on NGO, state, and private actors to enhance religious-secular dialogue.

In the West, an important obstacle to the development of a robust religious diplomacy has been what Luttwak (1994: 10) calls "a learned repugnance to contend *intellectually* with all that is religion or belongs to it." He cites the example of Western ignorance of Byzantine approaches to conflict resolution.

Obviously, the Byzantine ideal of *symphonia* provides a highly adaptable and historically significant framework for what these scholars are calling for, which is why it should be no surprise to anyone that the ROC is actively engaged in all of these arenas. Religious or faith-based diplomacy is thus one area where the West can learn from its Eastern brethren.

A second area where the ROC could help is by encouraging a broader and more sophisticated understanding of our common Byzantine heritage. As James H. Billington (1990) has observed, ignorance and neglect of Byzantium has been "a fixture of all the mistaken conventional wisdom" about Russia and Eastern Europe. This is no less true today than when he said it more than a quarter century ago. It will take a great deal of time and effort to change the conventional wisdom, but this is an essential undertaking, without which we will never be able to overcome the corrosive idea that some sort of mystical "values gap" permanently divides the two halves of European civilization.

We did not always think this way. Indeed, in the aftermath of the fall of the Berlin Wall, it was widely assumed that Russia would rejoin Europe. Unfortunately, the opposite happened. As NATO expanded eastward, Russia was pushed away from Europe both conceptually and practically, thus fulfilling émigré Russian cultural historian Vladimir Weidlé's (1952) warning of more than half a century ago that failure to see Russian culture as part of Western civilization would lie at the heart of both the West's inability to overcome the Cold War, and Russia's inability to overcome the Soviet era.

To avoid even greater tragedy in the future we should heed the warning of America's most venerated living specialist on Russia, the former Librarian of Congress James H. Billington (1997):

> If Americans cannot penetrate into the interior spiritual dialogue of other peoples, they will never be able to understand, let alone anticipate or affect, the discontinuous major changes which are the driving forces in history and which will probably continue to spring unexpected traps in the years ahead.

To put it another way, if we cannot learn to listen to others as they whisper their prayers, we may well confront them later on when they howl their war cries.

Some issues for further exploration

I have proposed an approach that takes seriously the role of the Church both as a political and an eschatological actor. Treating the ROC as nothing more than secular and political is misleading. Although it clearly is a political actor (as well as an economic actor, a legal actor, a cultural actor, an educational actor), we should never lose sight of the fact that the Church sees itself, first and foremost, as a *supernatural* actor, a tangible manifestation of the Holy Spirit in the world (Lossky, 1998).

This dualism explains the ability of the ROC to help resolve conflicts among Orthodox countries, as well as its failure to do so in Ukraine, where political issues have all but driven out eschatological concerns. It also limits the extent of cooperation between the state and Church authorities.

In looking at how this relationship is likely to unfold, therefore, I believe we must always bear in mind these two distinct contexts, political and religious. Aware of this distinction, scholars should periodically review the degree to which the ROC is becoming a source of tension or consolidation, both within Russian society and in Russia's relations with other countries.

This context has other interesting ramifications. If the popularity of the Russian leadership is, as I contend, partially the result of its utilitarian embrace of religious values, then that leadership and the political system is not only more stable than most Western analysts think, its behavior is also more predictable in the long term, if one includes the views of the ROC in those long-term calculations.

Finally, I would encourage a re-examination of the relevance of the Byzantine inheritance, both for political and international relations. In some respects that heritage diverges from the West, but in others there is considerable overlap. A more systematic appraisal of the inheritance that we share could encourage a reappraisal of Byzantine political ideals along lines suggested by scholars such as James H. Billington (1997), Antonie Carile (2000), Deno Geanakopolos (1976), Judith Herrin, Warren Treadgold, Helene Ahrweiler (1975), Silvia Ronchey, Sergei Ivanov, as well as, more classically, Sergei Averintsev, and Steven Runciman (1970).

The future may well depend on whether Europeans can once again learn to appreciate the values that once united these two, now estranged, parts of European identity.

Note

1 In this chapter the term "Church," when capitalized, refers to the entire Orthodox community. When uncapitalized, it refers to any other Christian religious denomination.

References

Ahrweiler, H 1975, *L'ideologie politique de l'Empire byzantine*, Presse universitaires de France, Vendome (France).
Anishyuk A 2011, 'Russian Orthodox Church Allowed to Enter Politics', *Reuters*, 3 February.
Appleby, RS 2003, 'Retrieving the Missing Dimension of Statecraft: Religious Faith in the Service of Peacebuilding', in D Johnston, (ed.), *Faith Based Diplomacy: Trumping Realpolitik*, pp. 231–258, Oxford University Press, New York.
Berdyaev, N 1926, 'Discord in the Church and Freedom of Conscience', *Put'* (October-November). Available from: www.holy-trinity.org/ecclesiology/berdyaev-discord.html. [15 November 2016].
Billington J 1990, 'Looking to the Past', *Washington Post*, 22 January 22, p. A11.
Billington, J 1997, 'Religion and Russia's Future', the Templeton Lecture on Religion and World Affairs, *FPRI Wire*, October 1997. Available from: www.fpri.org/articles/1997/10/religion-and-russias-future. [15 November 2016].
Blitt, RC 2011, 'Russia's "Orthodox" Foreign Policy: The Growing Influence of the Russian Orthodod Church in Shaping Russia's Policies Abroad', *University of Pennsylvania Journal of International Law*, 33(2), pp. 364–460.
Carile, A 2000, *Immagine e realta nel mondo bizantino*, Lo Scarabeo, Bologna (Italy).
Casanova, J 2003, 'What is a Public Religion?' in H Heclo & WM McClay, (eds.), *Religion Returns to the Public Square: Faith and Policy in America*, pp. 111–140. Johns Hopkins University Press, Baltimore, MD and London.
Curanović, A 2012, *The Religious Factor in Russia's Foreign Policy*, Routledge, New York.
Denysenko, N 2015, 'Civilization, Church, World: Competing Religious Narratives from Ukraine and Russia', *Bohdan Bociurkiw Memorial Lecture, Canadian Institute of Ukrainian Studies*, 11 February. Available at: https://lmu.academia.edu/NicholasDenysenko/Papers. [15 November 2016].
'Doklad Patriarkha Moskovskogo i vesya Rusi Kirilla na eparkhialnom sobranii gorod Moskvy' 2013, *Patriarchia.ru*, 20 December. Available from www.patriarchia.ru/db/text/3453393.html [15 November 2016].
Fagan, G 2013, *Believing in Russia: Religious Policy after Communism*, Routledge, Abingdon, UK.
Gvosdev, NK 2000, *Emperors and Elections: Reconciling the Orthodox Tradition with Modern Politics*, Troitsa Books, New York.
Johnston, D 1994, 'Introduction: Beyond Power Politics', in D Johnston & C Sampson (eds), *Religion, The Missing Dimension of Statecraft*, pp. 3–7, Oxford University Press, New York.
Kirill 2009 'Formirovanie sistemy tserkovno-gosudarstvennykh otnoshenii v sovremennoi Rossii,' *Religiya, Tserkov' v Rossii i za Rubezhom*, 4, pp. 21–27. www.patriarchia.ru/db/text/980244.html [15 November 2016].
Knox, Z 2004, *Russian Society and the Orthodox Church*. London: RoutledgeCurzon.
'Konferentsiya 'Pravoslavno-slavayanskie tsennosti – osnova tsivilizatsionnogo vybora Ukrainy' 2013, *Kremlin.Ru*, 27 July. Available at: www.kremlin.ru/news/18961. [15 November 2016].
'Krym imeet sakral'noe znachenie dlya naroda Rossii, zayavil Vladimir Putin' 2014, *Sedmitsa.ru*, 4 December. Available from www.sedmitza.ru/text/5266564.html [15 November 2016].
Lipich, O 2004, 'Patriarch Alexis II: Time to Re-Comprehend the Role of Orthodoxy in World History', *RIA Novosti*, 3 February. Available from *Johnson's Russia List* #8047. http://russialist.org.
Lossky, V 1998, *The Mystical Theology of the Eastern Church*, St. Vladimir's Seminary Press, Crestwood, New York.
Luttwak, E 1994, 'The Missing Dimension', In D Johnston & C Sampson, (eds), *Religion, The Missing Dimension of Statecraft*, pp. 8–19, Oxford University Press, New York.

Marsh, C 2004, *Burden or Blessing? Russian Orthodoxy and the Construction of Civil Society*, Institute on Culture, Religion, and World Affairs at Boston University, Boston, MA.
'Metropolit Kirill otvetil na voprosy frantsuzskogo zhurnala 'Diplomatie' 2005, *Pravoslavie.Ru*, 4 October. Available from: www.pravoslavie.ru/14744.html. [15 November 2016].
Meyendorff, J 1968, 'Justinian, The Empire and the Church', *Dumbarton Oaks Papers*, 22: 43–60.
Mite V 2004, 'Russia: Orthodox Church States Its Case for More Involvement in Foreign, Domestic Policies', *RFE/RL*, 6 February 6. www.interfax-religion.ru/gry/?act=news&div=33581.
Mitrofanova, AV 2005, *The Politicization of Russian Orthodoxy: Actors and Ideas*, Ibidem-Verlag, Stuttgart, Germany.
'Obmen "tserkovnymi poslami" otchasti vospolnit otsutstvie dipotnoshenii mezhdu Rossiei I Gruzii – patriarkh Kirill' 2009, *Interfax-Religiya*, 29 December. Available from: www.interfax-religion.ru/gry/?act=news&div=33581. [15 November 2016].
'Obshchestvennaya deyatel'nost pravoslavnykh khristian' 2011, *Patriarchia.ru*, February 2. Available from: www.patriarchia.ru/db/print/1400931.html. [15 November 2016];
Pankhurst, J & Kilp A 2013, 'Religion, the Russian Nation and the State: Domestic and International Dimensions', *Religion, State and Society*, 41(3), pp. 226–243.
Papkova, I 2011, *The Orthodox Church and Russian Politics*, Oxford University Press, New York.
'Patriarch Kirill challenges Church to "reset" people's minds' 2010, *Interfax*, 16 November. Available from Johnson's Russia List 2010-#215, www.cdi.org/russia/johnson/. [15 November 2016].
'Patriarkh Kirill: chetyre goda tserkovnogo sluzheniya' 2013, *VCIOM.ru*, February 6. Available from http://wciom.ru/index.php?id=515&uid=113626. [15 November 2016].
Payne, DP 2010, 'Spiritual security, the Russian Orthodox Church, and the Russian Foreign Ministry: collaboration or cooptation?' *Journal of Church and State*, 52(4), pp. 712–727.
Petro N 2016 'Historic Meeting in Havana Brings About 'Minor Breakthrough' on Ukraine', *Valdai Club*, 15 February. Available from http://valdaiclub.com/a/highlights/historic-meeting-in-havana-brings-about-minor-breakthrough-on-ukraine-. [15 November 2016].
'Praktika zayavalenii i deistvii ierarkhov, dukhovenstva, monashestvuyushchikh i miryan vo vremya predvybornykh kampanii' 2011, *Patriarchia.ru*, February 2. Available from: www.patriarchia.ru/db/print/1400896.html. [15 November 2016].
Prothero, S 2008, *Religious Literacy: What Every American Needs to Know – and Doesn't*, HarperCollins, New York.
Putin, V 2013, 'Zasedanie mezhdunarodnogo diskussionnogo kluba "Valdai",' *Kremlin.ru*, 19 September. Available from: http://kremlin.ru/news/19243. [15 November 2016].
Richters, K 2012, *The Post-Soviet Russian Orthodox Church: Politics, Culture and Greater Russia*, Routledge, London.
Romeo, F 2015, 'The Rebirth of the Patriarch of Moscow: Moscow Politics in Harmony with the Russian Orthodox Church?' *GlobalResearch*, 8 August. Available from: www.globalresearch.ca/the-rebirth-of-the-patriarch-of-moscow-moscow-politics-in-harmony-with-the-russian-orthodox-church/5467928. [15 November 2016].
Runciman, S 1970, *The Last Byzantine Renaissance*, Cambridge University Press, Cambridge, UK.
'Russia Church Says It Won't Claim Authority Over Rebel Georgian Regions' 2011, *Reuters*, 15 August. Available from: http://blogs.reuters.com/faithworld/2011/08/15/russia-church-says-it-wont-claim-authority-over-rebel-georgian-regions/. [15 November 2016].
'Russkaya pravoslavnaya tserkov. Dosye,' 2016, *TASS*, 12 February. Available from: http://tass.ru/info/2659249. [15 November 2016].
Ryabykh, P, 2010 'Russky mir – eto tsivilizatsionnaya obshchnost', 17 June, *Patriarchia.ru*. Available from: www.patriarchia.ru/db/print/26208.html. [15 November 2016].
'Slovo Svyateishego Patriarkha Kirilla posle Liturgii v novoosvyashchennom Uspenskom sobore Surozhskoi eparkhii' 2016, *Patriarchia.ru*, 16 October. Available from www.patriarchia.ru/db/print/4641740.html. [15 November 2016].
'Stenograficheskiy otchet o vstreche s delegatami Vserossiiskoi konferentsii prepodavatelei gumanitarnykh I obshchestvennykh nauk' 2007, *Kremlin.ru*, 21 June. Available from http://kremlin.ru/transcripts/24359 [15 November 2016].
Swidler L 1986, *Religious Liberty and Human Rights*, Hippocrene Books, New York.
Taksyur, Ya 2016, 'Vladyka Pavel: "Bratie, zhivite v mire!"', *Ritm Evrazii*, 30 April. Available from: www.ritmeurasia.org/news–2016-04-30–vladyka-pavel-bratie-zhivite-v-mire-23282 [15 November 2016].
Tsygankov A 2012, *Russia and the West from Alexander to Putin*, Cambridge University Press, New York.

'V zavershenie vizita v Velikobritaniyu Predstoyatel' Russkoi Pravoslavnoi Tserkvi otvetil na voprosy predstavitelei rossiiskhih i zarubezhnykh SMI' 2016, *Patriarchia.ru*, 19 October. Available from www.patriarchia.ru/db/print/4644339.html. [15 November 2016].

Vendley, W & Little, D 1994, 'Implications for Religious Communities: Buddhism, Islam, Hinduism, and Christianity' In D Johnston & C Sampson, (eds), *Religion, The Missing Dimension of Statecraft*, pp. 306–315, Oxford University Press, New York.

'Vsevolod Chaplin opredelil positsiyu RPTs' 2012, *Newsru.com*, 17 May. Available from: http://m.newsru.com/religy/17may2012/chaplin.html. [15 November 2016].

'Vystuplenie Svyateishego Patriarkha Kirilla na torzhestvennom otkrytii III assemblei Russkogo mira' 2009, *Patriarchia.ru*, 3 November. Available from: www.patriarchia.ru/db/print/928446.html [15 November 2016].

'Vystuplenie Svyateishego Patriarkha Moskovskogo i vseya Rusi Kirilla v Rossiiskoi akademii gosudarstvennoi sluzhby' 2009, *Patriarchia.ru*, 31 December. Available from http://www.patriarchia.ru/db/text/980244.html [15 November 2016].

Weidlé, V 1952, *Russia: Absent and Present* (translated by A. Gordon Smith), J. Day, New York.

Weir F 2011, 'Russia Emerges as Europe's Most God-Believing Nation', *Christian Science Monitor*, 6 May. Available from www.csmonitor.com/World/Europe/2011/0506/Russia-emerges-as-Europe-s-most-God-believing-nation. [15 November 2016].

Yannoulatos, A 2003, *Facing the World: Orthodox Christian Essays on Global Concerns*, St. Vladimir's Seminary Press, Crestwood, New York.

PART III

Directions

Andrei P. Tsygankov

Part III studies various regional and global directions of Russian foreign policy (RFP) reviewing its formation and implementation toward the United States, Asia, Europe, the Middle East, Eurasia, and the Arctic. Each contributor engages with the existing literature and asks (1) what role his/her assigned region has played in RFP relative to other regions; (2) how Russia's position vis-à-vis the region has evolved since the Cold War's end; (3) what helps to explain such evolution; and (4) whether Russia's engagement with a particular region has been on balance successful or not. This part reviews a considerable part of important geographic regions and directions in RFP. It is not meant to cover all existing regions and countries with which Russia maintains international relations. For example, it does not include Africa or Latin America or individual countries and sub-regions such as the Balkans or the Baltics. My hope is, however, that the provided coverage will give the reader a solid idea of Russia's international priorities and principles of foreign policy formation.

In her chapter about Russia's relations with the United States, Kari Roberts recognizes the global significance of the country for the Kremlin. She argues that these relations have evolved through several distinct stages corresponding with Russia's presidencies of Boris Yelstin, Vladimir Putin, Dmitri Medvedev, and the return of Putin. Each of the identified stages saw attempts to both cooperate and conflict over different issues. In the 1990s such issues included expansion of NATO, conflict in the Balkans, and arms control. The 2000s added to this list issues of counter-terrorism, democracy promotion, and stability in the Middle East. More recently, Russia and the United States have clashed over Ukraine, Syria, and the Kremlin's alleged interference with the U.S. presidential elections.

Roberts traces the identified patterns of cooperation and conflict to the U.S. paternalistic attitude, perception of Russia's weakness, and residual Cold War "baggage" as well as Russia's identity crisis and preoccupation with status. Each breakdown in Russia-U.S. relations was expressed in the U.S. accelerated pressures on the Kremlin to comply with the West's expectations over human rights at home and respect for Western global interests. For instance, the breakdown of "reset" during Medvedev's tenure was accompanied by the United States' continued expansion of NATO and development of the Missile Defense System in Europe, rejection of Russia's approach to resolving the crisis in the Middle East, and a growing criticism of Russia's flawed elections and handling of political protests. Roberts maintains that Russia-U.S. overall relations are of mixed accomplishment and leave future leaders with important enduring challenges. She concludes that the animosity over Russia's annexation of Crimea, the post-Cold War European order, and the Middle East that now permeates the bilateral relations may well endure and even "permanently polarize" the relationship.

Russia's relations with Asia demonstrate an entirely different trajectory moving in the direction of a greater cooperation since the 1990s. As Natasha Kuhrt shows, RFP evolved from its Euro-Western focus to an increased interest in China and the Asia Pacific region. Russia has built stronger economic, political, and military ties with China, improved relations with India and South Korea, preserved special ties with North Korea, and sought to resolve its territorial disputes with Japan. Kuhrt recognizes the growing intensity of Russia-Asia relations yet cautions against overestimating the potential of these relations. In particular, she identifies the risk of a growing dependence on China and suggests that the Kremlin's economic reliance on Beijing following the crisis in Ukraine resulted from necessity rather than a strategic choice. Kuhrt agrees with the view that the Kremlin-hailed cooperation between the Eurasian Economic Union and China's One Road, One Belt may come at the price of limiting Russia's influence in the region.

Kuhrt identifies three factors behind Russia's Asia turn: identity, considerations of status, and Russia's needs for economic and regional development. In identity terms the Asia turn results from Russia's frustration with the attitude of its Western other toward RFP. Russia also seeks to preserve a great power status by forming an informal alliance with China, while being wary of becoming dependent on Beijing's international priorities. Finally, by turning to Asia and seeking potentially lucrative deals and investors, Russia aims to address its growing development gap that is especially evident in Siberia and the Far East.

On the European direction, Russia's trajectory is similar to that of its relations with the United States although Russia-Europe ties are qualitatively stronger and more historically developed. As Tuomas Forsberg and Hiski Haukkala write, in the 1990s Russia's relations with the European Union progressed in the signing of the Partnership and Cooperation agreement in 1994, but then demonstrated a downward development evident in disagreement over Chechnya and the Balkans. In the early 2000s, Russia and the EU made a new effort to strengthen ties by signing in May 2003 the agreement about developing Four Common Spaces covering economics, politics, security, and education. However, subsequent disagreements over trade, security, and values made it impossible to renew the agreement. Finally, Medvedev's attempts to improve relations by employing the idea of modernization and concluding a Partnership for Modernization in 2010 did not progress and was abandoned with Putin's return to presidency. Russia-EU relations then further worsened over recognition of the Eurasian Customs Union and the Ukraine conflict.

Forsberg and Haukkala maintain that there is no consensus over interpretation of Russia's EU policy, but observers employ multiple factors responsible for the identified changes including domestic politics, ideology, and considerations of status. The authors' assessment of Russia's progress in relations with the EU stresses the Kremlin's considerable interest in developing economic ties, and lack of cooperation in security issues. Forsberg and Haukkala argue that overall the Kremlin bargained hard over terms of relations with the EU and has been generally successful in protecting Russia's sovereignty from European norms and principles.

Moscow has also sought to develop stronger economic and security relations with Central European and Eastern states, including those non-members of the EU. Dmitry Offitserov-Belskiy and Andrey Sushenstov argue in their chapter that Russia has been moderately successful in preserving economic ties and not successful on the security front. As Central and Eastern European states gradually moved from early integration experiments to the idea of an Eastern Partnership formulated in 2009, Russia's perception became centered on issues of sovereignty and security. Series of the West's actions and policies, including NATO's expansion, intervention in Yugoslavia in 1999 and Afghanistan in 2001, the U.S. invasion of Iraq in 2003, and support for colored revolutions in Eurasia and the coup in Ukraine in February 2014, served to strengthen Moscow's conviction that the West aims to limit Russia's influence in the region. As a result, even economic issues became subject to Russia-West competition with the Caucasus, Belarus, Moldova, and Ukraine affected. Offitserov-Belskiy and Sushenstov assess the Kremlin's use of various economic pressures to achieve political objectives as not very effective, but argue that the share of mutual economic dependence between Russia and the states of Eurasia remains considerable and may play an important role in the future.

In the Middle East, Russia progressed from being a relatively low key actor immediately following the end of the Cold War to having a much greater prominence since arrival of Yevgeni Primakov as the country's foreign minister in the mid-1990s, and especially since Putin's presidency. Today, following its military intervention in Syria since October 2015, Russia has emerged as a critically important player. Philipp Casula and Mark Katz document and assess the described progression of RFP in the region and attribute it to both strategic and identity factors. Strategic calculations of the Kremlin have to do with its perceived need to balance the influences of the West and protect Russia's own military presence and arms sales in the Middle East. The fact that Russia has well-developed relations with all major countries in the complex region speaks to the Kremlin's ability to tap into these countries' political and economic interests while steering away from forces of an ideological and religious nature. In addition, Russia's identity of a country with special ties to "the East" and its own historically strong school of Oriental studies has assisted Moscow in developing a culturally sensitive understanding of its partners in the region.

As a result, in Casula and Katz's assessment, Russia's diplomatic, economic, and military position in the region is much stronger than it has ever been. Moscow now is well placed to serve as a mediator in solving important political conflicts in the region. This, however, does not mean that the overall record of RFP in the Middle East is one of continuous success. Moscow has important disagreements with Saudi Arabia and other countries. The Kremlin has not been able to build a strong anti-terrorist coalition in the region, and its reputation as Assad's supporter continues to tarnish Russia's image in the West.

RFP in the South Caucasus has suffered from multiple problems and has been only modestly successful. As Maxim Suchkov writes, Russia has done much to pacify and stabilize this critically important region next to its southern border. Its relations with Armenia and Azerbaijan have improved in the 2000s. The situation with Georgia remains difficult following the Russia-Georgia military conflict in August 2008 and is partly dependent on the status of South Ossetia and Abkhasia being recognized by the Kremlin as independent states. Russia's difficulties are also linked to its own volatile Northern Caucasus that has suffered from separatism, poverty, and Islamic radicalism. Suchkov argues that Russia's problems in the Caucasus result from a combination of the region's instability, Moscow's sensitivity to what it views as U.S. meddling, and U.S. policies and misperceptions of Russia's motivations. In the author's assessment, future progress of RFP in the region will depend on the Kremlin's ability to engage the states of the region into mutually attractive economic and political projects.

Central Asia is another critically important region in Russia's south. Mariya Omelicheva argues that Russia has complex interests in the region including those of national security, geopolitical influence, and economic development. She identifies four prominent regional concerns that have shaped RFP since the arrival of Putin as the country's president – terrorism, energy, migration, and government practices. Omelicheva takes issue with mono-causal explanations of Russia's behavior such as geopolitics or cultural/civilizational imperialism and argues for complex understanding of the country's domestic and international predicaments.

In Omelicheva's assessment, Russia succeeded in establishing security cooperation with Kyrgyzstan, Tajikistan, and Kazakhstan thereby contributing to the region's stability. However, Uzbekistan and Turkmenistan continue to be less cooperative leaving a "major gap in the regional security architecture". Russia also succeeded in developing energy schemes in Eurasia that assume its centrality, although China has broken Moscow's monopoly and continues to challenge Russia's energy position. How Russia and China will harmonize their regional economic/energy priorities remains a critically important issue to watch. Russia continues to benefit from Central Asian migrants and successfully assured Central Asian like-mindedness of government practices (authoritarianism).

Finally, as a northern power, Russia has keen interests in the Arctic. Robert English and Andrew Thvedt challenge the notion of Russia presenting a threat to the West or fighting a new Cold War in the region. They maintain that Moscow has been a "responsible Arctic stakeholder" and that it is natural for Russia to have economic and security presence in the Arctic. Russia has concluded important agreements with other Arctic nations beginning with the creation of the Arctic Council (AC) in September 1996. Since then the AC made by the United States, Canada, Russia, Sweden, Norway, Finland, Denmark, and Iceland has successfully addressed a number of important issues that concern the region. As a rotating chair of the AC, Russia pushed for a Search and Rescue agreement which was concluded in 2011. Russia also settled with Norway competing claims to the Barents Sea and agreed to split evenly a contested zone of 175,000 square kilometers, opening the area to development of petroleum, minerals, fish, and other resources. As to claims of Russia building military bases in the Arctic, English and Thvedt assess that of the 12 to 15 of those identified as part of the Kremlin's "militarization", at least half are Search and Rescue centers, while others are airstrips with few additional constructions. Overall, Russian capabilities, facilities, and intentions are not intimidating and indeed lag behind those of NATO. English and Thvedt conclude by cautioning against a "narrative of rivalry and conflict" and by registering the solid record of international cooperation in the Arctic region.

14
THE UNITED STATES

Kari Roberts

MOUNT ROYAL UNIVERSITY, CANADA

Introduction

Concurrent, system-altering events shook the foundations of global order in 1991: the Soviet Union collapsed and the new Russian state was born. The Cold War ended, and Russian and US leaders faced a steep learning curve with respect to the new geopolitical reality. At times, the two nations have enjoyed a convergence of interests; however, their leaders have ultimately failed to normalize Russia-US relations (Sakwa, 2008; Roberts, 2014). The result is a record of mixed accomplishment, a relationship of both convergence and divergence, leaving enduring challenges for the next generation of Russian and US leaders.

Considerable analysis, much of it within the realist school of international relations, emphasizes the geopolitical nature of Russia-US relations: Russia pursues its place among the world's powers and increasingly resists the West's agenda, notably the expansion of NATO, which should come as no surprise (Mearsheimer, 2014). NATO's expansion brings the specter of US military power to Russia's doorstep; according to this narrative, US drive to expand its influence and Russia's defensive response are the key features that animate the relationship.

Another analysis of Russia-US relations is situated along a spectrum of blame in which attribution for the challenges in Russia-US relations are assigned to one or both nations. These accounts range from identifying the influence of anti-Russian sentiment in the United States (Tsygankov, 2009; Feklyunina, 2013), rendering its leadership incapable of fostering a measured relationship with Russia, to accusations that Russian leaders – particularly Putin – have deliberately fomented a new Cold War to project Russian power (Lucas, 2008). Other accounts consider the failings in the relationship against the backdrop of Russia's "backslide" from democracy (McFaul, 1997/98). Western hopes for democracy in Russia faded under President Boris Yeltsin, and disappeared with the ascendency of Vladimir Putin to the Kremlin. But understanding Russia through the lens of Western liberalism has its challenges; countless assumptions were made about the consolidation of democracy in Russia, and what it would mean for relations with the United States. A democratic Russia would join the liberal order, align its interests with the West, and be an asset to US global leadership. But this failed to materialize; Russian interests did not always align with the priorities of the West, and in some cases US and Russian interests were directly opposed, notably the decision to expand NATO into former Soviet territory, which has been a key point of contention since 1993.

This chapter recognizes the above contributions to the study of Russia-US relations, but aligns with the scholarship that privileges the interplay between structure and agency in the making of Russian foreign policy (Malcolm et al., 1996; Wallander, 1996; McFaul, 1997/98; Robinson, 2000; Donaldson and Nogee, 2009; Roberts, 2017). The structure in which decisions are made, and the agency of individuals within them, are essential to understanding foreign policy decisions. In short, ideas, individuals, and institutions matter. This is true for all foreign policy analysis, but is especially useful in understanding Russian foreign policy making, which features a constitutionally prescribed executive dominance (*Constitution of the Russian Federation*, 1993: Articles 80, 86). Russian "super presidential" powers dwarf the institutional presence of other foreign policy actors (Roberts, 2014). The foreign policy role of the President is important; he identifies Russian interests and enjoys the executive authority to pursue them. The concentration of decision power in the President's office, coupled with a culture of the popularity of strong leaders, enables the occupant to dominate Russian law and politics completely (Roberts, 2017). For this reason, it is not uncommon to see the phrases, "Putin's foreign policy" and "Russia's foreign policy" used interchangeably (Roberts, 2017). The execution of presidential authority has had an important impact upon relations with the West and therefore the post-Soviet presidencies of Yeltsin, Putin, and Dmitry Medvedev, are useful lenses through which to consider the stages of Russia-US relations since the end of the Cold War:

> Powerful personalities – Yeltsin and Putin and perhaps to a lesser extent Medvedev – have exercised a tremendous amount of personal discretion and influence when it comes to relations with Washington. Strong executive-centered institutions combined with weaker legislative ones accentuate the importance of the President, thereby revealing the magnitude of both structure and agency in Russian foreign policy making. Given the fluctuation in the tone and priorities of foreign policy toward the US under all three post-Soviet Presidents, it is fair to say that structure enables agency in important ways.
>
> (Roberts, 2013)

Appreciating the dominant role of Russian Presidents in foreign policy making, this chapter highlights the main achievements and challenges in Russia-US relations in four distinct presidential phases: the Yeltsin presidency (1991–1999), the first Putin presidency (2000–2008), the Medvedev presidency (2008–2012), and, finally, Putin's second presidency (2012–present). But before these phases can be considered, it is first important to explain the primacy of the West – notably the United States – in Russia's foreign policy calculus.

Why the United States matters

When the Cold War ended, Western governments were optimistic about democratic consolidation in Russia, and Russian leaders expected the West's help to cultivate the economic and political transition. Beyond this there was also the security relationship to think about. Many years and billions of dollars had been devoted to maintaining the geopolitical balance of power. Despite high expectations for Russia's political transformation, there was little consensus among Russian leaders about what its foreign policy stance would be. Residual competition from the Cold War, mounting resistance in Russia to the US assertion that they had "won" the Cold War, and fear that the loss of great power status might not be perceived as temporary, all influenced a crisis of identity in Russian foreign policy making that tested relations with the United States (Chafetz, 1996/97; Tolz, 1998). The result was an internal debate about with whom Russia's interests most naturally aligned. The relationship with the United States influenced Russian thinking about its place in the world, and also within the post-Soviet space.

Unfulfilled expectations of Western support for Russia's democratic transition coincided with a "paternalistic" tone from a US leadership that expected Moscow to adopt policies favorable to Washington, which would naturally be in Russia's own interest. Domestic political instability, coupled with the absence of clarity around Russia's role in the world, left Russian foreign policy adrift. The perception of Russian weakness, at home and abroad, fueled concerns among Russian leaders about its global power status. Therefore, a desire to "reverse the decline of Russia's international prestige," and to counter the narrative that Russia had lost the Cold War, began to animate foreign policy making (Roberts, 2010). Both Putin and Medvedev feared the emergence of US hegemony at the expense of Russia and identified this as a challenge to Russian interests (Monaghan, 2008; Roberts, 2010). The Cold War may be in the history books, but there is plenty of residual "baggage" that has influenced Russia-US relations, and which prompts Russian leaders to resist the narrative of Russia's diminished power status. This baggage has influenced each presidential era and persistently animates the relationship. The following sections highlight the key issues of record in the Russia-US relationship, some of which span the entire post-Cold War period. Perhaps given the legacy of the Cold War, it follows that security matters dominate the relationship.

The Yeltsin era (1991–1999): birth of a 'new' relationship?

Relations with the United States heavily influenced the internal policy debates during Yeltsin's first presidential term. Presidents Yeltsin and Clinton made efforts to sustain an open and cooperative dialogue between the two nations, but each faced domestic political opposition to this initiative. The shifting power balance between opinion groups in Russia (Bowker, 1997) enabled the presence of disparate foreign policy orientations, ranging from friendly alliance with the West, to overt isolationism, to expansionism with an eye to retaking Russia's rightful geopolitical space. These internal foreign policy debates are well documented (Tsygankov, 1997; Prizel, 1998; McFaul, 1999) and, coupled with the domestic challenges to Yeltsin's authority, as well as conflicting elite conceptions of the national interest, created enough political instability to impair a clear articulation of Russia's position on a host of key issues.

Shuffling off the Cold War mindset has been difficult for Russian leaders, especially given the perception that US power has confronted them at every turn. Despite the vigorous foreign policy debates among Russian elites, one thing they agreed upon was Russia's entitlement to primacy in the former Soviet space (Lynch, 2016). Perhaps it is little surprise that arms control and the new role for NATO have been identified by scholars as the two issues most symbolic of the new world order (Donaldson and Nogee, 2009), and the most conflictual.

NATO expansion

President Clinton drove the expansion of NATO following a 1993 meeting with Czech President Vaclav Havel and Polish President Lech Walesa. Russian leaders rejected the premise of NATO expansion and instead called for a European security framework with Russia's active participation. However, despite a US desire to support Russia's political transition, there was also a perceived need to "hedge their bets" against a resurgent Russia (Goldgeier, 1999: 94). Fears that Russia's past could destabilize its future were captured by US Secretary of State Madelaine Albright who described Russian Prime Minister Yevgeny Primakov as "he is what he was," implying that the Soviet legacy had a formative influence over its present leadership

(Perlez, 1999). Despite Clinton's assurances that NATO expansion would contain the "three no's" – no surprises, no rush, and no Russian exclusion (Talbott, 2002: 425) – enlargement moved ahead. Furthermore, the further Russia seemed to drift from democratic consolidation, the more intent upon membership some European nations became. Despite registering their opposition to NATO expansion, Russian leaders had little choice but to acquiesce and sought alternate ways of influencing the European security dialogue on US terms. Notwithstanding Russia's entreaties, NATO welcomed Poland, Hungary, and the Czech Republic in 1999 and Estonia, Latvia, and Lithuania in 2004. Membership in NATO's Partnership for Peace (PfP) initiative,[1] as well as the proposal to create a NATO-Russia Charter[2] were extended to Russia; however, these proposals were criticized as tokenism – a way to co-opt Russia, without extending it the meaningful partnership and recognition it sought as an essential pillar of the European security arrangement.

For Russian leaders, the expansion of NATO coincided with the loss of empire, domestic political instability, and a shifting geopolitical climate in which Russia's status was diminished. Russia remained a key nuclear power, but by any other metric its status as a major global power was in freefall. Russia was essentially denied reasonable opposition to NATO expansion on the grounds that, as an aspiring democracy, it had nothing to fear from a non-hostile alliance that could shoulder the burden of European security in an uncertain time. Russia was denied its rightful position of influence within the former Soviet space, or what some Russian leaders termed, "the Near Abroad," a designation that was understandably disconcerting to Russia's sovereign neighbors, as well as its right to consider the presence of US military power near its borders as a threat to its security interests. NATO's growth in post-Cold War Europe served as a symbol of Western accomplishment and Russian defeat.

There is some disagreement about whether early promises of non-expansion were ever made to Russia; nonetheless, Russia has consistently critiqued expansion as evidence that "the West is an unreliable partner" (Itzkowitx Shifrinson, 2016: 9) and that it failed to acknowledge "Russia's regional primacy" (Lynch, 2016). Furthermore, NATO's reimagined mandate, operationalized in its interventions in the Balkans, also represented a denial of the legitimacy of Russian interests in the former Soviet space. Interventions in Bosnia (1995) and Kosovo (1999) were met with Russian opposition, further testing the Russia-US relationship.

Kosovo

Conflict in the Balkans showcased the tensions in Russia-US relations. Russian leaders balked at NATO's involvement in Bosnia, and reluctantly partnered with NATO during its UN-sanctioned operation in Bosnia in 1995. Yeltsin, in support of Russia's Orthodox Serbian allies, feared a NATO intervention would escalate the conflict, but he directed Russian forces to participate in the NATO-led peacekeeping operation. However, this decision coincided with domestic instability in Russia which compromised Yeltsin's political leverage and rendered him virtually powerless to meaningfully oppose NATO actions there. Circumstances were different in 1999 when Russia vocally opposed NATO efforts to intervene in Kosovo without a UN mandate and obstructed UN decision making on Kosovo, taking umbrage with NATO's actions outside its traditional area of operation, within a region considered to be in Russia's orbit (Stent, 2014: 160).

Russia viewed NATO's drafting of the Rambouillet peace deal as a provocation – an excuse to bomb Serbia upon Belgrade's "bad faith" rejection of the deal. In fact, tensions were so high that Russian Prime Minister Yevgeny Primakov, en route to Washington, ordered his plane to be returned to Moscow in protest; soon afterward NATO air strikes in Kosovo began.

Yeltsin warned Clinton of potential Russian military involvement with the caution, "don't push Russia into this war!" (Talbott, 2003: 428). At the end of the war, Russia and NATO agreed to contribute peacekeeping troops to stabilize Kosovo, although there was some disagreement about just where and how Russian troops would be involved; this disagreement saw Russian troops ordered to the Pristina airport to ensure that Russia not be excluded from the post-war arrangement. The significance of this incident cannot be understated; while no direct conflict between Russian and NATO troops ensued, the incident revealed just how high tensions had become between the two sides. Kosovo was an important symbol of the deteriorating relationship. Russia was compelled to assert its entitlement to interests befitting a major power, and through this effort showed that Kosovo – still considered by Russia to be part of Serbia – fell within Russia's sphere of interest.

Arms control and missile defence

Arms control issues have understandably been a high priority for Russia and the United States. Highlights of these efforts were the containment of "loose nukes" through the Cooperative Threat Reduction Act,[3] the US abrogation of the Anti-Ballistic Missile (ABM) Treaty in 2002, the ratification of START II, and the signing of the 2010 New START Treaty. But the record of accomplishment on this file is mixed. Given the perceived decline of Russian power and prestige, it is perhaps understandable that arms control has been a Russian priority, in part because its nuclear arsenal has guaranteed it an enduring seat at the table during a time in which its voice has otherwise been muted.

Presidents Yeltsin and George HW Bush signed the START II Treaty in January 1993, promising a reduction in nuclear arsenals by about two-thirds, as well as the elimination of large multiple warhead missiles deemed less necessary in the new political climate; however, the deal met with resistance in a Russian Duma populated by communists and nationalists who resisted Russian acquiescence to the West. It was not ratified until 2000, and in fact it was used by Russian leaders, unsuccessfully, as a bargaining chip in the campaign to obstruct NATO expansion and also to prevent the United States from embarking upon a ballistic missile defence (BMD) program following their withdrawal from the 1972 ABM Treaty.

The ABM Treaty formed the backbone of strategic stability between the two countries in the 1970s and 1980s. The Treaty constrained the development of anti-missile technology, but the US leadership grew increasingly concerned about the proliferation of weapons of mass destruction (WMD) to rogue states and non-state actors, and this, combined with uncertainty about Russia, seemed to be enough to reanimate a discussion about the viability of a missile shield for the United States. In the wake of the 9/11 terrorist attacks, President George W Bush notified Russia of his intent to withdraw the United States from the ABM Treaty, enabling the pursuit of missile defence technology. Russia has categorized the potential placement of US missiles and defence systems in close proximity to Russia, as a security threat. As NATO continued its expansion closer to Russian territory, the proximity of missile defences has continued to be prioritized by President Putin.

Gore-Chernomyrdin Commission

The 1993 US-Russia Joint Commission on Economic and Technical Cooperation, known informally as the Gore-Chernomyrdin Commission, was tasked with managing some of the most difficult issues facing the two countries. The Commission contained a strategic stability group comprised of US Deputy Secretary of State Strobe Talbot and Russian Deputy Minister Yuri Mamedov. US Vice President Al Gore and Russian Prime Minister Victor Chernomyrdin sought to "institutionalize the concept of partnership," by convening a high-level mechanism of communication (Stent, 2014), as well as working groups in key areas such as energy, joint space exploration, and the environment. Yeltsin's leadership was increasingly confronted by domestic opposition; Clinton's decision to support Yeltsin politically (Talbott, 2003) required keeping the lines of communication open. The bi-national Commission was re-invigorated under Presidents Obama and Medvedev during the reset, in the form of the Russia-US Bilateral Presidential Commission.

Assessing the Yeltsin era

Ultimately, the Yeltsin era is best described as one of tentative, restrained cooperation between Russia and the United States. For Russia, its failure to consolidate democracy was influential in foreign policy making, especially with respect to relations with Washington (Lynch, 2016). The struggle to institutionalize the democratic process and the rule of law, in concert with the absence of effective leadership in these areas, left a vacuum in which an identity crisis, of sorts, flourished, and in which competing visions for Russian foreign policy clashed, culminating in a foreign policy based less upon ideology and more upon a pragmatic assertion of Russian national interests. For the Americans who wanted to support Russia's political transition, there was skepticism about whether democracy could truly take root there, which enabled an already latent fear of Russia to perpetuate. Some observers have suggested that mistrust of Russia manifested itself in a form of *Russophobia* (Tsygankov, 2009; Feklyunina, 2013), which is visible in some of the foreign policy decisions taken by the Clinton Administration, notably the expansion of NATO, the consideration of various missile defence platforms, and the denial of a role for Russia in the Balkan conflicts. The Cold War legacy loomed large and rendered interactions motivated less by common values and more by power calculations (Lynch, 2016).

The first Putin presidency (2000–2008): from partnership to break-up

When Vladimir Putin took office in 2000, he was not a new figure in Russian politics. His tenure as Prime Minister enabled his role as the chief architect of Russian opposition to NATO's occupation of Kosovo (Lynch, 2016). Putin viewed Russia's interests pragmatically, asserted them stridently, and rejected Western criticism of Russia's domestic affairs (Roberts, 2014). His consolidation of the vertical power structure enabled an emboldened assertion of his priority to restore Russia's rightful status among the world's powers. Credited at home with decisive action in Chechnya and able stewardship of the Russian economy, Putin could assert Russian interests more vigorously on the world stage. In the early 2000s, this took the form of seeking a strategic partnership with the United States, which enabled cooperation on terrorism and the advancement of an arms control agenda that was beneficial to both countries. However, despite an encouraging first meeting in which President Bush claimed to have looked into Putin's eyes and "saw his soul," relations between the two deteriorated in short order. An era that began with Putin's historic phone call to President Bush after 9/11, ended with heightened tensions and a need to reset the relationship.

9/11 and the counterterrorism agenda

The 9/11 attack on the US homeland, and Russia's brutal war in separatist Chechnya, led both nations to perceive a convergence of interests in the fight against terrorism. In fact, the early goodwill was so strong that Russia was asked to consider a possible military intervention in

Afghanistan, which they declined (Mankoff, 2009); however, this enabled intelligence cooperation, the opening up of Russian airspace, and Russia's diplomatic assistance in Central Asia to enable Afghanistan operations. Russia also assisted with search and rescue operations and arming anti-Taliban fighters in Afghanistan (Tsygankov, 2013). Given its ties with Uzbekistan and Kyrgyzstan, Russia could be an important conduit, which had the added benefit of giving Russia influence in US military operations there (Mankoff, 2009). Russia temporarily enjoyed a degree of influence befitting a great power, consistent with its psychology of *derzhava*, implying the inevitability of Russia's return to greatness and its challenge to presumptive US hegemony.

This military and civilian intelligence sharing enabled cooperation on other priorities such as dealing with WMD proliferation and the Iranian and North Korean nuclear programs. However, as Mankoff (2009) aptly observes, this cooperation was indicative only of overlapping interests, and not of a more profound commitment to meaningful civilizational or strategic convergence (2009: 115). Instead, 9/11 and its aftermath represented for Putin "an opportunity to achieve several long-standing aims of Russian foreign policy," but it was not an unconditional commitment to partnership (Mankoff, 2009: 115). Issue convergence enabled a short-lived cooperative phase in Russia-US relations but the common ground on counterterrorism did enable US goals of painless ABM withdrawal and the inclusion of the Baltic States in NATO; however, these resurfaced as items of contention when the rapprochement began to dissolve.

Arms control

The arms control agenda, embodied by the START agreements, underwent a transformation during Putin's first term. The Bush administration sought to retain a robust US nuclear arsenal capable of guarding against a nuclear threat from rogue nations (Stent, 2014). US withdrawal from the ABM Treaty enabled its plan for missile defence deployment, ostensibly aimed at rogue nations and not at Russia; however, despite repeated assurances, Moscow was unconvinced. Nonetheless, Putin did not mount serious resistance to the ABM withdrawal, probably because any protestations would have fallen on deaf ears anyway, which might have accentuated the limits of Russian influence. Instead, it appears a calculation was made that Russia might be able to pursue other priorities (such as keeping BMDs out of Europe, and slowing NATO's growth) in exchange for its muted response. Still, Russia did express concerns about missile defence, and Putin requested a new arms reduction agreement, which Bush was willing to consider, likely as a form of appeasement (Stent, 2014).

In 2002 Putin and Bush signed the Strategic Offensive Reductions Treaty (SORT), a minimalist treaty which, while committing both sides to overall reductions, did not oblige the destruction of stockpiles, nor impose a rigid system of compliance verification (Stent, 2014), and was silent on missile defence. This was a partial victory for Putin as it symbolized Russia's stature as an equal partner in weapons reductions and nonproliferation. SORT also brought Russia closer to parity with the United States at a time when budgetary constraints rendered the building of new offensive weapons impossible (Mankoff, 2009). Ultimately, despite some gains, the arms control agenda was derailed by Bush's insistence upon missile defence deployment in Europe, which intensified Putin's related concerns about NATO expansion, both of which brought the specter of US military power closer to Russia's doorstep.

NATO expansion, missile deployment, and the color revolutions

The accession of the Baltic States to NATO prompted Putin to express his expectation that NATO's expansion was now complete. Of special concern was the potential membership of

Georgia and Ukraine, viewed by Russia as historical allies, and well within the sphere of interest to which it was entitled. Political demonstrations in Georgia (2003) and Ukraine (2004), known as the color revolutions, and motivated in some measure by anti-Russian sentiment and a pivot toward the West, were met with US sympathy. Both revolutions saw the replacement of Russia-friendly leaders with pro-Western ones anxious to make overtures to a cautiously supportive West. US support for the color revolutions, as well as Russia's response to them, notably its 2008 military intervention in Georgia, precipitated a serious deterioration in the relationship, which did not rebound until 2009. Russia's actions in Georgia, in response to concerns of a NATO presence there, as well as a Georgian attack on South Ossetia,[4] prompted the White House to cut working level relations between the two nations, withdraw the agreement on peaceful nuclear energy cooperation from the Senate's consideration, and suspend the NATO-Russia Council (Charap, 2010: 281; Roberts, 2014).

This rift was further exacerbated by US outrage over Putin's domestic crackdown on political dissent, symbolized by the high profile deaths of Russian journalists critical of the Kremlin, and the prosecution of Russian billionaire Mikhail Khodorkovsky, as well as the gas supply and pricing standoff with Ukraine which had consequences for some European countries (Roberts, 2014). Emboldened by high oil and gas revenues, Russia's willingness to assert forcefully its security interests in the region effectively ended any serious talk of Georgian membership in NATO and muted the advocacy of an expanded NATO closer to Russian territory.

The perception in Russia was that NATO enlargement brought formerly Soviet countries into the West's orbit, sought to deny Russia its sphere of influence, and made possible the deployment of missile defence systems closer to Russia (Bush officials had discussed placing missile radar systems and interceptors in the Czech Republic and Poland). This served as a reminder to Russians that, not only had they lost the Cold War, but their influence did not hold the currency it once had. Its protests over enlargement seemed to have little impact, although they did drive NATO leaders to strike the NATO-Russia Charter, the effectiveness of which has been subject to the fluctuating tone of the relationship. Moreover, NATO's involvement in the Balkans, notably in Kosovo, operationalized a new European security arrangement that excluded Russia. Kosovo confirmed Russia's worst fears about NATO expansion: despite assurances to the contrary, NATO was prepared to take offensive action to defend against a perceived direct threat to a member state, even if against Russia's wishes, and they would be prepared to do so without a UN Security Council mandate (Lynch, 2016: 108).

Putin aired his grievances at the 2008 NATO Summit in Bucharest, calling upon NATO leaders to show restraint, to avoid pursuing their security at Russia's expense, and warning of possible retaliatory measures should expansion continue. Nonetheless, it was in Bucharest that Croatia and Albania were invited to join NATO, and talk of Georgian and Ukrainian membership was introduced. For Russia this symbolized the perceived decline of Russian power and the denial of its rightful interests.

The Munich speech

The frosty turn in Russia-US relations is best visible in Putin's speech to the 2007 Munich Security Conference in which he accused the United States of unilateral abuses of power, fomenting global instability, and selectively applying international law (Putin, 2007). Putin warned that US interventions, ostensibly to protect human rights, make things worse, as witnessed in Iraq, Afghanistan, Libya, Yemen, and Egypt (Kaylan, 2014: 15). The speech was a watershed moment in which Putin integrated Russia's long-standing concerns into "a structured broadside at a prestigious international gathering" (Stent, 2014: 149). For some, Putin's speech was an apt response to an earlier address by US Vice President Dick Cheney in Vilnius, in which he vowed to defend "the frontlines of freedom in the modern world," referenced the unfinished business of the color revolutions, and lectured about democracy, the rule of law, and free markets (Cheney, 2006). This was viewed as a rhetorical "shot across the bow" given his referencing of reform in Ukraine and Belarus, and his calling out of Russia's illiberal government. When the Munich speech followed, not quite a year later, it was met with musings about a "new Cold War" (Roberts, 2017). Putin doubled down with his own comparison of US presumption of hegemony to Hitler's Third Reich. The relationship had descended to an unprecedentedly low level. When Putin and Bush left office, relations were broken, and their predecessors perceived the need for a reset.

The Medvedev presidency (2008–2012): the reset

Presidents Obama and Medvedev seemed committed to a period of renewal in which the two nations could collaborate on missile defence, arms control, and re-establishing the United States and Russia Bilateral Presidential Commission. When Secretary of State Hillary Clinton presented her Russian counterpart, Sergei Lavrov, with a reset button in 2009, hopes were high for what the reset could accomplish. By many accounts, the reset enjoyed some successes. It is difficult to know for certain the nature of Medvedev's commitment to the reset due to the complexities of the tandem presidency; however, it appeared as though he was committed to pursuing the relationship. His public praise for neo-conservative icons Ronald Reagan and Margaret Thatcher fostered optimism in the West that he may be someone with whom they could cooperate.

For Russia, the reset enabled better engagement with NATO, movement on a New Strategic Arms Reduction Treaty (New START), and a return to membership talks with the World Trade Organization (WTO). From Russia it required supporting sanctions against Iran and greater cooperation generally in the UN Security Council, as well as cooperating with allies in Central Asia to facilitate NATO operations in Afghanistan. It also meant revival of the agreement on peaceful nuclear energy cooperation, which had been suspended in 2008, but which Obama successfully submitted to the US Senate for ratification in 2010. The warming of the relationship also awarded Russia the respect to which it felt entitled: President Obama acknowledged Russia as a key player on the world stage, without whose cooperation the United States' most significant national security interests and priorities would be less easily achieved (The White House, Office of the Press Secretary, 2010). Both countries benefitted from this renewed cooperation; the chief accomplishments of the reset are discussed below.

Bilateral Presidential Commission

The re-establishment of working level ties between the two governments symbolized its positive momentum. The United States and Russia Bilateral Presidential Commission was "dedicated to identifying areas of cooperation and pursuing joint projects and actions that strengthen strategic stability, international security, economic well-being, and the development of ties between Russian and American people" (United States and Russia Bilateral Presidential Commission, 2009). The Commission, co-chaired by the Presidents themselves, included key ties between Secretary Clinton and Minister Lavrov, as well as lower tier working groups in 15 policy areas: Policy Steering Group; Nuclear Energy and Nuclear Security; Arms Control and International Security; Terrorism; Drug Trafficking; Business Development and Economic Relations; Energy; Environment; Agriculture, Science and Technology; Space Cooperation; Health; Cooperation in Prevention and Handling of Emergency Situations; Civil Society; Educational,

Sport and Cultural Exchanges; and Military Cooperation (United States and Russia Bilateral Presidential Commission, 2009; Roberts, 2014). Just a few short years later, Obama suspended the Commission's work following Russia's 2014 actions in Crimea, diverting US funds for Commission operations to an aid package for Ukraine.

Arms control

START II, signed in 1993, was ratified by both countries, but was terminated when Putin announced Russia's withdrawal in 2002, in response to the US abrogation of the ABM Treaty. The Obama administration seemed to feel that reinvigorating the arms control agenda could reinforce the positive momentum of the reset, especially given that the 2002 SORT treaty was about to expire. New START sought to reduce deployed strategic nuclear weapons by half, and to establish new verification protocols (Roberts, 2014). Both sides agreed to strategic offensive weapons reductions and quickly ratified the treaty in 2010. Critics of new START felt it did not go far enough to restrict Russian development of new weapons technologies. On the Russian side, there was concern that New START was silent on missile defence, which was a key priority for Moscow. However, the agreement did reinvigorate the stalled arms control dialogue, which was integral to the credibility of each country's contributions to the non-proliferation regime (Roberts, 2014).

NATO expansion and missile defence

NATO welcomed Albania and Croatia during Medvedev's tenure, and recognized the membership aspirations of Georgia, Ukraine, Bosnia-Herzegovina, Macedonia, and Montenegro. NATO's Membership Action Plan for Georgia and Ukraine came on the heels of Georgia's 2008 military conflict with Russia, and was enacted in parallel with US efforts to suspend the NATO-Russia Council. These efforts were US driven and were understandably met with concern by the Russian leadership. In fact, the day after President Obama's election, and well before the reset, Medvedev gave a speech denouncing Georgia, condemning the presence of NATO warships in the Black Sea, and threatening to respond to US missile defence deployment plans in Europe with his own deployment of Iskandar missiles in Kaliningrad, perilously close to NATO territory (Stent, 2014).

Concerns about NATO's enlargement and the potential deployment of missile defences near Russia's borders were raised during the New START negotiations, but Obama gave assurances that the United States would reconsider the Bush-era plans for missile defence. To the disappointment of some European allies, he announced plans to abandon the placement of missile interceptors in Poland and the Czech Republic (Stent, 2014). Continental missile defence was not abandoned, but the United States sought to negotiate its plans, in cooperation with Russia, through the NATO-Russia Council (Stent, 2014). This prompted Medvedev to attend the Lisbon summit and though this momentum was positive, Russian leaders (notably Prime Minister Putin) remained suspicious about the real motivations behind missile defence deployment in Europe. Even Medvedev, upon receiving assurances from the United States that its missile defence systems would not target Russia, still threatened Russian withdrawal from New START and the possible counter-deployment of Russian missiles in Kaliningrad (Stent, 2014). The reset enabled a dialog between the two countries, but it was not enough to resolve the issues dividing them.

Assessing the reset

Resetting Russia-US relations was never as easy as the term implied (English, 2009); however, there did seem to be a desire to elevate shared interests above disagreements. For the

United States, benefits of the reset included Russian logistical support to NATO's International Security Assistance Force (ISAF) in Afghanistan, which involved enabling a supply line from Latvia through Russia, Kazakhstan, and Uzbekistan as an alternative to a route through Pakistan (Charap, 2010: 283; Roberts, 2014). As Charap (2010) notes, Moscow also agreed to support a proposal to enrich Iranian uranium, and even agreed to stronger sanctions against North Korea, and a new protocol on the disposal of weapons-grade plutonium (Charap, 2010: 283; Roberts, 2014). For Russia, the reset generated the investor confidence necessary to support the Russian purchase of 65 Boeing planes as well as a major investment commitment from Pepsi (Charap, 2010: 283; Roberts, 2014). The hope in Washington was that both members of the tandem presidency were on board with the reset and therefore the United States could expect policy continuity after Putin's 2012 re-election (Stent, 2014: 251). But this did not happen. Ultimately, the reset is probably best understood as a relic of the Medvedev presidency, quickly reversed upon Putin's return to the Kremlin.

The second Putin presidency (2012-present): the end of the reset

Russia's 2014 annexation of Crimea, just days after the Sochi Winter Olympics, was a transformational moment in Russia-US relations. The move prompted speculation about Putin's revanchist plans for the geopolitical order. Hillary Clinton likened Putin to Hitler in the 1930s (Rucker, 2014). While Crimea was undoubtedly a seminal moment, there were earlier signs of strain in the relationship, notably the revelation of a Russian spy ring in the United States and the WikiLeaks security breach, which involved the release of classified communications from the US Embassy in Russia which were of an incendiary nature. Additionally, the Justice for Sergei Magnitsky Act was gathering momentum in Congress. Passed in 2012, the Act instituted a travel visa ban for, and froze the assets of, Russian officials believed to be responsible for the unjust and inhumane treatment of Sergei Magnitsky, a Russian banker who had accused key Russian officials of tax fraud. He had been held in Russia, uncharged, for over a year, and subjected to inhumane incarceration, where he later died. For the Americans, the Magnitsky List was a form of protest of Russia's illiberal and authoritarian regime. Russia responded in kind, issuing a similar ban on high-level US bureaucrats. Putin lamented that the relationship had been "poisoned" (Stent, 2014).

The 2012 re-election of Putin marked a deeper divergence in Russia-US relations. Pro-democracy protests in Russia over allegations of voter fraud were said to be encouraged by Washington, and Putin swiftly reinvigorated his long-standing criticisms about NATO expansion, abuses of US power and the dangers of US unilateralism. In fact, Russia's 2014 military doctrine listed NATO as a direct threat to Russia, and asserted Russia's preparedness to defend its sphere of interest by any means necessary. This was a deliberate response to NATO's condemnation of Russian military aggression in Ukraine. Moreover, Putin's decision to grant asylum to NSA whistleblower Edward Snowden, who turned over classified documentation about US government surveillance programs to journalists in 2013, and is wanted in the United States for treason, reflected the growing wedge in the relationship. In his 2015 address to the UN General Assembly, Putin blamed the expansion of NATO for fomenting unrest in Ukraine (Putin, 2015). NATO enlargement had perpetuated the idea that Europe was divided, and it asked nations to choose between east and west, which has done little but destabilize the continent.

Since the beginning of Putin's third term, there have been no accomplishments of record in Russia-US relations. The relationship remains animated by concerns about the further expansion of NATO and its deployment of missile defences, but this climate of discord has given rise to other issues that have come to dominate the agenda and which have possibly set back the relationship irreparably: Russia's 2014 actions in Crimea and the ongoing civil war in Syria.

Crimea 2014–2015

US praise for Ukraine's 2004 Orange Revolution was a sore point for Putin, as were the overtures made to Ukraine in response to the 2013 Euromaidan movement which sought closer ties between Ukraine and Europe. Pressure from Russia caused Ukrainian president Victor Yanukovich to announce his withdrawal from a trade deal with the EU, which caused widespread pro-EU protests in western Ukraine in fall 2013. Protests continued throughout the Sochi Olympics, and within days of their conclusion, pro-Russian forces seized government buildings in Crimea, and Putin deployed Russian troops, ostensibly to stabilize the region. Russia's military presence quickly led to annexation, with Putin issuing a presidential decree recognizing Crimea to be sovereign and independent. A questionable referendum shortly followed, which saw Crimea residents vote to unify with Russia. This was met with stern reprisal from the West, which accused Russia of violating the sovereignty of Ukraine and of instigating unrest in Crimea; sanctions and travel restrictions were imposed upon key Putin officials (Roberts, 2017).

Putin claimed that Russian support to the legally elected sovereign government of Ukraine was within the bounds of international law and that Russia had an ethical and legal obligation to protect and defend the interests of Russians in Ukraine who were at risk of being persecuted by the Western leaning, nationalist impulses threatening to destabilize the country. The Russian Constitution of 1993 confers upon the President a responsibility to protect Russian speakers abroad, and Putin argued that he had a responsibility to prevent a looming humanitarian crisis in Eastern Ukraine, given the escalation of hostilities there. Putin reminded the West of its own humanitarian rationale for the illegal Kosovo intervention in 1999, absent a UN Security Council mandate. Moreover, Putin argued that:

> Russia's Black Sea Fleet was vulnerable to this regional instability, which constituted a strategic threat to Russian security and therefore Russia had the legal right to defend itself under Article 51 of the UN Charter. The US had made a similar case for its preemptive war of self defence against Iraq in 2003.
>
> *(Roberts, 2017)*

Putin seemed to be deliberately employing US rhetoric in making his case: human rights and national security were reasonable justifications for the use of force. But Western leaders did not see it this way.

The absence of President Obama and Secretary of State John Kerry at the 2015 70th Anniversary Victory Day military parade in Moscow's Red Square symbolizes the hostility that now permeates the relationship. Failure to commemorate Russia's sacrifice in liberating Europe from Nazi Germany was interpreted by some as a denial of Russia's sacrifice and its rightful place in the global power structure (Roberts, 2017). At present it seems as though Russia and the United States are locked in a "war of values" (Lynch, 2016: 101). Putin defends Russia's right to protect its borderlands, and accuses the West of denying Russia its rightful place as a regional power, and the defence of its diaspora. On a global scale, the events in Crimea reflect Russia's rejection of the supremacy of Western values and its interpretation of international law, proffering a Russian alternative for those who do not subscribe to Western hegemony. While Putin seemed to share with Yeltsin a desire to "square Russia's interests in profitable and harmonious relations with the Western world with its intense desire to be recognized as a great power" (Lynch, 2016: 108), the former could be sacrificed in favor of the latter. The priority continues to be that "Russia be granted the status of dominant power along its historical borderlands" (Lynch, 2016: 108). Russia's desire to be a respected regional and global power informs its actions both in its borderlands, and also in Syria, where it retains a powerful foothold due to its support for the Syrian regime. In these areas, key Russian and US interests are in conflict, and resolution does not appear to be on the horizon.

Syria 2011–2016

The continuing Syrian crisis illustrates the meaningful divergence of interests in Russia-US relations. Nonetheless, both seem to recognize the dangers of allowing Syria to bring them closer to the brink of conflict, and both have navigated the crisis carefully. Russia's backing of Bashar-al-Assad, its financial and military support of his regime, and its willful obstruction of a UN Security Council mandate to intervene in the civil war, have impeded the US objective of removing Assad from power. Western efforts to force him out, to support anti-Assad rebels in Syria, and to combat the Islamic State (IS) in a now destabilized Syria, have been impeded by Russian support for the regime and an unwillingness to risk further destabilization of Syria should Assad be forcibly removed. Putin was reluctant to support a UN Security Council mandate in Syria, given the manner in which he claims NATO used its mandate to patrol Libya's no-fly zone as an excuse to hunt Gaddafi. Putin was critical of US efforts to overstep the bounds of international law in a region whose instability was the consequence of US interference. In his 2015 UN address, Putin criticized those who presume to possess an "exceptional" entitlement to ignore international law and illegally circumvent the authority of the UN. He blamed the United States for meddling in the Middle East under the guise of democracy building when it is clear that the concern for human rights was a smokescreen for the pursuit of other interests (Putin, 2015). He connected the 2003 invasion of Iraq with the founding and growth of IS, and warned of the perils of working against Assad to combat terrorism (Putin, 2015).

A critical moment in the Syrian crisis occurred following Assad's use of chemical weapons in Damascus in 2013; Obama issued a weak ultimatum about the consequences of using chemical weapons. Putin stepped in with an offer to broker a deal to commit Assad to destroying his stockpile. This met with suspicion in Washington given that Russia was a key supplier of weapons to Syria in the first place. Putin's involvement inserted Russia into the resolution of the crisis and legitimized a regime that Western leaders sought to replace.

Prolonged civil war enabled IS to gain a foothold in a destabilized Syria, claiming a temporary caliphate in Aleppo in 2014 (though later reclaimed by government forces in December 2016). The intensified conflict between Assad and IS has further complicated the roles of Russia and the United States. With Russia supporting Assad, and both the United States and Assad fighting IS, cooperation between Washington and Moscow became necessary. When Russia announced a military operation to fight IS alongside Syria, matters were further complicated by the simultaneous presence of Russian and NATO troops in close proximity. In fact, concerns about battlefield contact were realized in March 2017 when Russian airstrikes accidentally bombed Syrian fighters being trained by the United States. Tensions continue as NATO allies and Russia define the conflict somewhat differently; they do not always perceive the same enemy, they disagree on tactics and also on precisely what the end goal should be. Despite a temporary ceasefire late in 2016, brokered by Russia and Turkey to enable the evacuation of civilians, the Syrian civil war remains a source of tension in Russia-US relations.

The 2016 US presidential election

The 2016 US presidential election campaign exacerbated the deteriorating relationship. In his bid for the White House, Donald Trump brought Russia to prominence as an election issue. His praise for Putin met with extreme criticism from Hillary Clinton, who repudiated Putin sharply for his illiberal leadership of Russia and his dangerous support for Assad; she also alleged that Russian hackers had been responsible for a security breach at the Democratic National Committee, which saw the release of numerous private emails embarrassing to the party's leadership. Clinton accused Russia of trying to orchestrate a Trump victory. Never has Russia figured so prominently in a US election; as a result, by November 2016, relations between Russia and the United States were arguably at their lowest point in the post-Cold War period. The 2017 inauguration of Donald Trump ushered in a promise to repair relations, and possibly lift sanctions against Russia. But despite these assurances, serious concerns persist about personal and/or business connections between White House officials (and Trump himself) and the Kremlin. In fact, a number of key White House officials came under fire after it was revealed that they had undisclosed conversations with Russian intelligence officials during the election campaign, and prior to Trump's inauguration. Just how deep these Russian connections go is as yet unknown; however, it is worth noting Trump's sharp reversal of President Obama's stance toward Russia. He avoided calling for an investigation into allegations of Russian interference in the 2016 presidential election, leading Congress to undertake this role. Trump has also talked of lifting sanctions on Russia, has celebrated better relations with Putin, has been publicly skeptical of NATO, and has blamed Russia's annexation of Crimea on Obama, forcefully warning that, if he (Trump) had been President, Putin would have stayed out of Ukraine (Bradner and Wright, 2016). As Congress investigates the depth of the Trump administration's ties to the Kremlin, Russia-US relations hang in the balance.

Russia-US relations: as good as it gets

Russian foreign policy toward the United States has been influenced by its leadership and by its diminishing global status. In response to the perception of US imperviousness to Russia's plight, evidenced by the forward march of NATO enlargement, the intent to deploy missile defences in Europe, and an overall failure to acknowledge Russia's regional power entitlements, Russia has pursued a reactionary foreign policy. Russian leaders felt as though the United States treated post-Soviet Russia like a defeated power, leaving it out of the post-Cold War European order. As Sakwa (2015) notes, Russia, treated as an enemy, eventually became one; the Crimea crisis can be viewed as the culmination of 20 years of exclusion and neglect. The animosity that now permeates Russia-US relations may well endure, in part because Russia today is better placed than it was in the 1990s to be taken seriously as a major power, and it is willing to act in support of this goal. Putin has been relatively successful at insulating Russia's borderlands from encroachment by other powers (Lynch, 2016); this is key to projecting power on the world stage. The stronger Russia perceives itself to be, the more emboldened it is to obstruct US initiatives. It is reasonable to expect an equally strident Russia in the future.

Ultimately, the record of post-Cold War Russia-US relations is mixed. A periodic convergence of interests has enabled some accomplishments (loose nukes, arms control, cooperation in counterterrorism), but long-standing irritants (NATO enlargement, missile defence, criticism of

Putin's leadership) have animated the relationship, perpetuating a discordant climate in which serious disagreements (Syria, Crimea) threaten to permanently polarize the relationship.

Perhaps Putin was right when he suggested that Russia-US relations were poisoned. Both nations have brought baggage to the relationship, some of it understandable given the relatively recent history of adversity. It does seem as though Russia's desire to be powerful, and relatedly, to offer a legitimate alternative to those who would resist US global dominance in so doing, has driven the two nations into a war of values. But, if the past 20 years offer any lessons, it is that the two countries will sometimes have to work together to accomplish their most important goals. Antagonism as an operating principle helps neither. Both must avoid lapsing into "new Cold War" rhetoric when relations are tested. The trick will be to find open channels of communication despite a meaningful divergence of values and interests. It is in both countries' interests to do so.

Notes

1 The 1994 Partnership for Peace program promoted bilateral cooperation and stable security relationships between NATO and other Euro-Atlantic area nations. The PfP was seen by potential countries desirous of NATO membership as a stepping stone to NATO entry. For NATO, the PfP was used to incentivize democratic reform, and also to build cooperation in key areas of defence planning, civil-military relations, joint military exercises, and emergency preparedness. Russia agreed to join the PfP in 1995.
2 Formally the 1997 *Founding Act of Mutual Relations, Cooperation and Security Between NATO and Russia*, the Charter sought to promote mutual trust and cooperation, and contained provisions for creating the NATO-Russia Permanent Joint Council, a mechanism for regular and emergency consultation and decision making chaired by the Secretary General of NATO. Russia established a permanent mission to NATO for consultation in security, conflict prevention, joint operations, information sharing, policy planning, arms control and proliferation issues, and terrorism. The Permanent Joint Council was suspended by NATO in 2014 after Russia annexed Crimea.
3 The 1991 US Cooperative Threat Reduction Act, also known as the Nunn-Lugar Act, provided American funding and training to assist in the retrieval, dismantling, and decommissioning of nuclear, biological and chemical weapons in the former Soviet Union.
4 South Ossetia, a breakaway republic in Georgia, is comprised of Russian speakers whose independence has long been disputed by the Georgian government. When President Mikhail Saakashvili ordered an invasion by Georgian troops in August 2008 Russia successfully intervened and officially recognized the independence of South Ossetia and Abkhazia.

References

Bowker, Mike. (1997) *Russian Foreign Policy and the End of the Cold War*. Burlington, VT: Dartmouth Publishing Company, Inc.
Bradner, Eric; Wright, David. (2016) Trump Says Putin is Not Going to Go into Ukraine, Despite Crimea. *CNN Politics*, August 1. Available at www.cnn.com/2016/07/31/politics/donald-trump-russia-ukraine-crimea-putin/.
Chafetz, Glen. (1996/97) The Struggle for a National Identity in Post-Soviet Russia. *Political Science Quarterly* 11, 4: 661–688.
Charap, Samuel. (2010) The Transformation of US-Russia Relations. *Current History* 729: 275–312.
Cheney, Dick. (2006) Vice President's Remarks at the 2006 Vilnius Conference. Office of the Vice President, May 6. Available at: https://georgewbush-whitehouse.archives.gov/news/releases/2006/05/20060504-1.html.
The Constitution of the Russian Federation. (December 12, 1993). English text available at: www.departments.bucknell.edu/russian/const/constit.html.
Donaldson, Robert H; Nogee, Joseph L. (2009) *The Foreign Policy of Russia: Changing Systems, Enduring Interests*, 4th Edition. New York: ME Sharpe.
English, Robert. (2009) A 'Reset' for Relations? Understanding Russian Grievances. *Global Dialogue* 11: 50–64.

Feklyunina, Valentina. (2013) *Constructing Russophobia, in Ray Taras, Russia's Identity in International Relations: Images, Perceptions, Misperceptions.* London: Routledge.

Goldgeier, James. (1999) *Not Whether But When: The US Decision to Enlarge NATO.* Washington, DC: Brookings Institution.

Itzkowitz Shifrinson, Joshua R., (2016) Deal or No Deal? The End of the Cold War and the U.S. Offer to Limit NATO Expansion. *International Security* 40, 4: 7–44.

Kaylan, M., (2014). Kremlin Values: Putin's Strategic Conservatism, *World Affairs* May/June, 9–17.

Lucas, Edward. (2008) *The New Cold War: Putin's Russia and the Threat to the West.* New York: Palgrave Macmillan.

Lynch, Allen. (2016) The influence of regime type on Russian foreign policy toward "the West," 1992–2015. *Communist and Post-Communist Studies.* 49: 101–111.

Malcolm, Neil; Pravda, Alex; Allison, Roy; Light, Margot. (1996) *Internal Factors in Russian Foreign Policy.* Oxford, UK: Oxford University Press.

Mankoff, Jeffrey. (2009) *Russian Foreign Policy: The Return of Great Power Politics.* Lanham, MD: Rowman and Littlefield Publishers, Inc.

McFaul, Michael. (1997/98) A Precarious Peace: Domestic Politics in the Making of Russian Foreign Policy. *International Security* 22, 3: 5–35.

McFaul, Michael. (1999) Russia's Many Foreign Policies. *Demokratizatsiya* 7, 3: 393–412.

Mearsheimer, John. (2014) Why the Ukraine Crisis is the West's Fault. *Foreign Affairs* (Sept/Oct): 1–12.

Monaghan, Andrew. (2008) 'An Enemy at the Gates' Or 'From Victory to Victory'? Russian Foreign Policy. *International Affairs* 84, 4: 717–733.

Perlez, Jane. (1999) Head to Head, Albright and Russia's Prime Minister Do Not See Eye to Eye, *New York Times*, January 26. Available at: www.nytimes.com/1999/01/26/world/head-to-head-albright-and-russia-s-prime-minister-do-not-see-eye-to-eye.html.

Prizel, Ilya. (1998) *National Identity and Foreign Policy Nationalism and Leadership in Poland, Russia and Ukraine.* Cambridge, UK: Cambridge University Press.

Putin, V. (2007) Speech at Munich Conference on Security Policy, *President of Russia*, February 10. Available at: http://archive.kremlin.ru/eng/speeches/2007/02/10/0138_type82912type82914type82917type84779_118123.shtml.

Putin, V. (2015) Address to the 70th Session of the United Nations General Assembly. *President of Russia*, September 28. Available at: http://en.kremlin.ru/events/president/news/50385.

Roberts, Kari. (2010) Jets, Flags and a New Cold War? Demystifying Russia's Arctic Intentions. *International Journal* LXV, 4: 957–976.

Roberts, Kari. (2013) Putin's Choice: The Russian President and the Reset. *St. Anthony's International Review*, 8, 2: 127–148.

Roberts, Kari. (2014) Détente 2.0: The Meaning of Russia's Reset with the United States. *International Studies Perspectives*, 15: 1–18.

Roberts, Kari. (2017) Understanding Putin: The Politics of Identity and Geopolitics in Russian Foreign Policy Discourse. *International Journal* 72, 1: 28–55.

Robinson, Neil. (2000) *Institutions and Political Change in Russia.* New York: St. Martin's Press.

Rucker, P. (2014) Hillary Clinton Says Putin's Actions Are Like 'What Hitler Did Back in the 30s', *Washington Post* (March 5). Available at: www.washingtonpost.com/blogs/post-politics/wp/2014/03/05/hillary-clinton-says-putins-action-are-like-what-hitler-did-back-in-the-30s/.

Sakwa, Richard. (2008) 'New Cold War' or 20 Years' Crisis? Russia and International Politics. *International Affairs* 2: 241–267.

Sakwa, Richard. (2015) The Death of Europe? Continental Fates after Ukraine. *International Affairs* 91, 3: 553–579.

Stent, Angela. (2014) *The Limits of Partnership: US-Russia Relations in the 21st Century.* Princeton, NJ: Princeton University Press.

Talbott, Strobe. (2002) *The Russia Hand: A Memoir of Presidential Diplomacy.* New York: Random House.

Tolz, Vera. (1998) Conflicting Homeland Myths and Nation State Building in Postcommunist Russia. *Slavic Review* 57, 2: 267–294.

Tsygankov, Andrei. (1997) From International Institutionalism to Revolutionary Expansionism: The Foreign Policy Discourse of Contemporary Russia. *Mershon International Studies Review* 41: 247–268.

Tsygankov, Andrei. (2009) *Russophobia: Anti-Russian Lobby and American Foreign Policy.* New York: Palgrave Macmillan.

Tsygankov, Andrei. (2013) *Russia's Foreign Policy: Change and Continuity in National Identity*. London: Rowman and Littlefield Publishers, Inc.
The United States and Russia Bilateral Presidential Commission (October 15, 2009). Fact Sheet, United States Department of State. www.state.gov/p/eur/ci/rs/usrussiabilat/index.htm.
Wallander, Celeste. (1996) *The Sources of Russian Foreign Policy After the Cold War*. Boulder, CO: Westview Press.
The White House, Office of the Press Secretary. (June 24, 2010) *The President's News Conference with President Dmitry A. Medvedev of Russia*. Available at: www.whitehouse.gov.

15
ASIA-PACIFIC AND CHINA

Natasha Kuhrt

KING'S COLLEGE LONDON, UK

Introduction

This chapter assesses the trajectory of Russia's policy towards Asia, principally Asia-Pacific, but will also touch on policy towards Central Asia and South Asia. It has been suggested that four 'old' regions are being 'pushed into one' (Central, South, Northeast and Southeast Asia), which facilitates the formation in the 'East Eurasian space' of a new geopolitical regional complex of 'Greater East Asia' (Sevastyanov, 2012). In defining the parameters of Asia therefore, a 'contest is emerging over how to define Asia conceptually, including choice of terminology' (Kuhrt, 2014a; Medcalf, 2016).

We first look at the evolution of Russia's policy in Asia, including attempts to craft an Asia-Pacific strategy, before outlining the aims and objectives of contemporary Russian policy in the region, including the role of the Russian Far East region (RFE), before detailing the trajectory of Russian bilateral relations with the key actors in the region: China, India, Japan and South Korea. Finally, we raise the question of how China's One Belt, One Road (OBOR) might reconfigure the international politics of the region, before drawing some conclusions regarding the success of the overall policy and outlining longer-term challenges.

The evolution of Russia's policy in Asia: wither the "pivot"?

Until the late 1990s, little scholarly attention was paid to Russia's Asia policy. In Russia, those working on Asia were sidelined, as Russian foreign policy focused principally on Europe and the US, reflecting the traditional emphasis on relations with the West during the Soviet period. The Ministry of Foreign Affairs (MFA) was criticized for 'continuing and even exaggerating its Soviet predecessors' "Euro-Americocentrism" and sidelining the South and the East' (Kuhrt, 2007:10). In the early 1990s, the MFA was headed by the pro-Western Andrei Kozyrev, who lacked expertise on China and Asia in general. This led to some embarrassing episodes which hampered Moscow's official China policy in these first years of Russian diplomacy. For example, there was an attempt to develop non-governmental links to Taiwan, which nearly threatened to derail relations with China at a time when the joint border remained undemarcated.

Furthermore, Beijing was fearful of the contagion of new Russian democratic and reformist ideas into China itself. Concerns in Beijing that Moscow might bring human rights considerations into bilateral relations went unrealized, however, as Moscow soon moved relations to a more pragmatic footing, and in 1995 refused to join the European Union in condemning China's human rights record, suggesting this might destabilize the internal situation in China. The same year it was declared that 'complete political unanimity' existed between China and Russia: Russia reaffirmed its adherence to the 'one China' policy while China expressed 'complete understanding of the actions taken by the Russian side to preserve the country's unity' (Kuhrt, 2007: 18). Kozyrev made it clear, however, that China was 'With all due respect . . . not a world economic leader for the time being' (Kuhrt, 2007: 9) and indeed, until 1993 the chief focus of economic efforts in the Asia-Pacific region was Japan.

Although relations with Japan continued to develop under Yeltsin, the furor over apparent plans to make territorial concessions to Japan in 1993 in exchange for investment, meant that relations became hostage to the territorial dispute, and even the 'summit without neckties' between Yeltsin and Hashimoto in 1997 failed to break the impasse. Research on the Russia-Japan relationship has tended understandably, to focus mainly on the history of the territorial dispute, and the lack of dynamism in these relations has inevitably meant fewer works on this topic in both Russia and the West.

The 2001 US intervention in Afghanistan focused global attention on Central Asia and saw the creation of the Shanghai Cooperation Organisation (SCO), which had evolved from confidence-building measures around border talks between Central Asian states, Russia and China, bringing the Eurasian region into sharper focus.

As Russia and China strengthened relations, principally with the declaration of a partnership aimed at strategic alliance in the twenty-first century, there was a growing recognition that the long neglected 'Asian leg' of Russian foreign policy was gaining in significance. Despite this, the focus remained squarely on the Sino-Russian relationship, rather than on Russia and Japan, or Russia and Asia more widely. Russian analysts generally provide 'optimistic' accounts, and this tendency has strengthened under Putin. However, in the 1990s, Russian scholarship on Russia-China relations had often been more alarmist – in particular regarding the Russian Far East and issues around territorial demarcation, Chinese migration and cross-border trade, reflecting real security fears as the Sino-Russian border opened up (Miasnikov, 1996; Gel'bras, 1997).

Since the start of the Ukraine crisis in 2014, Russia has intensified cooperation with China in an apparent 'pivot' to Asia. However, while this is presented in both Russia and the West as a sudden one, the broader context shows that this is more a gradual recalibration that has been taking place over several years. This must be seen in the context of the US pivot, or 'rebalancing', to Asia under Obama, and also in light of heightened rhetoric following the Ukraine crisis in 2014. This leads to the conclusion that the intensification of relations is partly designed to produce a reaction from the West and to highlight the dangers of isolating Russia.

The 'pivot' was declared by Putin in 2012 in the same year that Russia hosted the APEC summit. What does it entail?

At the discursive level, there is greater recognition of, firstly, the importance of regional powers, given the rise of China and India, arguably both more powerful in their respective regions, than as global powers (and reconfirmed by the 'BRICS' grouping); and, secondly, there has been some limited recognition by Russian academics and policymakers of one-dimensionality – that Russia's Asia policy had been overly focused on China in the post-Soviet period as a whole. In fact for much of this period, Russia's Asia policy was predominantly a China policy. Further, the Russian Far East was highlighted as a priority area.

The US 'pivot' or 'rebalancing' to Asia-Pacific, and Russia's growing rift with the West accounts at least in part, for the greater significance attached to relations with Asia-Pacific. This was borne out by the 2013 Foreign Policy Concept, and later reinforced in the 2016

Concept (Kuhrt, 2014a; FPC, 2016). A certain 'mirroring' of US language is evident – this plays a performative role – that true great powers (read the US, Russia) are capable of projecting power outwards and acting in more than one region simultaneously. In this scenario, Russia is not 'just one of the BRICS', i.e. mainly regional powers and 'not-quite' global powers, but rather a power that can act both regionally and globally, on a par with the US.

Is there really a pivot? The Russian approach to China is widely seen as a new, more accommodating one: the economic impact of sanctions and a falling oil price have forced Russia to yield economic positions to China.

However, in 2009, following the global financial crisis, Russia also talked of pivoting to Asia. Then too, Dmitry Medvedev suggested that Russia and China had been 'pushed together by the crisis'. It was at this time too that Moscow gradually began to cast around for alternative partners to reduce reliance on China. This demonstrates the fact that Russia is fully aware of the dangers of overreliance on China to the extent that it might forfeit foreign policy autonomy were it to pursue a formal alliance with China. Russia's China policy is a strategic partnership that is more than an 'axis of convenience' (Lo, 2008) or an alliance but that amounts to less than a full-blown alliance (Gelb and Simes, 2013; Bordachev, 2016) While alliances are significant phenomena in international relations, the Sino-Russian strategic partnership is more akin to an alignment than explicit alliance. There is no military component to the partnership, neither are there grounds to think it will evolve into such; furthermore, the disparities in the economic realm make full-blown alliance unlikely. Russia needs Chinese financial clout; the alignment with China acts as a force multiplier due to their status as P5 powers; the reinvigoration of the UN Security Council since the end of the Cold War in the context of increasing multipolarity acts to bolster Russia's great power status. Furthermore, Russia's increased 'othering' of the West at both domestic and foreign levels, means that powers like China assume increased significance in identity terms. In the wake of Ukraine, it seems that Russia's *economic* reliance on China is more about a lack of other options than a strategic choice.

The role of the Asia-Pacific in contemporary Russian foreign policy

Identity

In identity terms, the Ukraine crisis has helped to re-emphasize 'the importance of Russia's "Asia vector", and dramatized how "Other" the West is' (Wishnick, 2017). As Iver Neumann points out, the idea of Europe is 'the main "Other" in relation to which the idea of Russia is defined' (Neumann, 2017: 3). Yet the West/Europe is both self *and* other, for 'Russians, when they make out they discuss Europe, also discuss themselves' (Neumann, 2017: 3). Further, in engaging with Asia, Russia becomes once again *European* – i.e. in Asia it is perceived as European, not Asian, while in Europe, Russia tends to be viewed as unEuropean/non-Western (Kuhrt, 2014a). Thus turning to Asia helps paradoxically to *reinforce* Russia's Europeanness. Again, as Neumann suggests, Russia has sought recognition principally from the West of its great power status, and that while China, and possibly India, might be alternative centres from which to gain great power status recognition, 'the point when such recognition would make the recognition of Western powers superfluous for Russia to maintain its great power status remains a long way off' (Neumann, 2017: 188). Deep-seated historical fears have often been played on: Milan Hauner describes Russian ambivalence, encapsulated by the term 'Aziatchina', i.e. the almost unlimited capacity among Russians to identify themselves with Asia while showing their contempt for the Asian peoples and civilizations as 'utterly barbaric' (Hauner, 1990). This ambivalence still manifests itself in debates regarding the strategic partnership with China (Tsygankov, 2009; Kashin, 2013)

Sergei Karaganov has cautioned that following the 'Asian way of development will take us not to advanced Asia (we cannot go there), but to Africa . . . Either we move closer to Europe or go barbaric' (Karaganov in Kuhrt, 2014b: 101). Yet the pivot to Asia has in many respects become even more Sinocentric than before, threatening to undermine previous attempts at diversification of Russia's Asia policy declared ahead of the APEC summit of 2012. Paradoxically, however, this intensification of the Chinese part of the pivot has been accompanied by an acceleration of diplomacy with Japan, relations with which have been stagnating for many years – in fact, the acceleration could in part be explained by this very Sinocentrism.

Politics and status

Russian scholars explicitly depict the pivot as being at least in part driven by the advent of the 'new Cold War': 'Russia needs the turn towards Asia to gain more confidence and become less vulnerable to these aggressive attack' (Kanaev and Bordachev, 2017). Further, the development of Siberia and the Far East is a central part of Asia-Pacific policy, which is seen as preserving stability in the event of long-term confrontation with the West.

There is alignment between the two states on issues of sovereignty and self-determination within the regional agenda that is central to the SCO: the 'three evils' of religious extremism, separatism and terrorism. In this way the organization provides a potent ideological symbol of a multipolar world. Yet regarding Crimea, South Ossetia and Abkhazia, China appeared cautious in lending support to Russia.

At the global level, Russia and China ostensibly present a united front, with Russia, and to some extent China, both presenting their relationship as moving to a qualitatively new stage. They highlight the need to combat not only the Western order but also to defend their interests as members of the P5, where their opposition to issues such as regime change and 'coloured revolutions' provide points of convergence. China could be seen as a 'freerider' on Russia, due to Russia's greater diplomatic experience and 'clout', while China has only relatively recently begun to participate more actively in global affairs. Yet apart from Syria, where both have vetoed attempts at passing resolutions in an 'axis of obstruction' (Pei, 2014), they do not practice wholehearted solidarity. Indeed, China sometimes appears uncomfortable with Russia's actions, often preferring to exercise restraint (Snetkov and Lanteigne, 2014). Geir Flikke suggests the relationship is best viewed as one that is 'new, transformative, and mutually constitutive for both partners, arguing that the relationship is a mechanism for *upgrading* their status in international affairs as against Western-U.S. dominance' (Flikke, 2016). Certainly, the importance of status and resistance to Western hegemony, is indisputably at the core of the Sino-Russian partnership. However, the transformative potential of the relationship should not be overstated.

Russia and China also appear to agree that the events of Maidan in Ukraine are not evidence of a popular uprising against a corrupt authority, but rather the latest in a series of 'coloured revolutions', whose genesis can be traced back to the Orange Revolution of 2004 and of which the Arab revolutions are also part.

Russia and China increasingly stand together in international forums: for example, deputy Russian defence minister Antonov used the APEC summit to suggest that:

> No one can feel absolutely safe, entertaining the fact that 'color revolutions' have not come to the Asia-Pacific. The thing is, it may happen at any moment once the Western elites feel unhappy about the policy of a state and make a decision on the introduction of 'democratic' values. We recall the Umbrella revolution in Hong Kong. Who is next?

> World's leading countries should pursue responsible policy in the Asia-Pacific . . . In this context, we are concerned about the US policy in the Asia-Pacific given that it becomes more and more focused on systemic 'containment' of Russia and China.
>
> (Antonov, 2014)

This has prompted suggestions that there could eventually be an informal Sino-Russian alliance which Russia and China might use to escape what they see as a '"dual containment policy" by the West' (Gelb and Simes, 2013), what Alexander Gabuev calls a 'soft alliance' (Gabuev, 2015a). However, despite often rather optimistic analyses of bilateral relations, several voices in Russia are advising caution. Viktor Larin believes that China is deliberately changing the emphasis in bilateral relations from bilateral economic and political relations to global and regional security, asserting that Moscow often follows 'in the wake of Chinese initiatives' (Larin, 2014: 185). Another Russian scholar close to the Kremlin, emphasizes that:

> China and the Chinese leaders have played an exceptionally important role in the difficult period from 2014 to 2016 by making it easier for Russia to uphold its interests. However, at the same time he raises concerns that *'With this paradigm still in existence, Russia will never be able to take decisions interfering with the Chinese interests'*.
>
> (Bordachev, 2017; author's italics)

Thus Chinese support provides psychological comfort at a time when Russia has few friends. Yet it is clear also, that this comes at a price: for example, Moscow may be increasingly called upon to support China, including in territorial disputes in Asia-Pacific.

Economic and regional development

The area that has been consistently singled out by both sides as lacking in dynamism and failing to fulfil its potential, is the area of economic cooperation. In the 2013 Foreign Policy Concept, relations with China were singled out – it was noted that the 'scope and quality of economic interaction' should be brought into line with 'the high level of political relations' (MID, 2013).

The bilateral economic relationship is to some extent a 'hangover' from the 1990s when the opening of the joint border led to an upsurge in informal trade relations. As Larin notes, this 'created an ideology and infrastructure (including a social one) of relations that still influences both countries' and people's minds and actions' (Larin, 2014: 183).

Economics has long been the laggard of bilateral relations; while trade has shown a huge increase since the late 2000s, the pledge for trade to reach $100 billion in the year 2015 has yet to be attained.

The general trend has been for trade between the two countries to be on the decline: Chinese exports to Russia fell by 36% in the first half of 2014 and trade stalled at $90 billion. In 2015 the figure fell to around $64 billion and recovered only slightly to $66 billion in 2016. An economic slowdown in China meant less demand for key Russian goods such as metal and chemicals, while the share of oil and hydrocarbons in total exports to China increased from around 50% in 2008, to nearly 70% in 2013 (Federal Customs Service). Raw materials have long been the staple diet of Russia's exports to China, and while this has been heavily criticized even at the official level, the trend shows no signs of abating. The rents extracted from this trade remain a powerful disincentive to modernization and restructuring for those currently in power.

At the height of the Ukraine crisis in May 2014, a huge gas deal was signed with China – 'Power of Siberia'. Given that Russia and China had been in negotiations for nearly two decades over price issues, there was speculation that the crisis had spurred Russia to clinch the deal. Previously price had been an issue for Russia, but given the economic ramifications of the Ukrainian crisis, Moscow appeared to have run out of options, making China, with its huge economic potential, a far more attractive partner than before. Some suggested that the deal would barely cover Gazprom's costs. Gas prices also dropped significantly at this time. While on paper the deal looked impressive, on closer examination it appeared that the economic impact of sanctions was forcing Russia to yield economic positions to China. The launch was tentatively postponed from 2018 to 2019, possibly even to 2021, with the gas supply only reaching the agreed-upon amount by 2024 (Kuhrt, 2015b).

The dependence of the Russian economy on oil and gas revenues is particularly evident in Russia-China relations. The increasing asymmetrical dependence of Russia on China (rather than vice versa) remains a cause for concern. Russia's Energy Strategy has advocated increasing the share of Asia-Pacific energy markets from 3% to 30%, which may be achievable, but it also stated the long-term objective of reducing raw material exports from 64% to 34% by 2030, which seems far less so. The 2009 National Security Strategy characterized as potential threats *both* a failure to reduce Russia's dependence on raw materials *and* the loss of control over Russia's resources (Kuhrt, 2012: 487).

Oil is Russia's main export to China, indeed in 2015 Russia overtook Saudi Arabia as the biggest supplier of oil to China. Oil is pumped through the Eastern Siberia–Pacific Ocean pipeline as far as Daqing on the Chinese border, and then is shipped by rail further onwards, which has become a lucrative source of rents.

Russia has attempted to portray itself as a potential 'swing supplier' between Europe and Asia. However, the strategy is difficult because Europe has become quite an unstable market in energy terms. For this reason, then, the markets of East Asia, and China in particular, appear increasingly attractive to Russian energy companies. However, the amount of gas going to China is still only around one-quarter of what Russia supplies to Europe (Krutikhin, 2014: 64).

Russia risks becoming over-dependent on China in the energy sphere, while at the same time remaining a minor supplier in relative terms, with the chances of Russia becoming a 'swing supplier' between Europe and Asia remaining low. Yet, one encounters such optimistic scenarios as:

> Russian gas supplies to China alone are expected to equal those to Europe in 10 to 12 years, which will take the Russian-Chinese strategic partnership to a new level and consolidate Russia's and China's roles in the Asia-Pacific region and the world at large.
> *(Kanaev and Bordachev, 2017)*

Russian rhetoric regarding a switch of gas supplies from Europe to Asia should therefore be treated with caution. Supplying China will not substitute for the European energy market. It is widely expected that instead there will be a reorientation of Russian gas towards Europe (NSDR, 2016).

Russia is only one of a range of energy supply sources for many Asian states, including China. This fact has been described as a potential source of instability by regional leaders; for example, in the Khabarovsk Krai Social and Economic Development Strategy this was singled out as a negative factor in the longer term (Khabarovskii Krai Government, 2011: 37).

The creation of a Ministry for Far Eastern Development in 2012 appeared to signal a greater focus on the neglected RFE region, which is seen as a key component of Russia's Asia-Pacific policy. Yet despite the fact that as one Russian analyst notes, there is more attention paid to the RFE rhetorically than ever before, the region receives far less financial support and investment from the centre than other regions like the Arctic and Kaliningrad, which calls into question the priority that the Kremlin apparently devotes to it as part of its Asia-Pacific strategy. Further, the development plans for the Siberian regions have been dropped (Valdai, 2014) due to lack of resources but also a belated acknowledgement that the 'Soviet' approach of setting up megaprojects has been unproductive.

This region more than any other represents a 'litmus test' of Russia's Asia-Pacific policy. It has been suggested that a failure to integrate the region with broader integrative processes would consign the RFE to the status of a 'double periphery', i.e. a region on the periphery not only of the Asia-Pacific, but also of European Russia, thus making re-integration with the rest of Russia an urgent task. The socio-economic decline of the region has been marked by massive outflows of the local population. As noted in one report, the 'degree of the local population's fatigue is well seen in the mass emigration of retirees (usually less inclined to seek a better fortune elsewhere) to China' (Valdai, 2014: 37). Many in the RFE are also more likely to have visited China than their own capital.

In the 1990s, the growing dependence of the RFE on China was often securitized by governors seeking to make political capital in bargaining with the centre. Yet there remain whole *oblasts*, for example Amurskaya oblast, that are nearly wholly dependent on China for external trade. In 2014, 87.6% of exports went to China, and 84.9% of imports were from China, making China the biggest trading partner (Government of Amurskaya oblast, 2014). A report by the Valdai club in 2014 noted, however, that with the exception of Heilongjiang, due to the regional cooperation agreement with neighbouring provinces of the RFE, China does not intend to pursue 'intense economic relations with Russia' (Valdai, 2014).

This regional cooperation and development plan (approved 2009), linking Northeastern China and the RFE (Lee, 2013) has not gone smoothly, mainly due to a lack of coordination, although a commission was subsequently established, co-chaired by Yuri Trutnev, the presidential envoy to the RFE and Chinese Vice Premier Wang Yang. In order to boost interregional trade, transport infrastructure needs to be improved dramatically. This is why Russia has in recent years increasingly begun to participate in East Asian multilateral forums, signalled above all by Russia's hosting of the 2012 Asia–Pacific Economic Cooperation (APEC) summit in Vladivostok (Kuhrt, 2014a; Koldunova, 2016). The 2012 APEC summit was meant to provide a focus for such infrastructure projects, yet the projects were fraught with accusations of corruption and reports of bridges being built to 'nowhere' (Kuhrt, 2015a).

A promising new development is the establishment of regular meetings of the new 'Eastern Economic Forum' (EEF). Forums took place in 2015, 2016 and a third in 2017. The forum is attended by high-level political figures as well as business leaders (participants at the second forum included President Putin and Japanese Prime Minster Shinzo Abe). Various mechanisms have also been established for attracting foreign investment (most importantly the Advanced Special Economic Zones and the Free Port of Vladivostok (EEF, 2017). Japan had a significant presence at the 2016 Forum and various draft agreements were signed on possible plans for Japan to invest in the Northern Sea Route, amongst other energy projects (Kozinets and Brown, 2016).

As before, Russian analysts persist in seeing the RFE as a bridge, a view that has remained unchanged since the 1980s. Thus the Valdai report: 'It is also a bridge connecting Europe and Asia not only ideologically but also spatially' (Valdai, 2014: 41).

Russia in Asia-Pacific

A new body of Russian scholarship is now emerging that seeks to engage more robustly with work on regions and regionalism in relation to Asia-Pacific (Sevastyanov, 2012; Koldunova,

2016) This reflects the greater emphasis in general on the importance of integrative structures in Russian foreign policy, but also the emergence of comparative work at the scholarly level, prompted by the advent of the SCO, and interest in EU studies and 'non-Western IR'. The proliferation of regional organizations in Asia-Pacific also explains this interest.

Arms sales and the regional strategic balance

Russia's turn to Asia remains, above all, an embrace of China: yet Russia has also embraced China for lack of other viable partners in the region (Trenin, 2014). Furthermore, this 'wary' embrace (Lo, 2017) is fraught with security challenges, which means that Russia still needs to 'hedge' against a rising China where possible. While Russia has expressed support for the major Chinese initiatives in the sphere of trade liberalization in the Asia Pacific, the US abandonment of Trans-Pacific Partnership by the Trump administration also leaves China unchallenged in economic terms. However, the economic 'threat' is a far more tangible one in some ways than the military one.

While discussion of any military threat from China remains taboo, as Russian politicians never emphasize military and political deterrence of China (Kuhrt, 2007; Kashin, 2013; Valdai, 2014: 23), Russia has reinforced its Pacific Fleet and strengthened forces in the Far Eastern district close to the Chinese border. Furthermore, tactical nuclear weapons are viewed by Russia as being key in countering a potential threat from China. Thus while Russia does not openly acknowledge a threat from China, plans have been made to offset it to some degree. At the same time, China is one of Russia's best purchasers of weapons.

Russia has been selling weapons to China since the 1990s. At that time the Russian arms industry was largely unregulated, which led to some embarrassing episodes such as an attempt to sell arms to Taiwan (Kuhrt, 2007). Initially these arms deals were conducted on a barter basis rather than hard currency, in the so-called 'frying pans for submarines' scenario (Kuhrt, 2007). The rationale tended to be 'if we don't sell them someone else will'. Concerns began to be expressed, however, especially by the defence establishment, regarding the wisdom of selling arms to a former enemy and a rising power, and in the context of an undemarcated border.

It should be noted that Russia has traditionally ensured that the next generation of weapons systems were sold to India, rather than China (Kuhrt, 2007: 120). This policy appeared to continue under Putin (Blank, 2013), but then some began to advocate selling China the newer generation of Su-30 fighter jets, and lifting restrictions on the sale of multipurpose ships. It was even suggested that such a policy was the only means of ensuring the preservation of the Russian defence industry (Kuhrt, 2007: 121). This may have been prompted by discussions within the EU regarding a possible lifting of the arms embargo on China in 2005, which was ultimately kept in place.

While China and India together account for 56% of Russian arms exports in the years 2000–2016, it would be incorrect to conclude that China and India are the only two significant purchasers of Russian arms in Asia. Vietnam, Myanmar, Malaysia and Indonesia are also important customers, and Asia now makes up 70% of Russia's total arms exports in 2000–2016. In fact, Russia supplied nearly half of all arms exported to Asia-Pacific in the same period, at 43.1% (Connolly and Sendstad, 2017: 11).

Vietnam and other smaller Asia-Pacific countries will remain important customers, in particular as China and India continue to explore ways in which to build up their own weapons industry, either by means of reverse engineering, which leads to a loss of revenue for Russia, or by purchasing production licences. The effects of sanctions and the drop in oil price make the weapons industry an even more crucial source of hard currency than before. While China had obtained production rights and licences for some weapons systems, Russia continued to withhold more sophisticated technology, aware that China was engaging in reverse engineering.

Since the Ukrainian crisis, Russia has begun selling the more advanced Su-35 fighter jets to China in an apparent reversal of its previous policy to always sell India the latest models. One reason for this change of policy may be the fact that China has developed its own fighter (Tikhonov, 2014).

The sale of advanced weaponry to China, combined with an acceleration of military cooperation as evidenced by the increasing frequency of Sino-Russian joint military and naval exercises in the region since 2012, including 'Maritime Cooperation' and the Vostok exercises near Vladivostok, as well as in 2016 in the South China Seas, caused widespread alarm in the region. Russia has not, however, given unqualified support to China on territorial issues in the South China Sea. Thus Russian ambassador to the Philippines Kudashev affirmed that Russia shared concerns about freedom of navigation, provoking Chinese commentators to express concern about lack of support of China's 'nine-dash line' in the South China Sea and also Moscow's adherence to the 'freedom of navigation' debates (Kozyrev, 2015).

However, it is interesting to note that in China they frequently 'play up' Russian support, even when Russia has actually issued non-committal statements or statements of neutrality. Similarly, Russia also tends to exaggerate Chinese support on territorial issues such as South Ossetia and Abkhazia, and then the annexation of Crimea in 2014.

Russia-Japan relations

If the intention in Moscow behind such cooperation was to signal to Japan that its relationship with Beijing was moving to a higher level, then this was met with some success. Japanese voices, such as the Institute for Defense Studies (NIDS), stated explicitly that concern, even fear, of 'the potential dangers posed by this Russo-Chinese "united front against Japan" had prompted Tokyo to push for high level meetings with the Russian President' (NIDS, 2016: 223–224).

In the run-up to the APEC summit in 2012, some think tank circles had already recommended developing closer ties with Japan in order to maintain a 'flexible geopolitical posture' as concerns grew that Russia was hitching its wagon too closely to China.

Even before the Ukrainian crisis, Russia had begun to explore the potential for rebuilding relations with Japan. The Eastern Siberia–Pacific Ocean pipeline showed the dangers of Russian overestimation of Japan's oil thirst – Russia overplayed its energy hand by unsuccessfully attempting to play off Japan against China (Kuhrt, 2015a). After '3/11', Russia had hoped that Japan's need for alternative energy sources post-Fukushima would push it in Russia's direction. However, Russia had overestimated Japan's need for energy and the extent to which that might move it towards Moscow.

The Ukraine crisis led to the postponement of Putin's 2014 visit. The sanctions imposed by Japan, although far less punishing than those imposed by Western countries, were to Russia symbolic of Japan's tendency to follow the US's lead. Russia and Japan's trade turnover has long been miniscule and has traditionally consisted mainly of hydrocarbons and fish products; in fact, now trade is even less diversified.

Public opinion in Russia on the territorial dispute is unsurprisingly uncompromising, and since the annexation of Crimea has become more so. Nevertheless, there has been a huge increase in the diplomatic activity between Russia and Japan, including the drafting of an eight-point cooperation plan in December 2016, as well as meetings involving regional leaders and the Far Eastern Development Minister Galushka. In 2018 a summit is planned which will bring to an end a proposed 'Year of Japan in Russia and Russia in Japan' (MFA, 2017).

Talks on the peace treaty are ongoing, and there have been several rounds since 2014. However, the official Russian view is that 'progress can only be made if Japan fully recognizes the results of World War Two, including article 107 of the UN Charter' (MFA, 2017).[1] A not untypical view of relations with Japan suggests that:

> [t]he issue of territorial delimitation has already been decided by history, and any discussion of the matter should be concerned only with the conditions for using (including jointly) the territories in question without changing the status quo with regard to sovereign control over them.
>
> *(Shvydko 2017)*

As before, Japan will only sign a peace treaty once there has been agreement on territorial concessions, while Russia insists on signing a peace treaty first, and only then discussing territorial issues. Interestingly, however, there is much discussion of joint economic development of the islands, which was one of the proposals put forward during the Yeltsin years – although issues of sovereignty will make this difficult. Russia may be hoping that Japan will revert to the policy of the 1970s when it applied the notion of *sekei fukabun* or the 'inseparability of politics and economics', which in practice meant that despite the territorial issue Japan and the Soviet Union maintained a reasonably good economic relationship (see Kuhrt, 2007).

The Korean Peninsula

Relations with South Korea have improved steadily since normalization in the mid-1990s. Moscow and Seoul agreed on visa exemptions, and trade has maintained a steady, if unremarkable, trajectory. The normalization with Seoul initially came at the expense of relations with Moscow's erstwhile ally in the north, however, as in 1996 the DPRK designated Russia as an enemy state and relations stalled again in 2012 with the incumbency of Kim Jong-un (Shin, 2014: 133–135).

The whole peninsula has begun to take on a bigger role in Russia's Asian diplomacy, and since the Ukrainian crisis in 2014, bilateral relations between Russia and the DPRK have become more active. Like China, Russia has generally been reluctant to strengthen sanctions on Pyongyang, although the interests of China and Russia do not necessarily always coincide. Furthermore, Russia was somewhat taken aback when China joined the US in drawing up sanctions against the DPRK in 2015, which threatened Russian economic interests (Toloraya, 2016) As one Russian scholar suggests, Russia needs to ensure its economic and trade relations with the DPRK are not neglected, stressing the importance to Moscow of participating in 'the future opening up of North Korea' (Bordachev, 2014). This partly explains the Russian Duma vote to write off the DPRK Soviet era debt, and Russia's policy of continuing to supply oil to the DPRK despite the imposition of sanctions.

Russia tends to see the future of the peninsula in terms of a gradual integration of the North into the South (Ivashentsov, 2013). This is of course very different from the US policy of regime change, but also markedly different from China's policy which prefers to maintain the status quo of two Koreas (Zhebin, 2014).

Good relations with the DPRK are viewed as essential in ensuring Russian security in the Asia-Pacific. Given that Russia has a seventeen kilometre border with the DPRK near Vladivostok, instability on the peninsula would clearly threaten the RFE, perhaps leading to a refugee outflow over the border into Russia.

Russian plans involving the DPRK focus on construction of a Trans-Korean pipeline, which would benefit Pyongyang, as it would be able to charge transit fees. A further project seeks to build a railway across the peninsula. Some have mooted the idea of using North Korean labour in the RFE as North Koreans are perceived to be relatively skilled and 'well disciplined' (Valdai, 2014). It should be noted that there are already a large number of North Koreans working in the RFE, mainly in the logging industry.

Russia therefore has clear, if limited, economic interests in the Peninsula and is able to take advantage to some extent of the DPRK's isolation, by being a niche supplier.

South Korea has generally taken a positive view of Russia, but relations have been negatively affected by the Ukrainian crisis as well as Russia's condemnation with China of the THAAD missile deployment. While Seoul has not imposed sanctions on Russia, this is largely because its constitution does not allow it to do so, rather than for any other reason. Nevertheless, Russia and South Korea have a good, if modest, trade balance.

India

At the beginning of his third presidential term, Putin underlined the need for the restoration of the relations with former allies and geopolitical "friends" in Asia such as India, Iran and the DPRK.

In the 1990s, Evegniy Primakov had spoken of a *Russia-China-India strategic triangle*. The Indian vector was formalized by the 'Declaration on Strategic Partnership between India and the Russian Federation' in 2000, and the strategic partnership with China in 2001. Relations with China appeared to go from strength to strength, while by contrast the traditionally robust Russo-Indian relationship began to decline, to the extent that some Russian experts on India described it as 'stagnating' and even as an 'empty shell' (Trenin, 2010; Belokrentskiy, 2011).

The greater emphasis on 'Greater Eurasia' has emerged since the renewed interest in Afghanistan and Pakistan. Accordingly, the SCO is undergoing enlargement with the addition of Pakistan and India as full members. It might be suggested that because the SCO promotes illiberal norms, India's inclusion could be problematic, India being viewed as a democratic state, being groomed by the US as a beacon of democracy in East Asia. As Alexander Lukin notes, India's membership of the SCO is not 'problem free' (Lukin, 2015b); on the other hand, the inclusion of a traditionally non-aligned power such as India might help to assuage the fears of Central Asian states regarding Sino-Russian hegemony.

The US is widely seen as attempting to 'groom' India as its proxy in the East Asian Regional Security Complex as part of its rebalancing strategy, and India is increasingly being seen as an Asia-Pacific power, confirming Buzan's thesis of a more assertive China bringing India into East Asia to balance China (Buzan, 2012). With the rolling out of the OBOR, questions arise as to India's future stance. China seeks to reassure India of its motives by stressing that Indian participation in the OBOR will ensure the smoother running of the Maritime route in the Indian Ocean region. Yet Chinese reassurances have been rather unsuccessful so far, and India continues to see the Maritime Silk Route as a Chinese strategy to encircle India militarily.

Russia and, to a greater extent, China, view India's role in the Asia-Pacific region with ambivalence; however, Russia has brought India into the heart of Eurasia with the admission to the SCO as a full member, perhaps in an attempt to parry Chinese regional designs.

New challenges: China's OBOR

Putin's idea of a Greater Europe stretching from Vladivostok to Lisbon is countered by China's OBOR project, which envisions a 'Greater Eurasia' going from Shanghai to St Petersburg (Lukin, 2015a).

The May 2015 agreement on cooperation between the Eurasian Economic Union (EEU) and the OBOR project looked as if Russia was again making concessions to China. The OBOR is still a rather undefined project, but it also tends to highlight China and Russia's different approaches to regionalism, where China has seemed critical of the EEU for its exclusive approach, and as cutting off China from Central Asia. The process whereby a Russia-led Eurasian Economic Union together with the Chinese 'one belt, one road' in Central Eurasia, fuse together to form a 'Greater Eurasia' has been hailed by Aleksandr Lukin as a paradigm change in geopolitical terms (Lukin, 2015c), although he acknowledges the difficulties in coordinating within the SCO.

The lack of clarity on the content of this project is unsettling for Russia. At times Russian officials have appeared sanguine, but at others, have expressed concern that while Beijing does not present OBOR as an integration project, the reality will be rather different (Gabuev, 2015b). Thus Artyom Lukin and Rens Lee suggest that as part of the OBOR, the RFE would be just 'one piece in China's long-term geopolitical game aimed at creating zones of influence along its continental frontiers in Eurasia' (Lukin and Lee, 2015).

Conclusion

Some of the key longer-term challenges in the central Sino-Russian relationship are Chinese territorial claims in the Asia-Pacific, and the extent to which Russia might feel obliged to give China greater support in the longer term. The trajectory of China's OBOR initiative, which has the potential to transform Asia-Pacific, including Central Asia, is at the heart of Chinese strategy. Russia will need to be prepared for this. The development of the RFE will also remain key, although this region appears to be dropping off the domestic agenda. If Russia's Asia-Pacific policy is no longer driven by a desire to integrate the RFE, then what is driving it?

Russia has to proceed cautiously. If China is indeed preparing to take a more assertive role in global affairs rather than prioritizing 'short-term economic interests to promote development goals', and instead moving to promote national security interests (Zeng et al., 2015: 258), then Russia may find China less accommodating. Furthermore, while there is a certain amount of normative convergence in the political arena, in the economic field there is clear divergence: this is not just in terms of tensions between the two states regarding trade and spheres of influence, but also in terms of differing attitudes to globalization (Kaczmarski, 2017). Russia has increasingly railed against globalization and emphasized import substitution, not least as it needs to justify the current isolation from the rest of the world economy in the wake of sanctions.

It is true that the US and the West often 'underestimate rapprochement between China and Russia' (Kozyrev, 2015). On the other hand, there is also a tendency in Russia to overestimate the potential of this relationship to transform bilateral and regional ties (Lukin, 2015a). Elizabeth Wishnick takes a more balanced view, pointing out that Russia and China are 'partners of consequence' and that the relationship should not be undervalued (Wishnick, 2017).

The lack of clarity as to the substance of the relationship may also indicate the way in which the bilateral relationship is used discursively in both countries for domestic legitimation purposes, as well as externally to create uncertainty regarding intentions among neighbours. While Sinocentrism inhibits the diversification of Russia's Eastern 'pivot', could it be that Russia sees this Sinocentrism as the key to an Asia-Pacific strategy, i.e. that Sinocentrism acts as a force multiplier to make Russia more resilient, and thus better able to deal with the immediate security environment in Asia?

Neighbours such as Japan, with whom Moscow has sought a more cooperative relationship, may also be difficult to engage in the wider region. While Moscow may worry that aligning more closely with Beijing brings with it the associated risk of being drawn into Chinese territorial disputes, it may also be concerned lest rapprochement with Japan look as if it is aligning with Tokyo against China. Therefore, the transformative potential of the Sino-Russian relationship beyond bilateral relations is limited. Furthermore, Russia must ensure that it does not become cut off from integrative processes in Asia-Pacific. As a Valdai Club report warned:

[t]here is a risk that priority will be given to Eurasian integration. For Russia, this will mean not only huge untapped opportunities but also a danger of remaining on the periphery of global economic and political processes, whose center is moving to the Asia-Pacific.
(Valdai, 2014)

Note

1 Article 107 is the 'enemy state' clause in the UN Charter regarding Japan and Germany.

References

Antonov, Anatoly (2015) 'Deputy Defence Minister Anatoly Antonov gave speech in Singapore at the 14th Asia Security Summit "SHANGRI-LA DIALOGUE"', http://eng.mil.ru/en/mpc/news/more.htm?id=12037863@egNews, accessed 01.03.2017.
Belokrenitsky, Vyacheslav (2011) Russia-India-China: An Intricate Love Triangle to Counter the United States? http://www.geopolitica.ru/article/indiyskiy-pohod-vladimira-putina#, accessed 05.07.17.
Blank, Stephen (2013) 'The Context of Russo–Chinese Military Relations', *American Foreign Policy Interests*, 35(5), pp. 243–253.
Bordachev, Timofei (2016) 'Russia's Pivot to the East and Comprehensive European Partnership', Moscow, Valdai Discussion Club.
Bordachev, Timofei (2017) 'To Russia's Friends in Asia and Beyond', Moscow, Valdai Discussion Club.
Buzan, Barry (2012) *Asia: A Geopolitical Reconfiguration*, Paris: IFRI
Connolly, Richard and Sendstad, Cecilie (2017), *Russia's Role as an Arms Exporter: The Strategic and Economic Importance of Arms Exports for Russia*, London: Chatham House Research Paper.
Eastern Economic Forum, https://forumvostok.ru/en/main-page/, accessed 05.04.17.
Federal Customs Service of the Russian Federation, www.customs.ru/index2.php?option=com_content&view=article&id=24785:2016—&catid=125:2011-02-04-16-01-54&Itemid=1976, accessed 01.04.2017
Flikke, Geir (2016) 'Sino–Russian Relations Status Exchange or Imbalanced Relationship?' *Problems of Post-Communism* 63(3), pp. 159–170.
Gabuev, Alexander (2015a) 'A Soft Alliance? Russia-China relations after Ukraine', www.ecfr.eu/publications/summary/a_soft_alliance_russia_china_relations_after_the_ukraine_crisis331, accessed 20.11.2016.
Gabuev, Alexander (2015b) 'Post-Soviet States Jostle for Role in One Belt One Road Initiative', August 6, http://carnegieendowment.org/2015/08/06/post-soviet-states-jostle-for-role-in-one-belt-one-road-initiative/iel1, accessed 20.02.2017.
Gelb, Leslie and Simes, Dmitri (2013) 'A New Anti-American Axis?' *Council on Foreign Relations, July 6, 2013*. www.nytimes.com/2013/07/07/opinion/sunday/a-new-anti-american-axis.html.
Gel'bras, V (1997) Na vostochnom napravlenii', *Svobodnaya mysl'*, no. 11, November, pp. 45–55.
Government of Amurskaya oblast, 2014 Foreign Economic Activity in 2014, www.amurobl.ru/wps/portal/!ut/p/c5/rc1LDolwFADAs3gB3itSC...4p6sywGDtqpuQr-App24zSf4BBBayeTw!!/dl3/d3/L2dBISEvZ0FBIS9nQSEh/, accessed 14.12.2016.
Hauner, Milan (1990) *What Is Asia to Us? Russia's Asian Heartland Yesterday and Today*, London: Unwin Hyman.
Ivashentsov, Gleb (2013) 'Prospects for Russia-Republic of Korea Relations', in Ivan Ivanov, *Russia-Republic of Korea Relations: Revising the Bilateral Agenda*, Russian International Affairs Council: Moscow, Spetskniga.
Kaczmarski, Marcin (2017) 'Russia-China Relations and the West', *Working Papers*, http://transatlanticrelations.org/wp-content/uploads/2017/03/RBSG-Ostpolitik-2-track-2-book-Kaczmarski-final_website2.pdf, accessed 12.05.2017
Kanaev, Evgeny and Bordachev, Timofei (2014) 'Russia's New Strategy in Asia', *Russia in Global Affairs*, http://eng.globalaffairs.ru/number/Russias-New-Strategy-in-Asia-16997, last accessed 10.02.2017.
Kashin, Vasily (2013) 'The Sum Total of All Fears', *Russia in Global Affairs*, April–June, http://eng.globalaffairs.ru/number/The-Sum-Total-of-All-Fears-15935, last accessed 25.03.2016

Kashin, Vasily (2016) 'China's Power Projection Potential', *Russia in Global Affairs*, March 30, 2016, http://eng.globalaffairs.ru/number/Chinas-Power-Projection-Potential-18073, accessed 10.02.17.

Khabarovsk krai (2009) 'Strategiya sotsial'no-ekonomicheskogo razvitiya dal'nego vostoka i baikal'skogo regiona na period do 2025 goda', available at: http://gov.khabkrai.ru/invest2.nsf/General_ru/14FDC F99A4F6EEFACA25766B0024C2E5, last accessed 20.05.2013

Koldunova, Ekaterina. (2016) 'Russia's involvement in regional cooperation in East Asia', *Asian Survey* 56(3), pp. 532–554.

Kozinets, Andrei and Brown, James (2016) 'Russia's Turn to the East', *East Asia Forum*, www.eastasiaforum.org/2016/10/07/russias-turn-to-the-east/, accessed 01.02.17.

Kozyrev, Vitaly (2015) 'China and Russia multiply efforts in global agenda setting', Vol.15, Issue 19, October 2, https://jamestown.org/program/china-and-russia-multiply-efforts-in-global-agenda-setting/#.VwTZlFI4mu4ON, accessed 30.03.2017.

Kremlin (2009) 'O prigranichnom sotrudnichestve s Kitaem i Mongoliei i zadachakh razvitiya vostochnykh regionov Rossiiskoi Federatsii', *stenographic record of meeting held on 21 May 2009, 16:06*, Khabarovsk, available at: www.kremlin.ru/transcripts, accessed 15.01.16

Krutikhin, Mikhail (2014) in Kadri Liik ed., 'Can Russia reroute natural gas from Europe to Asia?' *Russia's Pivot to Eurasia*, (London, UK: European Council on Foreign Relations), pp. 91–95.

Kuhrt, Natasha (2007) *Russian Policy Towards China and Japan: the Eltsin and Putin periods*, London and New York: Routledge.

Kuhrt, Natasha (2012) 'The Russian Far East: "Dual Integration" or "Double Periphery"?' *Europe-Asia Studies*, 64(3), pp. 471–493.

Kuhrt, Natasha (2014a) 'Russia and the Asia-Pacific: Competing or Complementary Regionalisms? *Politics*, 34(2), pp. 138–148.

Kuhrt, Natasha (2014b) 'Russia and China: strategic partnership or asymmetrical dependence?', in Tsuneo Akaha and Anna Vasillieva eds., *Russia and East Asia: Informal and gradual integration*, London and New York: Routledge, pp. 91–108.

Kuhrt, Natasha (2015a) 'Russia and Asia-Pacific: Diversification or Sinocentrism?', in: David Cadier and Margot Light eds., *Russia's Foreign Policy: Ideas, Domestic Politics and External Relations*, Basingstoke, UK: Palgrave Macmillan, chapter 10, pp. 175–189.

Kuhrt, Natasha (2015b) 'Is Sinocentrism Putting Russia's Interests at risk?' *East Asia Forum*, 17 November 2015 www.eastasiaforum.org/2015/11/17/is-sinocentrism-putting-russias-interests-at-risk/, accessed 05.02.17.

Larin, Viktor (2014) 'Russia and China: New Trends in Bilateral Relations and Political Cooperation', chapter 14 in Rouben Azizian and Artyom Lukin eds., *From APEC 2011 to APEC 2012: American and Russian Perspectives on Security and Cooperation in the Asia-Pacific*, pp. 178–189. Honolulu, HI: Asia-Pacific Center for Security Studies; Vladivostok: Far Eastern Federal University Press.

Lee, Rensellaer (2013) "The Russian Far East and China: Thoughts on Cross Border Integration" *Foreign Policy Research Institute*, November 2013.

Lo, Bobo (2017) *A Wary Embrace: What the China-Russia Relationship Means for the World*, Sydney, Lowy Institute: Penguin Books.

Lukin, Alexander (2015a) 'Russia, China and the Emerging Greater Eurasia', August 18, www.theasanforum.org/russia-china-and-the-emerging-greater-eurasia/, accessed 10.02.2017.

Lukin, Alexander (2015b) "Shanghai Cooperation Organization: Looking for a New Role," Valdai Discussion Club Paper Special Issue, July 9, 2015 http://valdaiclub.com/publication/79220.html, accessed 10.02.2017.

Lukin, Alexander (2015c) 'Konsolidatsiia nezapadnogo mira na fone ukrainskogo krizisa: Rossiia i Kitai, SHOS n BRIKS', *Mezhdunarodnaia zhizn'*, February.

Lukin, Artyom and Lee, Rens, 2015 'The Russian Far East and the Future of Asian Security', *Orbis*, 59(2), pp. 167–180.

Medcalf, Rory (2016) www.theasanforum.org/reimagining-asia-from-asia-pacific-to-indo-pacific/ accessed 01.03.16.

Miasnikov, V. (1996) *Dogovornymi stat'iami utverdili: diplomaticheskii istoriya russok-kitaiskoi granitsy, XVII–XX vv.* Moscow: Institut dal'nego vostoka.

Ministry of Foreign Affairs of Russian Federation, 'MID' (2013), Foreign Policy Concept – Concept of the Foreign Policy of the Russian Federation *Approved by President of the Russian Federation V. Putin on 12 February 2013*, www.mid.ru/bdomp/brp_4.nsf/e78a48070f128a7b43256999005bcbb3/76389fec16 8189ed44257b2e0039b16d!OpenDocument, accessed 02.10.2016.

Ministry of Foreign Affairs of Russian Federation, 'MID' (2017) O sostoyanii i perspektivakh razvitiya rossiisko-iaponskikh otneshenii na sovremennom etape', www.mid.ru/perspektivy-rossijsko-aponskih-otnosenij, accessed 05.04.2017.

Pei, Minxin, "Why Beijing Votes with Moscow, *The New York Times*, February 7, 2012, http://www.nytimes.com/2012/02/08/opinion/why-beijing-votes-with-moscow.html?_r=0, accessed 15.02.2017.

National Institute for Defense Studies (NIDS) Japan (2016) *East Asian Strategic Review 2016*, Tokyo: The Japan Times.

Neumann, I.B. (2017) *Russia and the Idea of Europe. A Study in Identity and International Relations*. 2nd edition. London and New York: Routledge.

Sevastyanov, Sergei (2012) 'Ob institutakh integratsii v ATR', in: ATES ROSSIYA 2012, *Mezhdunarodnaya zhizn'* (International Affairs, Moscow) Special Issue on APEC 2012.

Shin, Beom-Shik (2014) 'Post-Cold War Russian Foreign Policy and the Korean Peninsula', in Tsuneo Akaha and Anna Vasillieva eds., *Russia and East Asia: Informal and Gradual Integration*, pp. 130–153. London and New York: Routledge.

Shvydko, Konstantin (2017) 'Russia-Japan Political Dialogue at the Highest Levels: Opportunities and Perspectives', http://russiancouncil.ru/en/analytics-and-comments/analytics/russia-japan-political-dialogue-at-the-highest-level-opportunities-and-perspectives-/, Russian International Affairs Council, 15 May 2017, accessed 15.05.17.

Snetkov, Aglaya and Marc Lanteigne (2014) '"The Loud Dissenter and Its Cautious Partner": Russia, China, Global Governance and Humanitarian Intervention', *International Relations of the Asia-Pacific* 15(1), pp. 113–146.

Tikhonov, Sergei (2014) 'Zachem Rossiya vooruzhaet Kitai', *Ekspert onlain*, http://expert.ru/2014/11/23/rossiya-i-kitaj/, accessed 05.12.16.

Toloraya, Georgy (2016) 'Russia's North Korea Conundrum', http://thediplomat.com/2016/03/russias-north-korea-conundrum/, accessed 11.11.16.

Trenin, Dmitri (2014) 'Russia's Break-out from the Cold War System: The Drivers of Putin's Course', *Carnegie Moscow Center*, December 22, 2014, http://carnegie.ru/2014/12/22/russia-s-breakout-from-post-cold-war-system-drivers-of-putin-s-course-pub-57589, accessed 02.10.2016.

Tsygankov, A. (2009) *What is China to Us? Westernizers and Sinophiles in Russian Foreign Policy*, Paris: IFRI, Russie NEI-Visions.

Valdai Discussion Club (2014) 'Towards the Great Ocean 2.0', id-1.rian.ru/ig/valdai/Twd_Great_Ocean_2_Eng.pdf, accessed 03.01.2017.

Wishnick, Elizabeth (2017) 'In Search of the "Other" in Asia: Russia–China Relations Revisited', *The Pacific Review* 30(1), pp. 114–132.

Zhebin (2014) *Rossiya i Koreya v menyaiushchemsya mire*, Moscow: IFES RAS.

16
THE EUROPEAN UNION

Tuomas Forsberg and Hiski Haukkala

UNIVERSITY OF TAMPERE, FINLAND

Russia's relationship with Europe – or the other European Great Powers and their alliances – has historically constituted the key direction of Russia's foreign policy shaping the identity of the country (Neumann, 2017). After the end of the Cold War, the EU has been Russia's most significant partner on a broad field of issues and has signified this historical continuity, although bilateral relations also exist and "Europe" remains bigger than the EU (Jonsson, 2012). Since the Ukrainian crisis in 2014, the relationship has become more confrontational and has arguably reached a watershed. The future remains uncertain, but for this reason it is important to revisit Russian policy towards the EU over this period. As we will discuss in this chapter, there is both continuity and change in Russian policy towards the EU. Russia's foreign policy towards the EU can also be explained through various approaches and theories, of which the most prominent can be related to power relations, domestic politics, culture and identities as well as psychological factors. Academic research on Russian foreign policy has progressed, but it remains a contested field and suffers from the political sensitivities associated with the topic.

Research on Russia-EU relations

During the more than 20 years that Russia-EU relations have existed in the institutional sense, the scholarly literature on the topic has expanded. To a large extent, research on Russia's policy towards the EU has been descriptive and/or prescriptive, and policy-oriented in nature. Much of the extant research offered up-to-date analysis of the changing agendas in Russia-EU relations, either after or before major summits or other significant events such as the Russo-Georgian war of 2008. Various think tanks and research institutes have been at least as visible in producing such knowledge as universities.

The research on Russia-EU relations has posited some general explanations related to the overall nature and development of the relationship focusing more often on the problems rather than on cooperation (Prozorov, 2006; Pursiainen, 2008; Haukkala, 2010; Sergunin, 2016). There are also many issue-specific attempts at explication related to fields such as security or energy cooperation. Although many theoretical perspectives have been applied to Russia's policy towards the EU, there is no single paradigm that currently guides the analysis. Analysts have focused on the power struggle and economic interdependence as well as identities and worldviews as the key factors influencing and shaping the relationship. Often such explanations are embedded in the analysis, but they are only rarely systematically developed, tested or contrasted with alternative explanations. The puzzle remains whether the same theory can explain both conflict and cooperation and the variation over time. Typically, explanations of Russian foreign policy towards the EU are singular, ad hoc, and related to events and political leaders rather than general patterns or complex mechanisms.

In general, the Russia-EU relations have often been approached more from the European than Russian perspective, and Russia has been seen as the object rather than the subject of various policies. Nevertheless, relations with the EU form a central part of research over Russian foreign policy. Historically, key schools of thought in Russian foreign policy have been distinguished on the basis of their views of Europe. Even today, Europe is at the core of Russian foreign policy formulation despite of its focus on the Eurasian Union or rhetoric of an Asian pivot and the importance given to BRICS cooperation. The issues of the enlargement, foreign policy and economic cooperation have dominated scholarly discussion in Russia. Russian EU studies have been characterized by their emphasis on empirics, realism and limited engagement with Western scholarly discourses (Romanova, 2015).

Evolution of Russian policy towards the EU

We can distinguish six periods or phases in Russian policy towards the EU (Forsberg and Haukkala, 2016; see also Thorun, 2009). These phases mostly correspond with the terms of the Russian presidents, but they also coincide with some major international events marking the shifts in policy.

The first period (1992-1994) was the formative phase of Russia's relations with the EU. At the time, Russia's foreign policy was oriented towards the West and one of the main priorities of Russia was to establish cooperative relations with the key Western actors on an institutional basis. During this phase Russia and the EU negotiated and finally agreed the contractual foundations of relations in the form of the Partnership and Cooperation Agreement (PCA). The Agreement was signed on June 24, 1994 on the fringes of the Corfu European Council. It was fundamentally different from the previous forms of agreement that the EU had had with the countries of the former Soviet Union. Although the PCA was primarily an economic agreement, it was much more wide-ranging and ambitious in its scope. In the agreement, the economic aspects of the relationship are complemented with a range of other sectors – including political dialogue; social and cultural cooperation; education, science and technology – with a view to providing a 'framework for the gradual integration between Russia and a wider area of cooperation in Europe' (PCA, Article 1). This was indeed a much more ambitious agenda for rapprochement and convergence compared with mere trade and cooperation as envisaged by the PCA. The Russians were driving a hard bargain, basically refusing to take any of the European Commission's (EC) proposals at face value. This was the case especially in the economic field where Russia repeatedly pushed for more trade concessions and a more generous long-term perspective in the form of a free trade area than what was envisaged in the Commission's original mandate. Further, the EC's insistence on political conditionality was a source of concern for the Russians, resulting in additional difficulties in the negotiation process. Second, the EC was less than forthcoming in meeting the Russian demands. Some member states in particular were slow to respond to the Russian requests and when they did so, it was usually in response to the domestic difficulties that the increasingly beleaguered President Yeltsin and his team of reformers were facing in Russia. In essence, the EC was constantly fearful of 'losing' Russia, which could have resulted in a rollback of Russian democracy and economic reforms in the country.

In the second phase (1994-2000), Russia's overall foreign policy started to change from the pro-Western orientation towards an emphasis on multiple partnerships. Not only did the importance of the West as a partner diminish on a general level, but the relationship with the EU faced serious concrete problems in putting the agreed mechanisms in place. Due to the First Chechen War, the ratification of the PCA was delayed by three years. At the same time, Russia had already started to question the very basis on which it was negotiated. In spite of this, cooperation with the EU was still seen as highly desirable. Even far-reaching objectives were not excluded at the time, as exemplified in the words of the then Prime Minister, Victor Chernomyrdin, who declared that "our entire scope of work is directed toward one objective – that Russia can become a member of the EU-Russia" (quoted in Forsberg and Haukkala, 2016: 22). Yet, in actual fact, the window to kick-start relations proved to be fleeting. In August 1998, the Russian economy was in free fall, forcing the Russian government to default on its debts and allowing the rouble to devalue in an uncontrolled manner. To all intents and purposes this setback was seen as a mortal blow to Russia's successful transition to a working and growing market economy. The Kosovo war in 1999 – although not a particular crisis between the EU and Russia per se (see Maass, 2016: ch. 1), as it was a NATO operation with the United States bearing the main responsibility – nevertheless burdened Russia's view of the West in general. A renewed break in the relations was caused by the Second Chechen War in 1999, as the EU regarded Russia's use of force as a violation of earlier commitments, disproportionate and hindering a political solution to the crisis.

The strains, however, soon dissipated and the third phase in Russia's policy towards the EU, coinciding with Putin's first term as President of Russia (2000-2004), was generally marked by optimism and progress in developing Russia-EU relations, particularly in the beginning. Putin's "European vocation" was perceived to be guiding his foreign policy orientation. The positive attitude towards the EU was plain, for example, in Putin's famous speech delivered in German at the *Bundestag* in 2001. "As for European integration", Putin declared, "we not just support[ing] these processes, but we are looking to them with hope". On this basis, Russia was eager to develop relations with the EU, and out of these efforts, the idea of Four Common Spaces that became the landmark of the relations was created. The negotiations over the content of the document started in 2001 and the document was accepted at the St. Petersburg Summit in May 2003:

1   The Common Economic Space, covering economic issues and the environment.
2   The Common Space of Freedom, Security and Justice.
3   The Common Space of External Security, including crisis management and non-proliferation.
4   The Common Space of Research and Education, including cultural aspects.

Discord started to increase again during Putin's second presidency (2004-2008), a period that can be seen as the fourth phase in the relations. As Dmitry Trenin (2006) declared in his *Foreign Affairs* article, "Russia's leaders have given up on becoming part of the West and have started creating their own Moscow-centered system". Surely, Russia was still interested in developing relations with the EU, but it was much more concerned that it should take place on the basis of equality and reciprocity in terms of searching for compromised solutions where both parties moved (Likhachev, 2006). The four "common spaces" were still elaborated at the Moscow Summit in May 2005, when the parties agreed on "road maps" on how these common spaces were to be put into effect, but the negotiations proved to be difficult. The problems manifested in trade disputes, security cooperation and clashes over values. As a result, the relations stagnated and the parties were not able to renegotiate the PCA that was meant to expire in 2007.

There is probably no single overwhelming reason why Russia's, and President Putin's attitude to be more precise, towards the EU started to cool after the initial years. The problems related to EU enlargement and the right of Russians to travel between Kaliningrad and the rest of Russia without visa was still solved on the basis of a compromise. Yet, the Russians started to feel that the European leaders and opinion builders were not treating Russia in a fair way, but were criticizing Russian conduct in all kinds of situations, be it the siege of the school in Beslan or the arrest of the leading oligarch of the time, Mikhail Khodorkovsky or other alleged human rights violations. One of the clearest disappointments related to foreign policy issues was in late 2003 when Putin's envoy, Dmitri Kozak, made an attempt to resolve the Transnistrian conflict by securing a Moldovan-Transnistrian agreement with the Moldovan President Vladimir Voronin, but the EU intervened and resisted the plan that would have entailed a federal structure for the country. Yet the biggest setback from the Kremlin's perspective was the Orange Revolution in Ukraine in the winter of 2004–2005. The EU's role, in particular, in that context was perceived as negative, because it had intervened in the electoral process and demanded new elections on the basis of election fraud, challenging the Russian blueprint for the future of Ukraine. The relations between the EU and Russia were further burdened by Russia's decision to impose an import ban on Polish meat in November 2005 due to a suspicion that Poland had exported meat to Russia from third countries, where the risk of animal diseases was high. The negative trends culminated in the Russo-Georgian war in 2008.

The Medvedev presidency (2008-2012) – the fifth phase in the evolution of Russian policy towards the EU – was not as strained as the previous period, but to a degree this had less to do with substance and more with the style of Medvedev himself as President. Although the start of Medvedev's presidency witnessed a crisis in Russia's relations with the West due to the war in Georgia, the relationship was normalized very swiftly, and the fact that Russia let the EU play a role as mediator and stabilizer in the conflict was seen as a positive element. Overall, Medvedev's key policy agenda was modernization as a response to Russia's persistent problems of economic backwardness, corruption and paternalistic attitudes, as Medvedev (2009) listed them in his agenda-setting "Go Russia!" article. Although Russia would not follow any foreign model in its reform policies, the EU was "in all respects Russia's most important partner for the purpose of modernisation" (Trenin, 2011: 20). During the Medvedev era, Russia concluded a Partnership for Modernisation in 2010 with the EU as well as a host of bilateral partnerships with EU countries. Trade relations flourished, and cultural and scientific cooperation were expanded, but there were also disappointments. One of the key objectives in Russian policy towards the EU was the abolishment of visas. Although negotiations progressed and technical readiness was improved, the final goal was not reached, and Russia accused the EU of politicizing the issue. Novel steps in cooperation were, however, taken in many issue areas, for example Russia for the first time participated in a EU-led crisis-management operation in Central Africa. Yet, no breakthrough in political relations followed. Most significantly, Medvedev's proposal for a new European Security Treaty did not succeed. Indeed, the reservoir of trust was not strengthened, but skepticism replaced earlier enthusiasm on both sides.

Putin's return to the presidency in 2012 started the sixth and so far the most contested phase in Russia's policy towards the EU, culminating in the rupture of relations in 2014 over the Ukraine conflict. The re-election of Putin as President was seen as disappointing by many EU leaders, and expectations were kept rather low on both sides. Putin's agenda was clearly becoming more assertive both internally as well as externally. This was visible at the otherwise rather amicable Russia-EU Summit in St Petersburg in June 2012 where Putin demanded that the EU should recognize the Eurasian Customs Union, and explained that it was now actually the right counterpart for the formal treaty negotiations between Russia and the EU. Yet, there were also some positive signs in the overall relations. For example, Russia's accession to the WTO in August 2012 was greeted as a progressive step by the West, and particularly before the Sochi Winter Olympic Games in February 2014, there seemed to be a short 'charm offensive' in the relations with the West. However, at about the same time, Putin had also started to propagate Russia's own 'traditional' and conservative values as representing the 'true Europe' and being superior to those prevalent in the liberal and increasingly decadent West (Putin, 2013). Before the Ukraine crisis, problems in Russia-EU relations were caused by a number of contentious issues ranging from the Russian anti-gay propaganda law and the sentencing of the Punk group Pussy Riot, to the civil war in Syria, to trade and energy issues as well as to the EU bailout of the Cypriot banks. The Ukraine crisis, however, became the most flammable topic on this mounting list of disagreements, partly because it was not a bilateral issue but because the events in Ukraine also had their own dynamics. Russia's annexation of Crimea and the warfare in Eastern Ukraine led the EU nevertheless to impose stepwise sanctions on Russia, with Russia replying by countersanctions applied to European imports. Although dialogue with European leaders continued in various bilateral and multilateral formats, political summit meetings on the EU level came to a halt. After three years of the Euromaidan events in Ukraine, not much has changed in Russia-EU relations, but a new confrontational normalcy has set in.

The basic story of the relations is rather familiar to the expert community, but some phases of this history of Russia-EU relations are more contested among researchers than others as interpretations are loaded with political implications. Overall, the relations have constantly evolved between more optimistic and more strained periods, rather than having been a steady linear story from a cooperative relationship towards conflict. Moreover, Russia has not been a mere object of EU policies. It has sometimes been claimed that the EU has imposed its rules and norms at the formative phase of the partnership when Russia was still a weak actor, but we argue that Russia bargained hard and successfully with the EU over the terms of the partnership. Perhaps unwittingly, the institutional framework received deeper forms of post-sovereign principles and the consequent expectation of political conditionality than Russia probably first realized. Another critical nodal point can be seen when Putin's "European vocation" of the early 2000s turned, first, into stagnation and then confrontation. There was clearly a certain accumulation of felt disappointments and frustration on both sides that contributed to the negative trajectory. However, non-linearity applies to this evolution too, since the Medvedev period was distinctively different from Putin's presidencies before and after him. Although no breakthrough in Russia's relations with the EU was achieved, escalating conflicts were avoided, and in many issue areas also steps towards expanding cooperation were taken. The future of the relations remains uncertain at this time of writing, but since the Ukraine crisis, a new normalcy consisting of political confrontation and sanctions but also of continued dialogue and even cooperation in some areas is taking place.

Making of Russian policy

Russia's 1993 Constitution granted the President of the country vast powers and autonomy in foreign and security policy, but the overall relations between Russia and the EU can be seen as consisting of various levels (Romanova, 2013). Although the making of Russian foreign policy is a collective business involving many actors, the President has been the key individual in Russian foreign policy decision-making and has decided over the nature of the relations with the EU. The most visible exception to this was under President Dmitri Medvedev (2008–2012), when the locus of decision-making and the consequent political power largely moved away from the President towards the government headed by Putin as the prime minister (see Lo, 2009). But even then, Medvedev played an essential role in shaping Russia's policy towards the EU.

The scholarly community seems to be in agreement that it is increasingly President Putin and a narrow circle of his colleagues in the Kremlin that take the key decisions (see Kryshtanovskaya and White, 2005; Lo, 2015). Obviously, a strong president-centric image of Russia's policy towards the EU is an oversimplification that does not bear serious scrutiny, but it does point to Putin's extraordinary role as the ultimate leader in Russia. In addition, it also alludes to the need to factor in the biography, psychological dispositions and even personal idiosyncrasies of the President (see Hill and Gaddy, 2015).

Be that as it may, we may nevertheless proceed from a fairly hierarchical understanding of the key players in Russian foreign policy decision-making that stands in stark contrast to the institutional cacophony so evident in the case of the EU. There is also some evidence that suggests the Ukraine conflict has resulted in a further reduction of the inner circle, where Putin and a very small group of trusted confidants make the essential decisions concerning Russian foreign policy at times even outside the formal decision-making structures and mechanisms (see Zygar, 2016). This has the unfortunate side effect of making it harder to gain reliable information about the workings of such closed and often informal groupings and the effect of this dynamism on decision-making in Russia. As to the formal institutions, the Presidential Administration is, in the words of Trenin and Lo (2005: 10), "the true national government", ultimately responsible for the strategic guidance of Russian policies, both domestic and foreign, and answerable only directly to the President. Another institution worth mentioning is the Security Council. Although originally intended to act as an executive tool in foreign and security matters, the Security Council has practically never played a key role in Russian foreign policy (Mankoff, 2009: 55). During Putin's tenure, however, the profile of the Security Council has been significantly upgraded.

The Foreign Ministry is in charge of the implementation of presidential foreign policy and plays a key role in the conduct of day-to-day affairs with the EU. The role of the Foreign Ministry is not always seen as progressive, but writing in the mid-2000s, the former External Relations Commissioner, Chris Patten (2005: 205), noted how the Ministry was the place where one could see the Soviet Union still in existence. Foreign ministers have, at times, become powerful figures in their own right, also in regard to the policy towards the EU. This was the case especially when Andrei Kozyrev and Yevgeny Primakov were foreign ministers. While Kozyrev was associated with the Western orientation in Russian foreign policy, Primakov's doctrine was 'multivectoral'. Sergey Lavrov, who had been serving as foreign minister since 2004, is popular at home and prominent abroad, but it seems that he is not so much driving as loyally executing as far as key decisions of foreign policy are concerned. Yet, especially when it comes to Russia's relations with the EU, the Foreign Ministry tends to have some important influence since it can offer specialists that have the kind of detailed knowledge about the EU that is often, and rather surprisingly, lacking in the highest echelons of Russian decision-making. The Mission of the Russian Federation to the EU plays a key role here, and its head, Ambassador Vladimir Chizhov, has occupied a very visible position in EU-Russia relations during his ten-year tenure.

Traditionally, prime ministers in Russia have been implementers of presidential directives rather than political leaders of their own. However, during Putin's tenure as prime minister, the authority and power of this office grew immensely, assuming a leading role in Russian politics, only to lose that position once Putin moved back to the Kremlin. Other sectoral ministers also have relevance for relations with the EU, such as economic development and trade and finance. This is due to the multi-sectoral nature of EU-Russia interaction itself, which has strongly emphasized economic issues and cooperation, giving the specialists in these ministries added significance compared with some other bread and butter issues of foreign and security policies. The Ministry of Economic Development, for example, is a very important actor in EU-Russia relations, with its own mission responsible for trade in Brussels, and often represents a more liberal attitude than the MID.

Although the Federal Assembly and its two chambers, the Council of the Federation and the State Duma, officially enjoy a respected role in constructing foreign policy, the parliament and its deputies have become increasingly marginalized in the actual making or even approving of the policy (Mankoff, 2009: 54). They have, however, an important role as the official talking shop of the country, and the representatives often support and explain Russian positions to the outside world. For example, the chair of the Duma's foreign affairs committee, Alexei Pushkov, has often publicly brought up Russian concerns in diverse fora related to relations with the EU or its member states. There are also direct linkages between the parliamentarians conducted in the framework of the EU-Russia Parliamentary Cooperation Committee.

A number of federal subjects – most of them being regions, some of them cities – that constitute the Russian federation have also played a role in Russia's overall relations with the EU. According to the Russian constitution, the federal subjects have some formal powers to influence foreign policy decisions within the federal system as well as to establish and carry out external policies of their own. They can conclude treaties, establish representative offices, make statements, attract foreign investments and tourism, and cooperate in many other ways with international bodies (Busygina, 2007; Sergunin, 2008). The federal subjects that were relevant, especially with regard to relations with the EU, were the regions adjacent to EU member states, in particular, Kaliningrad, Karelia and Pskov, which have participated in the so-called Euroregion schemes, such as Euregion Karelia across the Finnish-Russian border, Euregion Pskov-Livonia including the Lake Peipsi project across the Estonian-Russian border or Euroregion Baltic around Kaliningrad (see Roll et al., 2001; Aalto, 2002; Huisman, 2002; Browning and Joenniemi, 2004). The most active period of the involvement of the federal subjects in the external relations was in the 1990s and the early 2000s, after which such activities were curtailed rather effectively by the Kremlin. The regions nevertheless concluded hundreds of international agreements, and many of them sought tighter contacts with their foreign partners. Although the federal authorities have contested many of these agreements and replaced regional leaders who have been perceived as too independent, some forms of crossborder cooperation have continued. Crimea and Sevastopol are special cases in the list of the federal subjects because they have not been recognized by the EU as being part of Russia.

Traditionally, Russians have held very positive views of the EU (Tumanov et al., 2011: 141). At the same time, it is doubtful whether this positive image has ever really been based on any detailed understanding of what the EU entails, or whether the responses rather reflect the positive connotations connected with Europe in general (Semenenko, 2013). The popular support in Russia for EU membership – even if the question can be regarded as hypothetical – nevertheless declined from 50 per cent to under 30 in the early 2000s. Yet, according to the polls conducted by Pew Research Center (2015), in 2013 nearly two-thirds of Russians still felt favourably disposed towards the EU. The EU's image has been on a consistently higher level than that of the United States, not to mention NATO. Of the member states, Germany in particular deserves to be mentioned as it has traditionally been seen as the key player inside the EU. During the conflict in Ukraine, however, the perception of the EU, along with that of Germany and the United States, took a marked turn for the worse. In 2015 only about one-third of Russians (still) regarded the EU favourably. As a result, the image of the EU is now almost on a par with the traditional adversaries, the United States and NATO, whereas China is regarded as Russia's closest friend (see also VCIOM, 2014 and Levada-Center, 2015). The negative trend has also impacted Germany's image, which was perceived as being under the tutelage of the United States rather than being an autonomous actor (VCIOM, 2015). A poll conducted by Levada in November 2015 revealed that 75 per cent of respondents said that Russia should mend fences with the West. At the same time, 65 per cent of respondents saw that Russia should seek to accomplish this without undue compromises in its policies vis-à-vis the West (Hartog, 2015). The Russian media representations of the EU have also become more negative: the EU is seen as weak but still a competitor, and it is often de-personified as an entity (Chaban et al., 2017).

Russia's policy impact

There has been some discussion over Russia's influence on the EU and the policies of the member states. While Russia has had a degree of success in fostering its objectives with regard to the individual member states, its access and lobbying capacity at the EU level has been rather limited as exemplified by some key EU decisions in the energy sector. On the other hand, Russia has been rather effective in reasserting its great power status vis-à-vis the EU, and it has been difficult for the EU to influence Russia's position radically in any of the key issues on the agenda, a fact that should be seen in comparison with the sometimes major impact of EU policies in the states of its Eastern neighbourhood.

Since the mid-2000s, but particularly against the backdrop of the 2014 crisis and conflict in Ukraine, the debate over Russia's influence has concerned its 'soft power' in particular (Rutland and Kazantsev, 2016). Divergent views exist in this regard. On the one hand, some argue that Russia's soft power, tantamount to tactics of 'hybrid warfare', poses a danger to the EU and its member states, undermining common policies and creating undemocratic practices, for example through supporting right-wing groups (Schoen, 2016). Peter Pomerantsev and Michael Weiss (2014) see that "the Kremlin exploits systemic weak spots in the Western system, providing a sort of X-ray of the underbelly of liberal democracy". On the other hand, others hold that Russia's attempts to use soft power do not wield much influence. For example, Joseph Nye (2013) is sceptical about Russia's soft power: "although Putin has urged his diplomats to wield soft power, Russia does not have much". The debate has become sensitive since not all those opinions that are favourable to Russia and its behaviour, particularly in the Ukraine crisis, can be seen as evidence of Russian influence. What we know is that influence attempts exist; some support Russian views, but the majority of the EU populace has not been persuaded by the Russian positions and information campaigns. Russia's image has certainly not been enhanced, and very few believe in Russia's narrative of the Ukraine conflict, while the concrete decisions at the EU level have not been to Russia's liking. Although Brexit was mainly greeted in Russia, it cannot be counted as a success of Russian policy towards the EU.

Explaining Russian policy

For researchers interested in Russian foreign policy, the main question is often whether this policy is driven by power or ideology, as classically stated by George Kennan (1947) with regard to the Soviet Union or by such factors as geopolitics, security, economic interest, status or identity. It can be argued that all of these are enduring goals of Russia's foreign policy (Donaldson and Nogee, 2014), but there are also more nuanced discussions on the basis of which both temporal and geographical variation is explained. Russia's policy towards Europe has typically been indicative of its overall essence.

The old debate concerning Russian foreign policy was mostly framed between what – in IR parlance – are known as offensive and defensive realists, namely those who see hegemony and territorial expansion as the ultimate goal of Russia's foreign policy, and those who see Russia's interests more in terms of its defensive security needs. Alongside these two accounts, a growing number of scholars and pundits see Russia's foreign policy more in terms of maximizing economic gains rather than security. Some associate Russia's economic interest with the nation as a whole, some with the growth of the leading sector – gas and energy – while still others think that the economic interest is defined by an even smaller group of people who hold power and want to profit from it. In the words of Dmitri Trenin (2007), Russia's business is business. Sometimes this debate over the fundamental nature of Russian foreign policy can be simplified between two positions, namely between those who emphasize Russian national interest as a rational choice (Schleifer and Treisman, 2011), and those who think that various cultural, sociological and psychological factors play a significant role in Russian foreign policy formulation in a manner that obscures any straightforward notion of rationality (Forsberg and Pursiainen, 2017).

Domestic political explanations also surface quite often when Russian foreign policy is analysed. There are three basic variants. First, is the proposition that the regime type in itself affects Russia's relations with the Western powers (Lynch, 2016). Second, domestic political explanations may refer to the changes in the domestic constellations of power, and the policy shifts deriving from these changes. In the case of Russia, there have been no conspicuous changes of the governing elite, but alleged changes within the elite. The interests of the business elite were geared towards cooperation with Europe (Stowe, 2001). Hence, the relative decline of the liberal elite and the rise of the siloviki in the early 2000s potentially explains the shift in Russia's foreign policy away from the Western and European orientation (Kryshtanovskaya, 2008). Another variant of domestic political explanation would be the diversionary theory of conflict, whereby conflict is an outcome of power holders who have domestic difficulties and who want to increase or restore their popularity by creating an external conflict. This chimes quite well with Russia's behaviour to a degree, as Yeltsin started to adopt a critical stance towards the EU as his popularity waned. The recent phase of the conflict between the EU and Russia can be related to fears that Putin's regime might be challenged at home, but the more conflictual period started well before Putin had any problems with the support of the masses in Russia. Margot Light and David Cadier (2015) have nevertheless concluded that regime consolidation has been the main objective of Russia's contemporary foreign policy behaviour.

The sociological and psychological perspectives often start from the premise that Russian foreign policy is driven by identity concerns, since interests are defined on the basis of a certain identity (Hopf, 2002; Tsygankov, 2016; Neumann, 2017). Identity-based explanations typically emphasize that Europe has been Russia's most significant 'Other' and that Russia is a status-seeker trying to restore and strengthen its position as a great power and acquire recognition for it (Medvedev and Neumann, 2012; Leichtova, 2014; Schiffers, 2015), but they also have entailed Russia's desire to be regarded as a European country endowed with attributes like democracy and a market economy (Splidsboel-Hansen, 2002). Such explanations are sometimes discussed from the perspective of role theory (Grossmann, 2005). Identity-based theories often come close to domestic explanations when shifts in Russian identity are explained through the discursive preponderance of a certain school of thought. The traditional way of distinguishing between two intellectual groupings in Russia's foreign policy thinking, Westernizers and Slavophiles, has offered a powerful way of looking at this debate through lenses of identity (Neumann, 2017). Yet, changes in identity are often connected not simply to the intellectual debate but to the wider spectrum of discursive structural pressures (Clunan, 2009; Makarychev, 2014). Stephen White and Valentina Feklyunina (2014) have identified three basic identity discourses in Russia, arguing that the first discourse regarded Russia as a part of Europe, as defined by the West – a view that was predominant in the early 1990s. But subsequently, the mainstream view was based on the understanding that Russia was an equal and constituent part of the EU-centric Europe, while the third discourse emphasizing Russia's normative superiority vis-à-vis the EU-centric 'Europe' has been in the ascendancy recently. Moreover, negative images of the EU have also emerged and become sticky in the course of interaction of the two parties where various psychological mechanisms such as attribution error – the habit to interpret the behavior of the other on the basis of pre-formed negative conceptions – have led to the increasingly negative image of the EU in Russia (Casier, 2016).

Closely linked to identity and power, status is not always seen as a separate foreign policy motivation, but it is quite intriguing to take this perspective seriously with regard to Russia, given Russia's often expressed desire to be a great power respected as such by others (Clunan, 2009; Larson and Shevchenko, 2014; Tsygankov, 2012). Status theories may explain why Russia has been interested in creating and developing a partnership with the EU, since Russian leaders have seen Russia as a European power and cooperation with other European great powers has been a traditional reference group and symbolic arena of its diplomatic presence. At the same time, status theories can account for Russia's constant problems in its relations with the EU, since the EU has both questioned the Russian commitment to European values and relegated its position of a great power to that of a junior partner. Although Russia had the privileged status of a strategic partner, it was still a third party rather than equal to the EU when rules and norms were negotiated, and not even on a par with great powers inside the EU when decisions in Brussels were taken. Russia's identity thus changed, and it distanced itself from Europe as defined by the EU.

There is again no hard evidence to hand that would validate one account and disprove the others. They all offer relevant perspectives on Russia-EU relations. One means of combining them has been through neoclassical realism. As Elena Kropatcheva (2012: 38) has argued, in order to understand Russian foreign policy towards the West, "both the domestic context of action – material power capabilities, subjective self-perception and perception of international realities – as well as objective changes in the international context, that is the actions of the West, have to be taken into account". Typically, however, we would expect Russia to seek cooperation with Europe if defensive security, economic gain in the long term, or just European identity were the primary driving forces behind Russia's foreign policy. On the other hand, if Russia's foreign policy is driven by the goal of territorial expansion or the short-term economic interest of a particular ruling elite, we would expect conflict. We would also expect conflict if Russian foreign policy is driven by identity, if identity duly means that there is a growing need to underline that Russia is special in some way, and different from Europe (Neumann, 2017). Status – or honour – would, according to Andrei Tsygankov (2012), lead to cooperative behaviour if granted to Russia, but to conflict if status were denied, particularly when Russia itself is confident of its own status.

Although Russian foreign policy in general would be driven by all of the aforementioned goals, certain emphases in Russia's relations with the EU can be discerned. As the EU is not a fully fledged military actor, it is rather understandable that security concerns have not been primary in Russia's policy towards the EU. Most prominently, security concerns have emerged when Russia has assumed that EU enlargement would also lead to NATO enlargement. Yet security cooperation has been rather limited, even when the threat perception has been mutual. Economic interests have often predominated, but economic motives cannot provide an explanation for every political objective or trade dispute with the EU. Russia's identity position towards the EU has been contested in the Russian domestic debate. Russian leaders have emphasized both Russia's Europeanness and its distinctive features. Status often seems to be at stake. For example, foreign minister Sergey Lavrov (2013) very clearly indicated that the biggest problem in the EU's attitude towards Russia is that it does not treat it as an equal partner. Russia's willingness to establish a Eurasian Union comparable to the EU can also be seen as a sign of status politics.

Overall, Russian policy towards the EU has mainly pursued its economic interests. Russia has favoured partnership and cooperation, refraining from using energy as a weapon against the EU, but it has also safeguarded its sovereignty as well as its own economic benefits in various disputes. After the Ukraine crisis, attempts have been take towards reducing economic interdependence with the EU and some cultural distancing was already taking place before the crisis. Security questions entered into the relations when the eastern enlargement started to encroach on critical areas, Ukraine in particular, with Russia vehemently protecting its sovereignty in all fields. It is an open question to what extent EU presence in the Eastern European countries was seen as an irreversible step towards full Western integration with NATO (all countries that so far have joined NATO did so before joining the EU), or whether the EU neighbourhood policy rather challenged Russian regional leadership and its ambition to build a Eurasian Union. Status concerns can explain why Russia has been willing to cooperate with the EU, but has been disappointed and has protested when its status as an 'equal partner' or as a great power with its own sphere of influence has not been respected. Identity concerns and the representation of 'Europe' as an Other became gradually more visible after the Russian attempt to become accepted as legitimately and fully 'European' failed towards the end of Putin's first term as President. Yet, there is a lot of uncertainty when it comes to validating explanations for the true motivations behind Russian foreign policy since access to the decision-making process has been so restricted: the competition between two perspectives – domestic political motivation or the elite interests driving Russian foreign policy on the one hand, and national interests defined in terms of humiliating experiences, fears and strategic objectives on the other – are not easy to resolve.

Conclusions

Russian policy towards the EU has evolved in several phases. We have argued that the development has not been linear, but it has waned between more cooperative and confrontational relations. Overall, the relations have depended more on the general perception of the national interests and the role of the EU as a partner rather than on the specific issues. Russia's key interests were related to economy and identity, but in the 2000s, particularly after the Orange revolution in the Ukraine, they started to include security aspects too. The view of the EU as partner has been devalued, but it only changed clearly for the worse before the Ukrainian crisis and has stayed negative since. Nevertheless, Russia still sees the EU as a potential partner, though the EU is regarded as weak and decaying and harbouring bad intentions against Russia.

Research on Russian policy towards the EU has been fairly rich and comprehensive in the overall context of Russia's foreign policy, but much of that research has focused on policy issues and has been descriptive and often prescriptive in nature. At present, no single theory or approach dominates the field, but diverse theoretical schools and explanations coexist. Even within such theoretical approaches there is little consensus as to what direction Russian foreign policy is going to take in the longer run. Sadly, in the present situation, scholarly camps tend to be formed more on the basis of their political content than on theoretical grounds, which has confused theory development. Future research, however, should be able to distance itself from the dangers of presentism and political instrumentalism without losing the purpose of offering understanding as well as concrete proposals and guidance on how the relationship between Russia and the EU could be restored and improved.

References

Aalto, P. (2002) 'A European Geopolitical Subject in the Making? EU, Russia and the Kaliningrad Question', *Geopolitics*, 7(3): 143–74.
Browning, C. and P. Joenniemi (2004) 'Regionality Beyond Security? The Baltic Sea Region after Enlargement', *Cooperation and Conflict*, 39(3): 233–53.
Busygina, I. (2007) 'Russia's Regions in Shaping National Foreign Policy', in J. Gower and G. Timmins (eds), *Russia and Europe in the Twenty-First Century: An Uneasy Partnership* (London: Anthem Press).
Busygina, I. (2017) *Russia-EU Relations and the Common Neighborhood* (Abington: Routledge).
Casier, T. (2016) 'From Logic of Competition to Conflict', *Contemporary Politics*, 22(3): 376–393.
Casier, T. and Debardeleben, J. eds. (2018) *EU-Russia Relations in Crisis* (Abington: Routledge).
Chaban, N., Elgström, O. and Gulyaeva, O. (2017) 'Russian Images of the European Union: Before and After Maidan', *Foreign Policy Analysis*, 13(2): 480–499.
Clunan, Anne (2009) *The Social Construction of Russia's Resurgence: Aspirations, Identity and Security Interests* (Baltimore, MD: The Johns Hopkins University Press).
Ćwiek-Karpowicz, J. (2012) 'Limits to Russian Soft Power in the Post-Soviet Area', DGAP Analyse 8. Berlin: Deutsche Gesellschaft für Auswärtige Politik.
Donaldson, R. and J. Nogee (2014) *The Foreign Policy of Russia: Changing Systems, Enduring Interests*, 5th edn (Abingdon, UK: Routledge).

Forsberg, T and H. Haukkala (2016) *The European Union and Russia* (London: Palgrave Macmillan).
Forsberg, T and C. Pursiainen (2017) 'The Psychological Dimension of Russian Foreign Policy: Putin and the Annexation of Crimea', *Global Society*, 31(2): 220–244.
Grossmann, M. (2005) 'Role Theory and Foreign Policy Change,' *International Politics*, 4(3): 334–351.
Hartog, E. (2015) 'Russians Want Better Ties with West, But No Change in Policy: Poll', *Moscow Times*, December 2.
Haukkala, H. (2010) *The EU–Russia Strategic Partnership: The Limits of Post-Sovereignty in International Relations* (Oxford, UK: Routledge).
Hill, F. and C. Gaddy (2015) *Mr. Putin: Operative in Kremlin*, 2nd edn (Washington, DC: Brookings Institution Press).
Hopf, T. (2002) *Social Construction of International Politics: Identities and Foreign Policies, Moscow 1955 and 1999* (Ithaca, NY: Cornell University Press).
Huisman, S. (2002) 'A New European Union Policy for Kaliningrad', *Occasional Paper no. 33* (Paris: European Union Institute for Security Studies).
Jonsson, A. (2012) 'Russian and Europe', in G. Gill and J. Young (eds), *Routledge Handbook of Russian Politics and Society* (Abingdon, UK: Routledge).
Kennan, G [under the pseudonym X] (1947) 'The Sources of Soviet Conduct', *Foreign Affairs*, 25(4): 566–82.
Kropatcheva, E. (2012) 'Russian Foreign Policy in the Realm of European Security through the Lens of Neoclassical Realism', *Journal of Eurasian Studies*, 3(1): 30–40.
Kryshtanovskaya, O. (2008) 'The Russian Elite in Transition', *Journal of Communist Studies and Transition Politics*, 24(4): 585–603.
Kryshtanovskaya, O. and S. White (2005) 'Inside the Putin Court: A Research Note', *Europe-Asia Studies*, 57(7): 1065–75.
Larson D. and A. Shevchenko (2014) 'Russia Says No: Power, Status, and Emotions in Foreign Policy', *Communist and Post-Communist Studies*, 47(3–4): 269–279.
Lavrov, S. (2013) 'Russia-EU: Prospects for Partnership in the Changing World', *Journal of Common Market Studies*, 51 (Annual Review): 6–12.
Leichtova, M. (2014) *Misunderstanding Russia: Russian Foreign Policy and the West* (Farnham, UK: Ashgate).
Levada-Center (2015) 'International Relations', *Press Release*, 16 October, www.levada.ru/eng/international-relations-0, accessed 13 February 2017.
Light M. and D. Cadier (2015) 'Introduction', in Cadier, D. and M. Light (eds) *Russia's Foreign Policy: Ideas, Domestic Politics and External Relations* (London: Palgrave Macmillan).
Likhachev, V. (2006) 'Russia and the European Union', *International Affairs (Moscow)*, 52(2): 102–14.
Lo, B. (2009) 'Medvedev and the new European Security Architecture', *Policy Brief Paper* (London: Center for European Reform).
Lo, B. (2015) *Russia and the New World Disorder* (London and Washington, DC: Chatham House and Brookings).
Lynch, Allen (2016) 'The Influence of Regime Type on Russian Foreign Policy Toward "the West," 1992–2015', *Communist and Post-Communist Studies* 49(1): 101–111.
Maass, A.-S. (2016) *EU–Russia Relations (1999–2015): From Courtship to Confrontation* (Abingdon, UK: Routledge).
Makarychev, A. (2014) *Russia and the EU in a Multipolar World* (Stuttgart: Ibidem).
Mankoff, J. (2009) *Russian Foreign Policy: The Return of Great Power Politics* (Lanham, MD: Rowman & Littlefield).
Medvedev, D. (2009) *Go Russia!*, September 10, http://en.kremlin.ru/events/president/news/5413, accessed 28 May 2015.
Neumann, I. B. (2017 [1996]) *Russia and the Idea of Europe. A Study in Identity and International Relations* (London: Routledge).
Nye, J. (2013) 'What China and Russia Don't Get About Soft Power', *Foreign Policy Online*, April 29, http://foreignpolicy.com/2013/04/29/what-china-and-russia-dont-get-about-soft-power/.
Patten, C. (2005) *Not Quite the Diplomat: Home Truths about World Affairs* (London: Penguin Books).
Pew Research Center (2015) 'Russian Public Opinion: Putin Praised, West Panned', 10 June, www.pewglobal.org/2015/06/10/2-russianpublic-opinion-putin-praised-west-panned/, accessed 13 December 2015.
Pomerantsev; P. and M. Weiss (2014) 'The Menace of Unreality: How the Kremlin Weaponizes Information, Culture and Money', *The Interpreter*, 22 November, www.interpretermag.com/themenace-of-unreality-how-the-kremlin-weaponizes-information- cultureand-money/, accessed 13 December 2015.

Prozorov, S. (2006) *Understanding Conflict Between Russia and the EU: The Limits of Integration* (Basingstoke, UK: Palgrave).
Pursiainen, C. (2008) 'Theories of Integration and the Limits of EU–Russian Relations', in T. Hopf (ed.) *Russia's European Choice* (Basingstoke, UK: Palgrave Macmillan): 149–86.
Putin, V. (2001) Speech in the Bundestag, Berlin, 25 September.
Putin, V. (2013) 'Vladimir Putin Meets with Members the Valdai International Discussion Club', *Transcript of the speech and beginning of the meeting*, 20 September, http://valdaiclub.com/politics/62880.html, accessed 4 June 2017.
Roll, G., T. Maximova and E. Mikenberg (2001) 'The External Relations of the Pskov Oblast of the Russian Federation', *SHIFFE-Texte no. 63* (Kiel, Germany: Schleswig-Holstein Institute for Peace Research, Christian-Albrechts-University Kiel).
Romanova, T. (2015) 'Исследования отношений россии и евросоюза в нашей стране и за рубежом (1992-2015 гг.)' [The Russia-EU relationship research at home and abroad (from 1992-2015)]. *Современная Европа* 5: 100–114.
Romanova, T. (2017) 'EU-Russian Relations', in N. Tsvetkova (eds) *Russia and the World: Understanding International Relations* (London: Lexington Books), 357–373.
Rutland, P. and A. Kazantsev (2016) 'The Limits of Russia's "Soft Power"', *Journal of Political Power* 9(3): 395–413.
Schiffers, S. (2015) 'A Decade of Othering,' *East European Quarterly*, 43(1).
Schleifer, A. and D. Treisman (2011) 'Why Moscow Says No', *Foreign Affairs*, 90(1): 122–38.
Schmidt-Felzmann, A. (2015) 'European Foreign Policy Towards Russia,' in K.E. Jergensen, A. Kalland Aarstad, E. Drieskens, K. Laatikainen, and B. Tonra (eds) *The Sage Handbook of European Foreign Policy* (London: Sage)
Schoen, D. (2016) *Putin's Master Plan: To Destroy Europe, Divide NATO and Restore Russian Power and Global Influence.* New York: Encounter Books.
Semenenko, I. (2013) 'The Quest for Identity: Russian Public Opinion on Europe and the European Union and the National Identity Agenda', *Perspectives on European Politics and Society*, 14(1): 102–22.
Sergunin, A. (2008) 'Russian Foreign-Policy Decision Making on Europe', in T. Hopf (ed.) *Russia's European Choice* (Basingstoke, UK and New York: Palgrave Macmillan), 59–93.
Sergunin, A. (2016) *Explaining Russian Foreign Policy Behavior: Theory and Practice* (Stuttgart, Germany: Ibidem).
Smith, N. R. (2016) *EU-Russian Relations and the Ukraine Crisis* (Cheltenham, UK: Edward Elgar).
Splidsboel-Hansen, F. (2002) 'Russia's Relations with the European Union: A Constructivist Cut', *International Politics*, 39(4): 399–421.
Stowe, R. (2001) 'Foreign Policy Preferences of the New Russian Business Elite', *Problems of Post-Communism*, 48(3): 49–58.
Thorun, C. (2009) *Explaining Change in Russian Foreign Policy: The Role of Ideas in Post-Soviet Russia's Conduct Towards the West* (Basingstoke, UK: Palgrave Macmillan).
Trenin, D. (2006) 'Russia Leaves the West', *Foreign Affairs*, 85(4): 87–96.
Trenin, D. (2011) 'Modernizing Russian Foreign Policy', *Russian Politics and Law*, 49(6): 8–37.
Trenin, D. and B. Lo (2005) *The Landscape of Russian Foreign Policy Decision-Making* (Moscow: Moscow Center of the Carnegie Endowment for International Peace).
Tsygankov, A. (2016) *Russia's Foreign Policy: Change and Continuity in National Identity*, 4th ed. (Lanham, MD: Rowman & Littlefield).
Tsygankov, A. (2012) *Russia and the West from Alexander to Putin: Honour in International Relations* (Cambridge, UK: Cambridge University Press).
Tumanov, A., S. Gasparishvili and T. Romanova (2011) 'Russia–EU Relations, or How the Russians Really View the EU', *Journal of Communist Studies and Transition Politics*, 27(1): 120–41.
VCIOM (2014) 'Russia's Friends and Enemies in Time of Sanctions', *Press Release, No. 1681*, (Moscow: Vserossijski Centr Izuchenija Obshchestvennogo Mnenija), www.wciom.com/index.php?id=61&uid=1008, accessed 16 February 2016.
VCIOM (2015) 'Russia and Germany: From Partnership to Confrontation', September 18, (Moscow: Vserossijskij Centr Izuchenija Obshchestvennogo Mnenija), www.wciom.com/index.php?id=61&uid=1181, accessed 16 February 2017.
White, S. and V. Feklyunina (2014) *Identities and Foreign Policies in Russia, Ukraine and Belarus: The Other Europes* (Basingstoke, UK: Palgrave Macmillan).
Zygar, M. (2016) *All the Kremlin's Men: Inside the Court of Vladimir Putin* (New York: PublicAffairs).

17

CENTRAL AND EASTERN EUROPE

Dmitry Ofitserov-Belskiy

NATIONAL RESEARCH UNIVERSITY, HIGHER SCHOOL OF ECONOMICS, RUSSIA

Andrey Sushenstov

MGIMO UNIVERSITY, RUSSIA

Russian foreign policy in Central and Eastern Europe in the post-Cold war period followed the track of the evolution of its general foreign policy strategy. After the Second World War countries of Central and Eastern Europe were either Soviet republics or fell under the sphere of interests of the USSR. The following dissolution of the socialist bloc and the Soviet Union itself resulted in fundamental geopolitical changes in the region, erasing the solid military and political frontier that divided Europe on the borders of the GDR, Czechoslovakia and Hungary. New states took shape out of what was left of former socialist republics. The region became split and uneven politically. Moscow itself was no longer a political center for Central and Eastern Europe. It became the capital of a remote state that had no common borders with most of the Eastern European countries. Russia-NATO relations that used to be the basis of the continental politics lost their sense of certainty, having opened up room for experiments. Russia faced the challenge of shaping its foreign policy afresh, taking into consideration the changing environment on its western border.

The geopolitical configuration of Central and Eastern Europe is what makes this region especially important for Russian foreign policy. Its intermediate position in between Russia and the Euro-Atlantic makes it an arena for either cooperation or rivalry between the two power centers on the continent. Metaphorically put, this region may serve as a bridge over the chasm between Russia and NATO, or it may become a battlefield for the two. Apart from security concerns, there is also a factor of gas and oil transit via this territory, which explains Moscow's interest to ensure the safety of energy supply through Eastern to Western Europe, where its end consumers are.

Scholars of Russian foreign policy in Central and Eastern Europe largely disagree on its motives and goals. The key disagreement is between two approaches. One group of scholars argues that Russian policy inherently aims for expansion encouraged by imperial complexes (McFaul, 1998; Sherr, 2013; Umland, 2016) or ethnic and nationalist impulses (Rutland, 2014; Zevelev, 2014; Motyl, 2016). The other group believes that Moscow's primary concern is to ensure its national security and protect its values (Bogaturov, 2007; Mearsheimer, 2014; Tsygankov, 2015; Graham, 2017). Academic debates on issues of Russian foreign policy today are overly politicized. It is not clear how soon the academic sphere will break free from the extremes of the emotional load that is caused by the major conflict between Russia and the West over Ukraine.

Regional context: integration and disintegration in Central and Eastern Europe

There were different opinions on the end of the Cold War among the contemporaries, but these events undoubtedly came as a big shock. Formerly, all the countries in the region were integrated in economic, political and military spheres. The idea to preserve these ties had a positive response among the new Central and Eastern European states, especially with the establishment of the EU in Western Europe and the signing of the NAFTA agreement. In the early 1990s, international integration was perceived as inevitable. Russia expected to be a part of new European processes, yet was marginalized and later viewed as a threat.

The first result that came out of these integration experiments in the region was the Visegrad Group of Czechoslovakia, Poland and Hungary (February 1991). The member-states of the Group did not share a truly complex interdependence with each other. Within Soviet rigid hierarchical structures satellite states normally developed close ties with the leader of a bloc, but rarely did they have dependency among themselves. After the Socialist bloc was dissolved, its former members could hardly use their recent experience. Still, each of these counties had learnt from the socialist commonwealth how to cooperate within the framework of common interests. This experience influenced the perception of goals and means of European integration by the countries in the region. The Visegrad Group members proclaimed that the core aim of their integration project was joining the EU and NATO structures and refraining from formal institutionalization of the Group. Later on, the Visegrad countries demonstrated their inability to jointly assert their common interests in a united Europe. Russia was not focused on what was going on in the former socialist countries, but was irritated by their desire to join NATO and the EU.

Gravitation towards the West as a new center of power brought to life new forms of cooperation institutions in the post-Soviet space. They kept emerging in the shape of GUAM (Organization for Democracy and Economic Development for Georgia, Ukraine, Azerbaijan and Moldova), the Community of Democratic Choice and the Eastern Partnership. Yet only the latter managed to formulate a clear cooperation program, and it did little to fit with the real goals of the post-Soviet countries' elites.

The Eastern Partnership's grand architect was the Polish Foreign Ministry, which meant to make the program an extension to the European Neighborhood Policy. Building close ties between the EU and several former USSR member-states, namely Belarus, Ukraine, Moldova, Armenia, Azerbaijan and Georgia, was officially proclaimed the goal of the Partnership. The program defined by the European Commission included administrative reforms, training of state officials, measures to fight corruption, and development of civil institutions and independent media in the post-Soviet member-states. Other dimensions of the program included harmonization of the legislation of these states with that of the EU and establishment of free trade zones with the countries within the Partnership later – when they joined the WTO. European politicians expected that Western business would become an alternative for Russian state-controlled companies in the region, while the EU good governance programs would help eliminate corruption and weaken Russian influence. Other goals concerned diversification of energy sources and organization of their transit and supply bypassing Russia. In the long-term perspective, the program headed towards integration with the EU energy market. Liberalization of the visa regime between the EU and the Partnership member countries was another goal, so was the plan to take measures to curb illegal migration.

Moscow perceived the Eastern Partnership as potentially destabilizing, aiming to eliminate Russia's influence in the European part of the post-Soviet space by hindering Russia's own initiatives, such as the Union State of Russia and Belarus, Eurasian Economic Community, and Collective Security Treaty Organization. However, European and US diplomacy dismissed Russia's concerns over its inevitable decline of influence in the region.

Because of escalating rivalry between Russia and the West in the post-Soviet space, a series of clashes and crises emerged. A new frontier between the two gravity centers in Europe emerged, but this time it was of a political and economic nature, and its borders were closely adjacent to the Russian borderline. The countries that found themselves on the split line were especially fragile with their inexperienced elites and exacerbating instability caused by Russian-Western rivalry over them. Because of the EU's meddling, Russian attempt to settle the crisis in Transnistria (The Kozak Memorandum) failed in 2003. In 2005, Russia and the EU acted in support of the two opposing sides of the conflict in Ukraine's Maidan. Then in 2008 Georgia seemed to be trying to pull Russia and the US into confrontation on its territory when it tried to solve its problem of the two separatist republics by force. The culmination was the 2014 Ukrainian crisis, which was brought about by Western efforts to push Viktor Yanukovych's administration into signing Association Agreements with the EU first and then to refrain from the use of force in the public unrest in Kyiv. Western activity in integrating post-Soviet countries was no longer associated with restructuring. It now became a destabilizing factor in the region. Despite its clear reluctance to respond to escalation, Russia had to join the zero-sum game that the West had started with its expansion in Central and Eastern Europe (Charap and Colton, 2017).

Evolution and goals of Russian foreign policy in Eastern Europe

After the end of the Cold War, Russian foreign policy towards Central and Eastern Europe developed in three stages (Bogaturov, 2007).

In 1991–1996 Russia tended to identify its national interests with those of the West and refrained from setting its own priorities in foreign policy. For Central and Eastern European countries it meant Moscow's voluntary rejection of the integration legacy of the Warsaw Pact and Council for Mutual Economic Assistance, and reluctance to hinder Western plans to engage former socialist and post-soviet republics in its own integration projects. Russia did not oppose the 1993 US 'democratic enlargement' doctrine mistakenly considering itself among its beneficiaries. Moscow also supported establishment of new states on the territories of former Yugoslavia, in some cases pioneering the process. This approach reached its culmination with Russian support of NATO's intervention in Bosnia in 1995, which generated strong opposition to the Kremlin inside the country. By the mid-1990s, there was a strong sense of frustration and disappointment in Russia. The Western support for President Boris Yeltsin's controversial victory in the 1996 elections convinced the Russian elites that the EU and the US were willing to turn a blind eye to democracy to ensure a desired outcome.

In the meantime, the post-Soviet republics were trying to balance themselves between Russia and the US. For instance, Georgia launched a military cooperation program with the US, while Azerbaijan signed important contracts with Western companies to develop its oil fields. Increasingly, Russia perceived these developments through a security lens. The NATO-launched Partnership for Peace program in 1994 was meant to preserve cooperation with Russia, but the alliance was also actively developing military cooperation with other countries of Central and Eastern Europe preparing for another round of NATO enlargement. Russia opposed the process as aiming to isolate it, but was too weak to stop it. Feeling betrayed by his Western partners, at the Budapest meeting in December 1994 Yeltsin predicted the beginning of a 'cold peace' in Europe (Yeltsin, 1994), while the Russian military was discussing the idea of targeting Russian rockets at new members of the Alliance in case of its enlargement. In May 1995 Russia signed a separate partnership program with the Alliance hoping to develop a stronger voice in bargaining with NATO, but in practice accepting its further enlargement. In return for Russia's softening its position, Washington promised Russia assistance with joining the WTO and G7, as well as developing a basis for further Russia-NATO relations.

The new period of Russian foreign policy was marked by an increased vigor in asserting national interests. In 1996 a realist-minded Russian statesman Eugeny Primakov became the new Foreign Minister. He never doubted the importance of relations with the West, but not at the expense of Russia's national interests. Russia began to develop its own integration projects. In 1997 it signed the Treaty on friendship, cooperation and partnership with Ukraine, completing the process of normalization between the two countries. Russia also signed an agreement on establishing the Union State with Belarus. On October 10, 2000 Moscow signed the treaty establishing the Eurasian Economic Community with Belarus and Kazakhstan as additional members. The organization became the first success of Russian integration efforts, paving the way for its transformation into the Eurasian Economic Union in 2014.

Russian diplomacy continued to oppose NATO's enlargement. In order to make it more costly for the West, the Kremlin predicated its support on establishing special relations with Russia, restricting the number of candidates for the Alliance's membership to a minimum, placing limitations on arms deployment on new members' territories, and providing guarantees for non-deployment of nuclear weapons in these states. Other developments that affected Russian foreign policy at the time were the Alliance's intervention in Yugoslavia in 1999 and Afghanistan in 2001 and US intervention in Iraq in 2003. Following the Iraq invasion under the false reasoning of Saddam Hussein's plans to produce bacteriological and nuclear weapons, Moscow became convinced that US intervention in the affairs of the post-Soviet countries was highly likely, although the color revolutions came unexpectedly. Overall, it resembled the events of the late 1980s in Central and Eastern Europe when US political intervention destroyed the fragile trust between the US and Russia after the end of the Cold War.

The third stage of Russian foreign policy started in the mid-2000s and was based on a favorable economic performance. In 2006, during the meeting with Foreign Ministry officials, President Vladimir Putin called for Russia's political influence in the world to be adjusted in accordance with its newly acquired economic opportunities (Putin, 2006). The significant effect of the new approach for Central and Eastern European countries was in Moscow's yearning to decrease its dependence on transit oil and gas routes through unstable countries to Western Europe. Construction of the Nord Stream pipeline and plans to construct a similar pipeline in the Black Sea objectively reduced – although not eliminated completely – the transit value of the routes via Ukraine, Moldova and Belarus.

Paradoxically, the growing interdependence between Russia and Western European countries in the energy sphere did not help to ease their tensions over Eastern Europe. On the contrary, the tensions continued to be exacerbated by the EU pressuring the countries that were planning to sign the Association Agreement with the Union. Ukraine proved to be the most fragile and susceptible to this pressure. At the decisive moment, its leadership was paralyzed by the demands of Western politicians to refrain from using force against the armed protesters. The 2014 Ukrainian crisis became the greatest challenge to Russian foreign policy in Central and Eastern Europe. Russia was the last to revise its policy, and only after the EU and the US had expressed their support for the coup d'état in Kyiv.

Frozen conflicts and security issues

During the last years of the USSR, several serious ethnic conflicts emerged, and their scale was growing. Former Yugoslavia presented an even more depressing situation. None of the sides in a series of national conflicts had the capability to take over, and none was ready to admit its defeat. Pessimists saw the Yugoslavian scenario as one of the possibilities for Russia – if the worst were to happen. Due to both local reasons and Russia's role, the post-Soviet space registered a record number of frozen conflicts, as well as unrecognized or partially recognized states – Nagorno-Karabakh, Transnistria, South Ossetia and Abkhazia.

Even though in the early 1990s the Russian leadership lacked a clear political course, the overall logic in Russian actions was to curb ethnic conflicts and prevent their spreading to Russian territories. In particular, in the Caucasus, Russia assisted Azerbaijan in building its own military, yet at a later stage helped Armenia to preserve a military balance in the region.[1] Azerbaijan soon lost its military superiority. The Armenian forces' success in the Battle of Kalbajar had two important outcomes. First, it preconditioned involvement of the international community, and second, it created conditions for both sides to become interested in negotiations. Ceding to pressure, Levon Ter-Petrosyan approved the peace plan that was confirmed to Russia, the US and Turkey. The situation stabilized, and the conflict was frozen for years to come.

The Defense Ministry became the most active of Russian players in the Caucasus at that time. In the Transnistrian conflict the Russian army's role was even more noticeable. Major-General Aleksander Lebed, the Commander of the 14th Army stationed in Transnistria, was partly responsible for that. His appointment was due to his personal relations with the then Defense Minister, Pavel Grachev, and his experience in managing escalations of ethnic conflicts. He had broad powers in Transnistria, and had the right to take almost any decisions. On the night of June 8, 1992, when Moldovan and Romanian troops were on the offensive, General Lebed ordered a strike which caused the deaths of 2,500 people. This made Moldova join the negotiation table. Later on, Moldovan President Mircea Snegur tryied to stop General Lebed's transfer from Transnistria to make him stay as a 'guarantor of stability in the region' (Lebed, 2000).

In 2003 an effort of political conflict settlement was made. The Moscow-advocated Kozak Memorandum provided for the confederalization of Moldova, and Russia was to become the guarantor of this status with Russian peacekeeping troops deployed in Transnistria for 20 years to protect military warehouses. Russia aimed to bring Transnistria back to the Moldavian state, but with broad autonomy. This would give Moscow the opportunity to have more power over Kishinev and leverage the Moldovan leadership in case of emergency. Russia's principal role in conflict resolution without any Western mediators would be evidence of Russian leadership in the post-Soviet space. Yet, the EU's involvement made Kishinev decline Moscow's offer.

In late February 2006, Kishinev halted another round of negotiations on the Transnistrian conflict, which was one of the reasons for the crisis in Russian-Moldovan relations. One of the outcomes was a ban on Moldovan wine products imported to Russia. However, the relations between the two countries soon returned to normal after the two leaders met in November 2006. Some believe that Vladimir Voronin promised Vladimir Putin that Moldova would remain neutral and refuse to join NATO. This would grant the Moldovan authorities a reason not to unite with Romania, and at the same time help keep their hands free in relations with Russia, who had always felt unsafe about Transnistria's status (considering its Russian and Ukrainian population). As for Transnistria itself, there was no will to unite with Moldova, neither among the elites, nor among the majority of its population. And so they all expressed great concern over Moscow's plans to bring the unrecognized republic back into the Moldovan state.

Today's status of Moldovan-Transnistrian relations is not so much of a conflict, rather a political alienation. When Igor Dodon came to office in late 2016, Moldovan and Russian policies became more coherent on many issues, including Transnistria. Nonetheless, it does not imply that the chances to overcome the alienation between Kishinev and Tiraspol are now higher. To this end, there has to be some motivation to integrate Transnistria both from the part of the Moldovan president and the elites, which they lack so far. At the same time, there has to be a force in Transnistria interested in integration with Moldova, and this is lacking so far as well, even if this integration were to happen under the most favorable conditions for Tiraspol. The Transnistrian leadership in this respect is adamant.

Another important security issue for Russia was NATO's enlargement to the East. In October 2014, Russian Foreign Minister Sergey Lavrov said that Transnistria would have the right to political self-determination in case Moldova abandoned its neutral military and political status. Russia never used to doubt the Moldovan territorial integrity in the Transnistrian conflict. But balancing between the East and the West in the face of global Russia-Western confrontation will inevitably lead to the internal destabilization of Moldova, similar to what happened in Ukraine in February 2014.

The Ukrainian civil war is a typical example of a postponed conflict development. The new Kyiv authorities, who came to power as a result of the coup in February 2014, have abandoned the strategy of balancing between Russia and the West. Thus, they rejected the concept of Ukraine being a multination state located between the two centers of power. The core logic of the new Kyiv government was to take advantage of the historic chance to 'turn the country to the West' at all costs, even if it would lead to the country splitting.

Western interference in Ukrainian domestic affairs during Euromaidan made Moscow think that the goal of these actions was to harm Russian interests by means of granting Ukraine NATO membership and pushing out the Russian fleet from Crimea. The US leadership's comments that Russian actions in Crimea and Donbass caught it by surprise, left many in Moscow suspicious. In reality, Russian interests both in Crimea and Ukraine had been articulated to Europe and the US on more than one occasion. And it is not unreasonable to believe that the Russian message was received by the US government. Reports in February and May 2008 by the US embassy in Moscow published on Wikileaks contain a clear analysis of the Russian stance on Ukraine:

> GOR [Government of Russia] officials publicly and privately do not hide that their endgame is the status quo. Russia has accepted Ukraine's westward orientation, including its possible accession to the EU and closer ties with NATO, but NATO membership and the establishment of a U.S. or NATO base in Ukraine remain clear redlines. Ideally, Russia aims to secure a written neutrality pledge from Ukraine.
> *(Russell, 2008)*

The other report forecasts possible Russian reaction:

> Experts tell us that Russia is particularly worried that the strong divisions in Ukraine over NATO membership, with much of the ethnic-Russian community against membership, could lead to a major split, involving violence or at worst, civil war. In that eventuality, Russia would have to decide whether to intervene; a decision Russia does not want to have to face.
> *(Burns, 2008)*

Based on these facts, Moscow dismisses the possibility that the US was unaware of the probable consequences of their support for the coup in Ukraine. High-ranking officials as well as President Putin himself ('Meeting on Military Planning Issues', 2014) have repeatedly said that the US was deliberately trying to push Russia to protect its interests in Ukraine in order to drag it into a debilitating conflict. One can argue that Ukrainian NATO membership was off the table at that time, yet it is far more important the way the ordinary Ukrainians perceived it in 2014. Euromaidan proponents were advocating for the 'European future', which implies Ukraine's accession to NATO and the EU, while their opponents resisted the Western influence and called for protecting Russian-Ukrainian ties.

The issue of Ukrainian membership of NATO remains a subject of deep disagreement in Ukraine even after the Crimean cessation and the outbreak of the civil war in Donbass. According to Kyiv International Institute of Sociology, in September 2016 39% of Ukrainians were in favor of joining NATO, 31% of respondents were against it and the other 30% were in doubt or would refrain from voting were a referendum to take place ('Geopolitical Orientations of the Ukrainian Population', 2016).

In 2014 the new Ukrainian authorities held eight joint training sessions with NATO (with only three in the previous year), and soon after the civil war started became recipients of arms assistance from Alliance countries ('Kiev: postavki oruzhiia NATO', 2014). In 2015 the arms supply to Ukraine was no longer a secret, when the US introduced a special clause to the state budget to provide it.

In 2017 350 million USD was provided for that cause. The situation became even more complicated with the Ukrainian leadership lacking the desire to settle the conflict. There are several reasons for this. Kyiv is not ready to integrate territories with a pro-Russian population and is not capable of providing financial assistance to restore the destroyed economy of Donbass. Furthermore, it yearns to find excuses for the catastrophic effects of its economic policies and to postpone reforms, but at the same time it wants to keep receiving economic support from Western countries. In the meantime, the West keeps pressing Russia to fulfil the Minsk Agreements, abstaining from addressing Kyiv with similar demands ('Minsk agreement', 2015).

With the warring sides unready for de-escalation, the West refraining from pressing Kyiv authorities and little alternative to the use of force, it is safe to say that the conflict will continue for years to come.

Economic interdependence issues

Before the 2014 Ukrainian crisis, there was deep economic interdependency between Russia and the post-Soviet republics. This granted Moscow broad opportunities in foreign policy. After the crisis this interdependence was considerably decreased, but remained significant. The evolution of economic ties in the region shows in which cases there is a strategic vision of the future for relations, and in which cases merely a tactical rivalry over its influence with other powers.

After the Ukrainian Orange revolution in 2005 many of the post-Soviet elites decided to revise their relations with Russia, because they were convinced that its influence was fading. Many of the anti-Russian outbursts were rather provocative. Georgian President M. Saakashvili was the most prominent of such offenders. However, his conduct could hardly be considered completely irrational. As well as other politicians in Eastern Europe, he was counting on US support. This made him believe that anti-Russian rhetoric would receive approval in Washington and that if the Kremlin chose to respond in a harsh manner, his country would become a beneficiary of broader US military assistance. Washington watched his actions with understanding, but considered that in order to achieve true success in the post-Soviet space the country should fundamentally transform its political institutions, its elites, economic model and mentality. To this end, the US thought a nationalist project and alienation of all connections with Russia to be inevitable. At the same time, it gave Washington leverage to influence political processes in the region and create spots of tension in relations with Moscow.

Russia's economic leverage, however, was considerable. Economic pressure to ensure political loyalty has become a new element of Russian foreign policy since the mid-2000s. Moscow recognized the vital dependence of its neighbors on exports to Russia. For example, approximately 80% of Georgian and Moldovan wines went to the Russian market. Russia was the recipient of 35.8% of total Moldavan exports, most of which was wine products, and this made Russia one of the most important trade partners for Kishinev. In March 2006 Russia introduced a ban on importing Georgian and Moldovan wines based on sanitary requirements. The ban on Moldovan wine imports was lifted in autumn 2006, and in spring 2013 restrictions were halted for Georgian products (as a result of 2012 Georgian parliamentary elections, the government of Bidzina Ivanishvili came to power).

Russian trade restriction measures proved to be inefficient as a method of political pressuring, and considerably decreased the level of mutual economic interest and business loyalty to the idea of cooperation with Russia. In cases where the level of economic interdependency was initially high, Moscow usually refrained from pressuring its partners. These were cases when economic pressuring would not be sufficient for the country to experience real losses, or when it could lead to a symmetrical response and serious accusations of non-market policies. In situations of this kind, Russian policy was especially cautious. In certain cases, the Russian leadership started crediting or establishing preferential regimes for neighboring countries in exchange for loyalty. Preferential regimes and hidden subsidy mechanisms are especially convenient, because they allow flexibility in varying the level of support. These policies provided for an informal and selective attachment of major economic actors, especially those close to the authorities, in neighboring countries. An example of a hidden subsidy mechanism is in the transit of sugar, which has long been a major part of Belarussian exports to Russia, yet was purchased mainly from other countries.[2] Later on this was the strategy applied by Belarussian companies after Russia introduced restrictive measures on agricultural products from the EU. Today, Belarus still serves as an exporter of some European products to Russia.

Ukraine is a special example of the inefficient policies of Moscow in post-Soviet states. In its relations with Kyiv it has always preferred hidden subsidy mechanisms over debt schemes. Ukraine used to press for non-market principles in negotiations on gas prices with Russia. It was the last of the post-Soviet republics to start market relations with Gazprom in the gas sphere. Up until 2006, Russia sold gas to Ukraine at the extremely low price of 40–50 USD per cubic meter, and Ukraine received it in far greater volumes than what Germany and Italy together received from Russia. According to Russian estimates, in 1991–2013, because of the low gas prices, Ukraine managed to save more than 82.7 billion USD (Medvedev, 2014). Meanwhile the Ukrainian debt to Gazprom kept on growing, presaging crises of gas transit to the EU (2006 and 2009). Moscow's yearly subsidies in the form of gas price discounts, loans, submitting orders and functioning of the preferential trade regime, at the cost of Russian production, totaled 10–12 billion USD (Medvedev, 2014).

Before the coup in Kyiv, Russia was the major creditor to Ukraine. However, the total of the state and government-guaranteed debt seems insignificant compared to the share of Russian commercial companies in the Ukrainian debt market, which used to be 20% (Papchenkova et al., 2015). The majority of these companies were banks that bought Ukrainian government bonds. Ukrainian bonds equaling 3 billion USD with a due date of late 2015 made up a considerable part of the state's debt. Being the key creditor, Russia had all the capabilities to trigger a default in Ukraine, for the loan in 2013 was preconditioned by an early repayment obligation in case of external debt exceeding 60% of GDP (in summer 2015 it amounted to 96.5%). Russian President Putin noted in May 2015, that 'in response to the request made by Ukraine and [the] IMF we will not use this right in order not to make the difficult situation for our partners and neighbors even worse' ('Meeting with the Members of the Russian Government', 2015).

In 2013 Russia was the biggest trading partner of Ukraine (27.3%), while total trade turnover with the EU was only a little higher (31.2%). Although 2014 witnessed a major plunge in bilateral trade turnover by 40.2%, the growth in turnover with the EU by 12% obviously could not cover all the losses. Russian orders submitted to Ukrainian producers by the Russian Ministry of Industry and Trade in spring 2014, equaled 15 billion USD (8.2% of Ukrainian GDP), but in the last three years it has reduced tremendously. Apart from the political motives, the reduction was caused by a general decrease in Ukrainian industrial production, the destruction of Donbass' industry, a substantial growth in metallurgical exports to China (an important share of total Ukrainian exports) and the fall of the ruble, which raised the competitiveness of Russian products.

Russian companies used to submit orders for hundreds of industrial enterprises that worked together with Russian corporations on high-technology production of space rockets, ships, aircraft, helicopters, turbines and so on. Industrial production had been an important sphere of Russian-Ukrainian interdependence, especially in the military-industrial complex. Of samples of Russian arms and military equipment, 186 – including aircraft, helicopters, ships and rockets – used to have parts produced in Ukraine. The consequences of export restrictions for the Ukrainian high-technology industries will be tremendous. Russia, in its turn, has to carry out an urgent revision of its rearmament program by 2020. Moscow plans to overcome its technical dependency on Ukrainian produced components by 2018 ('Rogozin poobeshchal zameshchenie', 2015).

Critics of Russian policy towards Ukraine believe that Moscow aims to undermine the Ukrainian economy by dragging it into war and provoking capital flight from Ukraine (Bentzen, 2015). It would be true were it not for the fundamental economic interdependency, which makes Russia interested in Ukrainian stability. These ties are so strong that even the war in Donbass has very limited influence. Approximately 50% of Russian gas exports to the EU go through Ukraine, and security of this transit is Russia's vital interest, at least until the launch of the alternative route of a Black Sea pipeline.

In spite of the existing crisis in bilateral relations, important ties in finance and energy between Russia and Ukraine remain in place. The European market is not capable of substituting the Russian one in the short term. Unlike Moldova and Georgia, taking up a small niche in the European market will not be enough for Ukrainian producers. The size of the Ukrainian economy requires a massive market for its output. However, Ukraine's production competitiveness is low, and European producers and politicians are not ready to reduce their share in the common market. This produces certain obstacles, and they are already evident today.

Notwithstanding the tremendous drop in bilateral trade, Russian banks continue to play an important role in Ukraine's financial system. Three of them were in the top ten Ukrainian banks in terms of assets before the crisis, and today they maintain their position. They keep to their investment policies, and even managed to achieve some growth as compared to 2013 (6.8%). Considerable flows of Russian money come to Ukraine via Cyprus. There has been a recent decrease from 33.4% to 25.6%, mainly because of the performance of portfolio investments.[3]

Russian capital is still largely represented in Ukraine's electricity distribution networks. VS Energy International company owns 27 regional electricity providers. In addition, since 2014, Ukraine has been buying 1,500 megawatts of electricity from Russia with a total electricity consumption of 26,000 megawatt.

In the sphere of atomic energy, Russia and Ukraine have been strategic partners for decades. Ukraine inherited 4 atomic energy stations with 15 energy blocs from the Soviet Union (including the Zaporizhia Nuclear Power Plant – the biggest in Europe), with fuel coming from Russia. Construction of a fuel factory was planned in the Ukrainian Kirovograd region with Russian assistance; however, after the crisis erupted, the project has been paused. Instead, Ukraine started to experiment with using US fuel in the Soviet-era atomic energy blocs in the country's energy stations. Earlier there were experiments to replace Russian fuel with US fuel in Ukraine and the Czech Republic, and this turned out to be unsafe from a technological point of view. This pushed the Ukrainian authorities to seek agreements with Russia on nuclear fuel deliveries in 2015–2016.

In December 2014 Russia also started supplying Ukraine with 50,000 tons of coal per day without advance payment, based on internal Russian prices. Thus, Ukraine managed to escape the energy crisis in the winter of 2014–2015. In essence Russia acted as a mediator between the warring sides and sent Kyiv the coal it bought from Donbass. The deal, most probably, became part of the secret agreement on Ukrainian energy supplies to Crimea (in 2014–2015 Crimea received 70% of its electricity from Ukraine).

Despite the troublesome Russian-Ukrainian relations in the energy sphere, Ukraine remains an important consumer of Russian gas, oil and oil products. In 2014 the Ukrainian gas market consumed 42.6 billion cubic meters (bcm) of gas, thus becoming the fourth biggest market in Europe after Germany (86.2 bcm), Britain (78.7 bcm) and Italy (68.7 bcm). In 2015 consumption declined to 30.93 bcm ('Potreblenie gaza v Ukraine', 2015). The Russian gas share in total Ukrainian consumption in 2013 reached 85%, but since 2014 Kyiv has been decreasing the share coming from Russia and moved to reverse Russian gas deliveries from Slovakia, Poland and Hungary. Since 2016 Ukraine has stopped direct gas purchase from Russia and has been buying it in the EU, which does not change its origin but implies a different payment system.

Transit risks are still significant. The Ukrainian pipeline system is in a deplorable state and demands large investment for its reconstruction. Rather than providing such investment, Russia hopes to launch the Nord Stream-2 pipeline. The security of automobile and railway transportations is also being questioned, as are cargo transportations via Ukrainian ports. Russia needs to change the routes of its goods supplies to Central and Southern Europe. In 2015 construction of a railway was started, which will bypass Ukrainian territory to deliver goods between the Russian cities of Belgorod, Voronezh and Rostov-on-Don ('RZhD i Minoborony', 2015). Judging by the pace of construction, a political decision on this matter has been made.

The logic of transport communication development in Russia dictates avoiding transit through territories of post-Soviet republics. This strategy was not formed as a direct result of a Russian-Western conflict; however, the circumstances when it took shape are very much like the situation today. In 1999 Latvia, Lithuania and Estonia were among the first to join the EU's oil embargo against Yugoslavia, which was imposed in violation of the UN Charter. This was a clear sign that in critical situations Russia will no longer decide on the end points of its oil exports that go through these countries' territories – the US will. In the early 2000s Russia started shifting its transits to its ports. Huge investments in Russian port infrastructure made it possible to reduce cargo transit from Russia via Baltic ports, replacing them with the Russian ones of Ust-Luga, Primorsk and Novorossiysk. It is a tendency that will continue in the future.

Migrant labor is another vital sphere of Eastern European economies. Russia is the main destination for labor migrants from Moldova, Ukraine, Georgia and Belarus. The total amount of migrants in Russia is approximately 10 million people, one-third of them illegal migrants. Despite potentially tremendous losses, the new Ukrainian authorities have proposed lifting the current visa-free regime with Russia. Ukraine's withdrawal from the common labor market will affect 6 million seasonal workers and almost 400,000 highly qualified specialists. By Russian estimates, Ukrainians may lose approximately 11–13 billion USD a year (7% of GDP) if they stop working in Russia. The EU will have to absorb millions of Ukrainian workers because the current Ukrainian leadership has set the shift of the destination for migrant flow towards Europe as one of its goals.

Conclusion

Over the past 20 years Russian foreign policy in Central and Eastern Europe has lived through dramatic transformations. It has taken shape in conditions of shrinking geopolitical interests and a disastrous economic situation in the country. Short of the possibility opposing Western expansion to post-socialist countries, Moscow remained a passive observer for a long time. In the second half of the 2000s, Russian foreign policy gained a new momentum and found most Eastern European countries either deeply integrated into the EU and NATO structures, or willing to be a part of them.

The greatest achievement of Russian policy in Central and Eastern Europe is mostly a successful upgrade of the system of economic relations with the region. Bilateral agreements and new integration projects took the place of CMEA and the socialist bloc with its internal economic dynamics. Moscow has managed to decrease its dependency on transit countries and transform the economic chains inherited from the USSR, taking its internal market interests into account. Russia has finally formulated its own interests in foreign policy and has taken to asserting them.

Ukraine turned out to be a weak link in the foreign policy of Russia. Moscow failed to draw it towards its integrational projects. The separation process between the two closely connected economies, which had been planned with a long-term perspective in mind, was disrupted by the coup d'état in Kyiv in 2014. Threatened by the loss of vital interests, Moscow had to take drastic measures that cost it a lot in reputational and economic terms.

The future of Russian policy in Central and Eastern Europe depends to a great extent on the outcome of the Ukrainian crisis, whose perspectives are vague in the long term. Kyiv's adamant stance makes the realization of the Minsk Agreements highly unlikely. Russia will aim to normalize relations with Ukraine by halting politically motivated economic assistance and shifting trade and production relations onto a new non-preferential basis. In prospect is a pragmatism of ties that may lead to a recovery in relations and lead the way towards a tripartite trade regime between Russia, Ukraine and the EU. The EU has not yet come to realize the amount of yearly contributions that the stabilization of Ukraine will require if it is to come out from under Russian tutelage, and is not prepared to appropriate such funds. When the EU feels a tangible threat to its energy security, only then will the impulse towards the conclusion of a deal arise.

Acknowledgment

The research was carried out with support of the Russian Science Foundation grant (project No. 17-78-20170).

Notes

1 Chapter 19 returns to Russia's role in the Caucasus.
2 According to Belarussian customs service, in the first 6 months (January-June) of 2016 sugar export reached 187,000 tons, of which 160,000 tons went to Russia and 20,000 tons went to Ukraine. Raw sugar import equaled 234,000 tons, main importers were Brazil (121,000 tons) and Cuba (113,000 tons).

See: *'Sugar export and import in Belarus, January-June 2016'*, 2016, PRODUKT.BY, 31 August. Available from: http://produkt.by/news/eksport-i-import-sahara-v-belarusi-za-yanvar-iyun-2016-goda.

3 Estimates by 1 April 2016. See *'Priamye investitsii v Ukrainu vyrosli v 3 raza'* [Direct Investments to Ukraine Increased by 3], 2016, Ministry of Finance of Ukraine, 17 May. Available from: http://minfin.com.ua/2016/05/17/19237670/.

References

'Geopolitical Orientations of the Ukrainian Population: European Union, Customs Union, NATO (September 2016)', 2016, Kyiv International Institute of Sociology, 25 October. Available from: www.kiis.com.ua/?lang=rus&cat=reports&id=650&page=3.

'Kiev: postavki oruzhiia NATO na Ukrainu uzhe nachalis' [Kyiv: NATO Starts Arms Supply to Ukraine], 2014, *Vesti.ru*, 14 September. Available from: www.vesti.ru/doc.html?id=1968384.

'Meeting on Military Planning Issues', 2014, Official site of the President of the Russian Federation, 26 November. Available from: http://kremlin.ru/events/president/news/47098.

'Meeting with the Members of the Russian Government', 2015, Official site of the President of the Russian Federation, 20 May. Available from: http://kremlin.ru/events/president/news/49495.

'Minsk agreement on Ukraine crisis: text in full', 2015, The Telegraph, 12 February. Available from: www.telegraph.co.uk/news/worldnews/europe/ukraine/11408266/Minsk-agreement-on-Ukraine-crisis-text-in-full.html.

'Potreblenie gaza v Ukraine snizitsia do 34 kubov v etom godu - "Ukrtransgaz"' [Gas Consumption in Ukraine Will Decrease to 34 bcm This Year], 2015, RIA Novosti Ukraina, 25 June. Available from: http://rian.com.ua/economy/20150625/369551891.html.

'Rogozin poobeshchal zameshchenie ukrainskikh komplektuiushchikh v oboronke k 2018 godu' [Rogozin Promised to Replace Ukrainian Armory Parts by 2018], 2015, *Lenta.ru*, 1 July. Available from: http://lenta.ru/news/2015/07/01/oboronka/.

'RZhD i Minoborony podpisali dogovor o stroitel'stve dorogi v obkhod Ukrainy' [Russian Railway Service and Defence Ministry Signed an Agreement on Building a Railway Bypassing Ukraine], 2015, *Lenta.ru*, 30 June. Available from: http://lenta.ru/news/2015/06/30/railway/.

Bentzen, N, 2015, 'Ukraine's economic challenges. From ailing to failing?', *European Parliamentary Research Service, Members' Research Service*, June. www.europarl.europa.eu/thinktank/en/document.html?reference=EPRS_IDA(2015)559497.

Bogaturov, AD, 2007, 'Tri pokoleniia vneshnepoliticheskikh doktrin Rossii' [Three Generations of Russian Foreign Policy Doctrines], Mezhdunarodnye protsessy, vol. 5, no. 13, pp. 54–69.

Burns, WJ, 2008, 'Nyet Means Nyet: Russia's NATO Enlargement Redlines', Moscow Embassy #000265, Wikileaks, 1 February. Available from: https://cablegatesearch.wikileaks.org/cable.php?id=08MOSCOW265.

Charap, S & Colton, TJ, 2017, *Everyone Loses: The Ukraine Crisis and the Ruinous Contest for Post-Soviet Eurasia*, New York and London: Routledge.

Graham, T, 2017, 'Toward a New Equilibrium in U.S.-Russian Relations', *The National Interest*, 1 February. Available from: http://nationalinterest.org/feature/toward-new-equilibrium-us-russian-relations-19281?page=show.

Lebed, AI, 2000, 'Vremia sobirat' kamni' [It Is Time for Hard Work], I vozroditsia Rus', Moscow, pp. 197–198.

McFaul, M, 1998, 'A Precarious Peace: Domestic Politics in the Making of Russian Foreign Policy', *International Security*, vol. 22, no. 3, pp. 5–35.

Mearsheimer, J, 2014, 'Why the Ukraine Crisis Is the West's Fault', Foreign Affairs, September/October. Available from: www.foreignaffairs.com/articles/141769/john-h-mearshimer/why-the-ukraine-crisis-is-the-wests-fault.

Medvedev, DA, 2014, 'Rossiia i Ukraina: zhizn' po novym pravilam' [Russia and Ukraine: Living by New Rules], Nezavisimaia gazeta, 15 December. Available from: www.ng.ru/ideas/2014-12-15/1_medvedev.html.

Motyl, A, 2016, 'Putin's Russia as a fascist political system', *Communist and Post-Communist Studies*, vol. 49, no. 1, pp. 25–36.

Papchenkova, M, Smirnov, S & Overchenko, M, 2015, 'Putin: Rossiia uzhe mozhet trebovat' dolgs Ukrainy' [Putin: Russia Can Now Demand Debt Repayment From Ukraine], Vedomosti, 20 May. Available from: www.vedomosti.ru/economics/articles/2015/05/20/siluanov-ukraina-po-suti-obyavlyaet-defolt.

Putin, VV, 2006, Speech During the Meeting with Ambassadors and Permanent Representatives of the Russian Federation, 27 June. Available from: http://kremlin.ru/events/president/transcripts/23669.

Russell, DA, 2008, 'Russian-Ukrainian Relations Monopolized by Ukraine's NATO Bid', Moscow Embassy #001517, Wikileaks, 30 May. Available from: https://cablegatesearch.wikileaks.org/cable.php?id=08MOSCOW1517.

Rutland, P, 2014, 'A Paradigm Shift in Russia's Foreign Policy', *Moscow Times*, 19 May.

Sherr, J, 2013, *Hard Diplomacy and Soft Coercion: Russia's Influence Abroad*, Washington, DC: Brookings Institution Press.

Tsygankov, A, 2015, 'Vladimir Putin's Last Stand: The Sources of Russia's Ukraine Policy', *Post-Soviet Affairs*, vol. 31, no. 4, pp. 279–303.

Umland, A, 2016, 'Countering Russian Expansionism: Blueprints for a New Security Alliance', European Council on Foreign Relations, 18 April. Available from: https://ssrn.com/abstract=2775571.

Yeltsin, BN, 1994, Speech of the President of the Russian Federation in Budapest at the Plenary Session of the Conference on Security and Cooperation in Europe (CSCE), 5 December. Available from: http://yeltsin.ru/archive/audio/9035.

Zevelev, I, 2014, 'Granitsy russkogo mira' [The Borders of the Russian World], Rossiya v Global'noy Politike, 27 April. Available from: www.globalaffairs.ru/number/Granitcyrusskogo-mira-16582.

18
THE MIDDLE EAST

Philipp Casula

UNIVERSITY OF ZURICH, SWITZERLAND

Mark N. Katz

GEORGE MASON UNIVERSITY, USA

Introduction

Moscow's military intervention in Syria, beginning in September 2015, marked a sharp break from the much more reluctant, hesitant role that Russia had played in the region after the collapse of the Soviet Union. Not only was this Russia's first post-Soviet military intervention outside the former USSR, but its relative success in shoring up the Assad regime stood in stark contrast to the results that the United States and its allies achieved through military interventions in Afghanistan, Iraq, and Libya. This chapter will review the backdrop against which Russia's political and military involvement in Syria took place and review its relations to the Greater Middle East. It will scrutinize in detail Moscow's relations with selected countries in the region, which the authors deem to be crucial for post-Soviet Russia, and conclude with an outlook on key challenges, questions, and themes Russia will face in this region.

Russia and the Middle East: realism, constructivism or both?

As Western powers, especially the United States, are heavily engaged in the region, Russia cannot relate to the Middle East without relating to the West. In no other part of the world is Russia's foreign policy as "influenced by the development and behavior of Western nations" (Tsygankov, 2013: 1). This perspective implies a competition between Russia and the West *in* the Middle East as well as *for* the Middle East. The Middle East emerged as a place where the Soviet Union could and did act as a global power. For post-Soviet Russia, the region could play a similar role and, at least since Yevgenii Primakov's tenure as foreign minister, Russian foreign policy has become more "balanced" and "diverse" again (Tsygankov, 2013: 19), opening up to the Middle East as well. Hence, when coming to understand Russia's foreign policy in this region, questions of power and of power-balance vis-à-vis the West play a crucial role, and thus a "realist" approach seems very apt for analyzing these relations. Realism is the school of IR thought that is centered on nation-states, self-interest or "egoism" of states, "anarchy" in international relations, and "power politics" (Goodin, 2010: 133). Post-Soviet Russia seems to be engaging in such power politics again, to compete with the West for and in the Middle East.

Still, there is more to unravel: for Russia as for Western powers, the Middle East has been an area with a colonial legacy, of colonial exploitation or neocolonial ambitions. For the USSR, it has been a region in which socialism could potentially come true – at least this is what ideologues in Moscow believed and what some of the Middle Eastern leaders have declared. Historically grown images of the Orient played a powerful role in Moscow, London, and Washington alike. Furthermore, "the East" has traditionally played a special role in Russian culture. Moscow and St. Petersburg intellectuals have claimed to possess special access to "Russia's own Orient" in Central Asia (Tolz, 2011), deducing that this might also imply a special access to the "foreign East" (*zarubezhnii vostok*). How "Russia" sees itself in relation to the Middle East today cannot be disentangled from these legacies. Constructivism, addressing "the social and relational construction of what states are and what they want" (Goodin, 2010: 299), can take these issues into account.

We contend that together with power questions and balancing with the West, Russia's approach to the Middle East is highly "identity driven." In this sense, "history matters": a long history of Russian and Soviet interaction with the countries of the Middle East has shaped mutual expectations and interpretations. Contemporary Russian policy toward the Middle East implicitly builds on this tradition. Constructivism and realism emphasize two sides of the Russian-Middle Eastern entanglement and are equally instructive. Both will inform the approach followed in this chapter, which will strike a balance between constructivism and realism.

State of the art: Western and Russian perspectives

There is a very rich Russian literature on the Middle East, which experienced a marked spike after the events of the Arab Spring. However, there was no shortage of Russian accounts on this region beforehand. Especially after decolonization, many Middle Eastern states pivoted towards the Soviet Union. Conversely, "after a brief flirt with Israel, the Soviet leadership did many gestures of support for Arab countries . . . improving the image of the Soviet Union more and more" (Vasilev, 1993: 32, 65–67). From the 1950s to the 1970s, secular Arab regimes gained internal legitimacy and approval of the USSR by providing "mass education, health and other public services, industrialization and guarantees for employment, and social upward mobility, associated with independent initiatives and anti-imperialist postures" (Amin, 2016: 22). The ups and downs in Russian relations with the region also determined the quantity and quality of Russian literature produced on the region. Most recently, Soviet Oriental studies regained prominence and political relevance. The Middle East returned to university curricula with new textbooks such as Zviagelskaia's *Blizhnevostochnyi Klinch* focusing on Russian-Israeli relations and the Palestinian conflict, while Streltsov's *Rossiia i strany Vostoka* takes a look at the "the East" and Russia at large. From specialists of Russian Oriental Studies, however, there has always been a constant flow of publications (Belokrenitskii, 2010; Mamedova and Dunaeva, 2011), including retrospective analyses such as Medvedko and Medvedko (2009) or Primakov (2009), who scrutinize Soviet engagement in the Middle East.

Soviet policy toward the Middle East was a matter of intense interest to Western scholars during the Cold War, but Western interest in Russia's policy toward this region waned during the Yeltsin era, when Moscow was less active in the region. Russia's increased activity in the Middle East under Putin has resulted in a corresponding rebound in Western scholarly interest in examining it. Many of these studies have focused on Putin's policy toward individual countries or conflicts in the Middle East, or toward the region as a whole. Others have looked at Russian policy toward the Middle East in the broader context of Moscow's overall foreign policy, U.S.-Russian relations, or even the broader great power competition. Angela Stent (2014) examines U.S.-Russian cooperation and conflict in the Middle East in terms of the rise and fall of efforts to improve overall Russian-U.S. relations during each U.S. presidential administration since the end of the Cold War. Bobo Lo (2015) discusses Russia's policy toward the Middle East in terms of his overall argument that a "new world disorder" undermines all great power ambitions. Grygiel and Mitchell (2016) see Russia, China, and Iran as all working together to challenge the United States and its allies in various regions of the world, including the Middle East.

Role of the Middle East in Russian foreign policy

Cold War legacies in the Middle East

During the Cold War, the USSR entertained tight relations with many Middle Eastern countries. While relations with single states experienced ups and downs, all in all, the Soviet Union enjoyed a continuous presence in the region.

Especially tight relations developed between Egypt and the USSR: Nasser's Egypt became the Soviet Union's closest regional ally. Moscow supported Cairo politically, militarily, and economically. However, the problem with Egypt as with almost every other Middle Eastern state on good terms with the USSR was that they often suppressed their communist movements. Still, there were Soviet party officials who believed that at least some Middle Eastern countries could embark on a path to socialism. Indeed, many of these states pursued agrarian reforms and strengthened the state sector. South Yemen pushed "socialist" reforms furthest, receiving assistance from the USSR, the GDR, and Cuba. The Soviet Union's messianic stance was, however, soon to be replaced by a more pragmatic approach, as Vasilev (1993) suggests. With Egypt switching sides in the mid-1970s, the Soviet Union's main regional partner became Syria, which positioned itself at the helm of the anti-Sadat camp.

The late 1970s marked the decline of Soviet influence in the Middle East, both for internal and external reasons. Internally, economic and political stagnation left little enthusiasm for the Arab cause. Externally, the rise of Iran after the Islamic revolution in early 1979 brought a new player into the region that appealed not only to Shia populations. Additionally, the Soviet invasion of Afghanistan in December 1979 severely hurt Moscow's reputation in the Middle East. Vasilev (1993) shows how during the Cold War, relations with the Middle East were based – at least initially – on a presumed common identity: anti-imperialist and thus anti-Western, anti-Zionist and thus anti-Israel, and pro-socialist and thus anti-capitalist. All this resulted in the USSR not only having influence deriving from Soviet material assistance, but also originating in an identity-based alliance. However, this Soviet soft-power had its limits, as Mohamed Heikal already noted in the 1970s: "All the formative influences" of Arab leaders, that is:

> [t]he books they had read, the history they had learned, the films they had seen – had come from the West. The languages they knew in addition to their own were English or French – Russian was, and remained, a mystery to them.
> *(Heikal, 1978: 16)*

As for the Middle Eastern populations, Heikal complained that:

> [t]he Soviets have proved particularly inept in cultural exchanges . . . The Arabs are eager to read the works of Tolstoy . . . but these are not what they are offered. They would find at the Soviet Publishing House in Cairo the collected works of Lenin for as little as 30 piasters, but this is not what they want to buy.
> *(Heikal, 1978: 281)*

In another sense, the Soviet Union got it right. In contrast to Western interpretations at the time, Soviet officials soon understood that their Middle Eastern counterparts were *pragmatic* anti-imperialists. Unlike Western governments, the Soviet Union just delivered what their Middle Eastern counterparts demanded (Primakov, 2009: 18–21). Hence, pragmatism took increasing hold on both sides: Middle Eastern countries wanted to bolster their independence, and the Soviet Union wanted to keep their allies. Keeping them happy meant providing them with military support in their confrontation with Israel or in their struggle against "feudal" regimes, such as in Oman or Yemen. Primakov's *Russia and the Arabs* (2009) underscores how heavily the conflict with Israel shaped relations with the Arab Middle East. Soviet influence on conflict resolution, however, remained limited, as the USSR had severed diplomatic relations with Israel in 1967, and many rounds of secret and unofficial meetings afterward remained inconclusive and pushes within the Soviet leadership to restore relations failed internally (Primakov, 2009: 273–296).

The immediate aftermath of the Cold War was problematic both for Russia and the Middle East. Relations hit a low. Two major shifts occurred in post-Soviet Russia's relations with the Middle East. First, 9/11 heightened Russia's attention to the links between domestic terrorism inside Russia and possible links to the Middle East. In the Kremlin's eyes, the second war in Chechnya just confirmed what was already suspected: that Russian Muslim radicals were tied to Wahabism and that the Middle East played an ambiguous role in Chechnya. The Arab Spring marked the second major shift in Russia's relations with the Middle East and brought to Moscow's attention what it again perceived as the destructive role the West plays in the region. The Arab Spring and the West's reaction confirmed deeply seated beliefs about the negative influence the West plays in the Middle East. The campaign that the West conducted in Iraq (2003–2011) found no support in Moscow, and the Western stance on the revolutions in Tunisia, Egypt, Libya, and Syria found equally little approval in the Kremlin. While Russia stood aside in Iraq, supported Western troops in Afghanistan, and abstained from interference in Libya, Russia assumed a much more active stance in Syria, trying to live up to its self-perception as a global power, prevent regime-change in Damascus, and push back both Western influence as well as the influence of terrorism, broadly understood. Finally, the resurgence of political Islam, especially in its militant version (which we will label here "jihadism"), was perceived by Russia as a threat to be countered. Russian politicians, journalists, and scientists alike particularly blame the West for its rise and – in reminiscence of the plot during the Soviet war in Afghanistan – portray many conflicts in the Middle East as an oversimplified binary opposition between secular regimes and "jihadist" movements, the latter often seen as being sponsored by the West and the Gulf states (Dolgov, 2015: 27–29, 32).

Russia's foreign policy after the Soviet collapse

For Andrei Grachev (2008: 196), the events surrounding the first Gulf War symbolize the condition of Russian foreign policy shortly before and shortly after the collapse of the USSR. The rivalry between Foreign Minister Eduard Shevardnadze and Gorbachev's top adviser Yevgenii Primakov underlined the "chaos," "indiscipline," and "demoralization" that reigned in the Soviet Ministry of Foreign Affairs. Later, between 1992 and 1996, the Middle East was widely left out of the Russian foreign policy equation. During Andrey Kozyrev's tenure as Minister of Foreign Affairs, Russia adopted a clear pro-Western stance, aimed at maximum integration within Western organizations and institutions. For Kozyrev, "Arab leaders were a group of political riffraffs . . . to be kept at bay" (Posuvalyuk, 2012: 51–53).

Russian foreign policy toward the Middle East in this period was also determined by the changes taking place in the region itself. Also triggered by the end of the Cold War, the Middle

East underwent a transformation characterized by coups d'état (Algeria, Sudan), unification (Yemen), or open war (Iraq). The loss of legitimacy of the old, authoritarian, and secular regimes, a new tide of political Islam, the loosening of the opposition to Israel as a unifying factor, and the rise of new values, new players, and new demands (Streltsov, 2014: 32–33) changed the region profoundly and challenged the foreign policy of a post-Soviet Russia which was in disarray itself and, still stuck in Soviet ways of thinking, found it hard to cope with the new realities in the Middle East.

Given its economic condition in the early 1990s, Russia was particularly interested in the economic dimension of relations with the Middle East. Being a conflict-ridden region, the Middle East was a key buyer of Russian weaponry. Russia furthered these conflicts with weapons supplies and had an interest in keeping these conflicts alive. After the Cold War, Iraq and Syria – which still had huge debts vis-à-vis Moscow – became of key interest for post-Soviet Russia in the region. For Iraq, this meant that Russia pushed to end the sanctions imposed by the UN Security Council after the 1990 Iraqi invasion of Kuwait. Regarding Syria, which consolidated its international position after its support for the international coalition against Iraq in 1990, this meant a quick resumption of relations with Russia, not least in the military field.

Kozyrev's course had already started to lose momentum by 1993, with opposition to his pro-Western approach emerging within Yeltsin's team itself. The return of the Middle East in Russian foreign policy considerations, however, was instigated when Yevgenii Primakov took over the helm of the Foreign Ministry from Kozyrev. He questioned Russia's unconditional Western orientation and paid new attention to the Middle East.

Enter Yevgenii Primakov

Yevgenii Primakov became Russian Minister of Foreign Affairs in January 1996 and stayed in office until September 1998. His tenure had a double effect. First, Russia became more assertive in foreign policy, claiming back its status as a superpower and a global player; second, as a subplot to the aforementioned point, Russia became more involved in the Middle East, a region that Primakov had extensively travelled and studied as a scholar, journalist, and KGB operative since the 1960s (Andrew and Mitrokhin, 2005: 151).

With Primakov, the Israeli-Palestinian conflict received new attention. Primakov also tried to position Russia as a broker between Israel and Syria, especially in 1997 when Primakov toured the region. However, these efforts remained limited in their results. Primakov also brought a renewed pragmatism into relations with the Middle East, a pragmatism that Russia claims to represent nowadays too. It is a trend in Russian literature to speak of "pragmatism" (Vasilev, Primakov) or "de-ideologization" (Streltsov), and while it is true that there is no Soviet ideology anymore that influences the relationship with the Middle East, these terms themselves contain ideological axioms, such as economic efficiency or Russia being a great power.

Russia turns against the West

Relations between post-Soviet Russia and the West have never been easy. Under Primakov, Russia's stance had become more assertive. While relations briefly improved after 2001 in the context of the "war on terror," their ties mainly followed a long downward trend, marked by NATO's bombing of Yugoslavia (1999), the U.S.-led invasion of Iraq (2003), the 2004 dual enlargement of the EU and NATO, the "color revolutions" in Georgia and Ukraine (2003, 2004), the planning of a NATO missile defense system (2002/2007), and the intervention in Libya (2011). All these events caused relations with the West to sour, since in the Kremlin they were all perceived as manifestations of the West creeping closer to Russia's borders or as meddling in the affairs of sovereign states irrespective of Moscow's explicit objection, thus denying Russia its global role and refusing to acknowledge Russia's voice as an equal. The anti-Western turn in the mid-2000s culminated in Putin's well-known speech at the Munich Security Conference (Putin, 2007). Since then, many of the issues mentioned in this address resurfaced time and again in several of Putin's other speeches, particularly his address of March 18, 2014, commenting on the Crimean crisis.

Apart from the conclusion of the new START agreement in 2010, the "reset" of U.S.-Russia relations under Barack Obama and Dmitry Medvedev soon stalled, and relations between Russia and the West in general have remained strained during Putin's third term. Disagreements range from the Syrian civil war to the Ukraine crisis. At the same time, and despite being Russia's biggest trading partner, relations with the EU have stagnated, and European sanctions against Russia as well as European far-right parties' flirt with Russia further burdened bilateral relations. Russia opening up to Asia and the Global South, including the Middle East, must be seen with these developments in mind.

Global trends affecting Russian policy in the Middle East

Russian foreign policy toward the Middle East is also affected by factors other than Moscow's bilateral relations with the governments of the region or growing tensions between Russia and the West. One important trend has been the rise of the BRICS (Brazil, Russia, India, China, and South Africa). While Brazil and South Africa may not have much impact in the Middle East, China and India do. Unlike Russia, which competes with several Middle Eastern countries in the oil export market, China and India both import large quantities of oil from the region. Like Russia, both China and India want stability in the region and have good relations with all states there. Unlike Russia, though, they prefer to see lower petroleum prices. If Sino-Indian competition grows, the Middle East may become an arena in which both compete for influence – something that Russia and the West will both have to navigate somehow.

Another factor that affects the policy of Russia toward the region has been the rise of secessionist nationalism in the Middle East and many other regions of the globe. The Middle East has already witnessed de jure secession from Sudan (South Sudan) and de facto secession from Iraq (Kurdistan). While their strength and activity levels vary dramatically, secessionist movements also exist in Turkey (the Kurds), Iran (esp. Kurds, Azeris, Baluchis), Syria (Kurds), Yemen (the South), Libya (Cyrenaica), and Algeria (the Berbers). Like most established governments, Moscow generally opposes secession – though Russia has supported it in former Soviet republics it is at odds with (Georgia and Ukraine). On the other hand, Russia has had to adjust to the reality of South Sudan becoming independent and the Kurdish Regional Government being effectively so. The problem, of course, is that making exceptions for secessionists in some countries only serves to encourage similar forces elsewhere while complicating relations with governments feeling threatened by them.

A trend indigenous to the Middle East affecting Russia and others is the fierce rivalry that has emerged between Iran on the one hand and certain Sunni Arab states – most notably Saudi Arabia – on the other, which is being played out in Saudi-Iranian rivalry occurring in divided Sunni-Shi'a (or Sunni-Alawi) states such as Iraq, Syria, Lebanon, Bahrain, and Yemen. Moscow has backed the side supported by Iran in most of these cases, but sides with the Sunni monarchy in Bahrain and has largely remained neutral in Yemen. Moscow wants to have good relations both with Iran and with Sunni Arab states, but its support for the former has led some in the latter to see Russia as supporting Shi'as against Sunnis.

When it broke out in 2011, Russian observers saw the "Arab Spring" as a continuation of the "color revolutions" that led to the downfall of governments friendly to Russia and replacement by ones friendlier to the West in Serbia (2000), Georgia (2003), and Ukraine (2004). Moscow believed the West was pursuing similar aims not just in Libya and Syria, but even in Russia itself when demonstrations against Putin's plan to resume the presidency occurred in 2011–2012. Dolgov (2015: 33) claims, that "Islamist fighters" from Syria and Libya participated in the Euromaidan 2014 events, and that the EU and the United States aimed at repeating "the Syrian and Libyan scenario" in Ukraine in order to draw it into NATO. This Russian equation of the Arab Spring with the color revolutions underlies, among other factors, Putin's determination to defend the Assad regime in Syria.

While Russian annexation of Crimea in 2014 and promotion of secessionist forces in eastern Ukraine beginning that same year has deeply affected Moscow's relations with the West, it has had a remarkably limited impact on Russia's relations with the Middle East. The Arab states, Iran, and Israel have not expressed opposition to Russian policy toward Ukraine; they do not see it as affecting them. Turkey has been more concerned, but has not allowed this to get in the way of its recent restoration of good relations with Moscow that began in mid-2016.

Russia's return to the Middle East

Having largely retreated from the Middle East under Yeltsin in the 1990s, Putin set about restoring Russian influence in the region (Nizameddin, 2013). While Moscow made considerable efforts in this regard during the first decade of the 21st century, Russia still appeared to be a less important player there compared to the United States during the Bush Administration with its large-scale interventions in Afghanistan and Iraq and active pursuit of the "War on Terror" throughout the region. The relative U.S. disengagement from the region as well as fraying relations with several long time U.S. allies – including Saudi Arabia, Egypt, Turkey, and even Israel – during the Obama Administration combined with Putin's seemingly successful intervention in support of the Assad regime in Syria beginning in 2015, has led many to see Russian influence as being on the rise in the Middle East.

U.S. influence in the region, though, still remains strong. And even if it does further decline, this will not automatically result in its being replaced by Russia. The complexities of the Middle East that have stymied the United States affect Russia too. The opportunities and obstacles of Putin's efforts at increasing Russian influence in the Middle East from its Yeltsin-era low point can best be seen through an examination of Moscow's complex ties with the major states and actors in the region since the end of the Cold War.

Record of Russian foreign policy in the Middle East

Syria

Relations with Syria have always been important to the USSR and Russia. Soviet economic, military, and political support to Syria became a showcase for what the USSR could do for an Arab country. Also, the CPSU and the Baath-party had close contacts. These ties between Syria and the USSR became even more important after Egypt signed the U.S.-brokered Camp David Accords in 1978. Arm deliveries rose to new heights, and a Treaty of Friendship was signed in 1980, making Syria probably the closest of all Soviet allies in the Middle East.

Also, after the collapse of the USSR, Syria remained an important regional partner for Russia. First, Syria still owed a considerable debt to Russia. Russia wrote off roughly 70 percent of Syria's

13.4 billion USD debt in 2005 (El Din, 2013), but since then Russia has resupplied the regime with weaponry and most likely Syrian debts have risen again. Second, the Syrian army remained highly dependent on Russian weaponry and spare-parts. Finally, Syria continued to be an important country in the region, key to affecting the Palestinian conflict, and with stakes in Turkey and Iraq. In the 1990s, Syria briefly improved its international standing through participating in the 1991 Gulf War with the United States against Iraq. Russia renewed its economic (1993) and military cooperation (1994) shortly thereafter, and new arms' deliveries took place in 1998. The Syrian leadership sought a more strategic partnership with Russia under Bashar al-Assad; however, Moscow refrained from this due to Damascus' tense relations with Israel. In 2005, both countries settled their dispute regarding Syrian debts, and Syria allowed Russia to implement a variety of projects in the country. Russia and Syria also agreed on a long-term military partnership between 2005–2010 (Vasilev, 1993: 146; Streltsov, 2014: 35–36; Zviagelskaia, 2014: 21–24).

Under Bashar al-Assad, Syria underwent far-reaching neoliberal economic reforms, favoring the urban middle-classes and neglecting rural areas (Matar and Kadri, 2016), while political reforms remained cosmetic. When the Arab Spring engulfed the country, quickly spiraling down into civil war, Russia sided with the regime. From the beginning, Moscow opposed regime-change in Damascus. A narrative of foreign-sponsored "jihadists" and of a "media war" against Syria came to dominate Russian public discourse (Dolgov, 2015: 28–29). Yet while Russia kept a protecting hand over Assad's regime, it also sought to maintain contacts with what it called "moderate opposition." Moscow succeeded in averting Western air strikes against Damascus after the regime had used chemical weapons against the opposition in mid-2013, in exchange for reassurances that Damascus would surrender its chemical arsenal. Especially before Fall 2015, Russia intensified its diplomatic efforts to bring conflicting parties together, both internally and externally. But Moscow's attempts to convince foreign sponsors of the opposition to ease their support failed. This failure was also a result of Moscow's strained relations with many Gulf States and ultimately contributed to Russia's decision to step in militarily, triggering the largest and most protracted Russian post-Soviet military intervention outside of the former USSR. The intervention stabilized Damascus's position in the civil war, and led to the recapture of previously lost territory. It also allowed Russia to get a permanent foothold in Syria and dramatically increased its leverage on the Syrian regime. On the downside, Russia's military intervention damaged its already shaky standing as a broker in the conflict and further damaged its international reputation.

The new U.S. president, Donald Trump, called for Moscow and Washington to cooperate against the common enemy, ISIS, in Syria. Trump even seemed to accept Putin's logic that Assad was less worse than what would probably be a jihadist alternative to him. But when Trump launched an attack on a Syrian airbase in response to the Assad regime's use of chemical weapons against its opponents, Trump "completely changed" his position on Assad within days, and U.S.-Russian relations soured over Syria. It is still not clear whether Syria will prove to be a source of U.S.-Russian tension, an opportunity for U.S.-Russian cooperation, or both in the Trump era. Much will depend on whether the U.S. administration will come up with a strategy for the region, which Russia has but the United States still lacks.

Egypt

For the Soviet Union, relations with Egypt were of utmost importance. There were few international leaders who had more respect and more support from Moscow than Egypt's Gamal Abdel Nasser: "Nasser with his personal charisma, tact and caliber as a statesman" deeply impressed Soviet leaders (Vasilev, 1993: 67). Nasser received full support from Moscow despite his bad relationship with the Egyptian communists. When Nasser died in 1970, Soviet diplomacy did everything it could to preserve the legacy of Nasserism (Primakov, 2009: 133). However, under Anwar al-Sadat, Egypt pivoted to the West. Signing the Camp David accords with Israel, it alienated not only other Arab states but the USSR as well. Internally, Sadat initiated the policies of economic opening or *Infitah*. Soviet-Egyptian diplomatic ties were severed in 1981. Mubarak's reign was seen much more positively, both regarding international relations (Cold Peace with Israel) and domestic policies. Diplomatic relations were reestablished in 1984, and under Gorbachev, ties were normalized. Despite political disagreements, economic relations persisted throughout the period. With Putin's visit to Cairo and Mubarak's to Moscow, in 2005 and 2006 respectively, the relationship was fully reestablished, though Russia's influence was a shadow compared to the one it had under Nasser, and their renewed ties lagged far behind U.S.-Egyptian cooperation.

Mubarak's fall in February 2011 was met with deep skepticism in Russia, as was Mohammed Morsi's ascent. The Muslim Brotherhood was, at that time, still on a Russian list of terrorist organizations, and Russian commentators suspected that Egypt would pursue an "Islamic project" in the Middle East (Dolgov, 2015: 17). Nevertheless, Morsi visited Russia in April 2013, only months before his ousting, and arrangements were made for Russian participation in Egypt's civilian nuclear program, modernization of Soviet-built infrastructure, and an increase in Russian tourism, as Egypt's seaside resorts of Hurghada or Sharm-el-Sheikh had become one of Russians' favorite holiday destinations. All in all, Russia adjusted well to the fall of Mubarak and the rise of the Muslim Brotherhood to power.

The July 2013 Egyptian coup d'état, however, was hailed in Moscow. Despite the fact that Abdel Fatah al-Sisi belonged to a new generation of Egyptian officers with no ties to Russia whatsoever, as his military education had taken place in the West, he quickly found a connection to Russian President Putin and further boosted Russian-Egyptian ties. At the same time, relations between Egypt and the West cooled, given al-Sisi's increasingly authoritarian policies, leaving a void for Moscow to fill. For Russian observers, al-Sisi's power grab was a return to stability (Zviagelskaia, 2014: 73). Al-Sisi made Russia the first foreign country that he visited. He met with various Russian representatives and struck new arms deals, among them a US$3.5 billion contract in April 2015. Included in these contracts was an order of 46 MiG combat jets, diversifying its arsenal and providing a lifeline for this famed but crisis-stricken Russian aircraft producer. Egypt under al-Sisi thus signaled an end to a one-sided reliance on the United States, much to Russian satisfaction.

Iraq

Russian-Iraqi relations in the post-Soviet era have been largely dictated by Baghdad's strained relations with the international community between 1990 and 2003, and by the subsequent occupation by Western forces from 2003 to 2011, and the protracted internal strife which has continued. Formerly, in the 1970s, Iraq was an uneasy partner for the Soviet Union. Iraq signed an aid pact with the USSR in 1972, and this was, according to insiders, the culminating point of friendship. Afterwards, relations became more and more problem ridden. The "later Saddam" unleashed a campaign against the Iraqi communists in 1978, resumed the conflict with the Kurds, and then started leaning toward the United States (Primakov, 2009: 304–309). Also, his wars against Iran and Kuwait caused much displeasure in Moscow, as top diplomats bitterly recall. Former ambassador Viktor Posuvalyuk (2012: 110) even states that Iraq and the USSR had *never* been allies, as Saddam Hussein only wanted Soviet help to transform Iraq into the most powerful state in the Middle East.

The 1991 Gulf War has a special place in Russian-Middle Eastern relations for several reasons. To start, it marked the first time that Moscow and Washington were on the same side of a Middle Eastern conflict. Second, the Kremlin could test its clout in the region and act outside the Cold War logic. However, there was no unified approach in Moscow as to which position to assume in relation to Iraq, and a strong disagreement ensued between presidential representative Primakov and Foreign Minister Shevardnadze as well as between the higher echelons of the Foreign Ministry appointed by Gorbachev and the people running the day-to-day diplomacy (Grachev, 2008: 195–196), with one side unconditionally supporting Western military intervention and the other calling for restraint.

Between 1993 and 2003, relations evolved in the wake of the embargo imposed by the UN Security Council. Russia was skeptical about the usefulness of the embargo early on. Russia again tried to mediate between the United States and Iraq. Viktor Posuvalyuk, by then special presidential representative to the Middle East, argued that Russia did not only have economic interests in mind when it assumed a moderating role in 1998. For Posuvalyuk (2012: 191), Iraq was a matter of the principles of international relations, about the risk of setting an example according to which the United States would bypass the Security Council at will.

Thus, the 2003 invasion of Iraq represented for Russia the realization of all its nightmares, provoked harsh reactions, and had lasting repercussions for Russia's view of U.S. foreign policy. Beforehand, Russian companies had made small inroads into the Iraqi economy and were awarded a contract to restore Iraq's electric grid (Streltsov, 2014: 41; Zviagelskaia, 2014: 57). In 2008, Russia started cooperating more intensely with the new Iraqi government, debts of more than US$11 billion were cancelled, and Russian oil companies won tenders to extract oil in Iraq. Also, arms sales resumed. Additionally, a more strategic relationship between Iraq and Russia developed during the Syrian civil war, in which both countries sided with the Assad government. Intelligence is shared between Syria, Iraq, Iran, and Russia in joint information centers in Damascus and Baghdad.

Iran

Relations between Russia and Iran were difficult both in the Tsarist and the Soviet eras. Tensions date back to the early 19th century when Iran lost territory to the Russian Empire. Russia intervened militarily against Iran's 1905–1911 Constitutional Revolution. The Soviet Union supported the secession of the "Gilan Soviet" in northwestern Iran at the end of World War I, and of Iranian Azerbaijan and Kurdistan at the end of World War II. The Soviet Union and Britain occupied Iran during World War II; Joseph Stalin's initial refusal to withdraw Soviet troops led to one of the first crises of the Cold War. Soviet support for the Tudeh, Iran's Communist Party, angered both the monarchy and theocracy. Moscow completely miscalculated the character of the Iranian Revolution and had to rebuild ties from scratch (Shebarshin, 2012). The Soviet Union also armed and aided Iraq during its 1980–1988 war with Iran. Even nowadays, the Iranian press routinely refers to these events as reasons why Tehran should not trust Moscow.

Since 1989, however, cooperation has increased between Moscow and Tehran. Russia agreed to complete the nuclear reactor at Bushehr, which the German firm Siemens started working on during the monarchy, but stopped after the 1979 revolution. Russia also began selling weapons, including missiles, to Iran. Both countries supported the opposition Northern Alliance against the Taliban in Afghanistan during the 1990s. And along with China, Russia tried to weaken and delay U.S. and European efforts to impose UN sanctions on Iran over its nuclear program. All in all, Russian observers speak at times of a strategic partnership that is grounded in shared geopolitical interests and even in common cultural and "civilizational values" (Dunaev, 2015).

Yet, several issues continue to trouble relations. Russia's completion of the Bushehr reactor lagged years behind schedule. Moscow agreed to sell the S-300 air defense system to Iran, but then froze the deal in 2010, though Moscow reversed this decision in 2015. In addition, the two countries have been unable to resolve their differences over how to delineate the Caspian Sea, underneath which there are substantial quantities of petroleum. Iran has also been wary of Moscow's strong ties with Israel and its continued efforts to court anti-Iranian Arab states. And while it has acted to weaken them, Russia has frequently gone along with the West in imposing some UN sanctions on Iran.

Moscow and Tehran have both supported the Assad regime in Syria since opposition to it arose in 2011. Iranian forces were much more heavily involved in this effort until September 2015 when Russia deployed its air force to protect the Assad regime and attack its opponents. Yet even here, their cooperation is often fraught as was shown in August 2016 when Moscow's announcement that its bombers were flying missions over Syria from an Iranian air base led to anti-Russian criticism in Iran and the temporary cancellation of this program.

Israel

Although the USSR was one of the first countries to recognize Israel after it declared independence in 1948, in the mid-1950s Moscow aligned itself with the rising forces of Arab Nationalism, which were both anti-Western and anti-Zionist. Moscow broke diplomatic ties with Israel in the wake of the June 1967 war, in which Israel captured territory from and humiliated Egypt, Syria, and Jordan. Moscow sought to improve its ties to Arab countries generally through capitalizing on the unpopularity in the Arab world of U.S. support for Israel. But because the United States had ties to both Israel and most Arab states while the USSR did not have ties to Israel, it would be the United States which the belligerent parties in the Middle East would turn to in seeking peace efforts that largely sidelined Moscow.

Amidst improving Soviet-Western ties during the latter part of the Gorbachev era, Soviet diplomatic relations with Israel were restored in October 1991 – shortly before the dissolution of the USSR. Russian-Israeli ties improved during the Yeltsin era in the 1990s, when trade between the two countries grew and large numbers of Russian Jews immigrated to Israel. The relationship, though, was not especially cordial – particularly under the influence of the long-time advocate of close ties between Moscow and Arab Nationalist regimes, Yevgenii Primakov, when he was Yeltsin's Foreign Minister and then Prime Minister.

Since the rise of Vladimir Putin, Russian-Israeli relations have grown remarkably warm (Zviagelskaia, 2014: 117–135; Borshchevskaya, 2016). Several factors have contributed to this, including Putin's own personal regard for Jews, the close ties that Russian Jews in Israel have maintained with their motherland, Israel being a popular destination for Russian tourists, and growing bilateral ties not just in trade, but also in the military and security fields. Other contributing factors to better Russian-Israeli ties have been Israel's "understanding" for Putin's intervention in Chechnya at the beginning of his reign, Israel ending its arms sales to Georgia at the outset of the 2008 Russian-Georgian war, and Israel's refusal to go along with the United States and Europe in criticizing Russia's annexation of Crimea in 2014 and its policy toward Ukraine in general. Despite Israeli unhappiness about Moscow's close relations with its arch rival, Iran, the Netanyahu government has been remarkably uncritical of the Russian military intervention in support of Iran's ally, the Assad regime, in Syria (Barmin, 2016).

Saudi Arabia

The USSR was the first state to recognize the Saudi conquest in 1926 of Hejaz, the western part of which became Saudi Arabia, where the holy cities of Mecca and Medina are located.

In mid-1932, Prince Faisal visited Moscow. In mid-1938, though, the Soviets withdrew their diplomatic missions without explanation from Saudi Arabia and four other Middle Eastern countries. Unlike these others, however, Saudi Arabia refused to exchange embassies with the Soviet Union again until the very end of the Cold War in 1990.

During the Cold War, Saudi-Soviet relations were tense. Moscow did not appreciate how Saudi Arabia became so closely allied to the United States and was unwilling to have even normal diplomatic ties with the USSR. The Saudi government, for its part, felt threatened by Soviet support for its regional rivals – including Arab Nationalist regimes in Egypt, Syria, and Iraq, and Marxist-Leninist regimes in South Yemen, Ethiopia, and Afghanistan. During the 1980s, Moscow came to resent large-scale Saudi support for mujahideen groups fighting against the Soviet occupation of Afghanistan – a quagmire for Soviet forces, which Gorbachev ended up withdrawing them from in 1988–1989.

Despite the normalization of relations between Moscow and Riyadh in 1990, Saudi-Russian relations were relatively unfriendly during the 1990s and early 2000s. Russian officials and commentators regularly blamed Saudi Arabia for supporting Islamists in Chechnya and other Muslim regions of the former USSR (Melkumian, 2010: 149). Riyadh was unhappy that Russia would not cooperate with the Organization of Petroleum Exporting States (OPEC) in restraining oil production in order to lift prices in what was then a low oil price environment. In the immediate aftermath of 9/11, Vladimir Putin not only expressed his support for the United States, but frequently referred to the fact that 15 of the 19 bombers were Saudis in an effort to portray the United States and Russia as allies against a common Islamist threat which Moscow saw the Kingdom as supporting.

Saudi-Russian relations improved, though, in 2003 in the wake of the U.S.-led invasion of Iraq, which both Moscow and Riyadh disapproved of. Putin himself visited Riyadh in 2007, and Moscow had high hopes for greatly increased trade ties, as well as investment from, the Kingdom. But their relations turned sour again after the outbreak of the Arab Spring revolts in 2011 when Saudi Arabia aided the opponents of Russian-backed regimes in Libya and Syria. Riyadh is especially unhappy that Russia has sided with the Kingdom's arch-rival, Iran, in supporting Syria's Assad regime. Riyadh and Moscow continue to express hopes for improved relations, but achieving this goal has proven to be elusive.

Turkey

Russia and Turkey were regional rivals during the Tsarist and Ottoman eras. Relations between them improved after the early 20th-century revolutions in both countries. After the end of World War II, however, relations deteriorated when Turkey felt threatened by the Soviet Union and so turned to the United States for support and later joined NATO. During the Cold War, Turkey feared that Moscow was supporting the PKK – the Kurdish separatist movement that seeks to establish an independent Kurdish state in southeastern Turkey. Beginning in 1988, when conflict arose between Armenia and Azerbaijan even before the collapse of the Soviet Union, Russian support for Armenia and Turkish sympathy for Azerbaijan became an irritant to Russian-Turkish relations. Nevertheless, Russian-Turkish trade expanded dramatically beginning in the 1990s, and the countries started to cooperate in the energy sector (Ul'chenko, 2010: 24).

Russian-Turkish relations grew closer still in the early part of the 21st century. One factor leading to this was the U.S.-led intervention in Iraq beginning in 2003, which neither Moscow nor Ankara supported. Turkey feared that U.S. support for Iraqi Kurds would serve to strengthen Kurdish nationalists inside Turkey. Another factor was that Turkey's relations with the EU declined as it became increasingly clear that while Brussels was willing to accept

Eastern European and Baltic states that were formerly under Soviet domination as members, Turkey was not welcome. Yet another factor was that, like Putin, Turkey's leader Recep Tayyip Erdoğan became increasingly impatient with Western criticism over the state of democracy, human rights, and the rule of law in his country.

After the outbreak of the Arab Spring uprising in Syria in 2011, Russia and Turkey disagreed sharply over the fate of Syria's embattled ruler, Bashar al-Assad. Erdoğan called for him to go, while Putin insisted that he be allowed to remain in power. Still, Moscow and Ankara seemed to "agree to disagree" about Syria in the midst of an otherwise improving relationship. This changed, however, after Russia intervened militarily in Syria to defend Assad beginning in September 2015. In November 2015, Turkish forces shot down a Russian military aircraft in the Turkey-Syria border area. Putin reacted by imposing economic sanctions on Turkey. Furthermore, Moscow expressed support for Syrian Kurds, whom Ankara feared were allied with the PKK, fighting against Islamic State, which Moscow claimed Turkey was allowing to make use of Turkish territory.

Russian-Turkish relations dramatically improved, though, when in mid-2016 Erdoğan apologized for the shoot down incident and Putin agreed to lift sanctions. Their ties improved even more in the wake of the failed July 2016 coup attempt against Erdoğan, which Putin condemned more quickly than did Western governments – thus provoking not only Turkish resentment, but a Turkish belief that the West actually supported the coup. Yet despite the rebound in Russian-Turkish ties, Moscow and Ankara remain at odds over the fate of Assad in Syria (MacFarquhar, 2016). Their differences over the Azeri-Armenian dispute have not ended either.

Conclusions: future questions and themes

Russia in the Middle East today

Post-Soviet Russia in the Middle East today is in a much better diplomatic, economic, and military position than it has ever been. It has good relations with almost every regime and movement, even opposing ones. For example, it has good ties to Israel and to Iran, to Tel-Aviv and Ramallah; it has good relations with Turkey and with most Kurdish factions, even allowing a "representation" of the Northern Kurdish state, Rojava, to open in Moscow. Saudi Arabia is at odds with Russia on many issues, but Moscow has relatively good relations with other Arab Gulf states, including Oman, the UAE, Bahrain, and Kuwait. Hence, on the one hand, Moscow has the potential to be a major intermediary in the region. On the other, especially after its intervention in Syria, Russia's standing in the Middle East also appears damaged.

In its return to the Middle East, Russia has benefited from a long tradition of intense relations built during Soviet times. Albeit a vanishing generation, some senior Arab military personnel remain who have been trained in the Soviet Union and speak Russian, and who act not only as military but also as cultural intermediaries. In the case of Israel and due to emigration, the Russian language is one of the most widely spoken languages in the country, and key politicians have a Russian background. Still, Soviet and Russian soft power in the region is weak, mostly for the same reasons as in Soviet times: Russia does not offer a model to emulate. As Mohammed Heikal noted in the 1970s, good relations with Moscow are more pragmatic than heartfelt.

The Middle East turned out again to be a place where East-West rivalries are played out. However, the Cold War is hardly a good reference to understand Russia in the Middle East now. The picture has grown increasingly complex, with many new players determining the course of events in the region, not least Iran and Saudi Arabia, whose rivalry is increasingly influential in many conflicts (Syria, Yemen, Bahrain). Still, the Middle East is a place where Putin's Russia seems to be realizing its great power ambitions.

The West: Russia's friend or foe in the Middle East?

Relations between Russia and the West, especially the United States, have deteriorated in recent years over issues mainly unrelated to the Middle East, such as Georgia, Ukraine, the Baltics, NATO expansion, and EU enlargement, and EU regulations which Russian entities do not wish to comply with. In the Middle East, however, Russia and the West have shared some similar interests. Russia supported the U.S.-led campaign in Afghanistan against the Taliban and other jihadists. Russia also joined other major powers in negotiating a nuclear accord with Iran. While the Soviet Union supported or at least benefited from the overthrow of pro-Western governments in the Middle East during the Cold War, Putin's Russia has not sought their downfall. Indeed, the greatest differences between Putin and the West in the Middle East have been regarding Western efforts to further or support the downfall of authoritarian regimes Moscow has regarded as allies or partners in Iraq, Libya, and Syria.

Regarding Syria in particular, Moscow has sought to persuade Western governments that if the Assad regime falls, its most likely replacement will be a jihadist regime that is hostile to the West as well as toward Russia, and therefore it is in Western interests to join Russia in supporting Assad. Western governments, though, have not been persuaded by this argument, as they see the Assad regime's brutality as having given rise to the jihadist opposition instead. Yet despite their differences elsewhere as well as in the Middle East itself, Russia and the West do have a common interest in thwarting jihadists – something that Donald Trump seemed to recognize during his election campaign. But as serious U.S.-Russian differences over Syria and Iran in the short time since Trump became President have shown, having a common enemy does not guarantee that Moscow and Washington will be able to cooperate in the Middle East.

There could be serious consequences for Russia, though, if Russian ties to the West deteriorate further or just remain poor while Russian Muslim opposition to Moscow grows strong. Under these circumstances, it is not clear that the West would be willing, or even able, to help Russia against this "common threat," or that a proud but beleaguered Russian government would seek or welcome it.

The Middle East: Putin success or failure?

Whether Putin's policy toward the Middle East should be considered a success or a failure is not clear cut. Since he first came to power at the end of 1999, Putin has succeeded in re-establishing an important Russian presence in the region. Putin has also succeeded in establishing relatively good working relations with the governments of the region. There have been setbacks in some relationships – most notably between Russia and Turkey after the November 2015 Turkish shoot down of a Russian aircraft. But even this serious downturn was reversed in mid-2016. Further, the Russian military intervention in Syria that began in September 2015 has succeeded in propping up the Assad regime at relatively low cost to Moscow.

On the other hand, Putin has largely failed in building a coalition to join Moscow and Tehran in the fight against what Moscow sees as the common jihadist enemy; other states see the Assad regime, Iran, or even Syrian Kurds as too unreliable or as adversaries. This points to a larger problem for Moscow in the region: while Putin has succeeded in improving Russian ties with all the governments as well as some non-governmental actors in the region, he has not resolved or overcome the many differences among them. Indeed, Russian diplomacy has not so much tried to resolve differences among regional actors as take advantage of them.

What this means is that while Middle Eastern governments and other actors have been willing to increase their cooperation with Moscow, Russia's close ties to their adversaries limit the extent to which each actor is willing to trust or rely on Russia. Further, while Moscow has succeeded in gaining some acceptance from many Middle Eastern governments for Russian intervention in Syria to protect the Assad regime, public opinion in many countries of the region disapproves of Moscow's actions there. Putin, of course, may not be particularly concerned about this, but negative opinion about Russian actions in Syria could serve to limit the degree to which Middle Eastern governments either cooperate with Russia, or could even motivate them to cooperate with the United States and the West against it.

Finally, one has to assess the domestic repercussion of these policies. In terms of identity construction, especially Russia's intervention in Syria, they have bolstered the image of Russia as a resurgent superpower. Formerly, the Middle East was of little concern to the domestic audience, and by and large still is; however, due to Russia's involvement in Syria, it came back to public consciousness. Due to the West's reluctance to act decisively in the region, Russia could indeed strengthen her position in the Middle East. However, the West's dominance in the region is still undisputed, especially due to U.S. close diplomatic ties and military muscle in the Gulf region.

References

Amin, Samir (2016) "Egypt: Failed Emergence, Conniving Capitalism, Fall of the Muslim Brothers", in Ali Kadri (ed.) *Development Challenges and Solutions after the Arab Spring*. Houndmills, UK: Palgrave Macmillan, 19–38.

Andrew, Christopher and Vasili Mitrokhin (2005) *The Mitrokhin archive II. The KGB and the World*. London: Allen Lane.

Barmin, Yury (2016) "Russia Emerges as a Center of Gravity for Israel". *Al-Monitor*, November 6, www.al-monitor.com/pulse/originals/2016/11/russia-center-gravity-israel-palestine-mideast.html#ixzz4Q7khgXaM.

Belokrenitskii, V. Ya. (2010) *Rossija i islamskii mir*. Moscow: IVRAN.

Borshchevskaya, Anna (2016) "The Maturing of Israeli-Russian relations. *Washington Institute for Near East Policy*", www.washingtoninstitute.org/policy-analysis/view/the-maturing-of-israeli-russian-relations.

Dolgov, B.V. (2015) "Radikalnii islamism v kontekste obostreniia otnoshenii Zapada i Rossii", in Khazanov A.N. (ed.) *Vostok mezhdu Zapadom i Rossiei*. Moscow: IVRAN, 15–36.

Dunaev, E.V. (2015) *Rossiisko-Iranskoe otnoshenia. Problemy i perspektivy*. Moscow: IVRAN.

El Din, Yousef Gamal (2013) What's at Stake for Russia in Syria. *CNBC*, 3 September 2013, www.cnbc.com/id/101004539.

Goodin, Robert E. (2010). *The Oxford Handbook of International Relations*. Oxford, UK: Oxford University Press.

Grachev, Andrei (2008) *The Gorbachev Gamble*. Cambridge, UK: Polity Press.

Grygiel, Jakub J. and A. Wess Mitchell (2016) *The Unquiet Frontier: Rising Rivals, Vulnerable Allies, and the Crisis of American Power*. Princeton, NJ: Princeton University Press.

Heikal, Mohammed (1978) *The Sphinx and the Commissar. The Rise and Fall of Soviet Influence in the Middle East*. New York: Harper & Row.

Lo, Bobo (2015) *Russia and the New World Disorder*. London: Royal Institute of International Affairs.

MacFarquhar, Neil (2016) "Warming Relations in Person, Putin and Erdogan Revive Pipeline Deal", *New York Times*, October 10, www.nytimes.com/2016/10/11/world/europe/turkey-russia-vladimir-putin-recep-tayyip-erdogan.html?_r=0.

Mamedova, N.M. & E.V. Dunaeva (2011) *Politika RF i Irana v regional'nom kontekste*. Moscow: IVAN.

Matar, Linda and Ali Kadri (2016) "Investment and Neoliberalism in Syria", in Ali Kadri (ed.) *Development Challenges and Solutions after the Arab Spring*. Houndmills: Palgrave, 200–220.

Medvedko, Leonid I. & Sergey L. Medvedko (2009) *Vostok – delo bliskoe. Ierusalim – sviatoe*. Moscow: Grifon.
Melkumian, E.S. (2010) "Rossia i arabskie gosudarstva zaliva", in Belokrenitskii, V. et al. (eds.) *Rossija i islamskii mir*. Moscow: IVRAN, 144–160.
Nizameddin, Talal (2013) *Putin's New Order in the Middle East*. London: C. Hurst & Co.
Posuvalyuk, Viktor (2012) *Bagrovoe nebo Bagdad*. St Petersburg, Russia: Aleteiya.
Primakov, Yevgeny (2009) *Russia and the Arabs. Behind the Scenes in the Middle East from the Cold War to the Present*. New York: Basic Books.
Putin, Vladimir (2007) "Speech and the Following Discussion at the Munich Conference on Security Policy", February 10, http://en.kremlin.ru/events/president/transcripts/24034.
Putin, Vladimir (2014) "Address by President of the Russian Federation", March 18, http://en.kremlin.ru/events/president/news/20603.
Shebarshin, Leonid (2012) *Ruka Moskvy: Razvedka ot rastsveta do razvala*. Moscow: Algoritm.
Stent, Angela E. (2014) *The Limits of Partnership: U.S.-Russian Relations in the Twenty-First Century*. Princeton, NJ: Princeton University Press.
Streltsov, D. V. (2014) *Rossiia i strany Vostoka v postbipoliarnii period*. Moscow: Aspekt Press.
Tolz, Vera (2011) *Russia's Own Orient. The Politics of Identity and Oriental Studies in the Late Imperial and Early Soviet Periods*. Oxford, UK: Oxford UP.
Tsygankov, Andrei P. (2013) *Russia's Foreign Policy*. Lanham, MD: Rowman & Littlefield.
Ul'chenko, N. (2010) "Rossia i Turtsia: osnovnze etapy sotsial'no-politicheskogo razvitiia", in Belokrenitskii, V. et al. (eds.) *Rossija i islamskii mir*. Moscow: IVRAN, 17–28.
Vasilev, Alexei (1993) *Rossiia na Blizhnem i Srednem Vostoke*. Moscow: Nauka.
Zviagelskaia, Irina (2014) *Blizhnevostochnyi Klinch*. Moscow: Aspekt.

19
THE CAUCASUS

Maxim A. Suchkov

PYATIGORSK STATE UNIVERSITY, RUSSIA

Introduction

Whenever one is discussing Russia's insecurities and vulnerabilities, the Caucasus is frequently studied. The region has always had a special place in Russian history and geopolitics, and has been an inspiration for Russian literature from Alexander Pushkin to Mikhail Lermontov to Leo Tolstoy. A former part of the Great Silk Road, the Caucasus has historically been an arena for struggle and limited cooperation between three prime regional actors – Russia, Turkey, and Iran. The situation has been aggravated as great world powers turned their eyes to the region – first Great Britain (19th to 20th centuries), and Germany (during WWII) and later, the United States. In their struggle for control and influence in the region that possesses a colossal energy, logistics, and trade potential as well as overriding geostrategic significance, all of the contenders resorted to different means, leading at times to open confrontation.

Geographically, the Greater Caucasus Range divides the region into two parts – the Northern and the Southern Caucasus. But mountains here mean more than a geographic feature and a natural beauty. For centuries they have marked the borders for political entities, shaped cultural – and later political – identities, bred the sense of ethnic uniqueness that due to the natural barriers had to exist in isolation for millennia (Wertsch, 2013). Moreover, as nations in the region sought to revive their identities, some scholars introduced the geopolitical notion of "the Mountains" alongside those of "Sea" and "Land" (Ryabtsev, 2011: 19).

The rich cultural heritage of the region has been its blessing and its curse. There are about 50 peoples with distinctive cultures and languages (Topchishvili, 2011) while religion-wise, a very rough estimate of today's Caucasus say 57% are Christians (17 million people) and 43% are Muslims (13 million people).[1] This diverse plethora of actors on a relatively small territory of 400,000 sq km (40 million hectares) has inevitably led to their continuous social, cultural, and economic "interweaving." It also has a high conflict potential both in the North and the South of the Caucasus, earning the region the notorious title of the "knot of contradictions" (Sukhankin, 2014).

With the collapse of the Soviet Union, the Caucasus has become portrayed as a source of chronic instability (Ilyasov, 2012). Ethnic tensions, some of which stemmed into gory skirmishes and wars, growing Islamic radicalism, competition for access to the oil and natural gas reserves of the Caspian basin – these and some other factors have ensured that the region would become and remain a source of "significant international engagement and concern" (Nation, 2007).

For the newly independent states in the South Caucasus – Georgia, Armenia, and Azerbaijan – the break-up of the Soviet Union meant a promise of independence. For Moscow it signaled alarming prospects of a potential secession of some of its North Caucasus entities. Although there was – and still is – a sound Russian ethnic presence in the region, Dagestan, Chechnya, Ingushetia, Karachay-Circassia, Kabardino-Balkaria, North Ossetia-Alania, Adygea came to be referred to as "republics," meaning they were non-Russian ethnic areas in the Russian Federation.

To make matters worse, the conflicts in Nagorno-Karabakh, South Ossetia, and Abkhazia not only had an immediate devastating effect on Armenia, Azerbaijan, and Georgia but triggered a far-reaching impact on the Russian North Caucasus as well. Sergey Markedonov, Russia's leading authority on the Caucasus, scrutinizes the phenomenon of what he called the "intertwined conflicts" in his concise history of Eurasia in the first years after the collapse of the USSR (Markedonov, 2010a: 40–47).

Given the fact that most of the conflicts stem from the days of the Soviet Union – historians would argue some go back to even more ancient times – and the grave security implications the spread of the conflicts could have had on Russia's own "soft underbelly" of the North Caucasus, Moscow played a key mediating role in all of the conflicts. It eventually managed to bring the warring parties to the negotiating table to sign ceasefire treaties. The conflicts have never been resolved, ultimately making the Caucasus a home to three out of four "de facto" states in the post-Soviet space. Russian historians and political analysts still argue whether it was beyond Moscow's ability to make such a resolution happen given the maximalist demands of the local elites, politically galvanized societies, and the "memory politics" promoted by political parties and civic movements seeking a rather "winner takes all" solution than an acceptable compromise.

All these factors make it possible for scholars to adapt different approaches to the region. Some look into the regional dynamics and Russia's role here through the lens of Moscow's own insecurities (Blank, 2013) and the nature of Russian political regime. Others draw analogies with the past to explain Russia's contemporary phobias and interests in the region (King, 2011). Still others link the challenges Moscow faces in the Caucasus to Russia's broader security environment (Hahn, 2007; Markedonov, 2010a). This chapter takes these approaches into account and stresses internal drivers and external irritants that have shaped Russian policies in the Caucasus since the early 1990s.

Sources of Russia's concerns in the Northern Caucasus

Dominated for centuries by the Russian Empire and later the Soviet Union (Martin, 2001: 496), in the 1990s the Caucasus found itself in the "power vacuum." Regional and outside actors turned their eyes to the part of Eurasia to rediscover its geopolitical assets, natural resources, and logistical opportunities (Shaffer, 2009b: 131–142). Having serious problems with projecting its own power and ensuring control of the region, Moscow was especially susceptive to any real or hypothetical foreign influence over the region. The region's ethnic variety and territorial disputes were seen as pretexts for foreign states to encroach on Russia's "near abroad." Of all the array of states that sought to increase its regional presence, the United States seemed to be the prime irritant for Moscow. The reasons for such a sensitive reaction fall into three major problem areas.

First, the perception of each other's regional policies predominantly through the lens of the "zero-sum game": security stakes were – and still are – so high for Moscow in the Caucasus that virtually any U.S. initiative deemed to undermine Russia's security or status was viewed as a grave challenge for the other. The opposite was also true: Russia's policies to strengthen its position in its immediate neighborhood were perceived as a thinly veiled effort to "restore the Soviet Union" or chart out a "zone of influence."

Second, since the break-up of the Soviet Union, the dynamics of many regional processes in the Caucasus has been influenced by the United States – directly or circumstantially (Suchkov, 2013). With time, the fact that Moscow and Washington were frequently finding themselves on opposite sides of almost all regional developments only exacerbated the brewing contradictions: South Stream gas pipeline vs. the Nabucco pipeline, the GUAM Organization vs. the OCSA (Organization of Collective Security Agreement), Georgia vs. Abkhazia/South Ossetia, etc.

Finally, Moscow has always perceived the post-Soviet space (including the Caucasus region) as the zone of its vital security interests. Hence, virtually any U.S. – or, broadly, Western – initiative in the region was seen in Moscow as an attempt to exert more influence over Russia's most volatile region – the North Caucasus. The Kremlin soon concluded that the United States was not interested in security cooperation with Russia, but was rather oriented towards gaining influence in the post-Soviet space.

In this respect the war in Chechnya was a catalyst for Russia's perception. It was also then when the West formed its perception of Russia's regional policy. Fighting an extremely unpopular, bloody, and expensive war in the rebellious republic made Moscow especially susceptive to military activity near its borders let alone any foreign presence in and support for Chechnya. During the two wars, first separatist and then jihadist warlords found sympathy in Turkey and some Gulf states

Since the first Chechen war (1993–1996), the issue of the human rights abuses by the Russian federal security forces has become a popular theme among Western analysts, journalists, and human rights activists. Using the historical analogies, they were alluding to the Russian imperial practices of cracking down on the indigenous peoples of the North Caucasus (Applebaum, 1999). They also argued that under the pretext of fighting terrorism, Russia was strangling freedom in the most ethnically complex area of the country and thus the West – the United States in particular – should have their say on the cause. The idea that Russians were fighting "freedom fighters" rather than "violent jihadists" – as was claimed by Moscow – had been propagated at the top level. The notion was based on the premise that Russia exercised "brutal neo-colonialist" policy in the North Caucasus. The argument went that since "the rebels" fight back against "the suppression," Moscow can only blame itself for the chaos in the region.

Clearly, the Kremlin made and is still making a great number of strategic errors in the region. The cocktail of poverty, high unemployment rates, demographics, and migration statistics make it more prone to the extremist ideas. Being unable to manage it creates a temptation to hide behind the "terror threat" to justify a tightening-the-screws policy. Yet the different language used in U.S. and Russian discourse went far beyond their linguistic nuances, for it reflected divergent interpretations and created polar narratives.

Conceptually, it's still difficult for outside observers to think outside "the Chechen" paradigm and recognize other actors involved in the process. Until recently, many analysts rejected ties between the notorious Caucasus Emirate and Al-Qaeda, making U.S. decision-makers believe Russia and the United States were facing challenges of a different nature (Williams, 2007: 156–178). They insisted that while the United States and its allies had to deal with Islamist fundamentalist groups, separatism in the North Caucasus was of an ethno-nationalist character and was purely a "Russian problem."

In reality, the ethno-nationalist agenda in the North Caucasus and in Chechnya in particular exhausted itself in the 1990s and was rapidly replaced by radical Islamism (Markedonov, 2010b). By the time Vladimir Putin became President in 2000, the divide among Chechen leaders over the political future of Chechnya was palpable. Some welcomed the influx of foreign – predominately Arab – fighters, preachers, and emirs as they hoped it would further push Chechnya to the forefront of the global jihadi movement with more money and resources coming to the region. Others, however, believed the resistance was thus stripped of the initial idea and was moving Chechnya in the wrong direction. Putin discerned this trend and came to rely on one of the most powerful men in the "second group," Akhmat-Haji Kadyrov, the former mufti of the unrecognized Chechen Republic of Ichkeria and the father of current Chechen President Ramzan Kadyrov. Kadyrov proved to be instrumental in defeating the international terrorist groupings in Chechnya and was later elected the first president of the post-war republic. The phenomenon that later became known as the "Chechenization" of the Chechen conflict (Ware, 2009) was attributed as one of the key political successes of Vladimir Putin, cementing his authority in Russia.

In October 2002, Russia was shattered by the theater hostage crisis in Moscow that took the lives of 130 hostages (Yefimova, 2002). Two years after on September 1, 2004, the Beslan school hostage siege ended in at least 330 hostages killed, including 186 children. The crises pushed the Russian government to adopt security and political measures that many found excessive and abusive of civil rights. The terrorist attacks also triggered Moscow to act more decisively in the North Caucasus. The Kremlin dismissed the proposal on the peace talks from Chechen warlords and criticized Europeans heavily for harboring top Chechen leaders (Caucasus report, 2005). An ever bigger irritant for Moscow were U.S. public organizations monitoring Chechnya – such as the American Committee for Peace in the Caucasus – that Russian security forces saw as cover-ups for intelligence gathering. All of that amassed deep-seated grievances and made Russian leadership conclude that Europe and the United States still didn't seriously consider embracing Russia into the "Western camp," but rather saw it as a geopolitical adversary that needed to be weakened, if not "softly partitioned" (Hahn, 2011).

The negative vibes that reached the Caucasus in 1990s were a clear indication of the dangers associated with the geography of the region. Its very proximity to the Middle East and Central Asia burdened Moscow's security concerns with additional risks and forced Russia to be more watchful of the adjacent regions. And while the challenges Washington and Moscow were confronted with have a different pre-history and background, the ties between terrorist groups in the North Caucasus and in the Greater Middle East are obvious and well-proved – be it ideology, financial flows, or operational activity, Moscow lamented that this has barely been recognized by Western decision-makers which, in part, has shaped a respective narrative vis-à-vis the region in the United States. As a result, by the end of the 1990s, Russia and the United States had accumulated a heavy baggage of bitter disagreements.

Russia's evolving policies in the 2000s

The external risks for the Caucasus increased dramatically after the atrocities of September 11, 2001 that marked a major shift in U.S. foreign policy towards the Middle East and Eurasia. Seeking new geopolitical venues for operations in Afghanistan and Iraq, the Bush administration "re-discovered the Caucasus." Russia was among the first to show support for the U.S. tragedy, hoping for a change of heart in U.S. attitudes towards the situation in the North Caucasus. Indeed, The White House appreciated the Kremlin's sympathy and readiness to engage in anti-terrorist measures in Afghanistan. A narrow but promising window of opportunity for a fruitful cooperation appeared. Barely did it last for two years.

As the Bush administration declared the "war on terror," the military aspect of U.S. foreign policy augmented. The $100 million military exercises in the Caspian Sea were launched in the fall of 2003 to "defend key economic zones and conduct counter-terrorist operations." In fact, the Caspian Guard program did help monitor trade and transport routes around vital oil derricks. It involved not only state agencies of the United States and Azerbaijan but attracted a number of private military contractors (Abdullayeva and Shulman, 2004). While its prime target was to deter Iran, the drills triggered strong disapproval from Moscow, as it was wary of a larger foreign military presence in the Caspian.

By the mid-2000s, the United States and Russia didn't bother to create an illusion of a partnership in fighting terrorism. A series of landmark events – from the U.S. invasion in Iraq, to the "color revolutions" in the post-Soviet space – rolled the two countries back to "the Great Game" in Eurasia with antagonizing rhetoric coming from the two capitals. The aspirations for the two states to work productively towards joint efforts in securing the region gradually faded away leaving Washington and Moscow with even bigger grievances.

Feeling the need to enhance its power and control over the Caucasus, Russia tightened the screws in the North Caucasus and became more assertive regionally, making sure the South Caucasus states remained in its orbit of influence. The relations between Moscow and Washington in the second half of the 2000s went from bad to worse. The amount of bilateral disagreements over a number of issues in the post-Soviet space, as well as the way local leaders exploited these disagreements to their own political needs, culminated in the tragic five-day war in Georgia's breakaway republic of South Ossetia. Not only did it signal at the time the biggest crisis in U.S.-Russia relations since the end of the Cold War but it seriously transformed the security of the Caucasus.

Unlike the Bush administration, the Obama team in the first few years of his presidency made the U.S. presence less visible in the South Caucasus and more cooperative on the challenges threatening the North Caucasus. Partly it was due to the "reset" policy with Russia; partly because the administration itself set other priorities on its foreign policy agenda.

In any case, on May 26, 2011, the U.S. Department of State listed the Caucasus Emirate (CE) as a terrorist organization with its militant leader, Doku Umarov. The commendable initiative was welcomed by the Kremlin with the hope for further cooperation. Essentially, it was exactly the sign of support Russia sought from the United States, and the kind of action it had been waiting for for a long time (Markedonov, 2011). Many policy-makers, however, signaled moderate optimism as the decades-long experience made them more cautious about a "close cooperation" between the United States and Russia.

Another step Moscow expected from Washington on the issue was the shutdown of the CE prime information tool, the "Kavkaz-Center" website, which operated freely outside Russia. This entanglement of donors and sympathizers of the CE was the tip of the iceberg, but represented an important need that Russia communicated to the United States to pool their efforts so as to at least clamp down on information threats from extremist groups. Nonetheless the State Department initiative was a serious breakthrough as it demonstrated there was a more accurate understanding of the phenomenon at the state level and it potentially laid the grounds for productive cooperation in this area.

On April 15, 2013, the Caucasus came under yet another notorious international spotlight. The Boston marathon bombings shook the United States and left many with dubious conclusions on the degree of cooperation between Russian and U.S. security forces (or lack of thereof) and how quickly U.S. law-enforcement reacted to the signals (Ioffe, 2013). The attack opened a debate on whether the United States should reassess its policy toward extremism and whether the logic of "the enemy of my enemy is my friend" was pernicious when it came to preserving national security. But the tragedy also opened a second window of opportunity for U.S.-Russia cooperation on terrorism (Trenin, 2013). Unfortunately, that opportunity was smashed against the overall growing crisis in U.S.-Russia relations, with the reset policy swiftly exhausting itself and the gap on raging war in Syria growing.

Meanwhile, as Russia was preparing for the crucial event of the Sochi 2014 Olympics, new Caucasus-related thorny issues were raised with "the Circassian genocide" being at the top of the list. Complicated as it was, it played a contextual role in the expert debate in the West ahead of the Sochi Winter Olympics (Malashenko, 2013). At the official level, Moscow and Washington kept a relatively low profile on the issue. But as the Olympics approached, the information space was filling up with new feeds on it. The pressure was being mounted on the Russian leadership as various pundits, reporters, bloggers, NGO activists, and lobbying groups were raising awareness, calling on Western governments to use their powers and make Moscow address the legitimate concerns of the Circassian people living in the country and abroad (Bullough, 2012). Some U.S. academic venues launched research projects on the problem (most notable were the Johns Hopkins SAIS and the Rutgers University Center for the Study of Genocide, Conflict Resolution and Human Rights). The leading motive of the campaign was to hold Russians accountable for the mass killing of Circassian groups in the 19th century at the place where the Sochi Olympics was about to take place. Some even called for a boycott of the Olympics to showcase support for "the Circassian cause" (Richmond, 2013).

Needless to say, Moscow saw the debate as part of a coordinated effort to sabotage what was deemed to reboot Russia's international image. Some Russian analysts compared the criticism over the Circassian issue to the Tibet problem fueled in the wake of the Beijing Olympics in 2008 and insisted it was meant to test Russia. As the Olympics approached, the critical focus had shifted from "the Circassian issue" to the "inhumane treatment of guest workers" and the "crackdown on the LGBT community" to the billions squandered on the construction of the Olympics infrastructure and allegations of massive corruption (Grove, 2013).

Russia's policy in the South Caucasus: success or failure?

Relations with the states in the South Caucasus have been a mixed bag for Russia over the 25 years since their independence. Russia's attitude toward this part of the region has been overshadowed by concerns over a possible accession of Georgia, Azerbaijan, and Armenia to NATO. This pushed Moscow to seek its own geopolitical strongholds in the region.

Armenia came to be perceived as Russia's prime geopolitical beacon in the region, and rightly so. The Russia-Armenia "strategic partnership" was institutionalized through Armenia's membership in the Collective Security Treaty Organization (CSTO) from 1992, and the Eurasian Economic Union (EEU) from 2015 as well as through a number of bilateral formats. The Russian Federal Security Service for Border Protection guards Armenia's borders with Iran and Turkey together with the Armenian border patrol. The presence of the 102nd Russian military base stationed in Armenia's second biggest city of Gyumri in August 2010 was prolonged until 2044, which secured Russia a solid military presence in the middle of the South Caucasus at least until that time.

On the economic front, about 1,300 companies with Russian capital are operating in Armenia, which represents more than a quarter of all foreign-backed enterprises in the country. Up to 50% of all foreign investment in the Armenian economy comes from Russia, and Armenia enjoys close business links with more than 70 Russian regions (Markedonov, 2013: 30). One of the biggest assets of the bilateral relations is the Armenian diaspora: not only do Armenians represent the seventh largest ethnic group in Russia (1.18 million people), but they are active in the business world and other key spheres of social and political life in Russia.

Until 2001, Russia's relations with Azerbaijan were rather strained. Russia's military units had to be withdrawn from Azerbaijan in May 1993, and President Boris Yeltsin never paid an official visit to Baku. The normalization of bilateral relations with Azerbaijan started under President Putin, who visited Azerbaijan's capital in 2001.

As Sergey Markedonov correctly observed:

> In the case of Nagorno-Karabakh, Russia was faced not only with the issues of de-facto states and territorial secession but with a state-patron of secession that was interested, without serious preconditions, in cooperation with Moscow. This pushed the Russian leadership to "even" the level of its relationship with the South Caucasus countries. Those conditions (which could be defined as the first post-Soviet geopolitical status quo) predetermined Moscow's controversial policy approaches to Armenia.
> *(Markedonov, 2013: 32)*

Since then, Moscow has started to seek ways to reconcile Azerbaijan. One of the key principles Moscow chose to stick to was to avoid any decisions that could have tipped the balance in Nagorno-Karabakh either to favor Yerevan or Baku. Preserving the status quo was – and still is – seen as the best possible option under the given circumstances. Hence when Russia decided to help guard Armenian borders, it was a clear message to Azerbaijan. Yet, as an act of "geopolitical balancing" in 2007, Moscow supplied arms to Azerbaijan. Russia also saw Azerbaijan as instrumental in providing security for its turbulent Dagestan where the border area had been a major concern for both Moscow and Baku. Azerbaijan remained crucial in Russia's energy security and pipeline politics (Shaffer, 2009a), with Gazprom offering to buy more Azeri gas in 2010. The set of "leveling policies" on the part of the Kremlin triggered contradictions that shadow Russian-Armenian relations to this day.

Moscow too had its own grievances vis-à-vis Yerevan. It had to do with Armenia's response to the war in South Ossetia in 2008 where the Armenian government refrained from unequivocal support for Russia. Neither did Yerevan characterize the events as "the genocide of the Ossetian people" – the wording Moscow chose to label Saakashvili's reckless seizure effort – or express solidarity with Russia in recognizing the independence of Abkhazia and South Ossetia. On the contrary, after 2008 Yerevan pursued a rather constructive engagement with Tbilisi. It certainly wasn't a "sudden eye-opener" for the Kremlin, but a sign that there were clear and rigid limits to how far cooperation with even the closest allies might go.

Russian-Armenian relations have been remarkably dependent on the fractured perception of each other's policies stemming from frequently high expectations of one another. Armenians quite jealously react to any deals Moscow is seeking and striking with Azeris, especially when it comes to cooperation in the military-technical field. Russia, in its turn, often continues to operate on the inertia of "historic ties," expecting Armenia to show loyalty without an investment – political and financial – in this loyalty.

As for Azerbaijan, Dmitri Trenin, leading expert on Russia's Eurasian policies, argues that Baku managed "to play Russia extremely well." It virtually freed itself of the Russian military presence and subsequently replaced Soviet-era energy outlets with modern-day gas and oil pipelines "without irreparably damaging its relations with Moscow." A big part of these rather successful policies, according to Trenin, is that "Azerbaijan has long decided not to cross two red lines: seeking NATO membership and hosting U.S. military bases" (Trenin, 2011: 93–101).

This certainly wasn't the case with Georgia where aspirations for NATO membership heated the security agenda in the border area fueling Moscow's irritation with Georgian authorities.

During the Chechen War, international militants found a safe haven in the Georgian Pankisi Gorge. Even though Tbilisi had its traditional fears of the mountaineers who used to come down for hit-and-run raids, helping Chechens represented a poke in the eye for the Kremlin that Tbilisi couldn't resist given Moscow's own support for Abkhazia and South Ossetia. The Kremlin likened the harboring of Chechen militants by Georgia to the Taliban accommodating al-Qaeda. In 2002, Moscow "strongly warned" Tbilisi, using the language similar to that of the United States condemning al-Qaeda activities.

Not prioritized under the Yeltsin administration in the 1990s, Russia's overall policies toward Georgia were tainted by a genuine distrust most Russian decision-makers – especially among the security apparatus who managed most of the Caucasus activities – had vis-à-vis the then-president of Georgia, Eduard "the Silver Fox" Shevardnadze. Ironically, Moscow helped bring Shevardnadze to power in 1992. But since 1995, the Georgian president had charted the course towards a closer relationship with the United States as opposed to Russia. Therefore, Moscow regretted little when Shevardnadze himself was toppled in the Rose Revolution by a young and passionate Mikheil Saakashvili.

In 2004 Putin and Saakashvili established a fairly close relationship, which created an impression – at least in Moscow – that the two leaders could do a lot of mutually beneficial business together. One of the first "concessions" the Russians offered to Saakashvili, for the prospect of a long-term partnership, was Ajara. An autonomous republic of Georgia bordering Turkey, Ajara had long hosted a Russian military base, had assets from top Russian businessmen, and was ruled by a rebellious leader friendly with Moscow's movers and shakers. Letting Saakashvili take full control of the territory didn't make him thankful to Moscow, as was expected. On the contrary, the impulsive Georgian leader saw it as a green light to continue to ensure Tbilisi's jurisdiction over the other two break-away republics.

Contrary to the wide-spread view, it wasn't the attempt to restore Georgia's territorial integrity that made Putin snap. Experts and diplomats privy to the situation argue that the Russian President was prepared to cooperate on a step-by-step settlement of the conflicts. What concerned Moscow most was the way President Saakashvili wanted the conflicts resolved. Placating the domestic audience with populist promises to "return the lost territories" – in certain cases setting a specific timeline for the seizure of South Ossetia and Abkhazia – Saakashvili burned the political bridge with Moscow. A failure to deliver on those promises also meant the loss of political support among Georgians.

Since August 2004, when Saakashvili carried out a police raid operation in South Ossetia, relations between him and Putin were set on a steady path for a direct confrontation. Both sides exchanged hostile acts – the spy scandal in 2006, the subsequent deportation of Georgians from Russia, and the embargo on Georgian products. Both sides pursued independent policies towards South Ossetia and Abkhazia – Russia launched the "passportization policy" while Georgia started to create "governments in exile."

Remarkably, however, even at the highest peak of those crises, neither Russia nor Georgia went to recognize Abkhazia and South Ossetia as "independent states" – though the two were bombarding Moscow with visits and pledges for it – neither did it halt the drawdown of its troops from Soviet-era military bases in Georgia. The move was set to be a quid pro quo in return for Georgia's own pledge not to seek to join NATO. Moreover, the deals Russia offered to the Saakashvili administration on a peaceful settlement of Abkhazia and South Ossetia – the final one in the beginning of 2007 – were constantly declined.

By that time Saakashvili had made powerful friends in Washington and had been well-received in European capitals (King, 2004). Effectively playing the "Russia threat" card, he concluded that if he continued on a tough unilateral course of dealing with the Abkhaz and

Ossetians he'd have full Western support and Moscow wouldn't dare to resist. The dangerous game of continuous escalations and provocations against the backdrop of the NATO Bucharest Summit declaration that promised Georgia [and Ukraine] a membership "one day" resulted in Saakashvili's calculation to seize the moment of a power transition in Russia from Putin to Medvedev and up the ante by launching an offensive on Tskhinvali.

The August war ended in the defeat of the Georgian troops and Russia's recognition of Abkhazia and South Ossetia as independent states. The move came to be erroneously interpreted as Moscow's response to the Kosovo recognition. However, a more accurate analysis of the situation around the pre-war Abkhazia and South Ossetia suggests Russia's choice didn't have anything to do with the "cookie-cutter" approach. Should there not have been the Saakashvili attempt at the blitzkrieg seizure of Tskhinvali, both South Ossetia and Abkhazia might have still been in the "de facto" status.

The war in Georgia seriously shuffled the status quo in the region and put an end to any serious consideration of Georgia's NATO membership, at least within the near future (King, 2008; Philips, 2008). It also made Moscow more cautious of its southern flank and pushed it to beef up its security and military infrastructure along its perimeter. As part of the initiative, Russia signed some important security treaties with its new allies in Sukhumi and Tskhinvali.

Moscow's dealings with South Ossetia and Abkhazia, however, differed due to diverging agendas in the newly recognized republics. To this day South Ossetia remains a land-locked territory poor with resources and highly dependent on Russian financial aid and other support, with very bleak prospects of political existence as an independent entity. The two most frequently discussed options for the future status of South Ossetia are either its "entrance" into the Russian Federation as yet another [maybe even autonomous] republic, or its "accession" with North Ossetia as part of a united Republic of Ossetia. The options are politically and financially costly, and Moscow doesn't seem to be willing to push the developments voluntarily.

It's much more complicated with Abkhazia that set itself on a steady course for independence from Georgia and Russia alike. The Treaty on Alignment and Strategic Partnership between Russia and the Republic of Abkhazia, signed on November 24, 2014, won itself many opponents in Russia and Abkhazia. The Abkhaz opposition argued it would make the Republic more dependent on Russia, thus depriving it of long-sought-after independence. Russian critics, in turn, insisted it would put Moscow in a position of being an eternal donor to Abkhazia without any viable gains. Yet, the product of several previous drafts, the treaty covered bilateral, political, economic, and military cooperation and was an important signal of the direction Russian foreign policy was taking in the region.

Over the years since Russia and Abkhazia established diplomatic relations, the two have signed more than 80 bilateral agreements detailing practically every aspect of the relationship. In substance, the treaty helped Abkhazia to continue play its own game: it ultimately outsourced the Republic's social and economic policy to Russia thus leaving enough time and resources for the Abkhaz leadership to focus more on constructing a virtual ethnocracy. Ideally, Moscow might have wished to fully integrate Abkhazia into the Eurasian Union. But facing strong opposition from Belarus and Kazakhstan – as well as potential international repercussions – Russia was using tools available at the time to engage Abkhazia in bilateral cooperation. Therefore, the treaty had some practical value and was mutually beneficial at a tactical level.

Its long-term dimension with the emphasis on "strategic cooperation" signaled Moscow's strategic choice. As attempts to build a constructive dialogue with new Georgian authorities crashed against the stumbling block of the status of the disputed territories, both Moscow and Tbilisi foresaw little progress in dealing with each another. Subsequently, the Georgia-EU association agreement signed on June 27, 2014 and Georgia's new status as one of five "enhanced NATO partners" that was acquired in September, 2014, produced real concerns in Moscow over a potential beefed-up foreign military presence close to Russia's borders in the South.

There was also a West-related facet. Understanding that the crisis in the relations wouldn't get better any time soon, Moscow thought it was the right time to consolidate its volatile southern flank, no matter how bold the move would look. Moscow was acting out of the belief that since neither Russia nor the West was able to tailor the security pattern in the South Caucasus their way, both tried to secure as much geopolitical loyalty as they could. In a way, it was a reflection of what Putin alluded to during the NATO Bucharest Summit in 2008, when he boiled it down to a simple logic: "NATO status for Georgia will entail buffer zones in Abkhazia and South Ossetia."

In a nutshell, for the Kremlin, there was a strategic calculation as well as symbolism to the treaty with Abkhazia. It may all be quite pricey, but Russia couldn't afford the privilege of giving up on emerging geopolitical opportunities. This has been and will probably continue to be Moscow's predominant attitude towards the region.

New challenges: ISIS and the Ukraine crisis

"The Sochi effect" placed all of Russia's security services on their highest alert and helped stabilize the situation in the Caucasus for a couple of years after 2014. At the end of 2014, a factual decline in terrorist activity in the North Caucasus was observed with a total of 78 "crimes of a terrorist nature" taking place (24 Mir, 2014). It was three times less than in 2013 and four times less than in 2012. Even though the official statistics tend to paint a more optimistic picture, the progress was real: there was a lower incidence of "backlash" terror attacks in 2014 than in previous years.

The killing in March, 2014 of Doku Umarov, the head of the Caucasus Emirate and Russia's most wanted terrorist crowned the government-led anti-terrorist efforts. Although it didn't lower the overall threat, it was an important symbolic milestone for Moscow in the fight against jihadi extremists in the Caucasus. Yet, the attack in Grozny on December 4 of the same year and a subsequent skirmish in Kabardino-Balkaria's capital city of Nalchik seven days later was an indication that the extremists were not as inactive as they might have appeared in the tally of formal statistics, and they still remain a serious security challenge for Russia.

Internally, sources of conflict in the Caucasus, some of which have been pushing local people to join the ranks of terrorists, have to do with the following: spread of radical ideas and (pseudo)religious teachings; dissatisfaction with the performance of local legal and administrative systems, including "daily corruption" (бытовая коррупция); high unemployment rates and limited opportunities, especially for the youth; peculiarities of demographic and migration trends; improper balance of governance and power – massive abuses in some places, "power vacuums" in others; territorial and land ownership disputes overlapping with ethnic identity and religious fault lines; influence of traditional habits and life styles; and negative historic memory and deep-seated "hatred narratives" between some ethnic groups.

Externally, the sources of extremism include the rise of like-minded groups in the Middle East and the problems associated with inequality that globalization severed in these regions. The real concern for the Russian government was the potential impact of the Syrian crisis and the entire Middle East turmoil for the volatile North Caucasus. A core of the concern was a potential unleashing of hazardous politico-social movements able to exacerbate Russia's own radical Islamist problems. Moscow was using a mixture of tools to clamp down on the terror networks from deterring the "radical Salafi Islam" from the promotion of "traditional Islam," to fostering home-grown imams and secular pundits on Islam to fight the jihadist narrative of foreign preachers coming to the region (Yarlykapov, 2015).

The rise of ISIS threatened to re-energize these forces. The impact that ISIS had on the region was especially palpable in three key areas: ideological, social, and informational. Not only did it aggravate the region's conflict potential but in some areas triggered a return to the *regressive archaism* associated with religious fundamentalism.

Initially, the coming of ISIS divided the self-proclaimed CE fighters over loyalty to various like-minded groups in the Middle East. Although earlier some of the Emirate militants fought against Syrian President Assad alongside al-Nusra, in the spat between the group and ISIS, the CE chief commanders opted to support the latter. It further solidified channels linking the two extremist groups.

In 2013, ISIS acknowledged receiving funds from the CE. As ISIS accumulated power, it had the capacity to sponsor its fellow men in the North Caucasus. As Tomas De Waal, a prominent expert on the Caucasus, argued at the time: "If even a fraction of the vast amounts of money ISIS is said to have seized in Iraq makes a way back to the North Caucasus, it could boost the militants there" (Waal, 2014).

While terrorists in the Caucasus represent a regional group that claims to be a chain in the global jihadist link, ISIS positions itself as the centerpiece and driving force of global jihad. Paradoxically, against this background, it was ISIS that was in greater need of CE's back-up in an undeclared competition with its ideological rivals – Jabhat al-Nusra and the like – over influence on the umma.

For many outside observers, the ethnic component of ISIS fighters from Russia or wider Eurasia had become key. Indeed, many natives of the Caucasus made it to the top ranks of the ISIS leadership. However, what made both ISIS and CE more consolidated in substance and diverse in form was their strategic imperative which had to do with the religious rather than ethnic agenda. The ethnic card was rather effectively played out for the recruitment of more fighters, and it is where the ISIS social media strategy[2] proved efficient.

What worries Russian security experts to this day is not only ISIS's ability to recruit people through its sophisticated use of social media technologies, but also the influx of potential "jihadi returnees" to the Caucasus.[3] Addressing such "virtual radicalism" is something still to be addressed by the Russian government in the Caucasus.

The developments in Ukraine created an even more antagonizing framework for regional dynamics in the Caucasus from early 2014. In this regard, contradictory policies between Russia and the EU have never left the region. Now that the stakes are higher, and no party is willing to compromise its interests, the fragile balance between cooperation and confrontation has further swung to the latter.

First, a great deal of skepticism about the capability of European institutions to fix conflicts in the post-Soviet space is now prevailing among South Caucasian elites. Ironically, this understanding serves to deter violence in the region: responsible stakeholders in Tbilisi, Yerevan, and – to a lesser extent – Baku, have realized that if there should be serious warfare in the region there will be no international institutions powerful enough to stop it, or any great European powers ready for head-on military collision to defend their clients' interests.

At the same time, the South Caucasian states have found themselves between the devil and the deep blue sea: the Ukrainian crisis has shown that deciding between European and Eurasian integration comes at a high price, but that indecisiveness is an even worse path. Thus, the startling developments in Ukraine have triggered two opposite processes: on the one hand, they have accelerated Georgian efforts to integrate into Euro-Atlantic institutions. On the other, the Ukraine crisis has pushed Armenia to seek full membership of the Eurasian Union and encouraged Abkhazia and South Ossetia to forge closer ties with Russia.

The domestic support for Eurasian integration in Armenia, South Ossetia, and Abkhazia seems to have been spurred by a resurgence of national identity. All three have a common cause: historical reunification, an idea reenergized by "the Crimea precedent." Armenian supporters of Eurasian integration have projected "re-incorporation of the Crimea into Russia" onto the disputed territory of the Nagorno-Karabakh, suggesting that it is a precedent for reunification of Armenia's historical lands. Supporters of integration in South Ossetia hoped that it might use the same logic to reincorporate those territories into Russia.

When power politics are at play, smaller states often scramble to side with great powers. But those who expect the tit-for-tat game between Russia and the West to continue have opted to maneuver between the two. Azerbaijan has chosen this path, floating between East and West in its stance toward the crisis in Ukraine, and reaffirming its commitment to multi-vector diplomacy. Yet the time may come for Baku to make hard choices as well.

Finally, the crisis in Ukraine has had a remarkable impact on the South Caucasus. Although it may not yet be fully recognized, the transformed realities of Eurasian geopolitics have surely revived the idea that there are distinct geopolitical zones – daily bread for political and academic hardliners who love to ponder what this might mean for the Caucasus.

Conclusion

Describing the situation in the Caucasus, some analysts use the term "mutual insecurity" (Waal, 2013). That, in a way, underlies the argument that no actor can feel secure by creating threats for others. In the tangle-knot type of region such as the Caucasus, this is especially true. Regrettably, the situation in the Caucasus does not create a plethora of opportunities for cooperation between Russia and the West, but seizing up those few opportunities present is probably the key to surmounting that "mutual insecurity."

By the end of the Obama term, the U.S.-Russia relations were at their lowest point in modern history. The post-Soviet space has arguably remained the most uncompromised area for the two states. In the Caucasus and elsewhere in Eurasia, the status of ex-Soviet republics as well as the "frozen conflicts" and the de facto states they entailed are to this day the issues where any compromise, let alone progress, between Moscow and Washington can barely be imagined. Russia has a mixed record of successes and failures in the region, and, should the security situation deteriorate, would face uneasy choices – as in the balancing act between Armenia and Azerbaijan – or serious challenges – as when the jihadists start returning from Syria to the North Caucasus. It is also in pursuit of an adequate modus operandi vis-à-vis "those it tamed" – Abkhazia and South Ossetia – and a reasonable modus vivendi with Georgia.

The several months of the Trump presidency have dashed many hopes in Russia for a fruitful cooperation with the United States. Yet one thing that some seemed to have proved to be accurate is that President Trump expresses little interest in the Caucasus or the post-Soviet space outside Ukraine. This doesn't necessarily mean that the United States will abandon its allies in the region. But it may provide Russia with an opportunity to stabilize the region and engage with its states through mutually attractive projects. The question is whether Moscow takes advantage of the opportunity, or will the inertia of the political leadership continue to plague Russia's standing in the South Caucasus and push the North Caucasus further to the "internal abroad" mode.

Notes

1 There are also those practicing Judaism and Yezidism.
2 www.al-monitor.com/pulse/ru/originals/2014/08/is-clinton-atrocities-social-media-baghdadi-mccain.html.
3 www.theguardian.com/world/2014/jun/23/who-behind-isis-propaganda-operation-iraq.

References

Abdullayeva, S., and Shulman, V. January 26, 2004. U.S., Azerbaijan Begin 10-Day Naval Exercise. Itar-TASS.
Applebaum, A. December 20, 1999. Ethnic Cleansing, Russian Style. *The Weekly Standard*.
Blank St. 2013. Russian Defense Policy in the Caucasus. *Caucasus Survey*. Vol. 1, No. 1, pp. 75–89.
Bullough, O. May 21, 2012. Sochi 2014 Winter Olympics: The Circassians Cry Genocide. *The Newsweek Magazine*.
Caucasus Report: February 11, 2005. Vol. 8. No. 6. www.rferl.org/a/1341710.html.
Grove, T. February 21, 2013. Special Report: Russia's $50 billion Olympic gamble. *Reuters*.
Hahn, G. 2007. *Russia's Islamic Threat*. New Haven, CT, Yale University Press.
Hahn, G. 2011. *Getting the Caucasus Emirate Right*. Report of the CSIS Russia and Eurasia Program, Washington DC.
Ilyasov, M. 2012. Nestabilnost na Severnom Kavkaze: prichiny, factory i vozmozhnye posledstviya. *Kavkaz i Globalizatsiya*. Vol. 6, No. 3, pp. 57–69.
Ioffe, J. April 19, 2013. The Boston Bombing Suspects Were Reared by Both Chechnya and America, *The New Republic*. www.newrepublic.com/article/112971/boston-marathon-bombers-brothers-chechnya-forged-america.
King, C. 2004. A Rose Among Thorns: Georgia Makes Good. *Foreign Affairs*. Vol. 83, No. 2, pp. 13–18.
King, C. 2008. The Five-Day War. Managing Moscow after the Georgia Crisis. *Foreign Affairs*. Vol. 87, No. 6, pp. 2–11.
King, C. 2011. *The Ghost of Freedom. A History of the Caucasus*. Oxford, UK, Oxford University Press.
Malashenko, A. April 10, 2013. *Controversy and Concern over the Sochi Olympics*. Carnegie Moscow Center. http://carnegie.ru/publications/?fa=51456#.
Markedonov, S. 2010a. Turbulentnaya Evrazia: mezhetnicheskie, grazhdanskie konflikty, ksenofobia v novykh nezavisimykh gosadarstvakh possovetskogo porstranstva. *Moscow Bureau on Human Rights*.
Markedonov, S. 2010b. *Radical Islam in the North Caucasus: Evolving Threats, Challenges and Prospects*. Report of the CSIS Russia and Eurasia Program, Washington DC.
Markedonov, S. May 30, 2011. Emirat Poschitali. *Politkom.ru*. www.politcom.ru/12029.html.
Markedonov, S. 2013. "Russia and Armenia in the South Caucasus Security Context: Basic Trends and Hidden Contradictions", in *Armenia's Foreign and Domestic Politics: Development Trends*, ed. Mikko Palonkorpi and Alexander Iskandaryan, Yerevan, Armenia: Caucasus Institute and Aleksanteri Institute.
Martin T. 2001. *The Affirmative Action Empire: Nations and Nationalism in the Soviet Union, 1923–1939*. Ithaca, NY and London, Cornell University Press
24 Mir. 2014. FSB: v 2014 terrorism v Rossii snizilsya ppochti v tri raza. December 9, 2014.
Nation, C. 2007. *Russia, the United States and the Caucasus*. US Army War College, The Strategic Studies Institute.
Philips, D. September 2008. *Post-conflict Georgia: Policy paper*. The Atlantic Council of the United States, Washington DC.
Richmond, W. 2013. *The Circassian Genocide*. New Brunswick, NJ, Rutgers University Press.
Ryabtsev, V. 2011. *Geopoliticheskaya problematika Chernomorsko-Kaspijskogo regiona v trudakh uchenykh i spetsialistov Yuga Rossii*. South Federal University Press, Rostov-on-Don, Russia.
Shaffer, B. 2009a. *Energy Wars*. University of Pennsylvania Press, Philadelphia, PA.
Shaffer, B. 2009b. The Geopolitics of the Caucasus. *Brown Journal of Foreign Affairs*. Vol. XV, Issue II, pp. 131–142.
Suchkov, M. 2013. The Greater Caucasus in Russian-American Relations: Main Trends and Development Prospects. *Central Asia and the Caucasus*. Vol. 15, No. 4, pp. 18–29.
Sukhankin, S. November 2014. *"The Caucasus Knot": The New Lap of Violence*. Institut Català Internacional per la Pau, Barcelona.

Topchishvili, R. 2011. *Kavkazovedcheskie issledovaniya*. "Universal", Tbilisi.
Trenin, D. 2011. *Post-Imperium: A Eurasian Story. Carnegie Endowment for International Peace*. Washington, DC.
Trenin, D. April 19, 2013. Boston Common. *Foreign Policy*. www.foreignpolicy.com/articles/2013/04/19/boston_common_us_russia_cooperation.
Waal, de T. April 20, 2013. *The Search for Security in the Caucasus*, Keynote presentation at the Rose Roth Conference, Tbilisi. http://m.ceip.org/2013/04/29/search-for-security-in-caucasus/g2t2.
Waal, de T. July 7, 2014. Caucasus Emir Seeks a Re-Brand. *Carnegie Moscow Center*. http://carnegie.ru/commentary/?fa=56062.
Ware, R.B. 2009. Chechenization: Ironies and Intricacies. *The Brown Journal of World Affairs*. Spring/Summer. Vol XV, Issue II, pp. 157–168.
Wertsch, J. May 16, 2013. *Five Things Worth Knowing about the Caucasus*. Pulitzer Center for Crisis Reporting.
Williams B.G. 2007. Allah's Foot Soldiers: An Assessment of the Role of Foreign Fighters and Al-Qaida in the Chechen Insurgency. In: Gammer, M. (Ed) *Ethno-nationalism, Islam and the State in the Caucasus: Post-Soviet Disorder*. New York and London, Routledge.
Yarlykapov, A. 2015. *Islamskaya mozaika na Severnom Kavkaze: vyzovy dlya gosudarstvenno-konfessionalnykh otnoshenij*. Institut Etnologii i Antropologii, RAN, Moscow.
Yefimova, N. November 4, 2002. Duma Votes to Limit News Coverage. *Moscow Times*.

20
CENTRAL ASIA

Mariya Y. Omelicheva

UNIVERSITY OF KANSAS, USA

In December 2016, Russia's president Vladimir Putin signed a degree approving a new Foreign Policy Concept for the Russian Federation (2016). The document updates and amends the goals and directions of Russia's foreign policy in response to the changes in U.S. politics and international affairs. The main regional priorities remain, however, the same. Similarly to the previous foreign policy documents,[1] the new concept names regional integration within the Commonwealth of Independent States (CIS) and cooperation with CIS members as Russia's regional priorities. In a notable change to the 2013 Foreign Policy Concept, which listed Ukraine as Russia's "priority partner" in the CIS, the new document plays up the Eurasian Union comprised of the two Central Asian republics of Kazakhstan and Kyrgyzstan, Belarus, and Russia. Central Asia is also highlighted in the new document in yet another way. The 2016 Foreign Policy Concept stresses Russia's national interest in the Far East, where twelve regions of the Russian Federation share a nearly 7,000-kilometer-long border and strategically important infrastructure with Central Asia.

The region that encompasses the former Soviet republics of Kazakhstan, the Kyrgyz Republic, Tajikistan, Turkmenistan, and Uzbekistan, has always mattered to Moscow. The eighteenth-century Russian conquests of the nomadic and settled people of Turkic and Iranian origin had given the Tsars and, later, the Soviets, control of a vast landmass of striking topographic and human diversity. Historical legacy of Tsarist and Soviet domination has left an indelible mark on Russia's perceptions and attitudes toward Central Asia. The region's pivotal geopolitical location, coupled with security vulnerabilities and immense hydrocarbon resources, has been central to the Kremlin's foreign policy toward Central Asia.

The goals of this chapter are to review, assess, and explain Russia's foreign policy in Central Asia. It begins by providing an overview of the theoretical explanations dominating the thinking about Moscow's foreign policy. These explanations will be highlighted in the subsequent sections examining the key issue areas of Russia's foreign policy in Central Asia. These include security cooperation, energy cooperation, trade and economic relations, and Russia's effort to sustain its appeal as the foremost partner in Central Asia. Each of the sections will reflect on the record of Russia's successes and failures. The central argument of this chapter is that the dominant geo-political and ideological readings of Russia's relations with Central Asian states are limited in explaining Russia's foreign policy toward the region. I suggest examining Russia's engagement in Central Asia by looking at Russia's own geopolitical imagery. Such a critical geopolitical perspective shifts the discussion of foreign policy from an exclusively materialist and ideological foundation to the realm of discursive constructions, the so-called geopolitical visions about global politics and Russia's place in the world. These geopolitical visions provide Russia with a repertoire or descriptive and prescriptive ideas making certain foreign policies and their outcomes more or less possible.

Explaining Russia's foreign policy in Central Asia

The majority of publications on Russia's foreign policy have interpreted its international conduct through a lens of political realism (see, for example, Kubicek, 1997; Bohr 2004; Bohr, 2004; Blank, 2011; Cooley, 2012). Realist commentaries have also appeared under the rubric of classical geopolitics emphasizing the geostrategic importance of Central Asia to Russia, but also China, the United States, and other states.[2] From the vantage point of political realism, Russia's foreign policy in Central Asia represents one element of the renewed "Great Game," the geopolitical race for influence and control of the vast energy resources in the region (Menon, 2003; Marketos, 2009).[3] In the 1990s, U.S. and Chinese companies were in competition for the Central Asian gas and oil. In the wake of the 9/11 attacks, Central Asia assumed a marked geostrategic importance for Washington. The United States opened two military bases in Uzbekistan and Kyrgyzstan to facilitate the transfer of military supplies for the International Security Assistance Force (ISAF) troops in Afghanistan and increased its military assistance to Central Asia.[4] The direct security engagement of the United States in Central Asia has evoked strong Russian reaction. NATO's Partnership for Peace program activities in Central Asia invoked similar concerns. The Kremlin feared that over time this might diminish Russia's role in the post-Soviet territory and allow the United States and NATO to expand further southeast (Menon, 2015).

Russia has also been cast as an inherently expansionist empire, whose authoritarian political culture and entrenched imperialist outlook have shaped its policies toward its neighbors (for further discussion, see Tsygankov, 2012; Van Herpen, 2014; Omelicheva, 2016). Prominent historians studying the relationship of the Russian Empire to the non-Russian borderland underscored the role of its imperial ideology centered on its beliefs in "virility and power" and recognition by the Western states of Russia's expansionism (Pandey, 2007: 324). Russia's belief in its civilizing mission toward the backward people of the East was also named among the reasons behind Tsarist Russia's policies, and the Soviet institutional, cultural, and ideological frameworks of control established in Central Asia.[5] In contemporary scholarship, Moscow's imperialist ideology has been linked to diverse ideas and images about a cultural unity of peoples in the post-Soviet territory that Russia is predestined to preserve (Laruelle, 2012).

Russia's continuing quest to define and strengthen its national identity has given rise to explanations informed by constructivist assumptions (Hopf, 2002; Clunan, 2009; Tsygankov, 2013). The constructivist conceptions of Russia's foreign policy have highlighted the centrality of the idea of greatpowerness in Russia's understanding of the Self. Central Asia has been significant to Moscow principally because the region has been fundamental to Russia's self-perceptions as a great power state. Russia's global status has given it the ipso facto "right for involvement" in any matter Russia sees as important for its own interests (Lo, 2002: 53; Smith, 2016).

My contention is that neither perspective by itself suffices to provide a complete understanding of Russia's foreign policy. The factors that determined the Russian desire to dominate Central Asia have been complex, interrelated, and changing. They included economic and geopolitical motives, but also imperial ideology necessitating the extension and retention of state authority over diverse populations. A deeper understanding of Russia's foreign policy in Central Asia can be achieved through the application of an approach that integrates the insights from different theoretical perspectives, considers the context, and recognizes ways in which the Russian leadership, itself, views the world and Russia's place in it. A critical geopolitical perspective measures up to these expectations. It synthetizes orthodox geopolitics and geo-economic discourse to develop a new understanding of changing geopolitical images held by the nations (Zabortseva, 2012: 170). Instead of conceptualizing foreign policy as a product of imperial ideology or competition for power and resources, the critical geopolitical approach views it as a social, cultural, discursive, and political practice of "construction of ontological claims" (Kuus, 2010). These are the so-called "truths" of global politics constructed, defended, and experienced by the leadership of countries (Omelicheva, 2016). The examination of Russia's engagement with Central Asia through the lens of its own beliefs about power, ideology, and the nature of global affairs can enhance our understanding of Moscow's foreign policy in the region.

Security-related drivers of Russia's foreign policy in Central Asia

According to the government rhetoric and specific projects engineered by Russia in Central Asia, security-related considerations have been the primary drivers of Moscow's engagement with Central Asian states. For the Kremlin, the rise of religious extremism and terrorism in the predominantly Muslim nations has been the most alarming development in Central Asia. Consequently, Russia has sought to insulate itself from the threats associated with the activities of radical Islamic groups in Central Asia[6] and drug trafficking flows traversing the region from Afghanistan.[7]

To coordinate states' efforts in the fight against terrorism, the Russian leadership initiated the CIS Anti-Terrorist Center (ATC), which was established in Moscow in 2000. A structural subdivision of the ATC was opened in Bishkek, Kyrgyzstan. The intensified military and security cooperation of Russia with the former Soviet Union republics was institutionalized in the Collective Security Treaty Organization (CSTO), whose permanent military base was established in Kant, Kyrgyzstan, in 2002. The base hosts part of the Collective Rapid Deployment force (CRDF) designed to support "collective security" of the region. Another CRDF division is staged at the 201st Military Base in Tajikistan. This is Russia's largest military facility abroad with an estimated 7,500 military personnel in 2016 (Laruelle, 2008).

Concurrently, President Putin invested considerable time and effort to reenergize another security grouping, the Shanghai Cooperation Organization (SCO). The original mandate of the SCO was limited to the issues of border demarcation and demilitarization. By 2002, the organization had expanded its objectives to the fight against the "three evils" of terrorism, Islamism, and separatism to assuage security concerns of its founding members – Russia, China, Kazakhstan, Kyrgyzstan, Tajikistan, and Uzbekistan. The SCO's Regional Anti-Terrorism Structure (RATS) was established in Tashkent in 2004. Conjoint antiterrorist operations, military exercises, and security drills held under the auspices of the SCO and CSTO have become a regular feature of Russia-Central Asia security cooperation. The CSTO has also implemented the annual international counter-narcotics drills *Kanal* (Channel), and instituted the Collective Rapid-Response Force in 2009 to counter aggression, terrorist attacks, and drug trafficking operations (Omelicheva, 2011).

Russia has scored some success in its security and military affairs in Central Asia. In the defense, military, and security sectors, the region remains firmly anchored to Moscow. The Kremlin planners map out security cooperation with Kyrgyzstan, Tajikistan, and even Kazakhstan on the many aspects of these states' security and defense policies. These include joint military exercises, the purchasing and servicing of weapons and systems from Russia, sharing of intelligence information, cooperation over border control, and the training of military and security personnel (Omelicheva, 2011). Russia reinforced its military bases in Kyrgyzstan and Tajikistan and moved closer toward its goal of creating of a joint CSTO air defense system with Armenia, Belarus, and Kazakhstan (McDermott, 2012).

On the other hand, Russia has ignored the Central Asian states' internal dynamics conducive to political instability, terrorism, and organized crime. The Kremlin-led regional security projects have had a negligible impact on the root causes of security problems that continue to plague these states. A possible explanation for this inconsistency in the outcomes of Russia's military and security policies in Central Asia can be found in the arguments of political realism. According to the realist perspective, Russia's military and security engagement in Central Asia has been driven by geopolitical motives superseding its immediate concerns with regional security threats. Russia has sought regional domination under the banner of counterterrorist policy for countering U.S. hegemony and NATO's expansionism. In the 1990s, Russia's own economic, political, and military problems stymied the realization of Moscow's ambitions. By the turn of the twenty-first century, the global economic situation was favorable to the realization of Russia's geopolitical objectives. Russia's economic upturn coincided with Vladimir Putin's rise to power. The restoration of Russia's influence in international affairs was declared the chief priority for the Putin administration.[8]

While Russia's Central Asian policy cannot be understood outside the context of Russia-U.S. relations, as argued by political realism, the specific form that Russia's security and military policy has taken in Central Asia can only be discerned through the analysis of Russia's own geopolitical imagery of the region. The Russian views on Central Asia are rooted in historical memories of invasions that came from the Central Asian steppes. Improving the defenses of Russia's eastern frontiers became Moscow's strategic imperative. With the Central Asian territories fully absorbed by the Russian Empire and the Soviet Union, Russia enjoyed a strong defensive position, partly attributable to the topography of the region. The only exception was a small portion of the border with Afghanistan, where the difficult terrain made it virtually impossible to stage a large army. This led to a long-term Russian unease, with the threat in Afghanistan still playing out in the modern times. Russia's 201st Military Base, previously known as the 201st Motor Rifle Division in Tajikistan, is its largest military contingent abroad. The division constitutes the core of the CSTO's rapid deployment force and has been continually reinforced by the Kremlin with new armaments. Russia has been seeking to expand this military base by adding an air component to it. The largest military reconnaissance exercise to date under the auspices of the CSTO took place in Tajikistan in 2016, where about 1,500 servicemen from CSTO member states practiced a scenario of an army of insurgents crossing into Tajikistan from Afghanistan.

Although, there is little evidence that any state or non-state group intends to infiltrate Russia or Central Asia, from the Russian standpoint history is filled with uncertainties and changes of intent, particularly in the West. Against the backdrop of NATO and U.S. expansion along Russia's western flank, Russia cannot hope to survive without a good defense in Central Asia. Yet, as in the Tsarist and Soviet times, modern Russia lacks a clear security and military strategy for Central Asia, but seeks to mesh together geopolitical and security goals under the banner of counterterrorism.

Those examining Russia's foreign policy through the lens of its neo-imperial ideology argue that Tsarist and Soviet legacies of domination in Central Asia have shaped its security and military approaches in Central Asian states. Indeed, Russia has borne the costs of security initiatives in Central Asia, and its forces, doctrines, weapons, and technology have dominated the CSTO's exercises and training. Russia's political leadership has occasionally coached Moscow's engagement in the region in cultural, philosophical, and spiritual terms. However, there have been several inconsistencies between the expectations of neo-imperial ideology and Russia's foreign policy in Central Asia. Moscow did not seek, for example, to defend the sizeable Russian minorities in the region, despite the rise of ethnic nationalisms in all Central Asian states. It invested relatively few resources in the construction of Russian schools, universities, and military programs in the region that are so critical to the implantation of Russian culture into Central Asian states. The neo-imperial expansionism thesis has been further negated by the Kremlin's refusal to intervene in Kyrgyzstan during the ethnic riots in 2010, despite the appeals for Russia's help by Bishkek.

Russia's energy initiatives in Central Asia

Vladimir Putin's first two presidential terms (2000–2008) coincided with the period of high global prices on energy that encouraged his efforts at regaining state control over Russia's gas and oil enterprises. In 2005, the state became a major shareholder of Gazprom, a successor to the Soviet Ministry of Gas Industry exercising near monopoly on Russia's extraction, production, transport, and sale of natural gas. The Russian state also holds a controlling share of stock in Rosneft, one of the largest oil companies in the country, and owns two other companies – Transneft and Transnefteproduct – which operate all oil pipelines (except the Caspian Pipeline Consortium) (Goldman, 2008; Rutland, 2008).

In 2005, Vladimir Putin introduced a new concept of Russia as an "energy super-state" to describe Moscow's intent to use its dominant position in the energy market and near monopoly on the supplies of gas to multiple states for raising its international clout in relations with European countries and former republics of the Soviet Union (Kazantsev, 2010). This merger of Russia's energy and foreign policy appears to be consistent with the premises of political realism. The latter advocates the use of power for achieving national interest, and natural resources constitute an important element of national power.

Central Asia rich in natural resources has become drawn into Russia's energy schemes. Kazakhstan's Tengiz oil and gas field located along the northeast shores of the Caspian Sea is the sixth largest oil field in the world, and its proven gas reserves rank fifteenth in the world. Turkmenistan's gas reserves are second only to Russia's proven natural gas reserves. The Russian monopoly over the gas and oil transportation routes to and from Central Asia provided Moscow with a powerful bargaining chip in negotiations for lower import prices on Central Asian gas and oil. The resale of cheap Central Asian energy to Ukraine, Georgia, and European customers, and using the imported energy for the government-subsidized domestic consumption, afforded Russia considerable geopolitical and economic benefits at the time of high world energy prices. All in all, Moscow has regarded Russia's control over the production, sales, and transportation of energy resources in Central Asia as a vital strategic asset for enhancing its political and economic standing in the region (Kanet and Sussex, 2015).[9]

Moscow's energy policy in Central Asia has also demonstrated inconsistences with the realist expectations. Russia's energy initiatives in the region have been motivated by the goal of countering U.S. and EU influence in the energy sector. In 2007, for example, Russia, Kazakhstan, and Turkmenistan signed an agreement for the reconstruction and expansion of the western branch of the Central Asia–Center gas pipeline connecting the Caspian gas fields in Turkmenistan with the Russian natural gas pipeline system (Yesdauletova, 2009). The idea behind this new pipeline was to reduce the rationale for projects like Nabucco, which was designed to transport gas from the Caspian Sea to Europe bypassing Russia, backed by the EU and the United States. It is China, however, that has broken Russia's economic and energy monopoly in Central Asia. In 1997, the state-owned Chinese National Petroleum Company (CNPC) won a development and exploration contract for two of the richest oilfields in Kazakhstan. By the end of 2005, CNPC had completed the construction of a new pipeline bringing Kazakhstan's Caspian oil to China's Xinjiang (Fishelson, 2007). In December 2009, the Chinese president Hu Jintao welcomed the opening of the Turkmenistan-China natural gas pipeline, running from Turkmenistan through Uzbekistan and Kazakhstan to China. Also in 2009, the Kenkiaak-Kumkol section of the Kazakhstan-China oil pipeline became fully operational. The final stage of the pipeline, stretching nearly 3,000 km across Kazakhstan to the Caspian oil fields, was completed in 2011, but additional work on new pumping stations has continued to increase the pipeline's capacity (Weitz, 2008). The construction of the Central Asia–China gas pipeline system has lessened Russia's strategic importance for Turkmenistan, Uzbekistan, and even Kazakhstan in terms of energy politics. Although, Central Asia was potentially a hotbed for rivalry for regional hegemony between Russia and China, Moscow and Beijing have avoided political tensions over Central Asian states.

Furthermore, the realist perspective is unable to explain the nature of a statist geo-economic model based upon the principle of state control of economic policies, even at the expense of economic prosperity. Although, Russia has had several distinct traditions of foreign policy thinking,[10] statist beliefs have dominated Russia's foreign policy during Vladimir Putin's term. With its emphasis on the preservation of, and increase in, the role of the state in social, political, and international affairs, the statist ways of thinking encourage the consolidation of state control over economic relations rather than the development of market-based institutions and norms. In the context of Russia, statist beliefs have been juxtaposed on the framework of patron-client relations between political and economic elites which originated in the Soviet period. The ruling elites view society as their own private domain and appropriate public resources for personal gains in the form of rents from natural resources, among other things (Becker and Vasileva, 2017).

In Russia, a model of economic development designed to boost state power and feed particularistic interests has undermined its economic growth. Within this framework of statist thinking and client-patron relations, Russia's Gazprom has quickly depleted its old gas deposits, but has failed to divert its profits into substantial investments into the modernization of equipment and exploration of the new gas and oil wells. The business of re-selling Turkmen gas, whose prices increased more than 20 times throughout the 2000s, became unprofitable.[11] In 2008, Gazprom was forced to buy Turkmen, Uzbek, and Kazakh gas at the European price owing to growing Chinese competition. The geo-economic logic inspired by the concept of "energy super-state" has failed under the impact of the global financial crisis, the competition from liquified natural gas, and an increased volume of the shale gas projects in the United States and Europe.

Russia's economic engagement with Central Asia

The decade following the disintegration of the Soviet Union witnessed a flurry of efforts aimed at the institutionalization of economic cooperation of the newly independent states. The numerous treaties signed under the auspices of the CIS envisaged the creation of a common market and economic union, a free trade zone, and a space for free movement of people and capital. Economic projects uniting all CIS members were, however, unsuccessful in furthering integration, and Moscow sought to replace it with smaller regional projects. In Central Asia, these efforts led to the establishment of the Eurasian Economic Community (EurAsEc) in 2000 with the goal of promoting the creation of the Customs Union and a Single Economic Space between its members – Russia, Belarus, Kazakhstan, Kyrgyzstan, and Tajikistan. Russia also sought to strengthen its economic position in Central Asia by joining the Organization of

Central Asia Cooperation (OCAC) in 2004. Russia's hope was that the OCAC, established by the Central Asian republics in 1994 for coordinating their economic policies, would merge with the EurAsEc. The OCAC dissolved into the EurAsEc the following year, and Russia acclaimed the creation of a unified economic space with the Central Asian republics and Belarus as an important economic complement of the CSTO (Laruelle, 2008).

In practical terms, Central Asia has played a lesser role in Russia's economic policy compared to, for example, the EU, which has been Russia's first trading partner. The turnover of goods between Russia and Central Asia remained very low throughout the 1990s (US$6–9 billion annually), and constituted only 6.7% of Russia's total annual trade turnover in 2009. Trade turnover began growing in the post-2008 financial crisis period, but remained far behind Russia's trade volume with the European states.[12] It also retained the overall pattern of primary commodity orientation. The main products exported from Central Asia are raw materials, primarily gas and oil, but also minerals, agricultural products, and chemicals. Russia exports various manufactured goods to Central Asia. Russia's proportion of total foreign investment in the Central Asian republics also increased in the 2000s, but remained low compared to its share of foreign trade turnover in the same states (Sinitsina, 2012).

The ebbs and flows of Russia's internal economic situation have affected the fate of Russia's economic policies in Central Asia. The economic crisis of 1998, the financial crisis of 2008, and the recent economic recession sparked by the plummeting of oil prices and Western sanctions on Moscow have had a deleterious effect on the health of Central Asian economies. All Central Asian republics have sought to diversify their economic relations to decrease their dependence on Russia, and with the revitalization of Chinese economic relations with the region, Russia's economic standing in Central Asia has been reduced. Starting in 2008, China gradually displaced Russia as the largest trading partner with all of the Central Asian states, and became a major lender and investor in these countries, especially in the energy sector. Beijing has been supplanting Gazprom's presence in Turkmenistan by increasing its purchases of natural gas ever since 2009, and it has recently taken over in Kyrgyzstan as the builder and partner in two hydropower projects forsaken by Moscow (Kelly-Clark, 2016).

In 2013, Beijing proposed a new development strategy and framework involving Central Asia. The Silk Road Economic Belt is an initiative to integrate China with countries of Central and Southeast Asia into a cohesive economic area through building pipeline and railways infrastructure, broadening trade, and increasing cultural exchange. To counter this push by Beijing, Vladimir Putin announced the development of the Eurasian Economic Union (EEU), as a way to tie Central Asian republics to Russia. Developed from the Customs Union created by Russia, Belarus, and Kazakhstan in 2007 (which came into force in 2010), and the Single Economic Space established by the same states in 2012, the EEU came into effect in 2015, replacing the EurAsEc. The EEU seeks to eliminate non-tariff barriers and facilitate trade among the EEU members. It will also allow for the free movement of capital and labor, liberalization of services, and harmonization of the member-states' regulations. Armenia and Kyrgyzstan joined the EEU along with Russia, Kazakhstan, and Belarus.

Putin's thinking about the EurAsEc and the EEU as the "civilizational alternatives" to the EU have been cited as examples of Russia's imperial projects (Vasilyeva and Lagutina, 2016). Putin's appeals to Russia's "civilizational identity" and the "preservation of Russian cultural dominance" in the wake of the events in Ukraine (Putin, 2012) have also been used to testify to Russia's neo-imperial aims (Galeotti and Bowen, 2014). Upon closer inspection, the Kremlin perspectives on Eurasia are complex, diverse, and volatile. Vladimir Putin instrumentalized the various Eurasianist ideas and coached Russia's foreign policy in civilizational terms. He, nevertheless, has shied away from the most radical ideas promoted in the slogans of nationalist parties (e.g., the National Bolshevik Party led by Eduard Limonov) and writings of selected Eurasianist scholars such as Alexander S. Panarin and Alexander G. Dugin (Tsygankov, 2016).

By focusing on Russia's reactions to U.S. expansionism, realist perspectives have overlooked the nature of EU policies in Central Asia. It has been argued, for example, that Russia's foreign policy has partly proceeded from a reaction to EU structural power in the Central Asian states. The interpretation of EU policies in Central Asia and the choice of responses to them have been mediated by the domestic politics of Russia (Cadier, 2015). The EEU, in particular, has been connected in its goals and design to the EU, and its time of emergence has been tied to the development of EU programs in the post-Soviet territory. The EEU's emphasis on market integration through the harmonization of standards, norms, and regulations provides evidence to support EU influence on Russia's vision of its own structural power in Central Asia (Cadier, 2015).

"Soft power" in Russia's foreign policy in Central Asia

Neither the political realist theories nor the perspectives highlighting Russia's neo-imperial aims consider Russia's efforts to increase the appeal of Moscow's model of political and economic development in an effort to counter U.S. hegemony in the ideological realm. According to the Kremlin, a great power in international relations is supposed to flaunt an attractive model of development and exhibit moral greatness (Ziegler, 2012).

Although the Kremlin has never promoted its view on governance as actively as Western states and international organizations, it, too, has sought some convergence between Russia's own and other states' perspectives on governance and international relations by embedding its expectations into Russian foreign policies. Using regional organizations created in the post-Soviet space, Russia has pursued a new regional order through the definition and institutionalization of certain values and norms which operate in opposition to the accepted principles of liberalism, democracy, and freedom. Moscow's political discourse, for example, has emphasized the existence of multiple democratic models and paths to democratization, and called for recognition of this diversity and equality of the various forms of democratic rule. In this way, Russia has acted consistently with an expanded conception of a great power state which possesses soft power resources and is able to play the role of a normative architect of international relations. Moscow has formalized the concept of "soft power" in its foreign policy repertoire in Russia's 2013 Foreign Policy Concept as well as in the new Foreign Policy Concept approved in 2016.

The Kremlin based its ideological, image-making, and public relations campaign on a more effective use of electronic media. The Internet has become a cheap and convenient resource for disseminating Kremlin-backed information about Russia at home and abroad. Moscow's TV news and radio programming, in both English and Russian, have been systematically employed in an effort toward "regime branding" and legitimizing Russia's policy abroad (Lankina and Niemszuk, 2015). In 2005, the Russian government inaugurated its own grant-making scheme for delivering funds to the homegrown and foreign organizations loyal to Russia. This became part of the effort to create a network of state agencies, NGOs, think tanks and research institutions operating in Russia and abroad with the goal of promoting a positive image of the country and countering Western soft power (Omelicheva, 2015: 105). Moscow opened cultural and language offices in Central Asian states resembling Western projects, and organized youth exchanges and educational programs. Russia-backed and funded organizations have become actively involved in various international practices such as development financing and election monitoring, once exclusively controlled and administered by Western institutions (McGlinchey, 2011).

Conclusion

Russia's foreign policy in Central Asia has gone through a definite shift under the leadership of Vladimir Putin. Deserted by the Kremlin in the early 1990s, the region became an important strategic theater for Russia in the 2000s. Russia significantly expanded its economic cooperation with the Central Asian republics, tripling its trade with the region between 2003 and 2007. Moscow funded and implemented multiple industrial projects in the region, and retained its dominant position in the prospecting, production, and transportation of Central Asian gas and oil. In some measure, Russia has succeeded in keeping Central Asian republics in its orbit of influence by applying the traditional methods of strategic and economic manipulation and "soft power" tools. No other states surpass Moscow's military, defense, and security ties with Central Asia. Russia dominates the energy transportation routes and has the most diverse portfolio of investments in the region. Its political ideas and frameworks have been attractive to the leaders of Central Asian states. Russia's soft power has generated copycat versions of several Russian legislative initiatives by Central Asian governments.

The geopolitical loyalty of Central Asia to Moscow has come, however, at the expense of practical outcomes in regional affairs (Baev, 2005). Not only have Russia's bilateral and multilateral initiatives in Central Asia failed to effectively address the problems of drug trafficking, terrorism, and obstacles to regional economic integration, they have furthered the political malformations responsible for engendering them. Viewed in this light, Russia's foreign policy has had a damaging, if limited, effect in Central Asia.

The unveiling of the EEU coincided with a deep economic recession in Russia. The value of the Russian ruble plummeted in the wake of Western sanctions, Russia's counter-sanctions, and low oil prices. To avoid losing their competitiveness, the Central Asian EEU members have been forced to let their currencies weaken along with the ruble. Furthermore, Russian consumers' demands for imports from key Central Asian industries fell precipitously. Combined with the reduced purchases of gas by Gazprom, the drop in commodities' sales affected the volume of turnover trade between Central Asian countries and Russia. The fall in exports to Russia has had particularly harmful effects for the Central Asian members of the EEU, which joined the union to benefit from greater access to the Russian market. Before Kazakhstan allowed its currency to float, its citizens opted to buy the relatively cheap Russian goods in Russia, prompting the Nazarbayev government to call for negotiations to restrict the trade. According to statistics from the EEU, trade between Kazakhstan and Russia from January-November 2015 was down 25.6% compared to the same period in 2014, and between Kyrgyzstan and Russia down 19.4%. The trade turnover between Russian and Kazakhstan was lower by 26% in 2016 for the same period compared to the previous year, and down 6% with Kyrgyzstan (Eurasian Commission, 2017). The EEU's ability to mollify the systemic fault lines and international contradictions characterizing the EurAsEc were questioned by analysts. The current economic recession in Russia adds an additional level of uncertainty about the future of the EEU (Cadier, 2015: 169; Tarr, 2015).

Russia's economic decline has also affected the millions of Central Asian migrants working there whose earnings plunged, affecting the wellbeing of their families at home. Tajikistan, Kyrgyzstan, and Uzbekistan are among the most remittance-dependence states in the world, and the Central Bank of Russia has recorded two-fold drops in remittance transfers to these countries since the beginning of the crisis. For the Kremlin, the migration issue was a powerful instrument for inducing the entry of Tajikistan and Uzbekistan into the EEU. The Russian economy had also benefited from injections of low-paid Central Asian labor (Laruelle, 2008; Lo, 2015). The crisis, however, has unleashed virulent anti-migrant sentiments in Russia, prompting the Putin administration to introduce more stringent visa regulations for migrants. Restricting Central Asian migration to Russia has been compared to cutting foreign aid, with far more damaging consequences for the Central Asian people.

The important differences in the Central Asian states' political and economic potential[13] and differences in their foreign policy preferences have also affected Russia's foreign policy strategies in Central Asia. The Kremlin has approached Central Asia as a region, but has also focused on building and strengthening bilateral relationships of varying importance in different foreign policy sectors with individual Central Asian states (Oliphant, 2013; Lo, 2015). Kazakhstan has been viewed as Russia's most reliable and valuable partner, while Kyrgyzstan and Tajikistan have only mattered for Moscow's regional security interests and measures aimed at countering Western influences and democratization attempts. Uzbekistan has been a pivotal component of regional security, but very difficult to influence. Turkmenistan has played an important geo-economic role for Moscow, despite the recent row over the gas contract negotiations with Ashgabat. Reflecting these diverging priorities of the Russian Federation and the realities of Central Asia, Moscow's foreign policy in the region has often proceeded through bilateral rather than multilateral frameworks, and is likely to retain this "logic of hierarchy" that seeks to support selected states with more focused instruments in the near term (Cooley and Laruelle, 2013).

According to the critical geopolitics perspectives advocated in this chapter, Russia's perceptions of and interests toward Central Asia have been evolving and multilayered. The Kremlin has visualized Central Asia as a zone of geopolitical contestation with the West, a strategic location central to Russia's defense and reaffirmation as a great power (Sakwa, 2013: 174). Russia's economic and energy polices in Central Asia have been influenced by Moscow's statist thinking and the tradition of patron–client economic relations. The region has been featured in Russia's civilizational narratives highlighting its right, responsibility, and destiny to play a decisive role in regional politics, security, and international relations. In Russia's official discourse, references to geopolitical considerations have been intertwined with civilizational arguments. Russia's quest for great power status has been broached in practical as well as cultural and historical terms. Combined with the realist assessment of Russia's relative capabilities, this type of geopolitical-ideological reasoning has given rise to Russia's foreign policy in Central Asia being designed to close the gap between its ambitious self-perceptions and the uncomfortable realities of a rapidly changing world. The fusion of practical and ideological arguments allowed the Russian government to rely on an elastic, opportunistic, and pragmatic approach in its relations with Central Asia.

The place of Central Asia in Russia's foreign policy will continue to grow and will be dominated by political and security concerns. What changes may come will be driven by several factors, particularly the status of U.S.-Russia relations and the popular legitimacy of the Putin regime. Central Asia policy is far from being a top priority for the new U.S. administration. The region matters to the U.S. government in the context of broader U.S. policies, such as security in Afghanistan. The limited economic, security, and civil society engagement with Central Asia entertained in the past will remain in place or decline under the leadership of president Trump. At the same time, Central Asian regimes and people have become suspicious of the U.S. political agenda, and critical of its role in Eurasia and the Middle East. Central Asian governments will be hesitant to commit themselves to U.S. initiatives that go contrary to Russia's interests in Central Asian states, as the price would be too high and have an uncertain result. However, Russia will seek to strengthen its position in Central Asia, including in the economic realm, to compensate for the political independence of Ukraine and Georgia, and U.S. continued support for strengthening NATO and building European nuclear, cyber, and conventional defenses.

The "Great Game" in Central Asia, however, will be played between Russia and China. The changes in the energy market – rising costs of Central Asian gas and competition from the liquefied and shale gas projects in the Persian Gulf, United States, and Europe – will be the primary drivers of Russia's economic downsizing in Central Asian states, leaving more room for China's growing presence in the Central Asian states. Whether or not Moscow will feel threatened by China in Central Asia will depend on the extent to which Beijing will seek to translate its growing economic presence into political influence. Similarly to Russia, China has viewed the region as a second-order priority in its foreign policy and has not been eager to exploit its economic power for increased political clout in the region. China is pretty much the only external player to have made inroads in Central Asia, and the region has seen increased activity by Turkey, India, Iran, Pakistan, and the Middle Eastern states. Kazakhstan and Uzbekistan have tried to distance themselves from Russian-led integration, while reaching out to other external powers.

Notes

1. Vladimir Putin approved the 2000 and 2013 foreign policy concepts of Russia upon assuming the post of Russia's president. Dmitri Medvedev decreed the 2008 foreign policy concept following his inauguration as the Russian president.
2. Although, there are important differences between the classical geopolitics and realist traditions, there are also certain consistencies in their assumptions about the world, including state-centrism, the centrality of power, and pursuit of hegemony.
3. "The Great Game" is a phrase used to describe a political and diplomatic rivalry between the Tsarist Russia and British Empire in the nineteenth century over Central and Southern Asia.
4. Karshi-Khanabad (K2) airbase in Uzbekistan was shut in 2005 at the request of the Uzbek government. The Transit Center in Manas, Kyrgyzstan, was closed in 2014.
5. The Soviet Socialists republics of Kazakhstan, Kyrgyzstan, Tajikistan, Turkmenistan, and Uzbekistan were created in the late 1920–1930s by the Soviet nationality planners and became thoroughly integrated into the Soviet system (Rywkin, 1990; Crews, 2006).
6. The problem of Islamism in Central Asia has been associated with activities of the Islamic Movement of Uzbekistan (IMU), Hizb ut-Tahrir, and a number of less known radical Islamic movements, such as Akramiya and Tablighi Jamaat among others.
7. Because of its geographic position between the major narcotics producing territories of Afghanistan and the major narcotics markets in Europe and Russia, Central Asia serves as a transit area for drugs.
8. Vladimir Putin rose to Russia's leadership in 1999 having replaced ailing Russian president Boris Yeltsin.
9. Furthermore, Kyrgyzstan is completely dependent on Russia for energy import, and Tajikistan's all oil-based products are imported from Russia. Kazakhstan, where local oil refineries are unable to meet all the country's needs, also partly relied on the supply of oil from the Siberian refineries in Russia.
10. Among those philosophical traditions are Westernist, Civilizationalist, and Statist.
11. In 2003, Gazprom signed a contract with Turkmenistan which guarantees it a near monopoly over the purchase and exportation of Turkmen gas.
12. In 2011, for example, Russia exported to EU just under €200 million in goods and imported over €100 million (Nevskaya, 2016). The same year, Russia imported about US$10 million from Central Asian states, and exported about US$22 million (Sinitsina, 2012).
13. Kazakhstan is the region's economic engine and a destination for the labor migrants from other Central Asian states. Uzbekistan is the most populous republic and regional military strongman. Kyrgyzstan and Tajikistan are the resource-barren and weakest Central Asian states from an economic and political standpoint.

References

Baev, P 2005, 'Russia's Counterrevolutionary Offensive in Central Asia', *PONARS Policy Memo* 399 Available from: www.csis.org/media/csis/pubs/pm_0399.pdf [5 January 2017].

Becker, W & Vasileva, A 2017, 'Russia's Political Economy Re-conceptualized: A Changing Hybrid of Liberalism, Statism and Patrimonialism', *Journal of Eurasian Studies*, vol. 8, pp. 209–221.

Blank, SJ 2011, 'Challenges to Russia in Central Asia', *The Journal of the National Committee on American Foreign Policy*, vol. 3, no. 5, pp. 209–221.

Bohr, A 2004, 'Regionalism in Central Asia: New Geopolitics, Old Regional Order', *International Affairs*, vol. 80, no. 3, pp. 485–502.

Cadier, D 2015, 'Policies towards the Post-Soviet Space: The Eurasian Economic Union as an Attempt to Develop Russia's Structural Power', in D Cadier & M Light (eds.), *Russia's Foreign Policy: Ideas, Domestic Politics and External Relations*, pp. 156–174. Palgrave Macmillan, New York.

Clunan, AL 2009, *The Social Construction of Russia's Resurgence: Aspirations, Identity, and Security Interests*, John Hopkins University Press, Baltimore, MD.

Cooley A 2012, *Great Games, Local Rules*, Oxford University Press, Oxford, UK.

Cooley, A & Laruelle, M 2013, 'The Changing Logic of Russian Strategy in Central Asia: From Privileged Sphere to Divide and Rule?' *PONARS Eurasia Policy Memo 261*. Available from www.ponarseurasia.org/memo/changing-logic-russian-strategy-central-asia-privileged-sphere-divide-and-rule [3 January 2017].

Crews, RD 2006, *For Prophet and Tsar: Islam and Empire in Russia and Central Asia*, Harvard University Press, Cambridge, MA.

Eurasian Commission 2017, 'Express informatsiya: Ob itogah vneshnei i vzaimnoi torgovli tovarami Evrasiiskogo Ekonomicheskogo Soyuza, Yanvar' – Noyabr' 2016', Available from www.eurasiancommission.org/ru/act/integr_i_makroec/dep_stat/tradestat/analytics/Documents/express/November2016.pdf [16 January 2017].

Fishelson, J 2007, 'From the Silk Road to Chevron: The Geopolitics of Oil Pipelines in Central Asia', *Vestnik: The Journal of Russian and Asia Studies*, Available from: www.sras.org/geopolitics_of_oil_pipelines_in_central_asia [20 January 2017].

Galeotti, M & Bowen, AS 2014, 'How Russia's President Morphed from Realist to Ideologue – and What He'll Do Next', *Foreign Policy*, 21 April, Available from: www.foreignpolicy.com/articles/2014/04/21/putin_s_empire_of_the_mind_russia_geopolitics [3 September 2014].

Goldman, MI 2008, *Petrostate: Putin, Power and the New Russia*, Oxford University Press, Oxford, UK.

Hopf, T 2002, *Social Construction of Foreign Policy: Identities and Foreign Policies, Moscow, 1955 and 1999*, Cornell University Press, Ithaca, NY.

Kanet RE & Sussex M (eds.) 2015, *Russia, Eurasia and the New Geopolitics of Energy: Confrontation and Consolidation*, Palgrave Macmillan, Basingstoke, UK.

Kazantsev, A 2010, 'The Crisis of Gazprom as the Crisis of Russia's "Energy Super-State" Policy Toward Europe and the Former Soviet Union', *Caucasian Review of International Affairs*, vol. 4, no. 3, pp. 271–284.

Kelly-Clark, V 2016, 'Why is Central Asia dumping Russia for China?' *Global Risks Insights*, Available from: http://globalriskinsights.com/2016/05/why-central-asia-is-dumping-russia-for-china/ [4 January 2017].

Kubicek, P 1997, 'Regionalism, Nationalism and Realpolitik in Central Asia', *Europe-Asia Studies*, vol. 49, no. 4, pp. 637–655.

Kuus, M 2010, 'Critical Geopolitics', in R. Denemark (ed.), *The International Studies Encyclopedia*, pp. 683–670. Blackwell, Oxford, UK.

Lankina, T & Niemszuk, K 2015, 'Russia's Foreign Policy and Soft Power', in D Cadier & M Light (eds.), *Russia's Foreign Policy: Ideas, Domestic Politics and External Relations*, pp. 97–116. Palgrave Macmillan, New York.

Laruelle, M 2008, 'Russia's Central Asia Policy', Available from: http://isdp.eu/content/uploads/images/stories/isdp-main-pdf/2008_laurelle_russias-central-asia-policy.pdf [17 January 2017]

Laruelle, M 2012, *Russian Eurasianism: An Ideology of Empire*, John Hopkins University Press, Baltimore, MD.

Lo, B 2002, *Russian Foreign Policy in the Post-Soviet Era*, Palgrave Macmillan, New York.

Lo, B 2015, *Frontiers New and Old: Russia's Policy in Central Asia*', Available from: www.ifri.org/sites/default/files/atoms/files/ifri_rnv_82_central_asia_bobolo_eng_january_2015_0.pdf [5 January 2017].

Marketos, T 2009, 'Eastern Caspian Sea Energy Geopolitics: A Litmus Test for the U.S. – Russia – China. Struggle for the geostrategic control of Eurasia', *Caucasian Review of International Affairs*, vol. 3, no. 1, pp. 2–19.

McDermott, RN 2012, 'Kazakhstan-Russia: Enduring Eurasian Defense Partners', *Danish Institute for International Studies Report, Copenhagen*. Available from: www.diis.dk/files/media/publications/import/extra/rp2012-15-kazakhstan-russia_web.pdf [6 January 2017].

McGlinchey, E 2011, *Chaos, Violence, Dynasty: Politics and Islam in Central Asia* (Central Eurasia in Context), University of Pittsburgh Press, Pittsburgh, PA.

Menon, R 2003, 'The New Great Game in Central Asia', *Survival: Global Politics and Strategy*, vol. 45, no. 2, pp. 187–204.

Menon, R 2015, 'The Security Environment in the South Caucasus and Central Asia: Concept, Setting, and Challenges', in R. Menon, Y.E. Fedorov, and G. Nodia (eds.), *Russia, the Caucasus, and Central Asia: The 21st Century Security Environment*, Routledge, New York.

Nevskaya, A 2016, 'Russia-EU Economic Relations: Assessing Two Years of Sanctions', *Russia Direct*, Available from: www.russia-direct.org/analysis/russia-eu-economic-relations-assessing-two-years-sanctions [20 January 2017].

Oliphant, C 2013, 'Russia's Role and Interests in Central Asia', Available from: www.files.ethz.ch/isn/172941/russias-role-and-interests-in-central-asia.pdf [20 January 2017].

Omelicheva, M 2011, *Counterterrorism Policies in Central Asia*, Routledge, New York.

Omelicheva, M 2015, *Democracy in Central Asia? Competing Perspectives and Alternative Strategies*, University Press of Kentucky, Lexington, KY.

Omelicheva, N 2016, 'Critical Geopolitics on Russian Foreign Policy: Uncovering the Imagery of Moscow's International Relations', *International Politics*, vol. 53, no. 6, pp. 708–726.

Pandey, SK 2007, 'Asia in the Debate on Russian Identity', *International Studies*, vol. 44, no. 4, pp. 317–337.

Putin, V 2012, Russia: The Ethnicity Issue. *Nezavisimaya Gazeta Daily*, 23 January 2012. http://archive.premier.gov.ru/eng/events/news/17831/, accessed 3 September 2017.

Rutland, P 2008, 'Putin's Economic record: Is the Oil Boom Sustainable? *Europe-Asia Studies*, vol. 60, no. 6, pp. 1051–1072.

Rywkin, M 1990, *Moscow's Muslim Challenge: Soviet Central Asia*, M.E. Sharp, New York.

Sakwa, R 2013, 'Systemic Stalemate: Reiderstvo and the Dual State', in N. Robinson (ed.), *The Political Economy of Russia*, pp. 69–96. Rowman and Littlefield, Lanham, MD.

Sinitsina, I 2012, *Economic Cooperation Between Russia and Central Asian Countries: Trends and Outlook*, Working Paper 1, University of Central Asia, Institute of Public Policy and Administration, Bishkek, Kyrgyzstan.

Smith, H 2016, 'Putin's Third Term and Russia as Great Power', in M. Suslov & M. Bassin (eds.), *Eurasia 2.0: Russian Geopolitics in the Age of New Media*, pp. 125–149. Lexington Books, Lanham, MD.

Tarr, DG 2015, 'The Eurasian Economic Union among Russia, Belarus, Kazakhstan, Armenia and the Kyrgyz Republic: Can It Succeed Where Its Predecessor Failed?' Available from: https://ssrn.com/abstract=2185517 [2 December 2016].

Tsygankov, AP 2012, 'Assessing Cultural and Regime-Based Explanations of Russia's Foreign Policy: "Authoritarian at Heart and Expansionist by Habit"?' *Europe-Asia Studies*, vol. 64, no. 4, pp. 695–713.

Tsygankov, AP 2013, 'Moscow's Soft Power Strategy', *Current History*, vol. 112, no. 756, pp. 259–264.

Tsygankov, AP 2016, 'Uses of Eurasia: The Kremlin, the Eurasian Union, and the Izborsky Club', in M. Suslov & M. Bassin (eds.), *Eurasia 2.0: Russian Geopolitics in the Age of New Media*, pp. 63–80. Lexington Books, Lanham, MD.

van Herpen, MH 2014, *Putin's Wars: The Rise of Russia's New Imperialism*, Rowman & Littlefield, Lanham, MD.

Vasilyeva, N & Lagutina, M 2016, *The Russian Project of Eurasian Integration: Geopolitical Prospects*, Lexington Books, Lanham, MD.

Weitz, R 2008, *Kazakhstan and the New International Politics of Eurasia*, Central Asia-Caucasus Institute & Silk Road Studies Program, Washington, DC.

Yesdauletova, A 2009, 'Kazakhstan's Energy Policy: Its Evolution and Tendencies', *Journal of US-China Public Administration*, vol. 6, no. 4, pp. 31–39.

Zabortseva, Y 2012, 'From the "Forgotten Region" to the "Great Game" Region: On the Development of Geopolitics in Central Asia', *Journal of Eurasian Studies*, vol. 3, pp. 168–176.

Ziegler, C 2012, 'Conceptualizing Sovereignty in Russian Foreign Policy: Realist and Constructivist Perspective', *International Politics*, vol. 49, no. 4, pp. 400–417.

21
THE ARCTIC

Robert English and Andrew Thvedt

UNIVERSITY OF SOUTHERN CALIFORNIA, USA

Introduction

"Words are also deeds," not just in an abstract, philosophical sense, but in concrete acts as well. And at this tense juncture in US-Russia relations – with cyber intrusion now added to confrontations in Ukraine, Syria, and the Baltics – words are being spoken that could soon become deeds and spread that confrontation to the Arctic. Russia has for 20 years been a constructive partner in Arctic governance. Russia has also for nearly ten years been rebuilding its decrepit security infrastructure in the high north, in order to defend its sovereignty and guard against emergent threats at a time of rapid change in a region of great economic and strategic importance to Moscow. Yet since 2014 – reacting to conflict *elsewhere* – Western pundits, policy analysts, and politicians have abruptly recast Russia's Arctic activities as something ominous and requiring a determined response.

The new words are about "the scramble for the Arctic," with some even predicting "hot war in the cold north." The deeds that those sounding this alarm demand are a buildup in US-NATO Arctic capabilities across the board – land, air, and sea. And they nearly always begin with a call to close "the icebreaker gap." Simultaneously, the US and NATO have already stepped up military maneuvers and shows of force in the area, as has Russia, in what resembles a budding security dilemma. This is disturbing for a region that, since the Cold War's end, has been a model of positive interstate cooperation. Yet since this nascent rivalry has objectively little to do with actual threats – in most military measures, Russia is *behind* the US and NATO – one hopes for an easing of US-Russian tensions to halt an incipient Arctic arms race.

Russia, an Arctic power

Unfamiliarity often breeds alarm, and few US politicians or foreign-policy pundits have much familiarity with the Arctic – and certainly not with Russia's centuries-old traditions in the high north. Canadians, Norwegians, Finns, and other Nordic peoples naturally understand better what it means to be "an Arctic nation," though none matches Russia in the depth and complexity of their identification with the polar region. From distant forbears to modern pioneers, from sailors and soldiers to scientists, from ancient sagas to modern cinema – the *cultural* as well as economic and strategic significance of the Arctic to Russia is great. Consequently, though it hardly implies a literal claim, Russian politicians have sometimes waxed lyrical on the order of "the Arctic is ours!" in a manner that jars US ears (though similar rhetoric has also been heard from Canadian politicians).

Humans have inhabited the Russian Arctic since the end of the last Ice Age, the forbears of the Nenets, Saami, Chuchki, and other "indigenous peoples of the north." The first Slavic or "ethnic Russian" Arctic dwellers were the Pomors who migrated north from the Novgorod region in the 11th century and settled in the White Sea region (present-day Archangelsk). Fisherman, trappers, and traders, the Pomors explored the Urals, rounded the Kola peninsula, established trade with Norway, and may have even sailed to Spitsbergen (Laruelle, 2013).

From the expansion of Ivan the Terrible through the expeditions of Peter the Great, Russian conquest of Siberia, the Far East, and the Arctic lands above them was vital to the growth of the Russian Empire. It was Peter who sponsored the journeys of Vitus Bering, and it was Bering, with Aleksei Chirikov, who explored Alaska and the Aleutians. Semyon Cheluskin, Dmitry Laptev, and others had mapped most of Russia's Arctic coastline by the mid-18th century (Sale and Potapov, 2009). Opening a Northern Sea Route (NSR) was a key goal, with the development of Siberia and a foothold on the Pacific seen as economically as well as strategically vital (Josephson, 2014). Though Russia sold Alaska in 1867, the late 19th and early 20th centuries were notable for development from Spitsbergen and Novaya Zemlya (in the Barents and Kara Seas) to Kamchatka and Vladivostok (in the Northeast).

Russian zeal for the Arctic hardly flagged with the Bolshevik Revolution as the new Soviet regime launched intensive studies and development in the 1920s. Vladimir Lenin championed these pursuits, through the *Severekspeditsia* or Northern Scientific-Industrial Expedition. Later it was *Komseveroput* that managed the resource extraction vital for Joseph Stalin's Five-Year Plans through the mid-1930s (Josephson, 2014). With its coal (Vorkuta), metals (Kola), and oil (Uhta), Russia's Arctic would play a key role in industrializing the USSR. Later reorganized as *Glavsevmorput*, the Arctic administration of the later 1930s embodied the extremes of the time: glorious sacrifice in the service of the state, and brutal exploitation in Arctic GULAG camps from Vorkuta to Kolyma.

The public image of Stalin's Arctic was one of heroism – the pilots who pioneered polar aviation, and the icebreakers that plied the NSR, as the Red Arctic became "a central myth of Soviet popular culture" (Laruelle, 2013: 27). Adding to that myth was the Great Patriotic War, with the Arctic port of Murmansk being a vital lifeline – and one where Soviet and US sailors risked their lives – in supporting life-and-death struggles against the Nazis. Nearly 4 million tons of supplies came through Arctic convoys, something that left enduring memories of US friendship for many Soviet citizens even through the bitter Cold War years.

From Cold-War confrontation to post-Cold War collapse

The Cold War conjures up contrasting images of the Russian Arctic. One is of deadly nuclear confrontation across the North Pole – from the edge of space, to the ocean depths – while the other is of peaceful exploration and scientific research. One worked for the benefit of humanity, the other took humanity to the brink of annihilation. They coexisted, in the later Cold War years, with a third major pursuit, namely large-scale exploitation of Arctic energy resources. All three would retreat in the Cold War's aftermath, and all would return by the early 21st century.

Geography dictated that, as the US and USSR targeted bombers and missiles at each other, the Arctic would be their highway since the polar route between Moscow and Washington is the shortest. This was accompanied by construction of many northern installations – chiefly air bases and radar stations. The DEW Line (Distant Early Warning) across North America was matched by SPRN (*Sistema Preduprezhdeniia o Raketnom Napadenii* or Missile Attack Warning System) on the Soviet side (Åtland, 2008). In the 1960s another threat appeared – that of submarine-launched ballistic missiles (SLBMs) which, on the Soviet side, were based near Murmansk. So began a 20-year game of cat-and-mouse beneath the Arctic ice.

This was a fruitful time for Soviet Arctic research. "Drifting" ice stations contributed to fields from hydrochemistry and marine biology to geophysics and oceanography. Development of Arctic and West Siberian petroleum deposits began in the 1960s, followed by exploitation of fields on the Yamal peninsula and, in 1984, completion of the Urengoy-Uzhgorod pipeline to supply Europe with gas from the Yamal-Nenets region. Norilsk, second only to Murmansk as the world's largest city above the Arctic Circle, became the world's biggest nickel mining and smelting operation. In 1988, Soviet geologists discovered the Shtokman Field in the Barents Sea, and in 1989 the Prirazlomnoe Field in the Pechora Sea. The former holds 3.8 trillion cubic meters of natural gas, and the latter over 600 million barrels of oil. But their development, like so much else, was interrupted by the Soviet collapse of 1991.

This seemed unlikely in the early *perestroika* years, when Mikhail Gorbachev gave his 1987 "Murmansk Address" calling for the Arctic to be a "zone of peace" for international cooperation on research and resource development (Gorbachev, 1987). But in all three areas – military power, scientific research, and resource development – the Soviet collapse set Russia back sharply as the country descended into a decade of chaos and corruption. Arctic bases were shuttered as military spending was slashed. Scientific research suffered too – after decades of continuous manning, the last drifting ice station was closed in 1991 – as did investment not to expand but merely to maintain energy production. State support for Arctic housing, food, and fuel fell by 90 percent in the early 1990s, prompting an exodus of over one million people from the Russian far north (Heleniak, 2009).

Russia revived: a responsible Arctic stakeholder

In 1996, Russia was mired in depression under the stumbling Boris Yeltsin – the economy having shrunk by nearly half since 1992, and the oligarchs riding high after the "loans for shares" scandal gave them control of Russia's petroleum riches in return for financing Yeltsin's corrupt reelection. In retreat abroad, Russia was trying to extricate itself from a bloody conflict in Chechnya, while the US was preparing to expand NATO into the former Soviet bloc. At this dark juncture, a bright spot for Russian foreign policy was its role in the creation of the Arctic Council (AC) established by the Ottawa Declaration of September, 1996. For 20 years since, the AC has proved a most successful intergovernmental organization, operating by consensus among its eight members – the US, Canada, Russia, Sweden, Norway, Finland, Denmark, and Iceland – with the Arctic's indigenous peoples also represented as nonvoting "permanent participants" and a number of observer states as well. The AC addresses a wide range of issues concerning the region – excepting military security – by agreement of its founding members.

Russia held the chair of the AC in 2004–2006, and used it to advance a Search and Rescue (SAR) agreement that was concluded in 2011 (upon determination of each member-state's area of responsibility). This was the first legally binding agreement negotiated under the AC, aided by a task force on cooperative measures led by the US and Russia (Rottem, 2013). While SAR advanced, Russia was also negotiating with Norway to settle competing claims to the Barents Sea. In 2010, the parties agreed to split evenly a zone of some 175,000 square km and thereby open the area up to development of resources – petroleum, minerals, and fish (Amos, 2011).

By this time, Russia had bounced back thanks to a decade of rising oil prices and the strict management of Vladimir Putin (Appel, 2008). After a series of market reforms, Putin tightened tax collection and channeled revenues into reviving public services (health, education), creating reserve funds (c. one trillion dollars), and rebuilding crumbling infrastructure (including Arctic scientific and military installations). Polar research stations were reestablished after a 12-year absence, while energy investment soared – both vital for a region that by 2010 was generating 20 percent of Russia's GDP. Among the sources on Russia's Arctic shelf both on and offshore – in the Kara, Barents, and Pechora Seas – the Prirazlomnoe oil field came online in late 2013 and was soon producing 50,000 barrels daily from the world's first ice-resistant offshore rig.

It is ironic that while a large amount of the world's untapped petroleum (13 percent of oil, 30 percent of gas) lies in the Arctic, the alarmism that this evokes causes many to overlook another key fact – namely, that *over 80 percent of that petroleum lies in the undisputed national zones of the Arctic states* (Buchanan, 2016). These deposits are also, as a rule, much closer and more accessible than the remaining 20 percent, rendering competing claims to these distant zones much less urgent – and predictions of conflict still more unlikely. Equally salient is that the Arctic littoral powers have agreed to consensus action to abide by the UN Convention on the Law of the Sea (UNCLOS) in settling disputes. Most recently reaffirmed in the Ilulissat Declaration of 2008, this is downplayed if not overlooked altogether in alarmist commentary on states' rival claims. Russia claims the seabed beyond its 200-nautical mile offshore Exclusive Economic Zone (EEZ), extending to the North Pole – but so does Denmark, with a Canadian claim expected in 2018. A Google search of "Russia claims North Pole" produces over 32,000 hits, yet the same for Denmark yields fewer than 6,500.

Skepticism about Russia – more characteristic of foreign-policy pundits than Arctic specialists – stems as much from Russian swagger as any objectively aggressive actions. In 2007, a submarine expedition planted a Russian flag on the North Pole seabed – a seemingly irresistible trope to editorial writers, even though Moscow reassured that it was only a symbolic act of discovery (and no more one of conquest than 1969's planting of the US flag on the moon). In 2008 Moscow promulgated *Foundations of the Russian Federation's Policy in the Arctic Through 2020 and Beyond*. While emphasizing defense of Russia's sovereignty in the High North, its priorities remained – like those of the other Arctic powers – economic development, environmental protection, and a cooperative stance on regional issues (Heininen, 2014). Moscow has surely taken a hard line toward its indigenous peoples – united in the Russian Association of Indigenous Peoples of the North (RAIPON) – largely due to RAIPON's cooperation with foreign backers in protesting oil extraction in their homelands (Wallace, 2013). And some Russian officials have spoken provocatively about Arctic sovereignty (Lund, 2015). But this is largely rhetoric for a domestic audience, and Arctic experts generally credit Russia with a cooperative and constructive Arctic policy (Gorenburg, 2014).

Russia reviled: halos, horns, and the Arctic reconsidered

Since 2014, popular perceptions of Russia's Arctic policy have turned sharply negative. Western reporting and commentary have been marked, sometimes dominated, by rising concerns about "militarization" and Moscow's purported "aggressive new posture." The alarm in Western media – reflected in policy analyses and political debates as well – has seen notable threat inflation, dire predictions of the consequences of lagging behind, and so urging a match of any Russian buildup (Coffey 2014; Reterski 2014; Heritage, 2015; Holland, 2014; Stratfor, 2015; Gramier, 2017). Some commentary even raises parallels to such notorious episodes as the supposed bomber and missile gaps of the early Cold War, and the "window of vulnerability" of the late Cold War. Today, as then, Russian capabilities are exaggerated while the West's countervailing strengths – even superiority – are discounted. Today, as then, the actual context of Russian strategy and its attendant actions are broadly ignored so as to assign the direst possible interpretation. And so today, as then, scenarios of looming Russian aggression are distorted, even cartoonish, and far out of touch with reality. Unfortunately, they are also quite *in* touch with the reigning Russophobia of Western political elites and so raise the possibility of an incipient spiral of arms buildups in the region.

Already over 2008–2012 – as a direct result of two key events – some Western commentators began raising Arctic- and Russia-focused concerns more urgently. One of those was the planting of a Russian flag on the North Pole seabed in August, 2007. The second was the sharp melt-off of the polar ice cap over the summer of 2012, setting a new record low. The first, as already noted, was a purely symbolic act, but numerous pundits invoked dire consequences regardless. The latter event heightened environmental concerns, naturally, but many invoked a *strategic* threat. According to articles in the authoritative journal *Foreign Affairs*:

> While other powers are racing to carve up the region, the United States has remained largely on the sidelines... The region could erupt in an armed mad dash for its resources.
>
> *(Borgeson, 2008)*

> It's past time for the U.S. to close the icebreaker gap... Nuclear-powered icebreakers would also extend the Arctic reach... of U.S. Navy cruisers and destroyers... Competition over the positioning of military forces in the Arctic could soon intensify, and Russia's recent incursions into the northern European airspace and territorial waters may be an indication of things to come.
>
> *(Reterski, 2014)*

It is difficult to say what combination of concerns shapes media coverage of the Arctic. Already in 2012 there was a "spillover" effect from other critical coverage of Russia. For example, in 2011, US Secretary of State Hillary Clinton criticized Russia's elections and demanded a "full investigation of... fraud and intimidation" (Clinton, 2011). This sparked a backlash from Russian officials, and a spate of increasingly critical Western coverage through 2012, as it overlapped with the "Pussy Riot" scandal of that same year (the jailing of feminist punk-rock activists for a profane demonstration in a Moscow cathedral). And in 2013, Russia's image took another hit from the passage of the notorious law against "gay propaganda." This now-cascading critical coverage of Russia intersected with the Arctic again over the 2013 case of Greenpeace protestors who scaled a Russian oil platform in the Pechora Sea and were detained along with their vessel, *Arctic Sunrise*. Clinton herself argued the emerging consensus in a 2014 speech denouncing Russia's "heightened aggression" in the Arctic, noting that "they recently imprisoned several Greenpeace activists [and] have been aggressively reopening military bases" (Peritz, 2014).

Though she repeatedly employed the term "aggression," one could have as easily characterized both examples as defensive. Certainly, the Spanish Navy saw arresting Greenpeace protestors scaling *their* oil platform as a legitimate defensive act, since they did just that when the *Arctic Sunrise*'s next major protest struck a Spanish oil company (Mathiesen, 2014). Clinton and the myriad Western celebrities who denounced Russia's action in 2013, stayed silent upon the Spanish episode less than a year later. Similarly, the reopening of some Russian northern bases that were shuttered during the collapse of the 1990s (while NATO's northern presence remained strong) was not only just a step toward catching up, but rather leaping ahead. It was also something widely recognized as necessary given the new security and environmental problems caused by Russia's thawing Arctic. Indeed, US Admiral Robert Papp, Washington's senior Arctic officer, succinctly stated:

> Russia is doing those things we would be doing ourselves if there was an increase in traffic above our coast . . . One person might look at that and say "you are militarizing the Arctic," but another person might say you are doing reasonable things to make sure you have safety and security.
>
> (Jopson and Milne, 2015)

That "safety and security" refers to concerns arising from the predicted increase in traffic through the seas above Russia. For the inevitable oil or waste spills, there exist negligible spill management and cleanup assets. For poachers and smugglers, there are only modest patrol and interdiction forces. And for the scores of tankers, cargo, and cruise ships that will be transiting the NSR within a decade, there are few navigation and search-and-rescue facilities. Pursuant to the SAR agreement of 2011, Russia has assumed responsibility for the largest Arctic area that is simultaneously the least developed; at present, ships traverse hundreds of kilometers of treacherous seas between rescue, repair, and refueling facilities (Inozemtsev, 2016). Some future party of US tourists floundering north of the Bering Strait – because of engine trouble, a storm, or other calamity – will be glad of the new Russian SAR center at nearby Provideniya when the closest US Coast Guard base is in Kodiak, Alaska, over 2,000 kilometers distant.

Of the 12–15 "military bases" usually identified with Russia's Arctic "militarization," at least half are in fact SAR centers. Most of the rest are "air bases" – many just beginning construction, and only destined, even when complete, to be essentially an airstrip with a few outbuildings. And most are also located at such vast distances from the frontiers or facilities of other states that they will be ineffective for power-projection or intimidation purposes. Clearly, the rapid re-classification by Western observers of Russia's Arctic activities – from benign to belligerent – reflects a "halos and horns" effect. This is a cognitive bias where, if we see an actor as essentially nice (or nasty), we are predisposed to assess *all* of their actions positively (or negatively) based *not* on an objective assessment of the actions themselves but instead due to our underlying prejudice (Jervis, 1976). The "horns" effect for Russia, already growing after 2011 due to an authoritarian turn in domestic politics, sharpened dramatically after the Ukrainian-Crimean conflict of 2014. Of course, defense planners must assess an adversary's perceived *intent* as well as his or her objective *capabilities*. But the former should not be so exaggerated as to distort interpretation of the latter far beyond reason – as has occurred in the case of Russia's Arctic policies.

Oh no, the dreaded icebreaker gap!

The inflation of Russia's Arctic "threat" has, in both the media and many think-tank analyses, been so extreme as to raise parallels with the "missile gap" or "window of vulnerability" scares of earlier decades. Thus it is useful to review the elements of these threat assessments, and both scrutinize them in context as well as rebut their most exaggerated claims (MacDonald, 2015).

Arctic military bases. For multiple reasons, the facilities Russia is building across its Arctic do *not* represent the intimidating threat that they are portrayed to be. They are largely directed at coastal security and SAR missions. They generally do not support major power-projection capabilities, and are essentially *defensively* oriented (it is hard to see how *an air-defense system* could be used to invade Canada or seize a Norwegian oil platform, yet some analysts darkly note

Russia's possible placement of *air defense batteries* on its Arctic periphery as an aggressive step). What's more, even at the most optimistic pace, it will take a decade simply for Russia to regain the capabilities it had before its post-Cold War collapse (Klimenko, 2016; Wezeman, 2016). Further, when the aircraft and naval vessels that would use these bases are compared with their NATO counterparts, *it is the latter that have a decided edge*.

Icebreakers. Russia has a sizeable icebreaker fleet – and the US a very small one – because Russia has much greater need for their missions: resupply of icebound research stations or remote coastal communities, escort of commercial shipping through the perilous NSW, and SAR duties across Russia's vast Arctic area of responsibility. Some Russian icebreakers are also leased for polar cruises, or accommodating paying tourists on their research missions. Importantly, *icebreakers have minimal military utility*. Vessels that plod through multiyear sea ice at three knots (nautical miles per hour) are useless in any realistic scenario of naval combat. The image of icebreakers carving a path for frigates and destroyers (per Alaska Senator Dan Sullivan, "The highways of the Arctic are icebreakers . . . Russia has superhighways, and we have dirt roads with potholes") is simply ignorant (Reterski, 2014; Gramier, 2017). As noted, the number of icebreakers "doesn't relate at all to combat capability" (Stackpole, 2015). The modest Russian navy does not send its combat vessels out into Arctic ice behind icebreakers, and neither would the US Navy. That is why US icebreakers are operated by the Coast Guard; *because icebreakers support the missions of the Coast Guard*. In a mass of misunderstandings and distortions, perhaps none is so preposterous as that of an "icebreaker gap."

The Russian navy. A recent Heritage Foundation report on Russia's Arctic bases described a major shift of naval assets: "Russia has taken steps to militarize the Arctic. Russia's Northern Fleet, based at Severomorsk, accounts for two-thirds of the Russian Navy" (Heritage, 2015). In fact, this basing is *not* a step Russia has recently taken "to militarize the Arctic" since the Northern Fleet has been the largest part of the Soviet-Russian Navy *since the 1950s*. Yet many pundits accept Heritage's distortion and proceed from the "fact" of a major naval shift northward as proof of Russia's malignant designs. In reality, the Russian navy collapsed after the Cold War and is only now rebuilding. Their Northern Fleet includes some three dozen surface ships (only half of which are truly seagoing, rather than coastal-defense craft) and a similar number of submarines (many of which are Cold War relics and haven't put to sea in years). By contrast, the US Pacific Fleet numbers 60 vessels, and its Atlantic Fleet 190 – as well as over 1,500 carrier-based aircraft (Russia has no true aircraft carriers). Moreover, Russia's basing in the north *is not a sign of strength but a concession to weakness*. Each of Russia's other fleets – the Pacific, the Baltic, and the Black Sea – lack access to the open seas and must transit narrow passages (e.g., the Turkish straits) to exit tightly confined areas such as the Mediterranean, the Gulf of Finland, or the Sea of Japan. Only the Northern Fleet has relatively unfettered access to open ocean. Meanwhile, plans for Russia's first modern aircraft carrier have been delayed repeatedly. Russia *is* building some new vessels, such as the Gorshkov-class frigate – but this design has been decades in development and plagued by problems from faulty turbines to an air defense system 30 years out of date (Friedman, 2016). By *no* stretch of the imagination is Russia seriously challenging US naval dominance (Fedyszyn, 2016; Thomassen, 2016; Polmar and Kofman, 2017a).

Airpower in the Arctic. Here again is a critical area of decided US/NATO advantage. News stories paint a picture of a Russian threat, focusing on close encounters with fighter jets or bomber patrols that skirt NATO countries' airspace (*The Guardian*, 2015, 2016). But this is largely a sideshow, a ritual that both sides have long practiced and that NATO pilots – as opposed to NATO public-affairs officials – stress is "perfectly legal" and in fact a "welcome" practice routine (Posey, 2016). Moreover, bomber patrols have little to do with the Arctic per se; they are long-range aircraft that merely transit the Arctic, as do ours, while more fighter intercepts have occurred in the Baltic or Black Seas (Bamford, 2015; LaGrone, 2016). *When it comes to the actual balance of air power in the Arctic, Russia loses hands down.* The US has multiple squadrons – including fifth-generation F-22 and F-35 fighters – based in Alaska, while *Russia has no deployed fifth-generation fighters at all.* The lethality of this force is multiplied by the US's unmatched airborne warning and control systems (AWACS), while Russia's are primitive (McHale, 2012; McNaught, 2015). And even in areas where Russia has a local advantage – in numbers, though of older and less-capable aircraft – their reach is sharply limited. The US tanker fleet (in-air refueling) has nearly 500 aircraft while Russia has only about two dozen. Now count in the allies; Norway, Denmark, Sweden, and Canada add several hundred more combat aircraft to the Western arsenal, including the latest fourth-generation (F/A-18E, Typhoon Eurofighter) and fifth-generation (F-35A) fighter-attack jets. In sum, Russia can muster significant numbers of capable aircraft in its own backyard, which means essentially a *defensive* role. But in a large-scale offensive operation against the US and its allies, Russian air forces would be decimated.

Submarines and anti-submarine warfare. Here too US advantage is great. US attack submarines – the Los Angeles, Seawolf, and Virginia-class SSNs, known as "hunter-killers" – continue to patrol Arctic waters and track both Russian surface ships and ballistic-missile submarines (SSBNs) with near impunity. The latter are a key element of Russia's nuclear deterrent, especially as their bomber fleet ages and their land-based missiles have been reduced by treaty. Yet Russia's aging SSBNs have rarely put to sea in recent years, laying up at dockside instead of keeping their deterrent weapons hidden (Klimenko, 2016). It is not only the parlous condition of these nuclear-accidents-in-waiting, or the expense of deployment. They must also worry about both the shrinking icecap under which they have traditionally hidden, as well as about improving US and NATO ASW systems (Reterski, 2014; Clark, 2015; De Larrinaga, 2016; Osborn 2016, 2017). Meanwhile, the US has adapted some Ohio-class SSBNs to a land-attack role with new cruise missile and special forces delivery systems (Roblin, 2017). Despite recent hysteria about Russian subs in Scandinavian waters (Taylor, 2015), it is the US that has greatly increased its sub-based conventional-strike capabilities. (And with the acquisition of Wasp- and America-class amphibious assault ships, the US Navy's land attack power is truly fearsome.) The Russian navy is now beginning to deploy some new SSBNs as well as modern attack submarines, but remains far behind in this key dimension of the Arctic military balance (Axe, 2015). Indeed, the Russian submarine fleet is still "dwarfed" compared to its own Cold War-era force (Polmar and Kofman, 2017b).

What to do if the ice melts? Build icebreakers!

A US Navy report on *Naval Operations in an Ice Free Arctic* did indeed recommend that the US acquire more icebreakers (ONR, 2001). That would seem ill-advised – to put it mildly – except that at the time of the analysis the Arctic was not expected to be completely ice-free in the summer until at least 2050. Since then, accelerating loss of polar sea ice has caused some to predict the advent of an ice-free Arctic by 2025 or even sooner (SIPN, 2016), which indeed calls into question the wisdom of building vessels that cost at least $1 billion apiece and may not be completed until 2020. In any event, a cost-benefit analysis can be performed, based on different climactic predictions, to reach well-advised recommendations on procurement of some vessels that usefully support research, SAR, and law-enforcement needs.

What *is* clearly ill-advised are policy proposals – based on exaggerated assessments of "Russia's Arctic threat" – for US and NATO militaries. As seen, most alarm about Russia's "militarization" of the Arctic is overheated punditry and ignorant threat inflation. Ignorance is key, as lack of knowledge about the Arctic environment – and the military systems at issue – combine to make such canards as an "icebreaker gap" appear as real threats to the uninformed. (A Google search for "icebreaker gap" yields an astonishing 426,000 hits.) Of even greater concern to the defense analyst is the absence of *specific* threat scenarios – supporting *specific* policy responses – rather than a vague "the Russians are coming!" In contrast to the South China Sea – where territorial disputes are numerous, resource rivalries are urgent, and military forces collide in a crowded sea ringed by densely populated coastlines while key actors ignore international law – conditions could hardly be more different in the Arctic. What *exactly* will the Russians do, requiring *exactly* what US-NATO response?

Match whatever the Russians are doing. Most frequently seen are arguments to mimic Russian programs. If they have so many Arctic bases, or nuclear icebreakers, so must we. There is no real analysis of the supposed threat, and so no particular justification of the proposed response – there is only a vague Russian menace.

Respond to environmental disasters or cruise-ship emergencies. These are US Coast Guard SAR missions. While there may arise situations where US Navy vessels could assist, this is not their primary purpose and certainly not one prompted by "Russian militarization." In fact, what is described as Russia's "militarization" largely consists of *their* building up SAR bases and assets (Auerswald, 2015).

Go out and fight on the ice. Other proposals envision combat at sea – in particular, a clash of surface combatants. Because Russia has many icebreakers, they will dominate "the positioning of military forces in the Arctic" (Reterski, 2014) unless we procure our own to carve out "the highways of the Arctic" (Gramier, 2017) and so enable "U.S. Navy cruisers and destroyers . . . to quickly travel to [the Arctic] theater of operations [supporting] a true forward presence" (Reterski, 2014) that can "attack and defend isolated Arctic bases" (Mizokami, 2016). Such scenarios require ice-hardened combat ships, not just icebreakers, because "if you can only be on the surface where there is little or no danger of ice, then your presence is very restricted" (Johnson and De Luce, 2016). The silliness of this vision would not be worth rebutting, were it not so prevalent. Slow-moving icebreakers cannot possibly carve out "highways" upon which surface ships can rapidly maneuver; even ice-hardened ships (which adds a third to the cost of construction, and compromises other functions) are subject to hull breach even in loose ice; operating in Arctic conditions can also cause everything from weapons malfunction to superstructure icing with the risk of capsizing (Patch, 2009); above all, today's fantastically expensive naval vessels (Zumwalt-class destroyers cost nearly $1.5 billion each) would be sitting ducks for missile attacks if operating close to Russian strongholds in compromised Arctic conditions (Thomassen, 2016; Polmar and Kofman, 2017b).

Freedom of Navigation Operations. This refers to proactively asserting a right to operate in disputed waters, i.e., coastal areas that are regarded as international (under UNCLOS) when they are also claimed by the coastal state. The US Navy regularly conducts freedom-of-navigation operations (FONOP) that naturally seem aggressive to the state-claimant involved, such as recent missions near the Paracel and Spratly Islands contesting Chinese claims. Previous FONOP in the Gulf of Sidra, or the Black Sea, resulted in armed confrontations with Libya and the USSR. Some now call for asserting FON rights along the NSR, in areas Moscow claims as an inland waterway (just as Ottawa claims parts of the Northwest Passage that the US also does not recognize) (Foggo, 2016). While the US Navy sees this as a matter of principle, it is also provocative and risky, particularly in the current climate. As noted earlier, the one thing Russia's Arctic forces are well configured for is *defending* their territory. Add to that Russia's new air defense installations and emphasis on anti-access and area denial (A2/AD) capabilities, then provoking a confrontation close to their shores – and possible escalation – could go badly for the US.

Defend a threatened oil platform. Another scenario requires defense against seizure of an oil or gas platform (Auerswald, 2015). Why Russia would launch such an attack is unclear – Russia has no shortage of its own Arctic oil and gas, the resultant environmental catastrophe would devastate them as well, and why would Norway or Canada drill in disputed waters claimed by Russia in the first place? Still, the larger flaw in this scenario as justification for a major naval buildup is that the US-NATO already possesses the assets for just such a mission. Instead of a fleet of slow, vulnerable, ice-breaking surface combatants, it requires stealthy means of delivering firepower and troops in a surprise attack. *And this is a capability that the US already possesses*, with its SSNs and conventional-attack adapted SSBNs – converted Ohio-class nuclear ballistic missile submarines, now carrying cruise missiles and delivering special forces for stealthy infiltration (Moore, 2012). Combined with the unmatched US-NATO ability to bring stealthy long-range airpower to bear on Arctic targets, this unlikely scenario is nevertheless one that plays to US *strengths*, not weakness (Axe, 2015).

Can cooperation trump confrontation?

Russia's revised Arctic strategy highlights the region's economic and strategic importance. Since 2014, emphasis has been placed on protecting sovereignty and responding to threats, including those potentially posed by NATO (MID-Russia, 2016). Also since 2014, responding to the US-NATO buildup in the Baltics and Norway, Russia has taken such steps as increasing Arctic air patrols and conducting large-scale maneuvers (Klimenko, 2016). All the same, Russia has *not* significantly expanded upon the steady rebuilding of its decrepit Arctic security infrastructure begun a decade earlier. It has *not* deployed systems that challenge overall US-NATO dominance in the Arctic, and it has *not* deviated from the policy of consensus decision-making and negotiated resolution of regional disputes. Certainly, some belligerent rhetoric has been heard, though these words are largely directed at a Russian domestic audience. Russia's deeds, however, have not by any means lived up to the threats attributed to them (MacDonald, 2015; Wezeman, 2016).

In 2013, even before the Crimean crisis triggered a reassessment of all of Russia's military programs, there had begun a critique of Russia's "militarization" of the Arctic. At that time, the US Department of Defense itself warned:

> Being too aggressive in taking steps to anticipate future security risks may create the conditions of mistrust and miscommunication under which such risks could materialize. There is some risk that *the perception that the Arctic is being militarized may lead to an arms race mentality* that could lead to a breakdown of existing cooperative approaches to shared challenges.
>
> *(DoD, 2013; emphasis added)*

That mentality is not only visible, it is prominent among many Western, particularly US, media and think-tanks. Yet several factors slow the move from arms-race mentality to an actual arms race. One is the huge expense of the weapons systems touted (icebreakers cost over $1 billion each, ice-hardened surface combatants could top $2 billion). Another is the implausibility of the "threat scenarios" touted. And together these buttress a third restraining factor, which is that most military experts do not agree with the alarmist assessments and redirection of priorities toward acquisition of major new Arctic capabilities. From the caution of Admiral Robert Papp, to the pages of military journals where Arctic alarm remains low, to the words of the US Defense Department quoted earlier, the difference between professional military and civilian foreign-policy specialists is significant.

Nevertheless, history knows cases where the military is overruled and, in particular, where a new US presidential administration – acting on the advice of impassioned civilian analysts – launches a major new program or priority. The "Star Wars" or Strategic Defense Initiative of the Reagan Administration is just one such example. That program too began with the persistent elaboration of a Soviet threat, the so-called "window of vulnerability" to nuclear attack. In the case of the Arctic, elaboration of a new Russia threat is still at a relatively early stage. Nevertheless:

> Political rhetoric and press reporting about boundary disputes and the competition for resources may inflame regional tensions. Efforts to manage disagreement diplomatically may be hindered *if the public narrative becomes one of rivalry and conflict.*
>
> (DoD, 2013; emphasis added)

There has already emerged a "narrative of rivalry and conflict" on the Arctic, driven by determined policy advocates and abetted by careless journalists and politicians (some with vested interests). Whether this narrative grows, and the nascent "securitization" of the Arctic predominates, cannot be predicted. It could ultimately depend as much on the whims of a new US President as it does on the broader arc of US-Russian relations – the Crimea was where Russia's Arctic threat really began, in a critical sense – with the two closely linked in any case (Hoag, 2016; Yalowitz and Gallucci, 2016; Buchanan, 2016). A more pointless and wasteful venue for arms racing is difficult to imagine.

References

Amos, Howard. (2011) "Arctic Treaty with Norway Opens Fields," *The Moscow Times*. July 6, 2011.
Appel, Hilary. (2008) "Is It Putin or Is It Oil? Explaining Russia's Fiscal Recovery." *Post-Soviet Affairs*, vol. 24, no. 4, pp. 301–323.
Åtland, Kristian. (2008) "The Militarization of the Barents Region," *Barents Encyclopedia* 2007–2008. Access at: http://bar-enc.didaktekon.se/Editor/Sample-articles/Ex-Militarization-L-Atland-2011–09.pdf.
Auerswald, David P. (2015) "Geopolitical Icebergs: Hidden Dangers Lurk Beneath the International-Cooperation Surface in the Emerging Arctic." *USNI Proceedings*, vol. 141, no. 12, pp. 31–34.
Axe, David. (2015) "Russia and America Prep Forces for Arctic War." *Reuters*, October 5, 2015.
Bamford, James. (2015) "Frozen Assets: The Newest Front in Global Espionage is one of the Least Habitable Places on Earth – The Arctic." *ForeignPolicy.com*. Access at: http://foreignpolicy.com/2015/05/11/frozen-assets-arctic-espionage-spying-new-cold-war-russia-canada/.
Borgeson, Scott. (2008) "Arctic Meltdown: The Economic and Security Implications of Global Warming." *Foreign Affairs* vol. 87, no. 2, pp. 63–77.
Buchanan, Elizabeth. (2016) "Arctic Thaw: Arctic Cooperation and Russian Rapprochement." *Foreign Affairs*, 21 January 2017. www.foreignaffairs.com/articles/russian-federation/2016-01-21/arctic-thaw.
Clark, Bryan. (2015) *The Emerging Era in Undersea Warfare*. Washington, DC: Center for Strategic and Budgetary Assessments.
Clinton, Hillary. (2011) "Clinton Cites 'Serious Concerns' about Russian Election," *CNN*, 6 December 2011.
Coffey, Luke. (2014) "Russian Military Activity in the Arctic: A Cause for Concern." *Heritage Foundation Issue Brief* 4320. Access at: www.heritage.org/europe/report/russian-military-activity-the-arctic-cause-concern.
De Larrinaga, Nicholas (2016) "Farnborough 2016: UK orders P-8 Poseidon maritime patrol aircraft." *HIS Janes Defense Weekly*, access at: www.janes.com/article/62159/farnborough-2016-uk-orders-p-8-poseidon-maritime-patrol-aircraft.
DoD. (2013) *Arctic Strategy*, United States Department of Defense. Washington, DC, November 2013.
Fedyszyn, Thomas R. (2016) "Putin's 'Potemkin-Plus' Navy." *USNI Proceedings* May 2016, vol. 142, no. 5, pp. 1–6.
Foggo, James. (2016) "The Fourth Battle of the Atlantic." *USNI Proceedings*, vol. 142, no. 6, pp. 16–17.
Friedman, Norman. (2016) "World Naval Developments: What Was Behind Putin's Stalin-Style Purge?" *USNI Proceedings* Sept 2016, vol. 142, no. 9, pp. 4–7.

Gorbachev, M.S. (1987) "Award Ceremony Speech in Murmansk," *Foreign Broadcast Information Service Worldwide Report*, 14 December 1987, p. 75.

Gorenburg, Dmitry (2014) "How to Understand Russia's Arctic Strategy," *The Washington Post*.

Gramier, Robbie. (2017) "Here's What Russia's Military Buildup in the Arctic Looks Like," *Foreign Policy.com*, 25 January 2017. Access at: http://foreignpolicy.com/2017/01/25/heres-what-russias-military-build-up-in-the-arctic-looks-like-trump-oil-military-high-north-infographic-map/.

The Guardian. (2015) "Nato Reports Surge in Jet Interceptions as Russia Tensions Increase," *The Guardian*, 3 August 2015.

The Guardian. (2016) "Typhoon Jets Intercept Russian Planes That Committed 'Act of Aggression'," *The Guardian*, 13 May 2016.

Heininen, Lassi; Sergunin, Alexander; Yarovoy, Gleb Yarovoy. (2014) *Russian Strategies in the Arctic: Avoiding a New Cold War*. Moscow: Valdai. Access at: http://valdaiclub.com/files/11482/.

Heleniak, Timothy S. (2009) "Growth Poles and Ghost Towns in the Russian Far North," in E. Eilson Rowe, ed., *Russia and the North*. Ottawa: University of Ottawa.

Heritage Foundation. (2015) *Russia Fortifying Bases in Arctic Region*. Washington, DC: Heritage.

Hoag, Hannah. (2016) "Expert View: How the Outcome of the U.S. Election Affects the Arctic." *Arctic Deeply*, 9 November 2016. Access at: www.newsdeeply.com/arctic/articles/2016/11/09/expert-view-how-the-outcome-of-the-u-s-election-affects-the-arctic.

Inozemtsev, Vladislav. (2016) "Russia's Master Plan to Seize the Arctic." *The National Interest*. May 2, 2016. Access at: http://nationalinterest.org/blog/the-buzz/russias-master-plan-seize-the-arctic-16022.

Jervis, Robert. (1976) *Perception and Misperception in International Politics*. Princeton, NJ: Princeton University Press.

Johnson, Keith; De Luce, Dan. (2016) "US Falls Behind in Arctic Great Game." *Foreign Policy.com*, 24 May 2016. Access at: http://foreignpolicy.com/2016/05/24/u-s-falls-behind-in-arctic-great-game/.

Jopson, Barney; Milne, Richard. (2015) "US Urged to Assert Itself over Arctic." *The Financial Times*, 9 March 2015.

Josephson, Paul R. (2014) *The Conquest of the Russian Arctic*. Cambridge, MA: Harvard University Press.

Klimenko, Ekaterina. (2016) "Russia's Arctic Security Policy: Still Quiet in the High North?" *SIPRI Policy Paper 45*, Stockholm: SIPRI.

LaGrone, Sam. (2014) "Russian Fighter Buzzes US Destroyer in Black Sea." *USNI News*, April 2014.

Laruelle, Marlene. (2013) *Arctic Strategies and the Fate of the Far North*. New York: M.E. Sharpe.

Lund, Eric. (2015) "When Dmitry Rogozin Speaks, People Worry," *Arctic Journal*. Access at: http://arcticjournal.com/politics/1562/when-dmitry-rogozin-speaks-people-worry.

MacDonald, Adam. (2015) "The Militarization of the Arctic: Emerging Reality, Exaggeration, and Distraction." *Canadian Military Journal*, vol. 15, no. 3, pp. 18–28.

Mathiesen, Karl. (2014) "Greenpeace Ship Arctic Sunrise Detained in Spain." *The Guardian*, 19 November 2014.

McHale, John. (2012) "Polar Hawk USV to Perform HALE Security Missions for Canada's Arctic Territories." *Military Embedded Systems*, 4 June 2012.

McNaught, Jason. (2015) "The US Is Using Tech That Could Secure Canada's Arctic." *Vanguard Magazine*, 26 October 2015.

MID-Russia. (2016) *Foreign Policy Concept of the Russian Federation*. Ministry of Foreign Affairs, Moscow. November 30, 2016. Access at: www.mid.ru/ru/foreign_policy/news/-/asset_publisher/cKNonkJE02Bw/content/id/2542248?p_p_id=101_INSTANCE_cKNonkJE02Bw&_101_INSTANCE_cKNonkJE02Bw_languageId=en_GB.

Mizokami, Kyle. (2016) "How Russia is Fortifying the Arctic." *The Week*, 29 March 2016. Access at: http://theweek.com/articles/614075/how-russia-fortifying-arctic.

Moore, Brian. (2012) "Get Serious About the Arctic." *USNI Proceedings*, vol. 138, no. 8, pp. 27–29.

ONR. (2001) *Naval Operations in an Ice-Free Arctic*. Washington, DC: Office of Naval Research, Naval Ice Center, Oceanographer of the Navy.

Osborn, Kris. (2016) "The U.S. Navy's Underwater Robots Patrol the Arctic." *The National Interest*, 26 May 2016. Access at: http://nationalinterest.org/blog/the-buzz/the-us-navys-underwater-robots-patrol-the-arctic-16357.

Osborn, Kris. (2017) "Navy Plans Stealthier Attack Submarines, Citing Breakthrough Technology." *Warrior*. January 4, 2017. Access at: www.scout.com/military/warrior/story/1680206-navy-to-engineer-stealthier-attack-submarines.

Patch, John. (2009) "Cold Horizons: Arctic Maritime Security Challenges." *USNI Proceedings*, vol. 135 no. 5, pp. 6–9.

Peritz, Ingrid. (2014) "Hillary Clinton Warns Montreal Crowd of Russia's Increased Activity in the Arctic," *The Globe and Mail*, March 18, 2014.

Polmar, Norman; Kofman, Michael. (2017a) "'New' Russian Navy: Part 2." *USNI Proceedings* January 2017, vol. 143 no. 1, pp. 18–21.

Polmar, Norman; Kofman, Michael (2017b) "Russian Navy: Impressive Beneath the Waves." *USNI Proceedings* February 2017, vol. 143 no. 2, pp. 5–9.

Posey, Carl. (2016) "The Guard at NATO's Northern Gate." *Air and Space*, September 2016.

Reterski, Milosz. (2014) "Breaking the Ice: Why the United States needs Nuclear-Powered Icebreakers." *Foreign Affairs* December 11 2014. www.foreignaffairs.com/articles/united-states/2014-12-11/breaking-ice.

Roblin, Sébastien. (2017) "Why China and Russia Fear America's Killer Cruise Missile Submarines." *The National Interest*, 28 January 2016. Access at: http://nationalinterest.org/blog/the-buzz/why-china-russia-fear-americas-killer-cruise-missile-19221.

Rottem, Svein Vigeland. (2013). 'The Arctic Council and the Search and Rescue Agreement: The case of Norway." *Polar Record*, vol. 50, no. 3, p. 287.

SIPN. (2016) "2016: Post-Season Report." *Sea Ice Prediction Network*. Access at: www.arcus.org/sipn/sea-ice-outlook/2016/post-season.

Sale, Richard; Potapov, Eugene. (2009) *The Scramble for the Arctic: Ownership, Exploitation, and Conflict in the Far North*. London: Francis Lincoln Ltd.

Stackpole, Thomas. (2015) "The United States' Need for a New Icebreaker Doesn't Really Have Much to Do with Russia." *Foreign Policy.com*, 2 September 2015. Access at: http://foreignpolicy.com/2015/09/02/the-united-states-need-for-a-new-icebreaker-doesnt-really-have-much-to-do-with-russia/.

Stratfor. (2015) *Russia's Plans for Arctic Supremacy*. Access at: www.stratfor.com/analysis/russias-plans-arctic-supremacy.

Taylor, Adam. (2015) "It looks like Sweden Found a Sunken Russian Sub: But is it Putin's or the Czar's"? *The Washington Post*, 28 July 2015.

Thomassen, Daniel. (2016) "Russian Blue-Water Navy is a Pipe Dream." *USNI Proceedings* November 2016, vol. 142, no. 11, pp. 1–5.

Wallace, Ron. (2013) "The Case for RAIPON." *Canadian Defense and Foreign Affairs Institute*. February, 2013.

Wezeman, Siemon T. (2016) "Military Capabilities in the Arctic: A New Cold War in the High North?" *SIPRI Background Paper*. Stockholm: SIPRI.

Yalowitz, Kenneth; Gallucci, Vincent. (2016) "Can the U.S. and Russia Avoid an Arctic Arms Race?" *The National Interest*, 8 April 2016. http://nationalinterest.org/feature/can-the-us-russia-avoid-arctic-arms-race-15713.

PART IV

Organizations

Andrei P. Tsygankov

The final part of the volume addresses the issue of Russia's participation in international organizations. In studying Russia's experience with global governance, I selected some of the most important – although not all – organizations operating at both global and regional level such as the United Nations, G20, several pan-European and Asian organizations, as well as those limited to the post-Soviet Eurasia.

In addition to summarizing scholarship on the country's experience with selected organizations, each contributor assesses Russia's practical experience over time and in comparison with other organizations as generally successful or not in accomplishing Moscow's objectives. S/he also explains how Russia's perception and strategy within an organization have evolved and what has accounted for the change. Here, scholars seek to shed light on the question of whether Russia is guided primarily by national interests as it sees them or by wider global and regional concerns, or both. Finally, each chapter briefly reflects on a future role for a studied organization in RFP.

The first chapter analyzes Russia's experience with the UN. Alexander Sergunin argues that Russia's UN record has been largely positive. Russia views the UN as indispensable in preserving global peace and stability and has been a responsible actor within the organization by fulfilling multiple duties. It has been a critically important participant in the UN Security Council and exercised its veto power 13 times since the end of the Cold War. Russia has also contributed to the UN debate on sustainable development by promoting an approach that combines economic, social, and environmental dimensions. Furthermore, Russia has greatly contributed to the debate and practice of conflict management and peacekeeping. While accepting some principles of the R2P, Moscow criticized the concept's application in practice. Finally, Russia has been a prominent participant in discussing the issue of UN political, economic, and financial reform. According to Sergunin, the UN has been important to the Kremlin for both legitimacy and balancing objectives. Russia has worked hard to preserve the organization's unique legitimacy for providing global peace and security and to balance against U.S. attempts to dominate in global affairs. Sergunin maintains that Russia's future experience with the organization will continue to be guided by both considerations.

The other global organization of significance to Russia has been the G20. Andrej Krickovic writes that since the organization's establishment in 1999, Russia has been its consistent advocate and supporter although its interest in the G20 declined following the Ukraine crisis. Krickovic argues that both Russia's support and decline of interest can be attributed to Moscow's changing perception of international realities. Initially, Russia viewed the G20 as a potential force for boosting the country's status as a major power and addressing practical issues of replacing the dollar with a supranational currency, establishing new rules for global trade, investment, and macroeconomic policy. However, Moscow's status ambitions increased following Russia's confrontation with the West over the annexation of Crimea to go beyond political economy issues to address the fundamentals of security and international order and to reflect the Kremlin's desire for establishment of a modern day "Great Power Concert."

Russia also proved overly optimistic in expecting real solutions from the G20 forums. Although these forums were helpful in discussing the potential contribution of rising non-Western economies and possible shape of future global institutions such as the BRICS Development Bank and Asian Infrastructure Investment Bank, the G20 forums were not capable of tackling principal issues of global economic governance. In Krickovic's assessment, Moscow has been generally a good citizen within the organization by complying with 74% of its major G20 commitments – slightly more than the organization's average of 72% – and the organization will continue to be important in fulfilling Russia's goal of diversifying global political economy away from the West.

In addition to global organizations, Russia has participated in various regional institutions. Among those, Moscow has traditionally viewed as important European organizations responsible for the rule of law and human rights as well as regional security. As Hanna Smith writes, the Council of Europe (CoE) has represented the former, while the Organization for Security and Cooperation in Europe (OSCE) has been charged with the latter. Russia has had a challenging experience with both the CoE and OSCE. Moscow became a member of the CoE in 1996 expecting a greater integration with Europe despite the latter's growing criticism over Russia's conduct of the first Chechnya war. Moscow then grew increasingly disappointed with the CoE because of human rights problems in Chechnya, Russia's claims to have an exceptional role within the organization, and increasingly unpopular decisions by the European Court of Human Rights, a part of the CoE, to protect ordinary Russians against their own state.

Russia experienced a similar disappointment with the OSCE, which the Kremlin desired to become a European security umbrella alternative to NATO. Instead, in Russia's perception, since the organization's summit in Istanbul in 1999 the OSCE has grown intrusive in Russia's internal affairs and deviated from the original mission of peacekeeping by taking up the task of monitoring elections. President Putin later characterized the OSCE as "a vulgar instrument" for promoting "the foreign policy interests of one or a group of countries". Despite these tensions, Smith maintains that Russia remains interested in preserving relations with the pan-European organizations and hopeful that frank dialogue will lead to their improvement.

In Asia, Russia too became less interested in transregional multilateralism over time, although for different reasons than in Europe. Artyom Lukin provides a broad overview of Russia's Asian experience and demonstrates in his chapter how after an initially passive attitude in the 1990s Russia developed an active approach and presence in all major political and security institutions in Asia including ASEAN, Six Party Talks, the EAS, and others. However, having gained prominence in these institutions by 2011 and having hosted an important APEC summit in 2012 in Vladivistok, Russia began to scale down its trans-Asian activism in order to concentrate on Eurasian affairs. In Moscow's perception, the focus on Asia did not bring the sought after benefits of status and prestige, while strategically and economically the region remained too distant to merit a policy effort comparable with that toward Europe or the Middle East.

The new vision that motivates the Kremlin has become that of a "greater Eurasia" in which Russia is a major player, along with China and several other powers including, potentially, the

United States. Lukin describes various new formats in which Moscow has played a role to buttress the new vision such Shanghai Cooperation Organization (SCO), CICA, trilateral forums with the involvement of India, China, and Mongolia, and others. In developing the idea of greater Eurasia, Russia works in close cooperation with China and is motivated by compatibility of the two countries' interests, perception of threats, and norms of Westphalian sovereignty. In Lukin's assessment, Russia's preoccupation with establishing the concert-of-power arrangement in Eurasia is important yet challenging and potentially risky given the growing power differentials with China and India.

One prominent organization in the greater Eurasian region that Russia has supported and helped to develop is SCO. Maria Freire documents Russia's consistent efforts to promote the SCO – first as an organization to address in a multilateral format the vacuum of security and stability in Central Asia, and then as a more ambitious trans-Eurasian institution with participation of major powers including India, Pakistan, and others. Freire maintains that such evolution of Russia's position toward the SCO should be explained by several inter-related factors including a desire to contain the West's influence, preoccupation with security, and promotion of non-Western norms and values. Moscow is also concerned with the increasingly dominant role of China in the Eurasian region and seeks to involve other powers to offset China's influence. Freire assesses such effort by Russia as only partially successful given Beijing's growing economic weight and ambitions to play the central role in shaping the economic and institutional structure of the region.

In the effort to promote its own economic and security vision in the region, Russia also has sought to build institutions in which to act as the dominant power. As noted earlier in the chapter by Charles Ziegler (Chapter 7), Moscow is more open to global governance and multilateral cooperation in those areas that do not affect its vital security in the Eurasian region. In order to preserve its security and status in the immediate neighborhood, Russia has developed the Collective Security Treaty Organization (CSTO) and the Eurasian Economic Union (EAEU).

Mikhail Molchanov's chapter analyzes Russia's experience with the EAEU and argues that Russia has made a considerable progress in developing the organization institutionally, yet has been far less successful in delivering results defined as a growing volume of trade and investments. Although initially after its establishment in 2011 trade expanded during the first two years, it has been in decline since then. Molchanov explains Moscow's interest in developing the EAEU by mutual dependencies of its members (Russia, Kazakhstan, Belarus, and Kyrgyzstan) and by desire to adjust to neoliberal globalization in the increasingly regionally centered world. Even if Russia is a de facto dominant economic power, he maintains, participation in the organization brings long-term benefits to all members. In the light of the described economic problems and rising power of China, Molchanov's assessment is that Russia will have to adapt and eventually acquiesce. Recent efforts by Putin to integrate the EAEU, the SCO, China's "One Belt, One Road" project, and ASEAN into a "Big Eurasian Partnership" may be viewed as recognition of this reality.

Finally, in her chapter on the CSTO Ruth Deyermond describes how the organization has evolved from the initially limited Collective Security Treaty established in 1992 into the Organization with an expanded scope in 2002. In response to insecurities in Afghanistan and the U.S. military presence in Central Asia following the terrorist attacks on the United States on September 11, 2011, the CSTO began to develop various military and counter-terrorist capacities. Since the mid-2000s, the organization has built a Rapid Reaction Force and has been conducting many more military exercises. Finally, in response to the color revolutions, the CSTO adopted special provisions pledging to defend its members' (Russia, Belarus, Armenia, and Central Asian states) "constitutional order" from destabilization by various political, ideological, and informational means. Deyermond recognizes Russia's dominant position within the organization, but finds this explanation insufficient for understanding Moscow's motives. She draws the reader's attention to mutual security concerns and perceptions of its members. She further warns against overstating the domination/hegemony argument by pointing to limitations of Russia's power as expressed in its inability to keep Uzbekistan within the CSTO, as well as to Moscow's non-intervention in Kyrgyzstan's internal destabilization in 2010. Overall, Deyermond finds the organization to be an important yet limited vehicle for advancing RFP goals.

22
THE UNITED NATIONS

Alexander Sergunin

ST. PETERSBURG STATE UNIVERSITY, RUSSIA

Introduction

Russia succeeded to the Soviet Union's seat, including its permanent membership, on the UN Security Council after the dissolution of the Soviet Union in 1991. Eleven of the twelve members of the Commonwealth of Independent States (CIS) signed a declaration on December 21, 1991, agreeing that "Member states of the Commonwealth support Russia in taking over the USSR membership in the UN, including permanent membership in the Security Council." One day before the resignation of Soviet President Mikhail Gorbachev, Ambassador Y. Vorontsov forwarded to the UN Secretary-General Javier Pérez de Cuéllar a letter from the Russian President Boris Yeltsin stating that:

> [t]he membership of the Union of Soviet Socialist Republics in the United Nations, including the Security Council and all other organs and organizations of the United Nations system, is being continued by the Russian Federation (RSFSR) with the support of the countries of the Commonwealth of Independent States. In this connection, I request that the name "Russian Federation" should be used in the United Nations in place of the name "the Union of Soviet Socialist Republics." The Russian Federation maintains full responsibility for all the rights and obligations of the USSR under the Charter of the United Nations, including the financial obligations. I request that you consider this letter as confirmation of the credentials to represent the Russian Federation in United Nations organs for all the persons currently holding the credentials of representatives of the USSR to the United Nations.
>
> *(Yeltsin, 1991)*

The Secretary-General circulated the request among the UN membership. Since there were no major objections, the Russian Federation took the USSR's place. On January 31, 1992 President Yeltsin personally took Russia's seat at the Security Council meeting.

Russia's role and policies in the UN in the post-Cold War era is a rather vexed issue in the present-day scholarship. One group of researchers (Petro and Rubinstein, 1997: 283; Zaemsky, 2010; Belenkova, 2011; Dzhantaev, 2013; Kalyadin, 2016; Pacer, 2016: 119–120) believes that Russia is serious about the role of the UN in world politics, considers it the most significant international organization which is helpful in making the world a better and safer place, as well as views the UN as an important priority of Moscow's foreign policy.

On the other hand, there are authors (Lo, 2002: 87–90, 93–94; Cameron, 2008: 1; Oldberg, 2010: 32; Gowan, 2015; Shevchenko, 2015; Snetkov and Lanteigne, 2015) who think that the Kremlin's UN-first principle was not some abstract ideal to which Russia had a particular emotional or even intellectual attachment, but an instrument to be used selectively to promote specific policy aims. In the 1990s, this approach was a logical response to Russia's diminishing importance in the post-Cold War world and, at the same time, an effective tool to restrain U.S. power in the unipolar world. According to this school, currently, Moscow's UN-primacy line aims to ascertain Russia's great power status, promote its global ambitions, and prevent any anti-Russian moves of its political opponents.

This chapter aims at examining the following research questions:

- How can Russia's organizational behavior in the UN be explained? Is Russia guided primarily by national interests as it sees them or by wider global and regional concerns, or both?
- What role has the UN played in Russia's overall foreign policy relative to other regional and global organizations?
- What has been the record of Russia's UN membership since the Cold War end? How has Russia's role evolved? What have been some of the main issues, agreements, and disagreements?
- Has this been a record of success, failure, or a mixed bag? Has Russia accepted the rules as they are or tried to change or violate them?
- What future questions and themes are likely to arise in Russia' relations with the UN, including the much discussed reform of this organization?

The UN in the system of Russia's foreign policy priorities

For Moscow, the UN remains the key institution for regulating international relations, which can be traced in all Russian foreign policy documents and in multilateral and bilateral treaties and declarations. From Russia's point of view, the UN remains a unique universal format for the interaction of the states of the world. This organization has considerable potential for keeping international peace and security and offers every state equal rights to uphold its national interests. The UN is the foundation of a democratic world order which Russia publicly advocates.

For example, the UN is mentioned many times in Russia's 2016 foreign policy concept. In particular, its primacy in international relations is stressed in the sections on Moscow's foreign policy priorities as the most important one (subchapters "Shaping a just and sustainable world order" and "International law supremacy in international relations"). The paper emphasizes: "The UN which proved its indispensability and international legitimacy shall remain a centerpiece of the 21st century's world policy regulation and coordination" (Putin, 2016).

According to the Russian Foreign Minister Sergei Lavrov:

> First of all, the United Nations' legitimacy is unique. It is the only mechanism of international cooperation that relies on a solid foundation of international law and covers all spheres of human endeavor without exception: military-political, security, conflict resolution, development of economic and humanitarian cooperation and one more important function – modernization of international law.
>
> *(Cited in Khaspekova et al., 2015)*

First and foremost, the Kremlin views the UN as a backbone of the global security system. The UN Security Council (as well as some other UN specialized bodies) is a principal platform for conflict prevention, management, and resolution. With rare exception (such as some conflicts in the post-Soviet space), Moscow insists on UN involvement in preventive diplomacy, crisis management, peace-making, and post-conflict peace-building. This is explained by the UN's unique capabilities, including its unchallenged international legitimacy and authority as well as by its organizational and financial resources.

As part of its attempts to increase its role internationally, and as a permanent member of the UN Security Council, Russia presents itself as a guardian of international security. It demands that its opinion be sought, and its position respected, at times of crises. According to Minister Lavrov, the UN veto is an important instrument for avoiding the mistakes of the League of Nations, the precursor to the UN, which he suggests "collapsed because of [the] ignoring of the interests of the largest states" (Lavrov, 2012). In this respect, Russia views its UN veto as a special privilege that grants it a significant role internationally.

As far as the military aspects of international security are concerned, the Kremlin also values the UN role in developing arms control and the disarmament process, and maintaining/monitoring relevant regimes. Particularly, Russia favors international cooperation on strengthening the UN-born arms control and disarmament regimes, such as the 1968 Nuclear Non-Proliferation Treaty, the 1971 Convention on Prohibition of the Bacteriological (Biological) Weapons, the 1993 Convention on Prohibition and Utilization of the Chemical Weapons, and the 1996 Comprehensive Nuclear Test Ban Treaty.

Moscow also tends to use its seat at the UN Security Council to counter U.S. attempts to dominate world politics. Since the early 1990s, Russia has tried to use the Council to contain U.S. 'unipolarity' and Washington's alleged pretensions to the role of supreme arbiter who aimed to supplant the UN in this area. The great attraction of the UN for Russia was that it diffused power and authority among a greater number of international players – or at least gave the impression of doing so. To some extent, it compensated for the growing gap between the two former superpowers. It was therefore natural for Russia to insist on the UN Security Council's continuing role in international dispute settlement, because this forum was one of the few where it could aspire to a rough equality with the United States as well as claim major power status by 'right' and precedent.

The Kremlin is also serious about the use of the UN as an international norms and rules producer and guarantor. According to the 2016 Russian foreign policy concept, the UN should retain its leading role in the development of international law by codification of the customary law, producing new norms, eliminating collisions, and proper interpretation of disputable norms and principles (Putin, 2016). The document insists on the need to protect international law (first and foremost, the UN Charter) from any revisions to the benefit or interests of certain states. For example, Moscow strongly objects to some Western countries' attempts to interpret the 'responsibility to protect' concept as a right to intervene militarily in domestic affairs of 'rogue' states and/or oust 'undemocratic' regimes throughout the world.

Moscow believes that the UN is indispensable for solving some global problems of mutual concern for the whole of humankind. They can range from climate change and environment degradation to the world famine and demographic problems. On a number of occasions, President Putin has stressed the advantages of using the UN as the base for forging a global anti-terrorist coalition to solve this common problem. Despite the UN's importance the Kremlin believes that this global institution cannot properly work without the help of and coordination with other international organizations – global (World Trade Organization, Organization of

Economic Cooperation and Development), regional (e.g. the OSCE, EU, Council of Europe, CIS, ASEAN, African Union, etc.) and subregional (e.g. the Arctic Council, Barents-Euro-Arctic Council, Shanghai Cooperation Organization, etc.). As former Russian Foreign Minister Igor Ivanov rightly notes:

> For the United Nations to be more effective, we need supporting organizations. The UN will be unable to cope with contemporary security issues with its own forces. An interrelated network of regional institutions should "lend a shoulder" to the UN in the creation of a new security regime. However, these institutions should provide support to the UN without replacing it.
>
> *(Cited in Khaspekova et al., 2015)*

In general, Russia sees no alternative to the UN, although Moscow recognizes the fact that this organization is indeed in need of reform.

Russia's policies within the UN

Russia tries to be a responsible player in the UN. It is the 11th biggest contributor to the UN budget with its share under an approved scale being 2.438% (Khaspekova et al., 2015). Its total financial contribution in 2014, according to the Russian UN mission's information, amounted to some $325 million, including contributions not only to the regular budget, but to the budgets of peacekeeping operations as well as tribunals for the former Yugoslavia and Rwanda.

Being a UN Security Council permanent member, Russia tries to use its veto right in a responsible manner. It exercised its veto right 13 times in 1992–2015. To compare, in the same period, the United States used its veto 16 times, and China 8 times, of which 6 times jointly with Russia (Khaspekova et al., 2015). Russia has recently been using its veto right more frequently (four times in 2014–2015), because of the growing tensions with the West. The most conflictual issues related to the conflicts in the former Yugoslavia, the Middle East (Iraq, Libya, and Syria), and Ukraine.

Moscow believes that the veto right has always been crucial in terms of safeguarding international peace and security. Russia considers recent British, French, Polish, and Ukrainian proposals on modifying this instrument, aimed at restricting the Council's five permanent members' (P5) veto right, to be both unrealistic and detrimental to the stability of the UN system.

Sustainable development

Since the late 1980s, the USSR/Russia has contributed to the UN debate on sustainable development (SD). This discussion dates back to the 1987 UN Brundtland report, which defines SD as "development which meets the needs of the present without compromising the ability of future generations to meet their own needs" (United Nations, 1987).

Similar to their foreign counterparts, the Russian experts differ by their interpretation of the SD concept. One school, the 'economists', following the Brundtland report's approach believes that SD is a pattern of resource use that aims to meet human needs while preserving the environment so that these needs can be met not only in the present, but also for future generations. For this school, SD is an economy in equilibrium with basic ecological support systems. The 'economists' insist on the need to preserve its fragile ecological balance while exploring and developing a region's natural resources. They oppose unlimited economic growth and call for a mandatory ecological expertise for all developmental projects.

The 'green', environmentalist, school emphasizes SD's ecological aspects. The 'greens' believe that many ecosystems on the planet are both unique and – at the same time – fragile. For this reason, it cannot be sacrificed to successful economic development based on the exploitation of natural resources. They underline that Russia should avoid the so-called 'resource curse' and keep its ecosystems intact. They warn that if the economic activities in the environmentally fragile regions are not reduced to a reasonable minimum, the ecological implications will be catastrophic not only for Russia itself but also for the entire world. They note, for example, that Russian forests (taiga) produce a quarter of the planet's oxygen and its Arctic sector shapes not only regional but also global weather.

The third, 'anthropological'/human-centric, approach focuses on SD's social aspects, underlining the need to subordinate its economic and ecological components to the needs of human development. For this reason, it suggests concentrating on the 'human dimensions' of the UN's strategy – well-being, elimination of social inequality, healthcare, education, indigenous peoples, migratory processes, etc.

However, since the late 2000s, the so-called integrated approach to SD has gained a momentum both in the Russian and world academic communities. According to such an integrated approach, SD is conceptually broken down into three constituent parts: environmental, economic, and social (see Figure 22.1).

The *economic dimension* of the Russian SD strategy has the following priorities: sustainable economic activity; sustainable use of natural, including living, resources; development of transport infrastructure (including aviation, marine, and surface transport), information technologies, and modern telecommunications.

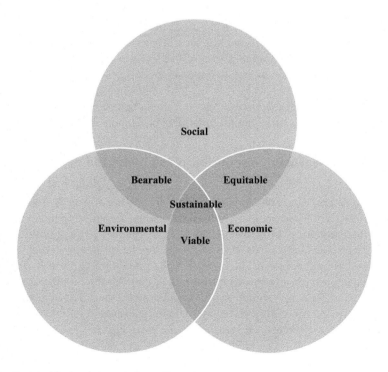

Figure 22.1 Sustainable development: three dimensions

The *environmental dimension* of Russia's SD strategy includes monitoring and assessment of the state of the environment; prevention and elimination of environmental pollution; biodiversity conservation; climate change impact assessment – globally and regionally, and prevention and elimination of ecological emergencies, including those relating to climate change.

Finally, the *social dimension* of the strategy focuses on the health of the people; education and cultural heritage; prosperity and capacity building for children and the youth; gender equality, and enhancing well-being, and eradication of poverty.

Russia has supported and vigorously participated in developing all the UN-related SD initiatives ranging from the Kyoto Protocol (1997) and Intergovernmental Panel on Climate Change reports (including the last one in 2014) to the International Maritime Organization's Polar Code (2014–2015), and Paris agreement on climate change (2015).

Together with other members of the international community, Russia worked hard to organize the UN Sustainable Development Summit held on 25 September 2015. The agreement by all 193 member countries of the UN General Assembly (GA) to approve the final document titled *Transforming our World: The 2030 Agenda for Sustainable Development* is unique as it applies to all countries. The UN formally adopted 17 Sustainable Development Goals (SDGs) with 169 targets. These goals and targets are ambitious, indivisible, and interlinked and focus on all three dimensions of sustainable development – economic, social, and environmental.

In particular, the SDGs include priorities, such as ending poverty in all its forms everywhere; eliminating hunger, achieving food security and adequate nutrition for all, and promoting sustainable agriculture; attaining a healthy lifestyle for all at all ages; providing equitable and inclusive quality education and life-long learning opportunities for all; attaining gender equality, empowering women and girls everywhere; securing water and sanitation for all for a sustainable world; ensuring access to affordable, sustainable, and reliable modern energy services for all; promoting strong, inclusive, and sustainable economic growth and decent work for all; promoting sustainable industrialization; reducing inequality within and among countries; building inclusive, safe, and sustainable cities and human settlements; promoting sustainable consumption and production patterns; promoting actions at all levels to address climate change; attaining conservation and sustainable use of marine resources, oceans, and seas; protecting and restoring terrestrial ecosystems and halting all biodiversity loss; achieving peaceful and inclusive societies, rule of law, effective and capable institutions; and strengthening and enhancing the means of implementation and global partnership for sustainable development.

Crisis management, responsibility to protect and peacekeeping

Russia believes that with all its shortcomings and contradictions, the UN system of conflict prevention and management as well as peacekeeping, based primarily on the legal principles and mechanisms of the UN Charter, is an effective mechanism for ensuring international security and world order. Particularly, Moscow insists that the UN should play a critical role in promoting normative frameworks to address issues of conflict resolution and peacekeeping.

Russia played an active role in discussing the Responsibility to Protect (R2P) concept, one of the most controversial initiatives introduced in 2001 by the International Commission on Intervention and State Sovereignty and later endorsed by the UN GA at the 2005 World Summit. R2P, often described as an emerging norm, essentially demands that states: (1) protect their populations from genocide, war crimes, ethnic cleansing, and crimes against humanity; (2) encourage and assist others to fulfill their responsibility; and (3) take timely and decisive action when necessary to and in accordance with the UN Charter to protect populations from these crimes.

R2P is premised on the idea that state sovereignty is not to be taken as a right, but as a responsibility, with the understanding that the most basic responsibility "for the protection of its people lies with the state itself" (International Commission on Intervention and State Sovereignty, 2001: 7). R2P has also been described as a contemporary way of framing humanitarian intervention and an innovative framework for the protection of human beings/communities from the abuse of state power and/or its failure to protect. Moscow, however, made some reservations on this point saying that R2P should not be interpreted as a right of certain states to interfere in internal affairs of countries with allegedly undemocratic regimes. The R2P principle should not be transformed from 'responsibility to protect' into 'right to punish.'

The endorsement of the R2P at the 2005 World Summit reflects a cautious, yet in essence an acceptance of its basic principles: responsibility to prevent, responsibility to react, and the responsibility to rebuild. While ultimately sanctioning the use of military interventions in the case of grave abuses of human rights that meet its designated 'threshold,' the R2P that emerged from the World Summit placed more emphasis on the importance of promoting a culture of prevention than previous conceptualizations of the principle (High-Level Panel on Threats, Challenges and Change, 2004).

The subsequent GA debate on the R2P further revealed the preference of the international community for pillars 1 and 2 of the R2P, which call for preventive measures and international assistance. Moscow notes that there has yet to emerge a clear consensus on the third pillar, which focuses on timely and decisive (military) response, largely due to concern about the implications of humanitarian intervention. In particular, a common issue raised by Moscow and many other governments is R2P's application, which could be based on unfair selectivity within the Security Council. The veto power of the P5 is central to these concerns because it guarantees that the Security Council is being a "neutral arbiter."

Moscow is sensitive to any international security crises where its voice, *via* the UN Security Council, is disregarded, and this leads to Russia returning to a much more vocal, obstinate, and obdurate position, as seen during the Kosovo (1998–1999), Iraq (2003), Libya (2011), and Syria (2011–) crises (Snetkov and Lanteigne, 2015). It thus remains very sensitive to events or circumstances in which its position as a great power is challenged or is seen to be undermined by other international actors, while embracing its role and position as a mediator in international disputes.

From the Russian perspective, controversies around R2P arise largely as a result of the way it is applied in practice, particularly by the West, rather than from the principle itself. Events such as Kosovo, Afghanistan, Iraq, Libya, and Syria have, for Russia, become precedents by which Western powers have 'instrumentalized' the principle of humanitarian intervention to further their own agendas internationally. Russia remains deeply suspicious of any proposal that appears to encourage regime change. For instance, the Kremlin refers to the Libyan case when the United States and NATO interpreted the UN Security Council resolution on establishing no-fly zones in a way as to legitimize first bombing the central government's troops and then ousting the Gaddafi regime.

Instead of the use of force, Russia advocates diplomacy as the best route for resolving civil crises, as in the case of the conflicts in Darfur (Sudan), Myanmar, Côte d'Ivoire, Libya, and most recently in Syria. In the latter case, Russia maintained its position that the Syrians should decide on their own future at the negotiation table with all the parties included.

In an attempt to raise its international profile, Russia has been willing to act as a mediator and engage in shuttle diplomacy between warring parties, as in the case of Libya, and most recently, Syria.

It should be noted that despite adopting its public role as a mediator for the regime, Moscow also emphasized that most mediation efforts should be undertaken either by the UN or regional actors. For example, in Syria, Russia backed the Arab League initiative which was better aligned with its version of how such humanitarian crises should be resolved. In this respect, Russia appeared to have come to accept the importance of the role that regional actors can and should play in such crises as foreseen within the 2005 R2P Convention.

As for the Russian contribution to peacekeeping operations, Moscow is among the top ten (eighth place with 3.15%) (Khaspekova et al., 2015). Russia's contribution is rather modest compared with the amounts allocated by the United States (first place, 28.38%) and Japan (second place, 10.83%). However, if one compares the contribution with the size of GDP, Russia's record is quite good, especially if one compares its contribution to that of another country comparable to the United States in terms of GDP calculated in accordance with the parity of purchasing power (PPP), e.g. China (6.64%). As of 2015, Russia had 66 servicemen (46 observers and 20 policemen) in the framework of the current 16 UN peacekeeping missions (versus 110 in 2014) (Khaspekova et al., 2015).

Moscow underlines that with the world facing new challenges, UN peacekeeping should evolve and be flexible. The Russian diplomats in the UN pose the following questions: How are peacekeeping missions established? Who funds them? How are they composed? Do regional institutions contribute to them? What is Russia's role in the present-day peacekeeping? What is the future of peacekeeping in general?

UN reform

The UN is usually criticized for its inability to quickly adapt to change and conduct relevant and timely reforms. The proponents of the UN reform believe that this organization was designed for the post-war and Cold War realities and its structure, procedures, and the way of functioning do not correspond to present-day needs.

First and foremost, such criticism is addressed to the UN Security Council. The reformist proposals concerning the Council boil down to five groups/'pillars':

- Council membership categories (number of permanent and non-permanent members; introduction of a third membership category; the possibility of immediate reelection for some non-permanent members, etc.).
- Veto right (status quo option, i.e. keeping the veto power only for the P5; providing other Council's members with the veto right; abolition of the veto right; introduction of limitations for the use of veto power in some circumstance such as, for example, the cases of genocide, crimes against humanity, mass human rights violations, and so on.
- 'Fair' distribution of the Council's seats among different regions.
- The Council's transparency and accountability.
- Its relations with the GA, including the Assembly's right to decision-making in the case of the Council's inability to act in critical situations.

Russia's official position on the Security Council's reform is rather general and lacks any specific details.

The efforts to reform the UN and adapt it to current realities should be aimed at safeguarding its intergovernmental nature and be in full compliance with the charter principle of labor division among its main bodies. The purpose of the reform of the UN Security Council is to achieve broader representation without damaging the effectiveness and efficiency of its work, and timely decision-making processes. It is necessary to keep searching for a compromise reform model which would enjoy the broadest support within the UN (The Permanent Mission of the Russian Federation to the United Nations, 2013).

On the other hand, it is known that Moscow's position on the Council's reform was not always the same and has evolved over time. In the 1990s and 2000s, when the neoliberal approach prevailed in Moscow's thinking on the UN, some Russian experts supported the Council's permanent membership for the 'group of four' (Brazil, Germany, India, and Japan) (Orlov, 2005) or even for five countries (Germany, Japan, and one state from each continent – Africa, Asia, and America) (Igor Ivanov, 2003). However, with the growth in tensions between Russia and the West, the Kremlin signaled that it favors permanent seats only for its two BRICS partners – Brazil and India – and, again, on the consensus basis (Khaspekova et al., 2015).

The Kremlin also believes that the veto right should not be modified and that only permanent members (existing and potential) should have it. As Yuliy Vorontsov, Russia's former representative in the UN, underlined, the Council's membership extension coupled with the abolishment or weakening of the veto right could make the Council a 'discussion club' rather than a decision-making body (Vorobyev, 2005). Similarly, Minister Lavrov (who has also served as Russia's representative in the UN from 1994 to 2004) objected to a veto system reform because it could make the Council even less efficient than now (Belenkova, 2011: 117).

Moscow supported two UN resolutions that made more difficult any hasty reforms of the Security Council. In 1998, the GA passed the resolution 53/30 that required 2/3 majority for any decisions related to UN reform. In 2008, another resolution (62/557) was adopted to introduce a 'package principle' for UN reform: all five 'pillars' should be approved by the GA at once. The proponents of UN reform heavily criticized these resolutions, trying to argue that they made any changes in the Security Council's composition and procedures virtually impossible.

At the same time, Russia's position on other aspects of UN reform is much more flexible. For example, in September 2015 Moscow supported a partial reform of the Secretary-General's election procedure. In particular, the principle of geographic rotation for Secretaries was abandoned; nomination of multiple candidates was welcomed; the public discussion of the candidates' political platforms was introduced; debates (including the televised ones) between the candidates were encouraged, etc. As a result of these innovations, the former prime minister of Portugal and UN High Commissioner on Refugees, António Guterres, was elected as a new Secretary-General in 2016.

The Russian UN mission actively participated in GA reform as well. In 1993, the initial GA committee system was changed, and the present six-committee structure was established. The GA procedures were also changed: it was decided that in addition to the fall three-month session, occasional spring and summer sessions can be convened, if needed.

Moscow upheld establishing new UN bodies to modernize its institutional structure. For example, the Kremlin assisted in creating a UN anti-terrorism committee in 2001. In 2006, Russia was helpful in transforming the UN Commission on Human Rights to a Human Rights Council with a higher status and broader powers.

Together with its BRICS partners (Brazil, China, India, and South Africa), Russia supports the idea of a substantial reform of the UN's economic and financial bodies, such as the Economic and Social Council, World Bank group, and the International Monetary Fund. Along with other emerging and developing countries, Russia believes that these UN institutions no longer reflect 'correlation of forces' in the world economic and financial systems trying to secure the dominance of Western powers in this sphere. Under Russian and Chinese pressure, an expert panel on the reform of the world financial-monetary system was created in 2009

(Gorelik, 2016). However, when this panel recommended establishing a Global Council on Economic Coordination under the auspices of the UN, the developed countries quietly put on hold this initiative. No surprise that the BRICS countries, which were disappointed with the lack of progress in this area, preferred to establish their own financial institutions' alternative to the Bretton-Woods system.

To sum up, Moscow favors UN reform but in a gradual way and on a consensus basis. The aim of the reform is to adapt the UN to present-day geoeconomic and geopolitical realities but, on the other hand, to not damage its effectiveness as a global governance institute.

Conclusions

In general terms, Russia's UN policies represent a combination – sometimes quite eclectic – of the pragmatic and ideational approaches. On the one hand, Moscow is guided by rather practical/material motives, viewing the UN as an efficient instrument for protecting and promoting its national interests – both regionally and globally. In particular, Russia tries to use the UN for conflict prevention, management, and resolution in its close geopolitical proximity. The UN (and especially its seat on the Security Council) is also important for the Kremlin in terms of ascertaining Russia's great power status and gaining international authority and prestige. Moreover, the UN is viewed by Russia as a rather useful tool for containing U.S. and other developed nations' hegemonic aspirations and shaping a more just and safer world order.

On the other hand, the UN is perceived by Moscow in civilizational terms. It is seen as a proper instrument to address the global problems that humankind currently faces as well as those looming ahead. The Kremlin aims to represent itself as a responsible international player that tries to contribute to making the UN an efficient global governance institute. Russia believes that the UN should play a crucial role in solving global problems, such as sustainable development (including the SDGs' achievement), conflict prevention and resolution, post-conflict peace-building, arms control and disarmament, climate change mitigation, fighting global crime and international terrorism, and so on.

Moscow aims at harmonizing UN activities with other global, regional, and subregional institutions to generate a synergetic effect in solving different international problems. However, if Russia's efforts to establish a division of labor between the UN and other international organizations in specific areas fail, Moscow does not hesitate to make a pragmatic choice between them. For example, when NATO intervened militarily in the Balkan conflicts in the 1990s, the Kremlin used the UN to prevent these interventions and later to maximally neutralize their negative implications. On the contrary, Russia has effectively blocked any UN attempts to interfere in the 2008 Georgia-Russia armed conflict and the 2014 Ukrainian crisis, preferring to manage these conflicts in the OSCE, CIS, 'Normandy,' and bilateral formats.

Russia's UN membership record since the end of the Cold War has been rather positive. Moscow has tried to use its veto right in a responsible manner, doing it less frequently than, for instance, the United States. However, with the start of the Ukrainian crisis, Russia's confrontation with Western countries in the UN Security Council increased, including its veto exercise. The so-called 'Arab awakening' and Ukrainian crisis were the most conflictual issues in the Council.

Russia is also a 'good UN citizen' in a sense that it contributes to the organization's budget on a regular basis and at a sufficient level. Moscow has also significantly contributed to UN discussions on all major issues ranging from sustainable development strategy and R2P to conflict resolution and fighting international terrorism and transnational crime.

Russia actively partakes in the ongoing debates on UN reform, including the Security Council. Moscow's position on this issue has evolved since the early 1990s from the rather favorable/liberal to the cautious/conservative one. The Kremlin is afraid of too radical changes in the UN system because it could weaken or make less efficient this organization and undermine Russia's global standing. Moscow wants to make sure that the suggested reforms will make this institution stronger and more adequate to the globalizing world, not the other way round. That's why Russia suggests a balanced approach to reform implementation based on consensus and incrementalism. At the same time, Moscow understands that to effectively meet the challenges of globalization, the UN should transform itself from a purely intergovernmental organization to a transnational body capable of functioning as a global governance institution.

Acknowledgment

This work was supported by the Russian Science Foundation (grant number 16-18-10315).

References

Belenkova, E 2011, 'Sovremennye discussii o reformirovanii Organizatsii Obyedinennykh Natsiy' [Contemporary discussions on the United Nations' reform], *Vlast'*, no. 12, pp. 115–117 (in Russian).

Cameron, F ed, 2008, *Russian foreign policy*, Special issue: The EU-Russia Center Review, no. 8. www.eu-russiacentre.org/wp-content/uploads/2008/10/review_viii_final_13_10.pdf.

Dzhantaev, HM 2013, 'Reforma prava veto v OON – prerogativa ego obladateley' [UN veto right is its possessors' prerogative], *Voprosy gumanitarnykh nauk*, no. 1, pp. 54–60 (in Russian).

Gorelik, A 2016, 'Pered smenoi na kapitanskom mostike' [On the eve of the shift on the captain bridge], *Russia in Global Affairs*, 9 September, www.globalaffairs.ru/print/number/Pered-smenoi-na-kapitanskom-mostike-18357 (in Russian).

Gowan, R 2015, 'Bursting the UN bubble: how to counter Russia in the Security Council', *European Council on Foreign Relations Policy Brief*, no. 137, www.ecfr.eu/page/-/Bursting_the_UN_bubble.pdf.

High-Level Panel on Threats, Challenges and Change 2004, *A more secure world: Our shared responsibility*, www.unrol.org/files/gaA.59.565_En.pdf.

'Igor Ivanov ne iskluychaet provedeniya zasedaniya SB OON na urovne glav gosudarstv srazu posle zaversheniya krizisa v Irake' 2003 [Igor Ivanov does not exclude the UNSC meeting at the level of the heads of the states immediately after the end of the Iraq crisis], *Pravda*, 22 March (in Russian).

International Commission on Intervention and State Sovereignty 2001, *The responsibility to protect*, International Development Research Centre, Ottawa, http://responsibilitytoprotect.org/ICISS%20Report.pdf.

Kalyadin, A 2016, 'V kakoi reforme nuzhdaetsya Sovet Bezopasnosti OON?' [What reform does the UN Security Council need?], *Mirovaya ekonomika i mezdunarodnye otnosheniya*, vol. 60, no. 7, pp. 48–59 (in Russian).

Khaspekova, D, Smekalova, M, Gurova, M, Sorokina, I, Teslya, A and D. Puminov 2015, *UN: Moving from peacekeeping to peace-building*, Russian International Affairs Council, Moscow, http://russiancouncil.ru/en/un#fiveplus.

Lavrov, SV 2012, Russian diplomacy and challenges of the 21st century, www.mid.ru/bdomp/Brp_4.nsf/arh/0BA48B6D0169152644257A830046F855?OpenDocument.

Lo, Bobo (2002) *Russian foreign policy in the post-Soviet era: reality, illusion and mythmaking*. Palgrave Macmillan, London and New York.

Oldberg, I 2010, 'Aims and means in Russian foreign policy', in Kanet, R (ed.), *Russian foreign policy in the 21st century*, Palgrave Macmillan, London and New York, pp. 30–58.

Orlov, A 2005, 'Kofi Annan podgotovil doklad o reformirovanii OON' [Kofi Annan prepared a report on the UN reform], *RIA 'Novosti'*, 20 March (in Russian).

Pacer, V 2016, *Russian foreign policy under Dmitry Medvedev, 2008–2012*, Routledge, Abingdon, UK.

The Permanent Mission of the Russian Federation to the United Nations 2013, *Position of the Russian Federation for the UN General Assembly*, http://russiaun.ru/en/russia_n_un/podkategorija_00.

Petro, N and A Rubinstein 1997, *Russian foreign policy: from empire to nation-state*, Longman, New York.

Putin, V 2016, *Kontseptsiya Vneshnei Politiki Rossiyskoi Federatsii* [The Foreign Policy Concept of the Russian Federation], November 30, http://publication.pravo.gov.ru/Document/View/0001201612010045?index=0&rangeSize=1 (in Russian).

Shevchenko, I 2015, 'Giving Russia the top job at the UN is an Orwellian nightmare and a betrayal of global peace efforts', *International Business Times*, September 4, www.ibtimes.co.uk/giving-russia-top-job-un-orwellian-nightmare-betrayal-global-peace-efforts.

Snetkov, A, Lanteigne, M 2015, 'The loud dissenter and its cautious partner: Russia, China, global governance and humanitarian intervention', *International Relations of the Asia-Pacific*, vol. 15, no. 1, pp. 113–146.

United Nations 1987, 'Chapter 2: towards sustainable development. A/42/427', in *Our Common Future: Report of the World Commission on Environment and Development*, United Nations, New York, www.un-documents.net/ocf-02.htm.

Vorobyev, V 2005, 'Sovbez ih poputal' [The Security Council confused them], *Rossiyskaya gazeta*, 14 September (in Russian).

Yeltsin, B 1991, *Letter to the Secretary-General of the United Nations from the President of the Russian Federation*, www.iaea.org/Publications/Documents/Infcircs/Others/inf397.shtml#att2.

Zaemsky, VF 2010, *Komu nuzhna reforma OON? V interesakh vsekh i kazhdogo* [Who need UN reform? In everyone's interests], Mezhdunarodnye otnosheniya, Moscow (in Russian).

23
THE G20

Andrej Krickovic

NATIONAL RESEARCH UNIVERSITY,
HIGHER SCHOOL OF ECONOMICS, MOSCOW

Ever since the Great Financial Crisis (GFC) of 2008–2009, the Group of 20 (G20) has emerged as one of the most significant international organizations. Most experts consider that it has eclipsed the Group of Seven (G7) when it comes to global economic and financial governance issues, signaling a dramatic shift in the world economy away from Western dominance (embodied in the G7) and the empowerment of the emerging powers of the developing world. According to Economist Barry Eichengreen (2009):

> Whether the task is developing ideas, reaching consensus on their desirability or moving from ideas to implementation, the G20 which has working groups active in all these areas is where the action is. The G7 is dead; may it rest in peace.

The G20 has also begun to expand its bailiwick to include high level discussions of some of the most intractable contemporary geopolitical and security issues, areas which have previously been dominate by the UN Security Council or the Group of 8 (G8).

Russia has been an active participant in the G20 since it was founded in 1999 and enthusiastically supported its expansion to include annual summit meetings of heads of states in 2008 in response to the GFC. Russia welcomed the strengthening of the G20 process as a natural response to larger changes in the global economy (Putin, 2015). Even though Russia was a member of the G8, it was excluded from the organization's discussions on economic and financial issues, with the other seven members of the G8 meeting separately as the G7 to discuss them without Russia. For Russia, the G20 serves as a vehicle for finally giving it a seat at the table where it can defend its interests as it continues its process of economic modernization and integration into the world economy (Kirton, 2016). In addition, the G20 has also been important to Russia for the prestige and status it confers. Exclusion from the G7 had been humiliating for Russia as it was deemed not to qualify as a "free market economy" (Tsygankov, 2016). The expanding role of the G20 validates Russia's status as a member of the club of the most significant world economies. As is true with its membership in the BRICS, it allows Russia to portray itself as one of the emerging economic powers that will dominate the future global economic and political order (Bratersky, 2012).

Nevertheless, though it continues to support and participate in the G20, Russia has begun to lose interest in the organization. It has grown increasingly frustrated with the slow progress that the organization has made in pushing forward significant global economic governance reforms and with the limited influence that Russia has been able to achieve over this process (Bratersky, 2017). It has also lost interest in the G20 as a vehicle for status seeking (Suslov, 2017). Membership in the group is not sufficiently exclusive to satisfy Russia's status ambitions. Russia sees itself as belonging to a much more exclusive group of great powers that includes the US, China and (up until recently) the EU. Moreover, as the G20 primarily focuses on economic issues – an area where Russia is still relatively weak – there are few opportunities for Russia to practice the kind of leadership that would demonstrate its power and boost its prestige.

Moreover, there is a growing belief among leaders and experts in Moscow that larger global political and economic trends are making multilateral institutions such as the G20 less relevant. They see the world entering a period of "de-globalization" characterized by growing economic nationalism and the division of the global economy into competing regional and trans-regional blocs (Karaganov, 2016). Under these circumstances global governance issues will be more effectively addressed on the regional level and through bilateral and "mini-lateral" agreements between the true great powers rather than in inclusive global multi-lateral frameworks such as the G20 (Suslov, 2016). The establishment of a modern day "Great Power Concert" would better serve Russia's status ambitions than more inclusive multilateral groupings. It would confer to it the level of status and prestige that Moscow feels it deserves. Russia's status would be fixed even if Russia's material power were to decline in the future – a prospect that greatly worries Russian leaders (Krickovic and Weber, 2017).

Though they may not expect much from it in the near term, they are not ready to give up on the G20 entirely. Russia will continue to actively participate in the G20, though the organization will take a back seat to Russia's engagement in other international fora. Russia acknowledges the important role that the organization played in getting the world out of the GFC, and Russian leaders want it to be able to play the same role in the future. They may question the organization's efficacy, but they still believe that it is important for Russia to maintain its presence in the organization in order to defend its interests. They recognize that the organization has tremendous long-term potential and that it is possible that it may one day transform itself into a truly effective forum for multilateral global governance that transcends contemporary political and economic divides. Finally, the G20 is still important for Moscow's status ambitions. The annual leaders' summit has become an important political and media event, giving Russian leaders an opportunity to meet with top Western leaders (which is not always easy to organize under present circumstances of growing tensions between Russia and the West) and to showcase the significant role that Russia plays in global politics.

The G20 in practice

The G20 was originally founded in 1999 in response to the 1998 financial crisis, and it has held regular annual meetings of finance ministers. Reportedly, US President George W. Bush asked, "What's the G20?" when his aides informed him that the French and British first introduced the idea to convene the organization as a response to the GFC (Postel-Vinay, 2016). The organization has only come to prominence since the 2008 GFC, when it was decided to expand the organization to include summit meetings of heads of state. As an international organization, the G20 is unique in that it combines two levels of governance (Cooper, 2010). At the first, "lower", level are the meetings of experts and finance ministers that have taken place regularly since the organization was officially formed after the 1998 Asian financial crisis. This level of the G20 is primarily focused on promoting technical issues related to international finance, trade and other economic issues. Among the issues where the G20 has made the most progress are the formation of international regulations to close loopholes to corporate tax evasion, the reallocation of IMF voting rights to better represent the emerging powers of the developing world, and (perhaps its most significant achievement to date) the coordination of member country's macroeconomic policies in response to the 2008 GFC (Luckhurst, 2016). At this level, the organization performs the kind of complex and multifaceted "networked diplomacy" described by liberal IR theorists such as Ann Marie Slaughter, which allows informed experts to transcend the traditional geopolitical divides that have often hampered inter-state cooperation (Slaughter, 2009; Luckhurst, 2016).

The second, "leadership", level consists of the annual summit meetings of heads of state from member countries as well as other countries invited to participate. The summit lends political support for the reforms being negotiated at the technical level. This support was especially important during the GFC, with high level meetings giving the political support necessary to push through some difficult and tricky policies needed to keep the international economy afloat (Cooper and Thakur, 2013; Drezner, 2014). Though in the beginning these discussions were largely devoted to problems related to the economic crisis, they have taken on a greater political dimension over time to include geopolitical and security issues, such as international terrorism and the crises in Ukraine and Syria. Meetings of the two tracks are regular with a member country appointed to the G20 presidency to oversee the agenda and host the meetings at the different levels. However, the institutional structure of the organization is minimal, and the organization largely works through informal practices (Cooper and Pouliot, 2015). The G20 has no permanent bureaucracy and even lacks an official charter to oversee and lay the groundwork of its work. Even membership is somewhat fuzzy. Though officially limited to 20 members, in practice other countries are invited to participate in G20 summits and given an indirect role in the countries' decision-making. Thus Spain has become a sort of "unofficial member" having attended all the G20 summits from the beginning (Cooper, 2010).

The two levels have often followed their own separate tracks and logics. Work on the expert/technical level has shown steady progress, though scholars are divided about the actual significance and impact of the reforms undertaken (Kirton, 2016). Discussions at the leadership level have grown increasingly tense as economic issues have been superseded by the contentious geopolitical crises of the day. The 2012 Summit in Cancun was dominated by discussions of the Eurozone crisis. The 2013 Summit in St Petersburg debated how to respond to the 2013 chemical weapons attack in Syria, which split the United States and its allies, who advocated military intervention, from the BRICS (led by Russia) who opposed it. The 2014 Summit in Brisbane was overshadowed by the downing of Malaysian Airlines Flight MH17 over Ukraine and by Russia's annexation of Crimea, And the 2015 Antalya summit by the November 2015 terrorist attacks in Paris and Russia's military intervention in Syria.

Western analysts are divided in their assessments of the efficacy and continued significance of the G20, especially since the GFC. Critics argue that, post GFC, the G20 has failed to establish the kind of political consensus needed to address the most glaring problems facing the world economy, such as massive debt imbalances, the continued liberalization of trade practices, and reforms to the world financial architecture to make it more representative (Bremmer, 2012; Blyth, 2013; Helleiner, 2014). Some critics go so far as to argue that the organization is nothing more than a "toothless talk shop" where participants are deeply divided by their diverging interests and world views (Vestergaard and Wade, 2012: 487). Proponents of the G20 give it tremendous credit for coordinating an unprecedentedly rapid response to the GFC and point to what they see as substantial progress having been made since the crisis on issues such as coordinating international financial regulations and expanding developing countries' voting rights in the IMF (which was agreed to at the G20 summit in Pittsburgh in 2009 but only ratified by US congress in 2015) (Cooper and Thakur, 2013; Kirton, 2016). Others offer a more balanced evaluation. While acknowledging the difficulties of coordinating policy between states and in reaching a larger consensus on economic policy issues, they still see the G20 as playing an important ideational role in challenging the established Western neo-liberal orthodoxies and introducing state-oriented models of capitalism favored by many developing countries into the larger debate (Luckhurst, 2016).

Russian attitudes towards the G20

Officially, Russia is an enthusiastic advocate for the G20, seeing it as an indispensable mechanism for maintaining stability in today's turbulent global governance. According to Russian President Vladimir Putin (2015), "Nowadays, [the] global economy is still unstable and cannot get onto a path towards sustainable and balanced development. In this context, the work that the G20 does is especially needed." Expert views about the organization are mixed. Scholars who specialize in global governance issues and who follow the work of the G20 primarily at the expert level generally offer a positive assessment of the G20's achievements and are optimistic about the organization's evolving role (Panova, 2011; Larionova et al., 2015). However, most Russian foreign policy experts are skeptical about the G20's ability to act as a vehicle for transformational change of, and downplay its importance to, Russian foreign policy. Though acknowledging the organization's success in helping to bring the world out of the GFC, many Russian observers feel that the organization has played a very limited role since. The organization is essentially perceived to be fulfilling cosmetic functions, and its activities are dismissed as no more than tinkering around the edges (Koshkin, 2013). The implementation of decisions made by the body on key issues such as the coordination and regulation of member state fiscal and macroeconomic policy, the improvement of developing world representation in decision-making bodies such as the IMF and World Bank, and the tougher banking standards and regulations have proceeded at an incremental pace and often faced setbacks. The interests of G20 member states are seen as being too diverse for its members to effectively agree on the reforms that are needed, and the United States and its Western allies are seen as jealously guarding its privileges (Lukyanov, 2016; Zubkov, 2017). As a result, Russian leaders and experts have come to believe that the "real issues", such as the composition of the global currency reserve, the rules that govern global trade and investment, and coordination of global macroeconomic policy, will not be addressed by the G20 in a meaningful way (Bratersky, 2017).

This was not always the case. Russia's leaders were very proactive in the early meetings of the G20 summit, actively pushing for transformational changes to the international financial architecture. Russian President Dmitry Medvedev seized the initiative at the 2009 Summits in London and Pittsburgh to call for the creation of a supranational currency to replace the dollar as the foundation of the international monetary system, to redistribute the voice in institutions such as the IMF and World Bank to increase representation from developing countries, and to push for the ratification of a new energy security charter that would take the interests of energy producers, as well as consumers, into consideration (Kirton, 2016). Russia tried to take advantage of the opportunities offered by the GFC to introduce radical reforms to the world financial architecture that would address the imbalances in the global economy that precipitated the crisis, and introduce new arrangements that would reflect the shift in the global balance of economic power towards developing countries, among which it saw itself as holding a special place (Kirton, 2016). It was hoped that the G20 would not only replace the G7 as the main forum for coordinating economic governance, but that it would introduce genuine changes that would make financial governance more representative and more responsive to the real needs of the world economy – ones which Western (and US) leadership had mismanaged and ignored (Bratersky, 2017).

These hopes for wide ranging, transformational change were soon dashed, and Russia's reform proposals in London and Pittsburgh were politely ignored by the other major players in the G20. Russia shelved many of the proposals it made soon after these summits when it became apparent that the Western members of the G20 were not prepared to take them seriously (Suslov, 2017). These failures also reflected the weakness of Russia's own economy and its lack of economic weight. According to Maxim Bratersky (2017), "Russia's initial approach to the G20 was absolutely naïve and it reflected a lack of understanding on the part of the leadership about how the world financial architecture really works." As a result, Russia has toned down its rhetoric and abandoned its hopes that the G20 could serve as a major vehicle for transformational change (Lukyanov, 2016). This change of attitude partly reflects Russia's negative early experience with the G20. But it is also consistent with Russian elite views about the nature of world politics. Russian experts and leaders are skeptical about the efficacy of multilateral institutions and the concept of "global governance" more generally, and believe that the most important global issues must ultimately be solved through great power politics (Grant, 2012). According to Alexei Bogaturov, "Sitting in the G20 is fine, but nobody thinks that key decisions are taken there or that resources will be put at the disposal of global governance . . . informal relations are more important than the formal relations of global governance" (Grant, 2012: 19).

Though Russia has often been forced to take a back seat to more powerful economies in setting the agenda within the G20, it has generally been a good citizen with the organization. Since the first G20 Summit in Washington DC, in 2008, Russia has complied with 74% of its major G20 commitments – slightly higher than the G20 average of 72%. For the most part, Russia has complied in areas where it has been easiest and painless for it to do so, such as commitments on macroeconomics, where its compliance score of 94% is above the G20 average of 80%.[1] Russia follows a policy of tight fiscal discipline and up until recently had a government budget surplus. Therefore the macroeconomic obligations do not represent all that much of a burden. It shirks compliance in areas where it does not really have a clear interest, such as commitments on trade liberalization, where its compliance rate of 17% is below the G20 average of 80%. Russia's exports are dominated by hydrocarbons and raw materials (which are usually not subject to tariffs), and most of its domestic industries are not competitive on the world market, instead relying on various forms of protection from foreign competition in order to survive (Kudrin and Gurvich, 2015).

From the Russian perspective, the G20 has not been without its achievements. It is through the G20 that the major developing countries have been able to increase their overall share of quotas within the IMF by 5%, with Brazil, Russia, India and China all entering the top ten countries by voting share (Weisbrot and Johnston, 2016). This success is important to Russia because the proposal for the BRICS countries to put forward a unified stance on quotas was first introduced at the first BRICS summit, an organization that was largely Russia's brainchild and which Russia played the decisive role in putting it together (Roberts, 2009). The G20 has also played an important role as the forum where alternative ("shadow") global economic institutions that are supported by Russia, such as the BRICS Development Bank and Asian Infrastructure Investment Bank (AIIB) can make their debut and gain legitimacy and traction. This was important, as in the past these kinds of non-Western initiatives have largely been marginalized (Lukyanov, 2014). Finally, like the SCO and BRICS, the G20 has important symbolic significance for Russia as a model for what future multipolar relations between states may look like, and where relations would be based not on common values and norms (as is the case with the G7 and other Western dominated institutions) but on concrete interests (Bratersky, 2012). Thus the G20 could serve as a sort of "incubator" for a more "rational" and less ideological post-Western model of global governance (Suslov, 2017).

Most Russian experts give much greater significance to the G20's summit level, which has served as an important forum for leaders to meet to discuss pressing geopolitical problems. The summits also offer a valuable opportunity for gauging Russia's status and taking stock of its relationship with other great powers (Lukyanov, 2014). The 2014 Summit in Brisbane, which came after Russia's annexation of Ukraine and subsequent suspension from the G8, was particularly difficult for Russia. There were even calls by some Western countries ahead of the summit to exclude Russia from the meeting altogether, though these were eventually beaten back. Australian Prime Minister and G20 host, Tony Abbot, promised that he would confront Putin openly about the downing of MH17, in which 38 Australian citizens perished. Abbott threatened he would "shirtfront Putin" – a reference to a move in Australian-rules football where one player openly charges into another in order to knock them down. Putin and Abbot avoided scandal and only exchanged cordial greetings when they met at the summit. Nevertheless, Canadian Prime Minister, Stephen Harper, was less diplomatic, bluntly admonishing Putin to "get out of Ukraine" during their meeting. Widely distributed photographs of Putin on the outer reaches of the G20 leader's group photo, and of him eating lunch alone at his table, seemed to suggest that the other leaders were shunning him and symbolized Russia's growing international isolation. Putin ended up leaving the summit early, citing his busy schedule, but many observers interpreted the move as stemming from his desire to avoid further Western criticism over Ukraine and his frustration with the low status accorded him at the Summit. According to popular Russian columnist Yulia Latynina (2014), "At the end of the G20 summit, we were discussing not the appearance of a new superpower in the world but why Putin did not stay for breakfast."

Putin's elevation to center stage was the main theme of the November 2015 summit in Antalya, which was dominated by the issue of terrorism after the terrorist attacks in Paris in October, and helped alleviate Russia's status anxieties, and demonstrated its continued relevance as a global player. Having improved his position on the issue of combating global terrorism after the military intervention in Syria, Putin held an intense impromptu meeting on the sidelines with Obama that was captured by the world's media (Sonne and Grove, 2015). Putin's treatment as "guest of honor" was one of the main stories of the 2016 Hangzhou summit. It drew attention to the burgeoning Sino-Russian relationship and contrasted with the alleged lapses in diplomatic protocol that lame-duck US President Obama was forced to endure during the summit (TASS, 2016).

Status considerations of this kind are a central concern in Russia's foreign policy. Russia is extremely sensitive about maintaining its status as a great power in the international system, which, given its relative decline, has been under threat throughout the post-Soviet period (Krickovic and Weber, 2017). Status has played a central role in Russia's engagement with the G20 from the very beginning. Russia's initial inclusion in the G20 in 1999, when it was still reeling from the effects of the 1998 financial crisis and had reached the nadir of its post-Soviet economic downturn, was an important affirmation of its status, despite its continual financial collapse and contrasted with its exclusion from the discussion of official issues within the G7 (Kirton, 2016). Russian observers have shown the greatest enthusiasm for the G20 as it demonstrates Russia's diplomatic successes and demonstrates Russia's status, rather than the more mundane progress the organization has made in tackling economic governance issues. Thus the G20 summits in St. Petersburg (2013), Antalya (2015) and Hangzhou (2016) were considered to be a success for Russia because of the diplomatic breakthrough that resolved the Syria Chemical

Weapons crisis (and whose groundwork was laid by Russia in St Petersburg) or for the respect and status that Putin and Russia have been accorded at these summits, rather than for the actual progress that they have made on concrete economic issues (Tkachenko, 2013).

Russia's Approach to The G20 Compared to Other International Organizations

Russia was initially eager to see the G20 eclipse the G8 as the preeminent multilateral forum for global economic governance. Though it is a member of the G8, Russia has been excluded from discussions on economics and finance, and G8 members meet separately to discuss these issues as the G7. Nevertheless, Russia still wanted to preserve the status and influence it held from its membership in the G8 and did not want to see the organization become marginalized. Russian leaders thus advocated for a sort of global division of labor, whereby economic and financial would become the purview of the G20, but issues of global security would remain the G8's domain (Panova, 2011).

In terms of its symbolic importance, Russia's membership in the G20 has taken on added significance since Russia's suspension from the G8 in 2014 over its annexation of Crimea. Russia's continued membership in the G20 shows that it is not isolated from the world community and has not become a pariah. Since being suspended, Russia has also looked to highlight the growing relevance of the G20 as opposed to the obsolescence of the G8 as the appropriate forum for discussing global governance issues. According to the new narrative, the G7/G8 has turned into a powerless institution that is incapable of resolving any of the existing international problems (Tsvetkov, 2016). Russian leaders announced that they will not look to reinstate their membership in the G8 in the future and that, from Moscow's point of view, the G20 has replaced the G8/G7. According to Dmitry Medvedev, "It is clear what this Group of Seven means without other major economies. Nothing" (Batchelor, 2017).

Russia's suspension from the G8 and estrangement from the West has made it more difficult for top Russian leaders like Putin to find fora where they can meet their Western counterparts to discuss pressing global issues such as Syria and Ukraine, and the G20 has come to serve this role. Under these circumstances, Russia favors the G20 because of the diversity of the membership. In institutions such as the G8 or OSCE and NATO-Russia Council, Russia often found itself feeling like the odd man out because of its domestic political system and the values it ascribed to diverge from "acceptable" Western norms. This made it difficult to defend its interests. It is easier for Russia to find allies among the developing nations of the G20 that also share some of Russia's skepticism about Western norms and values. According to Feodor Lukyanov (2014):

> Russia should give the G20 its full attention since it is a format in which Moscow will never standalone ... Officially, the G8 is no more due to Crimea, but the real reason is that Russia's involvement was long viewed as an intrusion ... That could never happen under the G20.

Russia's role in the G20 cannot be analyzed separately from its role in the BRICS. Since the 2009 summit failures, Russia has increasingly looked to coordinate its G20 agenda with other BRICS countries. In this way, Russia can compensate for some of its financial and economic weaknesses and also portray itself to the world community as a member of the group of rising economic powers. The most notable example was the coordination of the BRICS countries' stance on reforming the IMF and World Bank quotas ahead of the G20's 2009 Pittsburgh summit. Russia will continue this practice of leveraging its membership in BRICS to improve its position in the G20. It has largely abandoned the idea of presenting proposals independently of its BRICS partners, as it did during the earlier summits (Suslov, 2017).

G20 membership is important for satisfying Russia's status aspiration to be a member of the club of states that will decide the future of the global economy. Yet Russia's status ambitions go far beyond just being a member of this club. Moscow is also highly sensitive about its place at the top of the hierarchy among the most powerful states. The G20 is not an adequate vehicle for satisfying Russia's larger status ambitions because it is too inclusive (it includes 20 plus members), and because opportunities to demonstrate leadership within the organization are limited due to Russia's economic weakness (as well as the divisiveness within the group itself). Russia prefers to engage other states through bilateral or "minilateral" (combining three or more great powers) fora, especially when these arrangements give it the opportunity to engage countries that it truly regards to be members of its peer group, such as the United States and China, and to a lesser extent Japan, India and the EU, on an equal footing.

Russia is more enthusiastic about cooperation in international organizations where military and security issues are addressed more directly, and where Russia can demonstrate its leadership more effectively, for example regional organizations such as the Russian-led Collective Security Treaty Organization (CSTO) and the Shanghai Cooperation Organization (SCO), where it shares leadership with China. The most important multilateral organization for Russia continues to be the United Nations Security Council (UNSC), which it regards as the quintessential marker of its international status as one of the five great powers. Moscow jealously guards the privileges conferred by its permanent seat on the council and is wary of any multilateral institutions –including the G20 – that could potentially eclipse or devalue the UNSC (Grant, 2012).

Ideally, Russia would like to see the establishment of some form of 21st-century Great Power Concert (Karaganov, 2015). This preference is a reflection of Russia's acute status anxieties, which have shaped Russian foreign policy thinking throughout the post-Soviet period (Forsberg et al., 2014). Russia leaders worry about their country's ability to maintain its status as a great power over the long term as Russia struggles to keep pace economically and technologically with other great powers and grapples with demographic issues (Kuvshinova, 2013). A Great Power Concert would represent a kind of "shortcut to greatness" (Larson and Shevchenko, 2003) that would compensate for imminent decline. It would firmly establish Russia's status as one of the leading states in the international system – even if its ability to shape the material environment around it declines in the future (Krickovic and Weber, 2017).

Conclusion

Though it has adjusted its earlier expectations about the "transformational" potential of the G20, Russia still puts a priority on participation. It will continue to be engaged at both levels of the G20, as the costs of remaining engaged are relatively low and it still has much to gain from participation. First, it wants to be able to contribute to the reforms that are being undertaken so that it can defend its interests (lest changes be passed that would adversely affect Russia if it were absent). Second, Russia recognizes the important role that the G20 played in helping the global economy recover from the GFC. Of all the G20 countries, Russia was amongst the hardest hit and it wants to make sure that the institution is able to fulfill this important crisis management role in the future, should the need arise. Third, Russian leaders see the G20 as an embryonic form of what the future global governance architecture may evolve into. They want to be present and have a voice in this long-term process. Finally, and perhaps most importantly, membership in the organization is an important marker of Russia's status in the club of nations that are the major decisions about global economic governance – even as it recognizes that this reality more often than not falls short of the perception.

Nevertheless, when all is said and done, Moscow believes that it stands to gain more from engaging other great powers directly or indirectly, than through multilateral formats such as the G20. The preference is for the establishment of a 21st-century version of the Great Power Concert over more inclusive forms of global governance. In part, this is because Russian leaders are skeptical about the continued relevance of global governance as the world begins to enter what they see as a new era of fragmentation and de-globalization. But it also reflects Russia's loftier status ambitions, which it finds it cannot satisfy through the G20 alone, and which it believes can best be attained through more traditional forms of great power politics.

Note

1 I have calculated these statistics based on the University of Toronto – Russian Presidential Academy of national Economy and Public Administration's (RANEPA) reports on G20 compliance. For access to these reports, see www.ranepa.ru/eng/ciir-ranepa/research-areas/g20/analytics.

References

Batchelor, T. (2017) "Russia announces plan to permanently leave G8 group", *The Independent*, 13 January. www.independent.co.uk/news/world/politics/russia-g8-kremlin-crimea-ukraine-vladimir-putin-g7-g20-a7525836.html. [Accessed: 12 March 2017].

Blyth, M. (2013) "Paradigms and Paradox: The Politics of Economic Ideas in Two Moments of Crisis", *Governance*, 26(2), pp. 197–215.

Bratersky, M. (2012) "G20: Opportunities for a Dialogue between Groups of Countries at Different Poles of Imbalances in the Global Economy and Finance". In Timofeev, I. (ed.) *G20, G8, BRICS Development Momentum and Interests of Russia*, Moscow, Russian International Affairs Council, pp. 15–18.

Bratersky, M. (2017) Interview with Author, Moscow, 4 April.

Bremmer, I. (2012) *Every Nation for Itself: Winners and Losers in a G-zero World*. New York: Portfolio.

Cooper, A.F. (2010) "The G20 as an Improvised Crisis Committee and/or a Contested 'Steering Committee' for the World". *International Affairs*, 86(3), pp. 741–757.

Cooper, A. and Thakur, R. (2013) *The Group of Twenty (G20)*. New York: Routledge.

Cooper, A. and Pouliot, V. (2015) "How Much is Global Governance Changing? The G20 as International Practice". *Cooperation and Conflict*, 50(3), pp. 334–350.

Drezner, D. (2014) "The System Worked: Global Economic Governance During the Great Recession". *World Politics*, 66(1), pp. 123–164.

Eichengreen, B. (2009) "The G20 and the Crisis". http://eml.berkeley.edu/~eichengr/g20crisis_2-23-09.pdf. [Accessed: 2 April 2017]

Forsberg, T., Heller, R. and Wolf, R. (2014) "Status and Emotions in Russian Foreign Policy", *Communist and Post-Communist Studies*, 47(3), pp. 261–268.

Grant, C. (2012) *Russia, China and Global Governance*. London: Centre for European Reform.

Helleiner, E. (2014) *The Status Quo Crisis: Global Financial Governance After the 2008 Meltdown*. New York: Oxford University Press.

Karaganov, S. (2015). Venskii Koncert XXI Veka (A Vienna Concert for the 21st Century), *Rossiskaya Gazeta*, 3 June. https://rg.ru/2015/06/03/karaganov.html. [Accessed: 14 April 2017].

Karaganov, S. (2016) "S vostoka na zapad ili Bolyshaya Evraziya" (From East to West or Greater Eurasia), *Rossiskaya gazeta*, 24 October. https://rg.ru/2016/10/24/politolog-karaganov-povorot-rossii-k-rynkam-azii-uzhe-sostoialsia.html. [Accessed: 26 March 2017].

Kirton, J. (2016) *G20 Governance for a Globalized World*. London: Routledge.

Koshkin, P. (2013) "The G20: Effective Policy Group or Diplomatic Photo-op?", *Russia Direct*, 5 September. www.russia-direct.org/debates/g20-effective-policy-group-or-diplomatic-photo-op. [Accessed: 10 March 2017].

Krickovic, A. and Weber, Y. (2017) "Commitment Issues: The Syrian and Ukraine Crises as Bargaining Failures of the Post-Cold War International Order". *Problems of Post-Communism*, forthcoming. Early publication online. www.tandfonline.com/doi/full/10.1080/10758216.2017.1330660.

Kudrin, A. and Gurvich, E. (2015) "A New Growth Model for the Russian economy", *Russian Journal of Economics*, 1(1), pp. 30–54.

Kuvshinova, O. (2013) "Rossiya gotovitsya k desyati toshim godam" (*Russia prepares for ten thin years*), *Vedemosti*, 7 November. www.vedomosti.ru/newspaper/articles/2013/11/07/rossiya-gotovitsya-k-desyati-toschim-godam. [Accessed: 11 April 2017].

Larionova, M., Rakhmangulov, M. and Shelepov, A. (2015) "Assessing G7/8 and G20 Effectiveness in Global Governance". *The G8–G20 Relationship in Global Governance. London*. London: Ashgate, pp. 77–108.

Larson, D. W. and A. Shevchenko. (2003) "Shortcut to Greatness: The New Thinking and the Revolution in Soviet Foreign Policy". *International Organization*, 57(1), pp. 77–109.

Latynina, Y. (2014) "Rozhdenie sverxderzhavy" (Birth of a superpower), *Novaya Gazeta*, no. 131, 21 November, www.novayagazeta.ru/articles/2014/11/19/62014-rozhdenie-sverhderzhavy. [Accessed: 10 March 2017].

Luckhurst, J. (2016) *G20 Since the Global Crisis*. London: Palgrave Macmillan.

Lukyanov, F. (2014) "Sdelat' 'dvadtsatku' politicheskoi" (Politicizing the 'twenty'), *Rossiskaya Gazeta*, 12 November. https://rg.ru/2014/11/12/lukyanov.html. [Accessed: 24 March 2017].

Lukyanov, F. (2016) "Big 20 to Big Game: Power Politics Are Returning, Which Suits Russia", *Russia in Global Affairs*, 9 September. http://eng.globalaffairs.ru/redcol/BiG20-to-Big-Game-Power-Politics-Are-Returning-Which-Suits-Russia-18355. [Accessed: 16 March 2017].

Panova, V. (2011) "The G8 Role and Place in the Current International System and Its Future Development in the Context of External Challenges and Long-term Priorities of the Russian Foreign and Domestic policies". *International Organizations Research Journal*, 6(4), pp. 20–30.

Postel-Vinay, K. (2016) *The G20: A New Geopolitical Order*. London, Palgrave Macmillan.

Putin, V. (2015) Responses to Journalists' Questions Following the G20 Summit, 16 November, http://en.kremlin.ru/events/president/transcripts/press_conferences/50704. [Accessed: 2 April 2017].

Roberts, C. (2009) "Russia's BRICs diplomacy: Rising Outsider with Dreams of an Insider". *Polity*, 42(1), pp. 38–73.

Slaughter, A. (2009) *A New World Order*. Princeton, NJ: Princeton University Press.

Sonne, P. and Grove, T. (2015) "Vladimir Putin Suggests Russia's Isolation from the West Is Ending", *Wall Street Journal*, 16 November. www.wsj.com/articles/vladimir-putin-suggests-russias-isolation-from-the-west-is-ending-1447695525. [Accessed: 24 March 2017].

Suslov, D. (2016) "US–Russia Confrontation and a New Global Balance". *Strategic Analysis* 40(6), pp. 547–560.

Suslov, D. (2017) Interview with Author, Moscow, 6 April.

TASS (2016) "Putin Budet glavnim gostem na G20 v Kitaiskom Xanchzhou" (Putin Will Be the Guest of Honor at the G20 in Hangzhou, China), 3 August.

Tkachenko, S. (2013) "Once the G20 Summit became the Syrian Summit, Russia won", *Russia Direct*, 11 September, www.russia-direct.org/analysis/once-g20-summit-became-syrian-summit-russia-won. [Accessed: 8 March 2017].

Tsvetkov, I. (2016) "Was the G20 Summit in China Really a Success of Russian Diplomacy?", *Russia Direct*, 7 September, www.russia-direct.org/opinion/was-g20-summit-china-really-success-russian-diplomacy. [Accessed: 8 March 2017].

Tsygankov, A. (2016) *Russia's Foreign Policy: Change and Continuity in National Identity*, London: Rowman & Littlefield.

Vestergaard, J. and Wade, R. (2012) "The Governance Response to the Great Recession: The 'Success' of the G20". *Journal of Economic Issues*, 46(2), pp. 481–490.

Weisbrot, M. and Johnston, J. (2016) *Voting Share Reform at the IMF: Will it Make a Difference?* Washington, DC, Center for Economic and Policy Research (CEPR). http://cepr.net/images/stories/reports/IMF-voting-shares-2016-04.pdf. [Accessed: 8 April 2017].

Zubkov, I. (2017) "Svoboda Vypala iz teksta: SSha ne dali G20 osudit tergovie barery" (Freedom was cut from the text: The US Did Not Allow the G20 to Condemn Trade Barriers), *Rossiskaya Gazeta*, 19 March. https://rg.ru/2017/03/19/ssha-ne-dali-g20-osudit-torgovye-barery.html. [Accessed: 12 April 2017].

24
EUROPEAN ORGANIZATIONS

Hanna Smith

UNIVERSITY OF HELSINKI, FINLAND

Introduction

The Council of Europe (CoE) and the Organization for Security and Cooperation (OSCE) are the two most important institutions promoting European cooperation and collaboration that extend their membership beyond that of the European Union (EU). The two organizations have different histories, but their organizational identity is rooted in Europeanness. Both were created during the Cold War. The CoE was set up in 1949, at the very beginning of the Cold War. The Conference on Security and Cooperation in Europe (CSCE, the precursor of the OSCE) was negotiated in 1975, at the height of the Cold War. The Soviet Union was part of the process of creating the CSCE, but by contrast, the CoE was set up in order to counter communist regimes and so was directed against the Soviet Union in particular.

In Russian/Soviet interactions with Europe, being considered a part of Europe, and Europe's place as a reference point for Russia, have been important. The CoE and OSCE therefore figure strongly in Russian foreign policy, given Russia's wish to be a significant player in European affairs. This desire was expressed by President Putin when, paying respects to the late German Chancellor Helmut Kohl, he quoted him approvingly: "If we want to maintain our civilization in this tough and quickly changing world . . . Then naturally Europe and Russia need to be together" (Druzhinin, 2017). Since the fall of the Soviet Union, Russia has been especially keen on multilateral interaction in its foreign policy. Russia is active in multilateral frameworks like the G20, BRICS (Brazil, Russia, India, China and South-Africa) and (up until 2014) the G8, and multiple international organizations like the United Nations, the World Trade Organization (WTO), The Commonwealth of Independent States (CIS), etc. But the CoE and OSCE have a unique European dimension which the others lack. However, as a result of the deepening cooperation and widening geographical scope of the EU, understandings of Europeanness have been changing and Europe has become a disputed concept. The Russian foreign policy view is that both the CoE and OSCE represent wider Europe, or the pan-European concept. This leads to a mismatch between the EU's perspective that Russia is an outsider in Europe, and the perspective from the OSCE's and CoE's point of view that Russia is part of Europe.

In this chapter both organizations, the OSCE and CoE, are introduced. The origins and purpose of both are very important in tracing the evolution of Russia's relationship with the organizations today. Despite the deep differences between Russia and most other members in the two organizations, the need and usefulness of the organizations is still recognized by all members and at the grass roots level one can argue there have also been successes which could well prove to be significant in the future.

The Council of Europe

The CoE was created in 1949 as a means of giving Western Europe the upper hand in the battle of ideologies. Its aim was to hold up democracy in opposition to communism and fascism. It was considered very important at the time for the sake of European unity to promote some common norms and rules as well as define values in democracy, human rights and the rule of law – the holy trinity, as some CoE officials call them.

The initiative for forming an organization like the CoE came from France and Great Britain. Winston Churchill stated in Zurich in 1946 that the way forward for a prosperous Europe would be the creation of a United States of Europe:

> What is this sovereign remedy? It is to recreate the European fabric, or as much of it as we can, and to provide it with a structure under which it can dwell in peace, in safety, and in freedom. We must build a kind of United States of Europe.
>
> *(Churchill 1946)*

Churchill's idea was to ensure that West European unity would hold up against the communist "threat", as it was then seen. Some of the ideas of socialism were attractive for all societies. In order to counter them and to ensure that the rise of fascism would not be repeated, Western Europe needed mechanisms to enhance its own democratic institutions. Those institutions would also erect obstacles to belligerent acts by governments in any country. In other words, the central idea was to create the basis for strong West European soft power or cultural statecraft towards the East, while at the same time ensuring history would not repeat itself in the form of conflicts between European states.

One essential feature that continues to affect the organization's mechanisms and abilities was already decided back then. France and Great Britain differed slightly in their visions of the kind of organization they wanted. France even suggested the name "European Union", but this was rejected by the British on the grounds that the term was too loaded. The British view was that the new body would work better if it was more an organization that provided general guidelines and acted as a forum for the exchange of opinions than if it was able to force its decisions onto its members. The general feeling was that human rights, the rule of law and the understanding of democracy were too difficult subjects for an agreed substance to be imposed on different countries in the immediate aftermath of the Second World War in Europe and the rest of the world.

With the founding of the EU and its expansion in the 1990s, less attention has been focused on the CoE and its role in European cooperation. The EU has absorbed into its own agenda many of the issues that are at the core of the CoE's functions. This has created an interesting situation. The EU has 28 members (27 from the end of March 2019 following the UK's decision to leave) dealing with many of the same issues as the CoE. The CoE has 47 members, 19 of which do not belong to the EU, a majority of which are countries from the former Eastern bloc. This has opened up the possibility of dialogue between countries of the EU on the one hand and those countries that are members of the CoE but not EU members, of which Russia is the largest, on the other. This duality is both the CoE's strength and its weakness at the same time. By bringing together all European countries, the organization is able to some extent to paper over the distinction between the two Europes – the Europe made up of countries that are not members of the EU and the one made up of EU member countries. Thus it is a genuinely pan-European organization. On the other hand, the fact that its membership is dominated by one organized bloc weakens its credibility as a truly shared and democratic organization.

Russia became a member of the CoE in 1996. It was granted membership even though at the time there was a great deal of controversy over the first Chechen War, the use of the death penalty, and other shortcomings relating to the rule of law and human rights protection. Hence it has been argued that Russian membership was granted more on pragmatic grounds rather than on the basis that it was fully suitable for membership (Webber, 2000: 134). There were also two other noteworthy aspects of the application process: Russian understandings of its own exceptionalism, and the fact that there was such a high level of consensus among the Russian domestic public and elite opinion relating to Russian membership in the CoE (Webber, 2000; 135; Smith, 2014). The exceptionalism was part of Russia's great power identity, its self-perception as a great power even at a time when its material means and capabilities did not match the requirements of a great power. Regardless of whether Russia was a great power or not, this self-perception affected its attitude to CoE membership. Great powers often interpret common rules from their own perspective and are unwilling to accede if the common rules go against the great power's own interests. This great power self-perception explains much about Russia's behaviour in the CoE, once it had become a member. The consensus surrounding the application for membership was a rather unique factor in Russian foreign policy, at a time when there were strong divisions within the political establishment. At the beginning of the 1990s, Russia was seen as part of the West and part of Europe by a strong majority of Russians, which laid the basis for some unity in relation to foreign policy. This was clear in the views of both Andrey Kozyrev, Russian foreign minister from 1992–1996, and of Yevgeni Primakov, Russian foreign minister 1996–1999. They both saw Russian membership in the CoE as a concomitant of Russia's "rightful place in Western civilization as an equal partner" and as a "step towards a genuine unification of Europe" (Webber, 2000: 132, 134). These two factors paved the way for Russia joining the CoE. The first factor led to a Russian presumption that Russia would have an exceptional role inside the organization. The second factor linked membership with Russian integration with Europe in a broader sense. Each of the factors contained a high conflict potential, since both were grounded in the immediate expectations and perceptions of the time and therefore led to difficulties adapting to or preparing for what was to lie ahead.

The third factor that led to a high potential for conflict was the fact that the European Court of Human Rights (ECHR) was part of the membership package. On joining the CoE, Russia ratified and so recognized the compulsory jurisdiction of the ECHR and the right of individuals to sue Russia in that court over violations of the 1950 European Convention for the Protection of Human Rights and Fundamental Freedoms. This decision became increasingly unpopular, however, among the Russian political elite, while at the same time its popularity increased among ordinary Russians as well as with Russian judges (Trochev, 2009: 165). There seem to be three reasons for this. Since Russian joined the CoE, the number of cases brought against Russia in the ECHR has expanded rapidly. According to VTsIOM, in September 2001 only 2–3 percent of Russians saw the ECHR as a place to seek redress for justice over human rights. In 2003 the number had grown to 19 percent and by 2007, after a decade of Russian membership, 27 percent of respondents were ready to turn to the ECHR with a complaint against the Russian state about human rights violations (Trochev, 2009: 148). While the number of complaints against Russia grew, the number of judgements issued against Russia grew as well. The statistics are grim from a Russian perspective. There were 1,604 judgements issued against Russia in the period 1996–2014. This number is exceeded only by those for Turkey (3,095) and Italy (2,312), which have been subject to ECHR jurisdiction since its founding in 1959 (Newcity, 2015).

At the beginning of Russian membership, Russia was prepared for the fact that there would be judgements against it from the ECHR. Its record up to the 2010s for taking the complaints seriously, trying to work inside Russia to reduce the numbers of complaints, and paying up the fines the ECHR ordered was good. But while the number of complaints was growing, the work load to counter the complaints increased beyond the available resources and the level of fines also began to mount significantly. Another issue is the fact of Russian judges looking to the ECHR judgements as setting legal precedents has been a source of some concern for the Russian power elite. In 2015, President Putin signed a law which established the priority of national laws over the judgements of international court rulings. In response to a motion from the President or government, the Russian Constitutional Court has the right to recognize these rulings as unenforceable (Sinelschikova, 2015). This shows how decisions made a long time ago, in the mid-1990s, have become a problem for Russian political power, after judges and civil society made the ECHR the "most popular court" for Russians.

There are two decision-making mechanisms within the CoE. This leads to a certain duality for the whole organization. On the one hand, there is parliamentary oversight. The Parliamentary Assembly of the Council of Europe (PACE) consists of parliamentarians from each member state. They meet four times a year. The PACE elects the judges to the ECHR, the Commissioner for Human Rights, the CoE Secretary General and Deputy Secretary General as well as its own Secretary General. The PACE has eight committees and adopts recommendations for the Committee of Ministers, resolutions that express its own point of view and opinions relating to membership applications, draft treaties, etc. It can strip a member state of voting and participation rights. In Russia's case this has happened twice, in 2000 relating to the second Chechen War and in 2014 relating to the Russian annexation of Crimea.

The PACE's status has not always been considered high, and it has suffered from the reputation of being a home for 'second class parliamentarians'. This reputation, however, does not do justice to the PACE and its members. Its reports have been highly valued and well put together. In the process of monitoring the democratic progress of former socialist countries, including Russia, it has been essential for the process of European integration. The Russian PACE team has been made up of very senior Russian representatives, with not only a parliamentary background but also diplomatic training. Out of all the institutions of the Council of Europe, the PACE has had the most complicated relationship with Russia as a member state. It is in this forum that the consequences of the Russian annexation of Crimea were at their most visible. After the suspension of its voting rights, Russia announced in summer 2017 that it would not pay its membership fee in full since it was no longer to participate fully in the PACE. Despite such problems with the PACE, Russia has continued to participate in the activities of all the intergovernmental committees and monitoring bodies as well as the Ministerial Council (MC).

Real power in the Council of Europe lies with the Committee of Ministers (CM). Countries are represented on the CM by their foreign ministers. The CM can suspend cooperation and assistance programmes, or freeze or cancel membership altogether (CoE Statute, 1949: article 8). CM decisions are arrived at in three different ways, depending on the issue: unanimous vote, simple majority or two-thirds majority (CoE Statute, 1949: article 20). Furthermore, the meetings of the CM are private in nature and the CM decides what will become public from their meetings (CoE Statute, 1949: article 21). As a decision-making body, the CM fits well with the Russian understanding of how international relations should function, and its workings fall into the sphere of traditional diplomacy. Russian foreign ministers have had a much easier time with the CM than the Russian PACE delegation has in the PACE. On the occasion of the 20th anniversary of Russian membership in the CoE, its General Secretary Thorbjorn Jagland wrote, in reply to a letter from Russian foreign minister Sergei Lavrov, that "The council of Europe remains a crucial pan-European platform for dialogue and enhanced co-operation, and the Russian Federation is an indispensable member of this community" (CoE, 2016). Lavrov's letter also stressed the pan-European nature of the CoE and, just as former foreign minister Primakov had expressed in 1996, Lavrov stated that he also saw the CoE as working to remove the dividing lines inherited from the Cold War in Europe (Lavrov, 2016).

The CoE highlights the duality in Russian foreign policy. On the one hand, it wants to be part of Europe; on the other, it views Russia as a sovereign great power which cannot be bound institutionally on an equal basis with smaller powers. The CoE's pan-European nature is one of the major factors why the organization has been attractive to Russia. In the PACE the Russian delegation has come under fierce criticism and has responded by accusing the whole organization of double standards and Russophobia, questioning the usefulness of the organization and threatening to leave or withhold its membership fees. Inside Russia, opinions have also been divided about Russia's role in the organization. Then in the CM, Russia has been received in accordance with the traditions of diplomacy, and problems are discussed in diplomatic language, stressing the importance of open and frank dialogue and pan-Europeanness. This approach is appreciated in Russia and it is very much in line with Russian foreign policy's European orientation and its long-term policy aim of seeing a Europe without dividing lines. The ECHR has proven to be a challenge for Russia in ways that were not foreseen when Russia was applying to become a member of the CoE. The increasing number of judgements against Russia as well as some high-profile judgements related to cases like YUKOS and the cases launched against Russia by Georgia and Ukraine led to Russia turning against the ECHR and claiming that its activities had become politicized. In the cases where ordinary Russian citizens have filed against the Russian state after all legal mechanisms inside Russia have been exhausted, it has not been so easy to argue about the politicization of the ECHR. So the ECHR continues to have an impact in improving human rights conditions inside Russia, even if in a small and roundabout way.

The three different elements of CoE – PACE, MC and ECHR – all have something to contribute to the Russia-Europe dialogue in spite of strong differences of opinion and of interpretations of events. The CoE's role in a pan-European context is significant, and whether Russia will remain a member or not, its significance will only grow in the future when mechanisms of cooperation and European unity are set to become even more important.

The Organization for Security and Cooperation in Europe (OSCE)

The OSCE is the product of a Soviet initiative towards all-European security. Some analysts date its inception to February 10, 1954 when "Molotov's plan" was published; but others date this Russian desire for a pan-European collective security arrangement to as far back as the 1930s (Zagorsky, 2005: 22). The Helsinki Final Act of 1975 and the creation of the Conference for Security and Cooperation in Europe (CSCE), were two of the most important developments in Soviet-West and especially European relations:

> The road of multilateral preparations for the CSCE was not easy. The East and the West held very different concepts of European security. The NATO countries saw the armed forces and arms in Europe as the main issues. However, the Warsaw Pact countries wanted to have political consultations under the auspice of CSCE.
> *(Zagorsky, 2005: 43)*

Ultimately, the political aspects of the Helsinki Final Act were enormously significant for the future of European security and the fate of the Soviet Union.

The CSCE became an important balancing act in Soviet security thinking. Since relations between the superpowers took most of the foreign policy capital, Western Europe was left in the shadow of superpower politics. The CSCE kept Moscow involved in Europe, and by the mid-1980s "elements in the Soviet leadership realized that this policy (the concentration of Soviet-USA relations) had not just decreased Soviet security in Europe but had resulted in the Soviet Union's isolation from an increasingly dynamic group of states" (Lynch, 2000: 99–124). This factor, alongside Mikhail Gorbachev's new thinking policies with a greater focus on European affairs, meant the CSCE gained more attention in late Soviet security and foreign policy thinking.

Today the OSCE has 57 members and a wide geographical reach including North America, Europe and Asia. In this way, the organization has stretched the idea of "Europe" and today the OSCE is more frequently talked about in the context of East-West relations than European affairs. In comparison to the CoE, the OSCE acts as a bridging institution (Krastev and Leonard, 2014: 6), whereas the CoE is seen as a core European institution. The OSCE's main functions are as a security organization, but it involves a comprehensive approach to security with politico-military, economic, environmental and human dimensions considered as relevant. Issues like arms control, terrorism, good governance, energy security, human trafficking, democratization, media freedom and national minorities figure on the agenda of the organization. As with the CoE, the OSCE's highest decision-making body is the MC. It was established at the Paris Summit of the OSCE (then still the CSCE) in 1990. The Paris Treaty also stressed that the era of confrontation and division in Europe had ended and the unity of Europe was seen as of utmost importance (OSCE, 1990b). There was a high level of Soviet influence in drafting the charter. In this way the Soviet Union used the OSCE framework to transform existing European structures so that they related to a wider Europe, a Europe without dividing lines (Lynch, 2009: 5–13). As Mikhail Gorbachev stated:

> Great European minds have often dreamed of a united, democratic and prosperous Europe, a community and a commonwealth not only of nations and States but of millions of European citizens. It is up to our generation to tackle the task of making that plan an irreversible reality in the coming century.
>
> *(OSCE, 1990a)*

Gorbachev's statement fitted with the Soviet leadership's emphasis in the late 1980s and early 1990s that the OSCE could be used to create "a new European Community based on confidence, mutual understanding and an effective system of collective security" (Lynch, 2000: 102). It was also clear after the fall of the Soviet Union that Russia wanted to view the OSCE as a structure for dealing with security matters in Europe and as an alternative to NATO. "Its [Russia's] general line toward security matters in Europe has been to propose a collective security system based mainly on the OSCE structures" (Pursiainen, 1999: 144). The way the Russian leadership stressed the OSCE framework was visible in the Russian foreign policy doctrine of 1993, which mentioned the organization 13 times and where it "was seen as almost a panacea for all the problems facing Russia after the collapse of the Soviet Union" (Godzimirski, 2009: 126).

The Budapest summit of the OSCE (the last time it was known as CSCE, changing its name from 1 January 1995 OSCE), in December 1994, just before the first Chechen War, reflected the general mood in Russia-West relations. The old tensions that so many had hoped would have disappeared were back. The visible East-West rift overshadowed the important items that were agreed on in the summit, and in spite of Russia's continuing hopes relating to the OSCE, the idea of a new European collective security was given a back seat.

Since the 1994 OSCE Budapest summit, the concept of "Cold Peace" has been used to characterize Russia-West relations. Russian president Yeltsin first used the concept in his Budapest summit address:

> There should be no longer enemies, winners or losers, in that Europe. For this time in history, our continent has a real opportunity to achieve unity. To miss that opportunity means to forget the lessons of the past and to jeopardize our future . . . Europe, even before it has managed to shrug off the legacy of the cold war, is at risk of plunging into a cold peace.
>
> *(Talbott, 2002: 141)*

After issuing this warning about cold peace, Yeltsin suggested:

> A roadmap for Europe towards the 21st century . . . Its essence is the creation of a comprehensive European security system. In this room there are now the leaders of more than 50 countries in the world! CSCE is, in its coverage of countries and the potential of its participants, a unique structure. It is designed to be a strong and effective instrument of peace, stability and democracy.
>
> *(Yeltsin, 1994)*

Yeltsin's vision was that the programme would have been based on an agreement between NATO, the EU, the OSCE and the CIS. A major thrust of Russian diplomacy at that time was pushing such an option as an alternative to NATO's eastward expansion. For Russia it was important to promote an alternative to NATO enlargement, even if the indications coming from the former East European countries and the United States were that there was no stopping enlargement.

In order to further this end of promoting the OSCE's role as the main security organization in Europe, Russia was willing to accept a role for the OSCE in the first Chechen War. The first and second Chechen Wars did not help Russia in achieving European collective security, but the OSCE's role in the first Chechen conflict especially gave the organization experience of a new role in conflict management, which it also attempted to follow in the Second Chechen War and the war in Georgia in 2008. The two latter attempted interventions were not successful due to Russian dissatisfaction with the organization, and Russia's cooperation was essential if the OSCE was to have any meaningful role.

OSCE's summit in Istanbul in 1999 proved to be a watershed in Russian attitudes towards the OSCE. The new collective European security order failed to materialize and, in spite of the OSCE's constructive role in the First Chechen War, Russia was not happy about the way the OSCE criticized Russia. There was a long list of disagreements between Russia and, especially, Western member states. The Second Chechen War was a particularly hot topic for the OSCE, while Russia viewed it as an internal matter which the OSCE should not get involved in. Another issue was the adoption of a statement relating to Georgia which defined South Ossetia and Abkhazia as parts of Georgia. The Transnistria conflict was taken up and the normalization of Moldova-Transnistria relations was called for. A new treaty on conventional forces in Europe was signed which reflected the new realities of Europe, but the section that dealt with the Russian military presence in Georgia and Moldova was not as Russia would have wanted it. In the case of Georgia, Russia fulfilled the OSCE's requirements, but Moldova became a disputed issue. All of the issues discussed at the Istanbul summit developed into problems between Russia and the Western member states of the OSCE later on.

One further issue caused irritation in Moscow's eyes. In the 1990s the OSCE took up the monitoring of elections as one of its core functions. The OSCE's legitimization of elections to the Russian Duma and presidential elections is important for Russia. Even though shortcomings were always found, for a number of years the monitoring showed improvements in the election system. Nonetheless, the election monitoring was viewed in Russia as a measure directed against Russia and illustrating the double standards of the organization. At the time of the 2007 Duma elections, Russia decided to put limits on OSCE election monitoring, which then undermined the whole process of Russian elections and their legitimation. This created even more tension between the organization and Russia.

Such problems and disputes only increased during President Putin's first two presidential terms, 2000–2008. At the Munich security conference in 2007, Putin reflected on the situation from Russia's perspective:

> What do we see happening today [with the OSCE]? We see this balance [between the political-military, the economic and the human dimensions] is clearly destroyed. People are trying to transform the OSCE into a vulgar instrument designed to promote the foreign policy interests of one or a group of countries.
>
> *(Putin, 2007)*

While there were multiple problems relating to the OSCE, Russia was at the same time engaging in collective security arrangements in the East with the Collective Security Treaty Organisation (CSTO) and the Shanghai Cooperation Organization (SCO). These organizations fulfilled one aim of Russian foreign policy relating to collective security, but they did not satisfy the aspiration of Europeanness or ideas of pan-European cooperation with Russia as one of the strong and equal partners. When Dmitry Medvedev became president of Russia in 2008, he raised the idea of European collective security again. His proposal included the idea that all relevant security organizations – NATO, the EU, the OSCE, the CSTO and the CIS – should try to find a common framework for security matters in a pan-European way. As such, the Russian initiative did not get much support even though it aroused a good deal of interest. It was seen as Russia's own vision for European security and, in a positive sense, as a proactive move from Moscow to seek better relations between Europe and Russia. At that point relations were at a low point and Russia was seen as more interested in obstructing the interests of others than in advancing their own positive agenda (Lo, 2009). With this initiative, Medvedev was reviving the idea of the OSCE as a European security umbrella, only an umbrella that should be reformed according to Moscow's perspective. Even if the Medvedev initiative did not, ultimately, lead to any new security arrangements and the agenda was yet again pushed to the back seat at the beginning of Putin's third presidential term, events in Europe have proved that frameworks like the OSCE are essential when it comes to European security. With the Ukraine crisis, the annexation of Crimea and the war in Donbass, the role of the OSCE has yet again become important, but more in the format of its Helsinki 1975 role than in that of the 1990s.

The Russian foreign policy establishment has continued to bring up the need for collective European security. Even if Russian criticisms of the West have been stronger than ever within the framework of the OSCE, Russia has also taken the opportunity to remind everybody of the need for a common security framework. As Russia's permanent representative to the OSCE, Alexander Lukashevich, pointed out: "It is vital to start a strategic dialogue on the future of European security, understood in a broadest sense. The current system seems to reproduce confrontation" (Mid, 2017a). Foreign minister Lavrov, in his joint press conference with OSCE Secretary General Lamberto Zannier in Moscow in April 2017, pointed out that:

"Russia consistently advocates strengthening the OSCE and enhancing its role in the Euro-Atlantic region and in the international arena as a whole" (Mid, 2017b). Lavrov also talked once again about a true community with united and indivisible security that was part of the OSCE 2010 Astana summit declaration.

In this way the duality of Russian foreign policy is present in the OSCE as it is in the CoE. The OSCE is a complicated international organization. However, its history as a bridge between East and West still stands. The overall tensions in international relations, particularly between the East and the West, are very visible in the organization and can paralyze it in the worst case. However, the pan-European nature of the organization, together with a transatlantic dimension, is clearly in line with one side of Russia's foreign policy interests that sees integration in Europe as important. The fact that Russia sees the OSCE as the main international organization in the Ukraine conflict is an indication that, in spite of all of the Russian criticisms and objections, the organization has an important place in Russian foreign policy thinking.

Conclusion

The CoE and the OSCE are pan-European organizations. This feature makes them attractive from a Russian perspective. Russia's relationship with the two organizations has similarities and differences. The similarities are that both organizations view Russia as a challenging member, whereas Russia views both organizations as influenced by Russophobia. At the same time, both organizations are vital to Russia's interests relating to Europe and being part of Europe. Differences in Russia's relationship with the two organizations are down to their nature.

The CoE deals with questions on the rule of law and human rights. Its actions are based on the ECHR. Each of the members of the CoE subscribed to the 1950 European Convention for the Protection of Human Rights and Fundamental Freedoms. This also gave the CoE the mandate to monitor the application of that convention by its members and enabled the ECHR to make judgements in cases where domestic legal routes had been exhausted. In this way, Russia recognized along with 46 other states the jurisdiction of an international organization over its national law. This only changed in 2015 when President Putin sighed a law making it possible for the Russia President or government to question the decision of the ECHR and send the case to the Russian constitutional court. This change highlighted the growing rift between Russia and the West after events related to Ukraine in 2014.

Russian membership in the CoE brings a strong European dimension into Russian foreign policy. Despite deep dissatisfaction of the ECHR and PACE, Russia seems to value the overall framework of the CoE sufficiently that it is not ready to pull out of the organization. At the level of the Ministerial Council where traditional diplomacy is dominant, Russian Foreign Minister Lavrov feels much more comfortable, and relations, even during difficult times, emphasize the importance of open and frank dialogue.

The OSCE's focus on security issues fits not only with Russian foreign policy interests in the concept of a wider Europe, but also relates to Moscow's historical and long-term foreign policy aim of creating a European collective security architecture. This is as much to protect Russia's foreign policy interests as securing it as part of Europe. The activities of the OSCE that deal with issues other than security, like election monitoring, are less to Russian liking even if Russia benefitted greatly from OSCE election monitoring. The monitoring reports always included strong criticisms of the Russian system, but at the same time they legitimized the elections and highlighted some improvements in the process, making it easier for Russia to argue about the progress of democracy in Russia. Since 2007, when Russia started to limit the election monitoring process, talk about Russia as a democracy has also been decreasing rapidly.

With the events in Ukraine starting in 2014, OSCE has once again been given a significant role as a conflict management organization. This is not without problems, and in the worst-case scenario the organization's ability to act can be paralyzed if consensus cannot not found. In the long-term picture, from Helsinki 1975 until today, the organization has shown that it has an important place in European security architecture and as part of Russian foreign policy's pan-European dimension.

Russian interactions with both organizations show how difficult a partner Russia can be in a multilateral framework. Still, despite the existence of dividing lines, both organizations have succeeded in lowering East-West divisions.

References

Churchill, Winston, 1946, Speech delivered at the University of Zurich, 19 September, www.cvce.eu/content/publication/1997/10/13/7dc5a4cc-4453-4c2a-b130-b534b7d76ebd/publishable_en.pdf.

CoE, 2016, Lavrov, Jagland on Russian's membership in Council of Europe, 24 February, Secretary. www.mid.ru/en/foreign_policy/news/-/asset_publisher/cKNonkJE02Bw/content/id/2106003.

CoE Statute, 1949, available at www.coe.int/en/web/conventions/full-list/-/conventions/rms/0900001680306052.

Druzhinin, Alexei, 2017, Russia and Europe need to be together, Moscow is ready for this, said Putin, RIA Novasti, 17 June, https://ria.ru/politics/20170617/1496740090.html.

Godzimirski, Jakub M, 2009, Russia and the OSCE: From high expectations to denial? in Rowe Elana Wilson and Torjesen Stina (eds.), *Multilateral Dimension in Russian Foreign Policy*, London and New York: Routledge, pp. 121–141.

Ivan Krastev and Mark Leonard, 2014, The New European disorder, ECFR/117, November, www.ecfr.eu/page/-/ECFR117_TheNewEuropeanDisorder_ESSAY.pdf.

Lavrov, Sergei, 2016, Letter to Secretary General of Council of Europe, 24 February, Moscow, Russian Federation, Ministry of Foreign Affairs, translation from Russian, https://rm.coe.int/16805a2a6c.

Lo, Bobo, 2009, Medvedev and the new European Security architecture, Centre for European Reform, Policy Brief, July, www.cer.org.uk/sites/defoult/files/publications/attachments/pdf/2011/pbrief_medvedev_july09-741.pdf.

Lynch, Dov, 2000, Russia and the Organization for Security and Cooperation in Europe, in Webber, Mark (ed.), *Russia and Europe: Conflict or Cooperation*, Basingstoke, UK: Macmillan Press, pp. 99–124,

Lynch, Dov, 2009, The State of the OSCE, in Russia, The OSCE and the European Security, *EU-Russia Center Review*, issue 12, November, pp. 5–13.

MID, 2017a, Statement by the Permanent Representative of the Russian Federation to the OSCE Alexander Lukashevich at the OSCE Security Days Panel in Prague: The State of European Security today and prospects for the future, 23 May, Prague. www.mid.ru/en/foreign_policy/news/-/asset_publisher/cKNonkJE02Bw/content/id/2106003.

MID, 2017b, Foreign Minister Sergey Lavrov's remarks and answers to media questions during a joint news conference with OSCE Secretary General Lamberto Zannier, April 25, *Moscow*. www.mid.ru/en/foreign_policy/rso/osce/-/asset_publisher/bzhxR3zkq2H5/content/id/2763974.

Newcity, Michael, 2015, What's at stake if Russia turns its back on the Council of Europe, *Russia Direct*, 16 December, www.russia-direct.org/opinion/whats-stake-if-russia-turns-its-back-council-europe.

OSCE, 1990a, Speech by Soviet President Mikhail Gorbachev to the Second Summit of CSCE Heads of State or Government Paris, 19–21 November 1990. www.osce.org/mc/16155?download=true.

OSCE, 1990b, Charter of Paris for New Europe, www.osce.org/mc/39516?download=true.

Pursiainen, Christer, 1999, International Security regimes, OSCE and Chechnya, in Ted Hopf ed. *Understandings of Russian Foreign Policy*, Pittsburgh, PA: Penn State Press.

Putin, Vladimir, 2007, Speech and the following discussion at the Munich Conference on security, February 10 http://en.kremlin.ru/events/president/transcripts/24034.

Sinelschikova, Yekaterina, 2015, International courts' rulings no longer enforceable in Russia, Russia Direct, 10 December, www.russia-direct.org/russian-media/international-courts-rulings-no-longer-enforceable-russia.

Smith, H. 2014, Russian greatpowerness: foreign policy, the two Chechen wars and international organisations. Faculty of Social Sciences, University of Helsinki, Finland, PhD Thesis.

Talbott, Strobe, 2002, *The Russia Hand: A Memoir of Presidential Diplomacy*, New York: Random House.
Trochev, A. 2009, All Appeals Lead to Strasbourg? Unpacking the Impact of the European Court of Human Rights on Russia. *Demokratizatsiya: The Journal of Post-Soviet Democratization*, 17(2), pp. 145–178.
Webber, Mark, 2000, Russia and the Council of Europe, in Webber, Mark (ed.), *Russia and Europe: Conflict or Cooperation*, Basingstoke, UK: Macmillan Press, pp. 125–151.
Yeltsin, Boris, 1994, ОБЩЕЕ ПРОСТРАНСТВО БЕЗОПАСНОСТИ. ВЫСТУПЛЕНИЕ ПРЕЗИДЕНТА РФ БОРИСА ЕЛЬЦИНА НА ВСТРЕЧЕ СБСЕ В БУДАПЕШТЕ, *Rossiskaya Gazeta*, 06.12, No. 236, Moscow.
Zagorsky, Andrei, 2005, *Helsinkskii protsess*, Moscow, izdatelstvo: Prava Cheloveka.

25
ASIAN ORGANIZATIONS[1]

Artyom Lukin

FAR EASTERN FEDERAL UNIVERSITY, RUSSIA

Russia and Asia-Pacific institutions: declining engagement

Despite having two-thirds of its territory in Asia, Russia is a latecomer to Asian regional institutions. Due to the Cold War, the Soviet Union was shut out of regional cooperation in the Asia-Pacific that was dominated by the United States and its friends, having instead to rely on bilateral ties with a few Communist allies and quasi-allies such as Vietnam, Mongolia and North Korea. Moscow's only multilateral initiative at that time was the 1969 "Asian collective security" proposal.

The situation began to change under Mikhail Gorbachev, who, in his July 1986 speech in Vladivostok, announced Moscow's intention to shift emphasis from military buildup to diplomatic and economic engagement with the Asia-Pacific countries. In 1988, the Soviet government set up the national committee for Pacific economic cooperation and in the same year the Soviet delegation attended a meeting of the quasi-official Pacific Economic Cooperation Conference, the most prominent Asia-Pacific multilateral body at that time (Sneider, 1988).

Following the end of the bipolar confrontation, Russia joined the region's premier non-governmental forums, Pacific Economic Cooperation Council and Pacific Basin Economic Council, in 1992 and 1994 respectively. Yet acquiring the membership in the intergovernmental Asia-Pacific Economic Cooperation (APEC), which in the 1990s was widely seen as the main vehicle for region-wide integration, proved more difficult. For one thing, in the 1990s Russia's share of Asia-Pacific total exports stood at a meager 0.4 percent. This did not quite square with one of APEC's membership requirements that an applicant country have substantial economic ties to the Asia-Pacific. Another hurdle to Russia's membership was the apprehensions of some of the smaller and middle-sized APEC economies, such as Australia, that the addition of another big country would weaken their positions and raise the risks of great power domination within the forum. However, at the 1997 Vancouver summit Russia's APEC application was finally approved, along with Peru's and Vietnam's. Moscow's bid was supported by the United States, China and Japan, thus deciding the matter. In 1994 Russia became a founding member of the ASEAN Regional Forum (ARF) and in 1996 it was granted the status of a dialogue partner of ASEAN.[2]

Despite joining APEC and ARF, Russia, due to domestic turmoil, ceased to be a major factor in the Asia-Pacific during the 1990s. However, since 2000 Russia has managed to substantially improve its internal situation, enabling Moscow to embark on more pro-active policies in Asia, both on the level of bilateral relations and in multilateral settings. In 2003, Russia became one of the co-sponsors of the Six-Party Talks (SPT) on the North Korean nuclear issue. In 2007, Russia became the chair of one of the five working groups created within the SPT framework – the group on Northeast Asia peace and security mechanism – further raising Moscow's enthusiasm about SPT. In 2005, Russia sought membership of the East Asia Summit at its inaugural meeting in Kuala Lumpur, where President Vladimir Putin attended as a special guest. At that moment, the bid failed to gain consensus approval. Yet, in 2010, Russia, along with the United States, finally secured an invitation to join EAS (effective since 2011). In 2010 Russia joined the expanded ASEAN Defense Ministers' Meeting (ADMM-Plus), a platform bringing together defense officials from ASEAN and its eight dialogue partners.[3] The same year Russia was admitted into the Asia-Europe Meeting (ASEM).

Thus, by 2011, Russia secured membership of all the Asia-Pacific principal multilateral political and security bodies – SPT, ARF, ADMM-Plus, EAS and ASEM. Russia viewed its involvement in the Asia-Pacific diplomatic forums as confirmation of its standing as a major Asia-Pacific power.

While Russia attained full representation in the Asia-Pacific political institutions, in the economic arena its presence could be characterized as very modest at best. Russia was one of the very few economies in the Asia-Pacific that had no free trade agreements in the region.[4] APEC remained the only regional economic institution in which Russia had membership. That was one of the motivations for Moscow to invest considerable efforts and resources in hosting APEC events in 2012 when Russia acted as the forum's chair. The APEC summit in Vladivostok, held in September 2012, was a relative success (Martin, 2012). One of the major deliverables of the Vladivostok APEC Leaders' Meeting was an environmental goods and services agreement that called for the tariffs on 54 products, like solar panels, to be reduced to 5 percent or less. In hindsight, the APEC summit in Vladivostok was the high point of Russia's involvement in East Asia/Pacific multilateralism.

After 2012, Russia's interest in East Asian/Pacific multilateral economic institutions started to wane (Gabuev, 2014). Even in APEC, instead of following up on the achievements of the 2012 chairmanship, Russian officials and business leaders significantly scaled down their activities. This was as the result of several confluent developments.

First, in the realm of economic integration, Moscow decided to concentrate efforts on the promotion of the Eurasian Economic Union (EEU), a Russia-centered single market encompassing several former Soviet republics.[5] As Kirill Muradov points out, "having prioritised its own economic bloc within former Soviet borders, Russia drew a dividing line between itself and the emerging Pacific mega-regionals or even individual state members" (Muradov, 2013).

Second, by late 2012, it became obvious that APEC would not be the platform for Asia-Pacific trade liberalization and remain at best an OECD-type regional organization for functional cooperation in some niche areas. Instead, two competing integration projects emerged – the US-led Trans-Pacific Partnership and the Regional Comprehensive Economic Partnership (RCEP) championed by ASEAN and China. Russia was ready to join neither of them: most of its manufacturing industries were (and still are) too uncompetitive to seriously contemplate entering a region-wide FTA with Asia-Pacific economies. Even a "low-quality" FTA, such as RCEP, would be extremely problematic for many sectors of Russia's economy.

Third, a drastic deterioration in Russia's relations with the United States over Ukraine had an inevitable impact on their interaction in the Asia-Pacific. Whereas prior to the Ukraine crisis, Russian-US strategic dialogue and collaboration in the Pacific seemed possible (Japan-Russia-US Trilateral Conference, 2012), after the crisis it was out of the question. With the United States imposing sanctions on Russia, and its Pacific allies – Japan and Australia – following suit, Russia obviously could not hope for their support in the Asia-Pacific multilateral bodies.[6]

Having stalled on multilateral regionalism after 2012, Russia's only achievement in institutionalizing its economic links with the Asia-Pacific was the signing, in May 2015, of a bilateral FTA between the EEU and Vietnam, Russia's first in Asia. With a modest volume of bilateral trade and with many tariff lines exempted from liberalization, the FTA, which came into effect in October 2016, is mostly of symbolic and political value. The negotiations on another pilot FTA, with New Zealand, were frozen by Wellington in 2014 in response to Russia's actions in Crimea and eastern Ukraine.

As for political-security institutions in the Asia-Pacific, Russia has similarly shown a lackluster performance. SPT – the arrangement in which Moscow has a major interest and certain leverage due to the Korean Peninsula's proximity to Russian borders – has been stalled since 2009, mainly because of disagreements between Pyongyang and Washington. EAS, ARF and ADMM-Plus have continued to function, but Russia has mostly kept a low profile in these forums. One indication of Russia's unwillingness to invest much in East Asian institutionalism is Russian presidents' consistent failure to show up at the EAS annual meetings. Ever since Russia was admitted as a full member in 2011, no Russian leader has ever made it to the summit, which is seen as the region's premier security forum,[7] even while Moscow was paying lip service to EAS as the "key element in the construction of the new regional security architecture (Commentary of the Russian Ministry of Foreign Affairs, 2013). Similarly, ADMM-Plus has never been attended by a Russian minister of defense, who sends his deputies instead.

What are the reasons behind Russia's relative passivity within EAS, ARF and ADMM-Plus? For one, all of these bodies are ASEAN-centric and thus focused on Southeast Asia. Unlike Eastern Europe, Central Asia or the Middle East, this is a region remote from Russia, holding relatively little strategic importance for Moscow, and the one where Russia's leverage is limited. Second, EAS, ARF and ADMM-Plus remain toothless and feckless institutions. It is not them but rather the hub-and-spoke system of US alliances that underpins Asia-Pacific security and will continue to do so in the foreseeable future. Moscow has little motivation to invest its diplomatic resources in institutions whose influence is rather symbolic. Finally, in the last few years the South China Sea sovereignty disputes have emerged as one of the top agenda items for the three forums. Without a direct stake in the South China Sea, Moscow is not interested in tackling this issue or in backing any one side in the dispute, especially given the fact that China and Vietnam – the principal antagonists in the South China Sea – are both Russia's strategic partners. If it supported one, it would risk damaging relations with the other. The wisest course of action, then, is to pursue diplomatic neutrality and eschew commitments to any side of the argument. Thus, the lowered level of representation might be the most appropriate.

Despite Moscow's repeated pronouncements about the importance of the relationship with ASEAN, it seems that from the very beginning Russia's involvement in ASEAN-centric political-security forums has been largely determined by prestige considerations – formalizing Russia's status as a great global power and a major Asian player – rather than by the desire to pro-actively shape international politics in Southeast Asia. The third Russia-ASEAN summit hosted by Putin at Sochi in May 2016 was mostly a ritualistic event with few substantive deliverables.[8]

As Russia's interest in Asia-Pacific multilateralism has declined, Moscow is now prioritizing a different set of institutions – the arrangements that are less "Pacific" and much more "Asian," or "Eurasian," centered on the Moscow-Beijing strategic axis.

Russo-Chinese "strategic partnership" as an institutionalized quasi-alliance

China and Russia see their crucial national interests as mutually nonexclusive at the very least. As Dmitry Trenin observes, the Russia-China bond "is solid, for it is based on fundamental national interests regarding the world order as both the Russian and Chinese governments would prefer to see it" (Trenin, 2013: 6). Moscow is not inimical to China's rise as a great power, since this creates for Russia economic and political alternatives other than the West. For its part, China sees its security interests as generally compatible with those of Russia (Li, 2009). This convergence of basic interests constitutes the foundation for a strategic partnership. The existence of a common foe – the United States – may be transforming the partnership into an entente (Trenin, 2015). References to the Russian-Chinese relationship as a "de facto alliance" are increasingly being used by Russia's leading foreign policy experts (see, for example, Karaganov, 2014). A joint report by Russian and Chinese scholars sees "elements of a military-political alliance," albeit not legally binding, emerging between the two countries (Luzyanin et al., 2015a: 6). The report argues that, "if need be, the ties can be converted into an alliance relationship without long preparations" (Luzyanin et al., 2015a: 8).

Characterized by converging strategic interests, shared norms (especially the emphasis on the classic Westphalian sovereignty), extensive network of intergovernmental mechanisms and legal agreements, coordination of foreign, and increasingly economic, policies, the Sino-Russian relationship can be viewed as a bilateral institution of consequence for the global and Asian international order.

Moscow's pursuit of Eurasian continentalism

The Sino-Russian strategic partnership serves as the core for an emerging architecture of multilateral institutions in continental Eurasia.[9]

Shanghai Cooperation Organization

The SCO has been the most important institutional element of Eurasian continentalism. SCO was launched in 2001 and initially included six members – Russia, China, and four Central Asian republics (Kazakhstan, Kyrgyzstan, Tajikistan, and Uzbekistan).[10] SCO can best be defined as a multilateral strategic partnership (Luzyanin et al., 2015b: 9), modeled in many respects on the Sino-Russian strategic partnership, and the one in which Beijing and Moscow play the role of co-leaders. SCO's main areas of activities are regional security (with the emphasis on combating terrorism,[11] extremism, and drug trafficking), economic cooperation, and scientific and cultural exchanges.

So far SCO has mostly acted as a forum for consultation and coordination among Russia, China, and four Central Asian "stans." It has implemented relatively few tangible multilateral projects. For example, SCO has yet to deliver on any substantial economic cooperation. However, SCO's most significant contribution has been in maintaining security and stability in Central Asia. SCO has certainly made it easier for Moscow and Beijing to manage Central Asia in a constructive manner while avoiding direct competition and clashes of interest. SCO has been a stabilizing factor in an inherently unstable region made up of fragile states under the constant threat of the spread of militant Islamism from neighboring Afghanistan and the Middle East.

Alexander Lukin argues that, in addition to using SCO as an instrument of maintaining stability – in collaboration with China – in Central Asia, Moscow has seen it mostly as a political institution embodying Russia's ideological preference for a multi-polar world order and as an alternative to Western-dominated institutions (Lukin, 2015). This vision is in agreement with China's.[12] As a related and more specific objective, both Moscow and Beijing view SCO as a mechanism to limit what they see as the undesirable Western interference in Central Asia.[13]

Since 2001, SCO has developed to go well beyond Sino-Russian co-management of Central Asian security. One crucial indication of the organization's growth is the expansion of its membership from the initial six to eight (with the entry, in June 2017, of India and Pakistan as full members). SCO also has attracted four observer states (Iran, Afghanistan, Belarus, Mongolia) and six dialogue partners (Azerbaijan, Armenia, Cambodia, Nepal, Turkey, Sri Lanka). SCO's obvious appeal lies in its role as the only available institutional platform for multilateral interaction in Central Asia and the surrounding areas of continental Eurasia, especially on security issues.

Conference on Interaction and Confidence Building Measures in Asia (CICA)

This hitherto obscure forum started in the 1990s as a vanity project of Kazakhstani President Nursultan Nazarbayev. At present CICA brings together 26 participants from different parts of Asia and the Middle East, including Russia, India, South Korea, Iran, Pakistan, Turkey, and Egypt. Of note, the United States and its most loyal Asia-Pacific allies – Japan and Australia – are not among CICA's members.

In 2014 China took over the CICA presidency from Turkey and hosted the 4th summit in Shanghai in May 2014. The event became the group's largest ever, gathering 12 heads of state and government and 10 chiefs of international organizations, including the presidents of Russia, Iran, and the United Nations Secretary-General. Beijing's promotion of CICA may be aimed at forming a multilateral security system that covers most countries in Asia, but excludes "external forces," above all the United States and its main ally, Japan (Mu Chunshan, 2014).

Russia has yet to clarify its strategy toward CICA. On the one hand, Russia is a founding member and has been supportive of CICA. On the other, CICA, compared to SCO, is clearly of secondary importance to Moscow.

Russia-India-China (RIC) trilateral

The idea of a tripartite grouping, consisting of Russia, China, and India, was first voiced by Russian prime minister Evgeny Primakov in 1998. His vision of a strategic axis of the three largest powers in Eurasia acting as an effective counterbalance to the US hegemony has never got off the ground due to Sino-Indian rivalry and Delhi's lack of enthusiasm in associating itself with something that looked like an anti-Western coalition. A more modest version of Primakov's proposal was realized in the form of regular trilateral meetings of foreign ministers, the first of which was convened in Russia's Vladivostok in 2005. The latest (as of February 2017) 14th annual meeting of the three countries' foreign ministers, held in Moscow in April 2016, reiterated their common vision for "a more just and democratic multi-polar international system" as well as rejecting "forced regime change from the outside in any country" and emphasizing the "core principles" of respect for state sovereignty and non-interference into internal affairs of other states. Such language is in clear opposition to the Western liberal hegemony ("Joint Communiqué of the 14th Meeting of the Foreign Ministers of the Russian Federation, the Republic of India and the People's Republic of China," 2016). Of course, RIC forms the core of the BRICS grouping – the world's most significant non-Western arrangement.

Russia-Mongolia-China trilateral

Another Eurasian trilateral that has been recently taking shape includes Moscow, Beijing, and Ulan Bator. To some extent, Mongolia is being incorporated into the Sino-Russian entente. This was evidenced by the near-simultaneous visits by Xi and Putin to Ulan Bator (the Chinese leader came on August 21–22, 2014; Putin visited on September 5), followed by the first trilateral summit among China, Mongolia, and Russia held in Dushanbe on September 11, 2014 on the sidelines of the SCO meeting. The three presidents enunciated the vision of a "China-Mongolia-Russia economic corridor" (Campi, 2014). Annual trilateral summits were continued in 2015 and 2016, supported by the mechanism of regular meetings at vice-ministerial level. That said, Ulan Bator, politely deflecting Moscow's advice, is still in no hurry to join SCO as a full member and sticks with its "third neighbor" policy that seeks to hedge its dependence on China and Russia by maintaining active relations with the West, Japan, and India.

Russia and Chinese economic initiatives in Eurasia

The economic foundation of Eurasian continentalism is being formed by China-led multilateral projects, such as the Silk Road Economic Belt (SREB) and the Asian Infrastructure Investment Bank (AIIB). Collectively, they add up to a grand plan of creating a single – Sino-centric – economic space in Eurasia ("Vision and Actions on Jointly Building Silk Road Economic Belt and 21st-Century Maritime Silk Road," 2015). Russia was initially wary of these Chinese initiatives, fearing that they would compete with its own project of Eurasian Economic Union (EEU) that seeks to (re)integrate the post-Soviet space under Moscow's aegis. However, the conflict with the West and the deteriorating condition of Russia's economy has left Moscow with little choice other than bandwagoning with China's Eurasian schemes. In late March 2015, Russia joined AIIB, becoming the third largest AIIB shareholder after China and India ("Graphics: AIIB Voting Stakes," 2015). In May 2015, Putin and Xi agreed to coordinate their flagship economic initiatives in Central Asia – Russian-led EEU and China's SREB. In their joint declaration, the parties pledged "to make coordinated efforts toward the integration of constructing EEU and SREB," with SCO serving as the main platform for linking up the two Eurasian initiatives. The document also mentioned "a long-term goal of progressing toward a free trade zone between EEU and China" ("Joint Declaration by the Russian Federation and the People's Republic of China on the Coordination of the Construction of the Eurasian Economic Union and the Silk Road Economic Belt," 2015).

In June 2016, speaking at the St Petersburg International Economic Forum, Putin called for the formation of a "major Eurasian partnership" that would encompass EEU and other states in continental Eurasia, such as China, India, Iran, and Pakistan. Putin also announced the start of EEU-China negotiations on a comprehensive economic cooperation agreement, highlighting the central role Beijing is destined to play in Moscow's project of "Greater Eurasia" (Putin, 2016). However, the EEU-China economic partnership talks that were formally launched during Putin's visit to Beijing in late June 2016 are focused on trade and investment facilitation measures, not a full-fledged FTA. Russian officials recognize that the EEU member states "are not yet in a position for a deep market opening" with China (Fedorov, 2016). In addition, the glaring incompatibility in regulations, such as technical, veterinary, and phytosanitary standards, is a major barrier to be overcome if EEU and China are to achieve any meaningful level of economic integration (Fedorov, 2016). Even in its current bilateral format – between the Russian-led EEU and China – the Eurasian partnership negotiations are going to be a difficult and drawn-out process, let alone if this undertaking is to be subsequently joined by other proposed participants, such as India or ASEAN countries.

Composing a concert for Eurasia?

As always, Moscow's main game is political rather than economic. The Kremlin cannot but understand that in the trade and finance realm Russia's position in Eurasia is much weaker than that of China and probably even India. Russia's crucial strengths traditionally lie in the political-military and diplomatic domain. Hence Moscow strives for the role of the chief architect of a Eurasian political order that would reflect its own preferences and chime with the basic interests of the continent's major powers.

The kind of political order that Russia envisions for Eurasia is essentially one of a concert of powers – a model that puts a premium on relations among a few major powers.[14] These are Russia itself, China, and India, plus – with some qualifications – Pakistan and Iran. Accounting for the bulk of continental Eurasia's population, landmass, and military potential, the five big players could collectively manage security and economic affairs of the mega-region. Their collective governance would be based on, and legitimized by, a set of institutions, especially the Sino-Russian strategic partnership and SCO.

Russia aspires to be the main security and diplomatic broker in a concert of Eurasia, while leaving China with the role of the economic leader. This division of labor is already emerging in Central Asia, where, as Alexander Gabuev put it, "China would be the bank and Russia would be the big gun" (Standish, 2015). Such an arrangement might resemble the initial stages of the European Community when France acted as the political leader while West Germany was the economic engine.

Moscow's preference for a new Eurasian order is reflected in its diplomatic activism such as its leading role in securing Indian and Pakistani admission into SCO and advocacy for Iran's future membership. Moscow's interest in their participation in SCO partly stems from the desire to hedge against the rising influence of China. For all the friendship with China, Moscow is keen to prevent Beijing's domination of continental Eurasia. In this vein, when it comes to the game of institutions, instead of whole-heartedly subscribing to China's One Belt, One Road (OBOR) scheme, Moscow promotes its own vision of "a larger Eurasian partnership," or "Greater Eurasia," which is presented as a network of existing and emerging "integration formats" including EEU, OBOR, SCO, ASEAN, and potentially even the EU (Putin 2017).

Construction of a new security architecture for the Asia-Pacific: building a counter-narrative to US hegemony

Even though Russia has recently shifted its primary attention to institution-building in continental Eurasia, Moscow does have its own vision for an international order in East Asia and the Asia-Pacific, which it is promoting in the region's diplomatic forums. Such an order would be a "transparent, open, comprehensive, equal and indivisible security architecture, based on the primacy of international law, mutual trust, peaceful settlement of disputes, non-use of force." Moscow sees the East Asia Summit (EAS) as "the key element" in constructing the proposed security architecture (Russia's Ministry of Foreign Affairs, 2016). The crux of the Russia-proposed institutional architecture for the Asia-Pacific lies in its critique of "closed and semi-closed" security mechanisms, a thinly veiled reference to US-centric alliances and partnerships. These should be superseded by an "umbrella structure that must bring together all the Asia-Pacific states without exception, assuming the task of developing uniform rules of behavior for all participants on a non-bloc basis" ("Russian Foreign Minister S. Lavrov's remarks," 2016).

Pursuing this vision, in 2013 Russia initiated a series of consultations among the EAS members in order to "promote multilateral dialogue on the formation of the regional security architecture" (Russia's Ministry of Foreign Affairs, 2016). Moscow's initiative was supported by Beijing. As of February 2017, five rounds of consultations, in the format of workshops, have been held, hosted by Brunei (November 2013), Russia (April 2014), Indonesia (October 2014), Cambodia (July 2015; co-organized with India), and China (June 2016, co-organized with Laos). The 2017 host is Thailand.

That China backs Russia's pitch for a "new security architecture" is unsurprising. In 2010, Dmitry Medvedev and Hu Jintao issued a joint statement in which they came up with an "initiative to strengthen security in the Asia-Pacific." The 2010 initiative uses almost the same wording as found in the subsequent Russian proposals. In particular, the Sino-Russian statement called for "the creation in the Asia-Pacific region of an open, transparent and equal architecture of security and cooperation, based on the principles of international law, non-bloc approaches and respect for legitimate interests of all parties." It also emphasized that "it is important that all the states of the region renounce confrontation and do not cooperate against the third countries" ("Joint Statement of the Russian Federation and the People's Republic of China on comprehensive deepening of Sino-Russian relations of partnership and strategic interaction," 2010). The origins of this narrative can be traced to the second half of the 1990s when Sino-Russian strategic rapprochement was beginning to take shape. In the Russia-China Joint Declaration on a Multipolar World and Formation of a New International Order (1997), Boris Yeltsin and Jiang Zemin took a stand against "bloc politics" and "hegemony," calling for a "new comprehensive concept of security."

However, it would be incorrect to explain Moscow's security architecture initiative exclusively by the Sino-Russian strategic axis. In fact, Russia's proposals for the Asia-Pacific mirror its push for the European Security Treaty. The draft treaty, proposed in 2009 by the then Russian President Dmitry Medvedev, called for an "indivisible and equal security" in the Euro-Atlantic space. The core of the draft was the idea that the parties to the treaty must refrain from taking steps that could "significantly affect" the security of other participants. Moscow's proposal made very little progress, as it met with a cool response from most of the NATO and EU members, who interpreted the draft treaty as Russia's desire to gain a veto power over the matters of Euro-Atlantic security, such as admitting new countries to NATO.

Interestingly, the key reference to "indivisible security" found in Russia's proposals both for the Asia-Pacific and Europe is a flashback to the Soviet Foreign Minister Maxim Litvinov's famous dictum in the 1930s that "peace is indivisible." Now, as in the 1930s, the emphasis on indivisible security and opposition to political-military blocs reflects Moscow's sense of vulnerability and fear of isolation. In the 1930s, the Soviet Union was fearful that the Western powers would leave it on its own to face the Nazi aggression. Nowadays Moscow is struggling with the notion that it has to live with the powerful – and expanding – NATO alliance on its borders that marginalizes, and potentially threatens, Russia.

Russia's opposition to US-led alliances in the Asia-Pacific has never been as intense as its hostility to NATO's enlargement in Europe, because East Asia is largely not considered so vital for Russian security. Still, Moscow would prefer to have Washington's alliance system in the Asia-Pacific greatly diminished. The reasoning is simple: US alliances are indispensable for maintaining US global hegemony; hence the weakening of its alliances in a region as crucial as the Asia-Pacific would contribute to Moscow's professed goal of a multi-polar world free of the single superpower hegemony.

Moscow is under no illusion that its advocacy of a non-bloc security order for the Asia-Pacific is able to undermine the preponderance of US-centric alliances any time soon. Even in Europe, where Russia has a much bigger influence, the Kremlin's efforts to create a viable region-wide alternative to NATO as the main guarantor of security have so far failed. Rather, the primary goal of Russia's political campaign in the Asia-Pacific is a long-term one and involves building a narrative that counters the currently dominant discourse of US alliances as the cornerstone of the Asia-Pacific's stability and prosperity that "have underwritten regional peace and security" since the end of the World War II and must continue to do so (Clinton, 2011). This essentially constructivist effort to shape the ideational environment may bear fruit if and when strategic material conditions in the region change in the right direction. The rise in China's material capabilities and the resulting shifts in the balance of power in East Asia may give Moscow some grounds for optimism in this respect. Some US alliances in the region are showing visible cracks, with some of the junior allies and partners drifting away from Washington to Beijing (Thailand, Malaysia) or hedging their bets trying to maneuver between China and the United States (South Korea, the Philippines). At some point, the accumulated effects of the shifting power and loyalties, backed by an alternative security order discourse, could lead to significant transformations in the region's political landscape, possibly the emergence of new institutions replacing the current dominance of the US hub-and-spoke system.

It would be wrong to assume that Russia's pursuit of a new security architecture for the Asia-Pacific is motivated exclusively by its hostility to US hegemony. In fact, Russia is opposed to *any* hegemony, be it the United States' or China's. Like in Eurasia, Moscow's preferred vision for the Asia-Pacific is one of a concert of great powers, with Russia being a key participant. Other great powers in the Asia-Pacific Concert could include China, the United States, India, Japan, and potentially Indonesia and a unified Korea. Consolidated ASEAN, as a collective strategic actor, is essential for such a multi-polar order. In Russia's view, a strong ASEAN, capable of acting as one cohesive pole, can serve as a powerful counterweight to both US and Chinese attempts at hegemony in the Asia-Pacific, even though the China-hedging component of this vision is being kept implicit, for now.

Conclusion

The story of Russia's engagement with Asian and Pacific institutions can mostly be told in realist terms. Moscow has viewed regional bodies as instruments to promote national interests, secure Russia a seat at the decision-making table, or at least affirm Russia's status as a great Asia-Pacific power. In the same realist vein, Russia's main emphasis has been on institutions with a political-security agenda, while its participation in regional economic arrangements, such as FTAs, has been minimal.

While realism undoubtedly remains the main foundation of Moscow's strategic thinking, some constructivist elements have lately begun to feature more prominently, impacting Russia's approaches to Asian and Pacific institutions. This is noticeable in Russia's efforts to design and promote the vision of Eurasian continentalism, or "Greater Eurasia," which is institutionally based on the Moscow-Beijing strategic axis, SCO, and, implicitly, concert-of-power arrangements. To a significant extent, "Greater Eurasia" is being constructed as the antithesis to the Western-dominated liberal world order.

For all Moscow's infatuation with "Greater Eurasia," there are formidable difficulties involved in constructing the new order – from inherent fragility of many of its putative members to fraught relations between some of them. There is also a risk that, even if a concert of Eurasia takes shape, Russia may be overshadowed by its more powerful players such as China and later possibly India.

Even though Russia's interest in the Pacific dimension of the Asia-Pacific institutional architecture has since noticeably declined, having reached its high point at the Vladivostok APEC summit in 2012, Moscow still continues to have a stake in institutions that center on East Asia and the Pacific. Similar to continental Eurasia, Russia's vision for the Asia-Pacific order is essentially that of a concert of powers. To construct such an order, the entrenched structures of US hegemony in the Pacific need to be undone first. This is why Moscow is tirelessly promoting the narrative of a security architecture that should be "open, transparent, equal, non-bloc."

The Kremlin is well aware that its leverage in the vast East Asian/Pacific space is quite limited. Russia's geopolitical influence and vital interests are mostly concentrated in Northeast Asia/North Pacific, where Russia shares borders with China, Korea, Japan, and the United States. Significantly, Northeast Asia is characterized by an "organization gap" (Calder and Min Ye, 2010), essentially lacking regional institutions. Moscow has been actively advocating for the SPT, whose initial aim was to deal with the North Korea nuclear problem, to become the basis for a future multilateral mechanism in charge of political and security cooperation in Northeast Asia ("Remarks on the Developments on the Korean Peninsula and the Prospects for Re-launching of the Six-Party Talks," 2011). Moscow sees SPT as a concert-like arrangement that would help legitimize and solidify Russia's role as a key stakeholder in the region. The rising intensity of security problems in Northeast Asia, particularly those related to the Korean Peninsula, can make the idea of a Northeast Asian political-security institution even more relevant, providing Russia with an opportunity to realize its preferred institutional designs, at least in this part of the Asia-Pacific.

Notes

1 This chapter draws extensively upon the previously published chapter by Artyom Lukin ("Russia's institutional engagement with the Asia-Pacific: getting more Asian and less Pacific." In *Regional Institutions, Geopolitics and Economics in the Asia Pacific: Evolving interests and strategies*. Edited by Steven B. Rothman, Utpal Vyas, and Yoichiro Sato. Routledge, 2017).
2 That was upgraded from the status of a "consultative partner" of ASEAN that Moscow received in 1991.
3 The membership of ADMM-Plus exactly corresponds to EAS.
4 This was compounded by Russia's non-participation in WTO. Russian accession to WTO was not approved until December 2011.
5 As of February 2017, EEU includes Russia, Belarus, Kazakhstan, Armenia and Kyrgyzstan.
6 One of the casualties of the Ukraine crisis is Russia's prospective membership in the Asian Development Bank (ADB). Long before its present standoff with the West, Moscow applied to join ADB but was denied entry by Japan and the United States, the countries wielding the greatest decision-making power in the multilateral financial institution. Still there remained hope that sooner or later Russia would be admitted. The fallout from the Ukraine mess foreclosed this possibility.
7 In 2011–13, Russia was represented in EAS summit meetings by Foreign Minister Sergey Lavrov, while in 2014, 2015 and 2016 Prime Minister Dmitri Medvedev attended the summits. Incidentally, China's highest representative to EAS has always been the premier (number two) rather than the president (number one). It is telling that Moscow eventually followed Beijing's example in setting its own level of EAS representation.
8 The previous two summits took place in 2005 in Kuala Lumpur and in 2010 in Hanoi.
9 By "continental Eurasia" I mean the area more or less corresponding to Russia, Central Asia, China, Mongolia, South Asia, Afghanistan and Iran.
10 SCO's precursor had been "The Shanghai Five" (Russia, China, Kazakhstan, Kyrgyzstan and Tajikistan) who, in 1996 and 1997, signed two multilateral agreements on confidence building measures and troops reductions in their adjacent border areas.
11 SCO has a dedicated counter-terror arm, Regional Anti-Terror Structure, based in Tashkent, Uzbekistan.
12 That said, Beijing would like to enhance an economic integration component in SCO's activities, something that Moscow until recently was reluctant to do due to fears of losing Central Asia economically to China.
13 For example, in 2005 Russia and China initiated an SCO collective decision to call on the United States to withdraw its military forces from Central Asia.
14 According to Muthiah Alagappa, concert is joint management of international affairs by great powers on the basis of certain common goals, values and interests (Alagappa, 2003: 55).

References

Alagappa, Muthiah. (2003) "The Study of International Order." In *Asian Security Order*, edited by Muthiah Alagappa, 33–69. Stanford, CA: Stanford University Press.

Calder, Kent, Min Ye (2010) *The Making of Northeast Asia*. Stanford, CA: Stanford University Press.

Campi, Alicia. (2014) "Transforming Mongolia-Russia-China Relations: The Dushanbe Trilateral Summit." *The Asia-Pacific Journal*. November 10, 2014. www.japanfocus.org/-Alicia-Campi/4210/article.html.

Clinton, Hillary. (2011) "America's Pacific Century." *Foreign Policy*, October 11, 2011, http://foreignpolicy.com/2011/10/11/americas-pacific-century/.

"Commentary of the Russian Ministry of Foreign Affairs in connection with Foreign Minister Sergey Lavrov's Participation at the East Asia Summit." (2013) *Russian Ministry of Foreign Affairs*. October 8, 2013. http://mid.ru/bdomp/ns-rasia.nsf/3a0108443c964002432569e7004199c0/44257b100055e10444257bfe0043ae04!OpenDocument.

Fedorov, Gleb. (2016) "Interview with the the Eurasian Economic Union's Minister of Trade Veronika Nikishina." *RBTH*. August 8, 2016. http://rbth.com/business/2016/08/08/russian-automobiles-to-have-free-access-to-asean-via-vietnam-eaeu-minister_619053.

Gabuev, Alexander. (2014) "Russia's Performance in Multilateral Organizations: Pivot to Asia or Just to China?" *Carnegie Moscow Center*, November 6, 2014. http://carnegie.ru/publications/?fa=57144.

"Graphics: AIIB Voting Stakes." (2015) *Caixin Online*. July 3, 2015. http://english.caixin.com/2015-07-03/100825189.html.

"Japan-Russia-US Trilateral Conference on the Security Challenges in Northeast Asia." (2012) Moscow: Institute of World Economy and International Relations. June 16, 2012. http://imemo.ru/en/conf/2012/19062012/19062012_statement_M_EN.pdf.

"Joint Communiqué of the 14th Meeting of the Foreign Ministers of the Russian Federation, the Republic of India and the People's Republic of China." (2016) (Adopted in Moscow, April 18, 2016). *Ministry of External Affairs, Government of India*. http://mea.gov.in/bilateral-documents.htm?dtl/26628/Joint_Communiqu_of_the_14th_Meeting_of_the_Foreign_Ministers_of_the_Russian_Federation_the_Republic_of_India_and_the_Peoples_Republic_of_China.

"Joint Declaration by the Russian Federation and the People's Republic of China on the Coordination of the Construction of the Eurasian Economic Union and the Silk Road Economic Belt." (2015) *President of Russia Official Website*. May 8, 2015. http://kremlin.ru/supplement/4971.

"Joint Statement of the Russian Federation and the People's Republic of China on comprehensive deepening of Sino-Russian relations of partnership and strategic interaction." (2010) September 27, 2010, Beijing, http://kremlin.ru/supplement/719.

Karaganov, Sergey. (2014) "Mezhdunarodny krizis: izbezhat' Afghanistana-2 [International Crisis: avoiding a Second Afghanistan]." *Vedomosti*. July 28, 2014. www.vedomosti.ru/opinion/news/29501801/izbezhat-afganistana-2.

Li, Rex. (2009) *A Rising China and Security in East Asia*. New York: Routledge.

Lukin, Alexander. (2015) "Shanghaiskaya Organizatsiya Sotrudnichestva: v poiskah novoy roli [Shanghai Cooperation Organization: in search of a new role]." *Russia in Global Affairs*. July 9, 2015. www.globalaffairs.ru/valday/Shankhaiskaya-organizatciya-sotrudnichestva-v-poiskakh-novoi-roli-17573.

Luzyanin, Sergey et al. (2015a) *Rossiysko-Kitayskiy Dialog: model' 2015* [Russia-China Dialogue: 2015 Model]. Moscow: Russian International Affairs Council. http://russiancouncil.ru/inner/?id_4=5614#top-content.

Luzyanin, Sergey et al. (2015b) *Shanghaiskaya Organizatsiya Sotrudnichestva: model 2014–2015* [Shanghai Cooperation Organization: the model for 2014–2015]. Moscow: Russian International Affairs Council. http://russiancouncil.ru/paper21#top-content.

Martin, Michael F. (2012) *The Asia-Pacific Economic Cooperation (APEC) Meetings in Vladivostok, Russia: Postscript*. Washington, DC: Congressional Research Service. November 19, 2012.

Mu Chunshan. (2014) "What is CICA (and Why Does China Care About It)?" *The Diplomat*. May 17, 2014. http://thediplomat.com/2014/05/what-is-cica-and-why-does-china-care-about-it/.

Muradov, Kirill. (2013) "Russia's Pivot to Eurasia and the Battle for Ukraine." *East Asia Forum*. September 17, 2013. www.eastasiaforum.org/2013/09/17/russias-pivot-to-eurasia-and-the-battle-for-ukraine/.

Putin, Vladimir. (2016) "Transcript of the Speech at the Plenary session of St Petersburg International Economic Forum." *President of Russia Official Website*. June 17, 2016. http://en.kremlin.ru/events/president/news/52178.

Putin, Vladimir. (2017) "Speech at the One Belt, One Road International Forum." *President of Russia Official Website*. May 14, 2017. http://en.kremlin.ru/events/president/news/54491. Plenary session of St Petersburg International Economic Forum

"Remarks on the Developments on the Korean Peninsula and the Prospects for Re-launching of the Six-Party Talks." (2011) *Russian Ministry of Foreign Affairs*. February 4, 2011. www.mid.ru/bdomp/ns-rasia.nsf/3a0108443c964002432569e7004199c0/432569d80021985fc325782d0057a361!OpenDocument.

Russia's Ministry of Foreign Affairs. (2016) "Commentary in connection with the participation of Foreign Minister S. Lavrov in Russia-ASEAN, East Asia Summit and ASEAN Regional Forum meetings." July 23, 2016, www.mid.ru/regional-nyj-forum-asean-po-bezopasnosti-arf-/-/asset_publisher/0vP3hQoCPRg5/content/id/2366848.

"Russia-China Joint Declaration on a Multipolar World and Formation of a New International Order." (1997) (Adopted in Moscow, April 23, 1997). *Zakony Rossii*. Accessed August 31, 2016. www.lawrussia.ru/texts/legal_743/doc743a830x878.htm.

"Russian Foreign Minister S. Lavrov's remarks." (2016) Vientiane, Laos, July 26, 2016, www.mid.ru/ru/foreign_policy/news/-/asset_publisher/cKNonkJE02Bw/content/id/2370655.

Sneider, Daniel. (1988) "Soviets Hanker for Piece of Economic Action in the Pacific." *The Christian Science Monitor*. May 24, 1988. www.csmonitor.com/1988/0524/opac.html.

Standish, Reid. (2015) "China and Russia Lay Foundation for Massive Economic Cooperation." *Foreign Policy*. July 10, 2015. http://foreignpolicy.com/2015/07/10/china-russia-sco-ufa-summit-putin-xi-jinping-eurasian-union-silk-road/.

Trenin, Dmitri. (2013) *Russia and the Rise of Asia*. Moscow: Carnegie Moscow Center, November 2013.

Trenin, Dmitri. (2015) "From Greater Europe to Greater Asia: The Sino-Russian Entente." *Carnegie Moscow Center*. April 9, 2015. http://carnegie.ru/publications/?fa=59728.

"Vision and Actions on Jointly Building Silk Road Economic Belt and 21st-Century Maritime Silk Road." (2015) *National Development and Reform Commission (People's Republic of China)*. March 28, 2015. http://en.ndrc.gov.cn/newsrelease/201503/t20150330_669367.html.

26
THE SHANGHAI COOPERATION ORGANIZATION

Maria Raquel Freire[1]

UNIVERSITY OF COIMBRA, PORTUGAL

Introduction

This chapter looks at the Shanghai Cooperation Organization (SCO) and what has been Russia's role within and towards it. Centered around the idea of multilateralism sustained on the principles of sovereignty, territorial integrity, and mutual non-interference (Hantke, 2016), the 'Shanghai Spirit' became the cornerstone to the SCO's functioning, together with consensus decision-making and the politically binding character of decisions. The 'Shanghai Spirit' underlines a non-western approach to cooperation reinforcing its distinctive character in Eurasia. Russia's relative economic weakness has made the Kremlin initiatives to focus on the objectives of stability and security, whereas the Chinese agenda is more ideologically driven (Danilovich, 2013: 20).

The development of the SCO shows two interlinked trends, as argued here. Russia's positioning within the SCO is motivated mainly by considerations of regional stability, with a strong emphasis on the security agenda. However, Russia is only partially successful in advancing its stability-driven agenda given China's growing economic weight and preferences. In fact, Russia's enlargement policy, which has been part of the strategy to counter China, has revealed serious limitations. The chapter begins by mapping the literature on the SCO and Russia, identifying main approaches and issues, analyzing the role of Russia within SCO, as well as its expectations and limitations, and concludes by suggesting avenues for future research.

Mapping SCO-Russia relations

The literature available on the SCO generally touches upon Russia, as they are one of the big players within the SCO together with China, the latter often being described as the leading member state. Most of the works available take on a systemic or actor-oriented approach, though the works are not usually theoretically oriented. Geopolitics, regional security and integration, and the promotion of non(anti)-western values and norms, are the main axis around which the study of SCO-Russia relations has been organized.

Geopolitics are an overarching theme in approaching SCO-Russia relations. Several authors mention the balancing act against the west, in particular NATO enlargement and US involvement in Central Asia as a major drive. Some have labeled the organization as the "NATO of the East" (Stakelbeck, 2005) or "Eastern NATO" (Felgenhauer, 2011), whereas others have referred to it as having the potential to be a "counterrevolutionary alliance" (Silitski, 2010: 349), having an "anti-foreign influence" (Song, 2014: 86) or refusing US unilateralism (Eisenbaum, 2011: 152). However, as some underline, this does not mean 'against' the west, but instead constitutes an 'alternative' to western hegemony in international dynamics (Ambrosio, 2017: 133). Russia has itself voiced that the SCO is not developing in opposition to the west or as a rival to NATO (Hansen, 2008: 7; Lukin, 2015). Despite often being compared to NATO, some authors argue this comparison is not easy as "the SCO is described by both China and Russia as a partnership instead of alliance" (Economy and Piekos, 2015).

In this regard, some authors highlight the benefits arising from the composition of the SCO as allowing it to "streamlin[e] the emergence and development of Greater Eurasia" (Yefremenko, 2017). This has been the Russian approach. Russia has been promoting the idea of an "arc of stability in the north of Eurasia", which clearly contrasts with the "arc of instability along the SCO's southern rim – from the eastern Mediterranean through Iraq and Afghanistan to Pakistan and northern India" (Troitskiy, 2007: 44). This is most relevant in terms of stability promotion in the region, and understood by Moscow as the result of US "flawed policies of interven[tion]", such as in Iraq and Afghanistan (Troitskiy, 2007: 44). Russian Foreign Minister Lavrov commented on the "added prominence and appeal" (PressTV, 2017) of the SCO and its role in the new "polycentric world order" (Economy and Piekos, 2015). Lavrov further added that "Russia is not fighting against someone but for the resolution of all issues in an equal and mutually respectful manner" (Lavrov, 2016).

On a different tone, there are authors that highlight the limited reading coming out of this exclusionary approach being very much centered in advancing the SCO as a counter-weight exercise to the west or NATO. These works focus on the possibilities and limits of regional integration, looking at the need for an institutionalized forum to deal with matters of common concern, and the build-up of relations among the SCO's members, particularly China and Russia (Aris, 2009; Bordachev, 2016). Some authors talk about "shared hegemony" (Villalobos, 2012) and the benefits arising particularly for the biggest powers – China and Russia – from further integration in this format (Alvarez, 2009: 311). Others point to the convergence of views on the peaceful development of the Central Asian space (Vorobyov, 2012). Internal balancing between Russia and China is put forward as an element to be considered, and that might be parallel to the western counter-weight argument (Freire and Mendes, 2009). Others also point to the containing exercise of China and Russia by the other SCO members (see Song, 2014: 86).

On the normative debate, as Ambrosio (2017: 132) notes, in all SCO documents the only mention of 'democracy' pertains to the members' willingness to promote "a more democratic international order". However, this does not mean democratic order in the western liberal sense, but instead the normative shared understanding of equality in the international system as requiring a less hegemonic and unbalanced system. So, it refers to "a set of rules by which no state has the right to impose its interests and values on any other" (Cooley, 2015). This is pursued through the promotion of "development paths" that follow different avenues from the democratic ones – Ambrosio (2008), again highlighting the non-democratic nature of the regimes and how stabilization becomes in this context a key concept in cooperation as a way to avert any attempts at regime change. The recent addition of India to the Group, however, changes this regime approach. According to a Russian view, this enlargement shows that the SCO can "hardly [be] portrayed as a 'dictator's union'" (Lukin, 2015). In this same line, the 'colorful revolutions' in the post-Soviet space have been studied as part of externally induced processes for regime change, with the involvement of western powers, and particularly the US (Silitski, 2010). However, the idea moving Russian and Chinese policies is not that of "transforming" the states in Central Asia, but instead "stabilizing" the political regimes in these countries (Bordachev, 2016). When asked if the SCO was turning "anti-orange", Russian Foreign

Minister Lavrov answered that the organization was dedicated to political non-interference and the socio-economic development of the region (Lanteigne, 2007: 618).

The following section looks at the evolving agenda of the SCO and how Russia has been both an agenda-promoter and at times an obstacle to integration. It also links Russia's options within and towards the SCO with the broader Russian foreign policy agenda, particularly in the context where after the crisis in Ukraine relations with the west are still strained, and the 'Asia pivot' discourse has gained increased prominence.

Agenda-setting and -contesting: SCO's evolution and Russian politics

The institutional development of the SCO has been steady, and Russia has been a firm advocate of political consolidation.[2] The institutionalization of procedural rules such as decision-making by consensus, "informality" and the pursuit of "open regionalism" attest to the goals of "inclusiveness and nondiscrimination" (Lanteigne, 2007: 610). One of the first goals of the SCO as explicit in its Charter (SCO Charter, 2002) is to "maintain peace and strengthen security and confidence in the region", and this principle is enshrined in SCO documents, declarations and statements. This also points to the establishment of a formal structure where Russia and China might pursue collaboration instead of competition (Ambrosio, 2017: 131). Moreover, SCO documents make explicit reference to the UN principles as the overarching rules to be followed, particularly those on non-intervention and respect for the territorial integrity of states. This means the conservative trend in terms of the non-interference and sovereignty principles goes hand-in-hand with the radical trend of countering western hegemony in the international system.

Also, the "transformation into a political bloc" (Shibutov, 2016) includes the accession of new members, as well as the status of observer states and dialogue partners.[3] However, this was a process that took a long time to be defined, with the mechanism to formalize accession requests agreed only in 2010. The Regulations on the Admission of New Members (SCO Admission Procedures, 2010) included as criteria belonging to the Eurasian region, having diplomatic relations with all member states, having the status of observer or dialogue partner, maintaining active cooperation in all fundamental areas of actuation of the Organization, having no armed conflict with other states or committing to security principles not in line with the SCO ones, observing UN principles, and having no sanctions imposed by the UN Security Council. This last criterion was clearly directed at Iran, who has been seeking membership for a long time.

Iran submitted its application for membership in 2008, but the UN sanctions blocked any discussion about its eventual integration for many years. Russia has been supportive of Iran's application whereas China has been more cautious. In April 2017 Lavrov stated, "We hope that during their June summit in Astana, the heads of our states will be able to discuss the possibility of launching the procedure for admitting Iran into the organization as a full member" (RT News, 2017). But the SCO leaders were only able to agree on a declaration of support on the implementation of the "Joint Comprehensive Plan of Action to resolve the issue of the Iranian nuclear programme between the Islamic Republic of Iran and six international mediators plus the European Union" (SCO Press Release, 2017). Tajikistan was the main opponent to the Iranian bid after Teheran invited the leader of the banned Tajik Islamic Revival Party to attend a conference in 2015 (IFP, 2017). There are several issues on Teheran's motivation list to join the SCO, namely the understanding of the SCO as a counter-weight to the US, the fact that among Islamic countries it might raise its status, and the economic opportunities, particularly in energy terms this membership offers (Song, 2014: 99). Also, it is understood in

Moscow that "Iran blocks the western border of Afghanistan, and therefore it could become an outpost of the organization on the border with the militant groupings of ISIS" (Ibragimova, 2016), reinforcing the security agenda the SCO promotes.

In 2011, one year after the admission procedures were agreed, the SCO adopted a memorandum that concluded the procedures for membership request. Russia was one of the most active members in assuring all formalities for membership application were regulated. According to Lukin (2017, 2011) it was after Iran's membership request denial that this more proactive approach was developed. Moscow proposed the establishment of an experts' group to consider matters related to membership expansion to be discussed at the 2008 Summit, and it was this group that drafted the accession documents. This proactive approach shows Russia's commitment to reinforcing SCO's membership. In 2010, then President Medvedev was clear when he stated the relevance of enlargement as a way for the SCO to avoid becoming an "elite club" (Ferghana News Agency, 2011). Russia's understanding that the integration of a country like India would bring more balance to the growing economic weight of China was well-known. The policy of enlargement has been favored by Russia to respond to the "increasing gap between Russia and China's position in the world" (Davis, 2015) by bringing more countries to the table and in this way diluting China's influence (Davis, 2015). Moreover, expanding the group brings more room for balancing and diversification, especially for the Central Asia states. This might play favorably in terms of reinforcing multilateral dealings in parallel with the bilateral dynamics that have always been present in the region (see Hantke, 2016). It might also reveal limits by turning the SCO into a 'talk shop' with limited room for agreement (Gabuev, 2017).

According to Russian sources, "the advantages of accepting new members outweigh the drawbacks", and President Putin added that the inclusion of India and Pakistan marked the "beginning of a new chapter" (Maverick, 2015). These two new members will turn the SCO into a "much more powerful and influential international organization . . . represent[ing] a major portion of the non-Western world" (Lukin, 2015). Russian Deputy Foreign Minister Igor Morgulov commented that the inclusion of India and Pakistan "will improve the six-member grouping's economic and defense potential" (Financial Express, 2017). In fact, a free trade area "that involves China and India, let alone Russia, Pakistan and others is going to be of huge significance. It also absolutely determines where the bulk of China's Overseas Direct Investment is going to be heading – to Eurasia" (Romanova and Devonshire-Ellis, 2016). However, the Chinese 'go-it-alone' policy in financial terms has clear implications in this reading, as further analyzed later.

Despite Russian commitment to the enlargement policy, in Russian official documents the SCO does not get as much space as other regional organizations, such as the Collective Security Treaty Organization (CSTO), which is the preferred arrangement for military-security cooperation, and the Eurasian Economic Union (EAEU) which Moscow has been promoting as the economic driver of integration in the post-Soviet space. Nevertheless, the SCO has been gaining relevance in Russian official documents, in line with the changes in policy Russia had to operate in order to accommodate the growing power of China, as further analyzed in the next section. The 2000 Russian Foreign Policy Concept (Russian FPC, 2000) refers to the 'Shanghai Five' as a group created with active involvement from Russia. In 2008 when the new foreign policy concept was adopted, the SCO had already been established for a few years, but the mention it gets is brief and quite broad: "Further strengthening of the SCO, promoting its initiative for setting up a network of partner ties among all the integration associations in the Asia-Pacific Region occup[ies] a special place" (Russian FPC, 2008). The 2013 Foreign Policy Concept frames the SCO differently. It refers to the SCO as part of Russia's strategy of participation in different organizations for global development, along with the G20, the BRICS and others. The document recognizes the role of the SCO as one of "constructive influence on the situation in the region", committing to enhancing the SCO's regional role (Russian FPC, 2013: §77), including in relation to Afghanistan. The last foreign policy concept, from 2016, is clearly more inclusive, bringing together the partnership dimension that the security concepts highlight (Russian NSS 2020, 2009: §15; Russian NSS 2015), with the multilateral frameworks emphasized in the foreign policy documents. The document highlights Russia's goal to "strengthen SCO's role in regional and global affairs and expanding its membership", promoting trust and partnership and further cooperation among all states, independent of their status within the SCO (Russian FPC, 2016: §79). It also underlines the equal nature of cooperation and integration in the Asia-Pacific and Eurasian contexts (Russian FPC, 2016: §82) signaling discomfort with the big player that China has become in these contexts.

The reading of Russia's policy documents provides a brief mapping of how its relations with the SCO have been evolving. Clearly there has been an increased interest with the institutionalization process, including the SCO's enlargement. According to Moscow, the latter embodies the projection of the SCO's potential, particularly in security and economic terms, whilst assuring a more balanced membership. However, and despite this increase in interest, the rationale that has been present from early on of containing China and playing a counter-weight role to the west remains unchanged. Russia's effectiveness has thus been mixed, having managed to push forward the security agenda within limits, whereas failing in its attempts at containing China's rise.

The SCO agenda: a 'cart with two wheels'

The main issue on the agenda from the early days of the SCO has been security, with the very initial concern about settling border issues aligning with the non-traditional security agenda that has evolved. After the Andijan events in 2005 in Uzbekistan, the SCO quickly moved forward the anti-terrorist agenda and the non-interference principle, responding to what was understood as US involvement. Uzbekistan became a member of the SCO after these events, further underlining the relevance of regime stability and of the role attributed to the SCO in these political and security matters. The 'three evils' became a cornerstone of SCO's actuation, giving teeth to the Convention on Combating Terrorism, Separatism and Extremism (2001), later reinforced by the Convention on Counter-Terrorism (2009) and the Convention on Countering Extremism (2017) (see Julien, 2016: 10; SCO Press Release, 2017). Despite not having enforcement mechanisms, the SCO established formal instruments that have promoted cooperation in this area, and according to reports prevented hundreds of potential terrorist attacks. The creation of the Regional Anti-Terrorist Structure (RATS) in 2004 to coordinate information-sharing and promote confidence-building measures in the combat against the 'three evils' attests to the relevance of this dimension.

Russia has prioritized from day one this security-oriented agenda, in a context where US deep involvement in the region is not welcomed, and NATO maintains its enlargement strategy, regarded for long as a 'containment' strategy of an aggressive nature. Moreover, the fight against terrorism is in line with UN activities, with Russia promoting the role of the SCO as a multilateral forum contributing to international security (Facon, 2006: 29). In general, Moscow has been successful in pushing forward the security agenda, but has suffered a backlash with the SCO decision not to support its actions in Georgia in 2008. The wording of the Declaration is clear when urging the parties "to resolve the existing problems peacefully", including references to the territorial integrity principle and the condemnation of separatism, but not endorsing Russian actions in Abkhazia and South Ossetia (Antonenko, 2008;

Saivetz, 2012: 405). The same applies to Crimea, with no recognition of the territory as Russian by any of the SCO states. These interventionist moves from Russia challenged the 'Shanghai spirit' and the sovereignty-first principle, resulting in a mixed record for Russia as expressed in the lack of explicit support for its moves.

China also values the security dimension – this is clearly a shared issue among all SCO members – but it has been pushing for a bigger role of the economic agenda given the composition and regional span of the members and the potential the SCO offers as a market and as an energy hub – production, transit and supply. Moreover, China sees in the SCO a way to enter an area where Moscow has been the main power through a multilateral format. China positioned itself to promote the idea of an economically integrated project through the establishment of a "free trade zone, bank and fund for development and strengthening of transport cooperation. Of the four elements, only transport cooperation was partially successful; all other attempts to advance economic collaboration to some extent were not supported by Russia" (Shibutov, 2016).

Russia's resistance to further integration in economic terms, to a great extent motivated by the project of the EAEU, and the drive to restrain Chinese economic domination of Central Asia (Lukin, 2015), along with increased competition between Russia and the Central Asian states for energy supply to China, led Beijing to promote bilateral and out-of-SCO projects. These projects have increasingly become important also for Russia, especially after the 2008 financial crisis and Western sanctions. With Russia "experiencing a 7.9 percent fall of its GDP and an acute liquidity crisis, [it] was unable to give loans to its partners in Central Asia" (Gabuev, 2015). Moreover, with no SCO Bank or financial institution in place, "Central Asian countries have to turn to China for loans and negotiate with it one-on-one" (Gabuev, 2015).

The new international context, unfavorable to Russia, pushed for the 'Asia pivot' (Spanger, 2016; Lukin, 2017) approach and made of the Asia-Pacific region a most relevant space for Russia. Moreover, Russia itself has been benefitting from Chinese loans. Thus the accommodation of economic cooperation within the SCO became an imperative. Russia was becoming peripheral to a central project in energy transit, and it basically after "painful internal discussions . . . [had] to come to terms with the Silk Road project" (Spanger, 2016). Also, Moscow was feeling its "political clout in Central Asia could wane" (Economy and Piekos, 2015). This resulted from two differently oriented trends: on the one hand, Russia's limited capacity to respond to China's economic prevalence, and on the other, the recognition of the gains that further economic integration might bring to Russia itself. The Russian reasoning was thus that it had more to gain from deeper integration within the SCO than from the development of projects that simply bypass Moscow, such as the Chinese promoted Asian Infrastructure Investment Bank or the Silk Road Economic Belt project. In particular, the latter project is directed at integration of the Eurasian economies, and further bilateral projects with India are being developed under the "Act East policy" (Aneja, 2016).

Also, the SCO offers the potential for Russia to diversify its markets, particularly in face of difficult relations with the west. The suggestion coming from Russia to find a joint formula for the 'One Belt, One Road' Chinese project and the EAEU free trade area testifies to this understanding. Following extended talks, Russia and China signed a joint statement on 8 May 2015 on the cooperation of the Eurasian Economic Union and the Silk Road Economic Belt. According to President Putin, the two projects "complement each other very harmoniously", and the Joint Declaration "speaks precisely of these possibilities for integrating these models. Essentially, we seek ultimately to reach a new level of partnership that will create a common economic space across the entire Eurasian continent" (Putin, 2015). Yefremenko (2017) adds that the "initiative was partly defensive and designed to ease the tension that would otherwise have developed". Despite the Russian fears of becoming a "junior partner" or "resource appendix" of China, it is understood that partnership with China increases "Russia's position in the international arena as an independent centre of power" (Spanger, 2016). However, the independent course pursued by China in economic and financial terms proves that the SCO is not anymore understood in Beijing as a "useful instrument" (Gabuev, 2017).

Most analyses concur that Moscow did not have much alternative in face of the growing economic presence of China in global affairs. "Russia is acutely aware that it cannot, and will not try to, compete with China's growing global economic influence, even if this extends into Russia's traditional sphere of influence in Central Asia" (Lain, 2015). These developments led to the description of the SCO as a "cart with two wheels", an expression used by Jiang Zemin to show the relevance of security and economic cooperation within the SCO (Song, 2014: 93). Earlier, as Lanteigne (2007: 619) underlined, "the SCO 'bicycle' . . . best resembles a nineteenth-century penny farthing (large front wheel, miniature rear wheel)". This image clearly pictures the evolution of these issue-areas in the SCO agenda, with security dominating the agenda, but economics gaining increasing weight as pursued by China. Moreover, this direction has shown Moscow's failure in accommodating China's power within the SCO multilateral framework. Russia's disagreement with the establishment of an SCO financial institution and support for the inclusion of India, which meant as a trade off the accession of Pakistan, brings limits to the security role of the SCO on cooperation on counter-terrorism, particularly in view of difficulties regarding intelligence sharing between Delhi and Islamabad. "Moscow has turned a multilateral organization established to develop rules of the game for Eurasia into a useless bureaucracy. Now, the enervated SCO no longer has any sway over Beijing" (Gabuev, 2017). The Russian preference for regional security, where concrete successes have been achieved, has thus been overridden by its drive to contain China that led to options not favorable to Russia. To find a balance Russia became a strong supporter of the SCO enlargement policy and more receptive to economic initiatives, understanding its engagement as necessary so as to not remain outside fundamental processes taking place in the area. However, this approach has proved to be limited in its reach.

Final thoughts: questions and themes in Russia's relations with the SCO

Russia has always seen the SCO as a political organization, rather than an economic one, and envisaged it as "promot[ing] military and political cooperation through the CSTO", as the SCO was above all an "ideological symbol of a multipolar world" (Lukin, 2015). This political role for the SCO also means for Russia the legitimacy as a great power that it lost after Crimea in the west, and which SCO expansion might push forward (Economy and Piekos, 2015). The security rationale that was present at the time of the 'Shanghai Five' has been understood by Russia as the main focus area, specifically non-traditional security threats, such as terrorism and organized crime, meaning that there would not be room for overlap with the CSTO, a military-security organization led by Russia. Despite Russian efforts to contain Chinese attempts at boosting the economic dimension of the SCO's actuation, it ceded. However, and despite the institutionalizing process, as Lisa Martin (apud Song, 2014: 101) argues "there might be a well-established multilateral organization, but weak international multilateralism". This is very much linked to the triple function the SCO took on: as a multilateral forum, as a regional organization and as a vector for Chinese influence in an area that was not traditionally under its influence (Eisenbaum, 2011: 152).

Economic integration was not a priority until recently. Shifts in the international context, particularly in the aftermath of the Ukraine crisis and the annexation of Crimea, which led to the imposition of sanctions, along with the financial crisis and the lower price of oil, have led

Russia to change its positioning in the light of new Chinese initiatives outside an institutional framework. However, when the SCO describes itself as containing substantial economic potential, particularly in energy-related sources, it is positioning itself in a way that has not been matched by its actuation. Cooley (2010: 8) talks about "meager accomplishments" and failure to translate announcements into regional cooperation (Cooley, 2015). He adds that "despite its self-styled image as a 'new' type of regional organization, the SCO continues to be plagued by the perennial political concerns of its two key members, Russia and China, and their growing competition for influence in Central Asia" (Cooley, 2010: 8). But despite the well-known competition/cooperation relationship between China and Russia, and the difficulties that the enlargement process might bring to consensus finding, some claim it will constitute an "opportunity [for the SCO] to revolutionize itself into a more comprehensive institution capable of connecting and integrating a broad swath of Asia" (Economy and Piekos, 2015).

This means that the research agenda will keep focusing on the main players, but now in a different geopolitical context after the last enlargement. Whether this broader SCO is capable of projecting synergies or instead will end up tied up in institutional cumbersome and inefficient decision-making is an issue to be followed. This will determine how the SCO will position itself in Eurasia. In fact, the Greater Eurasia process is one of the most interesting dynamics ahead for Russia's relations with the SCO. Issues to watch here include Russia's readiness to promote the multilateral format and how this format will facilitate interests of Russia and other SCO members.

Notes

1 This research was conducted while the author was a Visiting Scholar at the Faculty of Social Sciences of the University of Leuven, with a Research Fund from the Portuguese Foundation for Science and Technology FCT SFRH/BSAB/128146/2016. The views expressed are the sole responsibility of the author.
2 Eight countries are currently full members – China, India, Kazakhstan, Kyrgyzstan, Pakistan, Russia, Tajikistan and Uzbekistan.
3 Afghanistan, Belarus, Iran and Mongolia have observer status and Azerbaijan, Armenia, Cambodia, Nepal, Turkey and Sri Lanka are dialogue partners.

References

Alvarez, José Manuel Saiz (2009) "La Organización de Cooperación de Shangai (OCS): Claves para la Creación de un Futuro Líder Mundial", *Revista de Economía Mundial*, 23, 507–526.
Ambrosio, Thomas (2008) "Catching the 'Shanghai Spirit': How the Shanghai Cooperation Organization Promotes Authoritarian Norms in Central Asia", *Europe-Asia Studies*, 60(8), 1321–1344.
Ambrosio, Thomas (2017) "The Architecture of Alignment: The Russia-China Relationship and International Agreements", *Europe-Asia Studies*, 69(1), 110–156.
Aneja, Atul (2016) "BRICS, SCO, EAEU Can Define New World Order: China, Russia", *The Hindu*, 1 April.
Antonenko, Oksana (2008) "A War with No Winners", *Survival*, 50(5), 23–36.
Aris, Stephen (2009) "The Shanghai Cooperation Organization: 'Tackling the Three Evils'. A Regional Response to Non-Traditional Security Challenges or an Anti-Western Bloc?", *Europe-Asia Studies*, 61(3), 457–482.
Bordachev, Timofey (2016) "The Great Win-Win Game", *Russia in Global Affairs*, 25 September, available at http://eng.globalaffairs.ru/number/The-Great-Win-Win-Game-18395. Accessed 16 May 2017.
Cooley, Alexander (2010) "Russia and the Recent Evolution of the SCO: Issues and Challenges for U.S. Policy", in Timothy Colton, Timothy Frye, and Robert Legvold (eds), *The Policy World Meets Academia: Designing U.S. Policy toward Russia*. Cambridge, MA: American Academy of Arts and Sciences.
Cooley, Alexander (2015) "Cooperation Gets Shanghaied: China, Russia, and the SCO", *Foreign Affairs*, 14 December, available at www.foreignaffairs.com/articles/china/2009-12-14/cooperation-gets-shanghaied. Accessed 16 May 2017.

Danilovich, Maryia V. (2013) "Approaches to SCO: China and Russia", in Rozanov, A. (ed) *The Shanghai Cooperation Organization and Central Asia's Security Challenges*, DCAF Regional Programmes Series n.16. Almaty, Minsk and Geneva: Geneva Centre for the Democratic Control of Armed Forces and Foreign Policy and Security Research Centre.

Davis, Andy (2015) "The New Eastern Bloc: China, Russia and India Are Joining Forces", *Newsweek*, 7 September.

Economy, Elizabeth C. and Piekos, William (2015) "The Risks and Rewards of SCO Expansion", *Council of Foreign Relations Expert Brief*, 7 July. www.cfr.org/expert-brief/risks-and-rewards-sco-expansion.

Eisenbaum, Boris (2011) "Négociation, coopération régionale et jeu d'influences en Asie centrale: l'Organisation de coopération de Shanghai", *Politique étrangère*, Printemps, 151–164.

Facon, Isabelle (2006) "L'Organisation de coopération de Shanghai Ambitions et intérêts russes", *Le Courrier des pays de l'Est*, 1055, 26–37.

Felgenhauer, Pavel (2011) "SCO Fails to Turn Into an 'Eastern NATO'", *Eurasia Daily Monitor*, 16 June, 8(116). https://jamestown.org/program/sco-fails-to-turn-into-an-eastern-nato/.

Ferghana News Agency (2011) "Russia: SCO Member States' Prime-Ministers to Discuss the Organization's Expansion", 8 November, available at http://enews.fergananews.com/news.php?id=2130&print=1. Accessed 16 May 2017.

Financial Express (2017) "India, Pakistan's Accession to Improve SCO's Potential: Russia", 25 April, available at www.financialexpress.com/india-news/india-pakistans-accession-to-improve-scos-potential-russia/642079/. Accessed 16 May 2017.

Freire, Maria Raquel and Mendes, Carmen Amado (2009) "*Realpolitik* Dynamics and Image Construction in the Russia-China Relationship: Forging a Strategic Partnership?", *Journal of Current Chinese Affairs*, 2, 27–52.

Gabuev, Alexandr (2015) "Taming the Dragon", *Russia in Global Affairs*, 19 March, available at http://eng.globalaffairs.ru/number/Taming-the-Dragon-17372. Accessed 16 March 2017.

Gabuev, Alexandr (2017) "Bigger, Not Better: Russia Makes the SCO a Useless Club", *Carnegie Moscow Center*, 13 June, available at http://carnegie.ru/commentary/71350. Accessed 16 June 2017.

Hansen, Flemming Splidsboel (2008) "The Shanghai Co-operation Organisation: Probing the Myths", *Royal Danish Defence College Brief*, December. https://pure.fak.dk/ws/files/5986814/The_Shanghai_Co_operation_Organisation_Probing_the_Myths.pdf.

Hantke, André (2016) "Will India and Pakistan Cripple the SCO?", 9 November, available at http://thediplomat.com/2016/11/will-india-and-pakistan-cripple-the-sco/. Accessed 16 May 2017.

Ibragimova, Galiya (2016) "After 15 Years, the SCO is Ready to Expand", *Russia Direct.org*, 30 June, available at www.russia-direct.org/analysis/after-15-years-shanghai-cooperation-organization-ready-expand. Accessed 16 May 2017.

IFP (2017) "Tajikistan Opposed to Iran's Full SCO Membership", *Iran Front Page*, 22 April, available at http://ifpnews.com/exclusive/tajikistan-opposed-irans-sco-membership/. Accessed 16 May 2017.

Lain, Sarah (2015) "Russia Gives Way to China in BRICS and SCO", *Lowy Institute*, 17 July, available at www.lowyinstitute.org/the-interpreter/russia-gives-way-china-brics-and-sco. Accessed 16 May 2017.

Lanteigne, Marc (2007) "*In Medias Res*: The Development of the Shanghai Co-operation Organization as a Security Community", *Pacific Affairs*, 79(4), 605–622.

Lavrov, Sergey (2016) "Russia's Foreign Policy in a Historical Perspective", *Russia in Global Affairs*, 30 March, available at http://eng.globalaffairs.ru/number/Russias-Foreign-Policy-in-a-Historical-Perspective-18067. Accessed 16 May 2017.

Lukin, Alexander (2017) *Pivot to Asia: Russia's Foreign Policy Enters the 21st Century*. Delhi: Vij Books India Pvt Ltd.

Lukin, Alexander (2011) "Should the Shanghai Cooperation Organization Be Enlarged?", *Russia in Global Affairs*, 22 June, available at http://eng.globalaffairs.ru/number/Should-the-Shanghai-Cooperation-Organization-Be-Enlarged—15245. Accessed 16 May 2017.

Lukin, Alexander (2015) "Shanghai Cooperation Organization: Looking for a New Role", *Russia in Global Affairs*, 10 July, available at http://eng.globalaffairs.ru/valday/Shanghai-Cooperation-Organization-Looking-for-a-New-Role-17576. Accessed 16 May 2017.

Maverick, Tim (2015) "Russia and China thumb noses at U.S.", *Wall Street Daily*, 4 September.

PressTV (2017) "Russia Backs Iran's Full Membership in SCO", 22 April, available at www.presstv.ir/DetailFr/2017/04/22/518979/Iran-SCO-membership-Russia-Lavrov. Accessed 16 May 2017.

Putin, Vladimir (2015) "Press Statements Following Russian-Chinese Talks", *President of Russia webpage*, 8 May, available at http://en.kremlin.ru/events/president/transcripts/49433. Accessed 16 May 2017.

Romanova, Marina and Devonshire-Ellis, Chris (2016) "China & Russia Propose Vast Eurasian Free Trade Zone & SCO Development Bank", *China Briefing*, 31 October.
RT News (2017) "Iran Ready for Shanghai Pact Full Membership: Russian FM Lavrov", 24 April, available at www.rt.com/news/385912-russia-backs-iran-shanghai-pact/. Accessed 16 May 2017.
Russian FPC (2000) *The Foreign Policy Concept of the Russian Federation*, Approved by the President of the Russian Federation V. Putin, 28 June. https://fas.org/nuke/guide/russia/doctrine/econcept.htm.
Russian FPC (2008) *The Foreign Policy Concept of the Russian Federation*, Approved by Dmitry A. Medvedev, President of the Russian Federation, 12 July. http://en.kremlin.ru/supplement/4116.
Russian FPC (2013) *Concept of the Foreign Policy of the Russian Federation*, Approved by the President of the Russian Federation V. Putin, 12 February. www.mid.ru/en/foreign_policy/official_documents/-/asset_publisher/CptICkB6BZ29/content/id/122186.
Russian FPC (2016) *Foreign Policy Concept of the Russian Federation*, Approved by the President of the Russian Federation V. Putin, 30 November. www.mid.ru/en/foreign_policy/official_documents/-/asset_publisher/CptICkB6BZ29/content/id/2542248.
Russian NSS (2015) *National Security Strategy – Appended text*, 31 December, available at www.ieee.es/Galerias/fichero/OtrasPublicaciones/Internacional/2016/Russian-National-Security-Strategy-31Dec2015.pdf. Accessed 16 May 2017.
Russian NSS 2020 (2009) *Decree of the President of the Russian Federation No. 537*, 12 May, available at http://rustrans.wikidot.com/russia-s-national-security-strategy-to-2020. Accessed 16 May 2017.
Saivetz, Carol R. (2012) "The Ties That Bind? Russia's Evolving Relations with Its Neighbors", *Communist and Post-Communist Studies*, 45, 401–412.
SCO Admission Procedures (2010) "Regulation on Admission of New Members to Shanghai Cooperation Organization", available at www.google.pt/search?q=SCO+Regulations+on+the+Admission+of+New+Members&ie=utf-8&oe=utf-8&client=firefox-b&gfe_rd=cr&ei=fEI5WaaOMYut8wfagYigDQ. Accessed 16 May 2017.
SCO Charter (2002) *Full text* available at file:///C:/Users/RAQUEL~1/AppData/Local/Temp/Charter_of_the_Shanghai_Cooperation_Organization.pdf. Accessed 16 May 2017.
SCO Convention on Combating Terrorism, Separatism and Extremism (2001) *Full text* available at www.fedsfm.ru/content/files/documents/conventions/the_20shanghai_20convention.pdf. Accessed 16 May 2017.
SCO Press Release (2017) "Press Release on the Results of the Shanghai Cooperation Organisation Heads of State Council Meeting", 9 June, available at http://eng.sectsco.org/news/20170609/289274.html. Accessed 16 May 2017.
Shibutov, Marat (2016) "SCO Transformation: Are There Any Prospects?", *The Astana Times*, 26 July.
Silitski, Vitali (2010) "'Survival of the Fittest': Domestic and International Dimensions of the Authoritarian Reaction in the Former Soviet Union Following the Colored Revolutions", *Communist and Post-Communist Studies*, 43, 339–350.
Song, Weiqing (2014) "Interests, Power and China's Difficult Game in the Shanghai Cooperation Organization (SCO)", *Journal of Contemporary China*, 23(85), 85–101.
Spanger, Hans-Joachim (2016) "Russia's Turn Eastward, China's Turn Westward", *Russia in Global Affairs*, 17 June, available at http://eng.globalaffairs.ru/number/Russias-Turn-Eastward-Chinas-Turn-Westward-18251. Accessed 16 May 2017.
Stakelbeck Jr., Fredrick W. (2005) "A New Bloc Emerges?", *The American Thinker*, 5 August.
Troitskiy, Mikhail (2007) "A Russian Perspective on the Shanghai Cooperation Organization", in Bailes, Alyson J. K.; Dunay, Pál; Guang, Pan and Troitskiy, Mikhail, *The Shanghai Cooperation Organization*, SIPRI Policy Paper No. 17, Sweden: SIPRI, May, 30–44.
Villalobos, Nidia Liseth Rodríguez (2012) "La organización de Cooperación de Shanghái: una herencia de la guerra fría", *Oasis – Observatorio de Análisis de los Sistemas Internacionales*, 17, 137–152.
Vorobyov, Vitaly (2012) "The SCO as a Rising Master of the Heartland", *Russia in Global Affairs*, 25 March, available at http://eng.globalaffairs.ru/number/The-SCO-as-a-Rising-Master-of-the-Heartland-15503. Accessed 16 May 2017.
Yefremenko, Dmitry (2017) "The Birth of a Greater Eurasia", *Russia in Global Affairs*, 13 February, available at http://eng.globalaffairs.ru/number/The-Birth-of-a-Greater-Eurasia-18591. Accessed 16 May 2017.

27

THE EURASIAN ECONOMIC UNION

Mikhail A. Molchanov

UNIVERSITY OF VICTORIA, CANADA

After some period of neglect, the literature on Russia's role in regional integration processes in Central Eurasia is burgeoning. The establishment of the Eurasian Economic Union (EAEU) in 2015 became an important landmark on the road from legacy organizations, such as the essentially post-Soviet Commonwealth of Independent States, to the emergence of a new type of regional integration entities throughout the continent. The nature of these new organizations and their potential and actual impact on the international order remain subject to an intense debate in academic and policy circles worldwide. The essence of this debate with respect to such great powers as Russia or China can be summarized as follows: is new regionalism in Eurasia an instrument of traditional power politics or a welfare-maximizing mechanism designed to benefit all of the participant states? Is it primarily about power or cooperation, geopolitics or regional development?

Existing approaches

Opinions on both sides have been offered. On the one hand, supporters of the *realpolitik* interpretation of Russia-EAEU relations described Russia's behavior as a manifestation of neoimperialist, hegemonic ambitions. According to this view, the EAEU emergence and development are best explained by Russia's bullying of smaller states into submission via a new form of alliance. On the other hand, students of international cooperation focused on mutually beneficial exchanges, regional trade in particular, and emphasized multilateralism and diplomacy in the EAEU inner workings.

While the first position is typically associated with various varieties of the realist school in international relations (IR) theory, the second appears influenced by the liberal institutionalist approach. The first interpretation was much helped by then U.S. Secretary of State Hillary Clinton's infamous presentation of Russia's efforts at creation of the EAEU as "a move to re-Sovietize the region" – an allegation that was staunchly denied by the Kremlin (UPI, 2012). A more benign reading of the Eurasian integration as a mutually beneficial endeavor animated by economistic, rather than hegemonist reasoning has been advanced by the Russian, Belarusian and Kazakh scholars. Recently, it has made forays into western academic literature, particularly in Europe (Vinokurov and Libman, 2012; Dutkiewicz and Sakwa, 2015; Lane and Samokhvalov, 2015; Czerewacz-Filipowicz and Konopelko, 2017).

The idea that any coming together of the former Soviet republics jeopardizes the interests of the United States and potentially endangers the world order dominated by western powers has been around since the early 1990s. Writing soon after the promulgation of Russia's first democratic Constitution, Zbigniew Brzezinski (1994: 76) decried as "proto-imperial" any plans for economic integration of the once-Soviet states for the sole reason that any "confederal arrangement" with Russia as its core "would prompt the reemergence of Russia as a mighty supranational state and a truly global power." For the whole generation of western analysts and policy makers coming to prominence in the last decades of the Cold War the only recipe for a "normal Russia" has always been a small, insignificant, inconsequential country. Thus, the only viable long-term strategy toward Russia and the region, from the western realist perspective, could be "*the consolidation of geopolitical pluralism within the former Soviet Union*" (Brzezinski, 1994: 79, emphasis in the original).

In practical political terms, that would mean thwarting attempts at formal multilateral institutionalization of economic and/or political ties between Russia and its neighbors and preventing the emergence of any supranational bodies with a real capacity to manage economic integration processes in the region. As Hillary Clinton opined, the concrete shape and form of the proposed regional integration organization (RIO) in Central Eurasia did not matter:

> It's going to be called a Customs Union, it will be called Eurasian Union and all of that. But let's make no mistake about it. We know what the goal is and we are trying to figure out effective ways to slow down or prevent it.
>
> *(UPI 2012)*

In the years leading to the establishment of the EAEU, Russia's regional integration attempts were often presented as a sneaky empire-building ploy aimed at restoration of "a position of strength vis-à-vis the West . . . by exercising power over dependent neocolonies, primarily the former Soviet states" (Wallander, 2007: 113). As both the Russia-led Collective Security Treaty Organization (CSTO) and the Shanghai Cooperation Organization, where Russia rubs shoulders with China and the Central Asians, were labelled "NATO of the East," alarms were raised about the start of the "new cold war" (Lucas, 2009). Presentations of Russia's foreign policy toward its neighbours as "neo-imperial" (Åslund, 2008; Ismayilov, 2011; Herpen, 2014) became a cliché.

Given the reality of the U.S. hegemonic decline, it comes at little surprise that such explanations were gaining strength since before Donald Trump's election as U.S. President, and even more so – after his victory. However, Eurasian economic regionalism is not about Russia's power projection abroad. It is noteworthy that the Foreign Policy Concept of the Russian Federation (2016) expresses skepticism about the ability of military alliances to answer global challenges of today. The EAEU is presented as an essential vehicle for the country's "steady development, comprehensive technological modernization and cooperation." Eurasian regionalism is called for to "enhance the competitiveness of the EAEU member States and improve living standards of their populations," as well as to help "establish a common economic and humanitarian space from the Atlantic to the Pacific by harmonizing and aligning interests of European and Eurasian integration processes." There is no indication that the EAEU's main purpose is military-security in nature.

Neither is there any evidence of Russia's alleged securitization of its economic cooperation policies. On the contrary, there is some evidence that regional integration in Central Eurasia has worked just as it was hoped – expanding trade-related benefits for its participants. In the first two years since the formation of the EAEU predecessor, the Customs

Union of Russia, Belarus, and Kazakhstan, internal trade turnover grew 10 percent, while the external trade increased by less than half that number (RIA Novosti, 2012). The early results of cooperation seemed encouraging. More benefits to trade could have been forthcoming had Russia not been sidelined by Ukraine's crisis, the Crimea conundrum, and the western sanctions that followed.

New regionalism

I have argued that the EAEU is an example of the so-called new regionalism in the developing world and is best understood through the prism of new regionalism approach (NRA) in international political economy (Molchanov, 2016). New regionalism emerged in response to neoliberal globalization and represents an adaptive reaction to it. It started as a new wave of regional cooperation agreements – neither fully closed nor fully open to outsiders; steering a third way between import substitution strategies and non-discriminatory trade liberalization. It is post-hegemonic in a sense of being, perhaps, the clearest manifestation of the world order moving beyond the U.S.-imposed unipolarity and toward a genuinely multipolar "world of regions" (Katzenstein, 2005; Telò, 2014).

New regionalism has been propelled to life by both difficulties and successes of globalization. On the one hand, it was a reaction to the WTO difficulties in resolving long-standing trade disputes, and on the other, to the success of the Single European Market and the U.S. conversion to regionalism. Be it as it may, new regionalism is regionalism of the global era, the feature of the "second great transformation" of the capitalist world economy.

According to the NRA founder Björn Hettne, new regionalism appears in a Polanyi-like "double movement" to check the excesses of market globalization. From this perspective, institutionalization of various RIOs throughout the world is nothing less than a political response to the threat that anarchic capitalism presents to the established structures of society. As an attempt to "manage the social turbulence" that the unfettered global expansion of the market forces brings in its wake, new regionalism becomes one of the forms of resistance to the destructive forces of global capitalism and neoliberalism. Restoration of regulative powers of the nation-state on a regional level not only signifies a much-needed "return of the political," but also promises "return of the social" and even "return of the moral" (Hettne, 2003: 32–33).

In practical-political terms, it means that new regionalist movements world-wide are as concerned about preservation of societies, identities, and cultures as they are about trade and development. Moreover, these newly emerging regions are not just arenas of action but actors themselves. "Through the lenses of IPE, as opposed to those of either economics or international relations, regions are not viewed simply as geospatial cartographic entities, but rather as socio-politically and economically constructed spaces" (Higgott, 2016). Of course, economic development is a primary goal that creation of preferential trade agreements and common economic spaces is supposed to achieve. New regionalism is where a modern developmental state meets globalization on the terms negotiated with other like-minded countries.

The origins of the modern "world of regions" can be traced back to the early post-war era. It was no one else but Karl Polanyi (1945: 87, 89) who observed that "the new permanent pattern of world affairs is one of regional systems co-existing side by side" and that regionalism offered "the alternative to the reactionary Utopia of the Wall Street." With regards to Russia's relations with its neighbours, he observed that "it is from the regionalism to which she is committed that Russia draws her greatest strength," and it is that regionalism that represents the "cure" for Eastern Europe's "three endemic political diseases – intolerant nationalism, petty sovereignties and economic non-cooperation" (Polanyi, 1945: 87–88).

The world financial crisis of 2008–2009 and the slow-moving collapse of the eurozone ignited a new search for the alternative models of economic integration world-wide. It had also boosted new regionalism in Eurasia, described by Russia's Foreign Minister Sergey Lavrov (2012) as an effective instrument of countering the negative effects of the global financial crisis. In keeping with the tradition of open regionalism, integration efforts in the post-Soviet space have not been aimed against integration processes elsewhere. The most recent proof of that is Russia's willingness to coordinate activities within the EAEU with China's One Belt, One Road initiative. Russian leaders have emphasized on numerous occasions that Moscow is keen on developing transregional relations and harmonizing integration processes between Europe, Eurasia, and Asia Pacific (Lavrov, 2016).

New regionalism has been characterized as distinct from regional integration à la European Union: it is "no longer conceived of as an instrument that is primarily intended to support national development strategies and policies, but as a developmental option in itself, promoting competitiveness and the effective insertion of economies into the international economy" (Abugattas, 2004: 3). This is definitely what Russia, Belarus, and the Central Asian economies, led by the EAEU member Kazakhstan, are seeking to achieve. However, economic development of Central Eurasia is not an end in itself, but just a stage in the evolutionary progression of its "regionness" from pre-existing regional space to the level of an international society, a regional community in the making and a regionally institutionalized polity (Hettne, 2005).

Since new regionalism is as much about societal cohesion, culture, and identity as it is about economic integration, the debate between international relations realists and IR liberals may simply miss the point. The question about the nature of the EAEU does not fit the Procrustean bed of economics vs. geopolitics (Podadera Rivera and Garashchuk, 2016). While the driving forces behind Eurasian regionalism very clearly cannot be reduced to "imperial nostalgia" (Krickovic, 2014), subsuming them under the rubric of a geopolitically "prudent" strategy for building power and capabilities is hardly an improvement if social dimensions of the problem are to be addressed in full. At the same time, a new regionalism approach, focusing attention on political and social aspects of region-building in addition to economic exchanges per se, seems best suited to addressing the complex experience of the post-communist states treading the uncharted waters of the deglobalizing postliberal capitalism.

EAEU: hopes and challenges

The idea of building a stronger Russia on the basis of political and economic integration with the former Soviet republics became one of the centerpieces of Russia's foreign policy with the start of Vladimir Putin's third presidential term. Putin (2011) made promotion of regional cooperation in Eurasia the cornerstone of his electoral campaign, promising the creation of a Eurasian Union as "a focal point for further integration processes" in his article "A new integration project for Eurasia: The future in the making." From the beginning, the Eurasian Union concept combined developmental and geopolitical aspects. The latter aspect linked to the idea of multipolarity and was evident in the description of the proposed Union as a "powerful supranational association capable of becoming one of the poles in the modern world" (Putin, 2011).

Soon thereafter, the outgoing president Dmitry Medvedev announced that an agreement to finalize preparations for a fully fledged economic union by 2015 had been made with the presidents of the other EurAsEC member states – Belarus, Kazakhstan, Kyrgyzstan, and Tajikistan. While snubbing the May 2012 G8 summit in Camp David, Putin conducted his first foreign visit upon re-election to Belarus, the country formally united with Russia by the Treaty on the Formation of a Union State since 1999. As a result of the visit, Lukashenko's struggling regime was promised the third instalment of a $3 billion loan from the EurAsEC anti-crisis fund, three-quarters of which was formed through Russia's federal budget allocations.

Putin's next visits, after a one-day stint in Germany and France, were to Uzbekistan and Kazakhstan. Uzbekistan, a principled long-time outsider, was brought on board via an agreement to join the free trade zone of the post-Soviet Commonwealth of Independent States (CIS) by the end of 2012. In Kazakhstan, the parties renewed the 20-year-old Treaty of Friendship, Cooperation and Mutual Assistance for the next ten years, making necessary provisions for the deepening of economic, political-military, and social integration, including new measures to promote free movement of citizens across their common border. The Kazakh-Russian nexus has re-emerged as the key for the success of the Eurasian integration, which Kazakhstan's Nazarbayev (2012) described as "the most promising process of the XXI century."

In September 2012, the Eurasian Economic Commission (EEC) approved an action plan on Kyrgyzstan's entry to the Customs Union and appointed a taskforce to prepare a "road map" for accession. Parallel to that, the EEC prepared a master document on the creation of the Eurasian Economic Union and presented it to the governments of Russia, Kazakhstan, and Belarus for adoption in 2013. The plan's purpose was to ensure that all necessary measures were being implemented for the formal launch of the EAEU on 1 January 2015. The treaty on creation of the EAEU, based on the EEC plan's recommendations, was signed by the leaders of Russia, Belarus, and Kazakhstan in the Kazakh capital Astana on 29 May 2014.

When the EAEU officially came into existence on 1 January 2015, it consisted of three member states: Russia, Belarus, and Kazakhstan. The earlier established Customs Union and the Single Economic Space were then expanded with the addition of Armenia and Kyrgyzstan. Armenia had joined the EAEU with a one-day's delay, and Kyrgyzstan in August 2015. The combined GDP of the member states, at $2.2 trillion, exceeded 3 percent of the world's total GDP in 2014, while the share of the industrial production ($1.3 trillion) was 3.7 percent of the global industrial production before the western sanctions struck. In May 2015, Vietnam and the EAEU signed a free trade agreement, which entered into force a year and a half later. In October 2015, the EAEU heads of state decided to coordinate activities aimed at aligning the development of the Eurasian Union with China's Silk Road Economic Belt initiative.

However, the rosy predictions of trade growth did not materialize, with intraregional trade, according to the EEC data, actually contracting by 6.5 percent in 2013 and by a further 10 percent in 2014. The years 2015 and 2016 proved equally disappointing. The share of the CIS trade in Russia's total foreign trade went down from 12.5 percent in 2015 to 12.1 percent in 2016. Although the share of the EAEU had slightly increased over the same period (from 8.0 percent to 8.3 percent), the actual volume of the Russia-EAEU trade shrank from $42.4 billion in 2015 to $39 billion in 2016 (Rosstat, 2017). In the year-on-year comparisons, the volumes of the mutual trade between EAEU member states in the first half of 2016 were 17 percent lower than the year before. Kazakhstan's trade with Belarus dropped twofold, and with Kyrgyzstan by nearly 60 percent. The Russia-Kazakhstan and Russia-Kyrgyzstan trade decreased by nearly 30 percent and 28 percent respectively. The volumes of the Armenia-Kazakhstan, as well as Belarus-Kyrgyzstan trade did not exceed 83 percent of their levels from a year before.

The sanctions that Russia incurred over the conflict in Ukraine cost its EAEU partners dearly. Their combined share of the world GDP dropped down to 2.2 percent. Intraregional trade, which stood at $65 billion in 2012 and 2013, shrank by more than 30 percent to $45 billion in 2015, and declined by 5.6 percent more, to $42.5 billion for 2016. The devaluation of the Russian ruble in 2014 made it cheaper by one-third in relation to the Kazakhstani tenge and Belarus's ruble, which, in turn, put a strain on these countries' exports. The tenge was devalued by 19 percent in February, and by 26 percent more in August 2015. The currency of Belarus lost 33 percent of its value over the same period, becoming the worst performer among more than 155 currencies tracked by Bloomberg (Kudrytski, 2015). Putin's idea of a Eurasian currency union was unequivocally rejected by Kazakhstan and found a conspicuously lukewarm reception in Belarus.

While the Russian Ambassador to the EU has been upbeat about the EAEU's future, seeing it as a vital instrument for the creation of a common economic space from "Lisbon to Vladivostok" (RT, 2016), Belarus's President Aleksandr Lukashenko decried the slow rate of progress toward creation of a common market with genuinely free movement of goods, services, capital, and labor. At the May 2016 meeting of the Supreme Eurasian Economic Council, Lukashenko noted unequal market access rights for EAEU members, the persistence of various barriers to trade, exemptions, and restrictions; the lack of support for national producers; the slow pace of integration in energy trade and in the creation of a common market of pharmaceuticals (Kozlik, 2016). The December 2016 EAEU summit in St. Petersburg proceeded without Belarus because of bilateral disagreements over the price of Russia's gas imports and Belarus cashing in on re-exportation of the EU goods sanctioned in Russia. Belarus refused to sign the EAEU Customs Code and withdrew its staff from the EAEU customs organs. In March 2017 Lukashenko threatened to retaliate if Belarus was forced to pay "European prices" for Russia's gas imports.

Pessimism about the Eurasian Union's chances of success goes up in inverse proportion to the intraregional trade going down. The western media notes "everyone's dissatisfaction." The EAEU second anniversary was met with the announcement that "2 years on, Eurasian Economic Union falls flat" (Michel, 2017). It seems that only Moscow still keeps the faith, even when some Russian economists have lambasted the Eurasian integration as a "nonsensical and disadvantageous (at least for Russia) endeavor" (Inozemtsev, 2016).

Pessimism was voiced even before the EAEU came into existence. Evgeny Vinokurov reported the "birth of Eurasiaskepticism" back in 2014, and attributed it to the uneven distribution of integration benefits and Russia's partner countries' unhappiness with non-tariff barriers that protect the Russian market (Vinokurov, 2014). Vasilyeva and Lagutina (2016: 118) distinguish between two kinds of the "Eurasian-skeptic" argument: one having to do with fears of Russia's "new imperialism" (Bugajski, 2004; Herpen, 2014) and another with the denial of objective endogenous factors and preconditions that could make Eurasian integration work. Inozemtsev (2016) raises concerns about the discrepancy in economic potentials of the member states, notes that more attractive partners are readily available, and decries the paucity of infrastructure or any other tangible foundations for the proposed regional integration project.

Researchers compared pre-integration conditions of the EAEU with early stages in the evolution of the European Economic Community and pointed out that difficulties arising from the larger distances, lower initial export levels, and more pronounced discrepancies in population and GDP did not work in the EAEU's favour (Blockmans et al., 2012). Success in implementation of common policies and the relative power of supranational institutions have also been found wanting. More criticism concerns decision making, which in the case of the EAEU is still dominated by the intergovernmental mode of governance.

The start-up conditions of the Eurasian integration process are indeed less favourable than those at the dawn of the European integration. To begin with, there is no external force even remotely comparable to the U.S. Army Europe that would ensure compliance with redistributional decisions and smooth over some of the inevitably arising tensions. It is a well-known fact that the U.S. military command in Europe facilitated a number of integrationist offers that the German government and business leaders could not afford to refuse. Russia's air defence installations notwithstanding, neither Minsk nor Astana feel in any way obliged to kowtow to

Moscow because of its scant military deployments abroad. While comparing to the EU's early history, one can hardly miss the fact that the Eurasian Union will have to do without an external arbiter or hegemon of a stature similar to that of the United States in post-war Europe.

The comparative sizes and distances are of essence, yet do not spell Eurasian integration's doom. Taking Mercosur as a comparison, the distance between Caracas and Buenos Aires is 1.7 times greater than the distance between Minsk and Astana. The Naypyidaw-Jakarta trek in ASEAN is 1.35 times more than the Moscow-Astana route. Brazil is 58 times larger than Uruguay in population size, and 53 times larger in the size of its GDP. The German economy is 15 times bigger than that of Portugal. France's economy is 125 times larger than Estonia's. A typical ratio of population sizes between Europe's smaller and bigger countries varies from 1:55 (Cyprus-Italy) to 1:95 (Malta-Poland). In population, Germany beats Denmark by roughly the same factor as Russia does Belarus. In GDP, Slovakia yields to Germany by a substantially larger margin than Belarus to Russia, and Kazakhstan comes closer to Russia than Portugal to France.

While the Eurasian Economic Commission may be weaker in its decision-making powers than the European Commission (EC) in its early days, the EC's own predecessor, the ECSC High Authority, was routinely ignored by the national governments. Moreover, the EU Commission itself was originally designed "as a European 'think-tank', whose role was precisely to propose legislation to the bodies with true legislative power" (Alesina and Perotti, 2004: 30).

The fact that decision making in the EAEU is dominated by the intergovernmental mode of governance comes as little surprise. Intergovernmentalism prevails across the majority of South-South and North-South trade blocs. Decision making in most regional integration organizations is by consensus, and enforcement mechanisms are weak or non-existent. Some trade blocs are more successful in integrating regional markets and some are less so. In most cases, the future of these organizations is found to be promising nonetheless. The existence of regional "hubs," such as Brazil in Mercosur or South Africa in SADC, is rarely seen as detrimental to regional cooperation efforts. Even if a dominant state may occasionally behave as an uncooperative "Rambo" seeking to maximize its own utility at the expense of its partners (Krapohl, 2017), expectations of long-term rewards of regional leadership typically return it to the course of cooperation.

EAEU and other regional and global organizations

According to Russia's strategic foreign policy pronouncements, strengthening and expanding integration within the EAEU is a key objective, a number one on the list of regional foreign policy priorities. In turn, the EAEU is seen as a key to further strengthening and promoting cooperation within the larger bounds of the CIS, with a view to "establish[ing] the Commonwealth as an influential regional organization" (Foreign Policy Concept of the Russian Federation, 2016).

Given all the criticism that the CIS has received over the years, including from Russia's own top leadership, such a view seems either atavistic or indicative of wishful thinking, or perhaps both. The CIS role, under the best of circumstances, was that of a caretaker, and could hardly be more than that (Molchanov, 2016: 24–31). Bureaucratization, incoherence, and the lack of meaningful cooperation between the CIS bodies and the national institutions of member states contribute to the widespread perception of institutional ineffectiveness. Decision making is often stalled by mutual disagreements. Implementation of the agreed-upon decisions has been lacking. Intraregional trade – the best indicator of the robustness of regional integration – has steadily declined. The annual summits became increasingly shallow, and at times, unfriendly. Georgia had cancelled its membership in 2008, and Ukraine limited its participation to a bare minimum after the "Maidan revolution" in 2014.

At the CIS October 2015 summit, Aleksandr Lukashenko lamented the organization's inability to facilitate a solution of frozen conflicts in Nagorno-Karabakh, Transnistria, and Ukraine. A year later, he added that the EAEU, which was conceived as a deeper form of integration, faced similar issues and expressed concern about both organizations' prospects (Sputnik, 2016). Vladimir Putin himself had second thoughts about CIS usefulness on more than one occasion and noted that its main purpose was to assist in a "civilized divorce" of the former Soviet states (Erkanyan and Strokan, 2005). Kazakhstan's Nazarbayev lamented the loss of his hopes on "a common defence space, free trade, free movement of people" and the readiness "to defend common values" (Informburo, 2016). It was indicative when, in September 2016, only seven of the eleven CIS member states sent their top leaders to the CIS's 25th anniversary summit in Bishkek.

Among several interstate organizations in Eurasia, the EAEU belongs to the developmental group, while the Collective Security Treaty Organization (CSTO) is a security-oriented alliance. The Kremlin views CSTO as one of the key elements of the current security framework in the post-Soviet space. The members of the CSTO are Armenia, Belarus, Kazakhstan, Kyrgyzstan, Russia, and Tajikistan. While international observers occasionally present the CSTO as "a kind of Eurasian counterpart to NATO" (Mankoff, 2012: 163), the organization protests such characterization.

Although the CSTO has been equipped with a 17,000 troops-strong Collective Rapid Reaction Force (CRRF), the organization is still trying to prove its usefulness. Joint military exercises happen periodically and, as of recent times, have been more commonly staged in the East European collective security region, that is, close to the borders of NATO countries. Yet critics charge that substantive military cooperation within the CSTO falls behind the demand, and the organization is more talk than action (Kucera, 2015).

A U.S. view is that the CSTO "most closely resembles a project to spread and deepen Russian influence, continue building upon preexisting dependencies on Russia, and prevent the entrance of other powers" (Keaney, 2017). The largely overlapping membership between the EAEU and the CSTO is not accidental. If the former serves to project Russia's economic interests, the latter amplifies Russia's military reach. The problem is, the CSTO lacks a clear operational mandate, is excessively dependent on Russia's contributions, and has failed to intervene in local conflicts in its direct sphere of responsibility. Unless it proves itself capable of forestalling such conflicts' emergence and escalation, its relevance will remain in doubt.

If Russian strategists can model the CSTO-EAEU relationship along the lines of NATO's interaction with the EU, the EAEU positioning vis-à-vis the Shanghai Cooperation Organization (SCO) is fraught with challenges. The SCO has existed since June 2001. The first document it adopted was called Shanghai Convention on Combating Terrorism, Separatism and Extremism. This happened three months before 9/11 and at the time reflected realities of the region more than anything else. The SCO Charter focused primarily on international and regional security, consensus building, and coordination of foreign policies of the member states; economic cooperation and cooperation in the use of natural resources appeared almost as an afterthought.

The evolution of the SCO serves as a textbook case of mission creep. While China used the organization as a vehicle for its entry into Central Eurasia, Russia had hopes it could contain and manipulate China's growing influence in the region. It has been an uphill battle for Moscow.

In 2003, with the adoption of the first programme of multilateral trade and economic cooperation, the SCO started moving beyond its original security mandate. During the 2004 summit Beijing left more than $1 billion on the table to promote its trade with Central Asia. In the following year, the SCO Business Council and Interbank Consortium were created and the Agreement on Inter-Bank Cooperation signed. At the Yekaterinburg summit in June 2009, China offered the SCO nations a credit of $10 billion, later increased to $13 billion, to help withstand the global economic crisis. Yet another $10 billion loan was pledged in 2012. By early 2016, the total sum of China's credit to the SCO member states was approaching $30 billion. Beijing was pressing hard for the establishment of an SCO development bank and the opening of a free trade zone.

Russia attempted to stall both proposals, but had little to offer in their place. The SCO Energy Club, long advocated by Moscow, was finally created in 2013, but did not grow into anything more than a platform for interstate dialogue. For some time, Russia promoted the Eurasian Development Bank and the Eurasian Business Council as an alternative to the SCO development bank, yet eventually gave up and signed up to the Chinese idea. The 2015 Ufa summit in Russia formally adopted the SCO Development Strategy Towards 2025. It proclaimed that the member states had no plans to establish a military alliance or a formal regional integration organization with supranational organs of governance. The SCO's main goals are to create a zone of peace and stability in the region and to facilitate economic collaboration on the basis of China's "Silk Road Economic Belt" proposal.

The question of the EAEU relevance inevitably emerges in this context. Chinese experts had argued that it is important to avoid the impression that the SCO means China, while the Eurasian Union is nothing more than Russia (Xin, 2013). Beijing is interested in boosting trade and investment with all countries of the Eurasian Union on a bilateral basis, while improving multilateral channels of interaction open to the SCO and championing its own "One Belt, One Road" (OBOR) project. The end objective is linking the Eurasia space fully to China's sphere of economic influence, which will also affect regional geopolitics.

Russia will have to acquiesce. The initiative on regional integration has already slipped away from Moscow, and the only thing remaining is, essentially, to play into China's hands with what may appear to be Russia's original proposals. Vladimir Putin's recent idea to integrate the OBOR, the EAEU, the SCO, and ASEAN into a "Big Eurasian Partnership" de facto advances China's agenda even if its primary impetus is to delay the creation of a China-dominated free trade zone in Central Asia (Romanova and Devonshire-Ellis, 2016).

References

Abugattas, L. (2004) *Swimming in the spaghetti bowl: Challenges for developing countries under the 'new regionalism.'* New York; Geneva: United Nations.
Alesina, A. and Perotti, R. (2004) The European Union: A politically incorrect view. *Journal of Economic Perspectives*, 18(4), 27–48.
Åslund, A. (2008) Putin's lurch toward tsarism and neoimperialism: Why the United States should care. *Demokratizatsiya*, 16(1), 17–26.
Blockmans, S., Kostanyan, H., and Vorobiov, I. (2012) *Towards a Eurasian Economic Union: The challenge of integration and unity.* CEPS Special Report No. 75 (December). Brussels: Centre for European Policy Studies.
Brzezinski, Z. (1994) The premature partnership. *Foreign Affairs*, 73(2), 67–82.
Bugajski, J. (2004) *Cold peace: Russia's new imperialism.* Westport, CT: Praeger.
Czerewacz-Filipowicz, K., & Konopelko, A. (2017) *Regional integration processes in the Commonwealth of Independent States: Economic and political factors.* Cham, Switzerland: Springer.
Dutkiewicz, P. & Sakwa, R. (Eds). (2015) *Eurasian integration: The view from within.* Oxford, UK and New York: Routledge.
Erkanyan, A., & Strokan, S. (2005). Vladimir Putin razocharovalsia v Sodruzhestve. *Kommersant*, 26 March, http://kommersant.ru/doc/557960.
Foreign Policy Concept of the Russian Federation. (2016) Approved by President of the Russian Federation Vladimir Putin on November 30, 2016. Available at www.mid.ru.
Herpen, M. van. (2014) *Putin's wars: The rise of Russia's new imperialism.* Lanham, MD: Rowman & Littlefield.

Hettne, B. (2003) The new regionalism revisited. In F. Söderbaum and T. M. Shaw (Eds.). *Theories of new regionalism: A Palgrave reader* (pp. 22–42). Basingstoke, UK: Palgrave Macmillan.

Hettne, B. (2005) Beyond the 'new' regionalism. *New Political Economy*, 10(4), 543–571.

Higgott, R. (2016) Regional worlds, regional institutions: Towards the regional economic institutionalisation of East Asia? *CSGR Working Paper 280/16*, Centre for the Study of Globalisation and Regionalisation, University of Warwick. Available at: www.warwick.ac.uk/csgr/papers/280-16.pdf.

Informburo (2016) Nazarbayev ob SNG: 'Vse poshlo ne tak, kak my hoteli.' Informburo.*kz*, 23 June, 16, 23, https://informburo.kz/novosti/nazarbaev-ob-sng-vsyo-poshlo-ne-tak-kak-my-hoteli.html.

Inozemtsev, V. (2016) Osobennosti natsionalnoi nostalgii. *The New Times/Novoe Vremia*, 7 (398), https://newtimes.ru/stati/temyi/cdcdb13bf62cbc2e57d851482ddbe259-osobennostu-nacuonalnoi-nostalguu.html.

Ismayilov, E. (2011) *How neo-imperial is Russia: Neo-imperialism in the foreign policy of Russia towards post-Soviet countries*. Saarbrücken, Germany: VDM Verlag Dr. Müller.

Katzenstein, P.J. (2005) *A world of regions: Asia and Europe in the American imperium*. Ithaca, NY: Cornell University Press.

Keaney, J. (2017) CSTO: A military pact to defend Russian influence. *American Security Project*, 1 February, www.americansecurityproject.org/csto-a-military-pact-to-defend-russian-influence/.

Kozlik, I. (2016) Dalshe razgvorov delo ne poshlo: Lukashenko raskritikoval EAES. *Komsomolskaya pravda*, 31 May, www.kp.ru/daily/26535/3553123/.

Krapohl, S. (Ed.) (2017) *Regional integration in the Global South: External influence on economic cooperation in ASEAN, MERCOSUR and SADC*. Cham, Switzerland: Springer International.

Krickovic, A. (2014) Imperial nostalgia or prudent geopolitics? Russia's efforts to reintegrate the post-Soviet space in geopolitical perspective. *Post-Soviet Affairs*, 30(6), 503–528.

Kucera, J. (2015) CSTO faces new wave of criticism over ineffectiveness. *Eurasianet.org*, 13 April, www.eurasianet.org/node/72956.

Kudrytski, A. (2015) Belarus ruble plunges to record low as Russia counterpart slides. *Bloomberg*, 24 August, www.bloomberg.com/news/articles/2015-08-24/belarus-ruble-plunges-to-record-low-as-russia-counterpart-slides.

Lane, D., & Samokhvalov, V. (Eds.) (2015) *The Eurasian project and Europe: Regional discontinuities and geopolitics*. Basingstoke, UK: Palgrave Macmillan.

Lavrov, S. (2012) Russian diplomacy and the challenges of the 21st century. *International Affairs: A Russian Journal of World Politics, Diplomacy & International Relations*, 58(5), 1–18.

Lavrov, S. (2016) Sergey Lavrov's remarks and answers to media questions at a news conference on Russia's diplomacy performance in 2015, Moscow, January 26, 2016. *The Ministry of Foreign Affairs of the Russian Federation*. Available at: www.mid.ru/en/foreign_policy/news/-/asset_publisher/cKNonkJE02Bw/content/id/2032328.

Lucas, E. (2009) *The new cold war: Putin's Russia and the threat to the West*. New York: Palgrave Macmillan.

Mankoff, J. (2012) *Russian foreign policy: The return of great power politics*. 2nd ed. Lanham, MD: Rowman & Littlefield.

Michel, C. (2017, January 11) 2 years on, Eurasian Economic Union falls flat. *The Diplomat*, http://thediplomat.com/2017/01/2-years-on-eurasian-economic-union-falls-flat/.

Molchanov, M.A. (2016) *Eurasian regionalisms and Russian foreign policy*. New York: Routledge.

Nazarbayev, N. (2012) Druzhba na veka [Friendship for centuries]. *Rossiiskaya gazeta*, No. 5903(230), 5 October, www.rg.ru/2012/10/05/nazarbaev-putin.html.

Podadera Rivera, P., & Garashchuk, A. (2016) The Eurasian Economic Union: Prospective regional integration in the post-Soviet space or just geopolitical project? *Eastern Journal of European Studies*, 7(2), 91–110.

Polanyi, K. (1945) Universal capitalism or regional planning? *The London Quarterly of World Affairs*, 10(3), 86–91.

Putin, V. (2011) A new integration project for Eurasia: The future in the making. *Izvestia*, 4 October, www.rusemb.org.uk/press/246.

RIA Novosti. (2012) [no byline] Sammit Evrazes v Moskve [The EurAsEC summit in Moscow], 19 December, http://ria.ru/trend/Moscow_EvrAzES_summit_19122012/.

Romanova, M., & Devonshire-Ellis, C. (2016) China & Russia propose vast Eurasian free trade zone & SCO Development Bank. *China Briefing*, 31 October, www.china-briefing.com/news/2016/10/31/42969.html.

Rosstat (Russia's Federal State Statistics Service). (2017) *Vneshniaya torgovlia*. Available from www.gks.ru/wps/wcm/connect/rosstat_main/rosstat/ru/statistics/ftrade/#.

RT (2016, 23 Sep) Europe & Russia will eventually have common economic space – envoy, www.rt.com/politics/360372-europe-and-russia-sanctions-envoy/.
Sputnik (2016, 28 Oct) Perspektivy SNG i EAES vyzyvayut v Belarusi trevozhnye nastroeniya. https://sputnik.by/politics/20161028/1025835086/aleksandr-lukashenko-perspektivy-sng-i-eaehs-vyzyvayut-v-belarusi-trevozhnye-nastroeniya.html.
Telò, M. (Ed.) (2014) *European Union and New Regionalism*. 3rd ed. Aldershot, UK: Ashgate.
UPI (2012) Moscow denies plans to 're-Sovietize.' December 7, www.upi.com/Moscow-denies-plans-to-re-Sovietize/38011354869000/.
Vasilyeva, N.A., & Lagutina, M.L. (2016) *The Russian project of Eurasian integration: Geopolitical prospects*. London: Lexington Books.
Vinokurov, E. (2014) The birth of Eurasiaskepticism. *Russia in Global Affairs, 1* (21 March), http://eng.globalaffairs.ru/number/The-Birth-of-Eurasiaskepticism-16498.
Vinokurov, E., & Libman, A. (2012) *Eurasian integration: Challenges of transcontinental regionalism*. Basingstoke, UK: Palgrave Macmillan.
Wallander, C. (2007) Russian transimperialism and its implications. *The Washington Quarterly*, 30, 107–22.
Xin, L. (2013) Kitai s odobreniem smotrit na plany Rossii po sozdaniiu Evraziiskogo soiuza [China approves of Russia's plans to create the Eurasian Union]. *Huanqiu Shibao*, 3 July 2013, trans. F. Kokorev, http://inosmi.ru/russia/20130705/210678606.html#comm.

28
THE COLLECTIVE SECURITY TREATY ORGANIZATION

Ruth Deyermond

KING'S COLLEGE LONDON, UK

The Collective Security Treaty Organization (CSTO) is a collective security organisation of post-Soviet states in which Russia is the dominant partner. Although it has often appeared to analysts to be more developed and effective on paper than in reality, and is frequently overshadowed by other organisations operating fully or partly in the post-Soviet space such as the Shanghai Cooperation Organisation (SCO) or the Eurasian Union, it has proved to be an important, if limited, vehicle for Russian foreign and security policy. The character of its development since the mid-2000s reflects Russian political and military predominance within the organisation, but also the growth of concerns shared by Russia and other member states about the twin threats to regional and regime security posed by the situation in Afghanistan and the normatively framed challenges from the West, above all the US. At the same time, the problems surrounding its development and its limited membership reflect the limits of Russian material and ideational capabilities when faced with the region's complex dynamics and the concerns about the threats posed by Russian domination. In this way, the CSTO can be seen as an interesting reflection of the capacity and limits of Russian regional hegemony.

Origins and development

The origins of the CSTO lie in the multilateral arrangements developed to manage the collapse of the Soviet Union – something reflected in a number of its key features and in the challenges it faces. The Collective Security Treaty (CST), signed in May 1992, aimed to retain a significant degree of military cooperation between a majority of the states of the Former Soviet Union (excluding the Baltic states), once initial attempts to establish a unified armed forces had failed. The Treaty committed the signatory states to security policy coordination, prohibited them from joining alliances hostile to other signatories, and declared that an attack on one signatory would be considered an attack on all (Collective Security Treaty Organisation, 2010a). The vague character of many of the Treaty's statements, and the scope this offered for potential intervention in signatory states' affairs by other signatories, above all Russia, raised questions about the intentions behind the Treaty and generated opposition to it in some post-Soviet states, including Ukraine (Deyermond, 2008: 43).

As with the broader Commonwealth of Independent States (CIS) framework of which it was a part, the CST was, at best, extremely limited in its functioning during the 1990s.

The organisations of the CIS generated an extensive framework of institutions and treaties, but these were widely regarded as virtual structures, not meaningfully connected to actual bilateral or multilateral interactions among member states. With the exception of the deployment of multinational peacekeeping forces in response to the conflict in Tajikistan, the CST appeared to provide little by way of collective security or foreign policy coordination. On the tenth anniversary of the CST, in May 2002, the signatories agreed to expand the scope of the CST, creating the CSTO. As Saat (2005: 4) notes, this development can be understood as a response by Russia to both the security threats posed by the post-2001 situation in Afghanistan and to the presence of the US in Central Asia as part of the 'Global War on Terror'.

Unlike the CST, which included Georgia and Azerbaijan for several years, the membership of the CSTO has never expanded beyond Russia, the Central Asian states, and Russia's two closest allies in the FSU outside Central Asia: Armenia and Belarus. Thus, although the CSTO is divided into three regions – European, Caucasus, and Central Asia, a structure inherited from the CST – the organisation is dominated by the interaction between Russia and the Central Asian states. Even within Central Asia, however, membership is limited to three of the region's five states: Kazakhstan, Kyrgyzstan, and Tajikistan. In keeping with its policy of neutrality, Turkmenistan has never joined the CSTO, or the CST before it. Uzbekistan, which was a signatory to the CST, did not initially join the CSTO, but became a member in 2006 after concerns about the potential threats to regime stability raised by both the 'colour revolutions' and Western responses to the 2005 Andijan massacre encouraged the Karimov government to seek a closer relationship with the region's other authoritarian governments. As widely noted, however (for example, Aris, 2010; Baev, 2014: 43; De Haas, 2016a: 206), Uzbekistan's membership of the CSTO was rendered problematic by its government's persistent concerns about Russian military and political domination. Uzbekistan's decision to withdraw from the CSTO in 2012 removed a potential counterweight to Russian dominance of the organisation and a source of institutional friction, but, as discussed later, this has created additional problems.

The structure of the CSTO has expanded since its creation, reflecting the emerging military and political priorities of the member states. The CSTO is headed by the Collective Security Council, comprising the heads of the member states, which the Charter specifies as the body responsible for setting the overall direction of the CSTO; below it are the Council of Defence Ministers, the Council of Foreign Ministers, and the Committee of CSTO Defence Council Secretaries (Collective Security Treaty Organisation, 2010b). Parallel to the ministerial councils, the CSTO Secretary-General heads the bureaucracy of the CSTO, the Secretariat and, since 2004, a CSTO Joint Staff. From its inception, the CSTO has had a Collective Rapid Deployment Force, which was intended to address the twin threats of terrorism and external aggression.

The institutional development of the CSTO accelerated in the second half of the 2000s, seemingly in response to both the nature of emerging security threats, particularly in the Central Asian region in the context of the conflict in Afghanistan, and concerns about US-led organisational and normative expansion into the post-Soviet space. As Weitz (2014: 3) suggests, it has evolved from its origins as a traditional collective defence organisation intended to facilitate a multinational force fighting a conventional war, into an organisation that aims to address a range of traditional and non-traditional threats including terrorism, drug- and human trafficking, peacekeeping, and emergency response. Several years into this evolution, then-CSTO Secretary-General Nikolai Bordyuzha stated that the CSTO's objectives were first, 'joint action by member states to reinforce stability'; second, to combat non-traditional security threats; and finally, to address traditional security threats such as interstate conflict or an attack on a member state (Bordyuzha, 2011). An additional, implicit, objective evident in the CSTO's development has appeared to be the countering of US-led Western influence through institutional mirroring or duplication. In 2007, the CSTO announced that it was creating a Parliamentary Assembly; an Anti-Terrorist Committee; anti-terrorist forces; and a Peacekeeping Force (Jackson, 2009). This, it has been suggested, was an attempt 'to at least symbolically occupy the position among its member states which NATO has assumed in the 1990s through its Partnership for Peace (PfP) programme' (Marat and Murzakulova, 2007). In 2009, most members of the CSTO agreed to the creation of a Rapid Reaction Force, although Belarus and Uzbekistan declined to participate. The CSTO has also agreed on the creation of a collective Air Defence System and, in 2013, Collective Aviation Forces; however, these have yet to be developed, and in that respect, they are symptomatic of a wider problem evident across most of the CSTO's existence: much of the CSTO's political coordination and structural development has been understood to exist only on paper. The creation of the Rapid Reaction Force was an attempt to address the problem that, as then-President Medvedev observed of the Collective Rapid Deployment Forces (playing on their name), 'of course they do deploy fast but they have never been deployed by anyone anywhere as yet. And these forces' value still exists on paper only' (Molchanov, 2015: 37).

The desire to give greater substance to the CSTO since the mid-2000s has been evident from the increase in frequency of military exercises conducted by CSTO forces. De Haas notes that military exercises were held annually in the period 2003–05, but increased to two or three times a year in most years during the period 2006–11, and rose to four to six per year in 2012–15 (2016b: 392). These have included the annual 'Rubezh' ('Frontier') counter-terrorism exercises, counter-narcotics, and the 'Unbreakable Brotherhood' peacekeeping exercises. Not surprisingly, the content of these exercises has reflected the current security preoccupations of member states: a counter-Islamic State (IS) exercise was held in Moscow in March 2015 and an anti-IS joint intelligence and reconnaissance exercise took place in Tajikistan in April 2016. In August 2014 the annual 'Interaction' exercise focused on cybersecurity and on information and psychological warfare (De Haas, 2016b: 399). The largest of the exercises, 'Tsentr' ('Centre'), held on several occasions since 2008, are conventional warfare exercises; in 2015, the 'Tsentr' exercise involved 95,000 troops and all branches of the armed forces (President of Russia, 2015).

The developing structure of the CSTO and the changing character of its military exercises have represented a response to internal, as well as external, challenges. Most significant of these was the violence in Kyrgyzstan in 2010, when the CSTO failed to provide assistance to the provisional government, despite the government's requests for support. In the aftermath of this failure, most member states agreed to expand the CSTO's scope to allow for interventions in member states' internal affairs, if those states were threatened by destabilising forces.

The remit of the CSTO has continued to develop in the period since this decision, as evidenced by the CSTO's most significant recent policy document, the Collective Security Strategy to 2025, released in October 2016. The strategy provides an indication of the extent to which member states' (perhaps most importantly Russia's) security concerns have expanded beyond the limits of conventional warfare and peacekeeping. In addition to the longer-standing concerns evident in the CSTO charter and later documents, prominent threats to member states identified in the strategy include attempts to destabilise a state's constitutional order; the use of media and the internet to achieve a 'destructive ideological and psychological' impact on member states' populations; the use of 'colour revolution' and hybrid war technologies; and the application of double standards by external states on matters of international law (The Collective Security Treaty Organisation, 2016). Thus, over the course of its fifteen-year existence, the CSTO has moved away from its early focus on more conventional military concerns, to a preoccupation with the challenges posed by new technologies and the normative conflict with the US and its European allies.

The CSTO literature

The CSTO has attracted comparatively little analytical attention compared with many other aspects of Russian foreign policy, perhaps because so much analysis since the late 2000s has been concentrated on Russia's relationship with the US, China, and Europe, though it has also received less attention than some other organisations wholly or partly located in the post-Soviet space, notably the Shanghai Cooperation Organisation (SCO) and the Eurasian Union.

Discussions of the CSTO have often been focused on attempting to clarify the structures, policies, and activities of what is generally agreed by Western analysts to be an opaque organisation (for example, Saat, 2005; De Haas, 2016b). Beyond this, analysis of the CSTO has often focused on two main aspects: its ineffectiveness, and the extent to which it acts as a vehicle for Russian hegemony in the post-Soviet space. As Kropatcheva (2016: 1527) notes, analysis by non-Russian scholars generally represents the CSTO as an instrument, successful or otherwise, of Russian regional domination, while Russian views are more diverse. Nikitina, for example, takes issue with what she regards as the consensus Western view, suggesting instead that 'Russia is less willing to be a regional security provider than outside observers usually assume', in part because 'Moscow does not want to continue to pay for its allies' loyalty' (Nikitina, 2012: 47). Many analysts, notably Allison (2004, 2008), Matveeva (2013), Pavel Baev (2014), Molchanov (2015), and Kropatcheva (2016) have questioned the capacities and effectiveness of the organisation in various aspects of its operation, although De Haas has suggested that its more recent structural developments and increase in military exercises indicate that 'the CSTO has become a professional security organisation' that 'forms a valuable military alliance for Central Asia' (De Haas, 2017: 12–13).

Another area of interest for some analysts has been the way in which the CSTO, together with other regional organisations, has provided normative solidarity, and thus a form of collective norm security for member states, which in turn has enhanced regime stability in a period when democracy-related challenges from the US and Western institutions appeared to threaten it. Thus, Roy Allison notes that 'regional coordination, cast in the grandiose language of regional integration . . . creates a basis for political solidarity between state leaders and their protection against or resistance to a perceived interventionist agenda of democracy-promotion by Western states' (Allison, 2008: 188).

The role of the CSTO in Russian foreign policy

Since its creation, the CSTO has occupied a significant, if limited, position in relation to wider Russian foreign policy. Successive Russian foreign policy concepts have identified the CSTO as central to regional security and as part of a broader framework of relations with the other states of the post-Soviet space. The 2016 Russian Foreign Policy Concept, like the previous Concept of 2013, identifies the CSTO as 'a key instrument to maintain stability and ensure security in the Organization's area of responsibility' and states that:

> Russia seeks to facilitate the development of the CSTO into a prominent multifunctional international organization capable of overcoming challenges and threats today's world is facing amid the growing pressure from various global and regional factors within the CSTO's area of responsibility and in the adjoining regions.
> *(Ministry of Foreign Affairs of the Russian Federation, 2016a)*

As this suggests, the CSTO appears to have both regional and wider significance for Russian foreign and security policy. At the regional level, most obviously, the CSTO is intended to act as a mechanism for addressing the significant security challenges that the Central Asian region poses for Russia. In particular, the complex range of threats arising from the situation in Afghanistan, notably those relating to terrorism, require cooperation with the states in Central Asia. As Kropatcheva suggests, cooperation on Afghanistan via the CSTO is particularly important given that 'Russia is not willing to take full responsibility for Afghanistan-related security problems [but] is interested in cost-/burden-sharing within the CSTO', (Kropatcheva, 2016: 1544).

Beyond this specific issue, the CSTO has clear importance for Russian security policy because it facilitates power projection and provides institutional legitimacy for the continued stationing of Russian forces in Central Asia – for example at the Kant base in Kyrgyzstan, where Russian troops form part of the Rapid Reaction Force. As a result of the CSTO, large areas of the post-Soviet space remain linked together through structures of security cooperation, while members are restricted by CSTO agreements in their ability to form security relationships with non-member states; this provides a greater degree of protection for Russian strategic interests in the region than it would otherwise be able to achieve without the umbrella of the CSTO.

This function of the CSTO is only really meaningful in relation to the Central Asian region, since the other two regions each include only one non-Russian member, and Russia's bilateral security relationships with Belarus and Armenia do not depend on the CSTO structure in any significant way. Nevertheless, the inclusion of these other two states, and therefore regions, in the CSTO is important for Russian foreign policy because it extends the scope of the organisation beyond a Central Asian sub-regional institution, creating an institution of wider international significance.

Globally, the CSTO performs a limited role in relation to other multilateral organisations, and thus its capacity to act as an international support for Russian power is restricted. For Russia's relationship to other powerful states, the role of the CSTO is arguably primarily preventive. In the case of Russia's complex and delicate relationship with China in Central Asia, the CSTO acts as a check on the possible further development of the SCO into security-related areas (Kacmarski, 2007). For more than decade the CSTO also appears to have performed a similar function in relation to the US. As Pop suggests, for instance, the creation of the Rapid Reaction Force can be understood as a mechanism to check NATO involvement in Central Asia during the first decade of the twenty-first century, underlining the greater reliability of Russia as a security partner for the region's states (Pop, 2009: 289) A second critical function relates to CSTO policy and, perhaps most importantly, the shared discourse of CSTO members on issues of stability and non-interference in states' internal affairs (see, for example, Ministry of Foreign Affairs of the Russian Federation, 2016b), which acts, as already noted, as a counter to perceived attempts at norm-driven intrusion, particularly on the part of the US.

The role of Russia in the CSTO

Since its creation, Russia has remained the unquestionably dominant state in the CSTO, politically, militarily, and in relation to the organisation's composition. To a significant extent, the CSTO is thus an expression of and a vehicle for the maintenance of Russian military hegemony in the post-Soviet space. The problems evident in the development of the CSTO, however, also indicate the limits of that hegemony.

At a practical level, Russian dominance within the CSTO has been inevitable given the huge disparity between the military capabilities of the Russian Federation and those of the other member states. Russian troops dominate the Rapid Reaction Force and the Peacekeeping Force; of the other member states, only Kazakhstan provides a numerically significant component of the Peacekeeping Force (De Haas, 2016b: 391). This dominance is equally evident within the CSTO's bureaucracy. In the period after its inception, for example, 50 per cent of the Joint Staff posts were occupied by Russian officers (Frost, 2009: 86). Most obviously, the dominance of Russia within the structures of the CSTO was both reflected and enhanced by the thirteen-year tenure of Nikolai Bordyuzha as CSTO Secretary-General, who occupied the post until the end of 2016 (after a delay of several months, Yuri Khatchaturov of Armenia was appointed as his successor in April 2017). Russian dominance is also sustained through the provision of goods to other member states. Russian arms are made available to CSTO members at reduced cost; for the poorer member states in particular, this has been a significant benefit. Perhaps more important over the long term is the training of CSTO officers in Russian military academies – as Frost notes, a Russian military education makes a Russian-inflected perspective on CSTO matters more likely among Central Asian officers (Frost, 2009: 86).

As this may suggest, the Russian troop presence and Russian military dominance of the CSTO is not necessarily unwelcome to the other member states – though in the case of some (notably Uzbekistan), it clearly has been so. Armenia and Belarus both have long-established, close security relations with Russia, while the two weakest states in Central Asia, Tajikistan and Kyrgyzstan, have a significant degree of energy and security dependence on Russia given the potential conflicts with other states in the region. In this respect, then, it can be argued that Russian dominance of CSTO bureaucracy and military structures reflects the classic understanding of hegemony in International Relations theory: Russia dominates materially and ideationally, but this domination provides collective goods to other states, in the form of security provision and a stabilising presence in the context of sub-regional tensions between Central Asian members.

If Russia is unquestionably the dominant state within the CSTO, it is nevertheless the case that the organisation's priorities reflect the concerns of member states more broadly. This is clear, for example, in the emphasis placed on the CSTO's counterterrorism and counter-narcotics functions. Terrorism and drug trafficking are very significant problems for the Central Asian member states as well as for Russia, particularly because of the proximity of Afghanistan and the difficulty in effectively securing borders to counter these threats. The prominence of both issues within the CSTO is reflected in policy documents, notably the 2016 Collective Security Strategy, which details the organisation's commitments to coordinated activity on both issues. It is also evident from the significant number of CSTO military exercises concerned with counterterrorism and counter-narcotics – as Hoffmann (2014) notes – that the majority of the CSTO's military exercises have addressed one of these two threats. Russian governmental statements on security policy priorities do not generally give the same degree of prominence to drug trafficking issues as they receive in the CSTO, suggesting that this is one area in which the organisation's agenda does not privilege Russian priorities over those of other members. It also indicates the extent to which, for most of its existence, the focus of the CSTO has reflected Central Asian security concerns and the security concerns of Russia in Central Asia rather than, for example, those of Belarus.

Other issues on the CSTO agenda do, however, reflect the security priorities of the membership as a whole. Arguably the most significant of these is the resistance to possible norms-driven external intrusion into member states. If the CSTO was, at least in part, a response to the presence in Central Asia as part of the 'Global War on Terror', both the US's adoption of a discourse of assertive democracy promotion under George W. Bush and the 'colour revolutions' which occurred in the same period encouraged member states to use the CSTO as a mechanism for resisting what they regarded as normatively framed threats to their security. Although the Russian government has, since the late 2000s, been the most vocal and prominent critic of what it has regarded as attempts to utilise the language of democracy promotion and human rights to advance national interests in the post-Soviet space, other CSTO member states have shown similar concerns, and this aspect of the CSTO's policy direction acts as an ideational glue binding members more closely together.

The limits of Russian power and influence in the CSTO

It is also clear that even if the CSTO demonstrates the scale of Russian capabilities and influence in relation to the other member states, it also shows their limits. This has been evident in several issues confronting the CSTO, notably the issues of Uzbek membership, the non-response to the violence in Kyrgyzstan in 2010, and the position of other member states on Russia's war in Georgia in 2008 and Ukraine in 2014.

As noted earlier, Uzbekistan is the only state to have joined and then left the CSTO. Both as a member and afterwards, its position has demonstrated a suspicion of Russian power and intentions, as well as a sub-regional rivalry with Kazakhstan. The government of Uzbekistan has resisted Russian political and military dominance of Central Asia throughout the post-Soviet period, seemingly keen to position itself as an alternative power centre in the region (Deyermond, 2009), and this has been reflected in its approach to the CSTO. Uzbekistan was one of two states not to support the creation of the Rapid Reaction Forces, opposing their potential use for resolving internal conflicts in member states (Tolipov, 2009) and had more generally opposed participation in combined military forces under Russian control, as well as participation in (Russian-led) CSTO military exercises (Aris, 2010). The Uzbek government has made it clear that it will not permit any foreign basing on its territory (De Haas, 2016a: 223), following the expulsion of US troops in the mid-2000s, and will also consistently oppose any CSTO policy or action that would involve the intervention in a member state's internal affairs – it was, for example, apparently instrumental in blocking any CSTO intervention in the 2010 crisis in Kyrgyzstan (Baev, 2014: 44). Both inside the CSTO and outside it, Uzbekistan has remained an obstacle to the CSTO's coherence and capacity to operate effectively as a collective security provider. The departure of Uzbekistan revived the problem previously identified by Roy Allison, that without it the CSTO is 'hollowed out in Central Asia' (Allison, 2008: 193), while Pavel Baev argued in 2014 that then-President Karimov was playing a spoiler role in relation to the CSTO, 'keen to demonstrate that the CSTO has no capacity to manage [Central Asia] conflicts and that Russia is only pursuing its own parochial agenda, making it impossible to trust as an impartial peace-maker' (Baev, 2014: 45). To the extent that the CSTO matters to Russian foreign and security in relation to Central Asia, the position of Uzbekistan remains a problem.

A different type of problem for Russia's CSTO policy was evident in the context of the Kyrgyzstan crisis of 2010. If the CSTO is intended by the Russian government to operate as an instrument of power projection both within and outside the region, any significant failure of the CSTO appears to reflect negatively on Russian capacities. In the case of Kyrgyzstan, the failure of the CSTO to intervene, despite the request of the Kyrgyz government to do so, raises questions about the effectiveness and purpose of the CSTO as a collective security organisation. Analysts have suggested various reasons for the failure of the CSTO to intervene, including opposition by Uzbekistan; the lack of strategic significance for Russia (Kropatcheva, 2016); dislike of the character of the new Kyrgyz government and the means by which it had come to power; and Russia's fear of international repercussions after the negative effects of the war in Georgia (Matveeva, 2013: 487). Whatever the reason, the consequence was that when confronted with its first significant challenge, the region's collective security organisation failed to act meaningfully to assist a member state in restoring order, despite the request of that state to do so. This has inevitably reflected on the credibility of both the CSTO and Russia as its leading member. As Matveeva argues:

> Conceived as a regional response to NATO, active in the post-Soviet periphery, [the] CSTO never proved itself in action, adding ammunition to the discourse that the organisation lacks the capacity to intervene properly in the first instance. [The] crisis in Kyrgyzstan may have been its golden opportunity, but instead showed it as an emperor with no clothes.
>
> *(Matveeva, 2013: 489)*

If the crisis in Krygyzstan exposed the limits of Russia's capacity or willingness to act as a security provider, through the CSTO, for other member states, the crises in Georgia and Ukraine demonstrated the limits of Russia's political influence. In both cases, the Russian government appears to have unsuccessfully sought an endorsement of its actions from other CSTO members, with little success; instead, CSTO members have provided a minimum of carefully worded support while withholding significant public agreement. Thus, the other member states agreed to condemn Georgian aggression in 2008, and offered limited support for Russian actions, but did not agree to recognition of South Ossetia and Abkhazia as independent states (in both cases, recognised by Russia). As Kropatcheva argues, 'the CSTO's half-hearted support [on Georgia] has not strengthened Russia's position internationally. On the contrary, it has revealed the weakness of Russia's position within the CSTO itself' (Kropatcheva, 2016: 1538).

Although the CSTO has expanded significantly in its policy scope, structure, and activities since its creation, it appears to remain an organisation with limited capacity either to act or to provide a clear, sustained degree of meaningful foreign policy coordination of the kind envisaged in its founding documents. Both its growth and its weakness are, to a significant degree, the consequence of Russian domination of the organisation but also of the limits of Russian capabilities and Russian interests in relation to it. While the CSTO will doubtless continue to evolve in its structure and policy, its emergence as a genuinely effective collective security organisation would depend on a much greater degree of commitment to that goal by Russia and by the other member states who appear to regard the bilateral relationship with Russia as more significant than the multilateral one. The CSTO thus seems likely to remain a politically useful but practically limited instrument of Russian regional power.

References

Allison, R. (2004). Regionalism, Regional Structures and Security Management in Central Asia. *International Affairs*. 80(3), 463–483.

Allison, R. (2008). Virtual Regionalism, Regional Structures and Regime Security in Central Asia. *Central Asian Survey*. 27(2), 185–202.

Aris, S. (2010). Russia's Approach to Multilateral Cooperation in the Post-Soviet Space: CSTO, EurAsEC and SCO. *Russian Analytical Digest*. 76(10), 2–5.

Baev, P. (2014). The CSTO: Military Dimensions of the Russian Integration Effort. In Starr, S.F., and Cornell, S.E., eds, *Putin's Grand Strategy: The Eurasian Union and its Discontents*. Washington, DC and Stockholm: Central Asia-Caucasus Institute Silk Road Studies Programme.

Bordyuzha, N. (2011). The Collective Security Treaty Organisation: A Brief Overview. In *OSCE Yearbook 2010*. Hamburg: Institut für Friedensforschung und Sicherheitspolitik an der Universität Hamburg.

Collective Security Treaty Organisation (2010a). *Dogovor o kollektivnoi bezopasnosti*. Available at: www.odkb-csto.org/documents/detail.php?ELEMENT_ID=126. Accessed 28 March 2017.

Collective Security Treaty Organisation (2010b). *Charter of the Collective Security Treaty Organisation*. Available at: www.odkb-csto.org/documents/detail.php?ELEMENT_ID=1896. Accessed 28 March 2017.

Collective Security Treaty Organisation (2016). *Strategiya kollektivnoi bezopasnosti Organizatsii Dogovora o kollektivnoi bezopasnosti na period do 2025 goda*. Available at: http://odkb-csto.org/documents/detail.php?ELEMENT_ID=8382. Accessed 30 June 2017.

De Haas, M. (2016a). 'Security Policy and Developments in Central Asia: Security Documents Compared with Security Challenges. *The Journal of Slavic Military Studies*. 29(2), 203–226.

De Haas, M. (2016b). War Games of the Shanghai Cooperation Organisation and the Collective Security Treaty Organisation: Drills on the Move!, *The Journal of Slavic Military Studies*. 29(3), 378–406.

De Haas, M. (2017). Relations of Central Asia with the Shanghai Cooperation Organization and the Collective Security Treaty Organization. *The Journal of Slavic Military Studies*. 30(1), 1–16.

Deyermond, R. (2008). *Security and Sovereignty in the Former Soviet Union*. Boulder, CO: Lynne Rienner.

Deyermond, R. (2009). Matrioshka Hegemony? Multi-Levelled Hegemonic Competition and Security in Post-Soviet Central Asia', *Review of International Studies*. 35(1), 151–173.

Frost, A. (2009). The Collective Security Treaty Organisations, the Shanghai Cooperation Organisation, and Russia's Strategic Goals in Central Asia. *China and Eurasia Forum Quarterly*. 7(3), 83–102.

Hoffmann, K. (2014). The Collective Security Treaty Organisation: A Multilateral Response to New Security Challenges? In Aris, S. and Wenger, A. eds, *Regional Organisations and Security: Conceptions and Practices*. Abingdon, UK: Routledge.

Jackson, A. (2009). Russian-led Military Block: A Real Counterweight to NATO? Caucasus Update, *Caucasian Review of International Affairs*, 22. Available at: http://cria-online.org/CU_-_file_-_article_-_sid_-_23.html. Accessed 28 March 2017.

Kaczmarski, M. (2007). Russia Attempts to Limit Chinese Influence by Promoting CSTO-SCO Cooperation. *CACI Analyst*. Available at: www.cacianalyst.org/publications/analytical-articles/item/11497-analytical-articles-caci-analyst-2007-10-17-art-11497.html. Accessed 28 March 2017.

Kropatcheva, E. (2016). Russia and the Collective Security Treaty Organisation: Multilateral Policy or Unilateral Ambitions? *Europe-Asia Studies*. 68(9), 1526–1552.

Marat, E. and Murzakulova, A. (2007). The CSTO Seeks to Build New Sub-Structures. *CACI Analyst*. Available at: www.cacianalyst.org/publications/field-reports/item/11490-field-reports-caci-analyst-2007-10-3-art-11490.html. Accessed 28 March 2017.

Matveeva, A. (2013). Russia's Changing Security Role in Central Asia. *European Security*. 22(4), 478–499.

Ministry of Foreign Affairs of the Russian Federation (2016a). *Foreign Policy Concept of the Russian Federation*.

Ministry of Foreign Affairs of the Russian Federation (2016b). *Joint statement by the member-countries of the Collective Security Treaty Organisation on ensuring comprehensive stability in the world in the First Committee of the 71st UN General Assembly, October 14, 2016*. Available at: www.mid.ru/en/foreign_policy/news/-/asset_publisher/cKNonkJE02Bw/content/id/2501032. Accessed 15 December 2017)

Molchanov, M.A. (2015). *Eurasian Regionalisms and Russian Foreign Policy*. Abingdon, UK: Routledge.

Nikitina, Y. (2012). The Collective Security Treaty Organization Through the Looking Glass. *Problems of Post-Communism*. 59(3), 41–52.

Pop, I.I. (2009). Russia, EU, NATO, and the Strengthening of the CSTO in Central Asia. *Caucasian Review of International Affairs*. 3(3), 278–290.

President of Russia (2015). *Strategicheskie komandno-shtabnye ucheniya 'Tsentr-2015'*. Available at: http://kremlin.ru/events/president/news/50329.

Saat, J.H. (2005). *The Collective Security Treaty Organisation*, Conflict Studies Research Centre Central Asian Series, 05/09. ISBN 1-905058-06-3.

Tolipov, F. (2009). CSTO: Collective Security or Collective Confusion? *CACI Analyst*. Available at: www.cacianalyst.org/publications/analytical-articles/item/11896-analytical-articles-caci-analyst-2009-9-1-art-11896.html. Accessed 28 March 2017.

Weitz, R. (2014). The Collective Security Treaty Organization: Past Struggles and Future Prospects. *Russian Analytical Digest*. 152, 2–4.

INDEX

Abbot, T. 372
Abkhazia: China and 257, 262; CSTO and 428; impact of conflict in 312; NATO and 111; OSCE and 383; recognition of 70, 127, 317; ROC and 225; Russian support for 318–320; SCO and 404; Ukraine crisis and 322
Abzalov, D. 209
"active measures" 156, 161–162
Adler, E. 5, 7
Adorno, T. 23
Afghanistan 109, 297, 306, 308, 328, 425
agency–structure problem 22
Ahrweiler, H. 229
Albright, M. 133, 239–240
Alexander Gorchakov Fund to Support Public Diplomacy 204
Alexander I 134
Alexander II 130
Allison, R. 424, 427
al-Qaeda 318
Altai 145–147
Althusser, L. 22
Ambartsumov, Y. 68
Ambrosio, T. 401
America's Strategy in World Politics (Spykman) 65
Anastasios, Archbishop 226
Anderson, J. 158
Anderson, R. D. 102
Andrew, C. 154
anti-Americanism 185–186
Anti-Ballistic Missile (ABM) Treaty 241, 243
Antonov, A. 257–258
Appleby, R. S. 228
Arab League 362
Arab Spring 188, 298, 301, 302, 306, 307
Arctic 338–348
Arctic Council (AC) 340

Armenia 286, 316, 317, 322, 414, 422, 426
Arms and Influence (Schelling) 176
arms control 241, 243, 246
arms sales 261–262
ASEAN Defense Ministers' Meeting (ADMM-Plus) 389, 390
ASEAN Regional Forum (ARF) 388, 390
Asia-Europe Meeting (ASEM) 389
Asian Infrastructure Investment Bank (AIIB) 393
Asia organizations 388–397
Asia-Pacific 254–266
Asia-Pacific Economic Cooperation (APEC) 260, 388–389
Assad, B. al- 111, 133, 249, 302, 305, 306, 307, 308, 309, 320–321
Association Agreements (AA) 71, 285
Astrov, A. 30, 31
Auty, R. M. 103
Averinstev, S. 229
Ayoob, M. 29
Azerbaijan 286, 317

Baev, P. 424, 427
Bakhtin, M. 22
Bakiev, K. 82
balance of power theory/strategy 44–45, 52, 64
Baluevsky, Y. 173
Baramidze, G. 111
Barr, M. 201
Barthes, R. 22
Basilesu 218
Belarus 413–415, 422, 426
Bering, V. 339
Berlusconi, S. 132
Beslan school hostage siege 272, 314
Biberman, Y. 130
Bilateral Presidential Commission 245–246

Index

Billington, J. H. 228, 229
Bismarck, O. von 63
Blakkisrud, H. 88
Bloomberg 174
Bogaturov, A. 68, 371
Boiko, Y. 144
Bolsheviks 25, 64, 219
Bordyuzha, N. 422, 426
Borogan, I. 161
Boston marathon bombings 315–316
Bourdieu, P. 13
Brandenburger, D. 82
Bratersky, M. 371
Breslauer, G. W. 102
Brest-Litovsk 63–64
Breuilly, J. 80
Brezhnev, L. 106–109, 112
Brezhnev Doctrine 66
BRICS 2, 36, 110, 126, 132, 191, 300, 363–364, 367, 371, 373–374
Brown, J. D. 102
Brundtland report 358
Brzezinski, Z. 66, 69, 109, 411
Budapest Memorandum 125
Bush, G. H. W. 69, 110, 241
Bush, G. W. 111, 126, 134, 241, 314–315, 368, 426
Buzan, B. 28
Byron, R. 229

Cadier, D. 88, 277
Camp David accords 303
capitalism 25
Carile, A. 229
Carter, J. 109
categorization 17
Caucasus 311–322
Caucasus Emirate (CE) 315, 320–321
causality 15
Central Asia 325–335, 405; *see also* Collective Security Treaty Organization (CSTO); *individual countries*
Central Europe 282–292
Charap, S. 176, 247
Chavez, H. 133
Chechnya 174, 298, 313–314, 383
Checkel, J. 8, 16
Cheluskin, S. 339
Cheney, D. 245
Chernomyrdin, V. 132, 241–242, 271
China: arms sales and 261–262; Central Asia and 329–330, 331, 335; conflict with 111; energy policy and 259–260; Eurasian economic initiatives and 393; main discussion of 254–266; natural gas and 145–147; norms and 13; rise of 48; SCO and 403–404, 405–406, 417–418; "strategic partnership" with 390–391; United States and 66

Chinese National Petroleum Company (CNPC) 329–330
Chirikov, A. 339
Chizhov, V. 274
Churchification 227
Churchill, W. 81, 378
"CIA project" 189
CIS Anti-Terrorist Center (ATC) 327
civilizational nationalism 89–90
Clinton, B. 69, 132, 239, 240, 241
Clinton, H. 182, 209, 246, 247, 250, 342, 410, 411
Clover, C. 67
club diplomacy 125
Clunan, A. L. 11, 29
coercive diplomacy 125, 129, 133–134
Cohen, Saul 66
Cohen, Stephen 208
"Cold Peace" 383
Cold War: Arctic and 339; constructivism and 5, 7; end of 238–239; geopolitics of 65–67; Middle East and 297–299
Colgan, J. D. 101
Collective Rapid Reaction Force (CRRF) 327, 417, 423, 425
Collective Security Strategy to 2025 423
Collective Security Treaty (CST) 421
Collective Security Treaty Organization (CSTO) 132, 316, 327, 374, 384, 403, 411, 417, 421–428
color revolutions 52, 70, 86, 91, 243–244, 257, 299, 422, 426
commonsense constructivism 14, 28
Comprehensive Nuclear Test Ban Treaty 357
Conference on Interaction and Confidence Building Measures in Asia (CICA) 392
Conference on Security and Co-operation in Europe (CSCE) 69, 381–382
conflict resolution, ROC and 228–229
Congress of Vienna (1815) 30–31, 32
constructivism 5–19, 23–24, 36, 43, 56, 83–84, 91, 296
containment consensus 65–66
contractual theory of international hierarchy 29
Convention on Combating Terrorism, Separatism and Extremism 404, 417
Convention on Prohibition and Utilization of the Chemical Weapons 357
Cooley, A. 407
Cooperative Threat Reduction Act 241
Correlates of War Project 101
Council for Mutual Economic Assistance 284
Council of Europe (CoE) 377, 378–381, 385
counter-hegemonic projects 36
counter-terrorism 161–162, 242–243, 404, 423
Crimea 81, 82, 86, 125, 127, 222–223, 248–249, 301, 405; *see also* Ukraine

Crimean War 49, 62–63
critical IPE 27–28
Critical Theory 23
crossborder cooperation 275
cultural diplomacy 203
cultural nationalism 89
culture, public diplomacy and 202–203
cyber norms 190–191
cyber power 182–194

Darwin, J. 61, 65
data encryption 186
defensive realists 45, 47, 276
De Haas, M. 423, 424
Delyagin, M. 26–27
Democratic Ideals and Reality (Mackinder) 61
Denysenko, N. 224
Deudney, D. 67
DEW (Distant Early Warning) Line 340
De Waal, T. 321
Deyermond, R. 13
diplomacy 123–135
Diplomatic Academy of the USSR 128
discourse analysis 16
discursive and institutionalist approaches 28–33
disinformation 134, 163, 185, 194, 201
diversionary theory of conflict 277
Dobrynin, A. 106, 108–109
Dodon, I. 287
Dolgov, B. V. 301
Dolinsky 202
Donbass 71, 86, 94, 113, 138, 163, 176, 177, 178, 222, 223, 287, 288, 290–291
DPRK 263–264
Draft Convention on International Information Security 191
Dual Alliance 63
dual containment policy 258
Dugin, A. 27, 68, 85, 87, 89–90, 332

East Asia Summit (EAS) 389, 390, 394
Eastern Economic Forum (EEF) 260
Eastern Europe 282–292
Eastern Partnership 283–284
economic interdependency 288–292
economic sanctions 72
Egypt 297, 302–303
Eichengreen, B. 367
election monitoring 384, 385
empire-building 46–48
energy policy/trade 49, 289–291, 306, 317, 329–330; *see also* petropolitics
energy security dilemma 139
English School 28–30
Erdoğan, R. T. 307
ethics, constructivism and 18
Etkind, A. 32

Eurasian continentalism 391–394
Eurasian Economic Community (EEC) 145, 285, 330, 414
Eurasian Economic Union (EAEU) 36, 264–265, 285, 316, 331–333, 389–390, 393, 403, 405, 410–418
Eurasian integration 36
European Convention for the Protection of Human Rights and Fundamental Freedoms 379, 385
European Court of Human Rights (ECHR) 379–380, 381
European organizations 377–386
European Security Treaty 395
European Union (EU) 10, 269–279, 378
Exclusive Economic Zone (EEZ) 341
expansion 23–24

Faisal, Prince 306
Federal Guards Service (FSO) 157
Feklyunina, V. 10, 16, 17, 201, 277
Fletcher, T. 202
Flikke, G. 257
Fominykh, A. 202, 203, 212
Foreign Intelligence Service (SVR) 157, 158–161, 163
Foreign Ministry, role of 274
Foreign Policy Concept (2013) 255, 258, 332, 403–404
Foreign Policy Concept (2016) 325, 332, 356, 357, 404, 411, 424
Forsberg, T. 12, 16
Foucault, M. 16, 22, 30–31
Founding Act on Mutual Relations, Cooperation and Security between NATO and the Russian Federation 69
Francis I, Pope 223
Frankfurt School 23
Frear, M. 94
freedom-of-navigation operations (FONOP) 346
Frontline Ukraine (Sakwa) 83
Frost, A. 426
FSB 157, 158–160, 161–162, 163

G20 367–375
Gabuev, A. 258, 394
Gadzhiev, K. 68
Galeotti, M. 160, 162, 163, 164
Garthoff, R. 156
gas, natural 138–148
Gazprom 138, 139, 141–148, 259, 289, 329, 330
Geanakopolos, D. 229
geo-economics 140–141
geopolitics 60–73, 81, 140–141
Georgia 111, 243–244, 246, 317–320, 383, 416, 428

Index

Georgian war (2008) 49, 50–54, 89–90, 127
Gerzsimov, V. 189
Gill, P. 155
Glazyev, S. 26–27
Global Council on Economic Coordination 364
Gody bol'shoi politiki (Primakov) 128
Golts, A. 159, 160
Gorbachev, M.: Afghanistan and 306; Arctic and 340; Asia and 388; coup and 157; diplomacy and 128; Egypt and 303; Japan and Germany and 16; KGB and 156; Malta Summit and 110; New Thinking of 11, 69, 128, 156; OSCE and 382; retrenchment and 101, 111–112; United Nations and 355
Gorchakov, A. 130–131
Gore, A. 132, 241–242
Gore-Chernomyrdin Commission 241–242
Götz, E. 51–52, 91
governmentality 30–32
Grachev, A. 298
Grachev, P. 172–173, 286
Gramsci, A. 14, 25, 27
Gray, C. 66
Great Financial Crisis (GFC) 367, 368, 369
"Great Game" 62
great power status 10–11, 19, 31, 33, 82, 110, 379
Gromyko, A. 106, 107, 108, 131
GRU 156, 157, 158–160, 163
Grygiel, J. 297
Gulf War 298, 302, 303–304
Guterres, A. 363
Guzzini, S. 5, 6, 18

Habermas, J. 23
Habsburg Empire 63
Hale, H. E. 86, 104, 105
Hansen, L. 16
Harper, S. 372
Hashimoto 255
Hauner, M. 256
Haushofer, K. 64, 65
Havel, V. 239
"Heartland" 61, 62, 64, 65, 66
hegemony, concept of 27, 34
Heikal, M. 297, 307
Heller, R. 12, 16
Helsinki Accords 69
Helsinki Final Act (1975) 381
Herrin, J. 229
Hettne, B. 412
Hillgruber, A. 64
Hirschman, A. O. 139
historical materialist approaches 25–28
Hitler, A. 64, 65
Hoffmann, K. 426
holistic model of nationalism 88–93

honor 12, 221
Hopf, T. 5, 9, 14, 15, 17–18, 28
Horkheimer, M. 23
Hosking, G. 32
Hu J. 330, 394
Hungarian Revolt 63
Huskey, E. 105
Hussein, S. 303
"hybrid warfare" 163, 179, 203
hypothesis testing 15
hysteresis 14, 16, 29

icebreakers 344, 345–346
identity: Asia-Pacific and 256–257; centrality of 83–84; constructivism and 7, 8–10; EU and 277, 278; management strategies for 11–12; recognition and non-recognition of 10–12; state 7
ideology, non-importance of 81–83
Ilulissat Declaration 341
image-projection 12
imperial geopolitics 60–62
imperial history 32–33
Imperial Russia 62–63
India 264, 401, 403
individualism 22
information, militarization of 186–187
"information aggression" 190
"information terrorism" 191
information warfare 121, 170–171, 182, 184–185, 186–187, 192, 201, 208, 211
Inozemtsev, V. 415
integration, international 283–284
intelligence 153–165
intergovernmentalism 416
Intergovernmental Panel on Climate Change 360
internal colonization 32–33
International Maritime Organization's Polar Code 360
international norms and identity 5–19
International Political Economy (IPE) 24
International Telecommunications Union (ITU) 190
Internet governance 185–186, 189
Internet Governance Forum (IGF) 190
intersubjectivity 6
Iran 297, 304–305
Iraq 285, 298, 299, 303–304
ISIS 320–322
Islamic State (IS) 249, 423
Israel 305
Ivanov, I. 123, 128, 129, 131, 133, 204
Ivanov, S. 174, 229
Izborsk Club 26–27

Jackson, P. 164
Jagland, T. 380–381

Japan 255, 262–263
Jessop, B. 27
Jiang Z. 395, 405
Johnston, D. 228
Jonsson, C. 124
Juneau, T. 55
Justice for Sergei Magnitsky Act 247
Justinian 218

Kadyrov, A.-H. 314
Kadyrov, R. 314
Kagarlitsky, B. 26
Kalbajar, Battle of 286
Kapustin, B. 28
Karabeshkin, L. 201
Karaganov, S. 61, 72, 257
Karagiannis, E. 50, 53–54
Karimov 427
Karl, T. 103
Kazakhstan 414–415, 425, 427
Keenan, E. L. 102
Kennan, G. 66, 276
Kennedy, P. 61
Kerry, J. 133, 248
KGB 153, 155–157, 158–159
Khanin 108
Khatchaturov, Y. 426
Khordorkovsky, M. 244, 272
Khrushchev, N. 106
Kievan Rus 62, 221–222
Kim J. 133
Kirill, Patriarch 219–220, 222, 223, 225, 226, 227
Kiseleva, Y. 201
Kiselyov, D. 204
Kissinger, H. 66, 69, 126, 131
Kjellen, R. 60, 64
Klotz, A. 15, 16
Kofman, M. 163
Kohl, H. 377
Kolstø, P. 88
Kondratyev, G. 172
Kordonsky, S. 26
Korea 263–264
Kosovo 127, 240–241
Kozak, D. 272
Kozak Memorandum 286
Kozyrev, A. 69, 123, 128–129, 130, 132, 172, 254, 255, 274, 298, 299, 379
Kramer, M. 162
Krickovic, A. 29, 30, 52
Kropatcheva, E. 48–49, 278, 424, 425, 428
Kryshtanovskaya, O. 105
Kryuchkov, V. 157
Kuboniwa, M. 108
Kudashev 262
Kukulin, I. 32
Kurdish nationalists 306–307

Kuzio, T. 87
Kyoto Protocol 360
Kyrgyzstan 414, 423, 426, 427–428

labor market 291–292, 333–334
Laclau, E. 34
Lagutina, M. L. 415
Lake, D. 29
Lambert, A. 61
Lanteigne, M. 13, 405
Laptev, D. 339
Larin, V. 258
Larson, D. W. 11–12
Laruelle, M. 83, 84, 88, 89, 90–91, 92, 94
Latynina, Y. 372
Lavrov, S.: after Russo-Georgian war 81; Council of Europe and 380–381; diplomacy style of 123, 274; EU and 278; Kerry and 133; Magnitsky Act and 127; NATO and 134; network diplomacy and 131–132; new regionalism and 413; OSCE and 384–385; reset and 245; on Russia's role 126, 204; SCO and 401–402; on Transnistria 287; United Nations and 356–357, 363
Lebed, A. 286
Ledeneva, A. V. 102, 105
Lee, R. 265
legal representation 124
Lenin, V. 25, 64, 339
Le Pen, M. 86
Lester, J. 27
Lévi-Strauss, C. 22
liberalism 84–87
Libya 299
Light, M. 88, 277
"linguistic turn" 24
Little, D. 228
Litvinenko, A. 162
Litvinov, M. 395
Lo, B. 274, 297
long-term national interest 221
Lucas, E. 86
Lukashenko, A. 384, 413–414, 415, 417
Lukin, A. 264, 265, 391, 403
Lukyanov, F. 205, 373
Luong, P. J. 104
Luttwak, E. 228
Lynch, C. 15, 16

Mackinder, H. 60–62, 64, 65, 67, 69, 72
Magnitsky Act 127, 247
Mahan, A. T. 60–62
Makarychev, A. S. 13
Malta Summit 110
Mamedov, Y. 241
managed nationalism 88–89, 92
Maness, R. 129

Mankoff, J. 49, 173, 243
Mann, M. 87
Manoilo, A. 204
March, L. 88, 89–90, 91, 92
Marcuse, H. 23
maritime doctrine 171, 172
Markedonov, S. 312, 317
Marten, K. 86, 104, 105
Martin, L. 406
Marx, K. 23, 25
Marxism-Leninism 82, 130
Matveeva, A. 424, 428
Mazepus, H. 94
McCloy 206
McFaul, M. 53
McGlinchey, E. 104
Mearsheimer, J. 50–51, 53, 71, 81
media 199–212
Medvedev, D.: Asia and 256; China and 394; CSCE and 423; cyber power and 188; diplomacy and 127; EAEU and 413; EU and 272, 273; on G7 373; G20 and 370; Georgia and 90; Gore-Chernomyrdin Commission and 242; military and 173, 174; Obama and 246, 300; public diplomacy and 204; Putin contrasted with 49; Russian Orthodox Church and 219; SCO and 403; on security matters 384; United States and 245–247
Medvedko, L. I. 296
Medvedko, S. L. 296
Membership Action Plan (MAP) 111
Merkel, A. 111, 132, 142
Middle East 295–309
migrant labor 291–292, 334
Migranyan, A. 68
militarized interstate disputes (MIDS) 101
military 163, 168–179
Military Doctrine of the Russian Federation 187
Military-Industrial Commission 173–174
Millennium Manifesto 82
Ministry of Internal Affairs (MVD) 157
Minsk Agreements 288, 292
missile defense 241
Mitchell, A. W. 297
Mitrofanov, A. 68
Mitrokhin, V. 155
Mitzen, J. 29
Molchanov, M. A. 424
Moldova 286–287, 383
Mongolia 392
Morgenthau, H. 44, 124
Morgulov, I. 403
Morozov, V. 10, 16, 17, 18
Morrison, K. M. 101
Morsi, M. 303
Moscovy 62

Moscow State Institute of International Relations (MGIMO) 128
Motyl, A. 53
Mouritzen, H. 50–51
Mubarak, H. 303
multi-polarity 205–210
Munich Security Conference 112, 127, 131, 244–245, 300
Munich speech 244–245, 300
Muradov, K. 389
Muslim Brotherhood 303

Nabucco project 142
Naftogaz 144
Nagorno-Karabakh 317, 322
Nartov, N. 68
Naryshkin, S. 157
Nasser, G. A. 297, 302–303
National Guard 157
nationalism 79–95
national security, power and 43–56
National Security Agency (NSA) 183, 188
national security strategy (NSS) 171
NATO: Arctic and 338, 344, 347; diplomacy and 126–127, 134; geopolitics and 69–71; Georgia and 111; maritime doctrine and 171; OSCE and 382, 383; practices and 13–14; Putin and 247; SCO and 400–401; semi-structured interviewing and 16–17; Ukraine and 287–288; United States and 239–240, 243–244, 246; weaponization of information and 208; Yeltsin and 285
natural gas 138–148
Nazarbayev, N. 392, 414, 417
Nazi-Soviet Non-Aggression Pact 64–65
neoclassical realism (NCR) 44, 45–46, 50, 52, 54, 55–56, 83
neo-Eurasianism 85
neorealism 23–24, 43, 45, 47–48, 51
network diplomacy 125, 131–132, 369
Neumann, I. 8, 9, 10–11, 14, 16, 29, 31, 32, 33, 256
New Cold War narrative 200, 208, 245, 251, 257
new regionalism approach (NRA) 412–413
New Russian Diplomacy, The (Ivanov) 128
New START Treaty 241, 246
New Thinking 11, 382
Nikitina, Y. 424
Nikolai I 82
9/11 242–243, 298, 306, 314
Nixon, R. 66, 130
no-first-use, doctrine of 170
Non-Proliferation Treaty 170
Nord Stream pipeline 120, 126, 142–143, 147, 285, 291
Northern Caucasus 312–314
Northern Sea Route (NSR) 339

Nougayrède, N. 207
Nuclear Non-Proliferation Treaty 357
Nusra, J. al- 321
Nye, J. 184, 203, 210, 276
Nygren, B. 44, 49

Obama, B., and administration of 127, 132, 190, 193, 242, 245–246, 248, 255, 300, 315, 372
offensive realists 45, 276
official nationality 89
oil *see* petropolitics
Oil Is Not a Curse (Luong and Weinthal) 104
One Belt, One Road (OBOR) 264–265, 394, 405, 413, 418
On Measures to Implement the Foreign Policy Course of the Russian Federation 204
ontological insecurity 29, 33
Operation Barbarossa 65
Orange Revolution 248, 272, 288
Organization for Security and Cooperation in Europe (OSCE) 377, 381–386
Organization of Central Asia Cooperation (OCAC) 330–331
Organization of Petroleum Exporting States (OPEC) 306
Others 7, 8, 9
Ottawa Declaration 340

Pacific Basin Economic Council 388
Pacific Economic Cooperation Conference 388
Panarin, A. S. 332
Pankhurst, J. 219
Papp, R. 343, 347
Paris climate agreement 360
Paris Treaty 382
Parliamentary Assembly of the Council of Europe (PACE) 380, 385
Parry, C. 61
Partnership and Cooperation Agreement (PCA) 270
Partnership for Peace (PfP) program 240, 284, 326, 423
patriotism, nationalism versus 80–81
patronal politics 104
Patrushev, N. 160, 174
Patten, C. 274
Paul, Metropolitan 222
peacekeeping missions, UN 362
Pérez de Cuéllar, J. 355
peripherality 27–28, 29, 62–63
personal diplomacy 132–133
Peter I 31, 219, 339
petropolitics 99–113
Petrov, N. 105
pipeline policy 141–142
Pivot Area 61

Pokrovsky, M. 25, 26
Polanyi, K. 412
political nationalism 89
political representation 124
Pomerantsev, P. 276
Ponomarev, B. 107
Pop, I. I. 425
postcolonial theory 32–33
poststructuralism 22
Posuvalyuk, V. 303, 304
Pouliot, V. 13–14, 15, 16–17, 29, 32
power 43–46
practice-focused framework 13–14
pragmatism 298, 299
Preobrazhenie (Kozyrev) 128–129
presidency, authority of 238
presidential elections, U.S. 193–194, 250
Primakov, Y.: Council of Europe and 379, 381; diplomacy style of 119, 123, 128, 129, 131, 274, 285; "Eurasianist" geopolitical consensus under 69, 70, 132; India and 264; Kosovo and 240; Kozyrev and 130; Middle East and 295, 296, 298, 299, 304, 305; MoD and 174; NATO and 239–240; RIC and 392; Russian business and 141; SVR and 158
Prizel, I. 8
Problem of Asia, The (Mahan) 60
process tracing 8, 16
Prokhanov, A. 27, 87
propaganda 201, 207
Prothero, S. 219
Prussia 63
public diplomacy 134, 199–212
Pushkov, A. 274–275
Putin, V.: Arctic and 341; ascension to power by 70; ASEAN and 390; Central and Eastern Europe and 285; Central Asia and 328, 329, 330–331, 333; China and 393, 405, 418; CIS and 417; "conservative turn" of 85, 86; Crimean annexation and 222–223; cyber power and 187–188, 189, 190; diplomacy and 123, 125–126, 127, 130–131, 132–134, 135; EAEU and 413–414, 415; East Asia Summit and 389; EU and 271, 272–274, 277; European organizations and 377; G20 and 370, 372–373; geopolitics and 70–72; Georgia and 54, 90; on great power status 82; international courts and 380; international economics and 141; Israel and 305; Medvedev and 49; Middle East and 296, 301, 303, 306, 307, 308–309; military and 168, 170, 173, 174, 175, 176, 178; Mongolia and 392; Munich Security Conference speech by 244–245, 300; NATO and 247; natural gas and 146; 9/11 and 306; norms and 13; opposition and 104; OSCE and 384; personal acquaintances of in government 105; petropolitics and 109–113; as prime minister 274; public

436

diplomacy and 204; religion and 226; Republican support for 209–210; reputation of 205, 209, 227; role of 83; *Russky mir Fund* and 222; Saakashvili and 318; SCO and 327, 403; security services and 153, 160, 162, 164; Ukraine and 51, 171, 224; United Nations and 357; United States and 242–245, 247–250
Putinism 49, 227

Q-methodology 19

Rambouillet peace deal 240
Rapallo, Treaty of 64
Ratzel, F. 64
Rawnsley, G. D. 201
Razumkov Centre 208–209
Reagan, R. 246, 348
realism 43–56, 81–83, 295, 326, 328, 396
Regional Anti-Terrorist Structure (RATS) 327, 404
Regional Comprehensive Economic Partnership (RCEP) 389
Reinsurance Treaty 63
"religious diplomacy" 228
reset, assessing 246–247
Reshetnikov, L. 161
resource curse theory 102, 104
Responsibility to Protec (R2P) concept 124–125, 357, 360–362
Rice, C. 133
Ripsman, N. M. 56
Robinson, N. 86
Rochlitz, M. 160, 163
Roeder, P. G. 106
Rogov, S. 68
Rogozin, D. 174
Ronchey, S. 229
Rose, G. 45, 48
Rosneft 146
Ross, M. L. 101, 103–104
Rossesr, A. 104
RT 207
Runciman, S. 229
Russia and the Arabs (Primakov) 298
Russia-China Joint Declaration on a Multipolar World and Formation of a New International Order (1997) 395
Russia/China/U.S. triangle 191–192
"Russia first" approach 51
Russia-India-China (RIC) trilateral 392
Russia-Mongolia-China trilateral 392
Russian Association of Indigenous Peoples of the North (RAIPON) 341
Russian Foreign Policy Concepts 205
Russian-Georgian war 12
Russian Institute for Strategic Studies (RISI) 160–161

Russian International Affairs Council 204
Russian navy 344
Russian Orthodox Church 217–230
Russia Today 204
Russkii mir 83, 90, 221–225
Russo-Japanese War 63

Saakiashvili, M. 54, 70, 177, 288, 318–319
Saat, J. H. 422
Sachs, J. D. 100
Sadat, A. al- 303
Sakhalin-1 consortium 145
Sakwa, R. 83, 250
Sanders, B. 182
Sarkozy, N. 111
Saudi Arabia 305–306
Saussure, F. de 22
Schelling, T. 176, 177
Schmitt, C. 32
Schröder, G. 132
Scott, L. 164
Search and Rescue (SAR) agreement 340, 343
Sechin, I. 146
Security Council 274
security services 153–165
semi-structured interviewing 16–17
Sending, O. J. 31
Serdyukov, A. 173
Sergunin, A. 201
shale revolutions 49
Shanghai Cooperation Organization (SCO) 132, 191, 255, 257, 264, 327, 374, 384, 391–392, 394, 400–407, 411, 417–418
Shaposhnikov, Y. 173
Shell, J. 207
Sherr, J. 135
Shevardnadze, E. 298, 304, 318
Shevchenko, A. 11–12
Shoygu, S. 173, 174, 189
Shuvalov, I. 141
Sikorski, R. 143
Silk Road Economic Belt (SREB) 331, 393, 405, 414, 418
Simes, D. 130
Sisi, A. F. al- 303
Six-Party Talks (SPT) 389
Sixth Novella (Justinian) 218
Skak, M. 160
Slaughter, A. M. 369
Smith, B. 104
Snegur, M. 286
Snetkov, A. 13
Snowden, E. 183, 185, 188, 194, 247
Snyder, J. 47–48
Sochi Olympics 5, 126, 247, 248, 272, 316, 320, 390

social constructivism 5, 7, 17; *see also* constructivism
Social Identity Theory (SIT) 11
social media 18
soft alliance 258
soft power 12, 18, 83, 186, 201, 276, 332–333
Soldatov, A. 160, 161, 163
SORM-II 188
South Caucasus 316–320
South Korea 263, 264
South Ossetia: Armenia's response to 317; China and 257, 262; CSTO and 428; impact of conflict in 312–313; NATO and 320; OSCE and 383; ROC and 225; Russian response to 50, 53, 70, 111, 127, 175, 176–177, 178, 235, 318–319; SCO and 404; Ukraine crisis and 322; United States and 244, 315
South Stream pipeline 143, 313
sovereign democracy 13
Soviet-German geopolitics 63–65
sovnarkhoz reforms 106
Splidsboel-Hansen, Flemming 52
SPRN (*Sistema Preduprezhdeniia o Raketnom Napadenii*; Missile Attack Warning System) 340
SPT 396
Spykman, N. 65
Stalin, J. 9, 64, 304, 339
START II 241, 246, 300
state corrosion argument 103
status aspirations 48–50
Steele, B. 29
Stent, A. 296–297
Sterling-Folker, J. 45
stigmatization 29, 31, 33
St. Petersburg Summit 271
Strategic Defense Initiative 348
Strategic Offensive Reductions Treaty (SORT) 243, 246
Strausz-Hupe, R. 66
Streltsov, D. V. 296
structuralism 22–38
structurationism 22
Stulberg, A. 102
subaltern empire 10, 16, 34–35, 37
submarines 345
summit diplomacy 126
Suslov, M. 107
sustainable development 358–360
symbolic representation 124
symphonia 219–220, 228
Syria: China and 13; diplomacy and 132–135; main discussion of 249–250; military force in 121, 174, 175–176, 177–178, 209, 235, 307; Putin and 4, 51, 101–102, 106, 109, 111, 168, 207, 308–309; retrenchment and 100; Russian relations with 297, 299, 301–302, 305; *see also* Arab League; Assad, B. al-

Tajikistan 426
Talbot, S. 241
Taliban 308
Tatar Yoke 62
Taylor, B. D. 160
Ter-Petrosyan, L. 286
terrorism 161–162, 318, 327
Thatcher, M. 246
"Third Rome" doctrine 219
Thrift, N. 22
Timofeev, I. 208, 209, 210–211
Tkachenko, S. 129, 133
trade: Asia-Pacific and 258; Central Asia and 330–332, 333; EAEU and 414–415; economic interdependency and 289–290
Transforming our World: The 2030 Agenda for Sustainable Development 360
Transnistria 286–287, 383
Trans-Pacific Partnership 261, 389
Treadgold, W. 229
Treaty of Friendship 301, 414
Treaty on Alignment and Strategic Partnership 319
Trenin, D. 68–69, 271, 274, 276, 317, 390–391
Triple Alliance 63
Trotsky, L. 25
Truman administration 66
Trump, D. 209, 250, 261, 302, 308, 322, 334, 411
Trutnev, Y. 260
Tsygankov, A. 9, 12, 29, 161, 200, 204, 208, 221, 278
Tsymbuskii, V. 68
Tsypkin, M. 160
Tucker, R. 82
Turkey 306–307, 308
Turkmenistan 422
Tymoshenko 144

Uffelmann, D. 32
Ukraine: Asia-Pacific and 256–257; CIS and 416; crisis in 50–54, 163–164, 171, 177–178, 208–209, 284, 285, 287–288, 292, 299, 320–322, 389; debt and 289–290; EU and 278; NATO and 243–244, 246; natural gas and 143–145, 147–148; *Russkii mir* and 221–225; *see also* color revolutions; Crimea
Ukrainian Greek-Catholic Church (UGCC) 224
Umarov, D. 315, 320
UN Commission on Human Rights 363
UN Convention on the Law of the Sea (UNCLOS) 341
"uneven and combined development" 25–26, 27, 33

unipolarity 140, 148, 357
United National Security Council (UNSC) 132, 244, 245, 248–249, 256, 299, 304, 351, 355, 357–358, 361–363, 364, 374, 402
United Nations 355–365
United States: Arctic and 338, 345–347; Caucasus and 312–313, 314–316; Central Asia and 326; geopolitics in 66–67; main discussion of 237–251; sanctions and 389
universalization 27
US-Russia Joint Commission on Economic and Technical Cooperation 241–242
Uzbekistan 414, 422, 427

Valdai Club 265–266
Valeriano, B. 129
values 12, 27, 34, 36, 80–81, 83, 85–86, 92, 121–122, 127, 199–200, 203–204
"values agendas" 218
"values gap" 227, 228
van Herpen, M. 87
Vasilev, A. 297
Vasilyeva, N. A. 415
Velikaya, A. 210–211
Vendley, W. 228
Vietnam 414
Vinokurov, E. 415
"virtual radicalism" 321
Visegrad Group 283
Volodin, V. 127
Voronin, V. 286
Vorontsov, Y. 355, 363

Walesa, L. 239
Walt, S. M. 51, 52
Waltz, K. N. 44–45, 47, 52
Wang Y. 260
war chest theory 100–102, 111–112
Warner, A. M. 100
War on Terror 299, 301, 314–315, 426
Warsaw Pact 284
Watson, A. 29
"weaponized information" 201, 208

"weapon" perspectives 139–140
Weidlé, V. 229
Weinthal, E. 104
Weiss, M. 276
Weitz, R. 422
Wendt, A. 6, 7, 22
White, S. 10, 17, 105, 277
WikiLeaks 182
Wilson, J. L. 201
Wishnick, E. 265
Wivel, A. 50–51
Wohlforth, W. C. 24, 44, 47, 48, 49, 50
Wolf, R. 12
world-system theory (WST) 24, 26–27
World Trade Organization (WTO) 129, 246
World War I 63–64
Worth, O. 28
Wuzhen World Internet Conference 193

Xi J. 133, 193, 392, 393

Yakdarbiyev, Z. 161
Yanukovych, V. 52, 71, 144–145, 163, 248, 284
Yefremenko, D. 405
Yeltsin, B.: Arctic and 340; Asia policy and 255; Caucasus and 317; China and 395; diplomacy style of 131, 132; EU and 277; G7 and 126; Kosovo and 240–241; MoD and 172; NATO and 285; OSCE and 383; presidency of 69–70; Putin and 109–110; security services and 157, 158; United Nations and 355; United States and 239–242; Western aid and 141
YouGov poll 205, 209
Yugoslavia 286, 299
Yushchenko 144, 147

Zannier, L. 384
Zarakol, A. 29, 30
Zevelev, I. 11
Zonova, T. 129
Zubok, V. 82
Zviagelskaia, I. 296
Zyuganov, G. 68

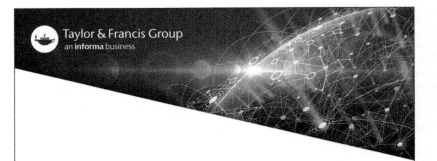